U0924200

“十三五”国家重点图书出版规划项目

“一带一路”建设中
国际贸易和投资风险防控
法律实务丛书

the legal series on prevention and control of risks
in international trade and investment under the construction
of the Belt and Road

总主编 张晓君

本丛书成果系教育部哲学社会科学研究重大课题攻关项目（项目批准号： 19JZD053）产出成果

国际商事争端解决法律实务

主编 徐忆斌 陈 方

厦门大学出版社
XIAMEN UNIVERSITY PRESS
国家一级出版社
全国百佳图书出版单位

图书在版编目(CIP)数据

国际商事争端解决法律实务/徐忆斌,陈方主编.—厦门:厦门大学出版社,2020.12
(“一带一路”建设中国国际贸易和投资风险防控法律实务丛书)
ISBN 978-7-5615-7355-6

Ⅰ.①国… Ⅱ.①徐…②陈… Ⅲ.①国际商事仲裁—研究 Ⅳ.①D997.4

中国版本图书馆 CIP 数据核字(2019)第 053159 号

出 版 人 郑文礼
责任编辑 李 宁

出版发行 厦门大学出版社
社 址 厦门市软件园二期望海路 39 号
邮政编码 361008
总 编 办 0592-2182177 0592-2181406(传真)
营销中心 0592-2184458 0592-2181365
网 址 http://www.xmupress.com
邮 箱 xmup@xmupress.com
印 刷 厦门集大印刷厂

开本 720 mm×1 000 mm 1/16
印张 35.25
字数 620 千字
版次 2020 年 12 月第 1 版
印次 2020 年 12 月第 1 次印刷
定价 98.00 元

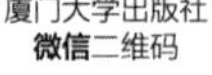
厦门大学出版社
微信二维码

厦门大学出版社
微博二维码

总　序

"一带一路"是新时代中国深化与世界各国全方位合作，努力实现全球共同发展的重要倡议。自2013年该倡议提出以来，七年间，"一带一路"从愿景转变为现实。国家主席习近平在2019年第二届"一带一路"国际合作高峰论坛发表的题为"齐心开创共建'一带一路'美好未来"的主旨演讲中强调，共建"一带一路"顺应了经济全球化的历史潮流，顺应了全球治理体系变革的时代要求，更是顺应了各国人民过上更好日子的强烈愿望。共建"一带一路"为世界经济增长开辟了新空间，为国际贸易和投资搭建了新平台。在共建"一带一路"的机遇之路上，中国与"一带一路"沿线国家的贸易投资交往愈加密切，中国企业的贸易投资活动更加积极。但机遇与挑战并存，"一带一路"沿线国家或地区存在政治体制、经济制度、法律体系与文化背景等方面的差异，国际贸易和投资关系错综复杂。值得注意的是，进入2020年，随着新冠疫情在世界范围内的广泛蔓延，有西方大国基于国内政治的考量，掀起单边主义和霸权主义的波澜，意图逆转全球化趋势，将正常的国际经贸交往政治化，为技术、商品、人员和资本的顺畅流动设置重重障碍，这不可避免地会传导到"一带一路"倡议的践行过程中，给中国与沿线国家的国际经贸关系施加了前所未有的严峻挑战。在此背景下，预防与控制国际贸易和投资的法律风险，成为推动共建"一带一路"行稳致远的重要保障。

本着这一问题意识，西南政法大学国际法学院、中国—东盟法律研究中心与深圳市前海国合法律研究院、泰和泰律师事务所等法律实务部门深入合作，结合教育部哲学社会科学研究重大课题攻关项目（项目批准号：19JZD053）"对'一带一路'沿线国家投资风险监测预警体系研究"，对我国企业在国际贸易投资中所面临的风险防控问题展开研究。"'一带一路'建设中国际贸易和投资风险防控法律实务丛书"就是我们深入合作开展系统研究结出的硕果，同时也是与国家安全学院开展跨学科研究的重要成果。丛书由具有较强科研能力的国际法学界和具有丰富国际贸易投资及争端解决经验的法律实务界人士联袂编著。

丛书围绕教育部哲学社会科学研究重大课题攻关项目（项目批准号：19JZD053），以"一带一路"国际贸易和投资中企业所面临的法律风险防控需求为导向，从国际网络贸易、跨境投资并购、国际知识产权保护、国际货物运输、国际税收、国际PPP、国际能源、商品进出口、国际信用证，以及国际投资争端解决、国际商事争端解决、涉外法律适用等实务性极强的领域出发，以丰富的实践案例和国际法律文书为基本内容，根据实务人员法律服务技能的实践性和涉外性特征，详述知识内涵，深度剖析裁判要旨，总结实践经验，提炼学习要点，对企业可能面临的法律风险展开极具针对性、前瞻性的研究，提出专业性、建设性和可操作性的风险防控措施建议。

西南政法大学国际法学院作为我国重要的国际法学研究和涉外法律人才教育培养基地，在服务"一带一路"建设的法治人才培养、学术研究和社会服务等方面具有强烈的责任担当，力图产出一批优秀学术成果，培养一批优秀法治人才。中国—东盟法律研究中心则是中国法学会首批法治研究基地、最高人民法院东盟法律研究基地。当今处于百年未有之大变局，在全球治理体系变革推进时期，国际法学院和中国—东盟法律研究中心心系天下，将以更大的担当和使命感，做好国际法治研究和国际法人才培养工作，为我国更高水平的对外开放和共建"一带一路"做出应有的贡献。

张晓君　教授、博士生导师
西南政法大学国际法学院院长、国际法学科负责人
中国法学会中国—东盟法律研究中心秘书长
2020年5月

编写说明

随着国际商事交流的不断发展，在此过程中产生的纠纷也与日俱增。如何解决国际商事争端一直是学界研究的重点。国际商事争端的解决方式可以分为诉讼性争端解决方式和非诉讼性争端解决方式两种。诉讼性争端解决方式主要是指司法诉讼，通过国际民事诉讼解决当事人之间的国际商事争端。但是，由于国际商事争端的复杂性，且诉讼本身的耗时长、程序烦琐等缺陷，因此在国际商事争端解决实务中，非诉讼性争端解决方式以其快速、便捷的特点更加受到当事人的认可。非诉讼性争端解决方法主要指以谈判、调解、仲裁等非诉方式解决纠纷，其中，调解与仲裁是替代性争端解决机制（Alternative Dispute Resolution，简称ADR）的典型代表，具有其他许多争端解决方式所不具备的特色优势，可以满足当事人的多种需求。此外，在国际商事争端解决领域，各国在逐步交往的过程中还发展出了开展贸易救济争端解决的国内反倾销、反补贴和保障措施（“两反一保”）程序，及世界贸易组织（WTO）多边争端解决机制，为国际双、多边商事交易的顺利进行和商事争端的成功解决提供了重要的依据和保障。

对于高水平涉外法律人才的培养，除了相关专业基础知识和语言能力的培养以外，更需要培养学生的法律逻辑思维。因而，在编选教材时就应当立足于案例，通过对案例的学习与解读，培养学生的思辨批判能力和实务运用能力。有鉴于此，本书在沿袭以章、节行文的传统编撰方法的基础上，对知识背景、学习要点进行阐释之后，列举与知识点相关的较为典型的案例，以便学生在学习知识点后立即结合案例进行思考，有利于加深学生对基础知识的理解并且加强其实务运用能力。同时，在章节之后加入延伸阅读部分，引导学生在课后继续就相关问题进行自主学习。

总体来说，本书力求突出实务性，书中所选的案例均为真实发生的，尽可能将国际商事交往过程中发生的争端及争端解决的程序呈现在书中，便于学生讨论实践中最有可能发生的争议点，帮助学生切实有效地将知识转化为运用法律解决实际问题的能力。此外，在案例之后，编者对案例进行简要评析，有助于学生快速掌握案件的要点，帮助其他读者读懂案例，并了解国际商事交往中的风险点，从而避免风险的发生。本书适宜于已具备法学基础知识的本科高年级学生和研究生，同样也适宜于学习国际商事争端解决的广大读者。

本书是西南政法大学国际法学院组织编写的"'一带一路'建设中国际贸易和投资风险防控法律实务丛书"之一。本书由西南政法大学、广东星辰（前海）律师事务所、武汉大学从事国际经济法律实务和研究的人员共同编写，是各位作者的研究与合作的成果。本书具体撰稿人及分工如下（以撰写章节先后为顺序）：

第一章：王颖（西南政法大学）、爱丽姆［广东星辰（前海）律师事务所］；

第二章：李文燕（西南政法大学）、刘群敏［广东星辰（前海）律师事务所］；

第三章：林俊（西南政法大学）、吴昊［广东星辰（前海）律师事务所］；

第四章：马小晴（西南政法大学）、刘群敏［广东星辰（前海）律师事务所］；

第五章、第六章：徐忆斌（西南政法大学）、吴昊［广东星辰（前海）律师事务所］；

第七章：徐忆斌（西南政法大学）；

第八章：董哲（武汉大学）。

由于时间和水平的限制，书中存在内容错误和疏漏之处是在所难免的，敬请各位读者惠予批评指正，以便我们在本书再版时修订完善。

编者

2020年3月

目录

第一章

国际商事争端谈判法律实务

【内容摘要】

本章要求掌握有关国际商事争端谈判的理论与实务，具体内容包括国际商事争端谈判的概念分类、国际商事争端谈判的过程、国际商事争端谈判的实务问题。本章采取理论与实践相结合的方式，确保读者能够深入了解国际商事争端谈判在实践中的具体情形，充分激发学习兴趣。

第一节　国际商事争端谈判的概述

【知识背景 / 学习要点】

一、国际商事争端谈判的概念

（一）谈判与国际商事争端谈判

谈判是用新的和解协议取代旧有合同，即争议双方基于各自利益以及某种需求，通过协商交涉、信息交换等方式，协调双方的利益关系，解决纠纷与争议。法律谈判分为广义与狭义，广义的法律谈判与谈判的概念相似，包括所有的民商事争端谈判和各种争端的协商活动。狭义的法律谈判，是指在谈判中运用法律思维，遵循一定的准则平衡谈判双方的利益，并能产生一定的法律后果的谈判。[①] 本章所指国际商事争端谈判是狭义上的法律谈判，是发生在国际商事领域，争端双方当事人以达成一系列合意为目的而进行的法律谈判。在具体的国际商事实践中，并非所有的法律谈判均以争端为前提，法律谈判是国际商事争端解决中的常见形式，同时也是其他争端解决程序的基础。[②] 本章所述的国际商事谈判为争端谈判。

（二）国际商事争端谈判的性质

1. 较强的灵活性

在具体的国际商事争端解决过程中，作为国际商事争端解决方式之一，国际商事争端有着许多其他争端解决方式所不具备的优势，比如灵活性就是其重要优势之一。灵活性主要表现为内容与过程等没有严格的规则束缚，可以满足当事人不同的利益需求。谈判的形式、方法，甚至时间与地点均可以自由地选择。因此，国际商事争端谈判实务中体现出较强的灵活性。

2. 对象特定性

国际商事争端谈判是在国际商事争端中，争议一方（谈判发起方）向另一方（谈判接受方）请求通过协商方式达成一定的合意。以国际商事争端中的和解谈判为例，谈判请求权的对象具有特定性，即谈判双方是相对且固定的，一旦谈判开始，谈判接受方不能与其他谈判申请方进行谈判。同样，谈判发起方也不能随意更换谈判接受方，争端谈判双方互相牵连。[③]

3. 自主选择性

国际商事争端谈判是一个自主选择的过程，国际商事谈判要求在尊重双方当事人的基础之上，充分保障当事人的意志自由，从而体现出自主选择性。自主选择性在实务中主要体现在两个方面。一方面，在国际商事争端谈判中，当

---

① 戴勇坚：《如何当好调解员：法律谈判的理论、策略和技巧》，湘潭大学出版社 2015 年版，第 18 页。

② Donald G. Gifford, *Legal Negotiation: Theory and Practice,* third edition, West Academic Publishing, 2017.

③ 对象特定性的例外：主要表现在国际商事合同违约谈判中，但关于对人身伤害和名誉损害等侵权案件的谈判，谈判双方当事人均不可变动。

事人为解决争端，可以自由选择是否通过谈判的方式解决争端。另一方面，若通过谈判的方式解决国际商事争端，则谈判解决争端的具体操作方式由当事方自主选择决定。

二、国际商事争端谈判的分类

（一）竞争型谈判与合作型谈判

1. 竞争型谈判

竞争型谈判又称零和谈判、对抗性谈判，是指在国际商事争端谈判中，当事人针对谈判对象做出大致相同的让步，一方所失（所得）与对方所得（所失）相加大致为零，方可取得谈判成果，国际商事争端法庭诉讼就是竞争型谈判的代表。在该状态下，因为双方利益资源有限而且谈判利益所得只能在两方之间分配，所以必然导致一输一赢。①

2. 合作型谈判

合作型谈判是指在国际商事争端中，谈判双方为了共同的目的探讨相应的解决方案，在此过程中兼顾双方的利益，为达到双赢结果而进行的谈判。在合作型谈判中，谈判能否成功关键在于双方的目标能否同时实现。合作型谈判以双方合作、互惠的态度为基础。在合作型谈判的过程中，双方开诚布公地进行信息交流，谈判各方真实地表达自己的意愿，并确切地了解对方的目标需要。确定双方的目标之后，寻找能实现共同目标的方法。②

（二）和解谈判与普通谈判

根据国际商事争端谈判是否诉诸法院进行分类，分为和解谈判与普通谈判。

1. 和解谈判

和解谈判是指在诉讼中进行国际商事争端谈判或如果国际商事争端谈判未

① 刘薇：《法律谈判实验教程》，中国政法大学出版社 2016 年版，第 7 页。
② 戴勇坚：《如何当好调解员：法律谈判的理论、策略和技巧》，湘潭大学出版社 2015 年版，第 13 页。

能达到预期效果可能诉诸法院的谈判。[①] 和解谈判不同于其他谈判，在和解谈判中，以律师为主的国际商事争端代理人在谈判中具有极其重要的地位。[②] 但在实践中，商事争端代理人和委托人之间的关系优劣可能会影响和解谈判的进程，因而在国际商事争端和解谈判中要调节好律师与当事人之间的关系。

2. 普通谈判

普通谈判是指所有和解谈判以外的谈判。普通谈判是国际民商事争端谈判的核心，也是国际民商事争端谈判中最为常见的谈判形式，不涉及法院诉讼中的谈判。

【案例摘录与评析】

西南非洲案 [③]

INTERNATIONAL COURT OF JUSTICE REPORTS OF JUDGMENTS,
ADVISORY OPINIONS AND ORDERS
SOUTH WEST AFRICA CASES
ETHIOPIA and LIBERIA
v.
SOUTH AFRICA;
PRELIMINARY OBJECTIONS
JUDGMENT OF 21 DECEMBER 1962

Preliminary question of existence of a dispute between the Parties. Origin, nature and characteristics of Mandates System. Mandate for South West Africa as an instrument of an

① The reasoning of this chapter generally applies to both settlement negotiation of disputes headed to litigation and settlement negotiation of disputes headed to arbitration. To avoid wordiness, however, the rest of this chapter is written entirely in terms of disputes headed to litigation.

② See generally Ronald J. Gilson & Robert H. Mnookin, Disputing Through Agents: Cooperation and Conflict Between Lawyers in Litigation, *94 Colum. L. Rev. 509* (1994). Agency law governs the circumstances under which a lawyer has the power to bind a client to a settlement. See § 3.40.

③ Joint Dissenting Opinion of Sir Percy Spender and Sir Gerald Fitzmaurice, https://www.icj-cij.org/en/case/46/judgments, 下载日期：2018 年 11 月 6 日。

international character. Question of registration of Mandate: Article 18 of Covenant. Article 7 of Mandate as treaty or convention within meaning of Article 37 of Statute. Dissolution of League of Nations and survival of Mandate. Essentiality of Article 7 of Mandate. Capacity to invoke that Article. Scope of Article 7 and interest of Member States in Performance Mandate. Rule of prior diplomatic negotiation and its applicability. Court's finding of jurisdiction.

...

Percy C. SPENDER.

G. G. FITZMAURICE.

Having regard to our view, stated under the preceding head, that the matters involved by the present Application are not of a kind① that are capable of settlement on the basis of a negotiation between the Applicants and the Respondent State, since these parties lack competence to settle such matters by a negotiation purely between themselves. The question of whether the present dispute is one that "cannot" be settled by negotiation hardly arises for us. We will consider it nevertheless, because certain points of principle are involved which seem to us important.

The Respondent has not denied that discussions have taken place in the United Nations, but has confined itself to contending that they did not take place in conditions that gave them any real chance of success, so that it cannot be said that the dispute is one that under circumstances could be settled by negotiation.

This contention involves questions of fact into which we do not propose to go because, in our opinion, there has not, properly speaking, been any negotiation at all in this case of the kind contemplated by Article 7.

Under Article 7, the dispute that cannot be settled by negotiation must be the dispute between the Mandatory and the other Member of the League concerned, i.e., the actual dispute between the parties to the proceedings before the Court, as such. This means that the negotiation required by Article 7 must relate to that dispute and no other. Now the Applications in this case were filed in November, 1960, and it is quite clear therefore that, up to that date, the Assembly proceedings on which the Applicants rely (even if they can not be called negotiation at all) had nothing whatever to do with the actual dispute between the Applicant States and the Respondent State, since this dispute did not then exist *as such*. All that existed up to that date was a disagreement between the Assembly (as an entity) and one of its Members—the Respondent

① Nor strictly does it exist now, since, as we pointed out under the preceding head, it cannot have been created merely by the institution of proceedings; and neither interchanges, outside the Assembly, or directly between the parties as such, have ever taken place.

State; and all that had taken place up to that date were sundry proceedings in the Assembly and its Committees, in which indeed the Applicants participated, but simply as Members of the Assembly. To attribute to these antecedent discussions the character of a negotiation relative to the present dispute (which only arose in November 1960, if even then) a negotiation conducted by the Applicants in and through the Assembly, or by the Assembly itself on behalf of the Applicants, seems to us wholly unrealistic.

We would not wish to exaggerate the extent of negotiation that may be required to establish that there has been the minimum necessary in the circumstances to make it clear that the parties cannot settle their dispute. But some negotiations must, we think, in fact have taken place between the actual parties to the proceedings before the Court, in their capacity as individual States. Furthermore, the negotiation must relate to the dispute (and no other) alleged to exist between the parties to the proceedings before the Court, which dispute must have existed antecedently to those proceedings. It is not sufficient for the negotiation (supposing it to have been one) to have related to a dispute which, at the time when this "negotiation" was taking place, did not exist specifically between the parties before the Court, but consisted merely in a general all round controversy pursued on the floor of an international Assembly.

We are not concerned to deny the propriety or utility of discussions in an international forum such as the Assembly of the United Nations. We do not think that, normally, such discussions can be regarded as an actual negotiation taking place between the parties before the Court, as we think Article 7 contemplated. Such discussions are, and necessarily must be, of too general and diffused a character to constitute a negotiation between the specific parties who eventually come before the Court in relation to a specific dispute between them as States. Be that as it may, what is clearly apparent to us is that a "negotiation" confined to the floor of an international Assembly, consisting of allegations of Members, resolutions of the Assembly and actions taken by the assembly pursuant thereto, denial of allegations, refusal to comply with resolutions or to respond to action taken there under, cannot be enough to justify the Court in holding that the dispute "cannot" be settled by negotiation, when no direct diplomatic interchanges have ever taken place between the parties, and therefore no attempt at settlement has been made at the state and diplomatic level. Since direct negotiations between the actual.

Parties to a dispute constitute the usual and normally indispensable method of attempting a settlement, we do not see how the Court can hold and adjudge the dispute (that any dispute) "cannot" be settled, when no recourse at all has been had to this method. We do not think it should be assumed or postidated that interchanges which have not succeeded in the Assembly or its subsidiary organs, might not, in different conditions, and amongst a restricted number of parties, stand some chances of success—at least a sufficient chance to make it not reasonably possible to affirm the contrary until this method has been attempted. Whether success would be achieved, must be a matter of opinion, but that is not the point; and to us, the failure to conduct, or even attempt, any direct negotiations between the parties to the present dispute in their capacity as such, appears (having regard to the terms of Article 7) to constitute a formal bar to the present proceedings.

In our opinion the fourth preliminary objection must accordingly be upheld.

We shall conclude by pointing out that requirements about "disputes" and "negotiations" are not mere technicalities. They appear in one form or another in virtually every adjudication clause that has ever been drafted, and for good reason. They are inserted purposely to protect the parties, so far as possible, from international litigation that is unnecessary, premature, inadequately motivated, or merely specious. Without this measure of protection, countries would not sign clauses providing for compulsory adjudication. This is an aspect of the matter to which we feel insufficient attention has been given. Our final conclusion on the whole case is that, for all of the reasons stated, and in relation to each of the objections raised, whether on the grounds actually advanced by the Respondent State or on other grounds, the Court is not competent in this case, and should refuse to assume jurisdiction.

【本案评析】

以上案例讲述的是在国际诉讼之前进行的外交谈判与诉讼之间的关系，在诉讼前进行争端谈判的目的是保护诉讼当事国免受不必要的国际诉讼的干扰，节约裁判资源，促进当事国顺利解决争端。国家间争端一般通过谈判的方式解决，在该案件中，由于国家间未能通过谈判获得成果，转而向国际法院进行诉讼。由此可见，谈判也是解决国家间争端的重要方式。

【延伸阅读】

相关学术论著

1. Stephen J. Ware, *Alternative Dispute Resolution,* West Academic Publishing, 2016.

2. J.G. Merrills, *International Dispute Settlement,* fourth edition, Cambridge University Press, 2005.

3. 刘薇:《法律谈判实验教程》,中国政法大学出版社 2016 年版。

4. Russell Korobkin, *Negotiation Theory and Strategy,* second edition, Aspen Publishers, 2009.

5. Larry L. Tepley, *Legal Negotiation in a Nutshell,* second edition, West Group, 2005.

6. Charles B. Craver, Effective Legal Negotiation and Settlement, eight edition, Carolina Academic Press, 2016.

7. Charles B. Wiggins & Randy Lowry, *Negotiation and Settlement Advocacy,* second edition, West Academic Publishing, 2005.

第二节　国际商事争端谈判的过程

【知识背景 / 学习要点】

谈判通常都是从谈判前的准备开始，然后再与对方谈判代表进行面对面交流，包括先交换信息后提出和解方案，谈判的最后有可能达成和解协议，也有可能宣布陷入僵局。虽然谈判过程通常遵循此类顺序进行，但在实务中也并非严格按照此类过程进行，谈判者完全可能以不同的顺序来完成谈判，比如谈判方可能会在交换信息之前就提出自己的要求，或者在交换信息过程中提出要求。因此，做好谈判前的准备是参与争端谈判的首要任务。

一、准备阶段

在实务中，在谈判准备阶段谈判人员主要解决的问题有三个：第一是明确自身的处境和所需要的利益，第二是了解对方的处境和希望获得的利益，第三是将双方需要争取的利益进行综合分析。只有通过以上三个方面的考量，才能够达到事先就对这场谈判的结果有一定的把控与预知的效果和目的。

（一）“内部”准备

谈判的“内部”准备，也是谈判人员在准备阶段需要解决的首要问题，明确谈判者自身的处境与所需要的利益需要了解以下几点：第一，希望从谈判中得到什么；第二，可接受的底线是什么；第三，谈判成功最大的障碍是什么。[①]

无论是个人之间简单的互动式谈判，还是复杂的商务磋商或法律谈判，谈判人员都须进行精心的“内部”准备。“内部”准备一般是由谈判人员通过事先评估其获得的所有信息进行的，因为这些信息及其变化都会影响该谈判人员对此次谈判策略的判断。但是在实务中，更为复杂的“内部”谈判往往要采取更加复杂的方法。例如公司间的并购谈判，当事方可能会花费大量的精力在谈判前的准备上，包括评估一系列不同的合作安排与合同条款等事项。

（二）“外部”准备

“外部”准备，亦即谈判人员对谈判对方可能的愿望要求及备选方案的评估预测。与“内部”准备一样，“外部”准备在很大程度上也取决于谈判的背景，包括争端法复杂性与处理事项的数量等等。

此外，作为“外部”准备的一部分，谈判人员通常也要考虑如何在本方的目标和对方的需求之间找到利益的共同点，以便有可能达成互益的和解协议，或者预测哪种可能的和解条款是双方都能接受的，但这往往需要事先制定包括实质性的和程序性的各种谈判策略。

谈判的实质性策略，就是要在谈判的“外部”准备阶段就做到“知己知彼”，使得谈判人员在谈判进行中能够获得谈判的主动权，及时有效地分析对方开出的条件、理解让步过程中的细微差别，以及实现其谈判的目标。通过前期扎实的准备工作，确定自身的需要并能理解对方的需要，是提高谈判成功率的关键。但是实际上影响谈判达到最优结果的因素还有很多，因此谈判者在实质性的谈判策略准备方面，不宜将目标定得过高，良好的“外部”准备工作意味着谈判者要事前对谈判结果做出客观的评估。

谈判的程序性策略是在谈判的“外部”准备中就做到“胸有成竹”，要尽可能地根据本方的目标和利益，运用一定的谈判技巧，透过双方理解的沟通方式

① ［美］罗伊·列维奇：《商务谈判》，王健等译，中国人民大学出版社 2015 年版，第 500~501 页。

清晰地表达给对方，找出满足双方需要的解决方案。当然，谈判者事前仔细规划谈判的程序性策略非常重要，但是也必须注意不必在谈判开始前对每一个谈判步骤的策略做过度的规划，因为谈判不一定按照你所设定的步骤进行，谈判的节奏也可能并不符合常规。因此，在实务中，谈判的程序性策略的重点是，谈判人员要清晰地认识到自身的优势和弱点，以及需求和利益，同时也要弄清对方的这些情况，以便能够随着谈判的进行及时有效地做出调整。有些时候，回避和妥协也可能是恰当的策略，成熟的谈判人员会识别这些情况并采取恰当的战略战术。

二、进行阶段

谈判进入进行阶段前一般有一个开场过程，在该阶段，双方谈判人员一般会将本方谈判意图进行概括介绍，目的在于初步沟通必要信息，缓和双方谈判态度，增进双方信任度。要注意的是，开场过程中不能将本方谈判的意图和盘托出，某些关键性的利益诉求也不能在此过程中较快地明确提及，较为适宜做一些原则性的介绍。这个过程时间较短，所以在语言上讲求简洁明了，语速也不宜过快，做到坦率而自信。

由于受到准备阶段的限制，彻底做好“外部”准备具有一定的难度，继而影响和限制“内部”准备的效果发挥。因此在谈判进行阶段，双方仍需进一步发掘对方的利益诉求，比如利用抛出的各种问题或针锋相对的立场观点与对方进行交换。实际上，谈判进行阶段就是交换信息的过程。在争端谈判实务中，交换信息至关重要的目的就是处理信息，而这主要包括两个方面，即获取信息和披露信息。

（一）获取信息

如前所述，谈判人员一般都在准备阶段做好对谈判对方需求目标以及替代方案的预设和评估，但是毕竟谈判无法直接从对方获取一手资料，更不可能精确地估算谈判的结果，而且谈判双方人员在价值观和偏好等方面也存在差异性，因此在谈判进行阶段进一步获取信息对于谈判的顺利进行极为重要。

在谈判进行阶段获取的信息主要包括三种。第一种是谈判相对方的目的或意图，即对方的真实期望是什么，比如在争端谈判中，对方是只想通过谈判解决争议还是另有通过诉讼程序的打算，抑或是不通过谈判而直接选择诉讼。第二种是对方可达成和解的替代方案，以及对不同替代方案的看法与意图。第三种是与有助于达成和解结果相关的有价值的各种信息。

在争端谈判实务中，直截了当地询问对方以及简单直白地透露所需信息，不但可能会影响谈判的进行，甚至还会降低和解的可能。因此，谈判进行阶段要能够有效获取信息，需要具备一些特殊的技巧与能力。这要求谈判人员能够善于运用开放式提问与策略式追问的技巧，并且具备洞悉秋毫与巧妙诠释语言背后深刻意涵的能力。

（二）披露信息

谈判人员也必须通过披露一定数量信息的方式，以信息交换信息，从而获取更多对方的信息。在实务中，谈判方除了披露信息以告知对方自身的需求和目标外，还可以公开某些信息以说服对方变更其立场，甚至做出一定的让步。当然，除交换信息外，谈判者也要交换提议的和解方案。因此，信息披露又可分为两个过程，即提出初始信息请求和提出争端和解方案。

在实务中，和解谈判要能够顺利达成谈判结果，提出谈判的和解替代方案必不可少，因为在无法达成和解协议时，谈判者往往都可能用到这种替代性的最佳选择方案。此外，为了避免谈判受挫或者被迫接受事后看起来并不满意的谈判结果，谈判人员除了必须准备、适时提出和不断调整本方的和解替代方案外，还要弄清楚谈判对方的和解替代方案，并与本方的替代方案进行比较做出恰当的判断。因为如果本方的替代方案条件优于对方，那么谈判时会对本方有利，但若相差不大则谈判结果没有多少回旋余地，替代方案可能还需要另做调整。

因此，对于已经获取的对方和解替代方案的信息，谈判人员需要始终密切关注对方的和解替代方案，以弄清和保持本方的谈判优势，而且也要通过一定的暗示方式，不断提醒对方，其和解替代方案相较于他的而言具有哪些独特的优势。

三、结束阶段

一次争端谈判的结束，主要包括两种情况，即一种是双方达成了相关协议，另一种是谈判陷入了僵局或没有达成任何协议结果。谈判结束的最好结果是达成和解或者签署和解方案中的相关协议，但是客观而言，参与谈判的意图是因事或因人而异的，无论采用何种谈判方法，也无论当事方和解意愿多么强烈，或者讨论多长的时间，争端谈判往往还是不可避免地会出现达不成和解而陷入僵局的情况。从谈判实务中来看，前述后一种情况也并非是一种最坏的情况，因为有可能没有达成协议比达成了协议更具有价值，或者双方虽然陷入了僵局，但这种僵局将会促使双方反思原因，并采用其他替代方式来推进争端的解决。谈判形成僵局的主要原因是双方利益没有得到满足，当然也有可能有其他的一些原因。

比如，一方或双方都没有达成和解的真正意图，谈判人员只是在为了收集在另一次谈判中可以使用的信息而进行谈判。又比如，谈判一方或双方过于坚持本方的谈判底线，不愿意做出一定的让步，更有甚者只专注于捍卫本方的立场，不愿意为推进谈判进行妥协。但是，无论谈判进程陷入僵局的确切原因为何，只要双方都对达成和解抱有希望，那么僵局就可以被视为谈判过程中的一种暂时停止的解决方法，因为僵局相对于不欢而散而言还带有和解的可能。

在实务中，谈判陷入僵局一般有两种途径可以化解，第一种途径即仍然在谈判中，通过加深认知、情感交流或者设置行动方案等方式处理谈判僵局。[①]首先，对于谈判中的主要问题已经解决而只是受到某些个别问题的影响而陷入僵局的情况，对替代解决方案的认知加深可以改变谈判方对谈判前景的看法，特别是

① Russell Korobkin, *Negotiation Theory and Strategy*, second edition, Aspen Publishers, 2009. pp.158~165.

如果建立起了求同存异的认知对双方僵局的解决更有帮助。其次，对由于受到强烈的负面情绪，比如不礼貌的举动，谈判气氛变得异常紧张而导致的谈判僵局，可以通过情感交流等方式，包括邀请参与活动或者赔礼道歉等，改变谈判双方对于彼此的既定态度和感觉，进而在一定程度上缓解僵局氛围。最后，对于因为缺乏信任而导致的谈判僵局，可以通过设置行动方案的方式，将促进冲突解决的执行机制、履行和解协议等的具体方式或流程明确细化，进而减缓双方因彼此的不信任而导致的谈判僵局。

第二种途径是考虑采用谈判以外的其他替代性程序，反向推动或者刺激谈判的进行。比如在争端谈判中引入国际商事调解的方式，通过第三方参与的方式协助当事方形成谈判和解方案。同时亦可在谈判中试探性地提出诉讼或者其他替代性争端解决方法（ADR），供陷入僵局而找不到出路的谈判相对方比较不同争端解决办法的优劣，从而使其能够直面僵局与困境，重新进行争端谈判。

【案例摘录与评析】

中日汽车索赔谈判①

我国从日本S汽车公司进口的大批FP148货车在使用时普遍发生了严重质量问题，致使我国蒙受巨大经济损失。为此，我国向日方提出索赔。

谈判一开始，中方简明扼要地介绍了FP148货车在中国各地的损坏情况，以及用户对此的反映。中方在此虽然只字未提索赔问题，但是已为索赔说明了理由和事实根据，展示了中方的谈判威势，恰到好处地拉开了谈判的序幕。日方对中方的这一招早有预料，因为货车的质量问题是一个无法回避的事实，日方无心在这一不利的问题上纠缠。日方为避免劣势，便不动声色地说："是的，有的车子轮胎炸裂、车窗玻璃炸碎、电路有故障、铆钉震断，有的车架偶有裂

① 段淑梅：《商务谈判》，机械工业出版社2016年版，第23~26页。

纹。”中方觉察到对方的用意，便反驳道：“贵公司代表都到现场看过，经商检和专家小组鉴定，铆钉不是震断的，而是剪断的，车架出现的不仅仅是裂纹，而是裂缝、断裂！而车架断裂不能用‘有的’或‘偶有’，最好还是用比例数据表达，更科学、更准确。”日方淡然一笑说：“请原谅，比例数据尚未准确统计。”“那么，对货车质量问题，贵公司能否取得一致意见？”中方对这一关键问题紧追不舍。“中国的道路是有问题的。”日方转了话题，答非所问。中方立即反驳：“诸位已去过现场，这种说法是缺乏事实根据的。在设计时就应该考虑到中国的实际情况，因为这批车是专门为中国生产的。”中方步步紧逼，日方步步为营，谈判气氛渐趋紧张。双方在谈判开始不久，就在如何认定货车质量问题上陷入了僵局。日方坚持说中方有意夸大货车的质量问题：“货车质量的问题不至于到如此严重的程度吧？这对我们公司来说，是从未发生过的，也是不可理解的。”此时，中方觉得该是举证的时候了，将有关材料向对方一推说：“这里有商检、公证机关的公证结论，还有商检拍摄的录像。如果……”“不！不！对商检、公证机关的结论，我们是相信的，我们是说贵国是否能够做出适当让步；否则，我们无法向公司交代。”日方在中方所提质量问题的攻势下，及时调整了谈判方案，采用以柔克刚的手法，向对方踢皮球，但不管怎么说，日方在质量问题上设下的防线已被攻克了。这就为中方进一步提出索赔要求打开了缺口。随后，双方对FP148货车损坏归属问题取得了一致的意见。日方一位部长不得不承认，这属于设计和制作上的质量问题。初战告捷，但我方代表意识到更艰巨的较量还在后面，索赔金额的谈判才是根本性的。

随即，双方谈判的问题升级到索赔的具体金额上。报价、还价、提价、压价、比价，一场毅力和技巧较量的谈判展开了。中方主谈代表擅长经济管理和统计，精通测算。他翻阅了国内外许多有关资料，甚至在技术业务谈判中他也不凭大概和想当然，认为只有事实和科学的数据才能服人。因此，他纸笺上的大大小小的索赔项目旁写满了密密麻麻的阿拉伯数字——这就是技术业务谈判，不能凭大概，只能依靠科学、准确的计算。根据多年的经验，他不紧不慢地提出："贵公司对每辆车支付的加工费是多少？这项总额又是多少？""每辆 6 万日元，计 5.84 亿日元。"日方接着反问道："贵国报价是多少？"中方立即回答："每辆 16 万日元，此项共计 9.5 亿日元。"精明强干的日方主谈人淡然一笑，与其副手耳语了一阵，问："贵国报价的依据是什么？"中方主谈人将车辆损坏后各部件需要如何修理、加固，花费多少工时等逐一报价。"我们提出的这笔加工费并不高。"接着中方代表又用了欲擒故纵的一招："如果贵公司感到不合算，派人员维修也可以，但这样一来，贵公司的耗费恐怕是这个数的好几倍。"这一招很奏效，顿时把对方将住了。日方被中方如此精确的计算所折服，自知理亏，转而以恳切的态度征询："贵国能否再压低一点？"此刻，中方意识到，具体数目的实质性讨价还价开始了。中方答道："为了表示我们的诚意，可以考虑贵方的要求，那么，贵公司每辆出价多少呢？""12 万日元。"日方回答。"13.4 万日元怎么样？"中方问。"可以接受。"日方回答。日方深知，中方在这一问题上已做出让步。于是双方很快就此项索赔达成了协议。日方在此项目费用上共支付 7.76 亿日元。

然而，中日双方争论索赔的最大数额的项目却不在此，而在于高达几十亿日元的间接经济损失赔偿金。在这一巨大数目的索赔谈判中，日方率先发言。他们也采用了逐项报价的做法，报完一项就停一下，看看中方代表的反应，但他们的口气却好似报出的每一个数据都是不容打折扣的。最后，日方统计可以给中方支付赔偿金 30 亿日元。中方对日方的报价一直沉默不语，用心揣摩日方所报数据中的漏洞，把所有的"大概""大约""预计"等含糊不清的字眼都挑了出来，有力地抵制了对方所采用的浑水摸鱼的谈判手段。

在此之前，中方谈判班子昼夜奋战，电子计算机的荧光屏上不停跳动着各种数字。在谈判桌上，我方报完每个项目的金额后，都讲明这个数字测算的依据，在那些有理有据的数字上，打的都是惊叹号。最后我方提出间接经济损失费 70 亿日元。

日方代表听了这个数字后，惊得目瞪口呆，老半天说不出话来，连连说："差额太大，差额太大！”于是，进行无休止的报价和压价。

“贵国提的索赔额过高，若不压半，我们会被解雇的。我们是有妻儿老小的……”日方代表哀求着。老谋深算的日方主谈人使用了哀兵制胜的谈判策略。

“贵公司生产如此低劣的产品，给我国造成多么大的经济损失啊！”中方主谈接过日方的话头，顺水推舟地使用了欲擒故纵的一招，“我们不愿为难诸位代表，如果你们做不了主，请贵方决策人来与我们谈判”。双方各不相让，只好暂时休会。这种拉锯式的讨价还价，对双方来说是一场毅力和耐心的较量。因为在谈判桌上，率先让步的一方就可能陷入被动。

随后，日方代表急忙用电话与日本 S 公司的决策人密谈了数小时。接着谈判重新开始了，此轮谈判一开始就进入了高潮，双方舌战了几个回合，又沉默下来。此时，中方意识到己方毕竟是经济损失的实际承受者，如果谈判破裂，就会使己方已获得的谈判成果付诸东流。而要诉诸法律，麻烦就更大。为了使谈判已获得的成果得到巩固，并争取有新的突破，适当的让步是打开成功大门的钥匙。中方主谈人与助手们交换了一下眼色，率先打破沉默说：“如果贵公司真有诚意的话，彼此均可适当让步。”中方主谈人为了防止由于己方率先让步所带来的不利局面，建议双方采用“计分法”，即双方等量让步。“我公司愿意付 40 亿日元。”日方退了一步，并声称：“这是最高突破数了。”“我们希望贵公司最低限度必须支付 60 亿日元。”中方坚持说。

这样一来，中日双方各自从己方的立场上退让了 10 亿日元，双方比分相等，谈判又出现了转机。双方界守点之间仍有 20 亿日元的逆差。但一个界守点对双方来说，都是虚设的。更准确地说，这不过是双方一道最后的争取线。该如何解决这“百米赛跑”最后冲刺阶段的难题呢？ 双方的谈判专家都是精明的，谁也不愿看到一个前功尽弃的局面。几经周折，双方共同接受了由双方最后报价金额相加除以 2，即 50 亿日元的谈判方案。

除此之外，日方愿意承担下列三项责任：第一，确认出售给中国的全部 FP148 型货车为不合格品，同意全部退货，更换新车；第二，新车必须重新设计试验，精工细作，并请中方专家检查验收；第三，在新车未到之前，对旧车进行应急加固后继续使用，日方提供加固件和加固工具等。

一场罕见的特大索赔案终于公正地交涉成功了。

【本案评析】

以上“中日汽车索赔谈判”案例，说明了以下几点问题：

在谈判开始前，中方做了充足的准备，从全局的角度去充分创造、比较与衡量最佳的解决方案。在谈判过程中，几次陷入了僵局，中方作为实际经济损失的承受者，充分认识到了自己的处境，一次次主动地克服障碍，使双方顺利地达成协议，令损失最小化。

中方胜利最关键的一点在于充分地收集整理信息，用大量客观的数据给对方施加压力，不仅收集了大量的证据，还精确计算出具体的报价，以严谨的科学态度使对方无法反击，对客观标准做了恰到好处的运用。当然，除这几个原因之外，中方的胜利还在于多种谈判技巧的运用。第一，在谈判前，大量的准备，证据的合理使用；第二，在谈判中，依靠数据掌握谈判主动权；第三，在具体报价谈判中留有余地。

第三节　国际商事争端谈判的实务问题

【知识背景 / 学习要点】

一、国际商事争端谈判中的欺诈与恶意谈判

（一）谈判中的欺诈

在实际谈判过程中，谈判者时常需要根据谈判的进度、谈判对手的现实需求及声誉做出合适的谈判策略以促成合作的达成或者争端的解决。但在一些情况下，谈判者的谈判技巧会造成违反法律或受道德谴责的后果。许多谈判者试图通过不披露甚至隐瞒信息的方式维护己方的利益，并且认为这种行为是正常

的谈判策略，虽然存在欺骗但是并不违反法律。然而，谈判涉及合同法、侵权行为法、刑法等法律领域，能够明确的是，刑法与侵权行为法明确禁止使用暴力或欺诈等谈判手段达成目的。①

欺诈是指一方当事人故意捏造事实，以使对方陷入错误的意思表示并从中获取利益的行为。但在谈判实务中，欺诈行为的实施主体并不一定局限于谈判当事双方本人，也可能是其指定的委托代理人或律师等。在谈判过程中，若一方当事人欺诈性地对相关信息作出了虚假陈述，以诱导对方依据虚假信息采取了错误行动或不作为，从而给对方造成损失的，则该方当事人应当承担相应的法律责任。

在竞争性谈判中，谈判双方为各自的利益各不相让，竭尽全力达到己方利益最大化的目的。在这种情况下，谈判者在一定程度上会失去理智，过度使用谈判技巧，使其成为虚假、欺诈或胁迫的手段，因而影响谈判双方的关系，不利于双方的合作。在争端解决谈判中，上述欺诈现象较少出现，谈判双方虽也有各自利益上的矛盾和分歧，但为了解决争端，其更强调开诚布公地谈论自己的想法和要求，甚至可以做到与对方共享重要信息以便找到解决双方问题的有效途径，使双方合作的价值得以最大化。

（二）恶意谈判

恶意谈判指的是行为人并无与对方达成合意的诚意，以损害对方或他人的利益为目的进行磋商的行为。恶意谈判严重违反诚实信用原则。在实务中，恶意谈判的案件非常少见，一方面，谈判者大都秉承着善意进行谈判，但尽管如此，谈判者也应当具备判断对方的意图的能力，以洞察对方是否有意愿达成交易或解决争端。另一方面，恶意谈判与欺诈不同，法律对恶意谈判行为规定较少，现今大多仅从道德角度进行约束，进而，恶意谈判案件很少在司法领域出现。，但是也有例外，例如《国际商事合同通则》第 2.14 条（2）就对这种行为进行了规制："以恶意（非善意）进行谈判或者以恶意（非善意）突然中断谈判的

① Russell Korobkin, *Negotiation Theory and Strategy,* second edition, Aspen Publishers, 2009.

一方当事人应对另一方当事人造成的损失承担责任。”

【案例摘录与评析】

一、国际商事争端谈判中的欺诈诉讼案例[①]

Cresswell v. Sullivan & Cromwell
668 F. Supp. 166 (S.D.N.Y. 1987)

JUDGE SWEET delivered the opinion of the Court ...

[Plaintiffs originally brought suit against Prudential–Bache in connection with a financial transaction. In preparation for a possible trial, the parties conducted discovery.] In January 1985, plaintiffs in this action entered into agreements with Prudential-Bache which resolved all their claims for approximately $1,600,000. Following execution of those agreements, this court entered a judgment and order dismissing plaintiffs' claims with prejudice on February 1, 1985 .

... [P]laintiffs now contend that during the pendency of the prior actions, Prudential-Bache and [its attorneys] Sullivan & Cromwell intentionally withheld production of documents which purportedly fell within the ambit of a document request served in December 1983. ...

The plaintiffs in this case are seeking damages for an alleged fraud committed upon them in the earlier actions, which they contend induced them to settle their claims for less than they otherwise would have been able to obtain. The issue raised on this motion is governed by Rule 60(b) of the Federal Rules of Civil Procedure. Rule 60(b) specifies the procedure for obtaining relief from a judgment when fraud or other misconduct has allegedly been committed in connection with obtaining the judgment. Under that Rule:

The court may relieve a party or his legal representative from a final judgment, order, or proceeding for the following reasons: ... (3) fraud (whether heretofore denominated intrinsic or extrinsic), misrepresentation, or other misconduct of an adverse party. ... The motion shall be made within a reasonable time, and ... not more than one year after the judgment, order, or proceeding was entered or taken ... This rule does not limit the power of a court to entertain an independent action to relieve a party from a judgment, order, or proceeding, ... or to set aside a

① Cresswell v. Sullivan & Cromwell, *United States District Court for the Southern District of New York*, July 31, 1987, Decided ; August 3, 1987, Filed, No. 87 Civ. 2685 (RWS).

judgment for fraud upon the court.

The Rule thus sets forth an express mechanism for a party seeking relief from a judgment. If plaintiffs' action fell under Rule 60, plaintiffs would essentially be suing for rescission and presumably would be required to tender back their part of the settlement to return to the status quo and possibly face preclusion from suing for damages. The plaintiffs here, however, are not seeking "relief" from a "judgment" within the terms of Rule 60(b). Instead, they seek to affirm the judgment of settlement, and sue for additional damages caused only by the fraud involving the failure to produce certain documents. Of course, in trying such a case, the merits of the prior actions will be relevant, but the issue will be different: whether the settlement value of the cases would have been higher without the fraud, and if so, by how much.

Defendants contend that Rule 60(b) is the exclusive remedy for a party claiming to have been defrauded into agreeing to a settlement leading to entry of a judgment or final order in a federal lawsuit. The proper avenue of redress for a party seeking relief from a judgment claiming fraud as grounds for relief is under Fed. R. Civ. P. 60(b) (3) .

... [N]othing in the language of Rule 60(b) supports the defendants' contention that it precludes an action for fraud in connection with a settlement. Rule 60(b) denotes instances when a court "may relieve a party ... from a judgment," but it does not purport to cover damages actions for fraud that seek to affirm or ratify a judgment rather than seek relief from a judgment. Its focus is on a specific remedy obtaining relief from a judgement—not on all available remedies for fraud. Neither party disputes that under New York law, a second action for damages rather than for rescission of the judgment or settlement may be brought when a state court judgment or settlement is allegedly procured by fraud. ... This result arises from the common law rule that a defrauded party can elect between rescission on the one hand and ratification and suit for damages on the other. ...

In Slatkin v. Citizens Casualty Co., 614 F.2d 301 (2d Cir.), cert. denied, 449 U.S. 981 66 L. Ed. 2d 243, 101 S. Ct. 395 (1980), the Second Circuit noted that New York law is "clear that one who has been induced by fraudulent misrepresentation to settle a claim may recover damages without rescinding the settlement." Id. at 312 (citing cases) ...

If all that will result from a misrepresentation is a new trial, then the party making it has everything to gain and nothing to lose. The plaintiffs would be placed at a disadvantage by a new trial: the defendants would not. If anything, defendants would benefit by having a preview of plaintiffs' case. ...

According to the defendants, a reasonable reading of Rule 60(b) would limit the plaintiffs to a suit to reopen the judgment to put plaintiffs and defendants back in the position they were in prior to settlement. ...

If this were the rule few plaintiffs would choose to enforce their claims of fraud in connection with a settlement. No matter how valid their cause of action. A plaintiff who must give up any benefit he has gained and risk receiving nothing in return will be reluctant to enforce his rights as a victim of fraud. Of course, he may ultimately gain more than he received in settlement the first time, either by going to trial this time around or settling for more, allowing negotiation to set a value on the second alleged instance of fraud. But this chance of receiving more does not justify the deterrent effect of requiring a plaintiff to give up the settlement he received for one claim of fraud to sue for further acts of fraud.

【本案评析】

上述案件表明，欺诈会引起合同无效与侵权责任。在合同法领域，谈判者的欺诈或重大失实陈述诱使对方进行交易，由此达成的合同无效。在侵权行为法领域，欺诈性失实陈述将引起因该虚假陈述造成损失的损害赔偿责任。在谈判中，律师也受到专业纪律的约束，防止其实施欺诈行为。值得注意的是，即使是无意的失实陈述也可能导致法律制裁，因此，在谈判过程中应当注意恰当地运用谈判技巧，以诚信为基础，不可将谈判变成虚假、欺诈和胁迫的手段。

二、恶意谈判诉讼案例①

Hoffman v. Red Owl Stores, Inc.
Judges: Currie, C. J.
Opinion by: Currie, C. J.

The instant appeal and cross appeal present these questions:

(1) Whether this court should recognize causes of action grounded on promissory estoppel as exemplified by sec. 90 of Restatement, 1 Contracts?

(2) Do the facts in this case make out a cause of action for promissory estoppel?

(3) Are the jury's findings with respect to damages sustained by the evidence?

Recognition of a Cause of Action Grounded on Promissory Estoppel.

---

① Hoffman v. Red Owl Stores, Inc. Supreme Court of Wisconsin February 5, 1965, Argued ; March 2, 1965, Decided No Number in Original.

Sec. 90 of Restatement, 1 Contracts, provides (at p. 110):

"A promise which the promisor should reasonably expect to induce action or forbearance of a definite and substantial character on the part of the promisee and which does induce such action or forbearance is binding if injustice can be avoided only by enforcement of the promise."

The Wisconsin Annotations to Restatement, Contracts, prepared under the direction of the late Professor William H. Page and issued in 1933, stated (at p. 53, sec. 90):

"The Wisconsin cases do not seem to be in accord with this section of the Restatement. It is certain that no such proposition has ever been announced by the Wisconsin court and it is at least doubtful if it would be approved by the court."

Since 1933, the closest approach this court has made to adopting the rule of the Restatement occurred in the recent case of Lazarus v. American Motors Corp. (1963), 21 Wis. (2d) 76, 85, 123 N. W. (2d) 548, wherein the court stated:

"We recognize that upon different facts it would be possible for a seller of steel to have altered his position so as to effectuate the equitable considerations inherent in sec. 90 of the Restatement."

While it was not necessary to the disposition of the Lazarus Case to adopt the promissory-estoppel rule of the Restatement, we are squarely faced in the instant case with that issue. Not only did the trial court frame the special verdict on the theory of sec. 90 of Restatement, 1 Contracts, but no other possible theory has been presented to or discovered by this court which would permit plaintiffs to recover. Of other remedies considered that of an action for fraud and deceit seemed to be the most comparable. An action at law for fraud, however, cannot be predicated on unfulfilled promises unless the promisor possessed the present intent not to perform. Suskey v. Davidoff (1958), 2 Wis. (2d) 503, 507, 87 N. W. (2d) 306, and cases cited. Here, there is no evidence that would support a finding that Lukowitz made any of the promises, upon which plaintiffs' complaint is predicated, in bad faith with any present intent that they would not be fulfilled by Red Owl.

Many courts of other jurisdictions have seen fit over the years to adopt the principle of promissory estoppel, and the tendency in that direction continues.① As Mr. Justice McFaddin,

① Among the many cases which have granted relief grounded upon promissory estoppel are: Goodman v. Dicker (D. C., D. C. 1948), 169 Fed. (2d) 684; Drennan v. Star Paving Co. (1958), 51 Cal. (2d) 409, 333 Pac. (2d) 757; Van Hook v. Southern California Waiters Alliance (1958), 158 Cal. App. (2d) 556, 323 Pac. (2d) 212; Chrysler Corp. v. Quimby (1958), 51 Del. 264, 144 Atl. (2d) 123, 144 Atl. (2d) 885; Lusk-Harbison-Jones, Inc., v. Universal Credit Co. (1933), 164 Miss. 693, 145 So. 623; Feinberg v. Pfeiffer Co. (Mo. App. 1959), 322 S. W. (2d) 163; Schafer v. Fraser (1955), 206 Or. 446, 290 Pac. (2d) 190, 294 Pac. (2d) 609; Northwestern Engineering Co. v. Ellerman (1943), 69 S. D. 397, 10 N. W. (2d) 879.

speaking in behalf of the Arkansas court, well stated, that the development of the law of promissory estoppel "is an attempt by the courts to keep remedies abreast of increased moral consciousness of honesty and fair representations in all business dealings." Peoples National Bank of Little Rock v. Linebarger Construction Co. (1951), 219 Ark. 11, 17, 240 S. W. (2d) 12. For a further discussion of the doctrine of promissory estoppel, see 1A Corbin, Contracts, pp. 187 et seq., secs. 193-209; 3 Pomeroy's Equity Jurisprudence (5th ed.), pp. 211 et seq., sec. 808b; 1 Williston, Contracts (Jaeger's 3d ed.), pp. 607 et seq., sec. 140; Boyer, Promissory Estoppel: Requirements and Limitations of the Doctrine, 98 University of Pennsylvania Law Review (1950), 459; Seavey, Reliance Upon Gratuitous Promises or Other Conduct, 64 Harvard Law Review (1951), 913; Annos. 115 A. L. R. 152, and 48 A. L. R. (2d) 1069.

The Restatement avoids use of the term "promissory estoppel," and there has been criticism of it as an inaccurate term. See 1A Corbin, Contracts, p. 232 et seq., sec. 204. On the other hand, Williston advocated the use of this term or something equivalent. 1 Williston, Contracts (1st ed.), p. 308, sec. 139. Use of the word "estoppel" to describe a doctrine upon which a party to a lawsuit may obtain affirmative relief offends the traditional concept that estoppel merely serves as a shield and cannot serve as a sword to create a cause of action. See Utschig v. McClone (1962), 16 Wis. (2d) 506, 509, 114 N. W. (2d) 854. "Attractive nuisance" is also a much-criticized term. See concurring opinion, Flamingo v. Waukesha (1952), 262 Wis. 219, 227, 55 N. W. (2d) 24. However, the latter term is still in almost universal use by the courts because of the lack of a better substitute. The same is also true of the wide use of the term "promissory estoppel." We have employed its use in this opinion not only because of its extensive use by other courts but also since a more-accurate equivalent has not been devised.

Because we deem the doctrine of promissory estoppel, as stated in sec. 90 of Restatement, 1 Contracts, is one which supplies a needed tool which courts may employ in a proper case to prevent injustice, we endorse and adopt it.

Applicability of Doctrine to Facts of this Case.

The record here discloses a number of promises and assurances given to Hoffman by Lukowitz in behalf of Red Owl upon which plaintiffs relied and acted upon to their detriment.

Foremost were the promises that for the sum of $ 18,000 Red Owl would establish Hoffman in a store. After Hoffman had sold his grocery store and paid the $ 1,000 on the Chilton lot, the $ 18,000 figure was changed to $ 24,100. Then in November, 1961, Hoffman was assured that if the $ 24,100 figure were increased by $ 2,000 the deal would go through. Hoffman was induced to sell his grocery store fixtures and inventory in June, 1961, on the promise that he would be in his new store by fall. In November, plaintiffs sold their bakery building on the urging of defendants and on the assurance that this was the last step necessary to have the deal with Red Owl go through.

We determine that there was ample evidence to sustain the answers of the jury to the questions of the verdict with respect to the promissory representations made by Red Owl, Hoffman's reliance thereon in the exercise of ordinary care, and his fulfilment of the conditions required of him by the terms of the negotiations had with Red Owl.

There remains for consideration the question of law raised by defendants that agreement was never reached on essential factors necessary to establish a contract between Hoffman and Red Owl. Among these were the size, cost, design, and layout of the store building; and the terms of the lease with respect to rent, maintenance, renewal, and purchase options. This poses the question of whether the promise necessary to sustain a cause of action for promissory estoppel must embrace all essential details of a proposed transaction between promisor and promisee so as to be the equivalent of an offer that would result in a binding contract between the parties if the promisee were to accept the same.

Originally the doctrine of promissory estoppel was invoked as a substitute for consideration rendering a gratuitous promise enforceable as a contract. See Williston, Contracts (1st ed.), p. 307, sec. 139. In other words, the acts of reliance by the promisee to his detriment provided a substitute for consideration. If promissory estoppel were to be limited to only those situations where the promise giving rise to the cause of action must be so definite with respect to all details that a contract would result were the promise supported by consideration, then the defendants' instant promises to Hoffman would not meet this test. However, sec. 90 of Restatement, 1 Contracts, does not impose the requirement that the promise giving rise to the cause of action must be so comprehensive in scope as to meet the requirements of an offer that would ripen into a contract if accepted by the promisee. Rather the conditions imposed are:

(1) Was the promise one which the promisor should reasonably expect to induce action or forbearance of a definite and substantial character on the part of the promisee?

(2) Did the promise induce such action or forbearance?

(3) Can injustice be avoided only by enforcement of the promise?[①]

We deem it would be a mistake to regard an action grounded on promissory estoppel as the equivalent of a breach-of-contract action. As Dean Boyer points out, it is desirable that fluidity in the application of the concept be maintained. 98 University of Pennsylvania Law Review (1950), 459, at page 497. While the first two of the above listed three requirements of promissory estoppel present issues of fact which ordinarily will be resolved by a jury, the third requirement,

---

① See Boyer, *98 University of Pennsylvania Law Review* (1950), 459, 460. "Enforcement" of the promise embraces an award of damages for breach as well as decreeing specific performance.

that the remedy can only be invoked where necessary to avoid injustice, is one that involves a policy decision by the court. Such a policy decision necessarily embraces an element of discretion.

We conclude that injustice would result here if plaintiffs were not granted some relief because of the failure of defendants to keep their promises which induced plaintiffs to act to their detriment.

Damages.

Defendants attack all the items of damages awarded by the jury.

The bakery building at Wautoma was sold at defendants' instigation in order that Hoffman might have the net proceeds available as part of the cash capital he was to invest in the Chilton store venture. The evidence clearly establishes that it was sold at a loss of $ 2,000. Defendants contend that half of this loss was sustained by Mrs. Hoffman because title stood in joint tenancy. They point out that no dealings took place between her and defendants as all negotiations were had with her husband. Ordinarily only the promisee and not third persons are entitled to enforce the remedy of promissory estoppel against the promisor. However, if the promisor actually foresees, or has reason to foresee, action by a third person in reliance on the promise, it may be quite unjust to refuse to perform the promise. 1A Corbin, Contracts, p. 220, sec. 200. Here not only did defendants foresee that it would be necessary for Mrs. Hoffman to sell her joint interest in the bakery building, but defendants actually requested that this be done. We approve the jury's award of $ 2,000 damages for the loss incurred by both plaintiffs in this sale.

Defendants attack on two grounds the $ 1,000 awarded because of Hoffman's payment of that amount on the purchase price of the Chilton lot. The first is that this $ 1,000 had already been lost at the time the final negotiations with Red Owl fell through in January, 1962, because the remaining $ 5,000 of purchase price had been due on October 15, 1961. The record does not disclose that the lot owner had foreclosed Hoffman's interest in the lot for failure to pay this $ 5,000. The $ 1,000 was not paid for the option, but had been paid as part of the purchase price at the time Hoffman elected to exercise the option. This gave him an equity in the lot which could not be legally foreclosed without affording Hoffman an opportunity to pay the balance. The second ground of attack is that the lot may have had a fair market value of $ 6,000, and Hoffman should have paid the remaining $ 5,000 of purchase price. We determine that it would be unreasonable to require Hoffman to have invested an additional $ 5,000 in order to protect the $ 1,000 he had paid. Therefore, we find no merit to defendants' attack upon this item of damages.

We also determine it was reasonable for Hoffman to have paid $ 125 for one month's rent of a home in Chilton after defendants assured him everything would be set when plaintiff sold the bakery building. This was a proper item of damage.

Plaintiffs never moved to Chilton because defendants suggested that Hoffman get some experience by working in a Red Owl store in the Fox River Valley. Plaintiffs, therefore, moved to Neenah instead of Chilton. After moving, Hoffman worked at night in an Appleton bakery but held himself available for work in a Red Owl store. The $ 140 moving expense would not have been incurred if plaintiffs had not sold their bakery building in Wautoma in reliance upon defendants' promises. We consider the $ 140 moving expense to be a proper item of damage.

We turn now to the damage item with respect to which the trial court granted a new trial, i.e., that arising from the sale of the Wautoma grocery-store fixtures and inventory for which the jury awarded $ 16,735. The trial court ruled that Hoffman could not recover for any loss of future profits for the summer months following the sale on June 6, 1961, but that damages would be limited to the difference between the sales price received and the fair market value of the assets sold, giving consideration to any goodwill attaching thereto by reason of the transfer of a going business. There was no direct evidence presented as to what this fair market value was on June 6, 1961. The evidence did disclose that Hoffman paid $ 9,000 for the inventory, added $ 1,500 to it and sold it for $ 10,000 or a loss of $ 500. His 1961 federal income-tax return showed that the grocery equipment had been purchased for $ 7,000 and sold for $ 7,955.96. Plaintiffs introduced evidence of the buyer that during the first eleven weeks of operation of the grocery store his gross sales were $ 44,000 and his profit was $ 6,000 or roughly 15 percent. On cross-examination he admitted that this was gross and not net profit. Plaintiffs contend that in a breach-of-contract action damages may include loss of profits. However, this is not a breach-of-contract action.

The only relevancy of evidence relating to profits would be with respect to proving the element of goodwill in establishing the fair market value of the grocery inventory and fixtures sold. Therefore, evidence of profits would be admissible to afford a foundation for expert opinion as to fair market value.

Where damages are awarded in promissory estoppel instead of specifically enforcing the promisor's promise, they should be only such as in the opinion of the court are necessary to prevent injustice. Mechanical or rule-of-thumb approaches to the damage problem should be avoided. In discussing remedies to be applied by courts in promissory estoppel we quote the following views of writers on the subject:

"Enforcement of a promise does not necessarily mean Specific Performance. It does not necessarily mean Damages for breach. Moreover the amount allowed as Damages may be determined by the plaintiff's expenditures or change of position in reliance as well as by the value to him of the promised performance. Restitution is also an 'enforcing' remedy, although it is often said to be based upon some kind of a rescission. In determining what justice requires, the court must remember all of its powers, derived from equity, law merchant, and other sources, as well as the common law. Its decree should be molded accordingly." 1A Corbin, Contracts, p. 221, sec. 200.

"The wrong is not primarily in depriving the plaintiff of the promised reward but in causing the plaintiff to change position to his detriment. It would follow that the damages should not exceed the loss caused by the change of position, which would never be more in amount, but might be less, than the promised reward." Seavey, Reliance on Gratuitous Promises or Other Conduct, 64 Harvard Law Review (1951), 913, 926.

"There likewise seems to be no positive legal requirement, and certainly no legal policy, which dictates the allowance of contract damages in every case where the defendant's duty is consensual." Shattuck, Gratuitous Promises-- A New Writ?, 35 Michigan Law Review (1936), 908, 912.①

At the time Hoffman bought the equipment and inventory of the small grocery store at Wautoma he did so in order to gain experience in the grocery-store business. At that time discussion had already been had with Red Owl representatives that Wautoma might be too small for a Red Owl operation and that a larger city might be more desirable. Thus Hoffman made this purchase more or less as a temporary experiment. Justice does not require that the damages awarded him, because of selling these assets at the behest of defendants, should exceed any actual loss sustained measured by the difference between the sales price and the fair market value.

Since the evidence does not sustain the large award of damages arising from the sale of the Wautoma grocery business, the trial court properly ordered a new trial on this issue.

By the Court. — Order affirmed. Because of the cross appeal, plaintiffs shall be limited to taxing but two thirds of their costs.

【本案评析】

上述案件是恶意谈判的典型案例，是少见的法院对恶意谈判进行责任划分的案例。由于被告未信守诺言，而这一行为使原告采取了使其利益受损的行动，不让原告得到救济是不公平的。可见，如若一方当事人无论出于何种目的（根本没有达成交易或解决纠纷的意愿或其他原因）违反诚实信用，恶意对另一方当事人的利益造成损害，应当对损害承担责任。

① For expression of the opposite view, that courts in promissory-estoppel cases should treat them as ordinary breach of contract cases and allow the full amount of damages recoverable in the latter, see note, 13 *Vanderbilt Law Review* (1960), 705.

二、国际商事争端谈判的保密

实现谈判目的的前提是谈判双方能够进行自由的信息沟通，而保障谈判双方能够毫无顾忌并畅所欲言的正是其交流内容的保密性，特别是只有向对方披露较为敏感信息时才能获得解决方案之时。因为有保密的约束和限制，使得谈判方无需考虑信息被泄露的问题，因此才更有可能向对方透露其核心利益诉求，从而利于谈判目的的实现。因此，在某种程度上，保密是谈判得以顺利进行的前提和基础。例如，世界贸易组织争端解决机制中的磋商程序，实际上就是一种充分利用保密原理设计的争端谈判，目的是通过这种必经的程序尽最大可能促成争端双方快速和解。

即使谈判方愿意向对方透露敏感信息，其亦会担心信息为第三人所知，如果信息被公开，将会给信息泄露方造成经济损失。因此，签署保密协议是谈判开始前或谈判期间需要进行的重要环节。

保密协议作为一种确保谈判中的信息不会“离开房间”的合同，在谈判开始时，谈判双方可进行商定，在谈判期间的任何信息均应保密。保密协议在一般情况下具有强制执行力，[①]但若谈判未达成和解，一旦进入诉讼程序，谈判方可以在诉讼中将保密信息作为证据提出。可见，诉讼中的相关要求较合同而言更具有强制力。此外，保密协议仅对签署协议者有约束力，其并不能完全杜绝任何第三人通过其他途径知晓保密信息。

为防止谈判期间的获得秘密作为证据在诉讼中被利用来损害到谈判方的利益，国内争端的双方当事人可申请法院对在谈判中披露的所有保密信息或材料予以密封存档，除非当事人有足够的证据证明其对保密信息有实质需要或申请未予以通过。当然在国际争端解决实务中，相关国际协定也可以通过程序规则对此予以规制，比如《关于争端解决规则与程序的谅解》第 4.6 条规定：“磋商应保密，并不得损害任何一方在任何进一步诉讼中的权利。”

① Wayne D. Brazil, *Protecting the Confidentiality of Settlement Negotiations*, 39 Hastings L.J. 955, 1026-29 (1988).

若双方当事人达成一致，签订和解协议解决纠纷，当事人双方在很大程度上会要求对和解协议的条款进行保密，[①] 大多数和解协议中都包含规定当事方、代理律师对和解协议的内容进行保密的条款。[②] 和解协议中的保密条款一般可以在因违反和解协议中的规定而提起的诉讼中强制执行，就和解协议作出判决可增加保密条款的可执行性。但即使在这种情况下，保密协议中的保密条款仍然不保护非当事人的信息披露。

【案例摘录与评析】

国际商事争端谈判中的和解协议的保密案例[③]

TES Franchising, LLC v. Feldman

Judges: Carmen L. Lopez, Judge.

Opinion by: Carmen L. Lopez

Opinion

MEMORANDUM OF DECISION APPLICATION FOR PRE-JUDGMENT REMEDY (# 113)

I. PROCEDURAL HISTORY

The plaintiff, TES Franchising, LLC (TES), based in Connecticut, operates a franchising business under the name "The Entrepreneur Source." Terry Powell is the founder and Chief Operating Officer of TES. The defendant, Richard Feldman, owned and operated a TES franchise in the state of California. A dispute arose between the parties and on February 2, 2005, the dispute was resolved by way of a settlement agreement.

On July 21, 2005, TES filed an application to show cause and a motion for exparte temporary injunction against the defendant (# 101). In this application, TES alleged that Feldman had violated the terms of the settlement agreement by disclosing confidential information. In addition, TES

① Blanca Fromm, Comment, Bringing Settlement Out of the Shadows: Information About Settlement in an Age of Confidentiality, 48 *UCLA L.Rev.* 663, 676 (2001).

② Laurie Kratky Dore, Secrecy by Consent: The Use and Limits of Confidentiality in the Pursuit of Settlement, 74 *Notre Dame L. Rev.* 283, pp.384~386 (1999).

③ TES Franchising, LLC v. Feldman, 2006 Conn. Super. Superior Court of Connecticut, Judicial District of New Haven, At New Haven February 2, 2006, Decided ; February 2, 2006, Filed CV05401319S.

filed a complaint seeking damages and injunctive relief.

On October 13 and 14, 2005, the court (Lopez, J.) held an evidentiary hearing on the application to show cause. The court granted [*2] the motion for a temporary injunction and ordered Feldman to abide by the terms of the settlement agreement, in particular the confidentiality provisions of the said agreement.

On October 13, 2005, while the application for a temporary injunction was being heard, TES filed an application for a pre-judgment remedy (# 112). In this application, TES is seeking to secure the sum of at least $ 245,000.00. The application for PJR was not presented or discussed during the evidentiary hearing on the application to show cause.

On January 9, 2006, the court held an evidentiary hearing on the application for PJR.

During this hearing, counsel for TES made an oral motion to increase the amount of the PJR sought from $ 245,000 to $ 500,000.

II. FACTS

Terry Powell is the founder and Chief Executive Officer of TES. He currently operates 280 franchises of this business throughout the United States. On July 11, 2002, he entered into a consultant franchise agreement with Richard Feldman. This agreement is a thirty-five-(35)-page document with three schedules attached and referred to as Schedules 1, 2 and 3. Pursuant to the terms of the franchise agreement, Feldman was permitted to do business [*3] as the Entrepreneurs Source, which is a federally registered trademark.

This agreement is a comprehensive document that sets forth the duties and obligations of the parties as well as their rights. Section ten of the agreement, entitled "Confidential Information," sets forth the restrictions on the use of confidential information. Essentially, the franchisee is precluded from divulging any "confidential information, knowledge or know-how concerning the operation, products, services, procedures, policies or customers of the Franchised Business or the TES System."

As part of the franchising agreement, the franchisee is given an Operations Manual, a CD Rom containing a confidential software package and a Pre-Training Manual. The franchisee is required to sign an acknowledgement indicating that he has received the material. This acknowledgement also contains a notice in large print that states that the material is confidential. There are three of these acknowledgments, each of which have been signed [*4] by Feldman.

Sometime in 2004 a dispute arose between the parties. This dispute was settled on February 2005, when the parties signed a "Settlement, Release, Confidentiality and Non Disclosure Agreement." The parties were each represented by counsel at the time that the settlement agreement was signed. The agreement is very comprehensive and describes in detail the course of conduct to be carried on by the parties after the separation.

Pursuant to the terms of the agreement, Feldman received a sum of money in exchange for a "full settlement and release and discharge" of TES "from any and all actions, causes of action, suits charges and obligations... covenants, contracts, controversies, agreements, promises, variances... claims and demands whatsoever, in law or equity, which against" TES, Feldman [*5] "ever had, now have or hereafter can, shall or may have for, upon or by reason of any matter, cause or thing whatsoever from the beginning of time to the date of this settlement agreement."

In paragraph 3d of the settlement agreement, Feldman agreed "not to make any disparaging remarks about," TES and TES agreed to not make any disparaging remarks against Feldman. This paragraph further sets forth that if Feldman is contacted by anyone concerning his departure from the company he should respond by saying, "I am in the process of exiting the TES system and after that will no longer be associated with TES. I feel that TES treated me fairly and we were able to work out a reasonable exit strategy for my business."

In the agreement, Feldman also agreed that he would not divulge any confidential information to anyone. Should he violate any of the terms of the agreement, for each violation he agreed to pay TES an amount equal to the current consultant initial [*6] franchise fee, which is currently $ 49,000.00.

On June 27, 2005, TES received a letter from the State of Michigan, Department of the Attorney General, Consumer Protection Division, Franchise Section. This letter advised TES that a complaint had been filed by Feldman with their office. The letter enclosed the complaint, which was contained in a copy of an email dated June 19, 2005. In this email, Feldman lists a number of grievances against TES. He also states that he "hired the law firm of Mario Herman ... to negotiate a settlement agreement ... I signed the settlement agreement under duress because I desperately needed the [money] being withheld to purchase an investment property."

The Michigan Attorney General asked TES to respond to the complaint within fifteen days of receipt of the letter. TES considered Feldman's complaint a violation of the settlement agreement.

In July 2005, TES learned that Feldman had sent emails complaining about TES to other state regulatory [*7] agencies throughout the United States. TES considered these communications additional violations of the settlement agreement. TES filed an application with the Superior Court for an injunction to enjoin Feldman from continuing to violate the settlement agreement.

During the hearing on the application for the injunction, Feldman testified that he had contacted at least thirty states to complain about TES practices. As stated in Part I of this memorandum, the court granted the temporary injunction and ordered Feldman to comply with the terms of the agreement.

TES claims that a PJR should issue in the amount of $ 500,000. This amount is based on at least ten separate violations of the settlement agreement. TES argues that each email sent to a regulatory agency is a violation which triggers the $ 49,000.00 penalty clause. In addition, TES has incurred several hundred thousand dollars of additional legal fees in connection with the complaints filed by Feldman around the country. TES has also incurred [*8] legal fees in prosecuting this pending complaint.

III. STANDARD OF REVIEW

General Statutes § 52-278d(a) provides in relevant part that a hearing on a prejudgment remedy "shall be limited to a determination of (1) whether or not there is probable cause that a judgment in the amount of the prejudgment remedy sought, or in an amount greater than the amount of the prejudgment remedy sought, taking into account any defenses, counterclaims or set-offs, will be rendered in the matter in favor of the plaintiff ... If the court, upon consideration of the facts before it and taking into account any defenses, counterclaims or set-offs ... finds that the plaintiff has shown probable cause that such a judgment will be rendered in the matter in the plaintiff's favor in the amount of the prejudgment remedy sought and finds that a prejudgment remedy securing the judgment should be granted, the prejudgment remedy applied for shall be granted as requested or modified by the [*9] court ... " Rafferty v. Noto Bros. Construction, LLC, 68 Conn.App. 685, 688, 795 A.2d 1274 (2002)

"Appellate review of a trial court's broad discretion to deny or grant a prejudgment remedy is limited to a determination of whether the trial court's rulings constituted clear error." State v. Ham, 253 Conn. 566, 568, 755 A.2d 176 (2000).

"The legal idea of probable cause is a bona fide belief in the existence of the facts essential under the law for the action and such as would warrant a [person] of ordinary caution, prudence and judgment, under the circumstances, in entertaining it ... Probable cause is a flexible common sense standard ... It does not demand that a belief be correct or more likely true than false ... " Morris v. Cee Dee, LLC, 90 Conn.App. 403, 411, 877 A.2d 899 (2005).

"Prejudgment remedy proceedings are not involved with the adjudication of the merits of the action brought by the plaintiff or with the progress or result of that adjudication. They are only concerned with whether and to what extent the plaintiff is entitled to have property of the defendant held in the custody of the law pending adjudication [*10] of the merits of that action." (Internal quotation marks omitted.) Morris v. Cee Dee, LLC, supra, 411-12.

IV. ISSUES IN DISPUTE

TES argues that a PJR should issue because Feldman has violated the terms of settlement agreement entered into between the parties on February 2, 2005. According to TES, Feldman has not only disclosed confidential information about TES and about the terms of the settlement agreement, but he has made disparaging remarks about TES. These actions, argues TES, are blatant violations of the settlement agreement and have caused TES to suffer damages.

TES further argues that it has established probable cause that a judgment will be rendered in its favor. In support of this argument, TES points to the fact that on October 14, 2005, the court granted a temporary injunction on the same facts as those presented in the PJR application. TES argues that since the court has already found likelihood of success on the merits on the application for the injunction, the court has necessarily found probable cause to establish a liability.

Feldman argues that a PJR cannot issue on the facts presented in this case. He argues that notwithstanding the existence [*11] of a settlement agreement setting forth the conditions under which any information about the settlement agreement or the operation of the business can be divulged by him, he has absolute immunity for any statements he has made. Feldman claims that since any disclosure made by him was made to regulatory and/or governmental agencies, he is immune from any liability.

Feldman asserts three additional reasons why a PJR should not be granted. First, Feldman denies that he has made any disparaging remarks about TES. Secondly, he claims that any information that he has divulged does not rise to the level of confidential information. Finally, Feldman asserts that the settlement agreement is invalid. In support of his claim that the settlement agreement is invalid, Feldman argues that TES breached the settlement agreement first and therefore he cannot enforce it against Feldman.

Feldman also argues that a PJR cannot issue because once the court takes into account his counterclaims, defenses as well as his setoff, the court will be precluded from entering judgment for the plaintiff.

V. DISCUSSION

A review of the defenses presented by Feldman, as well as his counterclaims, is necessary [*12] before the court can determine if there is probable cause to issue a prejudgment remedy. These defenses and counterclaims were presented orally and in a memorandum of law in opposition to the motion for prejudgment remedy.

First of all, Feldman does not deny that he made statements to regulatory agencies and to others about the terms of the settlement agreement as well as about TES. Nor does he deny that he initiated the contact with the agencies. At no time does he state that he was subpoenaed to respond to inquiries from a state agency. On the contrary, he states that the agencies contacted him only after he communicated with them. He maintains that in making these communications to governmental agencies, he is immune from liability because they were stated in the context of a quasi-judicial proceeding. Therefore, he maintains that the plaintiff will not be able to recover any damages from him when the trial on the merits is held.

In support of this position, he points to several appellate court cases 9Link to the text of the note holding that statements made during quasi-judicial proceedings are immune from damages claims. These cases are cases involving a plaintiff's attempt to collect damages for alleged [*13] defamatory statements made by defendants during administrative hearings such as unemployment compensation, internal affairs of a police department and/or the Attorney Grievance Committee.

None of these cases, however, involve a breach of contract claim. Feldman maintains that these cases support his position that although he entered into an agreement restricting his freedom to communicate with others concerning TES, he is immune from any liability because an individual cannot legally contract away his right to petition the government on a matter of public concern.

In addition to these claims, Feldman argues that the lawsuit filed by TES is a Strategic Lawsuit Against Public Participation, designed to retaliate against him for exercising his constitutional right to petition [*14] governmental authorities on matters of public concern. He admits that Connecticut does not have a statute addressing such lawsuits. He asks the court to look to other jurisdictions for guidance on this issue.

Feldman also claims that the settlement agreement is unenforceable because the clause providing for a payment of $ 49,000.00 for each time that the agreement is violated is a penalty and not a liquidated damages clause. He argues that a court cannot enforce a penalty clause in a contract.

Regarding his counterclaims, Feldman claims that TES violated the settlement agreement by not paying him certain monies owed to him for work performed during the pendency of the negotiations on the settlement agreement. Since TES violated the agreement first, Feldman believes that he was no longer obligated to uphold his end of the bargain. As a result, he is the one who is entitled to damages and not the plaintiff.

Finally, Feldman argues that a PJR should not issue because the actions of TES constitute a violation of the Connecticut Unfair Trade Practices Act, (CUTPA) General Statutes § 42-110a et seq. As a result of these violations, Feldman maintains that he [*15] is entitled to recover all monies paid to TES as well as to damages for emotional injuries incurred by him in defending the pending litigation.

VI. ORDERS

Having considered the defenses and the counterclaims presented by the defendant, the court finds that the plaintiff has established that probable cause exists to issue a pre-judgment remedy in the amount originally requested, that is $ 245,000.00, rather than the increased amount requested of $ 500,000.00. This amount is calculated to include coverage for the costs incurred for attorneys fees as well as for the loss of potential franchisees.

So ordered.

Carmen L. Lopez, Judge

【本案评析】

在上述案件中，双方当事人已通过谈判达成和解协议解决了争议，但一方当事人向法院提起诉讼表示另一方当事人不当披露保密信息违反了协议中的保密条款，要求另一方当事人赔偿损失并请求法院作出禁令保护机密信息不被披露。和解协议中的保密条款约束双方当事人对敏感信息“闭口不言”，若任一当事人违反保密条款，另一方当事人可向法院提起诉讼。

【延伸阅读】

一、相关学术论著

（一）经典文献

1. Micheal R. Carrell, Chriatina Heavrin, *Negotiation Essentials Theory, Skills and Practices, hibook,* 2010.

2.［美］珍妮·M.布雷特：《全球谈判》，范徵、王风华等译，中国人民大学出版社2005年版。

（二）著作类

1.［美］巴里·莫德：《国际商事谈判原理与实务》，中国人民大学出版社2016年版。

2. Stephen Ware, *Principles of Alternative Dispute,* West Academic Publishing, 2001.

3.［美］罗杰·费希尔、威廉·尤里、布鲁斯·巴顿著，王燕、罗昕译：《谈判力》，中信出版社 2012 年版。

（三）期刊类

1. 郝智伟:《浅析国际商事纠纷》, 载《中国商界》2012 年第 7 期。

2. 孔杰荣(柯恩)、蒋超翊:《解决与中国的国际商事争端: 过去与现在》, 载《北大法律评论》2014 年第 2 期。

二、相关网络资源

1. https://www.pon.harvard.edu/research_projects/harvard-negotiation-project/hnp/

2. https://www.coursera.org/lecture/negotiation-skills/a-dispute-resolution-el26b

第二章

国际商事调解法律实务

【内容摘要】

调解是一种传统的争议解决方式，其已在非洲、中国、远东等地实践多年。二十世纪中后期，替代性争议解决方式（ADR）于美国兴起，由于 ADR 能够弥补诉讼机制固有的缺陷及适应新时代的需求而逐渐风靡全球，成为国际商事主体解决商事争议的方式。调解作为一种争议解决方式，具有程序简便灵活、快捷高效、成本低廉等优势，完美展现了 ADR 的优势特点，因此，调解是现代社会公认的 ADR 中最具代表性的非诉讼机制。通过对本章的学习，了解何为国际商事调解，掌握国际商事调解的程序及和解协议等基础知识。同时更重要的是，结合案例熟悉国际商事调解过程中可能产生的各种纠纷，避免实践中出现错误或风险。

第一节　国际商事调解概述

【知识背景 / 学习要点】

一、国际商事调解的内涵与特点

（一）国际商事调解的含义

国际商事调解是指在国际商事交往中，各方当事人发生争议后，共同选择第三方作为调解员，由调解员通过说服、劝导等方式，使当事人之间的争议在自愿的基础上得到解决。[①]

联合国国际贸易法委员会在2002年提出的《国际商事调解示范法》中对“调解”及“国际调解”做出解释，并于2018年的《贸易法委员会国际商事调解和调解所产生的国际和解协议示范法》(以下简称2018年《示范法》)对其进行了修改。根据2018年《示范法》第1条第3款的规定，“调解”是指当事人请求一名或多名第三人(“调解员”)协助，其设法友好解决合同关系或者其他法律关系所产生的或者与之相关的争议的过程。而在第3条第2款中，《国际商事调解示范法》确定了国际调解的范围为：“调解如有下列情形即为国际调解：(a)达成进行调解的约定时，各方当事人的营业地在不同的国家；或者(b)当事人设有营业地的国家并非：(一)商业关系中相当一部分义务履行地所在国；或者(二)与争议事项关系最密切的国家。”[②]

同时，2018年《示范法》脚注中对“商事”一词进行了进一步的说明，“商事”应作广义解释，以涵盖由于一切商业性质关系而发生的事项，无论这种关系是否属于合同关系。可见，《示范法》尽可能地扩大了国际商事调解的适用范围，意在鼓励争议当事人选择调解解决纠纷，表明国际商事调解在商事解决纠纷中的作用。

(二)国际商事调解的特点

1. 自愿选择

双方当事人之间发生商事争议时，当事人仅凭意愿选择采用调解的方式加以解决，当事人通过合意解决其争议是调解的一个重要特征。当事人的自愿选

① Albert Fiadjoe, LLB (Hons) (Ghana), *Alternative Dispute Resolution:A Developing World, published in Great Britain 2004 by Cavendish Publishing Limited*, The Glass House, Wharton Street, London WC1X 9PX, United Kingdom, 2004, pp.57~58.

② 原文如下：A conciliation is international if: (a) The parties to an agreement to conciliate have, at the time of the conclusion of that agreement, their places of business in different States; or (b) The State in which the parties have their places of business is different from either:(i) The State in which a substantial part of the obligations of the commercial relationship is to be performed; or(ii) The State with which the subject matter of the dispute is most closely connected.

择权贯穿于调解程序的始终，任何一方当事人在调解过程中的任何时候都有权终止调解。也就是说，调解的启动、调解规则的适用、调解员的选定、调解程序的进行和终止以及调解结果的履行等都由当事人自己选择。虽然有些国家在诉讼法中规定，调解是进行诉讼的必经程序，但是任何一方当事人一经拒绝便不进行调解，而继续进行诉讼程序。

2. 第三方介入

与谈判相比，调解最大的特点在于第三方的介入与协助。在实践中，当事方往往难以通过直接协商达成协议，第三方介入协助解决争议，更容易使双方当事人互相妥协，并达成和解。第三方须在双方当事人之间保持中立，以取得当事人的信任，才有助于迅速达成和解、解决争议。在调解过程中，第三方还须积极地引导调解程序的进行，促使双方当事人积极沟通协调，达成和解。当事人有权选择第三人介入调解，第三方在调解过程中应遵守一定的行为规则，保证第三方的中立性。以香港特区为例，作为第三方的调解员必须公平地对待双方当事人，对任何和解协议的条款不得有任何个人利害关系，不得偏袒任何一方当事人，需要在合理的情况下应双方当事人的要求提供调解服务，并确保双方当事人均获告知调解程序。

3. 程序灵活性

调解作为 ADR 中的一种争议解决方式，可以弥补诉讼效率低下的不足，当然具有程序上的灵活性。调解程序是非正式的，在当事人主张、事实的证明责任及运作方式上都具有相当大的灵活性，双方当事人有权选择各自适用的程序。双方当事人可以根据自身的利益和条件进行协商，从而达成协议，解决争议。在调解适用规范上，除可依据现行有效的法律法规外，还可以以各种有关的社会规范作为解决争议的依据和标准。同时，调解员并不一定适用现行有效的法规来解决双方当事人的争议，还可以根据双方当事人提出的观点和要求制定调解方法，以达成妥协与和解。[①]总而言之，程序的灵活性是调解区别于其他

① ［英］罗杰·科特威尔：《法律社会学导论》，潘大松等译，华夏出版社 1989 年版，第 239 页。

争议解决方式的一个重要特征。

4. 契约性

调解是双方当事人对所产生的争议经过不断磋商的过程，最后对争议解决方案协商一致的结果。契约性这一特征贯穿于调解的整个过程，调解的启动、调解员的选任、调解规则的适用等事项，当事人均可以通过协商达成合意来处理。虽然第三方会介入调解过程，并影响调解的进行，但是其只能起到对双方当事人之间争议解决的一种主持、组织和促进的作用，当事人之间所达成的和解协议仍是建立在当事人合意的基础之上的，在本质上属于当事人之间的契约。

二、国际商事调解的类型

（一）司法调解

我国将调解制度作为在法律上的纠纷解决方式之一，此向来被西方国家推崇为"东方经验"。司法调解亦可被称为法院调解，国际商事司法调解是指双方当事人在法院的主持下，就所产生的国际商事争议进行平等、自愿的协商，达成一致协议，并经由法院确认产生一定法律效力的诉讼活动。在实践中，双方当事人一旦达成最终的调解协议，一般会由法院制作调解书，载明双方当事人的基本情况、争议事由、案件基本事实以及调解的结果，并由法院加盖印章，送达双方当事人时正式生效。调解书与判决书具有同样的法律效力，一旦当事人不履行，另一方当事人亦可申请法院强制执行。

相较于法院判决而言，调解则更关注人本身，可以更高效地解决国际商事纠纷。因此，司法调解的本质在于其体现一种谈判民主。[①] 谈判是指人与人之间为了满足需要、获取利益而采取的一种相互沟通行为，[②] 司法调解完全符合"谈判"这一范围。而民主，则是指调解是建立在自愿、平等的基础之上，同时

① 张莉：《多元调解机制下司法调解的本质解读》，载《中南民族大学学报（人文社会科学版）》2008 年第 2 期。

② 李明新、吴无其、汪达环：《现代谈判学》，中国社会科学出版社 1990 年版，第 39 页。

法院还要审查调解协议是否违背国家利益、公共利益或第三人合法权益。因此，在国际商事纷繁复杂的今天，司法调解在国际商事争议的纠纷解决途径中占有举足轻重的地位，其双方参与的自愿平等性、纠纷解决的快速性、双方对自身利益的相对满足性以及调解书的法律效力性等特点，使其能与诉讼机制相辅相成，更好地达到定分止争的作用，从而建立起纠纷的多元化司法解决方式，实现本国司法制度与国际商事活动的相恰。

（二）民间调解

民间调解与司法调解相对，是一种不需要法院参与的非诉讼调解方式，是引入民间的第三方进行的调解活动。根据所引入的第三方机构的不同，国际商事中的民间调解又可以分为两种具体形式。第一种是通过专门的调解组织所进行的国际商事调解，该类组织设立的专门目的即是主持双方当事人所提交的纠纷调解申请，从而通过调解方式解决国际商事争议，例如我国的国际商会调解中心、英国的“争议解决中心”（CEDR）等，均是属于专门的调解组织。第二种是国际商事争议解决机构中在通过其他方式处理争端时，同时运用调解方式解决纠纷，此主要是指国际商事仲裁机构所运用的商事调解，例如中国国际经济贸易仲裁委员会（CIETAC），在其出台的《中国国际经济贸易仲裁委员会仲裁规则（2015版）》中明确规定了实行仲裁与调解相结合。如果双方当事人愿意调解的，或一方当事人有调解意愿并经仲裁庭征得另一方当事人同意的，仲裁庭可以在仲裁程序中对案件进行调解；如果双方当事人愿意自行和解，仲裁庭在征得双方当事人同意后可以按照其认为适当的方式进行调解。仲裁与调解相结合制度的灵活性，便于迅速有效地解决双方当事人的纠纷。

三、国际商事调解的基本原则

基本原则是贯穿调解始终的、能反映适用对象客观需要及其规律的根本性准则。调解中具有根本性指导意义的准则是客观存在的，调解的立法与实践都必须遵循基本原则。为了使调解的当事人及调解人员在调解过程中均有章可循，许多调解机构都对调解的基本原则有所规定。

（一）合法性原则

在整个法律制度的设计中，合法性原则应是起点，因而调解制度当然需要遵循合法性原则。合法性原则在调解制度中应体现在三个方面：首先，调解的范围合法。《中华人民共和国民事诉讼法（2017修正）》规定，对于案件原则上均可以适用调解，但也规定了调解范围的例外情形，但这并未将国际商事争议排除在外，且国际商事争议作为一般商事争议的特殊情形，其纠纷性质可以适用调解，但这里需要注意的是，根据“意思自治”的理念，如果双方当事人在事前已经通过相关协议将纠纷解决方式之一的调解排除在外，那么此时将不属于调解的适用范围。其次，调解的内容合法。一般来说，调解所达成的内容不得损害国家利益、社会公共利益以及第三人的合法利益，否则所达成的调解协议应属无效。最后，调解的程序合法。正当程序理念已成为现代法治的应有之义，在调解中亦应遵守回避、告知等规则或义务，否则将构成程序违法。事实上，程序包含着决定成立的前提，存在着左右当事人在程序完成之后的行为态度的契机，并且保留着客观评价决定过程的可能性。[①]

（二）自愿性原则

调解作为私法行为，是在双方互谅互让的基础上达成一致，须以当事人的自愿为基础。当事人要在自愿的基础上达成调解协议，在调解程序、调解机构、调解员等方面都应当体现出当事人的意思自治，因此，自愿性原则应主要体现在两个方面：一是指程序上的自愿性，即双方当事人均自愿将争端事项通过调解方式解决，此亦是调解启动的前提条件，同时在法院调解中，一旦一方当事人不再愿意进行调解那么法院应尊重当事人的意愿，转为诉讼程序解决纠纷，自愿性原则伴随调解的整个过程。二是实体上的自愿性，虽然调解的特点是互谅互让，但是具体处分权应由当事人自己把握，对于达成何种调解内容以及如何

① 季卫东：《法律程序的意义——对中国法制建设的另一种思考》，载《中国社会科学》1993年第1期。

履行调解协议内容，均需双方自愿达成，不得有任何强迫。

（三）平等性原则

平等性原则是指在调解过程中双方当事人地位平等，不应因身份、国籍等进行差别对待。在调解过程中，只有在保障双方当事人平等的前提下，才可以为自愿协商、自由处分奠定基础。在国际商事纠纷中，不可避免地会因双方当事人的实力差异而致使实际地位具有一定的不平等性，在此情况下，调解主持方在调解过程中不得偏袒任一方，应在保持中立的前提下，使得双方当事人自由的表达意愿，公平公正的保护双方的合法权利或利益。因此，平等下的协商正是调解活动有效运作的精髓。以香港特区为例，调解员必须以公正无私的态度对待双方当事人。调解员若有可能或曾与任何一方当事人之间有任何从属、利害关系，须向另一方当事人披露，调解员必须在展开调解程序前取得双方当事人的书面同意。

（四）效率性原则

“时间就是金钱”是现代商业活动所普遍推崇的理念之一，一旦在国际商事活动中产生纠纷，所影响的不仅仅是纠纷本身的利益，同样会对未来的商事活动产生连锁效应。由此，尽快地解决纠纷应是双方当事人的共同“愿望”，而调解制度恰好符合这一特性，其无须像诉讼方式那样的漫长的裁判期间，在双方当事人达成调解协议时即意味着纠纷的解决。因此，在国际商事调解中遵循效率性原则要遵循两个方面：一是商事纠纷解决机构应当遵守“调判结合”“调裁结合”的原则，不能久调不决；二是双方当事人应当恪守诚信，以尽快解决纠纷为目的，不得假借调解之名，行拖延之实。

（五）保密性原则

调解不同于审判，审判一般要遵循公开原则，但调解是在双方自愿协商的基础上互谅互让，且国际商事纠纷涉及较多商业秘密，不可能“开诚布公”地进行。由此，非公开性原则应是国际商事调解的基本原则之一。在此原则的理念下，不但调解过程要私密进行，无关人员不得在场，而且双方当事人以及调解员对于调解过程中所获知的商业秘密以及私密信息，亦不得向他人或者社会披露。

四、国际商事调解程序

（一）调解程序的启动

1. 调解的申请

调解的启动需遵循自愿性原则，双方当事人达成调解的合意，这是国际商事调解开始的前提，亦是调解机构介入调解纠纷的依据。因此，国际商事调解程序的启动需要当事人正式提出调解申请。这种调解申请一般表现为书面调解协议，但实际上，调解机构并不严格要求存在书面的调解协议。如果是双方当事人共同申请或者事先有关于适用调解的约定，那么调解机构在收到申请后，应当及时审查申请是否符合受理条件。如果是由一方单独提起调解申请而又没有事前约定与调解相关的约定，那么调解机构在进行形式审查后应当向另一方发出调解的通知，如果对方明确拒绝调解，那么调解程序不得启动。也就是说，双方当事人可以在纠纷之前作出调解的合意，也可以在纠纷发生后作出。

2. 调解的受理

调解机构在对当事人的调解意愿以及申请材料进行审查后，应当对调解予以受理，在此时调解机构还要对被争议事项、调解的可能性以及案件是否已进入其他解决程序进行审查。如果符合调解的实质性条件，那么就对案件正式受理，调解程序正式开始。

（二）调解程序的进行

1. 调解员的选择

在国际商事调解程序中，调解员是指在案件中居中主持，促成当事人达成调解的专业人员。调解员在调解程序中非常重要，能够起到协助、引导、促成和解的作用。无论当事人以何种方式达成调解协议启动调解程序，调解员的确定是调解程序得以进行的关键环节。[①] 根据不同国家或者不同国际调解机构的规定，调解员的人数和选定都有具体的程序性规定。1980 年《联合国贸易法委员会调解规则》[②] 第 3 条规定，除非双方当事人协议应有两名或三名调解员，否则调解员应为一人。在实践中，调解机构通常会为当事人提供调解员名单以供其选择，调解员名单中的调解员均是经调解机构肯定后挑选出来的优秀人士。选定调解员是当事人的权利，除非当事人要求，调解机构和其他人不得干涉。

2. 调解会议的进行

调解会议是整个调解程序的核心，虽然不同国家或机构的国际商事调解规定有差异，但是会议一般包括确定争议焦点和协商谈判两个方面。确定争议焦点与法院正式开庭审理前归纳案件争议焦点类似，围绕主要争点进行陈述，理清纠纷的具体情况。经过各方当事人陈述后，调解员将对争点进行归纳，然后由双方当事人进行直接对话，调解员此时仅起到辅助作用，不能直接判定对与错，但可以在合理的范围内规劝双方当事人。在经过反复的谈判后，当事人在互相让步的情况下，使得争议差距逐渐缩小并最终趋于一致，从而取得调解的最终结果。

（三）调解程序的终止

国际商事调解程序在两种情况予以终结：一是双方当事人意见趋于一致，达成协议。经过双方当事人和调解员的共同努力后，双方当事人达成和解，解决纠纷，此时，当事人需要订立和解协议[③] 以终结调解程序。二是因最终意见分歧较大，难以形成统一而宣告调解失败。若在调解过程中，调解员或当事人任何一方认为调解无法进行，均可提出终止调解程序。调解程序终结后，当事人可以寻求其他途径解决纠纷，如申请仲裁或提起诉讼。

① 尹力：《国际商事调解法律问题研究》，武汉大学出版社 2007 年版，第 137 页。

② 联合国大会于 1980 年 12 月 4 日通过的第 35/52 号决议。

③ 各国对和解协议的形式规定不同，可以达成口头协议甚至通过电子邮件的等方式和解。

第二节　和解协议

【知识背景 / 学习要点】

一、和解协议的法律效力

和解协议是指在纠纷发生以后，为了解决纠纷，在第三人的主持下，当事人就他们之间的合同或其他非合同事项中的民事权利义务关系达成一致的意见。根据《联合国关于调解所产生的国际和解协议公约》第 1 条第 1 款的规定，和解协议在订立时由于以下原因之一而成为国际协议：“(a)和解协议至少有两方当事人在不同国家设有营业地；或者(b)和解协议各方当事人设有营业地国家并非：(一)和解协议所规定的相当一部分义务履行地所在国；或者(二)与和解协议所涉事项关系最密切的国家。”

要使调解达到解决纠纷的目的，只注重调解过程是不行的，还需要通过协议的形式将当事人双方达成的一致意思加以固定，促使当事人履行义务。[①]和解协议作为调解的结果，就是当事人双方终止争执、排除法律关系不明确之状态的约定。[②]在调解中，双方当事人可能仅达成口头协议，并不将调解内容制作成书面的和解协议，但这是很少见的情况。在通常情况下，调解当事人将签署书面和解协议作为对当事人之间争议解决的凭证。当事人可以选择在调解过程中，对争议解决达成一致当场签署和解协议，也可以在调解结束后由律师起草协议之后签署。[③]

在理论界中，关于和解协议具有法律效力问题不存在争议，各国或相关国

---

① 李祖军：《调解制度论：冲突解决的和谐之路》，法律出版社 2010 年版，第 327 页。

② 李双元、黄为之：《论和解合同》，载《时代法学》2006 年第 4 期。

③ Stephen J. Ware, *Alternative Dispute Resolution,* Third Edition, West Academic Publishing, 2016, p.575.

际组织也明确了和解协议的法律效力，[①] 但是对于和解协议的效力范围却有不同的观点。一种观点认为和解协议发生创设效力 [②]，双方当事人一旦达成和解协议，协议立即生效且其效力不因其他合同因素受影响，即使有新的证据证明协议所确定的法律关系与之前的基础关系不一致。第二种观点认为，和解协议发生认定效力，和解协议的达成只是确认之前的基础关系，如果有证据证明协议所确定的法律关系与之前的法律关系不一致，和解协议即无效。第三种是折中的观点，认为和解协议的效力应根据协议的具体内容而确定，即可以发生创设效力，也可以发生认定效力。

因此，既然和解协议具有法律效力，对当事人产生拘束力，那么当事人均应按照和解协议中的规定享有权利、履行义务。但在实践当中，仍然存在着对和解协议的效力产生疑问而发生诉讼的问题。

二、和解协议的强制执行力

和解协议的强制执行力与法律效力不同，指的是和解协议是否具有既判力 [③] 的问题。和解协议具有强制执行力需以和解协议具有法律效力为前提。在当前的国际商事调解立法上，已基本确定和解协议的法律效力，但在和解协议的强制执行力问题上，实践和立法仍不明确。也就是说，和解协议是否具有强制执行力在各个国家的立法与实践当中存在较大的分歧，但各国都未明确否定和解协议的强制执行力。

在实践中，有不少国家和国际组织对和解协议的强制执行力持肯定态度，

① 《联合国关于调解所产生的国际和解协议公约》第 3 条表明："本公约每一方当事人应按照本国程序规则并根据本公约规定的条件执行和解协议。如果就一方当事人声称已由和解协议解决的事项发生争议，公约当事方应允许该当事人按照本国程序规则并根据本公约规定的条件援用和解协议，以证明该事项已得到解决。"

② 创设效力指的是因和解协议而创设新的法律关系，使权利消灭或取得权利。

③ 既判力是一种诉讼概念，指的是作为诉讼标的之法律关系如果为终局的判决所确定，则当事人不得再就该法律关系提起诉讼，法院也不得再次审理该法律关系。该终局判决必须为当事人所履行，如果任何一力一不履行，则另一方可申请法院强制执行。

2002 年《国际商事调解示范法》[①]是确定和解协议的强制执行力的典型例子，2018 年修改之后仍然没有取消和解协议的强制执行力。除此之外，欧盟 2008 年《第 2008/52/EC 号关于民商事调解某些方面的指令》，意大利于 2003 年出台的一项调解法令及印度、新加坡、百慕大等国家的有关规定中也明确了和解协议具有强制执行力。

在有些国家和地区的立法当中则仅对和解协议的强制执行力持有条件的肯定，这种有条件的肯定是指和解协议并未直接从立法上获得强制执行力，而要由相关司法机构或仲裁机构认定后，才具有强制执行力。如德国 2000 年《德国民事诉讼法施行法》中规定，当事人需按照《德国民事诉讼法》的规定申请和解协议的强制执行。我国台湾地区、香港特别行政区的法律也同样规定和解协议的强制执行力需要经过法院的核定。

【案例摘录与评析】

一、和解协议相关条款争议诉讼案例[②]

Automated Ingredient Systems, L.L.C. v. Saft America, Inc.
No. 12-925-CV-W-DW

Signed 06/04/2013

Attorneys and Law Firms

Chad Lamer, Winco Foods, LLC, Boise, ID, Michael F. Saunders, Spencer Fane LLP, Kansas City, MO, for Plaintiff.

Colin R. Stockton, Robert Jenkins, Charlotte, NC, Kelvin J. Fisher, Wallace, Saunders, Austin, Brown &Enochs, Chartered, Overland Park, KS, James David Myers, Shaffer Lombardo Shurin,

① 其第 14 条规定："当事人订立纠纷和解协议的，该和解协议具有约束力和可执行性……颁布国可插入对和解协议执行方一法的说明，或提及关于执行方法的规定。" http://www.uncitral.org/pdf/chinese/texts/arbitration/ml-conc/04-90952_Ebook.pdf. 2018 年 9 月 30 日访问。

② Automated Ingredient Systems, L.L.C. v. Saft America, Inc. United States District Court, W.D. Missouri, Western Division.June 4, 2013Slip Copy2013 WL 12290248.

Kansas City, MO, for Defendant.

ORDER

Dean Whipple, United States District Judge

*1 Before the Court are Plaintiff's Motion to Enforce Settlement Agreement Under Seal with Suggestions in Support (Doc.32) and Defendant's Motion to Enforce Settlement Agreement or, in the Alternative, Motion to Resume Litigation (Doc. 34).

I. BACKGROUND

Plaintiff is a Missouri industrial equipment sales and design firm that specializes in the design, fabrication and installation of industrial and manufacturing products. Defendant is a designer and manufacturer of industrial batteries. Plaintiff and Defendant entered into a contract, wherein Plaintiff agreed to provide labor and materials toward construction of Defendant's battery production facility in Jacksonville, Florida ("the project"). Disputes arose between the parties regarding money owed and work performed. Plaintiff subsequently filed this lawsuit for breach of contract, unjust enrichment and quantum meruit.

On October 24, 2012, the parties participated in a full day mediation, which resulted in the parties executing a settlement document. The settlement document is titled "Settlement Offer Sheet," and is a standard typewritten form with various blanks that the parties completed by hand. The parties also lined through provisions of the form that they did not want to include in their agreement and circled terms where the form provides options. The document concludes by providing that the parties accept and agree to the terms of the settlement outlined above with the understanding that more formal settlement documents incorporating the above terms, dismissals, and any other documents necessary to effectuate the spirt and intent of the Agreement will be drafted by counsel for each settling party and signed by each settling party.

The general terms of the settlement agreement are not in dispute, however the parties disagree as to whether Plaintiff must provide lien releases① from two of its subcontractors that worked on the project—Aspen Automation, LLC ("Aspen") and Ronco Machine and Rigging, Inc. ("Ronco")—as a condition to receipt of Defendant's settlement payment.

II. DISCUSSION

A. Valid Settlement Agreement

The Court first must address whether the parties entered into a binding and enforceable settlement agreement on October 24, 2012.

A settlement agreement is a contract, and therefore the basic principles of contract law

① The parties use the terms "lien waiver" and "lien release" in their briefing; the Court will use the term "lien release" throughout this Order for the sake of consistency.

govern the enforcement of a settlement agreement. Washington v. Blunt, No. 08CV-4092-NKL, 2011 WL 2709833, at *2 (W.D. Mo. July 12, 2011). "The creation of a valid settlement agreement requires a meeting of the minds and a mutual assent to the essential terms of the agreement." Voyles v. Voyles, 388 S.W.3d 169, 172 (Mo. Ct. App. 2012). For the agreement to be enforceable, its essential terms must be sufficiently definite to enable a court to give them exact meaning. See id. Once the parties have settled a dispute and agreed to the terms of settlement, the parties cannot rescind their settlement agreement. Washington, 2011 WL 2709833, at *2.

*2 The Court finds that the settlement document contains the essential terms of the parties' settlement agreement. The document describes the amount of money to be paid, timing of payment, release of parties and claims, satisfaction of subcontractor claims, indemnification of Defendant, type of dismissal that will be filed with the Court and allocation of costs and fees. The Court further finds that the terms of the settlement document are sufficiently definite to enable the Court to give them exact meaning. Accordingly, the Court finds that the parties entered into a binding and enforceable settlement agreement on October 24, 2012.

Because the parties' settlement agreement is binding and enforceable, their dispute as to whether Plaintiff must provide subcontractor lien releases does not abrogate the settlement agreement. See Nwachukwu v. St. Louis Univ., 114 Fed.Appx. 264, 265-66 (8th Cir. 2004) (upholding enforcement of a settlement agreement even though the finalized settlement agreement contained more expansive and additional clauses compared to the initial handwritten agreement); Sheng v. Starkey Labs., Inc., 117 F.3d 1081, 1083 (8th Cir. 1997) ("The fact that the parties left some details for counsel to work out during later negotiations cannot be used to abrogate an otherwise valid agreement."); Voyles, 388 S.W.3d at 173 ("A contract will be valid and enforceable even if some terms may be missing or left to be agreed upon as long as the essential terms are sufficiently definite to enable the court to give them exact meaning.").

B. Disputed Lien Releases

Next the Court must address whether the disputed issue— the requirement that Plaintiff provide subcontractor lien releases—is part of the binding settlement agreement.

The following language in the settlement document is relevant to the lien release dispute. Section 3 addresses

"Consideration" and Section 3.iii contains the word "Release," followed by the option to select "full," "partial," or "whatever." The parties circled "full." Section 4 relates to "Claims Covered" and requests that the parties circle all claims that apply. The parties circled: "Specific identified claims," "All claims asserted in the suit," "All claims which could have been asserted in the suit," "All claims known or unknown," "All claims past, present, future" and "Project release."

Section 3.iv states: "[Plaintiff] agrees to satisfy the claims of subcontractors and suppliers of [Plaintiff] and indemnify and hold harmless [Defendant] for [Plaintiff] sub[contractor] claims." Section 13.vii states: "Parties will cooperate and will execute more formal settlement documents and any other documents (e.g. dismissals, lien releases, etc.) necessary or reasonably requested to effectuate the spirit and intent of this Agreement."

Plaintiff argues that under the agreement it is only required to satisfy subcontractor claims and indemnify Defendant for subcontractor claims; it is not required to provide lien releases from its subcontractors. Plaintiff maintains that lien releases from Aspen and Ronco are not necessary to effectuate the terms of the settlement agreement because Aspen and Ronco have no lien rights: they have not recorded mechanics' liens on the project within the time period required under Florida law, thus they are precluded from placing a lien on the project. Plaintiff requests that the Court order the settlement agreement be enforced without Plaintiff being required to obtain lien releases from Aspen and Ronco.

Defendant argues that Plaintiff agreed to provide lien releases from its subcontractors and Plaintiff is now attempting to eliminate the obligation because Plaintiff is having difficulty obtaining a lien release from Aspen.[①] Defendant requests that the Court order Plaintiff perform its obligations under the agreement by providing the lien releases so that the parties may execute the formal, finalized settlement documents.

*3 The Court finds that pursuant to the settlement agreement, Plaintiff must provide the requested lien releases. The settlement document specifically provides for the execution of lien releases to effectuate settlement in Section 13.vii and the parties did not line through or make modifications to that clause as they did with many other clauses in the form. Cf. Jake C. Byers, Inc. v. J.B.C. Invs., 834 S.W.2d 806, 816-17 (Mo. Ct. App. 1992) (noting that if the parties had a different intention than the one expressed in their contract, they would have included it in the contract).

Plaintiff's post-mediation actions also evidence that the parties agreed Plaintiff would obtain subcontractor lien releases. Within days after executing the settlement document, counsel for Plaintiff sent an e-mail to counsel for Defendant stating:

I am assuming you are preparing the lien releases for the subcontractors as part of the settlement agreement. Let me know if you already have the form of those and if so, you can send them to me prior to finalizing the formal settlement agreement? I would like to get those out to the subcontractors as soon as possible so that [Plaintiff] is not delayed in receiving payment from

① Plaintiff states that it requested a lien release from Aspen, however Aspen refused unless Plaintiff releases Aspen from all potential claims. Plaintiff maintains that it has claims against Aspen it is not willing to release.

[Defendant].

In this e-mail, Plaintiff acknowledges that obtaining subcontractor lien releases is part of the settlement agreement. Plaintiff also acknowledges its obligation to get the subcontractor lien releases as a condition of Defendant's settlement payment.

As further evidence of this agreement, Plaintiff requested and obtained lien releases from two of its subcontractors and attempted to obtain a lien release from Aspen. It was only Aspen's refusal to provide a lien release on terms favorable to Plaintiff that prompted the instant dispute and the filing of motions to enforce the settlement agreement. Although Plaintiff may have placed itself in a difficult position by agreeing to provide Defendant with subcontractor lien releases, it nonetheless agreed to do so, and cannot now remove that condition of the settlement agreement. See Visiting Nurse Ass'n, St. Louis v. VNA Healthcare, Inc., 347 F.3d 1052, 1055 (8th Cir. 2003) ("[T]he fact that a party decides after the fact that a contract is not to its liking does not provide a reason to ... release that party from its obligation.").

III. CONCLUSION

For the foregoing reasons, it is hereby ORDERED that:

(1) Plaintiff's Motion to Enforce Settlement Agreement Under Seal (Doc. 32) is DENIED;

(2) Defendant's Motion to Enforce Settlement Agreement (Doc. 34) is GRANTED;

(3) Plaintiff shall provide the requested subcontractor lien releases to Defendant as part of the settlement agreement within thirty (30) days; and

(4) The Court declines to award Defendant costs and fees as compensation for bringing its motion to enforce the settlement agreement and responding to Plaintiff's motion.

SO ORDERED.

【本案评析】

在上述案件中，双方当事人于调解过程中已达成和解协议，但对和解协议中的相关条款发生争议而诉诸法院。法庭审理后认定，双方当事人达成的和解协议条款内容清楚明确，对双方当事人具有法律约束力，应依据和解协议的规定享有权利并履行义务。在实践中，双方当事人虽达成和解协议，任何一方事后不满意和解协议当中的条款就可能提起诉讼，这时，法院将审查和解协议的内容，若不存在协议无效的情形，和解协议就具有法律效力，对双方当事人具有约束力。

二、口头和解协议法律效力与执行力诉讼案例[①]

STANDARD STEEL, LLC, and Douglas Westmoreland, L.P.

v.

BUCKEYE ENERGY, INC.

No. Civ. A. 04-538.

Sept. 29, 2005.

Attorneys and Law Firms

Kevin C. Abbott, Traci Sands Rea, Reed Smith, Pittsburgh, PA, for Plaintiffs.

Michael S. Delaney, Patrick Dougherty, Indiana, PA, Thomas E. Birsic, Thomas C. Ryan, Kirkpatrick & Lockhart Nicholson Graham, Pittsburgh, PA, for Defendant.

MEMORANDUM OPINION

CONTI, District Judge.

*1. On April 7, 2004, plaintiff Standard Steel, LLC ("plaintiff" or "Standard Steel"), commenced the above-captioned case seeking a declaratory judgment declaring the respective rights of Standard Steel and defendant Buckeye Energy, Inc. ("defendant" or "Buckeye") relating to certain agreements entered into between the parties for the sale of natural gas. On August 17, 2004, Douglas Westmoreland, L.P. ("Douglas"), was joined as a party-plaintiff.

On January 17, 2005, the parties submitted this case to private mediation presided over by mediator and former Chief Judge of the United States District Court for the Western District of Pennsylvania Donald Ziegler. On January 21, 2005, counsel for the parties advised the court that, after submitting the case to mediation, the case had settled. On that same day, the court ordered the case closed, but expressly retained jurisdiction in the matter to consider any issue arising during the period when settlement was being finalized, including but not limited to enforcing settlement. On February 4, 2005, new counsel entered a praecipe of attorney appearance for defendant. On February 11, 2005, defendant filed a motion to reopen the case. On February 25, 2005, plaintiffs filed a motion to enforce settlement. On July 27, 2005, this court heard evidence and argument during an evidentiary hearing on plaintiffs' motion to enforce settlement. On September 12, 2005, the parties filed proposed findings of fact and conclusions of law.

In order to decide the motions, the court must address (1) whether the parties reached an

---

① Std. Steel, LLC v. Buckeye Energy, Inc.,United States District Court for the Western District of Pennsylvania September 29, 2005, Decided ; September 29, 2005, Filed Civil Action No. 04-538.

oral agreement to settle the litigation; and, if so, (2) whether the oral settlement agreement is affected by a no-oral modification clause in one of the three underlying agreements at issue in the litigation and (3) whether there is a Statute of Frauds problem with enforcing the oral settlement agreement.

Pursuant to Federal Rule of Civil Procedure 52, this court makes the following findings of fact and conclusions of law.

I. FINDINGS OF FACT

1. On April 7, 2004, plaintiff Standard Steel filed a complaint seeking a declaratory judgment declaring the respective rights of Standard Steel and defendant Buckeye pursuant to certain agreements entered into between Standard Steel and Ter-Ex, Inc., Buckeye's predecessor in interest, for the sale of natural gas. Complaint at PP6-16; Complaint, Ex. A, B, C.

2. One of the three agreements underlying the litigation (the "Farmout Agreement") dated May 20, 1980, contains the following language: 7. The foregoing constitutes the entire agreement between Standard Steel and Ter-Ex [Buckeye's predecessor in interest]. No change, modification or alteration of this agreement shall be valid unless the same be made or specified in writing and signed by the parties hereto, their successors, and their assigns; provided, however, that neither this agreement nor the leasehold estate above mentioned may be assigned in whole or in part without first securing Standard Steel's written consent thereto, and further provided that any assignment hereafter executed shall specifically refer to and be made subject to the terms and conditions hereof.

*2. Respondent's Ex. 2 at 6, P7 (emphasis added).

3. The agreements underlying the litigation are contracts for the sale of goods valued at five hundred dollars or more. Complaint, Ex. A, B, C.

4. On May 14, 2004, defendant Buckeye filed an Answer, Defense and Counterclaim against Standard Steel seeking a declaratory judgement declaring the respective rights of Buckeye and Standard Steel regarding the same agreements and adding a counterclaim for breach of contract against Standard Steel. Answer at PP6-16.

5. On August 4, 2004, Buckeye filed a motion to compel joinder of Douglas pursuant to Fed. R. Civ. P. 19(a). Doc. No. 10. Standard Steel did not oppose the joinder. Doc. No. 11. The court ordered that Douglas be made a party-plaintiff to the litigation on August 17, 2004.

6. On December 6, 2004, the parties filed a joint motion to stay discovery pending mediation. Doc. No. 20. On December 9, 2004, the court entered an order staying proceedings pending the outcome of the mediation.

7. On January 17, 2005, the parties participated in private mediation before former Chief

Judge Donald Ziegler (the "mediation"). Transcript of July 27, 2005 Hearing ("Tr.") at 23-27.

8. Judge Ziegler previously served as a Judge in the Court of Common Pleas of Allegheny County for five years and as a United States District Court Judge for the Western District of Pennsylvania for twenty-five years. Since leaving the bench, Judge Ziegler had been engaged in private practice, doing primarily mediation and arbitration. Tr. at 23-24.

9. Present at the mediation were Judge Ziegler and counsel and client representatives for Standard Steel, Douglas, and Buckeye. Tr. at 24-25. Those present representing the parties had authority to make a binding agreement on behalf of the parties that day. Tr. at 25.

10. The primary issues being mediated concerned the past and future prices for the sale of natural gas. The five key issues being mediated were the amount that Standard would pay Buckeye for gas it had received in the past, the amount that Douglas would pay Buckeye for gas it would receive in the future, the surcharge that Douglas would pay Buckeye for gas it would receive in the future, the amount of gas that Douglas would take from Buckeye in the future, and the standard of merchantability for the gas if one were applied. See Tr. at 26 (testimony of Judge Ziegler) (emphasis added) as follows:

Q. What do you recall as being the key issue for the mediation?

A. Well, broadly speaking, it broke down to two issues, the amount that standard [sic] would pay Buckeye for gas it had received in the past and the amount that Buckeye would receive for gas sales in the future.

Now that second issue broke down into a number of subset issues. First we had the price that Buckeye would receive in the future from Standard for the sale of gas. The second aspect of that was a surcharge that Buckeye was demanding in addition to the base price. The third aspect of that was the amount of gas that Standard would take on an annual basis from one of the three wells. And then a final issue was whether or not the gas was to be merchantable in quality because one of the wells was producing natural gas that contained water.

*3 Melody Pritchard, President and CEO of Buckeye, confirmed that these were the key points discussed at the mediation. Tr. at 44, 51-52.

11. Judge Ziegler testified that it was his understanding that the parties reached an agreement to settle the litigation at the mediation:

Q. And, Judge Ziegler, did these parties reach an agreement to settle the litigation at the mediation that you were holding that day?

A. Yes, sir.

*** (objection by Buckeye)***

Q. Judge Ziegler, did the parties reach an agreement that day?

A. Yes, sir.

Tr. at 26-27 (emphasis added).

12. Judge Ziegler testified to his understanding of the content of the agreement to settle the litigation:

Q. What was the agreement that was reached that day?

A. The agreement was as follows: Standard would pay Buckeye $ 100,000 in four payments: $ 25,000 on March 31st, $ 25,000 on June 30th, $ 25,000 on September 30th, and $ 25,000 on December 31st.

Going forward, Buckeye would supply gas to Standard. It would sell it for a price on the market, and the parties would split that price fifty-fifty. Next, that Standard would pay Buckeye a surcharge of ten cents on each of the MCFs thousand cubic feet of natural gas.

Next, that the one well would produce at least one hundred thousand MCF on an annual basis. And that Standard would take up to one hundred thousand MCF from that well, which I believe was the Bearer well, although I may be in error what well of the three it was. I believe it was the Bearer well.

And, lastly, that this oral agreement would apply to the parties with respect to all three wells.

Q. Was there any agreement as to merchantability?

A. Yes, sir; there was. Ms. Pritchard specifically stated in Phase Three of the mediation when we were all together would Standard and Douglas please define merchantability. They did, and she said, "Very good, I understand. I agree."

Q. Judge Ziegler, when you said as to the future price that Buckeye would get one-half of what Douglas was selling it for on the market, was it your understanding that it would truly be one-half of whatever Douglas was getting for the gas?

A. Yes, sir.

Q. So there was no discussion about indexes or anything like that?

A. None whatsoever. And one of the main contentions going into the mediation was Standard was insisting upon the continuation of the fixed price. Buckeye was insisting on a variable going forward. And, therefore, by pegging it to the price that Douglas was able to sell the natural gas for in the future meant that the parties arrived at an agreement with which they could live.

That is, the price of natural gas in the future would vary and according with market conditions, and the parties would receive fifty percent of whatever that was. In addition, it also meant that both parties bore the risk going forward as well as the downside going forward in terms of market price.

Tr. at 26-29 (emphasis added).

*4 Q. Do you recall today, Judge Ziegler, on that merchantability issue what the Standard and Douglas representative said when Ms. Pritchard asked the question--

A. Related to the standard, I believe that Peoples Natural Gas had been receiving it.

Q. Was it your understanding that Douglas was, in fact, selling the gas into the Peoples Gas system?

A. Yes, sir.

Tr. at 31 (emphasis added).

13. Judge Ziegler testified that during the final stage of the mediation, "Phase III" in his parlance, he confirmed that each of the parties agreed to the material terms of the settlement agreement:

Q. Judge Ziegler, in your Phase Three, when the parties get back together, did you go over these material terms of the agreement with the parties together?

A. Yes, sir.

Q. And how do you do that-- how did you do that?

A. Well, I make notes after I perform my shuttled diplomacy in Phase Two, and I have the parties back in the Walter McGough room at Reed Smith. And I stated, "Now, the parties have agreed as follows: Standard will pay $ 100,000 in four annual payments to Buckeye. Is that correct?"

And the Standard representative said, "Yes."

And I turned to Ms. Pritchard and I said, "Is that correct?"

And she said, "Yes."

I turned to the second issue, which was the market price going forward of fifty-fifty, depending on whatever Douglas sold it for, and I said to the Douglas representatives, "Do you agree?"

And they said, "Yes."

And I turned to Ms. Pritchard and I said, "Do you agree?"

And she said, "I do."

And I turned to the third issue, which was the surcharge of ten cents. I repeated the same question Standard and Douglas. They agreed.

I turned to Ms. Pritchard, made the same statement to her. She said, "I agree."

I then turned to the fourth issue, which was a hundred thousand on the one well on an annual basis, repeated the question to Standard Douglas and said, "Do you agree?"

They said, "We do."

I turned to Ms. Pritchard and she said, "I agree."

And the final issue was merchantable quality. I said to Standard, "Do you agree that the oil--that the natural gas must be of merchantable quality?"

"Yes, sir."

And I turned to Miss Pritchard and I said, "Do you agree?"

And she said, "I have one question. Will they please define merchantable quality for me," which they did. And she said, "Yes, I agree."

And those all are the issues that were resolved. My notes were made contemporaneously with Phase Three, and all parties manifested an assent to all terms and conditions.

Tr. at 29-31 (emphasis added).

14. Melody Pritchard testified that she recalled Judge Ziegler going through these five key points at the end of the deposition and that she agreed with them. Melody Pritchard, however, testified that the agreement was only to "a general understanding of those key points." Tr. at 52-53. She clarified that position on cross-examination:

*5 A. Our position is that we had a general understanding of the points, of the key points, but we knew there was going to be a negotiated agreement that we would work on and execute that would detail those points.

Q. But you would agree with me that day you didn't tell Judge Ziegler or Standard or Douglas that there was going to be further negotiation, that "We're not agreeing to these five things."

A. I did not say that we weren't agreeing to the general key points, but I felt like everybody there knew we were going to have this agreement because we had already discussed it. We-- and I felt like everybody there was in agreement on that.

Tr. at 56 (emphasis added).

15. Counsel present at the mediation for Standard Steel and Douglas, Traci Rea, concurred with Judge Ziegler's testimony that the parties reached agreement on the five key points outlined by Judge Ziegler. Deposition Transcript of Traci Rea ("T. Rea Dep.") at 9-13.

16. On cross-examination, counsel present at the mediation for Buckeye, Michael Delaney and Patrick Dougherty, admitted that the parties agreed to the five key points outlined by Judge Ziegler, but maintained that there were still issues outstanding after the mediation was over:

Q. Okay. Do you recall at the end of the mediation Judge Ziegler going through with all the parties present and saying, "These are the terms, do you agree" to each party?

A. I remember-- I remember that, correct.

Q. And Buckeye agreed, right?

A. And Buckeye agreed to the items of understanding Judge Ziegler went through. I believe there were about five of them, which were the issues that we discussed that day.

Tr. at 75 (testimony of Michael Delaney) (emphasis added).

Q. Mr. Delaney, ... Is it your testimony that the parties reached an oral agreement at the mediation and agreed at the mediation that they would formalize that agreement in a written document?

A. That's not my testimony, Mr. Abbott.

Q. How is that wrong?

A. It's wrong that the parties reached a formal agreement during mediation. As I just stated, there were issues outstanding that still needed to be worked out.

Tr. at 74-75 (testimony of Michael Delaney) (emphasis added).

Q. Mr. Dougherty, do you agree at the end of the mediation that Judge Ziegler went through the five key points of the agreement?

A. Yes.

Q. And did both parties agree at that time that they were agreeable to those terms?

A. To the general concepts of the terms, yes.

Q. Did anyone say, "I'm only agreeable to general concepts," or did they just say, "I agree"?

A. No, I believe people did say, "I agree," and I believe it was also discussed that at that time a formal agreement would be placed in writing and that the parties would review those and sign once that was finalized.

Tr. at 66 (testimony of Patrick Dougherty) (emphasis added).

17. The parties disagree about whether an agreement was reached at mediation especially with respect to two issues: (1) what constituted "market price," and (2) what constituted "merchantability." In addition, the parties disagree about whether any oral settlement agreement reached was conditioned on a formal written agreement being negotiated and signed at a later date.

*6 18. Judge Ziegler testified that his understanding was that "market price" referred to the price that Douglas was receiving for selling the natural gas on the market:

Q. Judge Ziegler, when you said as to the future price that Buckeye would get one-half of what Douglas was selling it for on the market, was it your understanding that it would truly be one-half of whatever Douglas was getting for the gas?

A. Yes, sir.

Q. So there was no discussion about indexes or anything like that?

A. None whatsoever. And one of the main contentions going into the mediation was Standard was insisting upon the continuation of the fixed price. Buckeye was insisting on a variable going forward. And, therefore, by pegging it to the price that Douglas was able to sell the natural gas for in the future meant that the parties arrived at an agreement with which they could live.

That is, the price of natural gas in the future would vary and according with market conditions, and the parties would receive fifty percent of whatever that was. In addition, it also meant that both parties bore the risk going forward as well as the downside going forward in terms of market price.

Tr. at 28-29 (emphasis added).

19. Melody Pritchard, President and CEO of Buckeye, during her testimony at the hearing, assented to counsel's suggestion that the parties agreed that the price would be "in general a fifty-fifty of market price." Tr. at 45. Melody Pritchard testified, however, that the parties never discussed explicitly what would constitute "market price." Id. Melody Pritchard testified that at the time of the mediation she understood "market price" to mean "the Dominion prevailing price." Tr. at 46.

20. Counsel present at the mediation for Standard Steel and Douglas, Traci Rea, testified that she did not recall a specific discussion at the mediation about the definition of "market price," but that it was her understanding that it meant the price that Douglas was receiving for selling the natural gas on the market and that all parties understood that. T. Rea Dep. at 29-31. Traci Rea testified that Buckeye's previous settlement proposal had tied "market price" to what Douglas received when it re-sold the gas. T. Rea Dep. at 19-20, 31, 37-38.

21. Buckeye's previous settlement proposal defined "market price" as follows: "The definition of Market Price being the price Douglas negotiates for Buckeye produced gas if Douglas sells outside the Standard Steel system." Plaintiffs' Ex. 6 at 2. Buckeye's previous settlement proposal also discussed an index-based price if Buckeye gas stayed within the Standard Steel system and a minimum price. Id.

22. Counsel present at the mediation for Buckeye, Michael Delaney and Patrick Dougherty, did not recall any discussion at the mediation about the definition of "market price." Tr. at 61-62 (testimony of Patrick Dougherty), 70 (testimony of Michael Delaney).

23. Judge Ziegler testified that there was an agreement between the parties regarding what constituted "merchantability":

*7 Q. Was there any agreement as to merchantability?

A. Yes, sir; there was. Ms. Pritchard specifically stated in Phase Three of the mediation when we were all together would Standard and Douglas please define merchantability. They did, and she said, "Very good, I understand. I agree."

Tr. at 28 (emphasis added).

A ... And the final issue was merchantable quality. I said to Standard, "Do you agree that the oil-- that the natural gas must be of merchantable quality?"

"Yes, sir."

And I turned to Miss Pritchard and I said, "Do you agree?"

And she said, "I have one question. Will they please define merchantable quality for me," which they did. And she said, "Yes, I agree."

And those all are the issues that were resolved. My notes were made contemporaneously with Phase Three, and all parties manifested an assent to all terms and conditions.

Tr. at 31 (emphasis added).

24. Melody Pritchard testified that there was a discussion of what would constitute "merchantability" during the final phase of mediation while everyone was present. Tr. at 46-47. She testified, however, that she was not comfortable with the discussion of the term, there was a discussion that the engineers and attorneys would figure it out when they drafted the written agreement, and she assented to counsel's suggestion that it was her understanding that the "parameters of merchantability would be worked out by the engineers and lawyers as part of the final drafting of the agreement." Tr. at 46-48.

25. Counsel present at the mediation for Standard Steel and Douglas, Traci Rea, testified that, regarding "merchantability," the parties agreed that gas would be merchantable in accordance with the Peoples Gas standard of merchantability and that any question as to the Peoples Gas standard was clarified and consented to by Melody Pritchard at the mediation. T. Rea Dep. at 41-43.

26. Counsel present at the mediation for Buckeye, Michael Delaney and Patrick Dougherty, testified that the parties agreed that the gas had to be "merchantable," but the exact details of what that meant would be worked out later. Tr. at 62-64 (testimony of Patrick Dougherty), 70-71 (testimony of M. Delaney).

27. The court credits the testimony of Judge Ziegler as well as admissions from Buckeye's representatives and finds that the parties entered into an agreement during the mediation on January 17, 2005 with respect to the following five key terms:

(1) Standard Steel will pay Buckeye four quarterly installments of $ 25,000 each ($ 100,000 total) over the course of one year to settle Buckeye's claims for past gas sales.

(2) Douglas will pay Buckeye 50% of the price that Douglas receives when it resells the gas for gas sales occurring after January 17, 2005.

(3) In addition, Douglas will pay Buckeye a surcharge of ten cents per MCF for gas sales occurring after January 17, 2005.

(4) Douglas will take up to 100,000 MCF of gas annually for gas sales occurring after January

17, 2005.

*8(5) The gas sold by Buckeye must be merchantable as determined by the standard of Peoples Gas.

28. The parties agreed to formalize the oral settlement agreement in writing. Tr. at 31-32 (testimony of Judge Ziegler), 50 (testimony of Melody Pritchard), 65 (testimony of Patrick Dougherty), 71 (testimony of Michael Delaney).

29. Judge Ziegler testified that it was his understanding that the oral settlement agreement reached at the mediation was not conditioned on a formal written agreement to be entered into later. Tr. at 32, 34.

30. Judge Ziegler testified that, in his experience, parties to a mediation sometimes require a written agreement to be prepared and signed during mediation, but that no request was made, nor written agreement prepared, during the mediation at issue here. Tr. at 33-34.

31. Judge Ziegler testified that, in his experience, it is common for parties to reach an oral agreement during a mediation session. Tr. at 33.

32. Counsel present at the mediation for Standard Steel and Douglas, Traci Rea, testified that it was her understanding that, although all of the parties present at the mediation knew there would be a formal written document drafted reflecting the terms of the oral settlement agreement, the oral settlement agreement was not conditioned on a formal written agreement to be entered into later. She further testified that it was her understanding that everyone present knew that the oral settlement agreement reached at the mediation was a deal that would be enforceable. T. Rea Dep. at 38-39.

32. Melody Pritchard, President and CEO of Buckeye and client representative of Buckeye present at the mediation, and counsel for Buckeye present at the litigation, Michael Delaney and Patrick Dougherty, all testified at various times during the evidentiary hearing that they understood that the oral settlement agreement reached at the mediation was conditioned on a formal written agreement to be entered into later. Tr. at 50 (testimony of Melody Pritchard), 65 (testimony of Patrick Dougherty), 71 (testimony of Michael Delaney).

33. The court credits the testimony of Judge Ziegler and finds that though the parties contemplated that the oral settlement agreement would be reduced to writing, the parties did not condition the agreement on the execution of a written document.

II. CONCLUSIONS OF LAW

A. The parties entered into an enforceable oral settlement agreement at the mediation.

1. Oral settlement agreements are enforceable. The United States Court of Appeals for the Third Circuit has made clear that "an agreement to settle a lawsuit, voluntarily entered into, is

binding upon the parties, whether or not made in the presence of the court, and even in the absence of a writing." Green v. John H. Lewis & Co., 436 F.2d 389, 390 (3d Cir. 1970) [citing Good v. Pennsylvania R.R. Co., 384 F.2d 989 (3d Cir. 1967); Kelly v. Greer, 365 F.2d 669 (3d Cir. 1966); Main Line Theatres, Inc. v. Paramount, 298 F.2d 801 (3d Cir. 1962)]. "Settlement agreements are encouraged as a matter of public policy because they promote the amicable resolution of disputes and lighten the increasing load of litigation faced by courts." D.R. by M.R. v. East Brunswick Bd. of Educ., 109 F.3d 896, 901 (3d Cir. 1997).

*9 2. Settlement agreements reached through mediation are as binding as those reached during litigation. Id. ("We agree that reaching a settlement agreement during mediation, rather than during litigation, does not lessen the binding nature of the agreement on the parties.") [agreeing with D.R. by M.R. v. East Brunswick Bd. of Educ., 838 F.Supp. 184, 190 (D. N.J. 1993) ("The fact that this Agreement was reached during mediation does not in and of itself diminish the effect of the Agreement, or make it any less of a binding contract. To so hold would create a hierarchy of settlement agreements where some are deemed binding while others are not determinable merely by whether they were reached during mediation or during litigation. Such a rule would create confusion and indefiniteness as to the effect of a settlement agreement. Accordingly, it may have a chilling effect on the use of such agreements as parties would never know whether the matter was finally resolved.")].

3. Settlement agreements are interpreted as binding contracts. Orta v. Con-Way Transp., 2002 U.S. Dist. LEXIS 19302, 2002 31262063 (E.D. Pa. 2002) [citing Columbia Gas Systems, Inc. v. Enterprise Energy Corp., 50 F.3d 233, 238 (3d Cir. 1995)]. Thus, settlement agreements are construed according to traditional principles of contract law. Id. See also Coltec Industries v. Hobgood, 280 F.3d 262, 269 (3d Cir. 2002) [citing In Re Cendant Corp. Prides Litig., 233 F.3d 188, 193 (3d Cir. 2000) (Basic contract principles ... apply to settlement agreements ....)].

4. Pennsylvania law recognizes and enforces oral settlement agreements. See McDonnell v. Ford Motor Co., 434 Pa. Super. 439, 643 A.2d 1102, 1105-06 (Pa. Super.1994) ("It is well-established that 'the enforceability of settlement agreements is determined according to principles of contract law.'") [quoting Century Inn, Inc. v. Century Inn Realty, Inc., 358 Pa. Super. 53, 516 A.2d 765, 767 (Pa. Super. Ct. 1986)].

5. Pennsylvania law will enforce an oral settlement agreement if all of the material terms of the bargain are agreed upon, even if the parties intend to reduce the agreement to writing at a later date. Id. (citing Johnston v. Johnston, 346 Pa. Super. 427, 499 A.2d 1074, 1076) (Pa. Super. Ct. 1985) ("If parties agree upon essential terms and intend them to be binding, 'a contract is formed even though they intend to adopt a formal document with additional terms at a later date.'")

(citations omitted).

6. The intent of the parties is a question of fact which must be determined by the factfinder. Johnston, 499 A.2d at 1076 (citations omitted). If the existence and binding effect of the settlement agreement is contested by the parties, an evidentiary hearing exploring these matters is the appropriate procedure. McDonnell v. Ford Motor Co., 643 A.2d at 1105-06 [citing Limmer v. Country Belle Cooperative Farmers Corp., 220 Pa. Super. 171, 286 A.2d 669, 670 (Pa. Super. Ct. 1971)].

7. This court held an evidentiary hearing on July 27, 2005. The court heard evidence and argument concerning whether the parties entered into an oral settlement agreement during mediation on January 17, 2005, and what agreement, if any, was reached.

8. The court finds that the parties entered into a legally enforceable oral settlement agreement on January 17, 2005 with respect to five key issues: the amount that Standard would pay Buckeye for gas it had received in the past, the amount that Douglas would pay Buckeye for gas it would receive in the future, the surcharge that Douglas would pay Buckeye for gas it would receive in the future, the amount of gas that Douglas would take from Buckeye in the future, and the standard of merchantability for the gas if one were applied. In reaching this conclusion, the court credits in particular the testimony of Judge Ziegler, the neutral mediator presiding over the mediation that day. The court also notes that defendant and counsel representing defendant at the mediation, by their own admission at the evidentiary hearing before this court, testified that agreement was reached regarding the five key issues negotiated at the settlement. Further, defendant's party representative at the mediation, its President and CEO, manifested assent during the final phase of the mediation by answering "I agree" to each of these five key issues negotiated during settlement.

*10 9. The court finds that the five key issues negotiated during the settlement constitute the material terms of the settlement. As noted above, HN5 Pennsylvania law will enforce an oral settlement agreement if all of the material terms of the bargain are agreed upon, even if the parties later intend to reduce the agreement to writing at a later date. McDonnell v. Ford Motor Co., 434 Pa. Super.439, 643 A.2d 1102, 1105-06 (Pa. Super.1994). See also Johnston v. Johnston, 346 Pa. Super. 427, 499 A.2d 1074, 1076 (Pa. Super. Ct. 1985) ("If parties agree upon essential terms and intend them to be binding, 'a contract is formed even though they intend to adopt a formal document with additional terms at a later date.'") [citing Courier Times, Inc v. United Feature Syndicate, Inc., 300 Pa. Super. 40, 445 A.2d 1288, 1295 (1982); accord, Field v. Golden Triangle Broadcasting, Inc., 451 Pa. 410, 305 A.2d 689 (Pa. 1973), cert. denied, 414 U.S. 1158, 39 L. Ed. 2d 110, 94 S. Ct. 916 (1974); Bredt v. Bredt, 231 Pa. Super. 65, 326 A.2d 446 (Pa. Super. Ct.

1974); RESTATEMENT OF CONTRACTS (SECOND) § 27 (1979)]. In Field, the court explained, "the fact that additional provisions would enhance the position of both parties is not controlling. What is necessary is that the parties agree to all the essential terms and intend the [agreement] to be binding upon them." 305 A.2d at 694. See also Jasmine Exports v. New View Gifts, 2000 U.S. Dist. LEXIS 13251, 2000 WL 1286399, at *3-4 (E.D. Pa. 2000).

10. Here, there may well be gaps in the oral agreement reached by the parties. Nonetheless, so long as there was agreement as to essential terms, the oral agreement is enforceable. See id. Here the negotiation during mediation focused throughout every phase on the five key issues outlined by Judge Ziegler, the five key issues were agreed upon by every party, and the mediation was deemed concluded after each party specifically assented to terms necessary to resolve the five key issues. The record supports the court's determination that the terms resolving the five key issues constitute the essential terms of the agreement.

*11 11. The court will enforce the agreement that was reached regarding the terms resolving the five key issues found to be the essential terms of the agreement. The court, however, will not fill in gaps or interpret ambiguities, nor go beyond that which the evidence demonstrated that each party assented to, in enforcing the agreement. See Olson v. North Am. Indus. Supply, 441 Pa. Super. 598, 658 A.2d 358, 362 (Pa. Super.Ct. 1995).

12. The court finds, based on the findings of fact herein, that the parties' understanding of "market price" as regards the settlement agreement was that "market price" meant that price that Douglas receives when it resells the gas. The court does not take a position with respect to the dispute which arose later over "net price" and "gross price." The court finds, based on the findings of fact herein, that the parties' understanding of "merchantable" as regards the settlement agreement was that "merchantable" would be determined by the standard of Peoples Gas.

13. The parties contemplated that the oral settlement agreement would be reduced to writing. The parties, however, did not condition the settlement agreement on the execution of a written document. In such circumstances, the oral agreement is enforceable. As explained in Bush v. Internat'l Business Machines, HN6 "preliminary negotiations do not amount to a contract, ..." "if, however, all the material terms of a contract are agreed to and all that remains is to reduce this agreement to writing, an oral contract has been entered that is binding on the parties." Bush v. International Business Machines Corp., 1989 U.S. Dist. LEXIS 13473, 1989 WL 133644 (E.D. Pa.) *1 [citing RESTATEMENT (SECOND) OF CONTRACTS § 26 (1981); Kazanjian v. New England Petroleum Corp., 332 Pa. Super. 1, 480 A.2d 1153 (1984)]. The court in Bush clarified further that:

Likewise, an oral settlement agreement may be binding and enforceable absent a writing ...

In addition, the Restatement Second of Contracts provides: "Manifestations of assent that are in themselves sufficient to conclude a contract will not be prevented from so operating by the fact that the parties also manifest an intention to prepare and adopt a written memorial thereof; but the circumstances may show that the agreements are preliminary negotiations."

14. The court finds that the parties agreed at the mediation to the following essential terms comprising the settlement agreement:

(1) Standard Steel will pay Buckeye four quarterly installments of $ 25,000 each ($ 100,000 total) over the course of one year to settle Buckeye's claims for past gas sales.

(2) Douglas will pay Buckeye 50% of the price that Douglas receives when it resells the gas for gas sales occurring after January 17, 2005.

(3) In addition, Douglas will pay Buckeye a surcharge of ten cents per MCF for gas sales occurring after January 17, 2005.

(4) Douglas will take up to 100,000 MCF of gas annually for gas sales occurring after January 17, 2005.

*12(5) The gas sold by Buckeye must be merchantable as determined by the standard of Peoples Gas.

B. The no-oral modification clause in one of the contracts underlying the litigation has no effect on the oral settlement agreement.

15. The oral settlement agreement reached by the parties on January 17, 2005 is not affected by the no-oral modification clause in the Farmout Agreement, one of the three agreements underlying the litigation. Defendant submits that a no-oral modification clause, like the one in the Farmout Agreement, must be enforced unless plaintiffs meet their burden of showing that defendant specifically intended to waive its rights under the clause. Defendant cites Douglas v. Benson, 294 Pa. Super. 119, 439 A.2d 779 (Pa. Super.Ct. 1982), in support. Plaintiffs submit that, to the contrary, the agreement at issue before the court is the oral settlement agreement reached during mediation, not an agreement to amend one of the three underlying contracts containing the no-oral modification clause, and that therefore reliance on Douglas is inapposite. The court agrees with plaintiffs' characterization. Pending before the court is a motion to enforce settlement. The agreement at issue before the court is the oral settlement agreement reached by the parties at the mediation. The court in Douglas dealt not with the question of the effect of an oral settlement agreement to resolve a lawsuit, but with the question of the effect of negotiations to modify an agreement when parties were seeking to reach written agreement amending contract terms. Id. at 783-84.

16.Even if the oral settlement agreement were affected by the no-oral modification clause in the Farmout Agreement, the parties' assent to the essential terms worked after submitting to and participating in mediation in an effort to reach a settlement to resolve the underlying dispute indicates a clear waiver of the no-oral modification clause. HN7 Pennsylvania law recognizes that no-oral modification provisions are waivable by the conduct of a party to the contract. Somerset Community Hospital v. Mitchell, 454 Pa. Super.188, 685 A.2d 141, 146 (Pa. Super. Ct. 1996) ("An agreement that prohibits non-written modification may be modified by a subsequent oral agreement if the parties' conduct clearly shows the intent to waive the requirement that the amendments be made in writing."). See also Universal Builders v. Moon Motor Lodge, 430 Pa. 550, 244 A.2d 10, 15-16 (Pa. 1968). The court finds that defendant's conduct of submitting to and participating in the mediation before Judge Ziegler for the sole purpose of settling the litigation, and defendant's failure to object to notification of the court or the court order regarding settlement, constitute defendant's clear waiver of the no-oral modification clause.

C. The Statute of Frauds has no effect on the oral settlement agreement.

17. Though defendant argues that the natural gas agreements underlying the litigation are within the Statute of Frauds, and that therefore the proposed written settlement agreement is within the Statute of Frauds, the oral settlement agreement before the court is not within the Statute of Frauds. The oral settlement agreement is not a modification to the underlying natural gas sales agreements, but rather is a separate agreement to resolve the instant litigation. Though the effect of the oral settlement agreement may be to change the rights of the parties involved in the dispute going forward, the settlement agreement does not attempt to enforce the parties' obligations under the underlying contracts. See Springton Pointe Assocs. v. Ledbetter, 50 Pa. D. & C.3d 503, 507-08 (1989). Thus, defendant's Statute of Frauds defense is to no avail. The court notes, further, that HN8 the purpose of the Statute of Frauds is to prevent parties from escaping legal obligations. See id. ("The Statute of Frauds 'is not to prevent the performance or enforcement of oral contracts that have in fact been made; it is not to create a loophole of escape for repudiators.") (quoting 2 CORBIN ON CONTRACTS § 498). When, as here, the court credits Judge Ziegler's testimony, there is independent proof of the agreement between the parties. Under these circumstances, the normal concerns underlying the Statute of Frauds are not present.

*13 18. Even if there were a Statute of Frauds defense available, the parties' decision to submit to and participate in mediation in an effort to reach a settlement agreement to resolve the underlying dispute indicates a clear waiver of any Statute of Frauds defense. HN9 The Statute of Frauds defense can be waived for contracts for the sale of goods valued at five hundred dollars or more, which are covered by Article 2-201 of the UCC, codified in Pennsylvania at 13 Pa. C.S.A. § 2201. See H.B. Alexander & Son v. Miracle Recreation Equip., 314 Pa. Super. 1, 460 A.2d 343,

345 (Pa. Super.Ct. 1983); Duffee v. Judson, 251 Pa. Super.406, 380 A.2d 843, 846-47 (Pa. Super. Ct. 1977). See also Flight Systems v. Electronic Data Systems Corp., 112 F.3d 124, 127-28 (3d Cir. 1997). Assuming for the sake of argument that the Statute of Frauds did apply, the court finds that defendant's conduct of submitting to and participating in the mediation before Judge Ziegler for the sole purpose of settling the litigation, and defendant's failure to object to notification of the court or the court order regarding settlement, constitute defendant's clear waiver of any Statute of Frauds defense which might otherwise apply.

III. OTHER MOTIONS

Defendant's motion to reopen the case (Doc. No. 23) is DENIED AS MOOT.

IV. CONCLUSION

Plaintiffs' motion to enforce the settlement agreement (Doc. No. 24) is GRANTED. The parties are ordered to comply with the terms of the agreement made on January 17, 2005 as follows:

1. Standard Steel will pay Buckeye four quarterly installments of $ 25,000 each ($ 100,000 total) over the course of one year to settle Buckeye's claims for past gas sales.

2. Douglas will pay Buckeye 50% of the price that Douglas receives when it resells the gas for gas sales occurring after January 17, 2005.

3. In addition, Douglas will pay Buckeye a surcharge of ten cents per MCF for gas sales occurring after January 17, 2005.

4. Douglas will take up to 100,000 MCF of gas annually for gas sales occurring after January 17, 2005.

5. The gas sold by Buckeye must be merchantable as determined by the standard of Peoples Gas.

The parties are ordered to execute written documents formalizing this agreement and amending the underlying contracts as necessary.

V. ORDER

AND NOW, this 29th day of September, 2005, in accordance with this court's findings of fact and conclusions of law, the motion to enforce settlement filed by plaintiffs is GRANTED. It is hereby ordered, adjudged, and decreed that the oral settlement agreement entered into by the parties at the mediation on January 17, 2005 is enforceable and the parties shall comply with the terms of the agreement consistent with this opinion.

The clerk shall mark this case closed.

By the court:

Joy Flowers Conti

United States District Judge

【本案评析】

该案件主要涉及以下三个问题：第一，已交由法院审理的案件可以转为私人调解 (private mediation) 的问题；第二，对口头和解协议的法律效力问题；第三；口头和解协议的强制执行力问题。法庭认定，双方当事人就争议已达成和解协议，争议已解决。口头和解协议是当事人经调解达成的，对双方当事人均有约束力，且在了解口头和解协议的内容之后，认为协议内容清楚明确，具有可执行力的，双方当事人应遵守协议条款执行协议内容。

第三节　国际商事调解中的保密机制

【知识背景 / 学习要点】

一、国际商事调解的保密机制

国际商事调解的保密机制是调解得以盛行与广受好评的原因之一。在调解过程中，有关纠纷的一切信息未经当事人的明确同意均不得对外披露，这一机制有利于促成当事人之间的争议解决。因调解的保密机制，双方当事人在调解程序中更容易向第三方调解员披露敏感信息，不必担心在调解中表达的意愿、作出的陈述会被他方当事人知晓并于其他程序中恶意利用，也不用担心在调解中公开的商业秘密会被任何案外人知晓。同时，双方当事人的开诚布公能帮助调解员快速了解案件争议点及解决争议的入手点，从而有效地解决纠纷。

保密机制作为调解程序的重要保障，主要体现在以下三个方面：(1)保密是当事人之间以及当事人和调解员构建信任的基础。信任是达成合作的基础，当事人之间的纠纷解决需要双方互相信任，重新建立契约，化干戈为玉帛；当事人与调解员之间同样需要信任，有助于调解员开展工作，促成当事人的和解。(2)保密是当事人之间充分交流的保障。调解的保密性剥夺了纠纷当事人利用调解中获得的信息损害他方当事人的能力，在相对未受威胁的环境下当事人之间可进行意义深刻的交流。[①] 因此，调解程序的保密促使当事人坦诚地表达其真实需求和意愿，从而增进了和解的可能性。(3)保密是调解员中立的保证。保密性要求调解员对一切非当事人和其他程序保持沉默以保证其不偏不倚的中立地位，使得调解员在调解程序之中或之后免于披露的压力而能增强其公正性，从而保全调解员的声誉。

二、国际商事调解保密信息的范围

为了保障调解程中的信息不被泄露，各国的立法和调解规则中大都有关于调解信息保密的规定，但各国所采用的立法方式不同，对保密信息的范围规定不同，在此仅列举两种普遍的立法模式。

第一种模式是将所有和调解有关的信息都作为保密的范围。例如 2018 年《示范法》第 10 条规定："除非当事人另有约定，与调解程序有关的一切信息均应保密，但按法律要求或为了履行或者执行和解协议而披露信息的除外。"[②] 示范法使用宽泛的措辞将应予保密的信息涵盖了与调解程序有关的所有内容，不仅包括与争议事项相关的信息，还包括当事人在调解中披露的个人情况、经营状况等信息。WIPO 调解规则也明确规定，介入调解程序的一切人，包括调解员本人、争议方、争议方代表和顾问以及独立的专家都应遵守调解程序的保密性并不得向任何第三方泄露有关程序的情况或在程序进行过程中获取的信息，除非双方当事人另有规定。[③] 这种规定使调解更具吸引力。以香港特区为例，调解员必须将调解过程所产生或与调解工作有关的所有资料保密，但如果法律规定或基于公共政策理由而被强制披露的情形除外。对于任何一方当事人在机密的情况下向调解员披露的资料，在未取得事先准许的情况下不得向另一方当

① 肖建华、唐玉富:《论法院调解保密原则》，载《法律科学》2011 年第 4 期。

② 原文如下：Unless otherwise agreed by the parties, all information relating to the conciliation proceedings shall be kept confidential, except where disclosure is required under the law or for the purposes of implementation or enforcement of a settlement agreement.

③ 尹力:《商事案件调解保密规范解析》，载《东方法学》2008 年第 6 期。

事人披露。不过，如果这些资料包含对人身安全构成实际或潜在威胁的内容，则不受前述内容限制。

第二种模式是将应保密的信息事项一一列举。如《美国仲裁协会商事调解规则》第 12 条规定的，在调解过程中，当事人或证人向调解员披露的机密情况，调解员不应泄露。调解员对在任职期间收到的所有记录、报告或其他文件应当保守秘密。[①]

除上述不得披露信息的情形之外，各国还规定了相关的例外情形，如在当事人同意、法律另有规定或为了履行和解协议的情况下，调解员或当事人可以披露有关信息。总之，各国在法律规定和实践中原则上要求调解员、证人、当事人、当事人的代理人或律师及参与调解的任何第三人遵守保密规则，但在例外情形下可以依法披露有关信息。

三、国际商事调解保密的方式

国际商事调解中的保密并不仅仅指的是单纯的向外泄露调解中的信息，更重要的是指调解中披露的与案件有关的信息不得在其他程序中作为证据加以采用。在调解程序中，双方当事人会发表意见和表达自己的意愿，若达成和解则案件了结，若未达成和解，任一方当事人均可提起诉讼或仲裁，那么，在调解过程中的双方当事人的意见、意愿等表示都可能对当事人造成损害。因此，各国在调解规则中通常都规定了确保信息保密的内容。

调解员、当事人等调解参加人不应泄露调解程序所涉信息，不应在任何诉讼、仲裁或其他程序中援引或引证调解中发表的意见、建议及作出的陈述，将调解所涉观点、陈述、人员等作为证据或证人；同时，法庭、仲裁庭或其他行政机关不得强迫调解员、当事人等泄露这些信息。2018 年《示范法》第 11 条第 1

① 尹力：《商事案件调解保密规范解析》，载《东方法学》2008 年第 6 期。

款[1]中对应予保密的事项作了详细的规定："调解程序的一方当事人、调解员或者任何第三人，包括参与调解程序管理的人在内，不得在仲裁程序、司法程序或类似程序中依赖于下列任何一项、将其作为证据提出或就其提供证言或证据：（1）一方当事人关于参与调解程序的邀请，或者一方当事人曾经愿望参与调解程序的事实；（2）一方当事人在调解中对可能解决争议的办法所表示的意见或提出的建议；（3）一方当事人在调解程序过程中作出的陈述或承认；（4）调解人提出的建议；（5）一方当事人曾表示愿望接受调解人提出的和解建议的事实；（6）完全为了调解程序而准备的文件。"

【案例摘录与评析】

违反调解保密性诉讼案例[2]

Foxgate Homeowners' Assn.

v.

Bramalea California, Inc.

No. S087319.

I. BACKGROUND

The underlying litigation is a construction defects action in which the defendants are the developers Bramalea, Ltd. (now Bramalea, Inc.), a Canadian corporation, and its subsidiary

① 原文如下：A party to the conciliation proceedings, the conciliator and any third person, including those involved in the administration of the conciliation proceedings, shall not in arbitral, judicial or similar proceedings rely on, introduce as evidence or give testimony or evidence regarding any of the following: (a) An invitation by a party to engage in conciliation proceedings or the fact that a party was willing to participate in conciliation proceedings; (b) Views expressed or suggestions made by a party in the conciliation in respect of a possible settlement of the dispute; (c) Statements or admissions made by a party in the course of the conciliation proceedings; (d) Proposals made by the conciliator; (e) The fact that a party had indicated its willingness to accept a proposal for settlement made by the conciliator; (f) A document prepared solely for purposes of the conciliation proceedings.

② Foxgate Homeowners' Assn. v. Bramalea California, Inc., Supreme Court of California,July 9, 2001, Decided,No. S087319.

Bramalea California, Inc., a California corporation (collectively Bramalea), and various subcontractors. The plaintiff is a homeowners association made up of the owners of a 65-unit Culver City condominium complex developed and constructed by defendants. In a comprehensive January 22, 1997 case management order (CMO), made pursuant to Code of Civil Procedure section 638 et seq.① the superior court appointed Judge Peter Smith, a retired judge, as a special master to act as both mediator and special master for ruling on discovery motions. Judge Smith was given the power to preside over mediation conferences and to make orders governing attendance of the parties and their representatives at those sessions. The CMO specifically provided that Judge Smith was to "set such ... meetings as [he] deems appropriate to discuss the status of the action, the nature and extent of defects and deficiencies claimed by Plaintiffs, and to schedule future meetings, including a premediation meeting of all experts to discuss repair methodology and the mediation ..." Defendants were ordered to serve experts' reports on all parties prior to the first scheduled mediation session. The order confirmed that privileges applicable to mediation and settlement communications applied. ②

The parties were ordered to make their best efforts to cooperate in the mediation process.

Bramalea, Ltd. was (and continues to be) represented by Ivan K. Stevenson, who also acted as co-counsel for Bramalea California, Inc. The record reflects that, on the morning of September 16, 1997, the first day of a five-day round of mediation sessions of which the parties had been notified and to which the court's notice said they should bring their experts and claims representatives, plaintiff's attorney and nine experts appeared for the session. Stevenson was late and brought no defense experts. Subsequent mediation sessions were cancelled after that morning session because the mediator concluded they could not proceed without defense experts.

Plaintiff filed its first motion under Code of Civil Procedure section 128.5, for the imposition of sanctions of $ 24,744.55 on Bramalea and Stevenson (Bramalea/Stevenson) for their failure

---

① Code of Civil Procedure section 638 now provides in part: "A referee may be appointed upon the agreement of the parties filed with the clerk, or judge, or entered in the minutes or in the docket, or upon the motion of a party to a written contract or lease that provides that any controversy arising therefrom shall be heard by a referee if the court finds a reference agreement exists between the parties: "(a) To hear and determine any or all of the issues in an action or proceeding, whether of fact or of law, and to report a statement of decision thereon. (b) To ascertain a fact necessary to enable the court to determine an action or proceeding." Code of Civil Procedure section 639, subdivision (a) (5) permits the court, without agreement of the parties, "to appoint a referee to hear and determine any and all discovery motions and disputes relevant to discovery in the action and to report findings and make a recommendation thereon."

② The order stated: "Any and all documents and/or communications to which a privilege may be claimed or may attach in regard to mediation and settlement negotiations shall be subject to California Evidence Code, § § 1152 and 1152.5, and any other applicable law."

to cooperate in mediation. The sanctions sought reflected the cost to plaintiff of counsel's preparation for the sessions, the charges of plaintiff's nine experts for preparation and appearance at the mediation session, and the payment to the mediator, which was no longer refundable. Plaintiff's memorandum of points and authorities and declaration of counsel in support of the motion for sanctions recited a series of actions by Bramalea and Stevenson that, plaintiff asserted, reflected a pattern of tactics pursued in bad faith and solely intended to cause unnecessary delay. The actions described included objections to the schedule and attempts to postpone the mediation sessions, and culminated with Stevenson's appearance without experts at the mediation session at which architectural and plumbing issues were to be discussed. The motion recited that when asked by plaintiff's counsel if he would have expert consultants present for the future mediation sessions, Stevenson replied that "I can't answer that." When asked why he had arrived without expert consultants, Stevenson replied: "This is your mediation, you can handle it any way you want. I'm here, you can talk to me." In an ensuing conversation Stevenson said that regardless of settlement between plaintiff and the subcontractors, who had not appeared in the case, Bramalea would not allow the subcontractors to get out of the case and, in a cross-complaint, sought indemnity from them.

On September 18, two days after the aborted mediation session, Judge Smith filed the report that is the object of this dispute with the superior court. The report recited that on June 13, 1997, plaintiff's counsel requested that the mediation be continued to a later date to accommodate Stevenson. It was then continued to the September 16-22 dates. On July 16, 1997, the mediator denied as untimely a request by Stevenson for changes to the CMO and for another postponement. On August 15, 1997, Stevenson challenged the mediator pursuant to Code of Civil Procedure section 170.6. The superior court struck the challenge on September 8, 1997, and on September 15, 1997, Stevenson sought a writ of mandate in the Court of Appeal. That court denied Stevenson's request for stay two days later and subsequently summarily denied the petition.

The report of the mediator stated: Mr. Stevenson has spent the vast majority of his time trying to derail the mediations scheduled for September 16 through 22, 1997.Mr.Stevenson has refused to make demands on the sub-contractor/cross-defendants who were sued by Bramalea defendants. [P] On September 16, 1997, Mr. Stevenson arrived 30 minutes late. Even though the purpose of the mediation session was to have Bramalea's expert witnesses interact with plaintiff's experts on construction defect issues, Mr. Stevenson refused to bring his experts to the mediation. Mr. Stevenson stated on several occasions that he did not need experts because of his vast knowledge in the field of construction defect litigation.

"Mr. Stevenson also stated that 'he was not going to dump on the subs' (subcontractors), nor did his client Bramalea have any responsibility for the construction of the project since they did not 'pound any nails or swing any hammers.'" [P] Mr. Stevenson claims to have express indemnity agreements with all the sub-contractors/cross-defendants. If this is correct, no sub-contractor can settle with plaintiff without the consent of Bramalea. [P] Towards the end of the morning of the first mediation session of September 16, 1997, it became apparent that Mr. Stevenson's real agenda was to delay the mediation process so he can file a Motion for Summary Judgment. Mr. Stevenson asserted that he has a valid Statute of Limitations defense to plaintiff's entire claim. Mr. Stevenson wants to open discovery in order to bolster his position. The special master has no idea whether Mr. Stevenson's Statute of Limitation contention is valid. However, it has been the experience of the mediator, in past mediations, that this tactic can be used to cut the amount of plaintiff's claims.

Mr. Stevenson has had adequate time to file a Motion for Summary Judgment since the case was filed around May 18, 1993.

"As a result of Mr. Stevenson's obstructive bad faith tactics, the remainder of the mediation sessions were canceled at a substantial cost to all parties ..."

The mediator's report recommended, inter alia, that Bramalea/Stevenson be ordered to reimburse all parties for expenses incurred as a result of the cancelled September 16-22 mediation sessions.[①]

Bramalea/Stevenson opposed the motion on numerous grounds, advising that a new mediator had been agreed upon, but in claiming that the motion was improper did not assert confidentiality of the mediation sessions as a basis for the opposition. They objected to the declaration of plaintiff's counsel regarding events during the mediation session on grounds of hearsay (§ 1200) and on the basis that the declarant offered no foundation for how he was able to recall the statements exactly. They objected to the content of the report of the mediator, but again did not assert the confidentiality of mediation, instead giving their own version of the events during mediation. The confidentiality provisions of former section 1152.6 (now § 1121; see

① The mediator also recommended that the court grant leave to any aggrieved party to file a motion for sanctions; that Stevenson be ordered to serve written demands for contributions on all subcontractors forthwith; that Bramalea and Stevenson be ordered to have its experts attend mediation sessions if so ordered by the mediator; that a new mediator/special master be appointed as Judge Smith was no longer willing to serve; and that an existing stay of discovery be maintained until a new mediator was appointed. Judge Smith then resigned as of the September 18, 1997, date of his report.

pp. 10-11, post) were not asserted.[①]

The superior court denied this first motion without prejudice, as Bramalea, Ltd., was then in a Canadian bankruptcy proceeding. After one mediation session, the new mediator advised the court that further mediation would not be constructive and recommended that the discovery stay be lifted. Bramalea filed a motion seeking return of mediation fees to be paid to Judge Smith, asserting that the mediator was biased and had done nothing during the mediation process to further the mediation, again describing events during the mediation. A new declaration by Judge Smith was offered in support of an opposition to that motion. This declaration stated that Stevenson had aborted the September 1997 mediation session by refusing to participate in good faith.

Plaintiff filed a new motion for sanctions in May 1998, seeking $ 30,578.43, based on the same grounds as the first motion and supported by the same declaration of its counsel and the initial report of Judge Smith.

In their opposition to this motion Bramalea/Stevenson asserted the same reasons put forth in the original opposition, adding an objection based on section 1121. Bramalea/Stevenson's opposition to this motion objected that "under mediation statutes, which became effective as of the first of this year, this motion and the events that occurred at the mediation which plaintiff is revealing in its moving papers, are not admissible and not a proper basis for seeking and/or imposing sanctions." They also argued that the "act" of Judge Smith was "especially inappropriate in that the Legislature recently enacted Evidence Code, Section 1121, which provides: 'Neither a mediator nor anyone else may submit to a court ... and a court ... may not consider, any report, assessment, evaluation, recommendation, or finding of any kind by the mediator concerning a mediation conducted by the mediator, other than a report that is mandated by court rule or other law ... .' " They also objected on the basis of "section 1115 et seq." to consideration of the statements attributed to Stevenson by plaintiff's attorney.

Plaintiff's second motion for sanctions was granted by the superior court on May 26, 1998. Bramalea/Stevenson filed a timely notice of appeal.

II. COURT OF APPEAL

On appeal, Bramalea/Stevenson contended, inter alia, that the superior court violated the confidentiality of mediation when the judge considered the report of the mediator in assessing the events and communications that occurred during the September 1997 mediation in imposing

① Plaintiff noted the confidentiality guaranteed by section 1152 and former section 1152.5 (repealed by Stats. 1997, ch. 772, § 5), in asserting lack of merit in Bramalea's attempt to assert the work product privilege as justification for failing to produce experts.

sanctions on them.

The Court of Appeal reversed the sanctions order and remanded the matter to the superior court because that court had not complied with the requirement of Code of Civil Procedure section 128.5, subdivision (c), that the court enter an order that "recite[s] in detail the conduct or circumstances justifying the order." Because the issue was one of great importance whose determination was necessary to a final resolution of the matter, and to give guidance to the superior court as to the matters it could properly consider on remand, the Court of Appeal addressed and rejected appellant's claim that the mediator was barred by section 1121, which prohibits most reports regarding mediation and consideration by the court of such reports, from reporting conduct during mediation to the court.

The Court of Appeal concluded that the rule precluding judicial construction of an unambiguous statute [Code. Civ. Proc., § 1858; Hughes v. Board of Architectural Examiners (1998) 17 Cal. 4th 763, 775 (72 Cal. Rptr. 2d 624, 952 P.2d 641)] should not apply here. It invoked instead the rule that permits judicial construction of an apparently unambiguous statute where giving literal meaning to the words of the statute would lead to an absurd result or fail to carry out the manifest purpose of the Legislature. [Times Mirror Co. v. Superior Court (1991) 53 Cal. 3d 1325, 1334, fn. 7 (283 Cal. Rptr. 893, 813 P.2d 240)]. With regard to the latter, the court acknowledged that the purpose of the confidentiality mandated by section 1119, which makes evidence of anything said during mediation inadmissible and undiscoverable, is to promote mediation as an alternative to judicial proceedings and that confidentiality is essential to mediation. The Court of Appeal reasoned, however, that it should balance against that policy recognition that, unless the parties and their lawyers participate in good faith in mediation, there is little to protect. It concluded that the Legislature did not intend statutory mandated confidentiality to create an immunity from sanctions that would shield parties who disobey valid orders governing the parties' participation.The Court of Appeal also expressed doubt that section 1121 was intended to preclude a report to the trial court if the parties engaged in improper conduct by attacking or threatening to attack an opposing party. In sum, section 1121 was not intended to shield sanctionable conduct.

Relying on the statement of purpose offered by the California Law Revision Commission at the time the section was proposed, the Court of Appeal concluded that section 1121 served to preserve mediator neutrality and prevent coercion of the parties. The Law Revision Commission Comment on Evidence Code section 1121 to which the Court of Appeal referred states in pertinent part: "As Section 1121 recognizes, a mediator should not be able to influence the result of a mediation or adjudication by reporting or threatening to report to the decision maker on the merits of the dispute or reasons why mediation failed to resolve it. Similarly, a mediator should not have authority to resolve or decide the mediated dispute and should not have any function for the adjudicating tribunal with regard to the dispute, except as a nondecisionmaking neutral." [Rep. on Chapter 772 of the Statutes of 1997 (Assembly Bill 939), com. on Evid. Code, § 1121 , 27 Cal. Law Revision Com. Rep. (1997) 595, 602.]

The Court of Appeal acknowledged that it was creating a non-statutory exception to the confidentiality requirements. The court described the exception as narrow, permitting a mediator or party to report to the court only information that is reasonably necessary to describe sanctionable conduct and place that conduct in context. The report in this case was not so limited. It included extraneous information, recommendations and conclusions, and it characterized the conduct and statements reported, all matters for argument by the parties, not a report by a neutral. The Court of Appeal cautioned: "The report should be no more than a strictly neutral account of the conduct and statements being reported along with such other information as required to place those matters in context." The Court of Appeal directed the trial court to disregard any portions of the report or the declarations submitted by the parties that did not conform to this limitation.

Bramalea/Stevenson claim that any exception that permits reporting to the court and sanctioning a party on the basis of a mediator's report of conduct orstatements allegedly undertaken in bad faith during mediation violates the statutes that guarantee confidentiality of mediation.①

And, notwithstanding the limited scope of the exception the Court of Appeal believed it had created, numerous amici curiae with an interest in alternative dispute resolution urge the court to enforce the statutory rule of absolute confidentiality.

III. DISCUSSION

At the time Judge Smith submitted his September 18, 1997 report to the superior court, former section 1152.6 (Stats. 1995, ch.576, § 8) provided: "A mediator may not file, and a court may not consider, any declaration or finding of any kind by the mediator, other than a required statement of agreement or non-agreement, unless all parties in the mediation expressly agree otherwise in writing prior to commencement of the mediation. However, this section shall not apply to mediation under Chapter 11 (commencing with Section 3160) of Part 2 of Division 8 of the Family Code."

① The parties do not argue that Code of Civil Procedure section 128.5 is inapplicable to conduct during court-ordered mediation. We therefore assume, without deciding, that the court that ordered mediation may impose sanctions under that section based on conduct during the mediation.

The report was not authorized by former section 1152.6, but, as noted above, no party objected, either before or at the hearing on plaintiff's first motion for sanctions, to the superior court's consideration of the report.①

When the motion for sanctions at issue here was heard, former section 1152.6 had been repealed and replaced by section 1121 (Stats. 1997, ch.772, § 3), which retains and enlarges the substance of former section 1152.6. Section 1121 provides: "Neither a mediator nor anyone else may submit to a court or other adjudicative body, and a court or other adjudicative body may not consider, any report, assessment, evaluation, recommendation, or finding of any kind by the mediator concerning a mediation conducted by the mediator, other than a report that is mandated by court rule or other law and that states only whether an agreement was reached, unless all parties to the mediation expressly agree otherwise in writing, or orally in accordance with Section 1118."

Section 1119, subdivision (c), enacted at the same time (Stats. 1997, ch. 772, § 3) provides: "All communications, negotiations, or settlement discussions by and between participants in the course of a mediation or a mediation consultation shall remain confidential." Sections 1119 and 1121 became effective on January 1, 1998. [Cal. Const., art. IV, § 8, subd.(c).]

The language of sections 1119 and 1121 is clear and unambiguous, but the Court of Appeal reasoned that the Legislature did not intend these sections to create "an immunity from sanctions, shielding parties to court-ordered mediation who disobey valid orders governing their participation in the mediation process, thereby intentionally thwarting the process to pursue other litigation tactics." The court therefore crafted the exception in dispute here. As stated and as applied, the exception created by the Court of Appeal permits reporting to the court not only that a party or attorney has disobeyed a court order governing the mediation process, but also that the mediator or reporting party believes that a party has done so intentionally with the apparent purpose of derailing the court-ordered mediation and the reasons for that belief.

(1a) Appellants contend that the legislative policies codified in sections 1119 and 1121 are absolute except to the extent that a statutory exception exists. The only such exception they

① Failure to object to admission of evidence of events occurring during a prior mediation has been held to constitute a waiver. [Regents of University of California v. Sumner (1996) 42 Cal. App. 4th 1209 (50 Cal. Rptr. 2d 200)]

acknowledge is the authority of a mediator to report criminal conduct.①

They argue that the report of the mediator, which plaintiff submitted to the court with its motion for sanctions and which the court considered, was a form of testimony by a person made incompetent to testify by section 703.5,② and violated the principle that mediators are to assist parties in reaching their own agreement, but ordinarily may not express an opinion on the merits of the case. In permitting consideration of any part of the report, the Court of Appeal has created a vague and inconsistent exception to the mandate of confidentiality, one that the Legislature did not authorize.③

Respondent Foxgate Homeowners' Association, Inc., which has elected to rely on the brief it filed in the Court of Appeal [see Cal. Rules of Court, rule 29.3(a)], argues that section 1119 is inapplicable in as much as Judge Smith submitted his report to the superior court in 1997, prior

---

① Amici curiae Beverly Hills Bar Association and Ron Kelly, a mediator, suggest that the trial court and Court of Appeal need not have considered Judge Smith to be acting as a mediator when he submitted his report. Had he been classified as a special master ordered to report to the court, his report would not have been subject to the mediation confidentiality statutes and would be governed by the parties' agreement to the CMO provision for reporting. The superior court CMO states: "Judge Peter Smith . . . is appointed as Special Master pursuant to Code of Civil Procedure § 638 et seq., and shall act as mediator for settlement conferences and as discovery referee. The Special Master shall rule on all discovery disputes, shall assist in the implementation of this Order and shall preside over mediation conferences and make any orders governing the attendance of parties and their representatives thereat." Amicus curiae Association of Southern California Defense Counsel suggests that Judge Smith acted as though he was conducting a settlement conference and asks this court to clarify the differences between a settlement conference at which a court may, on its own motion, sanction a party for not participating (Code Civ. Proc., § 177.5) and mediation, as does amicus curiae California Dispute Resolution Council. We have no occasion to do so here. It seems clear from the record, and the parties appear to agree, that the proceeding about which Judge Smith reported was a mediation proceeding and the judge was acting as a mediator.

② Section 703.5: "No person presiding at any judicial or quasijudicial proceeding, and no arbitrator or mediator, shall be competent to testify in any subsequent civil proceeding, as to any statement, conduct, decision, or ruling, occurring at or in conjunction with the prior proceeding, except as to a statement, or conduct that could (a) give rise to civil or criminal contempt, (b) constitute a crime, (c) be the subject of investigation by the State Bar or Commission on Judicial Performance, or (d) give rise to disqualification proceedings under paragraph (1) or (6) of subdivision (a) of Section 170.1 of the Code of Civil Procedure. However, this section does not apply to a mediator with regard to any mediation under Chapter 11 (commencing with Section 3160) of Part 2 of Division 8 of the Family Code."

③ Appellants also contend that the decision of the Court of Appeal violated the separation of powers doctrine (Cal. Const., art. III, § 3), and that, even if the mediation privilege is disregarded, the trial court abused its discretion in imposing sanctions on them. These claims are not reasonably encompassed within the issues stated in the petition for review on which review was granted and will not be addressed for that reason. [See Cal. Rules of Court, rule 29.2(b)]

to the date on which section 1119 went into effect. Foxgate also argues that section 1152, on which Bramalea/Stevenson rely, is inapplicable as it governs only offers to compromise, and that an exception found in former section 1152.5 did apply. Subdivision (a)(4) of former section 1152.5 [Stats. 1996, ch. 174, § 1, see now § 1122, subd. (a)(1)] created an exception to the confidentiality requirements governing mediation when all of the parties who conducted the mediation or participated in it consented. Foxgate claims that this exception was made applicable by the parties' agreement that Judge Smith was to "have the authority to establish discovery stays, revise discovery stays in place, hear and determine any and all motions seeking to revise the Case Management Order, report his finding to the Court, and make recommendations to the Court." It also contends that the report was exempted from section 1119, barring submission to, or consideration by, the court of a mediator's findings or recommendations, by the introductory clause of that section making its provisions applicable to mediation "[e]xcept as otherwise provided in this chapter," a provision that brings into play the consent exception of section 1121.

Regardless of whether it would have been proper for the court to consider the report of Judge Smith when it was initially transmitted to the court, it was not proper when submitted by plaintiff in support of the second motion for sanctions. We reject Foxgate's assumption that the date on which Judge Smith submitted his report to the superior court is relevant. The motion for sanctions made at that time was denied. At the time Foxgate made its May 1998 motion for sanctions, submitting therewith a copy of that report and a declaration by its attorney about the mediation session in issue, section 1121 was in effect and barred both a mediator from submitting any report like that of Judge Smith and anyone else from submitting a document that revealed communications during mediation and barred the court from considering them. Bramalea objected to consideration of the report and the declaration of Foxgate's attorney, citing sections 1119 and 1121.

Foxgate also argued below that the parties' agreement to the CMO giving the mediator the power to report to the court encompassed the report sent by Judge Smith. The Court of Appeal rejected that argument because the parties had also expressly reserved all mediation privileges. We agree with the Court of Appeal's interpretation of the parties' agreement. Other than a report regarding the success of the mediation or lack thereof and findings related thereto, reports to the trial court concerning the events, communications, and occurrences during the mediation retained their confidential status.

Thus, we consider only the second motion and must determine if the mediation confidentiality statutes then applicable admit of any exceptions.

We do not agree with the Court of Appeal that there is any need for judicial construction of sections 1119 and 1121 or that a judicially crafted exception to the confidentiality of mediation they mandate is necessary either to carry out the purpose for which they were enacted or to avoid an absurd result. The statutes are clear. Section 1119 prohibits any person, mediator and participants alike, from revealing any written or oral communication made during mediation. Section 1121 also prohibits the mediator, but not a party, from advising the court about conduct during mediation that might warrant sanctions. It also prohibits the court from considering a report that includes information not expressly permitted to be included in a mediator's report. The submission to the court, and the court's consideration of, the report of Judge Smith violated sections 1119 and 1121.

Because the language of sections 1119 and 1121 is clear and unambiguous, judicial construction of the statutes is not permitted unless they cannot be applied according to their terms or doing so would lead to absurd results, thereby violating the presumed intent of the Legislature. [Diamond Multimedia Systems, Inc. v. Superior Court (1999) 19 Cal. 4th 1036, 1047 (80 Cal. Rptr. 2d 828, 968 P.2d 539); California School Employees Assn. v. Governing Board (1994) 8 Cal. 4th 333, 340 (33 Cal. Rptr. 2d 109, 878 P.2d 1321).] Moreover, a judicially crafted exception to the confidentiality mandated by sections 1119 and 1121 is not necessary either to carry out the legislative intent or to avoid an absurd result.

The legislative intent underlying the mediation confidentiality provisions of the Evidence Code is clear. The parties and all amici curiae recognize the purpose of confidentiality is to promote "a candid and informal exchange regarding events in the past ... This frank exchange is achieved only if the participants know that what is said in the mediation will not be used to their detriment through later court proceedings and other adjudicatory processes." [Nat. Conf. of Comrs. on U. State Laws, U. Mediation Act (May 2001) § 2, Reporter's working notes, P 1; see also Note, Protecting Confidentiality in Mediation (1984) 98 Harv. L.Rev. 441, 445. ("Mediation demands ... that the parties feel free to be frank not only with the mediator but also with each other ... Agreement may be impossible if the mediator cannot overcome the parties' wariness about confiding in each other during these sessions.").]

As all parties and amici curiae recognize, confidentiality is essential to effective mediation, a form of alternative dispute resolution encouraged and, in some cases required by, the Legislature. Implementing alternatives to judicial dispute resolution has been a strong legislative policy since at least 1986. In that year the Legislature enacted provisions for dispute resolution programs, including but not limited to mediation, conciliation, and arbitration, as alternatives to formal court proceedings which it found to be "unnecessarily costly, time-consuming, and complex" as contrasted with noncoercive dispute resolution. (Bus. & Prof. Code, §§ 465, 466.) Thereafter, by a 1988 amendment of Evidence Code section 703.5 (Stats. 1988, ch. 281, § 1, p. 977), the Legislature made arbitrators as well as judges incompetent to testify about proceedings over which they presided, and, as noted above, a 1993 amendment added mediators as persons incompetent to testify. (Stats. 1993, ch. 114, § 1, p. 1194.) In 1993 the Legislature gave further impetus to the policy of encouraging mediation when it enacted Code of Civil Procedure section 1775 et seq. (Stats. 1993, ch. 1261, § 4, p. 7323), which created a mandatory arbitration or mediation pilot project for Los Angeles County. Statements made by parties during mediation were expressly made subject to the confidentiality provisions of the Evidence Code. (Code Civ. Proc., § 1775.10.) The Legislature extended the same confidentiality to statements made during mediation provided for in a recently enacted early mediation pilot program. (Code Civ. Proc., §§ 1730, 1738.)①

(1b) To carry out the purpose of encouraging mediation by ensuring confidentiality, the statutory scheme, which includes sections 703.5, 1119, and 1121, unqualifiedly bars disclosure of communications made during mediation absent an express statutory exception.②

Heretofore the only California case upholding admission, over objection, of statements made during mediation in which no statutory exception to confidentiality applied, was Rinaker v. Superior Court (1998) 62 Cal. App. 4th 155 [74 Cal. Rptr. 2d 464], a case that is clearly distinguishable. There, a juvenile court judge conducting a jurisdictional hearing in a delinquency matter (Welf. & Inst. Code, § 602) ordered disclosure by a volunteer who had mediated a civil harassment action between the victim and juveniles who had engaged in a rock throwing incident. The minors who were the subject of the hearing claimed that the victim's statements at the mediation session differed from his testimony at the delinquency hearing. The Court of Appeal held that, although a delinquency proceeding is a civil action within the meaning of Evidence Code section 1119 and the confidentiality provisions were applicable, that statutory right must yield to the minor's due process rights to put on a defense and confront, cross-examine, and impeach the victim witness with his prior inconsistent statements. { Pennsylvania v. Ritchie (1987) 480 U.S.

① Corresponding confidentiality provisions may be found in Business and Professions Code section 6200, subdivision (h) (attorney fee dispute arbitration); Code of Civil Procedure section 1297.371 (conciliation in international commercial disputes); Food and Agricultural Code section 54453, subdivision (b) (agricultural cooperative bargaining associations); Government Code sections 11420.10-11420.30 (administrative adjudication), 12984-12985 (conciliation, etc., in housing discrimination complaint), 66032-66033 (land use mediation); Insurance Code section 10089.80 (earthquake claim mediation); and Labor Code section 65 (labor dispute mediation).

② The request of amici curiae that the court take judicial notice of documents they describe as legislative history of Assembly Bill No. 1757 (1993-1994 Reg. Sess.), which added mediations to the testimonial immunity privilege of section 703.5, is granted.

39, 51-52 [107 S. Ct. 989, 998-999, 94 L. Ed. 2d 40]; Davis v. Alaska (1974) 415 U.S. 308, 315-319 [94 S. Ct. 1105, 1109-1102, 39 L. Ed. 2d 347].} To maintain confidentiality to the extent possible, however, the Court of Appeal stated that the juvenile court judge should first have held an in camera hearing to weigh the minors' claim of need to question the mediator against the statutory privilege to determine if the mediator's testimony was sufficiently probative to be necessary. (Rinaker, supra, 62 Cal. 4th at pp. 169-170.)

Although criticized [see Reuben, Strictly in Confidence, Cal. Law. (Sept. 2000) p. 31], Rinaker is consistent with our past recognition and that of the United States Supreme Court that due process entitles juveniles to some of the basic constitutional rights accorded adults, including the right to confrontation and cross-examination. [See Alfredo A. v. Superior Court (1994) 6 Cal. 4th 1212, 1225 (26 Cal. Rptr. 2d 623, 865 P.2d 56), and cases cited.] In this matter, however, plaintiffs have no comparable supervening due-process-based right to use evidence of statements and events at the mediation session.

In the only other reported case arising in California in which a mediator's testimony about events during mediation was compelled and admitted, a federal magistrate judge, Wayne Brazil, an expert in mediation law, ruled that the testimony of a mediator could be compelled notwithstanding sections 703.5 and 1119, which were held tobe applicable (Fed. Rules Evid., rule 501, 28 U.S.C.), because the evidence was necessary to establish whether a defaulting party had been competent to enter into a settlement that another party sought to enforce. [Olam v. Congress Mortg. Co. (N.D.Cal. 1999) 68 F. Supp.2d 1110.] There the plaintiff had waived confidentiality and the defendant had agreed to a limited waiver of confidentiality, and the agreement in question fell within the exception of section 1123 for settlement agreements resulting from mediation if the agreement provided that it was enforceable. Nonetheless, the magistrate judge was not satisfied that the waivers were an adequate basis on which to compel the mediator's testimony, as the mediator had not waived the mediation privilege. After considering Rinaker, in which the magistrate judge noted the mediator had not invoked section 703.5, the magistrate judge concluded that a similar weighing process should be used to determine if the parties' interest in compelling the testimony of the magistrate outweighed the state's interest in maintaining confidentiality of the mediation. After doing so, the magistrate judge concluded that the testimony was the most reliable and probative evidence on the issue, and there was no likely alternative source, the testimony was crucial if the court was to be able to resolve the dispute and was essential to doing justice in the case before him. (Olam, at p. 1139.)

That case, too, is distinguishable, as Bramalea/Stevenson have not waived confidentiality.

The mediator and the Court of Appeal here were troubled by what they perceived to be a failure of Bramalea to participate in good faith in the mediation process. Nonetheless, the Legislature has weighed and balanced the policy that promotes effective mediation by requiring confidentiality against a policy that might better encourage good faith participation in the process. Whether a mediator in addition to participants should be allowed to report conduct during mediation that the mediator believes is taken in bad faith and therefore might be sanctionable under Code of Civil Procedure section 128.5, subdivision (a), is a policy question to be resolved by the Legislature. HN6 Although a party may report obstructive conduct to the court, none of the confidentiality statutes currently make an exception for reporting bad faith conduct or for imposition of sanctions under that section when doing so would require disclosure of communications or a mediator's assessment of a party's conduct although the Legislature presumably is aware that Code of Civil Procedure section 128.5 permits imposition of sanctions when similar conduct occurs during trial proceedings.①

Therefore, we do not agree with the Court of Appeal that the court may fashion an exception for bad faith in mediation because failure to authorize reporting of such conduct during mediation may lead to "an absurd result" or fail to carry out the legislative policy of encouraging mediation. The Legislature has decided that the policy of encouraging mediation by ensuring confidentiality is promoted by avoiding the threat that frank expression of viewpoints by the parties during mediation may subject a participant to a motion for imposition of sanctions by another party or the mediator who might assert that those views constitute a bad faith failure to participate in mediation. Therefore, even were the court free to ignore the plain language of the confidentiality statutes, there is no justification for doing so here.

Plaintiff's motion for sanctions and the trial court's consideration of the motion and attached documents violated both sections 1119 and 1121. The motion had attached both the report of Judge Smith and a declaration by plaintiff's counsel reciting statements made during the mediation session. Section 1121 prohibits the submission by anyone to a court and consideration by the court of "any report, assessment, evaluation, recommendation, or finding of any kind by the mediator concerning a mediation conducted by the mediator." Plaintiff violated this section,

---

① The conflict between the policy of preserving confidentiality of mediation in order to encourage resolution of disputes and the interest of the state in enforcing professional responsibility to protect the integrity of the judiciary and to protect the public against incompetent and/or unscrupulous attorneys has not gone unrecognized. [See Kentra, Hear No Evil, See No Evil, Speak No Evil: The Intolerable Conflict for Attorney-Mediators Between the Duty to Maintain Mediation Confidentiality and the Duty to Report Fellow Attorney Misconduct (1997) BYU L.Rev. 715; Irvine, Serving Two Masters: The Obligation under the Rules of Professional Conduct to Report Attorney Misconduct in a Confidential Mediation (1994) 26 Rutgers L.J. 155.] As noted, however, any resolution of the competing policies is a matter for legislative, not judicial, action.

as did the court. Plaintiff also violated subdivision (c) of section 1119 in counsel's declaration and by submitting the report. Both documents included communications in the course of the mediation.①

The court violated subdivision (a) of section 1119 when it admitted in evidence at the sanctions hearing "anything said ... in the course of ... mediation."

The remedy for violation of the confidentiality of mediation is that stated in section 1128: "Any reference to a mediation during any subsequent trial is an irregularity in the proceedings of the trial for purposes of Section 657 of the Code of Civil Procedure. Any reference to a mediation during any other subsequent noncriminal proceeding is grounds for vacating or modifying the decision in that proceeding, in whole or in part, and granting a new or further hearing on all or part of the issues, if the reference materially affected the substantial rights of the party requesting relief."②

In as much as the superior court's sole basis for imposing sanctions on Bramalea/Stevenson was allegations in and the material offered in support of the motion for sanctions, it is clear that reference to the mediation materially affected their rights and that the Court of Appeal did not err in setting aside the order imposing sanctions. If, on remand, plaintiff elects to pursue the motion, the trial court may consider only plaintiff's assertion and evidence offered in support of the assertion that Bramalea engaged in conduct that warrants sanctions. No evidence of communications made during the mediation may be admitted or considered.

IV. DISPOSITION

The judgment of the Court of Appeal is affirmed.

【本案评析】

上述案件表明，在诉讼过程中披露调解中的相关信息作为证据，那么，审判程序就存在违规行为，如果该行为使双方当事人的实质性权利产生重大影响，那么可以全部或部分撤销或修改裁决。若没有法律规定的例外情形，调解员、当事人、

① To the extent that the declaration of counsel stated that the mediator had ordered the parties to be present with their experts, there was no violation. As noted earlier, neither section 1119 nor section 1121 prohibits a party from revealing or reporting to the court about noncommunicative conduct, including violation of the orders of a mediator or the court during mediation.

② See also Code of Civil Procedure section 1775.12: "Any reference to the mediation or the statement of nonagreement filed pursuant to Section 1775.9 during any subsequent trial shall constitute an irregularity in the proceedings of the trial for the purposes of Section 657."

当事人的代理人或律师等任何调解参与人不得披露调解程序中的信息，且与案件相关的信息不得作为证据由诉讼或仲裁程序所采用。

【延伸阅读】

一、相关学术论著

（一）著作类

1. Goldberg, Stephen B., *Dispute Resolution Negotiation, Mediation, Arbitration, and Other Processes,* Published by Wolters Kluwer Law & Business in New York, 2012.

2. Karl Mackie and others, *The ADR Practice Guide: Commercial Dispute Resolution,* Butterworths (2nd ed.), 2002.

3. Louise E. Dembeck, International Mediation—The Art of Business Diplomacy, *The Hague—London–Boston, Kluwer Law International,* 2000.

4. Harold I. Abramson, Mining Mediation Rules For Representation Opportunities And Obstacles, *The American Review of International Arbitration,* 2004.

5. 范愉：《非诉讼纠纷解决机制研究》，中国人民大学出版社 2000 年版。

（二）论文类

1. UNCITRAL Model Law on International Commercial Conciliation: Adopted 24 June 2002, *Year book Commercial Arbitration,* vol.27, 2002.

2. 章武生：《司法 ADR 之研究》，载《法学评论》2003 年第 2 期。

二、相关网络资源

1. http://www.uncitral.org.

2. http://www.china-arbitration.com.

3. http://lab.ccpit.org.

第三章

国际商事仲裁法律实务

【内容摘要】

本章内容将国际商事仲裁理论与实际紧密联系，通过对国际商事交往中可能出现纠纷的相关理论知识的系统介绍，辅助相关案例的呈现与解析，尽可能全面地反映国际上和我国的涉外商事仲裁相关理论与实践的发展。本章的重点在于，国际商事仲裁协议、国际商事仲裁裁决的承认与执行以及撤销国际商事仲裁裁决的理论概述与实践指引，对于深入了解国际商事仲裁中的正义、秩序、自由和效率价值具有重要的指导意义，同时对于我国商事仲裁制度改革实践及“一带一路”商事纠纷解决机制的构建探索也具有启发作用。

第一节　国际商事仲裁概述

【知识背景／学习要点】

一、国际商事仲裁的定义及其优势

（一）国际商事仲裁的定义

法律意义上的国际商事仲裁是指在争议产生之时，双方当事人依据自愿达成的仲裁协议或者虽未订立仲裁协议但一致同意以仲裁的方式解决争议，将争议提交仲裁协议中规定的仲裁机构或双方一致选择的独立的、非政府性质的仲裁机构进行仲裁，且最终裁决结果对双方当事人均具有拘束力。[①] 在世界范围内，国际商事仲裁已成为解决国际商事争端的一种既定方法。

国际商事仲裁是由争议双方当事人依据意思自治原则自主选择的争端解决方式，且无需诉诸法院。[②] 但国际商事仲裁是在不同国家的当事人之间进行的，当事人代表不同的法律和文化背景，因此国际商事仲裁在实践中也不存在国家主权的干预因素，其有时更像是举行的一次国际商务会谈，而不具有较为正式和严格的法定程序。

（二）国际商事仲裁的优势

1. 中立性

国际商事争端若在不同主权国家的法院进行审理时，往往会受到当事人所在国家法院地的某些保护主义因素影响，从而造成偏袒一方的情况或非中立的审理结果。但是，国际商事仲裁作为解决争端的一种方式给予每一争端当事方自主选择的机会，当事人不仅可以选择第三方国家进行仲裁审理，还可以根据不同的专业领域和行业特点来选择仲裁员。而且仲裁员本身也是独立于任何一方当事人或任何国家或国际机构，其丰富的经验和专业的知识能够在仲裁过程中较快地掌握争议案件事实或其中相关的法律问题，从而既为当事人节省了成本和开支，也能为他们提供合理的仲裁结果。此外，仲裁庭的作用也是持续性的。仲裁庭被指定处理一个特定的案件时，其将会从头到尾追踪处理整个案件，这使得仲裁庭能够迅速且深入地了解当事人、律师和案件的情况，进而为当事人解决纠纷。[③]

2. 效力性

国际商事仲裁裁决具有法律意义上的强制约束力，仲裁庭将以裁决的形式

---

① Gary B Born, *International Commercial Arbitration: Commentary and Materials. 2nd ed.* Kluwer Law International, 2001, p.6.

② Julian D.M Lew, Loukas A. Misteilis, Stefan Kroll. *Comparative International Commercial Arbitration.* Kluwer Law Internatinal, 2003, p.8.

③ Gary B Born. *International Commercial Arbitration: Commentary and Materials.2nd ed.* Kluwer Law International, 2001, p.12.

作出裁决结果。具体而言，仲裁程序的最终结果是一项具有约束力的裁决，参与仲裁的当事人既不可随意拒绝或者接受相关内容建议，同时其一般也不会和法院判决一样走上诉程序，仲裁裁决具有一裁终局的性质。因此，这也意味着仲裁裁决在国际商事仲裁中一旦做出，可以直接获得被执行的效力。目前为止，已经有 165 个国家加入了《承认及执行外国仲裁裁决公约》（简称《纽约公约》），这就要求各缔约国应承认仲裁裁决具有拘束力，并依援引裁决的程序规则及公约所规定的各条所载规定执行仲裁裁决。①

3. 高效性

相较于国内司法诉讼而言，国际商事仲裁在程序上并不是非常正式和刻板的，当事方可以更为自由地就仲裁规则和程序达成一致，比如协商仲裁程序具体阶段，选择仲裁员等。在仲裁案件审理中，当事方和仲裁员也可以较为灵活地选择最适合其所涉特定争端具体情况的程序步骤。而仲裁程序的自由与灵活，不但不会影响争端解决的进度，反而会使得仲裁更加高效，毕竟当事方对程序问题的考虑都会从时间和经济成本的角度出发。

4. 保密性

仲裁程序的保密性往往被视为仲裁的重要优势之一。司法程序中，新闻媒体和公众一般有权了解法院诉讼程序的细节，但是国际商事仲裁程序则是保密的。相较于司法程序来说，国际商事仲裁的保密性通常在提交申请、证据审查和最终裁决方面做得更好。这不仅可以保护商业秘密，而且还通过减少向公众开放的程序促进争议的加快解决，因为和国际商业谈判类似，仲裁的保密性会更有助于双方当事人尽可能在仲裁进程中交换意见，而这将会更有利于实质争议问题的暴露，以期实现仲裁公正。

二、国际商事仲裁的发起

与诉讼程序不同，仲裁程序的适用，以当事人达成合意并明确加以选择为

① 参见《承认及执行外国仲裁裁决公约》第三条的规定。

前提。及时达成仲裁协议、确保其完整有效，是保障仲裁程序顺利进行、仲裁裁决得以被承认和执行的基础。

（一）国际商事仲裁协议的达成

国际商事仲裁协议，是指国际商事关系中的双方当事人合意签订的自愿将他们之间业已发生或将来可能发生的商事法律争议交付中立的第三方仲裁解决的一种书面协议。①

首先，在争议发生前，当事人双方就可以在基础合同协商草拟时，通过拟定仲裁条款的方式，明确约定仲裁机构、使用语言、仲裁地点等事项，将仲裁机制约定为争端解决的方式。这样做的目的在于为当事人提供事前的防范，因为是否发生争议是无法确定的，但一旦订入了争议解决条款，就可以为当事人提供一种及时和有效的解决路径，从而确保当事人之间的争议能够在很大程度上得以处置，因此其也在一定程度上为合同双方的履行提供了约束和保证。

此外，争议发生以后，双方仍可以通过合意方式选择仲裁方式解决争议，但此时当事人之间可能已经进入了争议僵持的状态，或者双方在持续的磋商中无法取得对争议解决办法的一致看法，这就导致仲裁方式的选择相较争议发生前要更为困难和不确定。我国《民事诉讼法》规定，在没有仲裁协议，或者仲裁协议无效的情况下，如果一方当事人先行向法院起诉，法院有权依法予以受理。因此，若未能确定选择仲裁方式，则当事人将不得不面临采用国内司法诉讼程序来解决其争议。

（二）特设仲裁庭和常设仲裁庭

仲裁庭的组成，直接影响着仲裁的进行、裁决的效力，甚至决定了裁决能否顺利得以承认与执行。在国际商事仲裁中，仲裁庭依照组成方式的不同，可以分为特设、常设两种。②

双方当事人可以在争议发生之后，任命仲裁员、即时组成仲裁庭进行仲裁。

---

① 邓瑞平：《国际商事仲裁法学》，法律出版社 2010 年版，第 58 页。

② 许杰：《国际商事仲裁实务》，法律出版社 2017 年版，第 9 页。

之所以称为“特设”仲裁庭，是因为该仲裁庭独立于仲裁机构。特设仲裁庭存在的唯一意义即在于本案一旦审理终结，裁决作出，仲裁庭即告解散。与此相对，当事人也可以选择某一家专业的常设国际仲裁机构，并选择适用该机构拟订公布的仲裁规则管理仲裁进程，此为常设机构仲裁。

特设仲裁不属于任何一个专门的仲裁机构，没有既定的管理流程。在这种情况下，案件的保密性较高，也具有很高的灵活性。然而，特设仲裁庭的“灵活”是一把双刃剑：没有专属仲裁机构，没有固定的仲裁规则，也没有统一的管理流程，一切皆取决于当事人的安排，这意味着提交仲裁的协议需要准备得相当完备。而在实务中，仲裁协议通常以条款的形式，简明扼要地出现在基础合同的后半部分，绝不会长篇大论去讨论仲裁的流程细节。如果仲裁协议中没有相应的规定，双方当事人最好选择有经验的仲裁员，或者选择适用某一仲裁机构的规则。

【案例摘录与评析】

涉及国际商事仲裁管辖权、国际商事仲裁裁决撤销与执行案例[①]

MACTEC, INC., Plaintiff–Appellant,

v.

Steven GORELICK, Defendant–Appellee.

Nos. 03–1290, 03–1378.

Oct. 26, 2005.

EBEL, Circuit Judge.

This case involves a contract dispute over payment of royalties for a patented invention. The parties to the contract differed as to the meaning of a contractual term and, pursuant to the agreement,arbitrated their dispute. After a hearing, the arbitrator found for Defendant Gorelick

① MACTEC, Inc. v. Gorelick.United States Court of Appeals, Tenth Circuit.October 26, 2005427 F.3d 82177 U.S.P.Q.2d 1097 (Approx. 15 pages).

and awarded $4.5 million. Plaintiff MACTEC, Inc. filed an application in district court to vacate the arbitration award pursuant to the Federal Arbitration Act, 9 U.S.C. § 10 (2000) ("FAA"). Along with that application, MACTEC filed a declaratory judgment action on the grounds that the arbitrator's interpretation of the disputed contractual term constituted illegal patent misuse. In separate orders, the district court denied the application to vacate and dismissed the declaratory judgment action. MACTEC appealed both decisions to this court, and we consolidated the appeals for a hearing before a single panel.

As a matter of first impression in this circuit, we conclude that a non-appealability clause in an arbitration agreement that forecloses judicial review of an arbitration award beyond the district court level is enforceable. Due to the presence of such a clause in the instant arbitration agreement, we hold that we lack jurisdiction over MACTEC's appeal from the district court's denial of the application to vacate the arbitration award and DISMISS the case.

Regarding MACTEC's appeal from the dismissal of its declaratory judgment action, we conclude that the doctrine of res judicata bars the suit and we AFFIRM the district court's dismissal.

BACKGROUND

I. Factual history.

A. Development and assignment of the NoVOCs technology

While a professor at Stanford University, Defendant–Appellee Steven Gorelick ("Gorelick") and one of his colleagues, Haim Gvritzman ("Gvritzman"), developed a new method for removing volatile organic contaminants from groundwater ("the NoVOCs technology"). What was unique about this technology is that it was designed to remove the contaminants in situ, or while the water was still underground, by using processes known as vapor stripping and gas pumping.

In 1991, Gorelick and Gvritzman assigned "any right, title, and interest," in the NoVOCs technology to Stanford, including the right to seek a patent. In return for their assignment, Gorelick and Grivtzman each received a one-sixth share of net royalty income, with the remaining two-thirds royalty going to the university. Stanford subsequently applied for, and received, a patent for the NoVOCs technology and has owned that patent ever since.

In 1992, Gorelick formed a company called NoVOCs, Inc., ("NoVOCs") with the intention of developing profitable wells that used the NoVOCs technology. To that end, NoVOCs obtained an exclusive license from Stanford to use the patented technology in exchange for a series of annual royalties. Gorelick was the sole shareholder and manager of NoVOCs.

In 1994, Gorelick sold all of his shares in NoVOCs to a company called EG & G, pursuant to a stock purchase agreement. In return for the stock, EG & G agreed to pay Gorelick an upfront payment of just under $3.3 million. In addition, EG & G agreed to give Gorelickinstallment payments of (1) twenty-five percent of future revenue derived from licenses or sub-licenses of the NoVOCs technology; and (2) $3000 for each well EG & G drilled using the NoVOCs technology. By acquiring all of Gorelick's stock, EG & G became the exclusive license holder of Stanford's patent and thereby assumed NoVOCs' obligations to pay royalties to the university. The stock purchase agreement provided that all disputes arising under the agreement would be governed by California law and would be subject to arbitration. Two aspects of the stock purchase agreement are particularly relevant to this appeal: First, the agreement specifically excluded from the scope of arbitrable issues any disputes relating to patent invalidity or infringement. Second, the agreement provided that any judgment upon the award rendered by the arbitrator would be final and nonappealable.

B. Entrance of MACTEC and subsequent re-negotiations

In 1997, EG & G agreed to sell certain of its assets to Plaintiff–Appellant MACTEC,Inc. ("MACTEC") including its stock in NoVOCs (and, by implication, NoVOCs' license to Stanford's patent over the NoVOCs technology).In a separate written instrument, MACTEC became the successor-in-interest to the stock purchase agreement between EG & G and Gorelick, expressly assuming all of EG & G's payment obligations to Stanford and Gorelick.

In 1998, MACTEC, through one of its LLC subsidiaries, began using a different method of in situ groundwater treatment in some of its wells, known as "UBV" technology.Because the NoVOCs and UBV technologies overlapped, MACTEC was unsure as to whether the use of the UBV technology would trigger the $3000 per-well royalty obligation to Gorelick it had assumed in the stock purchase agreement.As a result, MACTEC approached Gorelick with the intention of re-negotiating the royalty payments.The parties eventually agreed in writing to reduce Gorelick's royalty payment to $1500 for each "remediation well" that was installed by the LLC. For remediation wells not installed by the LLC, but rather by another entity under the MACTEC umbrella, Gorelick would continue to receive his original $3000 payment. The term "remediation well" is defined in the document as "any hole that (i) has been dug, drilled, or otherwise installed, or (ii) which existed and has been converted in use, and that is employed or intended for the partial or complete removal treatment of subsurface contaminants." Nowhere in the written agreement did MACTEC condition Gorelick's payment on a given well's use of NoVOCs or UBV technology.

C. Royalty payment dispute

For the next two years, Gorelick received occasional payments from MACTEC, ranging from $1500 to $4500. Gorelick received the final payment on November 15, 2000. One month later,

Gorelick learned from Stanford that MACTEC had canceled its licensing agreement for the NoVOCs technology.Gorelick then called executives at MACTEC who stated that since their relationship with Stanford had terminated, they no longer had royalty obligations to Gorelick.

Gorelick responded that his agreement with MACTEC was a separate legal obligation which he expected MACTEC to honor. In addition, Gorelick asked MACTEC for specific information regarding remediation wells for which he was entitled to receive payment because he felt that there had been inadequate reporting throughout the whole process. MACTEC did not provide the requested information, and instead alleged that the NoVOCs technology had caused the company as much as $3 million in damages.

II. Procedural history.

On August 6, 2001, Gorelick filed a demand for arbitration to recover payments under the stock purchase agreement. During discovery, Gorelick became aware of a number of wells that MACTEC drilled but for which it never paid him royalties under the contract. These wells eventually became the central issue in the controversy. MACTEC maintained that these wells were drilled using only public-domain technology, not the NoVOCs or UBV technology. As a result, it argued that it was not required to pay Gorelick the royalty payments. Gorelick responded by pointing to the plain language of the 1998 amendment to the stock purchase agreement, which makes no distinction between NoVOCs wells and other types of wells.

A. Preliminary issues before the arbitrator

At the arbitration, MACTEC sought to introduce extrinsic evidence of the parties' intent over the meaning of the term "remediation well" to support its position that the royalty payments only applied to wells involving NoVOCs or UBV technology. Both sides briefed and argued the issue before the arbitrator. The arbitrator felt that extrinsic evidence of intent was only relevant if one of the contract terms was ambiguous. Finding no ambiguity in the contract, the arbitrator excluded all extrinsic evidence of the parties' intent.

MACTEC also raised two affirmative defenses in its hearing brief (which was filed only a few days before the actual hearing). First, MACTEC claimed that Gorelick's interpretation of the contract constituted patent misuse under Zenith Radio Corp. v. Hazeltine Research Inc., 395 U.S. 100, 136, 89 S.Ct. 1562, 23 L.Ed.2d 129 (1969). Second, MACTEC argued that Gorelick's patent was effectively invalid because the European Patent Office concluded that the technology was not based on an "inventive step."

Gorelick, in his hearing brief, filed a motion to strike these two defenses. Gorelick argued that the defenses were not timely raised because they were not included in MACTEC's specification of defenses, filed on April 1, 2002 (pursuant to the arbitrator's scheduling order). After hearing argument, the arbitrator issued the following oral ruling:

[T]he motion to strike is granted on several bases. Number one, we had a clear scheduling order. And I believe, if I'm accurate, that all claims and defenses had to be asserted in writing by April 1st of this year. That was not done.

Secondly, even if it weren't an issue of failure to specify on time, you can't bring up new defenses in a case where there's been as much discovery and motions as there have been in this case. You can't bring up new defenses a week or five days before trial.

And thirdly, invalidity of the patent is beyond my jurisdiction. That's a federal issue, and we're not going to decide the patent issues here. If there was an invalidity of the patent, you've got a right to file a lawsuit in federal court. Those two issues are out of this case, period, okay?

B. Arbitrator's award and district court review

At the conclusion of the four-day hearing, the arbitrator found for Gorelick and awarded approximately $4.5 million in damages.Pursuant to the stock purchase agreement, MACTEC sought review before a federal district court and filed an application to vacate the arbitrator's award pursuant to the FAA, 9 U.S.C. § 10. In support of its application, MACTEC advanced three primary arguments: (1) it was improper for the arbitrator to exclude extrinsic evidence relating to the intent of the parties; (2) the court should not have struck the patent misuse defense; and (3) enforcement of the award would be patent misuse and would therefore be illegal. These actions, MACTEC argued, required vacatur under 9 U.S.C. § 10(a)(3) and on public policy grounds.

After considering MACTEC's arguments, the district court held that: (1) the arbitrator did not violate 9 U.S.C. § 10(a)(3) by either (a) granting the motion to strike the defense of patent misuse, or (b) refusing to hear evidence of the parties' intent; and (2) it was not a patent misuse (or a violation of public policy) to enforce the arbitration award.

C. The declaratory judgment action

Two weeks after filing its application to vacate the arbitration award, MACTEC filed a complaint in the same district court seeking a declaratory judgment that Gorelick's (and, by implication, the arbitrator's) interpretation of the contract constituted patent misuse. Gorelick moved pursuant to Fed.R.Civ.P. 12(b)(1) and (6) to dismiss, arguing, inter alia, that (1) the action was barred by res judicata; and (2) MACTEC failed to state a claim. In a one-page order issued the day after denying MACTEC's application to vacate the arbitration, the district court dismissed the declaratory judgment action with prejudice. The court did not expressly give its reasoning, stating only that it was acting for the reasons set forth in the earlier order denying MACTEC's application to vacate.

MACTEC subsequently appealed both decisions to this court.2 In addition to his opening brief, Gorelick has filed a motion to dismiss for lack of appellate jurisdiction, which is a matter of initial concern before the court.

DISCUSSION

I.Gorelick's motion to dismiss the arbitration appeal for lack of appellate jurisdiction.

Ordinarily, this court's jurisdiction to consider an appeal from a district court's confirmation of an arbitration award arises under 28 U.S.C. § 1291 and 9 U.S.C. § 16(a)(1)(D). The jurisdictional problem in this case arises from the fact that in the stock purchase agreement, the provision dealing with arbitration contained a non-appealability clause. It states, in relevant part:

Judgment upon the award rendered by the arbitrator shall be final and nonappealable and may be entered in any court having jurisdiction thereof.

Therefore, the question before us is whether such a provision is enforceable and, as a result, deprives this court of appellate jurisdiction.

As a general rule, judicial review over an arbitration award is very limited. The FAA, 9 U.S.C. § 10(a), lists only four situations in which it is appropriate at the district court level to vacate an arbitration award: (1) where the award was the product of corruption or fraud; (2) where there was evident partiality or corruption on the part of the arbitrator; (3) where the arbitrators were guilty of misconduct in refusing, upon sufficient cause shown, to postpone the hearing or hear pertinent and material evidence; and (4) where the arbitrator exceeded his powers. In addition, the Supreme Court has held that vacatur is also appropriate when the arbitrator demonstrates a "manifest disregard" for the law. Wilko v. Swan, 346 U.S. 427, 436–437, 74 S.Ct. 182, 98 L.Ed. 168 (1953), overruled on other grounds, Rodriguez de Quijas v. Shearson/Am. Express, Inc., 490 U.S. 477, 485, 109 S.Ct. 1917, 104 L.Ed.2d 526 (1989); see also Hoeft v. MVL Group, Inc., 343 F.3d 57, 64 (2d Cir.2003). As for appellate review, the FAA merely provides that decisions made under § 10(a) may be appealed. 9 U.S.C. § 16. The statute is silent on whether such an appeal is barred if the parties agree that the district court's judgment confirming or vacating the award is to be non-appealable.

This court considered a similar issue in Bowen v. Amoco Pipeline Co., 254 F.3d 925 (10th Cir.2001). In that case, the parties, pursuant to a prior agreement, arbitrated a dispute over damages caused by an oil pipeline leak. Id. at 927–28, 930. The arbitration panel found for the plaintiff and awarded damages. Id. at 930. Thereafter, the plaintiff sought, and received, a confirmation of the award from the district court. Id. The defendant appealed, claiming that the arbitrators exceeded their powers and acted in manifest disregard of the law. Id. at 930, 932.

The plaintiff moved to dismiss the appeal for lack of jurisdiction, citing a provision in the arbitration agreement that stated that the district court's ruling on the award was to be "final."

Id. at 930. We noted in dicta that "although parties to an arbitration agreement may eliminate judicial review by contract, their intention to do so must be clear and unequivocal." Id. at 931 [citing Dep't of Air Force v. Fed. Labor Relations Auth., 775 F.2d 727, 733 (6th Cir.1985); Aerojet–Gen. Corp. v. Am. Arbitration Ass'n, 478 F.2d 248, 251 (9th Cir.1973)]. We held that the parties' agreement to make the district court's judgment "final" did not clearly evince an intent to waive all appellate review, stating:

In fact, the very statute from which we derive our jurisdiction, 28 U.S.C. § 1291, grants appellate courts jurisdiction from "all final decisions of the district courts." Hence, by agreeing that the district court's ruling shall be final, the parties have merely reinforced the appellate jurisdiction conferred by § 1291.

Bowen, 254 F.3d at 931. As a result we denied the plaintiff's motion to dismiss the appeal. Id. at 930.

In the instant case, the stock purchase agreement states not only that the district court's judgment shall be final, but also that it shall be "nonappealable". As a result, Gorelick relies heavily on our dicta in Bowen to argue that the instant clause should be held to have waived all judicial review over the district court's confirmation of the arbitration award.

In a separate portion of Bowen, however, we held that the parties may not contractually expand the standard of judicial review to allow the district court to vacate the award for insufficient evidence. 254 F.3d at 935, 937. In so doing, we noted that "[w]hen Congress passed the Act in 1925, it did so with the primary goal of changing the judiciary's refusal to enforce arbitration clauses in private contracts." Id. at 933. This policy notwithstanding, we refused to enforce the parties' agreement to permit judicial review of an arbitrator's decision based on sufficiency of the evidence. Id. at 935, 937. Our decision was rooted in another policy goal of the FAA: "[B]y agreeing to arbitrate, a party trades the procedures and opportunity for review of the courtroom for the simplicity, informality, and expedition of arbitration." Id. at 935 (alteration in original) (quotation omitted).

We would reach an illogical result if we concluded that the FAA's policy of ensuring judicial enforcement of arbitration agreements is well served by allowing for expansive judicial review after the matter is arbitrated.... Contractually expanded standards, particularly those that allow for factual review, clearly threaten to undermine the independence of the arbitration process and dilute the finality of arbitration awards. ...

Id. We ultimately framed our Bowen holding in broad terms: "We agree and hold that parties may not contract for expanded judicial review of arbitration awards." Id. at 937.

From this holding, one might argue that if Bowen expressly forbade private expansion of judicial review, it might also, by implication, prohibit private restriction (or elimination) of judicial review. After all, to justify our refusal to enforce the parties' contractual provisions expanding judicial review, we described the Supreme Court's jurisprudence in this area as suggesting "that the FAA is more than a collection of default rules, which parties may alter with complete discretion." Id. at 935. But to make such an argument ignores our dicta in the jurisdictional section of the decision, that "parties to an arbitration agreement may eliminate judicial review by contract" so long as they clearly and unequivocally indicate their intention to do so. Id. at 931.

How, then, do we reconcile our stated willingness to accept private restrictions on judicial review with our express holding that private expansions on judicial review are unenforceable? Fortunately, the panel in Bowen solves this dilemma: "The key question is whether the alternate rule conflicts with the federal policies furthered by the FAA." Id. at 935. If the fundamental policy behind the FAA is to reduce litigation costs by providing a more efficient forum, it makes sense to uphold contractual provisions that support that aim while striking down provisions that subvert it.

This is not to say that we would uphold any and all private restrictions on judicial review over an arbitrator's award. In Hoeft, the parties' agreement provided that the arbitrator's decision was not "subject to any type of review or appeal whatsoever." 343 F.3d at 63. After the arbitrator found for the plaintiff, the defendant successfully persuaded the district court to vacate the award on the grounds that the arbitrator manifestly disregarded the law. Id. at 61, 63. On appeal, the plaintiff argued that the non-appealability clause should have barred the district court from examining the substance of the arbitrator's decision because the parties had expressly agreed that the arbitrator's award would not be subject to any sort of judicial review. Id. at 63. The Second Circuit held that a non-appealability provision cannot deprive the federal courts of the ability to apply the standards set forth in 9 U.S.C. § 10(a) or Wilko. Hoeft, 343 F.3d at 66. The court noted that the plaintiff's position was internally inconsistent: the plaintiff essentially argued that he should be entitled to the benefits of judicial confirmation of the award without incurring the risk of vacatur under § 10(a)(3). Id. at 64. This would, the court argued, turn the district court's involvement with the case into nothing more than a rubber stamp of the arbitration award. Id. The court's overarching concern was that if the federal courts were to give the stamp of legitimacy to the arbitrator's decisions (by confirming his award), they must also retain the right to abrogate that award (if his conduct falls within the narrow parameters for vacatur). See id.

There is a fundamental difference between the instant case and Hoeft. In Hoeft, the non-appealability clause applied to a district court's review of the arbitrator's award. 343 F.3d at 63. Here, on the other hand, the clause applies only to an appellate court's review of the district court's judgment (presumably confirming or vacating the arbitrator's award). As a result, none of the policy concerns implicated by Hoeft are present in this case. The agreement here preserves district court review under 9 U.S.C. § 10(a)(3), and while an unsatisfied defendant would not be able to appeal a district court order denying his application to vacate the award, so too would an unsatisfied plaintiff be unable to contest a district court's vacatur of an arbitration award in plaintiff's favor. From the parties' perspective, *830 then, the risks of a negative outcome resulting from the non-appealability clause are borne equally by both sides. What we have here is something less than full judicial review of the arbitrator's decision; but we do not have a situation in which there is no judicial review at all, nor a situation where a court is asked to enforce an arbitration award without being given the authority to review compliance of that award with the FAA. It is, in a sense, a compromise whereby the litigants trade the risk of protracted appellate review for a one-shot opportunity before the district court.Indeed, courts routinely enforce agreements that waive the right to appellate review over district court decisions. See 15A Charles Alan Wright et al., Federal Practice and Procedure 3901, at 18–19 (2d ed.1992) [hereinafter "Wright & Miller"]. We see no reason to treat district court decisions concerning arbitration awards differently than any other kind of district court judgment.

Thus, consistent with our dicta in Bowen, we hold that contractual provisions limiting the right to appeal from a district court's judgment confirming or vacating an arbitration award are permissible, so long as the intent to do so is clear and unequivocal. Here, the parties' contract expressly provided that the district court's judgment would be both "final" and "nonappealable" While use of the term "final" would not, by itself, be enough to convey an intent to eliminate appellate rights, see Bowen, 254 F.3d at 931, inclusion of the term "nonappealable" serves this purpose.

Accordingly, Gorelick's motion to dismiss the arbitration appeal for lack of jurisdiction is GRANTED. This leaves only our consideration of the declaratory judgment appeal.

II. Whether MACTEC's declaratory judgment appeal is barred by the doctrine of res judicata.

As noted above, in addition to its application to vacate the arbitration award, MACTEC contemporaneously sought, in a separate legal proceeding before the same district court, a declaration that Gorelick's (and, by implication, the arbitrator's) interpretation of the contract permitted Gorelick to collect royalties on unpatented technologies and therefore constituted patent misuse.Although framed as an illegality of contract issue, MACTEC originally raised this argument at the arbitration. That is, MACTEC claimed that Gorelick's interpretation of the contract would *831 amount to patent misuse and as a result, would be an illegal contract which would be unenforceable under basic contract law principles. The arbitrator ruled that MACTEC could not assert a patent misuse defense because (1) MACTEC failed timely to file its defense; and (2) because issues of patent invalidity were, by the terms of the arbitration agreement, beyond the scope of arbitrable issues.

MACTEC then re-asserted this argument before the district court in its application to vacate the arbitration award, arguing that since the arbitration award permitted patent misuse, it must be vacated on public policy grounds. See Denver & Rio Grande W. R.R. Co. v. Union Pac. R.R. Co., 119 F.3d 847, 849 (10th Cir.1997) (noting that courts may vacate arbitration awards that violate public policy). The district court considered and rejected this argument, based on its conclusions that Gorelick was never a patent holder of the NoVOCs technology, the payments were voluntary, and the agreement was not a patent license.

When MACTEC filed its declaratory judgment action, Gorelick moved to dismiss under Fed. R.Civ.P. 12, arguing, inter alia, that the suit was barred by res judicata. Although the district court did not base its dismissal of the suit on res judicata,we nevertheless consider it as an alternate ground of affirmance because it was adequately raised below. See Blum v. Bacon, 457 U.S. 132, 138 n. 5, 102 S.Ct. 2355, 72 L.Ed.2d 728 (1982).

Thus, the precise issue before our court is whether the arbitration award itself (or the district court's subsequent confirmation of the award) precludes MACTEC's subsequently-filed declaratory judgment action. The application of res judicata is a question of law which we review de novo. Satsky v. Paramount Communications, Inc., 7 F.3d 1464, 1467–68 (10th Cir.1993).

The doctrine of res judicata, or claim preclusion, will prevent a party from relitigating a legal claim that was or could have been the subject of a previously issued final judgment. Id. at 1467. Under Tenth Circuit law, claim preclusion applies when three elements exist: (1) a final judgment on the merits in an earlier action; (2) identity of the parties in the two suits; and (3) identity of the cause of action in both suits. Wilkes v. Wyo. Dep't of Employment Div. of Labor Standards, 314 F.3d 501, 504 (10th Cir.2003). If these requirements are met, res judicata is appropriate unless the party seeking to avoid preclusion did not have a "full and fair opportunity" to litigate the claim in the prior suit. Yapp v. Excel Corp., 186 F.3d 1222, 1226 n. 4 (10th Cir.1999).

Here, it is undisputed that the parties to the arbitration and the declaratory judgment were the same. As for finality, a valid and final award by arbitration generally has the same effect under the rules of res judicata as a judgment of a court. Restatement (Second) of Judgments § 84(1) & cmt. b (1980). Indeed,

[i]f any party dissatisfied with the award were left free to pursue independent judicial proceedings on the same claim or defenses, arbitration would be substantially worthless. Unless the express terms of the agreement or the peculiar custom of a trade dictate otherwise, therefore, subsequent judicial proceedings on the same claim or defenses ordinarily should be

precluded. And so the courts rule.

Wright & Miller, supra,4475.1 at 509; but cf. McDonald v. City of West Branch, 466 U.S. 284, 292, 104 S.Ct. 1799, 80 L.Ed.2d 302 (1984) (holding that in an action under 42 U.S.C. § 1983, a federal court should not afford res judicata effect to an arbitration award brought pursuant to a collective-bargaining agreement because of the special federal rights that a § 1983 action is designed to protect).

Here, MACTEC has not challenged whether the arbitration award (or the district court's confirmation thereof) was final, but rather whether the award may be appealed to this court. The appealability of a judgment, however, does not hinder its preclusive effect. See 18A Wright & Miller, supra,4433, at 78–85 (noting general rule that a final judgment from a lower court carries res judicata effect even though it is still subject to review by an appellate court).

Identity of the cause of action is also present in both suits. Wilkes, 314 F.3d at 504. To determine what constitutes a "cause of action" for preclusion purposes, this court has adopted the "transactional approach" found in the Restatement (Second) of Judgments Petromanagement Corp. v. Acme–Thomas Joint Venture, 835 F.2d 1329, 1335 (10th Cir.1988). Under this approach, a cause of action includes all claims or legal theories of recovery that arise from the same transaction. Id. A contract is generally considered to be a "transaction" for claim preclusion purposes. Id. at 1336.

Here, MACTEC's allegations of patent misuse clearly arise out of the same contractual transaction as the underlying arbitration—the execution of the stock purchase agreement between Gorelick and MACTEC (as EG & G's successor-in-interest) and the subsequent renegotiation of the agreement's terms in 1998. Thus, the third prong of claim preclusion is met.

However, MACTEC contends that it did not have a full and fair opportunity to raise the patent misuse defense at the arbitration. This is because, according to MACTEC, the arbitrator refused to allow MACTEC to present a patent misuse defense because it ruled that such issues were beyond the scope of the arbitration. Because the arbitrator was jurisdictionally barred from considering its patent misuse defense, MACTEC argues that it never had the opportunity to litigate this claim.

But this argument ignores the fact that MACTEC had a second chance to assert its patent misuse theory before the district court in its application to vacate the arbitration award. Indeed, MACTEC took advantage of this opportunity, arguing in its written motion that the arbitrator's award permitted patent misuse and should thus be vacated on public policy grounds. Furthermore, the district court considered and rejected this argument on the merits. Once the district court issued its decision, any subsequent litigation raising patent misuse was precluded. As we have noted above, the district court's decision to confirm the arbitration award (over

MACTEC's patent misuse objections) was nonappealable. Accordingly, the declaratory judgment action is barred by res judicata.

CONCLUSION

For the reasons stated above, the arbitration appeal (No. 03–1378) is DISMISSED for lack of jurisdiction. As to the declaratory judgment appeal (No. 03–1290) we AFFIRM the judgment of the district court dismissing the case.

【本案评析】

本案涉及对专利发明的特许权使用费支付的合同纠纷。主要反映了仲裁实务中的撤销仲裁裁决、法院对仲裁裁决之裁定进行审查的管辖权、仲裁裁决的可执行性几个问题。在案件中，上诉人 MACTEC 是同被上诉人 Gorelick 签订的股份买卖协议的利益继受者。该协议要求 MACTEC 向 Gorelick 支付使用 Gorelick 专利技术的专利费。协议中仲裁条款约定："对仲裁员所作裁决之判决是最终的和不可上诉的。"后双方当事人之间就专利费支付产生争议。争议提交仲裁，仲裁裁决的结果是裁决 MACTEC 支付 450 万美元的损害赔偿。MACTEC 在美国科罗拉多地区法院根据《联邦仲裁法》第 10(a)(3)条请求撤销上述裁决。随后，MACTEC 提起了一个独立的诉讼，要求一份宣告性判决，判定 Gorelick 对合同的解释构成专利权的滥用。地区法院裁定该裁决是可执行的，拒绝了 MACTEC 的专利有效性的主张并且驳回了两起诉讼。MACTEC 因此提起了上诉。

美国第十巡回上诉法院认为，作为优先考虑事项，其缺乏对确认仲裁裁决之裁定进行审查的管辖权，理由是当事人间的仲裁条款清楚明确地排除了对地区法院判决的上诉。法院区分了其他限制当事人扩大或者限制司法审查能力的先例，并且裁定其所审理的条款是可执行的，因为符合通过地区法院为当事人提供充分保护的同时支持有效审查裁决的联邦政策。法院认定 MACTEC 在仲裁程序中以及其撤销仲裁裁决的申请中都提出了滥用专利的问题，故以案件已产生既判力为由维持了地区法院对宣告判决诉讼的驳回裁定。

第二节　国际商事仲裁协议部分

【知识背景 / 学习要点】

一、国际商事仲裁协议的有效性

国际商事仲裁协议的有效性对仲裁程序具有重要的意义。这个问题出现在许多国际仲裁中，并可能对仲裁程序的进程产生决定性的影响。改为：国际商事仲裁的有效性分为形式有效性和实质有效性。

（一）形式有效性

从国际层面来看，主要涉及国际商事仲裁的国际公约，包括一些区域性的国际公约，均要求仲裁协议应采用书面方式订立。比如《纽约公约》第 2 条即要求各缔约国应承认，当事人以书面协定承诺彼此间所发生或可能发生的一切或任何争议，如涉及可以仲裁解决事项的确定法律关系，应提交仲裁，而无论其是否为契约性质。而且该条还将“书面协定”规定为，当事人所签订或在互换函电中所载明的契约仲裁条款或仲裁协定。此外，世界银行集团旗下达成的《解决国家与他国国民间投资争端公约》中也有对于投资仲裁类似的规定，公约第 25 条即要求在争端解决国际中心（ICSID）主持下进行仲裁的协议应符合书面形式。

从国内层面来讲，虽然有些个别例外，但是大多数国家的仲裁法规中也包含了“书面形式”的相关要求，以作为仲裁协议形式有效性上的法定纪律。这些“书面形式”要求在大多数国家法律制度以及许多国际文件中都有着较为深厚的历史渊源联系。 比如 1985 年《联合国国际贸易法委员会国际商事仲裁示范法》第 7 条第（2）款规定，“仲裁协议应为书面形式”。

（二）实质有效性

与一般的合同类似，国际商事仲裁协议不仅存在形式有效性的问题，同样也有实质性效力的问题。比如《纽约公约》第2条第3款规定，当事人就诉讼事项订有本条所称之协定者，缔约国法院受理诉讼时应依当事人一造之请求，命当事人提交仲裁，但前述协定经法院认定无效、失效或不能实行者不在此限。《联合国国际贸易法委员会国际商事仲裁示范法》第8条(1)规定，就仲裁协议的标的向法院提起诉讼时，如当事一方在不迟于其就争议实体提出第一次申述时要求仲裁，法院应让当事各方交付仲裁，除非法院认定仲裁协议无效、不能实行或不能履行。

一些国家仲裁立法中所载的仲裁协议实质性无效的范围，一般仅限于仲裁协议出现通常适用的合同法中规定的无效的情况，例如严重误解、欺诈行为、显失公平和胁迫、履行不能、放弃权利或情势变更等。但是，在某些国家或地区，其仲裁立法中也可能会规定特殊的无效规则，如处理不同类型合同的仲裁协议时，某些无效的要求只适用于某些类别的争端。下面具体说明如下：

1. 显失公平和胁迫

大多数国家或地区的合同法中都基本上会规定显失公平的协议或通过胁迫获得的协议是无效的。当出现在国际商事争端实务中时，当事人有时会提出争辩，认为包含仲裁条款或仲裁协议本身的合同是显失公平的，要求排除对此类仲裁条款的执行。

2. 欺诈行为

欺诈使一切行为无效，因此无论是通过直接诱导的方式进行欺诈，还是通过虚构事实的方式欺诈所订立的协议均是无法律效力的，当然此类仲裁条款和协议也是不可强制执行的。

3. 履行不能和履约受挫

一般各国的合同法律制度都承认履行不能（当事人自身的原因导致合同无法履行）或履约受挫（当事人以外的原因导致无法履行合同，也有国家称为“不可抗力")是可以不履行合同义务的合法理由。因此尽管实际上它们很少被适用，但是在原则上，履行不能和履约受挫同样也是适用于国际仲裁协议效力的认定的。

4. 违法性协议

违法性的协议，也即协议本身的条款和内容违反法律的规定，是不受合同法律保护的，因此此类协议一般也是无效的，仲裁协议具有违法性也不例外。实务中，仲裁协议违法性的依据主要包括不符合竞争政策、有违金融监管或受到贸易制裁限制等合同原因所导致的问题，但在有的情况下，违法性也包括在一些特定的领域，国家不允许采取仲裁的方式处理纠纷，比如涉及消费者权益或劳动权益合同等情况。当然，由于不同国家的法律制度不尽相同，因此在处理此类的仲裁协议的违法性问题时，也会存在各种不同的情况。

5. 能力和资格

限制行为能力或无行为能力的人，无法作出正确的判断，各国立法基本都规定，其不能对诸如诉权等重大权益作出处分行为。订立仲裁协议是重大的法律行为，其涉及当事人间重要的争议事项，因此不具有完全行为能力的自然人及不具备资格的法人和其他组织，其订立的仲裁协议并不当然具有法律效力。同样地，由于资格和能力问题，其所签订的仲裁协议不仅无效，而且根据该协议作出的裁决也将因此而无法得到法院的承认与执行。比如《纽约公约》第 5 条第 1 款第 1 项规定："协定之当事人依对其适用之法律有某种无行为能力情形者，或该项协定依当事人作为协定准据法之法律系属无效，或未指明以何法律为准时，依裁决地所在国法律系属无效者。"这就是把确定的标准交由各国国内法决定。

6. 放弃仲裁权

与其他的合同权利一样，仲裁权也是可以放弃的。一些国家的立法中也规定，对仲裁权的放弃可以作为对仲裁协议的抗辩理由之一。[①]

① Gary B Born, *International Commercial Arbitration,* Kluwer Law International, 2009, pp.736~743.

二、国际商事仲裁协议独立性

在国际范围内，仲裁条款一般被推定为可从基础合同中“分离”或“分割”出来而具有其独立性。这种独立性具体由国家仲裁立法或由来自世界各地几乎所有司法管辖区的司法裁决，以及主要的机构仲裁规则所规定。这一推定在国际商事贸易和投资中同样得到承认。

仲裁协议的独立性同时表明即使通过了一项与基础商事合同具有密切联系的仲裁协议，该协议也可推定为一项独立的协议。根据一项主要的国际仲裁裁决：“国际判例法的若干决定维护了仲裁条款的自治原则或独立性。”分析理由是，当事人的仲裁协议包涵了当事人之间给予的与基础合同内容不同的且独立的承诺：“通常当事人间的相互承诺是独立于基础合同的，并使得该仲裁协议形成可分离和可执行的部分。”

这种独立性通常被认为对仲裁程序产生重大影响：“国际仲裁条款的自主性是国际仲裁中的概念基石。除非另有规定，仲裁协议独立性表明了仲裁条款的持续有效性（尽管当事人的基础合同有缺陷），并允许将不同的实体法适用于当事人之间的仲裁协议和基础合同。”

三、国际商事仲裁协议的法律适用

国际商事仲裁协议的法律选择是一项复杂但极为重要的内容，但在当前国际仲裁领域关于仲裁的法律选择却引起了广泛的争议与法律选择的混乱，而这与简化、高效和合理化解决争端的国际仲裁的目标不相称。然而，当前，该法律选择的问题作为一个实践问题，首要前提就是必须理解当代冲突法理论的复杂性，并通过有益的探索减少国际仲裁法律选择的混乱状况。

仲裁协议的法律选择方式主要包括以下几个部分：（a）各当事方明示或默示地选择适用于仲裁协议本身的法律；（b）仲裁地法律；（c）适用于基础合同的法律；（d）寻求对仲裁协议进行司法执行的法院所在地的法律。仲裁庭、法院或陪审员在作出法律选择时几乎没有统一的做法。

在国际商事仲裁过程中，仲裁的法律适用因受到《纽约公约》和内国法的共同规制可能会产生不同的法律后果，具体而言，《纽约公约》和内国法的相关法律规则会对国际商事仲裁协议的法律选择提供依据，而在《纽约公约》和内国法之间找到关于准据法的确定方式和其他实质性规则的选择办法的平衡点是极其困难的。

【案例摘录与评析】

一、国际商事仲裁协议有效性案例[1]

KAHN LUCAS LANCASTER, INC., Plaintiff–Appellee,

v.

LARK INTERNATIONAL LTD., Defendant–Appellant.

No. 97–9436.

Argued June 12, 1998.

Decided July 29, 1999.

PARKER, Circuit Judge:

Defendant–Appellant Lark International, Ltd., ("Lark") appeals from a judgment of the United States District Court for the Southern District of New York (Denise L. Cote, Judge), entered August 15, 1997, granting Plaintiff–Appellee Kahn Lucas Lancaster, Inc.'s("Kahn Lucas") motion under 9 U.S.C. § 206 and the Convention on the Recognition and Enforcement of Foreign Arbitral Awards, Jun. 10, 1958, 21 U.S.T. 2517, 330 U.N.T.S. 3(entered into force with respect to the United States, Dec. 29, 1970) (the "New York Convention" or the "Convention"), as implemented, 9 U.S.C. §§ 201–08, to compel arbitration. The judgment was entered in accordance with an Opinion and Order of the district court, dated August 6, 1997, which held that arbitration clauses in certain purchase orders sent by Kahn Lucas to Lark were enforceable under the Convention and bound Lark, despite the fact that Lark had not signed the purchase orders.

We reverse.

---

① Kahn Lucas Lancaster, Inc. v. Lark Intern. Ltd..United States Court of Appeals, Second Circuit. July 29, 1999186 F.3d 210 (Approx. 12 pages).

I. BACKGROUND

A. Facts

Lark is a Hong Kong corporation which acts as a purchasing agent for businesses seeking to buy and import clothing manufactured in Asia. Kahn Lucas is a New York corporation, with its principal place of business in New York, NY, engaged in the children's clothing business, primarily in reselling imported clothing to major retailers.

Kahn Lucas and Lark enjoyed a business relationship which began in 1988 and pursuant to which Lark would assist Kahn Lucas in arranging for overseas manufacturers to make garments ordered by Kahn Lucas. As part of this relationship, Lark processed KahnLucas's purchase orders and invoices. Pursuant to the terms of the purchase orders, as well as the parties' standing practice, the manufacturers would issue Kahn Lucas a seller's invoice for payment once the ordered garments were completed. Lark would then issue a separate invoice to Kahn Lucas for its commission, usually a set percentage of the amount charged by the manufacturer, on the order. Kahn Lucas paid both of these invoices through draw-downs on an existing letter of credit on which Lark was the named beneficiary. Lark would then remit payment to the manufacturer.

The dispute in this case arises from two purchase orders Kahn Lucas issued in early 1995 for children's fleece garments, manufactured in the Philippines, that it was to resell to Sears Roebuck, Inc. (the "Purchase Orders").

The Purchase Orders stated that the garments were "ordered from" Lark, listed "Lark International (Agent)" as seller, and were signed by Kahn Lucas. They were not signed by Lark. The Purchase Orders also clearly indicated that they contained a number of additional terms printed on the reverse side, and were made conditional upon the seller's acceptance of those terms. Included in these terms were clauses relating to arbitration, which stated:

Any controversy arising out of or relating to this Order ... shall be resolved by arbitration in the City of New York.... The parties consent to application of the New York or Federal Arbitration Statutes and to the jurisdiction of the Supreme Court of the State of New York, and of the United States District Court for the Southern District of New York, for all purposes in connection with said arbitration....

(the"Arbitration Clauses"). Lark accepted the Purchase Orders without objection.

In July 1995, the manufacturers issued final invoices relating to the ordered garments, and Lark issued its commission invoice. But citing defective garments and failed deliveries, Kahn Lucas refused to release funds to Lark to pay either the seller's invoices or Lark's commission invoice.

B. Proceedings Below

Unable to achieve a satisfactory settlement with Lark and the manufacturers, Kahn Lucas sued Lark in the United States District Court for the Southern District of New York, invoking diversity jurisdiction and alleging breach of contract, breach of warranty, negligence, and breach of fiduciary duty. Lark responded to the complaint with a motion to dismiss for lack of personal jurisdiction. Kahn Lucas responded by asserting numerous bases upon which to premise personal jurisdiction, including transient jurisdiction (as one of Lark's officers had been served while in New York) and the New York long arm statute, N.Y. C.P.L.R. § 302(a)(1). In an Opinion and Order dated February 24, 1997, the district court held that it did not have personal jurisdiction over Lark to adjudicate the then-pending claims, but also held that, given the Arbitration Clauses, it would have personal jurisdiction over Lark if Kahn Lucas were to seek to compel arbitration. See Kahn Lucas Lancaster, Inc. v. Lark Int'l Ltd., 956 F.Supp. 1131, 1139 (S.D.N.Y.1997) ("Kahn Lucas I"). Accordingly, the district court conditionally dismissed Kahn Lucas's claims, but stayed the dismissal to afford Kahn Lucas the opportunity to bring a motion to compel arbitration.

By motion brought pursuant to 9 U.S.C. § 206 and the Convention, Kahn Lucas converted its complaint into a motion to compel Lark to arbitrate the dispute in accordance with the Arbitration Clauses.Kahn Lucas also filed a demand for arbitration with the American Arbitration Association. Lark opposed the motion to compel arbitration. Lark argued that it was not bound by the provisions of the Purchase Orders because the Purchase Orders were directed towards the sellers of the garments to which they related, namely the manufacturers, and not towards Lark. Lark also argued that the Arbitration Clauses were not enforceable under the Convention because Lark had not signed the Purchase Orders.

In an Opinion and Order dated August 6, 1997,the district court granted Kahn Lucas's motion to compel arbitration. Kahn LucasLancaster, Inc. v. Lark Int'l Ltd., No. 95 CIV. 10506, 1997 WL 458785 at (S.D.N.Y. Aug.11, 1997) ("Kahn Lucas II "). The district court first noted that subject matter jurisdiction could only be properly based on section 203 of the implementing statutes of the Convention, 9 U.S.C. § 203, which provides an independent basis for subject matter jurisdiction; it could not be based on diversity. Id. at [citing Matimak Trading Co. v. Khalily, 118 F.3d 76 (2d Cir.1997) (holding that Hong Kong corporations are not citizens of a foreign state for purposes of diversity jurisdiction)]. Section 203 states that "[a]n action or proceeding falling under the Convention shall be deemed to arise under the laws and treaties of the United States." 9 U.S.C. § 203.

The court next focused on whether the Arbitration Clauses were enforceable under the Convention so as to vest the court with jurisdiction under section 203. The Convention provides that "[e]ach Contracting State shall recognize an agreement in writing under which the parties undertake to submit to arbitration all or any differences which have arisen or which may arise between them ... concerning a subject matter capable of settlement by arbitration." New York Convention art. II, § 1. The Convention goes on to define "agreement in writing" to include "an arbitral clause in a contract or an arbitration agreement, signed by the parties or contained in an exchange of letters or telegrams." New York Convention art. II, § 2. Although Lark had not signed the Purchase Orders, the district court held that the Purchase Orders represented an "arbitral clause in a contract," and therefore an "agreement in writing" to arbitrate sufficient to bring the dispute within the Convention. In holding that an arbitral clause in a contract need not be signed by the parties to be enforceable under the Convention, the district court relied on the only appellate case interpreting this section of the Convention, Sphere Drake Ins. PLC v. Marine Towing, Inc., 16 F.3d 666, 669 (5th Cir.1994) [outlining, without much analysis, article II, section 1 of the Convention as including "(1) an arbitral clause in a contract or (2) an arbitration agreement, (a) signed by the parties or (b) contained in an exchange of letters or telegrams"), and declined to follow Sen Mar, Inc. v. Tiger Petroleum Corp., 774 F.Supp. 879, 882 (S.D.N.Y.1991)] ("An arbitration clause is enforceable only if it is found in a signed writing or an exchange of letters.").

The district court then turned to Lark's argument that it should not be bound by the Arbitration Clauses because it was not the seller of the garments.

The district court held that the Purchase Orders embodied "an agreement between Kahn Lucas and Lark for the sale of goods, as opposed to an agreement between Kahn Lucas and the manufacturers." Kahn Lucas II, 1997 WL 458785 at *5. The district court relied on the fact that Kahn Lucas and Lark were the only parties mentioned on the Purchase Orders, and on the fact that Kahn Lucas was to pay Lark directly for the garments ultimately delivered under the Purchase Orders. See id. Finally, the district court found that Lark was bound to the terms of the Purchase Orders despite the fact it did not sign them because it manifested assent to the Purchase Orders by performing under them, and that the subject of the dispute was therefore within the scope of the Arbitration Clauses. See id. at *6.

Lark then moved pursuant to Fed.R.Civ.P. 59 to alter or amend the district court's judgment, but the district court promptly denied this motion. Lark timely appealed.

II. ANALYSIS

On appeal, Lark advances largely the same arguments that it did below. First, it argues that in order to be enforceable under the terms of the Convention, any agreement to arbitrate, be it an "arbitral clause in a contract" or an "arbitration agreement," must be signed by the parties or contained in an exchange of letters or telegrams. Because the Purchase Orders were not signed by both parties, the argument continues, they are not "agreements in writing" enforceable under the Convention. Second, Lark argues that the district court erred in finding that it was bound by the terms of the Purchase Orders, including the Arbitration Clauses, because it was not the seller of the garments.

For the reasons that follow, we hold that the definition of "agreement in writing" in the Convention requires that such an agreement, whether it be an arbitration agreement or an arbitral clause in a contract, be signed by the parties or contained in a series of letters or telegrams. Therefore, the Arbitration Clauses are not enforceable under the Convention, and both the district court and this Court lack subject matter jurisdiction over the dispute. Because of this holding, we need not consider Lark's second argument, and we accordingly reverse the judgment of the district court and dismiss Kahn Lucas's motion to compel arbitration for lack of subject matter jurisdiction.

A. Applicable Principles of Construction

Treaties are construed in much the same manner as statutes. See United States v. Alvarez–Machain, 504 U.S. 655, 663, 112 S.Ct. 2188, 119 L.Ed.2d 441 (1992); see also Sale v. Haitian Ctrs. Council, Inc., 509 U.S. 155, 177–83, 113 S.Ct. 2549, 125 L.Ed.2d 128 (1993). The district court's construction of the Convention, like the construction of any statute, is a matter of law which we review de novo. See Stuart v. United States, 813 F.2d 243, 246 (9th Cir.1987), rev'd on other grounds, 489 U.S. 353, 109 S.Ct. 1183, 103 L.Ed.2d 388 (1989); see also Koreag, Controle et Revision S.A. v. Refco F/X Assocs., Inc., 961 F.2d 341, 347–48 (2d Cir.1992). Statutory construction is a "holistic endeavor" and must account for the statute's "full text, language as well as punctuation, structure and subject matter." United States Nat'l Bank v. Independent Ins. Agents of Am., Inc., 508 U.S. 439, 455, 113 S.Ct. 2173, 124 L.Ed.2d 402 (1993) (internal quotations omitted). Thus, the obvious starting point in construing a treaty is its text. See Eastern Airlines, Inc. v. Floyd, 499 U.S. 530, 534, 111 S.Ct. 1489, 113 L.Ed.2d 569 (1991). And the plain meaning of a text "will typically heed the commands of its punctuation." United States Nat'l Bank, 508 U.S at 454, 113 S.Ct. 2173; see also United States v. Ron Pair Enters., Inc., 489 U.S. 235, 241–42, 109 S.Ct. 1026, 103 L.Ed.2d 290 (1989) (holding that the "grammatical structure of the statute," specifically the placement of commas, mandated a specific construction).

Among the rules of punctuation applied in construing statutes is this: When a modifier is set off from a series of antecedents by a comma, the modifier should be read to apply to each of those antecedents. See Bingham, Ltd. v. United States, 724 F.2d 921, 925–26 n. 3 (11th Cir.1984); see also Elliot Coal Mining Co. v. Director, Office of Workers' Comp. Programs, 17 F.3d 616, 630 (3d Cir.1994) (noting that the "use of a comma to set off a modifying phrase from other clauses indicates that the qualifying language is to be applied to all of the previous phrases and not merely the immediately preceding phrase"). As stated by the Eleventh Circuit, this rule is a "supplementary 'rule of punctuation,' " to the "doctrine of the last antecedent," which states that a modifier generally applies only to the nearest, or last, antecedent.1 See Bingham, 724 F.2d at 925–26 n. 3 [citing Quindlen v. Prudential Ins. Co. of Am., 482 F.2d 876, 878 (5th Cir.1973)]. Of course, "these doctrines are not absolute rules," id. at 926 n. 3, and in applying them we are mindful of the Supreme Court's admonition that "a purported plain-meaning analysis based only on punctuation is necessarily incomplete and runs the risk of distorting a statute's true meaning." United States Nat'l Bank, 508 U.S. at 454, 113 S.Ct. 2173.

In addition to utilizing rules of punctuation, we are aided in our plain-meaning analysis by the fact that the Convention exists in five official languages—French, Spanish, English, Chinese, and Russian—of equal authenticity. See New York Convention art. XVI, § 1. Because one purpose of the Convention is to unify the standards under which international agreements to arbitrate are observed, Scherk v. Alberto–Culver Co., 417 U.S. 506, 520 n. 15, 94 S.Ct. 2449, 41 L.Ed.2d 270 (1974), we should, if possible, adhere to an interpretation consistent with all of the official languages. That said, some of the official languages provide more insight into the drafters' intent than others: Of the five official languages, English, French, and Spanish were the working languages of the United Nations Conference on International Commercial Arbitration, which drafted the Convention. See Rules of Procedure, U.N. Conference on Int'l Commercial Arbitration, Rule 32, E/Conf.26/5/Rev.1 (1958)(hereinafter "Rules of Procedure "); see also Eastern Airlines, 499 U.S. at 536, 111 S.Ct. 1489 (considering language employed by drafters to gain insight into intent of parties). All records of Conference meetings were kept in these working languages. Rules of Procedure at Rule 36.

Finally, to the extent the drafters' intent is unclear from the text of the multiple versions of the Convention, we may turn to the Convention's legislative history for guidance. Eastern Airlines, 499 U.S. at 535, 111 S.Ct. 1489 (treaty history and negotiations may be consulted in construing difficult or ambiguous treaty passages).

B. Construction of the New York Convention

As noted above, article II, section 1 of the Convention provides that each contracting state (including the United States, China, the United Kingdom, and Hong Kong) "shall recognize" an "agreement in writing" to arbitrate a given dispute. Article II, section 2, in turn, defines the term "agreement in writing" to include "an arbitral clause in a contract or an arbitration agreement, signed by the parties or contained in an exchange of letters or telegrams." Lark contends that the modifying clause "signed by the parties or contained in an exchange of letters or telegrams," modifies both: (1) "an arbitral clause in a contract" and (2) "an arbitration agreement" and, as a result, the dispute between the parties is not arbitrable due to the absence of Lark's signature on the Purchase Orders. Kahn Lucas contends, and the district court held, that "signed by the parties" modifies only the clause immediately preceding it, "an arbitration agreement," and not the previous clause. Thus, in Kahn Lucas's view, the unsigned Purchase Orders constitute an "agreement in writing" to arbitrate enforceable under the Convention.

As an initial matter, we must determine the meaning of the two elements in the series, namely "an arbitral clause in a contract" and "an arbitration agreement." We find the meaning of "an arbitral clause in a contract" to be self-evident. We also find that the phrase "an arbitration agreement," because it is used in conjunction with the phrase "an arbitral clause in a contract," refers to any agreement to arbitrate which is not a clause in a larger agreement, whether that agreement is part of a larger contractual relationship or is an entirely distinct agreement which relates to a non-contractual dispute. The parties agree that the Arbitration Clauses each constitute "an arbitral clause in a contract" and not "an arbitration agreement" under the Convention.

We turn, then, to the plain meaning of the English-language version of the Convention. Taking its lead from the Fifth Circuit's analysis in Sphere Drake, 16 F.3d at 669–70, Kahn Lucas argues that the grammatical structure of section 2 compels the conclusion that its dispute with Lark falls within the Convention. We disagree. Section 2 takes the structure "A or B, with C." This structure is exactly that to which the "supplementary rule of punctuation" expressed in Bingham applies. Grammatically, the comma immediately following "an arbitration agreement" serves to separate the series ("an arbitral clause in a contract or an arbitration agreement") from the modifying phrase ("signed by the parties or contained in an exchange of letters or telegrams"), and suggests that the modifying phrase is meant to apply to both elements in the series. Indeed, this comma can serve no other grammatical purpose. As a result, Kahn Lucas's reading of the statute would render the comma mere surplusage, a construction frowned upon. Cf. Trichilo v. Secretary of Health & Human Servs., 823 F.2d 702, 706 (2d Cir.1987) ("we will not interpret a statute so that some of its terms are rendered a nullity").

Although the grammatical structure of the English-language version of the Convention suggests that the parties' dispute is not arbitrable, we are hesitant to use punctuation as the sole guide to the meaning of the text. See United States Nat'l Bank, 508 U.S. at 454–55, 113 S.Ct. 2173. But in this case, other available interpretive tools strongly support the conclusion the punctuation suggests.

First, the plain language of the other working-language versions of the Convention compels the conclusion that, in order to be enforceable under the Convention, both an arbitral clause in a contract and an arbitration agreement must be signed by the parties or contained in an exchange of letters or telegrams. In the French- and Spanish-language versions, the word for "signed" appears in the plural form, "signes " and "firmados " respectively. New York Convention, 21 U.S.T. 2524, 2538. Because each of the two antecedents is couched in the singular, the modifier unambiguously applies to both of them. If, as Kahn Lucas argues, only an arbitration agreement need be signed by the parties, the French-language version would utilize the verb "signe " and the Spanish "firmado".

The non-working official-language versions of the Convention do not offer similarly clear-cut support for this interpretation, but do not weigh strongly against it either. The Chinese-language version, like the English-language version, cannot utilize a uniquely plural form of the verb for "signed." Nor does it contain punctuation helpful to our task. However, in the Chinese-language version, the modifier "signed" precedes, rather than follows, the objects it modifies. New York Convention, 21 U.S.T. 2529. Therefore, if the modifier were construed to apply only to one of the objects, it would apply to "arbitral clause in a contract," rather than "arbitration agreement," offering no comfort to Kahn Lucas in this case. The Russian-language version uses the singular form of the verb "signed" (transliterated as "PODPECANOYE"), suggesting that it modifies only "arbitration agreement." New York Convention, 21 U.S.T. 2533. But because the plain meaning of the French- and Spanish-language versions of the Convention unambiguously supports the conclusion that the modifier applies to both antecedents, the structure of the English-language version suggests such an interpretation, and the Chinese-language version is susceptible of such an interpretation, we are reluctant to allow the seemingly contradictory Russian-language version to dictate a different result. See Eastern Airlines, 499 U.S. at 536, 111 S.Ct. 1489 (giving controlling weight to meaning of language in which treaty was drafted). This is particularly so in light of the stated purposes of the Convention, one of which is to "unify the standards by which agreements to arbitrate are observed and arbitral awards are enforced in the signatory countries." Scherk, 417 U.S. at 520 n. 15, 94 S.Ct. 2449 (citing the Convention).

Finally, to the extent the plain meanings of the non-English language versions of the Convention do not resolve any ambiguity that exists in the English-language version, the legislative history of article II puts the matter to rest. The text of article II, as reported by the Conference's Working Group, and subject only to modification by the Drafting Committee for form, not substance, Summary of the 23d Meeting, U.N. Conference on Int'l Commercial Arbitration, U.N. ESCOR, E/Conf.26/SR.23 at 4, 7 (Sept. 12, 1958), reverses the terms "arbitration agreement" and "arbitration clause in a contract." The Working Group text thus reads: "The expression 'agreement in writing' shall mean an arbitration agreement or an arbitration clause in a contract signed by the parties, or an exchange of letters or telegrams between those parties." Consideration of the Draft New York Convention on the Recognition and Enforcement of Foreign Arbitral Awards, U.N.

Conference on Int'l Commercial Arbitration, U.N. ESCOR, E/Conf.26/ L.59, Agenda Item 4, 2 (June 6, 1958). Therefore, unless the modifier "signed" in the Convention applies to both antecedents, the Drafting Committee's editorial changes would amount to an unintended, and unauthorized, substantive amendment to article II, section 2.

Accordingly, although we are cognizant that the Convention "should be interpreted broadly to effectuate its recognition and enforcement purposes," Bergesen v. Joseph Muller Corp., 710 F.2d 928, 933 (2d Cir.1983), the rules governing our construction do not allow us to follow the Fifth Circuit's interpretation of article II, section 2 as expressed in Sphere Drake. Upon review of the Convention's text, punctuation and subject matter, as well as an examination of the Convention's legislative history, we hold that the modifying phrase "signed by the parties or contained in an exchange of letters or telegrams" applies to both "an arbitral clause in a contract" and "an arbitration agreement."

C. Application to the Facts

Having determined that the Convention requires that "an arbitral clause in a contract" be "signed by the parties or contained in an exchange of letters or telegrams," we turn to the application of the Convention to the facts of this case.

As noted above, the Arbitration Clauses were contained in the Purchase Orders which were signed only by Kahn Lucas, and not by Lark. There is therefore no "arbitral clause in a contract ... signed by the parties." Further, Kahn Lucas does not contend that the Purchase Orders, even together with Lark's Confirmation of Order forms, represent "an arbitral clause in a contract ... contained in an exchange of letters or telegrams." As a result, there is no "agreement in writing" sufficient to bring this dispute within the scope of the Convention.

Because the dispute in question does not fall within the Convention, subject matter jurisdiction cannot properly be premised on 9 U.S.C. § 203. The district court and this Court thus lack subject matter jurisdiction over this dispute. The judgment of the district court is reversed, and Kahn Lucas's motion to compel arbitration is dismissed with prejudice.

III. CONCLUSION

For the foregoing reasons, the judgment of the district court is reversed, and Kahn Lucas's motion to compel arbitration is dismissed with prejudice for lack of subject matter jurisdiction.

【本案评析】

本案反映了仲裁实务中仲裁协议形式有效性的问题。在案件中，Kahn Lucas Lancaster, Inc. 起诉 Lark International, Ltd.，指控其违反合同义务。美国纽约南区地方法院根据《关于承认和执行外国仲裁裁决的公约》作出强制仲裁决定，Lark

International, Ltd. 提出上诉。本案的争议焦点在于双方仅有买方签署，卖方并未签署的买卖合同，其中约定的仲裁条款是否构成仲裁协议的形式有效性要件。上诉法院巡回审判法官 Parker 认为：(1)根据公约的规定，仲裁协议以及合同中的仲裁条款必须由当事人签字或包含在信函交换中；以及(2)仅由买方 Kahn Lucas Lancaster, Inc. 签署的采购合同中包含的仲裁条款并不足以构成将当事方的争议纳入公约范围的书面仲裁协议，强制仲裁的决定因此被驳回。

二、国际商事仲裁协议实质有效性案例[①]

Rizalyn BAUTISTA, Individually and as Personal Representative of the Estate of Mari–John Bautista, and all claiming by and through her, Plaintiff–Appellant,

v.

STAR CRUISES, Norwegian Cruise Line, Ltd., Defendants–Appellees.

No. 03–15884.

Jan. 18, 2005.

RESTANI, Chief Judge:

The S/S NORWAY's steam boiler exploded on May 25, 2003, while the cruise ship was in the Port of Miami. Six of the crewmembers represented in this action were killed and four were injured.Each crewmember's employment agreement with Defendant NCL includes an arbitration clause, which the district court enforced pursuant to the United Nations Convention on the Recognition and Enforcement of Foreign Arbitral Awards, opened for signature June 10, 1958, 21 U.S.T. 2517, 330 U.N.T.S. 3 (the "Convention"), and its implementing legislation, 9 U.S.C. §§ 202–208 (2002) (the "Convention Act").

See Bautista v. Star Cruises, 286 F.Supp.2d 1352 (S.D.Fla.2003).Plaintiffs' appeal presents an issue of first impression in this Circuit: whether the crewmembers' employment agreements were shielded from arbitration by the seamen employment contract exemption contained in section 1 of the Federal Arbitration Act, 9 U.S.C. §§ 1–16 (2002) (the "FAA").2 Because the FAA seamen exemption does not apply and the district court had jurisdiction to compel arbitration, we affirm.

---

① Bautista v. Star Cruises.United States Court of Appeals, Eleventh Circuit.January 18,2005.396 F.3d 1289.2005 A.M.C.372.18 Fla.L.Weekly Fed.C 177 (Approx. 17pages).

BACKGROUND

I. THE SUITS AGAINST STAR CRUISES AND NCL

Following the explosion aboard the NORWAY, Plaintiffs filed separate but nearly identical suits in Florida circuit court against Defendant–Appellee NCL, owner of the NORWAY, and Defendant–Appellee Star Cruises, alleged by Plaintiffs to be the parent company of NCL. The complaints sought damages for negligence and unseaworthiness under the Jones Act, 46 U.S.C.App. § 688, and for failure to provide maintenance, cure and unearned wages under the general maritime law of the United States.

NCL removed the ten cases to federal district court pursuant to section 205 of the Convention Act, which permits removal before the start of trial when the dispute relates to an arbitration agreement or arbitral award covered by the Convention. See 9 U.S.C. § 205.3 In the notices of *1293 removal filed with the district court, NCL described how the crewmembers were bound by employment agreements that include an arbitration provision covered by the Convention.

II. THE CREWMEMBERS' EMPLOYMENT AGREEMENTS INCORPORATE AN ARBITRATION PROVISION

At the time of the explosion, each crewmember's employment was governed by the terms of a standard employment contract executed by the crewmembers and representatives of NCL in the Philippines between August 2002 and March 2003. The Philippine government regulated the form and content of such employment contracts, as well as other aspects of the seamen hiring process, through a program administered by the Philippine Overseas Employment Administration ("POEA"), a division of the Department of Labor and Employment of the Republic of the Philippines ("DOLE").

Each crewmember signed a one-page standard employment agreement created by the POEA, with some variations according to the position for which the crewmember was hired. Each agreement sets forth the basic terms and conditions of the crewmember's employment, including the duration of the contract, the position accepted, and the monthly salary and hours of work. Additional terms and conditions are incorporated by reference: Paragraph 2 provides that the contract's terms and conditions shall be observed in accordance with POEA Department Order No. 4 and POEA Memorandum Circular No. 9. Department Order No. 4, in turn, incorporates the document containing the arbitration clause: The Standard Terms and Conditions Governing the Employment of Filipino Seafarers On Board Ocean–Going Vessels (the "Standard Terms"). Section 29 of the Standard Terms requires arbitration "in cases of claims and disputes arising from [the seaman's] employment," through submission of the claims to the National Labor Relations Commission ("NLRC"), voluntary arbitrators, or a panel of arbitrators. Standard Terms, sec. 29; R.3.60, p. 1.5

A POEA official verified and approved the execution of the employment contract by the crewmembers and NCL representatives. Although Plaintiffs dispute that the crewmembers saw the arbitration provision or had it explained to them, see Pls.' Mot. for Remand, Exs. 1–8, copies of the Standard Terms provided to the district court by NCL indicate the crewmembers initialed or signed the Standard Terms. See Defs.' Resp. to Pls.' Mot. for Remand, Exs. D–F; R–3–60. NCL also provided affidavits from managers at various manning agencies licensed by the POEA to *1294 recruit seamen. In the affidavits, the managers attest that (1) they explained the employment documents to the seamen in their native language; (2) the seamen had an opportunity to review the documents; and (3) the seamen were required to attend a Pre–Departure Orientation Seminar for seamen, which was conducted in both the English and Filipino languages and which reviewed, among other subjects, the Standard Terms and the dispute settlement procedures provided for in the employment contract. Id. at Exs. C–F; R–3–60.

III. THE DISTRICT COURT COMPELS ARBITRATION

In an order issued on October 14, 2003, the district court granted NCL's motion to compel arbitration and denied Plaintiffs' motion to remand the case to state court. In disposing of the case, the district court ordered that the parties submit to arbitration in the Philippines pursuant to Section 29 of the Standard Terms and retained jurisdiction to enforce or confirm any resulting arbitral award. Plaintiffs appeal.

JURISDICTION

A case covered by the Convention confers federal subject matter jurisdiction upon a district court because such a case is "deemed to arise under the laws and treaties of the United States." 9 U.S.C. § 203. Defendants removed these cases from state court pursuant to 9 U.S.C. § 205, which permits removal of disputes relating to arbitration agreements covered by the Convention. See, e.g., Notice of Removal, R1–1–3. Plaintiffs claim that this case is not covered by the Convention, and thereby challenge the district court's jurisdiction. We discuss this challenge below. Assuming the district court exercised jurisdiction appropriately, its order is final and appealable because, by compelling arbitration of the dispute, it "dispos[ed] of all the issues framed by the litigation and [left] nothing for the district court to do but execute the judgment." See Employers Ins. v. Bright Metal Specialties, Inc., 251 F.3d 1316, 1321 (11th Cir.2001).6

STANDARD OF REVIEW

We review de novo the district court's order to compel arbitration. Employers Ins., 251 F.3d at 1321.

DISCUSSION

In deciding a motion to compel arbitration under the Convention Act, a court conducts "a very limited inquiry." Francisco v. STOLT ACHIEVEMENT MT, 293 F.3d 270, 273 (5th Cir.2002), cert. denied, 537 U.S. 1030, 123 S.Ct. 561, 154 L.Ed.2d 445 (2002); DiMercurio v. Sphere Drake Ins.' PLC, 202 F.3d 71, 74 (1st Cir.2000); Ledee v. Ceramiche Ragno, 684 F.2d 184, 186 (1st Cir.1982). A district court must order arbitration unless (1) the four jurisdictional prerequisites are not met, Std. Bent Glass Corp. v. Glassrobots Oy, 333 F.3d 440, 449 (3d Cir.2003);or(2) one of the Convention's affirmative defenses applies. DiMercurio, 202 F.3d at 79; see also Czarina, L.L.C. v. W.F. Poe Syndicate, 358 F.3d 1286, 1292 n. 3 (11th Cir.2004) ("jurisdictional prerequisites to an action confirming an award are different from the several affirmative defenses to confirmation").

Two jurisdictional prerequisites are at issue here. First, we must determine whether the arbitration agreement arises out of a commercial legal relationship. Second, we ask whether there exists an "agreement in writing" to arbitrate the matter in dispute. Lastly, we consider Plaintiffs' purported affirmative defenses that the arbitration provision is unconscionable under U.S. law and incapable of being arbitrated under the law of the Philippines. In analyzing these arguments, we are mindful that the Convention Act "generally establishes a strong presumption in favor of arbitration of international commercial disputes." Indus. Risk Insurers v. M.A.N. Gutehoffnungshutte GmbH, 141 F.3d 1434, 1440 (11th Cir.1998) [citing Mitsubishi Motors Corp. v. Soler Chrysler–Plymouth, Inc., 473 U.S. 614, 638–40, 105 S.Ct. 3346, 3359–61, 87 L.Ed.2d 444 (1985)]. Plaintiffs' arguments fail.

I.PLAINTIFFS' EMPLOYMENT CONTRACTS ARE COMMERCIAL LEGAL RELATIONSHIPS UNDER THE CONVENTION ACT, REGARDLESS OF THE FAA SEAMEN EXEMPTION

We have yet to determine whether the FAA exemption for seamen's employment contracts applies to arbitration agreements covered by the Convention Act.8 The district court determined that it does not. This conclusion is consistent with that of the Fifth Circuit—the only court of appeals to decide this issue—and several district courts. See Freudensprung v. Offshore Tech. Servs., Inc., 379 F.3d 327 (5th Cir.2004); Francisco v. STOLT ACHIEVEMENT MT, 293 F.3d 270 (5th Cir.2002), cert. denied, 537 U.S. 1030, 123 S.Ct. 561, 154 L.Ed.2d 445 (2002); Acosta v. Norwegian Cruise Line, Ltd., 303 F.Supp.2d 1327 (S.D.Fla.2003); Adolfo v. Carnival Corp., No. 02–23672, 2003 WL 23829352, 2003 U.S. Dist. LEXIS 24143 (S.D.Fla. Mar. 11, 2003); Amon v. Norwegian Cruise Lines, Ltd., No. 02–21025, 2002 U.S. Dist. LEXIS 27064 (S.D.Fla. Sept. 26, 2002).

As we take up this issue of statutory interpretation, the first step is to determine whether the statutory language has a plain and unambiguous meaning by referring to "the language itself, the specific context in which that language is used, and the broader context of the statute as a whole." Robinson v. Shell Oil Co., 519 U.S. 337, 341, 117 S.Ct. 843, 846, 136 L.Ed.2d 808 (1997). The inquiry ceases if the language is clear and "the statutory scheme is coherent and consistent."

Id. at 340, 117 S.Ct. 843 [quoting United States v. Ron Pair Enterprises, Inc., 489 U.S. 235, 240, 109 S.Ct. 1026, 1030, 103 L.Ed.2d 290 (1989)]. Such is the case here. The statutory framework of title 9 and the language and context of the Convention Act preclude the application of the FAA seamen's exemption, either directly as an integral part of the Convention Act or residually as a non-conflicting provision of the FAA.

A. The FAA Seamen Exemption Does Not Apply to the Convention Act Directly

1. Overview of the Convention and the Convention Act

The Convention requires that a Contracting State "shall recognize an agreement in writing under which the parties undertake to submit to arbitration all or any differences which have arisen ... between them in respect of a defined legal relationship, whether contractual or not, concerning a subject matter capable of settlement by arbitration." Convention, art. II(1).9 When the United States acceded to the Convention in 1970, it exercised its right to limit the Convention's application to commercial legal relationships as defined by the law of the United States:

The United States of America will apply the Convention only to differences arising out of legal relationships, whether contractual or not, which are considered as commercial under the national law of the United States.

Convention, n. 29.10 Plaintiffs assert that the United States national law definition of "commercial" resides in section 1 of the FAA, which defines "commerce" and provides that "nothing herein contained shall apply to contracts of employment of seamen." 9 U.S.C. § 1. Although section 1 clearly exempts seamen's employment contracts from the FAA, see Circuit City Stores, Inc. v. Adams, 532 U.S. 105, 109, 121 S.Ct. 1302, 1306, 149 L.Ed.2d 234 (2001), the exemption's application outside the FAA is restricted by the second and third chapters of title 9.

2. The Statutory Framework of Title 9 of the United States Code

The three chapters of title 9 are closely interrelated, but, contrary to Plaintiffs' argument, they are not a seamless whole. As indicated, the FAA and the Convention Act comprise Chapter 1 and Chapter 2, respectively. Chapter 3 contains the legislation implementing the Inter–American Convention on International Commercial Arbitration, Jan. 30, 1975, 14 I.L.M. 336 (entered into force June 16, 1976). 9 U.S.C. §§ 301–307 (the "Inter–American Act"). Within the general field of arbitration, each act has a specific context and purpose. Congress, as it added the Convention Act and then the Inter–American Act to title 9, anticipated conflicts among these treaty-implementing statutes and the FAA. Congress addressed potential conflicts in two ways, each of which limits the degree to which title 9 may be considered a single statute.

The first is general in nature. The FAA applies residually to supplement the provisions of the Convention Act and the Inter–American Act. Rather than put the Convention Act and the Inter–

American Act on equal footing with the FAA in the field of foreign arbitration, Congress gave the treaty-implementing statutes primacy in their fields, with FAA provisions applying only where they did not conflict. See 9 U.S.C. § 208 (the Convention Act residual provision); 9 U.S.C. § 307 (the Inter–American Act residual provision). This hierarchical structure accords with our understanding that, "[a]s an exercise of the Congress' treaty power and as federal law, 'the Convention must be enforced according to its terms over all prior inconsistent rules of law.' " Indus. Risk Insurers, 141 F.3d at 1440 [quoting Sedco, Inc. v. Petroleos Mexicanos Mexican Nat'l Oil Co., 767 F.2d 1140, 1145 (5th Cir.1985)].

The second technique for reconciling title 9's chapters is more specific. Certain provisions of the Convention Act and the Inter–American Act refer explicitly to specific sections of other chapters of title 9. Section 302 of the Inter–American Act, for example, directly incorporates several sections of the Convention Act: "[s]ections 202, 203, 204, 205, and 207 of this title shall apply to this chapter [9 U.S.C. §§ 301–307] as if specifically set forth herein." 9 U.S.C. § 302. Most relevant for the instant case is the reference in section 202 of the Convention Act to section 2 of the FAA.

3. Section 202 of the Convention Act

In contrast to the Inter–American Act's direct incorporation of several Convention Act sections, section 202 does not incorporate section 2 of the FAA as an exhaustive description of the Convention Act's scope. Rather, section 202 uses section 2 as an illustration of the types of agreements covered by the Convention Act.

In articulating the Convention's commercial scope under the laws of the United States, section 202 of the Convention Act provides that an agreement falls under the Convention if it "aris[es] out of a legal relationship, whether contractual or not, which is considered as commercial, including a transaction, contract, or agreement described in section 2 of this title [9 U.S.C. § 2]." 9 U.S.C. § 202 (emphasis added).11 Section 2 of the FAA makes valid and enforceable "[a] written provision in any maritime transaction or a contract evidencing a transaction involving commerce *1298 to settle by arbitration." 9 U.S.C. § 2 (emphasis added).

The Convention Act's reference to section 2 does not indicate an intent to limit the definition of "commercial" to those described in section 2 of the FAA as modified by section 1; the expansive term "including" would be superfluous if the FAA provided the full and complete definition. "Including" demonstrates that, at the very least, Congress meant for "commercial" legal relationships to consist of contracts evidencing a commercial transaction, as listed in section 2, as well as similar agreements. See Federal Land Bank v. Bismarck Lumber Co., 314 U.S. 95, 100, 62 S.Ct. 1, 4, 86 L.Ed. 65 (1941) ("the term 'including' is not one of all-embracing definition, but connotes simply an illustrative application of the general principle."); Argosy Ltd. v. Hennigan, 404 F.2d 14, 20 (5th Cir.1968) ("The word 'includes' is usually a term of enlargement, and not of limitation.... It therefore conveys the conclusion that there are other items includable, though not specifically enumerated by the statutes.").

We therefore understand the reference to section 2 of the FAA to be generally illustrative of the commercial legal relationships covered by section 202. The illustration rendered by section 2 includes employment agreements and makes no mention of the section 1 seamen exemption. Cf. Circuit City Stores, 532 U.S. at 113, 121 S.Ct. at 1308 (construing section 2 and rejecting the proposition that an employment contract is not a "contract evidencing a transaction involving interstate commerce"). Accordingly, the terms of the Convention Act do not provide that we read section 1 into section 202.

Plaintiffs cite committee testimony in the legislative history in the hope of demonstrating that Congress intended section 202 of the Convention Act to incorporate the FAA seamen exemption. Ambassador Richard Kearney, Chairman of the Secretary of State's Advisory Committee on Private International Law, testified before the Senate Foreign Relations Committee that the definition of commerce contained in section 1 of the original Arbitration Act is the national law definition for the purposes of the declaration. A specific reference, however, is made in section 202 to section 2 of title 9; which is the basic provision of the original Arbitration Act.

S. Comm. on Foreign Relations, Foreign Arbitral Awards, S.Rep. No. 91–702, at 6 (1970). Although it is plausible to infer from Ambassador Kearney's comments that he believed the section 1 exemptions should apply to the Convention Act, his views as a single State Department official are a relatively unreliable indicator of statutory intent. See Circuit City Stores, 532 U.S. at 120, 121 S.Ct. at 1311 ("Legislative history is problematic even when the attempt is to draw inferences from the intent of duly appointed committees of the Congress."); Francisco, 293 F.3d at 276 (quoting Circuit City Stores to discount Ambassador Kearney's testimony). Plaintiffs nevertheless claim that, according to Udall v. Tallman, 380 U.S. 1, 16, 85 S.Ct. 792, 801, 13 L.Ed.2d 616 (1965), his views are entitled to "great deference." Pls.' Op. Br. at 27. Udall, however, accords such deference only to "the officers or agency charged with [the statute's] administration," 380 U.S. at 16, 85 S.Ct. at 801, and there is no indication that the State Department is so charged. Even if the above testimony were owed some deference, it could not alter the plain terms of the Convention Act. See Barnhart v. Sigmon Coal Co., 534 U.S. 438, 457, 122 S.Ct. 941, 954, 151 L.Ed.2d 908 (2002) ("Floor statements from two Senators cannot amend the clear and unambiguous language of a statute."). Rather than directly incorporate an FAA provision that Congress did not, we adhere to the framework Congress provided and evaluate the applicability of an unmentioned

FAA section according to the Convention Act's residual application provision.

B. The FAA Seamen Exemption Does Not Apply Residually

As noted above, section 208 of the Convention Act provides that non-conflicting provisions of the Arbitration Act apply residually to Convention Act cases:

Chapter 1 [9 U.S.C. §§ 1 et seq.] applies to actions and proceedings brought under this chapter [9 U.S.C. §§ 201 et seq.] to the extent that chapter is not in conflict with this chapter [9 U.S.C. §§ 201 et seq.] or the Convention as ratified by the United States.

9 U.S.C. § 208 (emphasis added); cf. 9 U.S.C. § 307 (providing for residual application of the FAA to the Inter–American Act). Under this residual provision, the issue is whether the FAA seamen exemption conflicts with the Convention Act or the Convention as ratified by the United States.

A conflict exists between the FAA seamen exemption, which is narrow and specific, and the language of the Convention and the Convention Act, which is broad and generic. Plaintiffs, under the impression that an FAA term may only be contradicted by name, argue that no conflict exists because section 202 of the Convention Act is silent as to seamen's employment contracts. According to this logic, a statutory provision pertaining to persons above the age of eighteen would not conflict with a provision that exempts thirty year-olds. Because the Convention Act covers commercial legal relationships without exception, it conflicts with section 1, an FAA provision that exempts certain employment agreements that—but for the exemption—would be commercial legal relationships. The Fifth Circuit came to the same conclusion in Francisco:

In short, the language of the Convention, the ratifying language, and the Convention Act implementing the Convention do not recognize an exception for seamen employment contracts. On the contrary, they recognize that the only limitation on the type of legal relationship falling under the Convention is that it must be considered "commercial," and we conclude that an employment contract is "commercial."

293 F.3d at 274. We see no reason to diverge from the sensible reasoning of our sister Circuit.

Indeed, to read industry-specific exceptions into the broad language of the Convention Act would be to hinder the Convention's purpose:

The goal of the Convention, and the principal purpose underlying American adoption and implementation of it, was to encourage the recognition and enforcement of commercial arbitration agreements in international contracts and to unify the standards by which agreements to arbitrate are observed and arbitral awards are enforced in the signatory countries.

Scherk v. Alberto–Culver Co., 417 U.S. 506, 520 n. 15, 94 S.Ct. 2449, 2457 n. 15, 41 L.Ed.2d 270 (1974) (emphasis added); see *1300 also Indus. Risk Insurers, 141 F.3d at 1440 (identifying additional purposes of the Convention, such as relieving congestion in the courts and providing an expedient alternative to litigation). In pursuing effective, unified arbitration standards, the Convention's framers understood that the benefits of the treaty would be undermined if domestic courts were to inject their "parochial" values into the regime:

In their discussion of [Article II(1)], the delegates to the Convention voiced frequent concern that courts of signatory countries in which an agreement to arbitrate is sought to be enforced should not be permitted to decline enforcement of such agreements on the basis of parochial views of their desirability or in a manner that would diminish the mutually binding nature of the agreements.

Scherk, 417 U.S. at 520 n. 15, 94 S.Ct. at 2457 n. 15. This concern is addressed by the broad language of section 202 of the Convention Act. Considering the language of the Convention Act in the context of the framework of title 9 and the purposes of the Convention, we find no justification for removing from the Convention Act's scope a subset of commercial employment agreements. The crewmembers' arbitration provisions constitute commercial legal relationships within the meaning of the Convention Act.

II. PLAINTIFFS' EMPLOYMENT AGREEMENTS WERE AGREEMENTS IN WRITING, WHICH VESTED THE JURISDICTION OF THE DISTRICT COURT

Finding no error in the district court's determination that instant arbitration provisions are commercial legal relationships, we turn to the other relevant jurisdictional prerequisite, i.e., that the party seeking arbitration provide "an agreement in writing" in which the parties undertake to submit the dispute to arbitration. Convention, art. II(1); see also Czarina, 358 F.3d at 1291. Agreements in writing include "an arbitral clause in a contract or an arbitration agreement, signed by the parties or contained in an exchange of letters or telegrams." Convention, art. II(2).

NCL supplied the district court with copies of the employment agreement and the Standard Terms signed by each crewmember. See Defs.' Resp. to Pls.' Mot. for Remand, Exs. D–F; R–3–60. Although Plaintiffs claim the crewmembers did not have an opportunity to review the entirety of the Standard Terms before signing, Plaintiffs do not dispute the veracity of the signatures. See Pls.' Op. Br. at 36 n.1. Accordingly, this documentation fulfills the jurisdictional prerequisite that the court be provided with an agreement to arbitrate signed by the parties. Plaintiffs try in vain to identify three reasons why the signed documents fail to constitute agreements in writing.

First, Plaintiffs impugn the incorporation of the Standard Terms into the employment agreement, citing decisions of other Circuits that interpret Article II(2) to require inclusion of an arbitration provision in a signed agreement or an exchange of letters or telegrams. See Std. Bent Glass, 333 F.3d at 449; Kahn Lucas Lancaster, Inc. v. Lark Int'l Ltd., 186 F.3d 210, 218 (2d Cir.1999);

cf. United States Fidelity & Guar. Co. v. West Point Constr. Co., 837 F.2d 1507, 1508 (11th Cir.1988) (finding that, under the FAA, the incorporation of an arbitration provision expressed an intent of the parties to arbitrate). This argument fails to address the fact that the crewmembers signed the Standard Terms, the document containing the arbitration provision.

Second, Plaintiffs assert that, in order to satisfy the agreement-in-writing requirement, NCL bears an "evidentiary burden" *1301 of establishing that the crewmembers knowingly agreed to arbitrate disputes arising from the employment relationship. See Pls.' Op. Br. at 42. The parties disagree as to whether the crewmembers were specifically notified of the arbitration provision, and each side supports its position with affidavits. See Pls.' Mot. for Remand, Exs. 1–8; Defs.' Resp. to Pls.' Mot. for Remand, Exs. C–F; R–3–60. Plaintiffs also emphasize the general solicitude for seamen reflected in the Jones Act and Garrett v. Moore–McCormack Co., 317 U.S. 239, 243–44, 63 S.Ct. 246, 249–50, 87 L.Ed. 239 (1942). Plaintiffs, however, offer no authority indicating that the Convention or the Convention Act impose upon the party seeking arbitration the burden of demonstrating notice or knowledgeable consent. To require such an evidentiary showing in every case would be to make an unfounded inference from the terms of the Convention and would be squarely at odds with a court's limited jurisdictional inquiry, an inquiry colored by a strong preference for arbitration. See Francisco, 293 F.3d at 273. It is no better to style Plaintiffs' defective notice claim as an affirmative defense, as virtually every case would be susceptible to a dispute over whether the party resisting arbitration was aware of the arbitration provision when the party signed the agreement. In the limited jurisdictional inquiry prescribed by the Convention Act, we find it especially appropriate to abide by the general principle that "[o]ne who has executed a written contract and is ignorant of its contents cannot set up that ignorance to avoid the obligation absent fraud and misrepresentation." Vulcan Painters v. MCI Constructors, 41 F.3d 1457, 1461 (11th Cir.1995).

Third, Plaintiffs' argue that the agreement-in-writing prerequisite remains unfulfilled because NCL did not attach the signed copies of the Standard Terms to its notices of removal to the district court. NCL was under no such obligation. The agreement-in-writing prerequisite does not specify when a party seeking arbitration must provide the court with the agreement in writing. The Convention Act's removal provision states that "[t]he procedure for removal of causes otherwise provided by law shall apply, except that the ground for removal provided in this section need not appear on the face of the complaint but may be shown in the petition for removal." 9 U.S.C. § 205. Section 205 does not require a district court to review the putative arbitration agreement—or investigate the validity of the signatures thereon—before assuming jurisdiction: "The language of § 205 strongly suggests that Congress intended that district courts continue to be able to assess their jurisdiction from the pleadings alone." Beiser v. Weyler, 284 F.3d 665, 671 (5th Cir.2002); cf. 28 U.S.C. § 1446 (requiring only "a short and plain statement of the grounds for removal"). NCL's notices of removal met procedural requirements by identifying the relevant documents and describing how they bind the Plaintiffs to arbitration. See, e.g., R1–1–3; see also Whole Health Chiropractic & Wellness, Inc. v. Humana Medical Plan, Inc., 254 F.3d 1317, 1321 (11th Cir.2001) ("The law disfavors court meddling with removals based upon procedural—as distinguished from jurisdictional—defects").

III. PLAINTIFFS' AFFIRMATIVE DEFENSES FAIL

The Convention requires that courts enforce an agreement to arbitrate unless the agreement is "null and void, inoperative or incapable of being performed." Convention, art. II(3). Plaintiffs do not articulate their defenses in these terms, claiming instead that the arbitration provision is unconscionable and the underlying dispute is not arbitrable. For purposes of analysis, we style the former as a "null and void" claim and the latter as an "incapable of being performed" claim.

A. The Arbitration Provision Is Not Null and Void

"[T]he Convention's 'null and void' clause ... limits the bases upon which an international arbitration agreement may be challenged to standard breach-of-contract defenses." DiMercurio v. Sphere Drake Ins. PLC, 202 F.3d 71, 79 (1st Cir.2000). The limited scope of the Convention's null and void clause "must be interpreted to encompass only those situations—such as fraud, mistake, duress, and waiver—that can be applied neutrally on an international scale." Id. at 80.

Plaintiffs do not claim fraud, mistake, duress or waiver. Instead, Plaintiffs, allege that the crewmembers were put in a difficult "take it or leave it" situation when presented with the terms of employment. See Pl's Op. Br. at 43. Plaintiffs argue that state-law principles of unconscionability render the resulting agreements unconscionable. They support this position by citing the Supreme Court's opinion in First Options of Chicago, Inc. v. Kaplan, 514 U.S. 938, 944, 115 S.Ct. 1920, 1924, 131 L.Ed.2d 985 (1995) ("courts generally ... should apply ordinary state-law principles that govern the formation of contracts"). In Kaplan, however, the Court applied the FAA, not the Convention. See id., 514 U.S. at 941, 115 S.Ct. at 1922. Domestic defenses to arbitration are transferrable to a Convention Act case only if they fit within the limited scope of defenses described above. Such an approach is required by the unique circumstances of foreign arbitration:

concerns of international comity, respect for the capacities of foreign and transnational tribunals, and sensitivity to the need of the international commercial system for predictability in the resolution of disputes require that we enforce the parties' agreement, even assuming that a contrary result would be forthcoming in a domestic context.

Mitsubishi Motors Corp. v. Soler Chrysler–Plymouth, Inc., 473 U.S. 614, 629, 105 S.Ct. 3346,

3355, 87 L.Ed.2d 444 (1985)

While it is plausible that economic hardship might make a prospective Filipino seaman susceptible to a hard bargain during the hiring process, Plaintiffs have not explained how this makes for a defense under the Convention. It is doubtful that there exists a precise, universal definition of the unequal bargaining power defense that may be applied effectively across the range of countries that are parties to the Convention, and absent any indication to the contrary, we decline to formulate one.13

B. The Arbitration Provision is Not Incapable of Being Performed

Plaintiffs argue that, under the law of the Philippines, the seamen's claims are not considered "claims arising from this employment" pursuant to Section 29 of the Standard Terms and therefore are not subject to arbitration in that country. To support this claim, Plaintiffs rely on Tolosa v. N.L.R.C. (2003) G.R. No. 149578 (Phil.). Tolosa involved a claim against a deceased seaman's employer for the grossly negligent acts of his shipmates when the he fell ill. Id. at 6. Because the complaint focused primarily on the tortious conduct of the shipmates rather than a claim "arising from employer-employee relations," the Philippine Supreme Court held that neither the labor arbiter nor the national labor relations body had jurisdiction. Id.

Here, a similar result is not foreordained. Plaintiffs have options beyond tort claims; they complain that NCL failed in one of its central duties as an employer and shipowner, i.e., to provide a seaworthy vessel. Accordingly, the holding in Tolosa is an insufficient basis from which to conclude that this dispute cannot be arbitrated in the Philippines.

CONCLUSION

The district court properly granted NCL's motion to compel arbitration. The plain language of the Convention Act, 9 U.S.C. §§ 201–208, precludes application of the exemption for seamen's employment agreements set forth in 9 U.S.C. § 1, and there are no impediments to the district court's jurisdiction to compel arbitration. Furthermore, the agreement to arbitrate is not null and void or incapable of being performed.

AFFIRMED.

【本案评析】

本案涉及国际商事仲裁协议实质有效性问题。案件中，菲律宾游轮上的蒸汽锅炉于2003年5月25日爆炸，6名船员因此死亡，4人受伤。每名船员与被告NCL的雇佣协议包括一项仲裁条款，地区法院根据《承认和执行外国仲裁裁决公约》执行该条款。菲律宾游轮船员或其家属在州法院对船东提起诉讼，请求因蒸汽锅炉爆炸造成死亡或受伤的损害赔偿。被告将案件上诉至联邦法院并请求强制仲裁。上诉法院首席法官 Restani 认为：(1)《联邦仲裁法》(FAA)第一部分中关于海员雇佣合同的豁免条款并不适用于本案中，船员雇佣协议；并且(2)船员雇佣协议中的仲裁条款是有效的且是可执行的。

三、国际商事仲裁协议独立性案例[①]

Premium Nafta Products Limited (20th Defendant) and Others

v.

Fili Shipping Company Limited (14th Claimant) and Others

With that background, I turn to the question of construction.Your Lordships were referred to a number of cases in which various forms of words in arbitration clauses have been considered. Some of them draw a distinction between disputes "arising under"and "arising out of" the agreement. In Heyman v. Darwins Ltd. [1942] AC 356, 399 Lord Porter said that the former had a narrower meaning than the latter but in Union of India v. EB Aaby's Rederi A/S [1975] AC 797 Viscount Dihorne, at p.814, and Lord Salmon, at p.817, said that they could not see the difference between them. Nevertheless, in Overseas Union Insurance Ltd. v. AA Mutual International Insurance Co. Ltd. [1988] 2 Lloyd's Rep 63, 67, Evans J said that there was a broad distinction between clauses which referred "only those disputes which may arise regarding the rights and obligations which are created by the contract itself" and those which "show an intention to refer some wider class or classes of disputes". The former may be said to arise "under"the contract while the latter would arise "in relation to" or "in connection with" the contract. In Fillite (Runcorn) Ltd. v. AquaLift (1989) 26 Con LR 66, 76 Slade LJ said that the phrase "under a contract" was not wide enough to include disputes which did not concern obligations created by or incorporated in the contract.Nourse LJ gave a judgment to the same effect. The court does not seem to have been referred to Mackender v. Feldia AG [1967] 2 QB 590, in which a court which included Lord Denning MR and Diplock LJ decided that a clause in an insurance policy submitting disputes "arising there under" to a foreign jurisdiction was wide enough to cover the question of whether the contract could be avoided for nondisclosure.

I do not propose to analyse these and other such cases any further because in my opinion

① 林一飞：《最新商事仲裁与司法实务专题案例》(第八卷)，对外经济贸易大学出版社 2012 年版，第 5~8 页。

the distinctions which they make reflect no credit upon English commercial law. It may be a great disappointment to the judges who explained so carefully the effects of the various linguistic nuances if they could learn that the draftsman of so widely used a standard form as Shelltime 4 obviously regarded the expressions "arising under this charter" in clause 41(b) and "arisen out of this charter" in clause 41 (c)(1)(a)(i) as mutually interchangeable. So I applaud the opinion expressed by Longmore LJ in the Court of Appeal (at paragraph 17) that the time has come to draw a line under the authorities to date and make a fresh start. I think that a fresh start is justified by the developments which have occurred in this branch of the law in recent years and in particular by the adoption of the principle of separability by Parliament in section 7 of the 1996 Act. That section was obviously intended to enable the courts to give effect to the reasonable commercial expectations of the parties about the questions which they intended to be decided by arbitration. But section 7 will not achieve its purpose if the courts adopt an approach to construction which is likely in many cases to defeat those expectations. The approach to construction therefore needs to be re-examined.

In my opinion the construction of an arbitration clause should start from the assumption that the parties, as rational businessmen, are likely to have intended any dispute arising out of the relationship into which they have entered or purported to enter to be decided by the same tribunal. The clause should be construed in accordance with this presumption unless the language makes it clear that certain questions were intended to be excluded from the arbitrator's jurisdiction. As Longmore LJ remarked, at para 17: "If any businessman did want to exclude disputes about the validity of a contract, it would be comparatively easy to say so."

This appears to be the approach adopted in Germany:see the Bundesgerichtshof's Decision of 27 February 1970 (1990) Arbitration International,vol.6,No 1,p79:

"There is every reason to presume that reasonable parties will wish to have the relationships created by their contract and the claims arising therefrom,irrespective of whether their contract is effective or not,decided by the same tribunal and not by two different tribunals."

If one adopts this approach,the language of clause 41 of Shelltime 4 contains nothing to exclude disputes about the validity of the contract,whether on the grounds that it was procured by fraud,bribery,misrepresentation or anything else.In my opinion it therefore applies to the present dispute.

【本案评析】

本案涉及国际商事仲裁协议独立性的问题，涉及原告与被告之间签订的租船合同。原告称其有权提起诉讼，因为其主张租船合同系受贿达成，而有关受贿的争议并非源于租船合同，因此不能适用租船合同中的仲裁条款。

法院对 Disputes Arising under 和 Disputes Arising out of 的区别进行了界定。有关仲裁协议是由《仲裁法》第 7 条的独立原则决定的。[①] 仲裁条款的建立须由理性的当事人愿意将现有或将来的争议提交给同一个仲裁庭。条款的解释须依照这个前提，除非有文字明确规定排除有关合同仲裁员对某些特定问题的管辖。在租船合同中的仲裁条款并没有排除有关合同效力的争议，无论是欺诈、误解、受贿或其他原因。因此，仲裁条款适用该争议。仲裁法的独立原则意味着主要合同的无效或撤销并不必然意味着仲裁条款的无效或撤销。主合同因受贿达成，并不意味着仲裁协议也是因受贿达成。两个协议应被视为分别达成，且仲裁协议只有存在与它本身有直接关联的理由时才可能生效，而不是主要合同无效的必然结果。

四、国际商事仲裁协议适用法律案例[②]

FILANTO, S.p.A., Plaintiff,
v.
CHILEWICH INTERNATIONAL CORP., Defendant.
789 F.Supp. 1229
United States District Court,
S.D. New York.

BRIEANT, Chief Judge.

By motion fully submitted on December 11, 1991, defendant Chilewich International Corp. moves to stay this action pending arbitration in Moscow. Plaintiff Filanto has moved to enjoin arbitration or to order arbitration in this federal district.

This case is a striking example of how a lawsuit involving a relatively straightforward international commercial transaction can raise an array of complex questions. Accordingly, the

① 1996 年英国《仲裁法》第 7 条规定："除非当事人另有约定，构成或旨在构成其他协议（无论是否书面）一部分的仲裁协议不得因其他协议无效、不存在或失效而相应无效、不存在或失效。为此目的，仲裁协议应视为不同的协议。"

② Filanto, S.p.A. v. Chilewich Intern. Corp.United States District Court, S.D. New York.April 14, 1992789 F.Supp. 1229 (Approx. 17 pages).

Court will recount the factual background of the case, derived from both parties' memoranda of law and supporting affidavits, in some detail.

Plaintiff Filanto is an Italian corporation engaged in the manufacture and sale of footwear. Defendant Chilewich is an export-import firm incorporated in the state of New York with its principal place of business in White Plains. On February 28, 1989, Chilewich's agent in the United Kingdom, Byerly Johnson, Ltd., signed a contract with Raznoexport, the Soviet1 Foreign Economic Association, which obligated Byerly Johnson to supply footwear to Raznoexport. Section 10 of this contract—the "Russian Contract"—is an arbitration clause, which reads in pertinent part as follows:

"All disputes or differences which may arise out of or in connection with the present Contract are to be settled, jurisdiction of ordinary courts being excluded, by the Arbitration at the USSR Chamber of Commerce and Industry, Moscow, in accordance with the Regulations of the said Arbitration." [sic]

Ex. C to July 19 Simon Chilewich Affidavit. This contract was signed by Byerly Johnson and by Raznoexport, and is sometimes referred to as "Contract No. 32–03/93085".

The first exchange of correspondence between the parties to this lawsuit is a letter dated July 27, 1989 from Mr. Melvin Chilewich of Chilewich International to Mr. Antonio Filograna, chief executive officer of Filanto. This letter refers to a recent visit by Chilewich and Byerly Johnson personnel to Filanto's factories in Italy, presumably to negotiate a purchase to fulfill the Russian Contract, and then states as follows:

"Attached please find our contract to cover our purchase from you. Same is governed by the conditions which are enumerated in the standard contract in effect with the Soviet buyers [the Russian contract], copy of which is also enclosed."

Ex. A to September 16 Melvin Chilewich Affidavit. The next item in the record is a letter from Filanto to Chilewich dated September 2, 1989. Ex. D to October 29 Filograna Affidavit. This letter refers to a letter from Chilewich to Filanto of August 11, 1989, which "you [Chilewich] sent me with the contracts n 10001–10002–10003." These numbers do not correspond to the contract sued on here, but refer instead to other, similar contracts between the parties.2 None of these contracts, or their terms, are in the record, both parties having been afforded ample opportunity to submit whatever they wished.

The last paragraph of the September 2, 1989 letter from Filanto to Chilewich states as follows:

"Returning back the enclosed contracts n 10001–10002–10003 signed for acceptance, we communicate, if we do not misunderstood, the Soviet's contract that you sent us together with your above mentioned contract, that of this contract we have to respect only the following points of it:

–n 5 Packing and marking

–n 6 Way of Shipment

–n 7 Delivery—Acceptance of Goods

We ask for your acceptance by return of post." [SIC]

Ex. D to October 29 Filograna Affidavit. The intent of this paragraph, clearly, was to exclude from incorporation by reference inter alia section 10 of the Russian contract, which provides for arbitration. Chilewich, for its part, claims never to have received this September 2 letter. In any event, it relates only to prior course of conduct.

It is apparent from the record that further negotiations occurred in early 1990, but the content of those negotiations is unclear; it is, however, clear that deliveries of boots from Filanto to Chilewich were occurring at this time, pursuant to other contracts, since there is a reference to a shipment occurring between April 23, 1990 and June 11, 1990. Ex. H to December 4 Simon Chilewich Affidavit.

The next document in this case, and the focal point of the parties' dispute regarding whether an arbitration agreement exists, is a Memorandum Agreement dated March 13, 1990. This Memorandum Agreement, number 9003002, is a standard merchant's memo prepared by Chilewich for signature by both parties confirming that Filanto will deliver 100,000 pairs of boots to Chilewich at the Italian/Yugoslav border on September 15, 1990, with the balance of 150,000 pairs to be delivered on November 1, 1990. Chilewich's obligations were to open a Letter of Credit in Filanto's favor prior to the September 15 delivery, and another letter prior to the November delivery. This Memorandum includes the following provision:

"It is understood between Buyer and Seller that USSR Contract No. 32–03/93085 [the Russian Contract] is hereby incorporated in this contract as far as practicable, and specifically that any arbitration shall be in accordance with that Contract."

Ex. A to July 24 Simon Chilewich Affidavit. Chilewich signed this Memorandum Agreement, and sent it to Filanto. Filanto at that time did not sign or return the document. Nevertheless, on May 7, 1990, Chilewich opened a Letter of Credit in Filanto's favor in the sum of $2,595,600.00. The Letter of Credit itself mentions the Russian Contract, but only insofar as concerns packing and labelling. Ex. A to December 4 Simon Chilewich Affidavit.

Again, on July 23, 1990, Filanto sent another letter to Chilewich, Ex. D to October 23 Filograna Affidavit, which reads in relevant part as follows:

"We refer to Point 3, Special Conditions, to point out that: returning back the above-mentioned contract, signed for acceptance, from Soviet Contract 32–03/93085 we have to respect only the following points of it:

–No. 5—Packing and Marking

–No. 6—Way of Shipment

–No. 7—Delivery—Acceptance of Goods."

It should be noted that the contract referred to in this letter is apparently another contract between the parties, as the letter refers to "Sub. Contract No. 32–03/03122", while the contract sued on in the present action is No. 32–03/03123.

This letter caused some concern on the part of Chilewich and its agents: a July 30, 1990 fax from Byerly Johnson, Chilewich's agent, to Chilewich, mentions Filanto's July 23 letter, asserts that it "very neatly dodges" certain issues, other than arbitration, covered by the Russian Contract, and states that Johnson would "take it up" with Filanto during a visit to Filanto's offices the next week. Ex. G to December 4 Simon Chilewich Affidavit.

Then, on August 7, 1990, Filanto returned the Memorandum Agreement, sued on here, that Chilewich had signed and sent to it in March; though Filanto had signed the Memorandum Agreement, it once again appended a covering letter, purporting to exclude all but three sections of the Russian Contract. Ex. A to December 11 Filograna Affidavit.

There is also in the record an August 7, 1990 telex from Chilewich to Byerly Johnson, stating that Chilewich would not open the second Letter of Credit unless it received from Filanto a signed copy of the contract without any exclusions. Ex. C to December 4 Simon Chilewich Affidavit. In order to resolve this issue, Byerly Johnson on August 29, 1990 sent a fax to Italian Trading SRL, an intermediary, reading in relevant part:

"We have checked back through our records for last year, and can find no exclusions by Filanto from the Soviet Master Contract and, in the event, we do not believe that this has caused any difficulties between us.

We would, therefore, ask you to amend your letters of the 23rd July 1990 and the 7th August 1990, so that you accept all points of the Soviet Master Contract No. 32–03/93085 as far as practicable. You will note that this is specified in our Special Condition No. 3 of our contracts Nos. 9003001 and 9003[illegible]."

Ex. D to December 4 Simon Chilewich Affidavit. Filanto later confirmed to Italian Trading that it received this fax. Ex. G to December 4 Simon Chilewich Affidavit.

As the date specified in the Memorandum Agreement for delivery of the first shipment of boots—September 15, 1990—was approaching, the parties evidently decided to make further efforts to resolve this issue: what actually happened, though, is a matter of some dispute. Mr. Filograna, the CEO of Filanto, asserts that the following occurred:

"Moreover, when I was in Moscow from September 2 through September 5, 1990, to inspect

Soviet factories on an unrelated business matter, I met with Simon Chilewich. Simon Chilewich, then and there, abandoned his request of August 29, 1990, and agreed with me that the Filanto–Chilewich Contract would incorporate only the packing, shipment and delivery terms of the Anglo–Soviet Contract. Also present at this meeting were Sergio Squilloni of Italian Trading (Chilewich's agent), Kathy Farley, and Max Flaxman of Chilewich and Antonio Sergio of Filanto."

December 11 Filograna Affidavit at 5.

Mr. Simon Chilewich, in his sworn affidavit, does not refer to this incident, but does state the following:

"In fact, subsequent to the communications and correspondence described above, I met with Mr. Filograna face to face in Paris during the weekend of September 14, 1990. During that meeting, I expressly stated to him that we would have no deal if Filanto now insisted on deleting provisions of the Russian Contract from our agreement. Mr. Filograna, on behalf of Filanto, stated that he would accede to our position, in order to keep Chilewich's business."

December 4 Simon Chilewich Affidavit at ¶ 25. Plaintiff does not address or deny defendant's version of the Paris meeting. Filanto's Complaint in this action alleges that it delivered the first shipment of boots on September 15, and drew down on the Letter of Credit. Complaint at ¶ 8.

On September 27, 1990, Mr. Filograna faxed a letter to Chilewich. This letter refers to "assurances during our meeting in Paris", and complains that Chilewich had not yet opened the second Letter of Credit for the second delivery, which it had supposedly promised to do by September 25. Ex. B to December 4 Simon Chilewich Affidavit. Mr. Chilewich responded by fax on the same day; his fax states that he is "totally cognizant of the contractual obligations which exist", but goes on to say that Chilewich had encountered difficulties with the Russian buyers, that Chilewich needed to "reduce the rate of shipments", and denies that Chilewich promised to open the Letter of Credit by September 25. Ex. C to December 11 Filograna Affidavit.

According to the Complaint, what ultimately happened was that Chilewich bought and paid for 60,000 pairs of boots in January 1991, but never purchased the 90,000 pairs of boots that comprise the balance of Chilewich's original order. Complaint at ¶¶ 9–11. It is Chilewich's failure to do so that forms the basis of this lawsuit, commenced by Filanto on May 14, 1991.

There is in the record, however, one document that post-dates the filing of the Complaint: a letter from Filanto to Chilewich dated June 21, 1991. This letter is in response to claims by Byerly Johnson that some of the boots that had been supplied by Filanto were defective. The letter expressly relies on a section of the Russian contract which Filanto had earlier purported to exclude—Section 9 regarding claims procedures—and states that "The April Shipment and the September Shipment are governed by the Master Purchase Contract of February 28, 1989, n 32–03/93085 (the 'Master Purchase Contract')." Ex. H to December 4 Simon Chilewich Affidavit.

This letter must be regarded as an admission in law by Filanto, the party to be charged. A litigant may not blow hot and cold in a lawsuit. The letter of June 21, 1991 clearly shows that when Filanto thought it desirable to do so, it recognized that it was bound by the incorporation by reference of portions of the Russian Contract, which, prior to the Paris meeting, it had purported to exclude. This letter shows that Filanto regarded itself as the beneficiary of the claims adjustment provisions of the Russian Contract. This legal position is entirely inconsistent with the position which Filanto had professed prior to the Paris meeting, and is inconsistent with its present position. Consistent with the position of the defendant in this action, Filanto admits that the other relevant clauses of the Russian Contract were incorporated by agreement of the parties, and made a part of the bargain. Of necessity, this must include the agreement to arbitrate in Moscow. In the June 21, 1991 letter, Mr. Filograna writes:

"The April Shipment and the September Shipment are governed by the Master Purchase Contract of February 28, 1989 N. 32–03–93085 (the 'Master Purchase Contract') The Master Purchase Contract provides that claims for inferior quality must be made within six months of the arrival of the goods at the USSR port."

Ex. H to December 4 Simon Chilewich Affidavit.

Against this background based almost entirely on documents, defendant Chilewich on July 24, 1991 moved to stay this action pending arbitration, while plaintiff Filanto on August 22, 1992 moved to enjoin arbitration, or, alternatively, for an order directing that arbitration be held in the Southern District of New York rather than Moscow, because of unsettled political conditions in Russia.

Jurisdiction/Applicable Law

Plaintiff bases subject matter jurisdiction in this action on diversity of citizenship, as Filanto is an Italian corporation with its principal place of business in Italy, while Chilewich is a New York corporation with its principal place of business in New York, thereby invoking New York law and choice of law rules, under Erie R. Co. v. Tompkins, 304 U.S. 64, 58 S.Ct. 817, 82 L.Ed. 1188 (1938).

This Court, however, finds another overriding basis for subject matter jurisdiction which will affect our choice of law: chapter 2 of the Federal Arbitration Act, which comprises the Convention on the Recognition and Enforcement of Foreign Arbitral Awards and its implementing legislation, codified at 9 U.S.C. § 201 et seq. (West Supp.1991). The United States, Italy and the USSR are all signatories to this Convention, and its implementing legislation makes clear that the Arbitration Convention governs disputes regarding arbitration agreements between parties to international commercial transactions:

"An arbitration agreement or arbitral award arising out of a legal relationship, whether contractual or not, which is considered as commercial, including a transaction, contract, or agreement described in section 2 of this title, falls under the Convention. An agreement or award arising out of such a relationship which is entirely between citizens of the United States should be deemed not to fall under the Convention ..." 9 U.S.C. § 202 (West Supp.1991).

The Arbitration Convention specifically requires courts to recognize any "agreement in writing under which the parties undertake to submit to arbitration...." Convention on the Recognition and Enforcement of Foreign Arbitral Awards Article II(1). The term "agreement in writing" is defined as "an arbitral clause in a contract or an arbitration agreement, signed by the parties or contained in an exchange of letters or telegrams". Convention on the Recognition and Enforcement Of Foreign Arbitral Awards Article II(2).

The Convention's implementing legislation also provides an independent basis of subject matter jurisdiction:

"An action or proceeding falling under the Convention shall be deemed to arise under the laws and treaties of the United States. The district courts of the United States ... shall have original jurisdiction over such an action or proceeding, regardless of the amount in controversy." 9 U.S.C. § 203 (West Supp.1991).

Thus, although defendant has moved for a stay under Chapter 1 of the Arbitration Act, 9 U.S.C. § 3 (West 1970), this case actually falls under Chapter 2 of that title—the Convention and its implementing legislation.

This independent jurisdictional basis is of some importance to this litigation. On a motion pursuant to the Arbitration Act, federal law governs issues relating to the arbitrability of a dispute. Moses H. Cone Hospital v. Mercury Construction Corp., 460 U.S. 1, 24, 103 S.Ct. 927, 941, 74 L.Ed.2d 765 (1983) (Act "creates a body of federal substantive law of arbitrability, applicable to any arbitration agreement within the coverage of the Act"); Prima Paint v. Flood & Conklin Mfg. Co., 388 U.S. 395, 404–05, 87 S.Ct. 1801, 1806–07, 18 L.Ed.2d 1270 (1967)(application of federal arbitration law in diversity case permissible notwithstanding Erie since Arbitration Act was enacted pursuant to Congressional commerce power); McPheeters v. McGinn, Smith & Co., 953 F.2d 771, 772 (2d Cir.1992) ("Federal law ... governs the current dispute as to the scope of the agreement") (citation omitted); Genesco, Inc. v. T. Kakiuchi & Co., Ltd., 815 F.2d 840, 845 (2d Cir.1987) (same); Coenen v. R.W. Pressprich & Co., 453 F.2d 1209, 1211 (2d Cir.) ("Once a dispute is covered by the Act, federal law applies to all questions of interpretation, construction, validity, revocability and enforceability"), cert. denied, 406 U.S. 949, 92 S.Ct. 2045, 32 L.Ed.2d 337 (1972).

However, the focus of this dispute, apparent from the parties' submissions, is not on the scope of the arbitration provision included in the Russian contract; rather, the threshold question is whether these parties actually agreed to arbitrate their disputes at all. In such a situation, where the issue is whether there is any arbitration agreement between the parties, there is authority for the proposition that state, rather than federal law, should be applied. Recold, S.A. de C.V. v. Monfort of Colorado, Inc., 893 F.2d 195, 197 n. 6 (8th Cir.1990) ("In addressing the issue of whether a party has entered into an agreement to arbitrate under the Arbitration Act, courts are to apply general state law principles....") (citation omitted); Supak & Sons Mfg. Co., Inc. v. Pervel Industries, Inc., 593 F.2d 135, 137 (4th Cir.1979) ["Section 2 (of the Act) dictates the effect of a contractually-agreed upon arbitration provision, but it does not displace state law on the general principles governing formation of the contract itself"]; Astor Chocolate Corp. v. Mikroverk, Ltd., 704 F.Supp. 30, 33 (E.D.N.Y.1989) ("While federal law governs the issue of the scope of the arbitration clause, state law governs the issue of whether or not the clause is part of the contract"); Cook Chocolate Co. v. Salomon, Inc., 684 F.Supp. 1177, 1182 (S.D.N.Y.1988) ("At the same time, however, § 2 of the Act preserves general principles of state contract law as rules of decision on whether the parties have entered into an agreement to arbitrate"); Duplan Corp. v. W.B. Davis Hosiery Mills, Inc., 442 F.Supp. 86, 87–88 (S.D.N.Y.1977) (Congress in passing Arbitration Act did not intend "to create a federal law of contract formation"). Indeed, the Supreme Court has recently indicated that this analysis is correct, at least with respect to cases controlled by chapter 1 of the Arbitration Act:

"Thus, state law, whether of legislative or judicial origin, is applicable if that law arose to govern issues concerning the validity, revocability, and enforceability of contracts generally".

Perry v. Thomas, 482 U.S. 483, 492 n. 9, 107 S.Ct. 2520, 2527, 96 L.Ed.2d 426 (1987) (emphasis in original). See also Volt Information Sciences v. Leland Stanford, Jr. University, 489 U.S. 468, 475, 109 S.Ct. 1248, 1253–54, 103 L.Ed.2d 488 (1989) (same).

Plaintiff at one point did contend that state law applied, for an understandable reason: New York law arguably imposes a heavier burden on a party seeking to compel arbitration than does its federal counterpart. Compare Schubtex, Inc., v. Allen Snyder, Inc., 49 N.Y.2d 1, 399 N.E.2d 1154, 424 N.Y.S.2d 133 (1979) (retention without objection by buyer of seller's printed forms containing arbitration clause insufficient basis to compel buyer to arbitrate) and Matter of Marlene Industries Corp., 45 N.Y.2d 327, 333, 380 N.E.2d 239, 242, 408 N.Y.S.2d 410, 413 (1978) (parties "will not be held to have chosen arbitration as the forum for the resolution of their disputes in the absence of an express, unequivocal agreement to that effect") with Pervel Industries, Inc. v. TM Wallcovering Inc., 675 F.Supp. 867, 869–70 (S.D.N.Y.1987) (agreement to arbitrate may be inferred from parties' course of dealing), aff'd, 871 F.2d 7 (2d Cir.1989). There is, however, some authority in this Circuit that federal law applies to contract formation issues when the existence of an agreement to arbitrate is in issue. David L. Threlkeld & Co., Inc., v. Metallgesellschaft Ltd., 923 F.2d 245, 249 (2d Cir.) (applying federal law of contracts to dispute regarding existence of agreement *1236 to arbitrate), cert. dismissed, 501 U.S. 1267, 112 S.Ct. 17, 115 L.Ed.2d 1094 (1991); Genesco, supra, at 845 ("Hence whether Genesco is bound by the arbitration clause of the sales confirmation forms is determined under federal law, which comprises generally accepted principles of contract law") (footnote omitted); Fisser v. International Bank, 282 F.2d 231, 233 (2d Cir.1960) (same); In re Midland Bright Drawn Steel Ltd., 1989 WL 125788, 1989 U.S. Dist. Lexis 12368 (S.D.N.Y.1989) (applying federal law to contract formation issue in case governed by Arbitration Convention). See also Matter of Ferrara, S.p.A., 441 F.Supp. 778, 780–81 (S.D.N.Y.1977), aff'd without opinion, 580 F.2d 1044 (2d Cir.1978). Cf. Fahnestock & Co., Inc. v. Waltman, 935 F.2d 512, 517–19 (2d Cir.) (upholding under state law vacatur of punitive damages element of arbitrator's award), cert. denied, 502 U.S. 942, 112 S.Ct. 380, 116 L.Ed.2d 331 (1991).

This Court concludes that the question of whether these parties agreed to arbitrate their disputes is governed by the Arbitration Convention and its implementing legislation. That Convention, as a treaty, is the supreme law of the land, U.S. Const. art. VI cl. 2, and controls any case in any American court falling within its sphere of application. Thus, any dispute involving international commercial arbitration which meets the Convention's jurisdictional requirements, whether brought in state or federal court, must be resolved with reference to that instrument. See Black & Pola v. The Manes Organization, Inc., 72 A.D.2d 514, 421 N.Y.S.2d 6 (1st Dep't 1979) (federal law determines whether parties have agreed to arbitrate if underlying dispute involves interstate commerce), aff'd, 50 N.Y.2d 821, 407 N.E.2d 1345, 430 N.Y.S.2d 49 (1980). See also Threlkeld, supra, at 250 (holding Convention and Arbitration Act preempt Vermont statute requiring inter alia that arbitration agreement be signed by both parties).4 But see McDermott International v. Lloyds Underwriters of London, 944 F.2d 1199, 1210–11 (5th Cir.) (noting conflicting authorities on whether state courts must apply Arbitration Act and stating that "state courts do not necessarily have to stay litigation or compel arbitration under the Convention either"), reh'g en banc denied, 947 F.2d 1489 (5th Cir.1991). This Court believes that the Fifth Circuit is clearly wrong on this in light of Article VI of the Constitution, not therein mentioned; the Second Circuit also apparently disagrees with that court's conclusion. Corcoran v. Ardra Insurance Co., Ltd., 842 F.2d 31, 35 (2d Cir.1988).

Accordingly, the Court will apply federal law to the issue of whether an "agreement in writing" to arbitrate disputes exists between these parties.

Courts confronted by cases governed by the Arbitration Convention must conduct a limited, four-part inquiry:

"1) Is there an agreement in writing to arbitrate the subject of the dispute. Convention, Articles II(1), II(2).

2) Does the agreement provide for arbitration in the territory of a signatory country? Convention, Articles I(1), I(3); 9 U.S.C. § 206; Declaration of the United States Upon Accession, reprinted at 9 U.S.C.A. § 201, Note 43 (1990 Supp.)

3) Does the agreement arise out of a legal relationship, whether contractual or not, which is considered as commercial? Convention, Article I(3); 9 U.S.C. § 202.

4) Is a party to the contract not an American citizen, or does the commercial relationship have some reasonable relation with one or more foreign states? 9 U.S.C. § 202."

Ledee v. Ceramiche Ragno, 684 F.2d 184, 186–87 (1st Cir.1982); Sedco v. Petroleos Mexicanos Mexican National Oil Co., 767 F.2d 1140, 1145 (5th Cir.1985); Tennessee Imports, Inc. v. Filippi, 745 F.Supp. 1314, 1321 (M.D.Tenn.1990); *1237 Corcoran v. Ardra Insurance Co., Ltd., 657 F.Supp. 1223, 1227 (S.D.N.Y.1987), aff'd, 842 F.2d 31 (2d Cir.1988).

In this case, the second, third and fourth criteria are clearly satisfied, as the purported agreement provides for arbitration in Moscow, the Chilewich–Filanto relationship is a "commercial" relationship, and Filanto is an Italian corporation. The central disputed issue, therefore, is whether the correspondence between the parties, viewed in light of their business relationship, constitutes an "agreement in writing".

Courts interpreting this "agreement in writing" requirement have generally started their analysis with the plain language of the Convention, which requires "an arbitral clause in a contract or an arbitration agreement, signed by the parties or contained in an exchange of letters or telegrams", Article I(1), and have then applied that language in light of federal law, which consists of generally accepted principles of contract law, including the Uniform Commercial Code. See, e.g., Genesco, supra, at 845–46 (holding under "general contract principles" that buyer agreed to arbitrate disputes arising under unsigned sales confirmation forms due to parties' course of dealing and buyer's signatures on related sales confirmation forms); Sen Mar, Inc. v. Tiger Petroleum Corp., 774 F.Supp. 879, 883–84 (S.D.N.Y.1991) (denying seller's motion to compel arbitration since arbitration clause not in signed writing or in exchange of letters); Midland Bright Drawn Steel, supra, 1989 WL 125788, at 4, 1989 U.S.Dist.Lexis 12368, at 3–4 (holding seller entitled to stay of arbitration since arbitration clause represented material alteration of contract not accepted by seller); Beromun Aktiengesellschaft v. Societa Industriale Agricola, Inc., 471 F.Supp. 1163, 1171–72 (S.D.N.Y.1979) (denying seller's motion to compel arbitration since no contract ever formed between parties). But see Astor Chocolate, supra, at 33–34 (applying state contract law in case governed by Convention). See also Zambia Steel & Building Supplies Ltd. v. James Clark & Eaton Ltd., 2 Lloyd's Rep. 225 (1986) (United Kingdom) (seller's oral assent to sales note containing arbitration clause sufficient under Convention to compel arbitration).

However, as plaintiff correctly notes, the "general principles of contract law" relevant to this action, do not include the Uniform Commercial Code; rather, the "federal law of contracts" to be applied in this case is found in the United Nations Convention on Contracts for the International Sale of Goods (the "Sale of Goods Convention"), codified at 15 U.S.C. Appendix (West Supp.1991). This Convention, ratified by the Senate in 1986, is a self-executing agreement which entered into force between the United States and other signatories, including Italy, on January 1, 1988. See Preface to Convention, reprinted at 15 U.S.C. Appendix (West Supp.1991). Although there is as yet virtually no U.S. case law interpreting the Sale of Goods Convention, see Taylor & Crisera, "U.N. Pact Has Wide Application", Nat.L.J., Dec. 23, 1991 at 23, it may safely be predicted that this will change: absent a choice-of-law provision, and with certain exclusions not here relevant, the Convention governs all contracts between parties with places of business in different nations, so long as both nations are signatories to the Convention. Sale of Goods Convention Article 1(1)(a). Since the contract alleged in this case most certainly was formed, if at all, after January 1, 1988, and since both the United States and Italy are signatories to the Convention, the Court will interpret the "agreement in writing" requirement of the Arbitration Convention in light of, and with reference to, the substantive international law of contracts embodied in the Sale of Goods Convention.

Not surprisingly, the parties offer varying interpretations of the numerous letters and documents exchanged between them. The Court will briefly summarize their respective contentions.

Defendant Chilewich contends that the Memorandum Agreement dated March 13 which it signed and sent to Filanto was an offer. It then argues that Filanto's retention of the letter, along with its subsequent acceptance of Chilewich's performance under the Agreement—the furnishing of the May 11 letter of credit—estops it from denying its acceptance of the contract. Although phrased as an estoppel argument, this contention is better viewed as an acceptance by conduct argument, e.g., that in light of the parties' course of dealing, Filanto had a duty timely to inform Chilewich that it objected to the incorporation by reference of all the terms of the Russian contract. Under this view, the return of the Memorandum Agreement, signed by Filanto, on August 7, 1990, along with the covering letter purporting to exclude parts of the Russian Contract, was ineffective as a matter of law as a rejection of the March 13 offer, because this occurred some five months after Filanto received the Memorandum Agreement and two months after Chilewich furnished the Letter of Credit. Instead, in Chilewich's view, this action was a proposal for modification of the March 13 Agreement. Chilewich rejected this proposal, by its letter of August 7 to Byerly Johnson, and the August 29 fax by Johnson to Italian Trading SRL, which communication Filanto acknowledges receiving.

Accordingly, Filanto under this interpretation is bound by the written terms of the March 13 Memorandum Agreement; since that agreement incorporates by reference the Russian Contract containing the arbitration provision, Filanto is bound to arbitrate.

Plaintiff Filanto's interpretation of the evidence is rather different. While Filanto apparently agrees that the March 13 Memorandum Agreement was indeed an offer, it characterizes its August 7 return of the signed Memorandum Agreement with the covering letter as a counteroffer. While defendant contends that under Uniform Commercial Code § 2–207 this action would be viewed as an acceptance with a proposal for a material modification, the Uniform Commercial Code, as previously noted does not apply to this case, because the State Department undertook to fix something that was not broken by helping to create the Sale of Goods Convention which varies from the Uniform Commercial Code in many significant ways. Instead, under this analysis, Article 19(1) of the Sale of Goods Convention would apply. That section, as the Commentary to the Sale of Goods Convention notes, reverses the rule of Uniform Commercial Code § 2–207, and reverts to the common law rule that "A reply to an offer which purports to be an acceptance but contains additions, limitations or other modifications is a rejection of the offer and constitutes a counter-offer". Sale of Goods Convention Article 19(1). Although the Convention, like the Uniform Commercial Code, does state that non-material terms do become part of the contract unless objected to, Sale of Goods Convention Article 19(2), the Convention treats inclusion (or deletion) of an arbitration provision as "material", Sale of Goods Convention Article 19(3). The August 7 letter, therefore, was a counteroffer which, according to Filanto, Chilewich accepted by its letter dated September 27, 1990. Though that letter refers to and acknowledges the "contractual obligations" between the parties, it is doubtful whether it can be characterized as an acceptance.

More generally, both parties seem to have lost sight of the narrow scope of the inquiry required by the Arbitration Convention. Ledee, supra, at 186. All that this Court need do is to determine if a sufficient "agreement in writing" to arbitrate disputes exists between these parties. Cf. United Steelworkers of America v. Warrior & Gulf Co., 363 U.S. 574, 582, 80 S.Ct. 1347, 1352–53, 40 L.Ed.2d 1409 (1960) (party cannot be required to submit to arbitration absent agreement). Although that inquiry is informed by the provisions of the Sale of Goods Convention, the Court lacks the authority on this motion to resolve all outstanding issues between the parties. Indeed, contracts and the arbitration clauses included therein are considered to be "severable", a rule that the Sale of Goods Convention itself adopts with respect to avoidance of contracts generally. Sale of Goods Convention Article 81(1). There is therefore authority for the proposition that issues relating to existence of the contract, as opposed to the existence of the arbitration clause, are issues for the arbitrators:

"The district court reasoned that an arbitrator can derive his or her power only from a contract, so that when there is a challenge to the existence of the contract itself, the court must first decide whether there is a valid contract between the parties. Although this appears logical, it goes beyond the requirements of the statute and violates the clear directive of Prima Paint, 388 U.S. at 404, 87 S.Ct. at 1806 ..." Republic of Nicaragua v. Standard Fruit Co., 937 F.2d 469, 476 n. 9 (9th Cir.1991), cert. denied, 503 U.S. 919, 112 S.Ct. 1294, 117 L.Ed.2d 516 (1992).

The Standard Fruit court is technically correct in its interpretation of the Prima Paint case, which drew a distinction between a challenge to the validity of the contract itself and a challenge to the validity of the arbitration clause; the former, in the Court's view, was a question for the arbitrators, while the latter was a question for the court. Prima Paint, supra, 388 U.S. at 404, 87 S.Ct. at 1806.

However, there are often limits to how many angels can dance on the head of a pin—even when the performance is choreographed by the distinguished courts just cited. There seems, for example, to be some confusion in the Ninth Circuit itself about the proper application of the Prima Paint rule, as a case decided six months prior to Standard Fruit shows. See Three Valleys Municipal Water District v. E.F. Hutton & Co. Inc., 925 F.2d 1136, 1138–42 (9th Cir.1991) (holding whether contract containing arbitration clause formed initially question for court). There are numerous cases in the Second Circuit where the court has-out of necessity—adjudicated relevant contract issues on motions to stay or compel arbitration. See, e.g., McPheeters, supra, at 773 (holding that defendant seeking arbitration not third-party beneficiary of underlying agreement); Genesco, supra, at 846 ("We focus not on whether there was subjective agreement as to each clause in the contract, but on whether there was objective agreement with respect to the entire contract") (citation omitted); Maria Victoria Naviera, S.A. v. Cementos Del Valle, S.A., 759 F.2d 1027, 1030 (2d Cir.1985) (holding that contract containing arbitration clause was not modified by later agreement); Midland Bright Drawn Steel, 1989 WL 125788 at 2–4, 1989 U.S.Dist.Lexis 12368 at 3 (resolving date when underlying contract formed and holding that contract did not include arbitration clause); Beromun Aktiengesellschaft, supra, at 1172 (denying motion to compel arbitration since "no contract ever existed between parties").

Since the issue of whether and how a contract between these parties was formed is obviously related to the issue of whether Chilewich breached any contractual obligations, the Court will direct its analysis to whether there was objective conduct evidencing an intent to be bound with respect to the arbitration provision. Cf. Matterhorn, Inc., v. NCR Corp., 763 F.2d 866, 871–73 (7th Cir.1985) (Posner, J.) (discussing cases). See also Teledyne, Inc. v. Kone Corp., 892 F.2d 1404, 1410 (9th Cir.1990) (arbitration clause enforceable despite later finding by arbitrator that contract itself invalid).

The Court is satisfied on this record that there was indeed an agreement to arbitrate between these parties.

There is simply no satisfactory explanation as to why Filanto failed to object to the incorporation by reference of the Russian Contract in a timely fashion. As noted above, Chilewich had in the meantime commenced its performance under the Agreement, and the Letter of Credit it furnished Filanto on May 11 itself mentioned the Russian Contract. An offeree who, knowing that the offeror has commenced performance, fails to notify the offeror of its objection to the terms of the contract within a reasonable time will, under certain circumstances, be deemed to have assented to those terms. Restatement (Second) of Contracts § 69 (1981); Graniteville v. Star Knits of California, Inc., 680 F.Supp. 587, 589–90 (S.D.N.Y.1988) (compelling arbitration since party who failed timely to object to salesnote containing arbitration clause deemed to have accepted its terms); Imptex International Corp. v. Lorprint, Inc., 625 F.Supp. 1572, 1572 (S.D.N.Y.1986) (Weinfeld, J.) (party who failed to object to inclusion of arbitration clause in sales confirmation agreement bound to arbitrate). The Sale of Goods Convention itself recognizes this rule: Article 18(1), provides that "A statement made by or other conduct of the offeree indicating assent to an offer is an acceptance". Although mere "silence or inactivity" does not constitute acceptance, Sale of Goods Convention Article 18(1), the Court may consider previous relations between the parties in assessing whether a party's conduct constituted acceptance, Sale of Goods Convention Article 8(3). In this case, in light of the extensive course of prior dealing between these parties, Filanto was certainly under a duty to alert Chilewich in timely fashion to its objections to the terms of the March 13 Memorandum Agreement—particularly since Chilewich had repeatedly referred it to the Russian Contract and Filanto had had a copy of that document for some time.

There are three other convincing manifestations of Filanto's true understanding of the terms of this agreement. First, Filanto's Complaint in this action, as well as affidavits subsequently submitted to the Court by Mr. Filograna, refer to the March 13 contract: the Complaint, for example, states that "On or about March 13, 1990, Filanto entered into a contract with Chilewich ..." Complaint at ¶ 5. These statements clearly belie Filanto's post hoc assertion that the contract was actually formed at some point after that date. Indeed, Filanto finds itself in an awkward position: it has sued on a contract whose terms it must now question, in light of the defendant's assertion that the contract contains an arbitration provision. This situation is hardly unknown in the context of arbitration agreements. See Tepper Realty Co., v. Mosaic Tile Co., 259 F.Supp. 688, 692 (S.D.N.Y.1966) ("In short, the plaintiffs cannot have it both ways. They cannot relay on the contract, when it works to their advantage, and repudiate it when it works to their disadvantage").

Second, Filanto did sign the March 13 Memorandum Agreement. That Agreement, as noted above, specifically referred to the incorporation by reference of the arbitration provision in the Russian Contract; although Filanto, in its August 7 letter, did purport to "have to respect" only a small part of the Russian Contract, Filanto in that very letter noted that it was returning the March 13 Memorandum Agreement "signed for acceptance ". Exhibit A to November 28 Filograna Affidavit (emphasis added).

In light of Filanto's knowledge that Chilewich had already performed its part of the bargain by furnishing it the Letter of Credit, Filanto's characterization of this action as a rejection and a counteroffer is almost frivolous.

Third, and most important, Filanto, in a letter to Byerly Johnson dated June 21, 1991, explicitly stated that "[t]he April Shipment and the September shipment are governed by the Master Purchase Contract of February 28, 1989 [the Russian Contract]". Exhibit H to December 4 Simon Chilewich Affidavit. Furthermore, the letter, which responds to claims by Johnson that some of the boots that were supplied were defective, expressly relies on section 9 of the Russian Contract—another section which Filanto had in its earlier correspondence purported to exclude. The Sale of Goods Convention specifically directs that "[i]n determining the intent of a party ... due consideration is to be given to ... any subsequent conduct of the parties", Sale of Goods Convention Article 8(3). In this case, as the letter post-dates the partial performance of the contract, it is particularly strong evidence that Filanto recognized itself to be bound by all the terms of the Russian Contract.

In light of these factors, and heeding the presumption in favor of arbitration, Moses H. Cone, supra, at 24–26, 103 S.Ct. at 941–42, which is even stronger in the context of international commercial transactions, Mitsubishi Motors Corp. v. Soler Chrysler–Plymouth, Inc., 473 U.S. 614, 631, 105 S.Ct. 3346, 3356, 87 L.Ed.2d 444 (1985), the Court holds that Filanto is bound by the terms of the March 13 Memorandum Agreement, and so must arbitrate its dispute in Moscow.8

Remedy

Having determined that the parties should arbitrate their disputes in accordance with their agreement, the Court must address the question of remedy. As this action is governed by the Convention and its implementing legislation, the Court has specific authority to order the parties to proceed to arbitration in Moscow. 9 U.S.C. § 206 (West Supp.1991) ("A Court having jurisdiction under this Chapter may direct that arbitration be held in accordance with the agreement at any place therein provided for, whether the place is within or without the United States"). Defendant has not sought this remedy, since it would likewise be the defendant in the arbitration. However, it would be clearly inequitable to permit the party contending that there is an arbitration agreement to avoid arbitration. In the interests of justice, the Court will compel the parties to arbitrate in Moscow. Cf. Tennessee Imports, supra, at 1322 n. 4 (treating defendant's motion to dismiss as request to refer parties to arbitration).

There may be some theoretical question as to whether the remedy defendant does seek—a stay under 9 U.S.C. § 3—is available in a case falling under the Convention. The problem here is that Chapter 2 of the Act—the Convention and its implementing legislation—does not expressly grant the Court authority to stay an action pending arbitration. Chapter 1 of the Arbitration Act, which governs arbitration agreements relating primarily to interstate commerce, does make a stay available, 9 U.S.C. § 3 (West 1970). Furthermore, 9 U.S.C. § 208, the final section of the statute implementing the Convention, states that Chapter 1 of the Act applies to Chapter 2 cases when not in conflict with Chapter 2.

Some courts have suggested that the language of Article II(3) of the Convention, which states that a court "shall refer the parties to arbitration" once the requirements of the Convention have been satisfied means, by negative implication, that a stay is not permitted. According to these courts, the proper remedy in a Convention case is to refer the parties to arbitration and dismiss for lack of subject matter jurisdiction. McCreary Tire & Rubber Co. v. CEAT S.p.A., 501 F.2d 1032, 1037 (3d Cir. 1974) (dismissal required); Astor Chocolate, 704 F.Supp. at 35 (same); Siderius, Inc., v. Compania de Acero del Pacifico, SA, 453 F.Supp. 22, 25 (S.D.N.Y.1978) (same). This is facially absurd because the enabling legislation gives the district court the power at least to compel arbitration. How could even this limited power be exercised without subject matter jurisdiction?

Other courts, have concluded that granting a stay pending arbitration is permissible in Convention cases. E.g., Rhone Mediterranee Compagnia Francese Di Assicurazioni E Riassicurazoni v. Lauro, 712 F.2d 50, 54 (3d Cir.1983). Our own Court of Appeals seemed to adopt this position, as it recently countenanced an injunction in aid of arbitration in a Convention case, Borden, Inc. v. Meiji Milk Products Co., Ltd., 919 F.2d 822, 826 (2d Cir.1990), cert. denied, 500 U.S. 953, 111 S.Ct. 2259, 114 L.Ed.2d 712 (1991). In a more recent case, though, with facts closer to those in the instant case, another panel of that court expressly declined to follow Borden, or resolve the issue of whether a stay or dismissal is appropriate, Threlkeld, supra, at 253 n. 2. See also Tennessee Imports, supra, at 1323–25 (reviewing cases and holding that stay and dismissal are both permissible methods of referral under the Convention); Restatement (Third) of the Foreign

Relations Law of the United States § 487(2) (1980) (same).

This Court agrees in theory with those courts which have held that retaining jurisdiction but staying the action is consistent with the commands of the Convention. However, to do so in this case would serve no purpose, since the entire controversy between these parties is subject to and will be resolved by arbitration. Accordingly, it is appropriate that a final judgment issue here containing a mandatory injunction to arbitrate in accordance with the Convention and what this Court finds to be the agreement of the parties.

Lastly, the plaintiff contends that if this Court does order arbitration, the Court should take judicial notice of the unsettled conditions in Moscow and order arbitration to proceed in this judicial district. The language of section 206 is concededly permissive: the Court "may direct that arbitration be held in accordance with the agreement at any place therein provided for". 9 U.S.C. § 206 (West Supp.1991). These parties, though, did agree to arbitrate their disputes in Moscow. Compare Oil Basins Ltd. v. Broken Hill Proprietary Co., Ltd., 613 F.Supp. 483, 486–87 (S.D.N.Y.1985) (section 206 furnishes sole authority for court to order arbitration outside its judicial district) with Bauhinia Corp. v. China National Machinery & Equipment Import & Export Corp., 819 F.2d 247 (9th Cir.1987) (ordering arbitration before American Arbitration Association when parties' agreements ambiguous as to arbitration site).

Plaintiff relies on cases which have stated or held that forum-selection clauses may be invalidated when the chosen forum has become seriously inconvenient or dangerous. The Bremen v. Zapata Off–Shore Co., 407 U.S. 1, 16, 92 S.Ct. 1907, 1916–17, 32 L.Ed.2d 513 (1972) (noting that invalidation of forum-selection clause appropriate when chosen forum "seriously inconvenient") (emphasis in original); Rockwell International Systems, Inc. v. Citibank, N.A., 719 F.2d 583, 587–88 (2d Cir.1983) (no adequate remedy in courts of post-revolutionary Iran). Whatever the applicability of these cases in the arbitration context, the chosen forum in this case does have a reasonable relation to the contract at issue, as the ultimate purchaser of the boots was a Russian concern and the Russian Contract was incorporated by reference into Filanto's Memorandum Agreement with Chilewich. Furthermore, though conditions in the Republic of Russia are unsettled, they continue to improve and there is no reason to believe that the Chamber of Commerce in Moscow cannot provide fair and impartial justice to these litigants.

Settle a final judgment on five (5) days notice.

SO ORDERED.

【本案评析】

本案涉及的主要法律问题在于国际仲裁协议有效性的认定及其应当适用的

法律。本案涉及的仲裁协议是买卖皮靴合同中的仲裁条款。国际商事合同的仲裁条款是当事人之间达成的关于如何解决合同争议的协议。此项协议具有契约的性质，可以得到法院的强制执行。当事人可以在合同中的仲裁条款中对该仲裁条款的适用法律，作出专门的规定。如果当事人未能就该仲裁条款应当适用的法律作出规定，按照各国普遍适用的决定国际商事合同适用法律的最密切联系原则，决定该仲裁协议的适用法律。按此原则，一般应当认定仲裁地所在国的法律，与仲裁协议有着最为密切的联系。

第三节　国际商事仲裁裁决的承认与执行

【知识背景 / 学习要点】

一、国际商事仲裁承认与执行简介

（一）承认与执行的含义

国际商事仲裁裁决的承认即内国法院对仲裁机构所作的具有约束力的裁决予以许可和确认，并赋予其强制执行力的司法行为，裁决的承认是一种静态行为。同时裁决的承认是仲裁裁决取得执行力的必须过程，是使仲裁裁决在法院地国取得如同内国法院之终局判决一样的法律效力的过程。

国际商事仲裁裁决的执行是在承认仲裁裁决的基础上，使已经发生法律效力并取得了执行力的仲裁裁决得以强制实施。相比较而言，仲裁裁决的执行则是动态的司法行为，必须是内国法院通过司法权的强制力使当事人履行或实现其权利和义务。原则上当事人双方同意以仲裁方式解决纠纷，那么对于裁决结果就应该心悦诚服才是。但有些当事人在不利的裁决作出之后，会有所不平，甚至不自动履行该裁决，而在非裁决地国执行该裁决会增加很多困难。裁决一经作出，仲裁庭所负法律责任即告结束，其没有权力去执行该裁决，而要持裁决到裁决地国以外的国家来执行该裁决，必须依靠法院的权威或国际公约或国内法的规定。总之，仲裁裁决的承认与执行是国际商事仲裁裁决获得法律约束力和实现或满足债权人权益和利益的保障性程序制度，是在主权平等和互惠基础上通过有关国家法院提供承认和执行仲裁裁决的司法协助来完成和实现的。因此，它鲜明地体现出司法对仲裁的支持和救济。说明国际商事仲裁的有效进行不可能完全脱离特定的国家的法律体系，国际商事仲裁裁决的承认与执行也有赖于特定国家法律的强制性。

国际商事仲裁裁决承认和执行的程序随国内法而有所不同。一般而言，任何外国裁决要在内国取得执行力都必须首先得到内国法院的承认；然而，并非所有的裁决都要经过执行程序，只有含有给付内容的而且履行方未自动履行的仲裁裁决才需要执行。换言之，某些仲裁裁决并不需要经过执行这一步骤，例如基于确认之诉所作出的仲裁裁决仅获得法院承认即可在法院地国发生类似已决判决的法律效力。当然，绝大多数的裁决是既需要承认也需要执行的，仅需要单纯承认的仲裁裁决属于极少数情况。

（二）仲裁裁决的执行

国际商事仲裁的最终目的是仲裁裁决能够得到良好执行。当前，无论是各国内国法还是国际仲裁规则均对仲裁裁决效力进行了相应规定。比如《贸易法委员会规则》第 32 条第（2）款规定：“仲裁裁决应是终局的，对当事方具有约束力……”。而在国际商事仲裁裁决执行实践中，大多数裁决的执行大多数是当事人自愿执行，仲裁庭无权干涉仲裁裁裁决的后续执行。仲裁案件中的败诉方在执行仲裁裁决方面大多采取以下四种方式应对裁决：第一，败诉方按自愿执行仲裁裁决。第二，败诉方将该裁决作为谈判基础与胜诉方进行谈判，减少自身应偿付的金额。第三，对仲裁裁决提出异议。第四，拒不执行仲裁裁决。

（三）国际商事仲裁裁决的执行方式

如果一方未执行仲裁裁决或者未按约定执行仲裁裁决，仲裁相对方可采取以下方式执行仲裁。第一，给败诉方施加压力。可以以其他措施进行反向规制，该措施包括商业压力、外交压力等方式，督促其执行。例如，如果当事人涉及政府或国家机构，胜诉方可能会采取外交手段施加压力。如果一个相关公司作为败诉方无法执行仲裁裁决，胜诉方施加的压力可能指向其商业信用。现今，GAFTA（谷物与饲料贸易协会）的相关规则对该类内容有相关的条款规定。[①] 但是，采取该类措施助推国际商事仲裁裁决的执行效果较弱。[②] 第二，向有管辖权的法院申述，强制执行裁决。[③]

国际上，向法院对于仲裁裁决的执行的方式包括以下四种：第一，仲裁裁决在法院登记或存放，即可强制执行仲裁裁决。[④] 第二，不需登记存放，直接可获得执行。第三，先向法院申请仲裁裁决承认，得到承认后才可强制执行。[⑤]第四，将裁决作为主合同的证据起诉，并要求败诉方将履行该裁决作为一项合同履行的义务。在司法实践中，具体执行程序会因国家和法院的要求不同而变化。

申请法院执行仲裁协议，执行对象主要针对财产类标的。[⑥] 即申请执行方在向法院申请强制执行令前，需对被执行方资产进行系统追查——包括银行账户和商业资产中的资金等，如果被执行人拒绝执行，申请执行人可以向法院申请清算被执行人的资产，强制执行。

二、拒绝承认与执行国际商事仲裁裁决的理由

根据《纽约公约》的规定，在有下列原因的情况下可以拒绝承认与执行外国仲裁裁决，即被请求执行国家的法院可以依照被诉人的请求拒绝对外国仲裁裁决承认与执行。

第一，原仲裁协议的当事人，根据对他们适用的法律，存在某种无行为能力

① GAFTA Form 125, Arbitration Rules (effective for contracts dated from January 1, 2003 onwards), Art. 22.1.

② Alan Redferm, M Hunter, Nigel Blackaby, Constantine Partasides. *Law and Practice of International Commercial Arbitration.* fourth edn. Sweet & Maxwell, 2004, p.505.

③ Julian D. M. Lew, Loukas A. Mistelis, Stefan Kroll. *Comparative International Commercial Arbitration.* Kluwer Law International, 2003, p.688.

④ 参见 English Arbitration Act 1996, s.66.

⑤ 参见 France under the Code of Civil Procedure 1981, Art.1498.

⑥ Elder. The case against arbitral awards of specific performance in transnational commercial disputes,13 Arbitration International 1, 1996.

的情况，或根据仲裁协议所选定的准据法，该项仲裁协议无效。

第二，被诉人未接到关于指定仲裁员或进行仲裁程序的适当通知，或者由于其他情况未能对案件进行抗辩。

第三，裁决所处理的事实，不包括在仲裁协议之内或超出了仲裁协议的范围。

第四，仲裁庭的组成或仲裁程序与双方当事人的协议不相符，或者当事人之间的协议没有约定时与进行仲裁国家的法律不符。

第五，仲裁裁决对当事人还没有发生约束力，或者裁决已经由作出裁决的国家或据其法律作出裁决的国家的管辖当局撤销或停止执行。

第六，如果被请求承认与执行仲裁裁决的国家的管辖当局查明依照该国的法律不可以仲裁或调解或该裁决的承认与执行将和该国家的公共秩序相抵触时，也可以拒绝执行。

三、国际商事仲裁裁决的撤销

（一）申请撤销国际商事仲裁裁决的含义和要求

所谓申请撤销仲裁裁决是指对符合法定应予撤销情形的仲裁裁决，经法院组成合议庭审查核实，裁定撤销仲裁裁决的行为。国际商事仲裁实行一裁终局制，仲裁裁决一经作出，即发生法律效力，当事人不能就同一纠纷再向仲裁机构申请仲裁，也不能就同一纠纷向法院起诉或上诉。一裁终局制度的确立，充分体现了尊重当事人意愿的原则和仲裁方式快捷性的优点。然而，由于受到各种因素的影响，有些仲裁裁决也不可避免地可能出现不同程度的偏差或错误。因此各国和国际文件中均规定在特定理由存在的情况下可以申请撤销仲裁裁决，对确保仲裁裁决的合法性和正确性，具有非常重要的意义。

撤销国际商事仲裁裁决需符合以下要求才可成立。第一，撤销国际商事仲裁裁决的申请必须由当事人提出，一般情形下法院不得依职权撤销仲裁裁决。但法院认定该裁决违背社会公共利益的，应当裁定予以撤销。第二，撤销国际商事仲裁裁决是法院或仲裁机构的职权，即只能由法院或仲裁机构作出裁定予以撤销，任何其他机构和个人均无权撤销仲裁裁决。第三，法院或仲裁机构必须对当事人提出的撤销仲裁裁决的申请进行审查核实。仲裁裁决只有符合法定予以撤销的情形时，法院才能作出撤销仲裁裁决的裁定，将仲裁裁决予以撤销。

（二）申请撤销仲裁裁决的理由

1. 实体法理由

申请撤销国际商事仲裁裁决的实体法理由包括事实错误和法律错误两种。第一，事实错误。仅有少数国家允许当事人以事实发生错误为理由提出撤销仲裁裁决，以事实错误为理由撤销仲裁裁决会影响国际商事仲裁的有效性和仲裁庭的权威性。第二，法律错误。一些国家在国内法中作出法院可以审查法律错误的规定。

2. 程序法理由

申请撤销国际商事仲裁裁决的程序法理由包括以下几个方面。第一，仲裁协议不存在。仲裁协议是当事人申请仲裁和仲裁机构受理当事人的仲裁申请的前提和基础。对于没有仲裁协议而申请仲裁的，仲裁委员会不予受理，更不能对案件作出裁决。若仲裁机构对没有仲裁协议的纠纷案件予以受理并作出裁决，则违反了当事人自愿的原则，该仲裁裁决也就是违法裁决，当事人有权向人民法院申请撤销此裁决。第二，仲裁事项超越仲裁协议范围或仲裁庭缺乏管辖权。当事人申请仲裁的事项，必须是仲裁协议确定的事项，仲裁机构也只能就仲裁协议范围内的争议事项作出裁决。如果当事人申请仲裁的事项超出仲裁协议约定的范围，而仲裁机构仍予以受理并作出裁决，或者虽然当事人确定了申请仲裁的范围，但是仲裁机构所作出的仲裁裁决超出了当事人的请求范围，那么仲裁庭管辖权存在瑕疵，此仲裁裁决也应予以撤销。第三，仲裁庭组成或仲裁程序违反法定程序。根据各国国内法和仲裁机构的规定，仲裁庭是由 3 名仲裁员组成，还是由 1 名仲裁员组成，由双方当事人约定，仲裁员应当由当事人选定或者委托仲裁委员会主任指定。只有当事人没有在规定的期限内约定仲裁庭组成方式或者选定仲裁员时，才由仲裁委员会依照职权指定。当仲裁庭的组成违反了仲裁法的规定，则由该仲裁庭所作出的仲裁裁决应予以撤销。另外，仲裁必须按法定的程序进行。如果仲裁机构没有按照仲裁程序规则所规定的期限将全部文件或材料送达双方当事人，或者当事人未能在仲裁程序中获得充分的陈述或辩论的机会，或者有关仲裁员有法定回避情形而未予回避等等，均是违反仲裁程序的做法。在违背法定仲裁程序基础上所作出的仲裁裁决，属于法定被撤销的理由。第四，仲裁员在仲裁该案时有索贿受贿、徇私舞弊、枉法裁决等不法行为。如仲裁员在仲裁案件的过程中非法索要或非法接受当事人财物或其他不正当利益，或为了谋取私利或为了报答一方当事人已经或承诺给予自己的某种利益而弄虚作假，或在仲裁案件时颠倒是非甚至故意错误适用法律，都是仲裁过程中的严重的违法行为。这些行为必然影响案件的公正审理和裁决，损害一方当事人的合法权益。在此基础上作出的仲裁裁决应当予以撤销。第五，违反公共政策和社会公共利益。如果仲裁裁决违背各国国内法中的公共政策或社会公共利益，法院也应当裁定撤销该仲裁裁决。

四、中国对域外仲裁裁决的承认与执行

（一）对外国仲裁裁决执行的法律框架

1982 年以前，我国法律中没有关于承认和执行外国仲裁裁决的规定，这些裁决完全是当事人自愿的、以非正式的方式执行的。[①]在1978年和1983年之间，中国政府与众多国家签订了相互保护海外投资的双边协议，这些协议都没有解决中国承认和执行外国仲裁裁决的问题。

1982 年，《审判民事诉讼法》颁布生效，后来被《民事诉讼法》所取代。《民事诉讼法》第 204 条申明，外国仲裁裁决可以通过司法协助的方式，根据有关双边协定或互惠性规则得到承认和执行。要在中国承认和执行外国的仲裁裁决，以下规则必须遵守：首先，该裁决必须被视为在其管辖区内作出的最终裁

① Cheng Dejun, Moser Michael, and Wang Sheng chang, *International Arbitration in the People's Republic of China: Commentary, Cases & Materials,* Butterworths, 2000, p.123.

决；其次，当事人的直接申请承认和执行的请求不被接受的，当事人必须向外国法院申请由外国法院代表当事人寻求确认和执行；最后，人民法院可以拒绝执行外国裁决，理由是该裁决违反了基本的中国法律原则，或违背了中国的国家利益和社会利益。

在1986年12月2日，中国正式加入《纽约公约》，并在互惠条款上作了保留。在1987年4月10日，最高人民法院发布关于我国加入的《承认及执行外国仲裁裁决公约》的通知。该通知规定了有关互惠保留和商业保留的解释和规则，相关法院管辖区对公约裁决的承认和执行，以及提交承认和执行申请，拒绝承认和执行的理由与《纽约公约》规定的相同。《纽约公约》于1987年4月22日在中国生效。同时，中国还与其他国家政府缔结了许多司法援助双边条约，这些条约毫无例外地规定：根据《纽约公约》的规定，仲裁裁决应在双边条约缔约国同时是《纽约公约》缔约国时才予以承认和执行。

（二）中国香港特区、澳门特区和中国台湾地区的仲裁裁决的认可和执行

1. 香港特区仲裁裁决的认可与执行

从1841年至1998年，香港是英国的受保护国。在1977年，香港加入了《纽约公约》，所以在中华人民共和国恢复对香港的主权之前，香港与内地相互执行仲裁裁决，均受《纽约公约》的规制。

1997年7月，根据中英联合声明，中国恢复对香港及有关领土的主权，更名为香港特别行政区（以下简称“香港特区”）。这项改变不但标志着一个时代的终结，而且还引起了关于认可和执行香港与内地之间仲裁裁决的问题。简而言之，香港回归祖国后，香港特区作出的裁决再也不能归类为《纽约公约》规制范围内的裁决。[①]

回归近两年后，内地与香港特区于1999年6月21日签署了一份谅解备忘

① 在1997年7月1日恢复对香港的主权后，中国政府将《纽约公约》的领土适用范围扩大到香港特别行政区，但须遵守中国在加入《公约》时最初的声明和保留。因此，在其他缔约国作出的仲裁裁决将根据《纽约公约》在香港得到承认和执行，反之亦然。

录。《中国内地与香港相互执行仲裁裁决谅解备忘录》为香港法院认可及执行内地仲裁机构的仲裁裁决及内地法院根据《香港仲裁条例》认可及执行在香港作出的仲裁裁决提供法律依据。

根据《谅解备忘录》第 2 条的规定，如任何一方未能遵从仲裁裁决，无论该裁决是在香港特区作出或在内地作出的，寻求强制执行的一方均可向该违约方所在地的有关法院申请执行裁决，或在违约一方的财产所在的地方申请执行裁决。内地有关法院指的是有关的中级人民法院，香港指的是高等法院。如果违约方在两个司法管辖区拥有财产，申请人不得同时向两个司法管辖区的有关法院提出申请。如果有关法院在一个司法管辖区执行裁决未能收回全部债务，那么申请人可向另一司法管辖区的法院申请执行该裁决，以期收回未清偿的余额。

根据《谅解备忘录》第 3 条的规定，向有关法院申请执行在内地或香港作出的裁决，申请人须向法院提交一份执行书面申请、一份仲裁裁决及一份仲裁协议。

根据《谅解备忘录》第 7 条的规定，如果寻求强制执行的一方能够证明本条所列的某种情况存在，或者有关法院决定该事项在争议的范围内，不能通过在执行地方适用的法律进行仲裁解决，或者如果内地法院裁定在内地执行裁决会违反内地的公共利益，或者香港法院决定在香港作出的终裁裁决会违反香港的公共政策。拒绝认可和执行《谅解备忘录》规定的仲裁裁决的理由与《纽约公约》第 5 条所规定的完全相同。

2. 澳门特区仲裁裁决的认可和实行

虽然《澳门民事诉讼法》规定承认和执行外国仲裁裁决，包括认可在内地作出的仲裁裁决，但是在澳门作出的裁决在内地进行执行在过去一直是有问题的，它缺乏明确的法律依据，原因是中华人民共和国于 1999 年恢复对澳门的主权。[1] 对于这种情况的补救的讨论始于2006年9月，内地与澳门特别行政区就相互认可和执行仲裁裁决作出安排（澳门安排）最终于2007年10月30日签署，并于2008年1月生效。

澳门安排的大部分条文，例如有关申请认可或执行所需文件的条文、拒绝认可及强制执行的理由和有关的法庭及时限与内地与香港特区之间的《谅解备忘录》相同。

但与内地与香港特区的《谅解备忘录》不同的是，澳门安排载有有关暂停、终止及恢复执行程序的条文。根据澳门安排的规定，如果一方向内地或澳门特别行政区的法院申请执行裁决，而另一方却向另一司法管辖区的法院申请撤销裁决，则执行法院须裁定暂停执行程序，条件是被要求执行的一方申请暂停，并提供充分的担保。当事人申请中止执行的，应当向法院提供另一法院接受申请撤销裁决的法律文件。执行法院应根据一项认可的判决裁定终止执行程序或裁定撤销仲裁裁决。撤销裁决的申请无效的，执行法院应当裁定恢复执行程序。

3. 中国台湾地区仲裁裁决的承认和执行

最高人民法院于1998年1月15日颁布了《人民法院对台湾地区法院民事判决的认可规定》。《人民法院对台湾地区法院民事判决的认可规定》不仅适用于认可法院在台湾地区作出的民事判决，而且还应认可和执行在台湾地区作出的仲裁裁决。[2] 在此之前，位于台湾地区的仲裁机构作出的仲裁裁决在大陆并没有得到认可和执行。《人民法院对台湾地区法院民事判决的认可规定》授权台湾地区作出的仲裁裁决的一方仲裁机构，向大陆人民法院申请认可和执行。作为先决条件，该项裁决的一方当事人的居所或惯常居所，或债务人财产的所在地，须位于大陆。[3] 如所有要求均获满足，该裁决将由大陆法院认可及执行。

根据《人民法院对台湾地区法院民事判决的认可规定》，台湾地区仲裁机

① 2005年7月19日，中国宣布《纽约公约》适用于澳门特区，但须遵守中国在加入《公约》时原先作出的声明和保留。

② 参见《人民法院对台湾地区法院民事判决的认可规定》第19条的规定。

③ 参见《人民法院对台湾地区法院民事判决的认可规定》第2条的规定。

构申请认可和执行仲裁裁决的期限是在裁决生效之日之后一年。[①] 在申请人住所或惯常居所所在地，或者在被申请执行的当事人的财产所在地的中级人民法院，对台湾地区仲裁裁决的认可和执行具有管辖权。[②]

根据《人民法院对台湾地区法院民事判决的认可规定》，大陆人民法院在以下六种情况下将拒绝认可和执行台湾地区的仲裁裁决，第一，未确定所要求认可的裁决的有效性；第二，被要求认可的裁决是在未被依法传唤的被告未出庭情况下作出的，或在被告处于行动障碍的情况下没有适当代表人代替出庭时作出的；第三，案件由内地人民法院专属管辖；第四，大陆人民法院曾就该案件作出判决；及第五，某外国或某地区的法院已作出判决，而该判决已获大陆人民法院认可；第六，被要求认可的裁决违反了中国法律或社会公共利益的基本原则。[③] 如不存在任何上述情况，该裁决将由大陆人民法院认可和执行。

最高人民法院于 2015 年 6 月 2 日颁布了《关于认可和执行台湾地区仲裁裁决的规定》，废除了《人民法院对台湾地区法院民事判决的认可规定》对台湾地区仲裁裁决的认可和执行的适用。根据《关于认可和执行台湾地区仲裁裁决的规定》，在台湾地区作出的仲裁裁决的任何一方均可向人民法院申请认可和执行。[④]

申请认可和执行台湾仲裁裁决的期限为两年，从该裁决所指明的最后一次执行日期开始起算。[⑤] 申请人应当向申请人、被申请人住所所在地、惯常居住地或者财产所在地中级人民法院或者专门人民法院提交申请，[⑥] 该申请需附上原仲裁协议和仲裁裁决或经适当证明的副本。[⑦] 法院应接受申请或裁定在七日内

---

① 参见《人民法院对台湾地区法院民事判决的认可规定》第 17 条的规定。

② 参见《人民法院对台湾地区法院民事判决的认可规定》第 3 条的规定。

③ 参见《人民法院对台湾地区法院民事判决的认可规定》第 9 条的规定。

④ 参见《关于认可和执行台湾地区仲裁裁决的规定》第 1 条的规定。

⑤ 参见《关于认可和执行台湾地区仲裁裁决的规定》第 19 条的规定和《中华人民共和国民事诉讼法》第 239 条的规定。

⑥ 参见《关于认可和执行台湾地区仲裁裁决的规定》第 4 条的规定。

⑦ 参见《关于认可和执行台湾地区仲裁裁决的规定》第 7 条的规定。

不接受申请，申请人可就法院的不接受申请的裁定提出上诉。

法院决定认可仲裁裁决的，应当在两个月内作出裁定。只有在第 14 条所列的某种情况存在时，法院才能裁定不认可或执行裁决。法院裁定不认可和执行裁决或者裁定驳回申请的，应当在两个月内向最高人民法院报告。

【案例摘录与评析】

一、撤销国际商事仲裁裁决和不予执行仲裁裁决案例①

INTERNATIONAL TRADING AND INDUSTRIAL INVESTMENT COMPANY (f/k/a/ International Trading and Investment Company), Petitioner,

v.

DYNCORP AEROSPACE TECHNOLOGY et al., Respondents.

Civil Action No. 09–791 (RBW).

Jan. 21, 2011.

REGGIE B. WALTON, District Judge.

Currently before the Court is an amended petition filed by petitioner International Trading and Industrial Investment Company, formerly known as International Trading and Investment Company ("International Trading"), to confirm an arbitral award (the "Award") rendered in its favor and against respondents DynCorp Aerospace Technology and its affiliated companies under the Federal Arbitration Act, 9 U.S.C. § 207 (2000) (the "FAA"),and the Convention on the Recognition and Enforcement of Foreign Arbitral Awards, June 10, 1958, 21 U.S.T. 2517, 330 U.N.T.S. 38, available at 1970 WL 104417 (the "New York Convention" or the "Convention"), which was ratified by Congress and codified at 9 U.S.C. §§ 201–08 (2000). Amended Petition for Confirmation of Foreign Arbitral Award (the "Am. Pet.") at 1. On December 1, 2010, the Court held a hearing on the merits of International Trading's petition, at which time the Court issued an oral ruling granting the petition and informed the parties that it would issue a short order thereafter. Upon further reflection, however, the Court believes that the issues presented in this case compel a more thorough written analysis and explanation regarding the Court's rulings, and

① International Trading and Indus. Inv. Co. v. DynCorp Aerospace Technology.United States District Court, District of Columbia.January 21, 2011763 F.Supp.2d 12 (Approx. 24 pages).

this memorandum opinion reflects the Court's efforts in that regard.

I. Background

The following facts in this case are undisputed unless otherwise noted. "DynCorp ... is an American company that ... provides logistical support and security services to the [United States] Armed Forces in Qatar."

Resp'ts' Opp'n at 3. On July 17, 1998, DynCorp entered into an agreement (the Agreement or 1998 Agreement) with International Trading, "under which [International Trading] was appointed as [a] service agent for the purpose of establishing, operating[,] and maintaining a licensed branch office [for DynCorp] in the State of Qatar." Am. Pet.24. International Trading's specific "duties under the Agreement included assisting DynCorp in obtaining all licenses and permits required to establish a branch office; advising it regarding importing and exporting equipment, spares[,] and stores; and advising and assisting it in dealings with government ministries, departments, and agencies," id. 26, so that ultimately DynCorpcould "obtain ... contracts to provide security services in Qatar," id. 27. The Agreement was written in both Arabic and English, Resp'ts' Opp'n at 4; Pet'r's Reply at 11, with the Arabic version controlling in the event of a conflict between the two versions, although consideration must be given to the English Terms as well, see Resp'ts' Opp'n, Ex. A (the 1998 Agreement) at 19.

The duration of the contract was governed by Section 9. 1, which stated the following:

[T]his Agreement shall be for a period of [s]ixty months from the date of signature and shall continue thereafter unless and until terminated by either party giving to the other not less than 90 ... days prior notice expiring on or any time after the first anniversary of the date hereof.

Id., Ex. A (the 1998 Agreement) at 12. On September 24, 2001, DynCorp sent a letter to International Trading evincing its intent to terminate the agreement on December 23, 2001. Am. Pet. ¶ 30. International Trading disputed DynCorp's ability to terminate the agreement because it believed that "the Agreement could not be terminated until after the expiration of the base period of sixty months," which would not have been until July 20, 2003. Id. DynCorp's position was that "the maximum term of the Agreement was sixty months, and that either party could terminate [the Agreement] upon ninety days notice one year after the ... Agreement was signed." Resp'ts' Opp'n at 5.Unable to resolve this dispute on their own, International Trading initiated arbitration proceedings before the International Chamber of Commerce (the "ICC") under Section 13.1 of the Agreement.Am. Pet. ¶ 31.

Pursuant to the ICC Rules, the ICC selected Paris, France as the site for the arbitration, id. ¶34, to which neither party objected, see id. 35. The parties also agreed that Qatari law governed the resolution of any substantive questions in the case, and that the ICC Rules would apply to any procedural issues that arose during the proceedings. Id. On May 29, 2006, the arbitrator issued a written decision in which he concluded that DynCorp breached the Agreement because Section 9.1 required the Agreement to remain in effect "for a period of 'sixty months from the date of signature and shall continue thereafter, unless and until terminated,' i.e., the initial term of the Agreement is 60 months and the Agreement will continue after the initial term until terminated by either party," Pet'r's Mem., Ex. A [May 29, 2006 Arbitral Award ("the Award")] at 23 (emphasis omitted in part), and DynCorp had announced its intention to terminate the agreement prior to that date, Am. Pet. ¶ 41. The arbitrator rejected DynCorp's position to the contrary, noting that:

[i]f the intention of any of the parties was to allow the other to terminate the Agreement as of the date of its first anniversary only, the Agreement would have been drafted and signed initially for a period of one year, renewable yearly. But, upon signature of such Agreement, the intention of both parties was clear: it was initially drafted for a period *18 of sixty months, and after sixty months, it was automatically renewable unless and until terminated by either party (by a prior notice).

Pet'r's Mem., Ex. A (Award) at 24. As a result of the breach, the arbitrator concluded that International Trading was entitled to $1,107,764.95 for damages, Am. Pet. 45, $40,000 for costs, and interest of 5% per annum, id. 46.

On July 23, 2006, DynCorp pursued a stay of the Award before the Qatari Court of First Instance, arguing that "the [a]rbitration suffered from procedural defects," but was denied relief, Resp'ts' Opp'n at 8. DynCorp then appealed to the Qatari Court of Appeal, which concluded that the dispute "was resolved on correct, suitable, and accepted ... law," id., Ex. D (Decision of Qatari Court of Appeal) at 12–13, but while the court upheld the arbitrator's award of damages and costs, it vacated the award of 5% interest, Resp'ts' Opp'n at 9. Soon thereafter, DynCorp appealed to the Qatari Court of Cassation, which is the court of last resort in the State of Qatar. Id. After consideration of the matter, the Court of Cassation concluded "that the arbitrator failed to follow Qatari law by improperly interpreting the 1998 Agreement in light of the parties' intentions." Id. at 10. The Court of Cassation found that the arbitrator's interpretation of the Agreement "goes against the apparent meaning of the contract conditions," and that the arbitrator's reading of the Agreement was a "misinterpretation of facts," as well as "error [regarding] the implementation of the law." Id. According to DynCorp, International Trading did not object to jurisdiction before any of the Qatari tribunals and voluntarily participated in the proceedings. See id. at 8–10.

On April 30, 2009, International Trading filed its petition in this Court, which it later amended on May 22, 2009, requesting that the Court confirm the Award pursuant to 9 U.S.C. § 207, as well as Article IV of the New York Convention. Am. Pet. at 1. In response, DynCorp moved on July 31,

2009, to have the Court deny confirmation of the Award, arguing that the Court of Cassation "was a valid authority to set aside the Award," and that in any event, recognition of the Award should be denied "under Chapter 2 of the FAA."Resp'ts' Opp'n at 1. Because DynCorp also initiated proceedings before the courts of France to set aside the Award on the same day it filed its cross-motion in this Court, DynCorp also requested a stay of the proceedings under Article V(1)(e) of the New York Convention, id., which states that where "an application for the setting aside ... of [an] award has been made to a competent authority referred to in Article V(1)(e), the authority before which the award is sought be relied upon may ... adjourn the decision." The Court denied the motion for a stay without prejudice on July 28, 2010, "in light of the parties' agreement that the motion should be held in abeyance pending resolution of" the matter before the French courts. Order, Int'l Trading and Indust. Invest. Co. v. DynCorp Aerospace Tech., Civil Action No. 09–791(RBW) at 1. On November 4, 2010, the Paris Court of Appeal rejected DynCorp's action to set *19 aside the Award, Pet'r's Supp. Mem. at 1, and subsequently, at the December 1, 2010 hearing, this Court entertained the parties' arguments as to whether the Award should be confirmed.

II. Standard of Review

Pursuant to 9 U.S.C. § 207, the Court is required to "confirm the award unless it finds one of the grounds for refusal or deferral of recognition or enforcement of the award specified in the [New York] Convention." Those specified grounds can be found under Article V of the Convention. Specifically, Article V(1) authorizes the Court to deny confirmation of the arbitral award under the following circumstances:

(a) The parties to the agreement ... were, under the law applicable to them, under some incapacity, or the said agreement is not valid under the law to which the parties have subjected it or, failing any indication thereon, under the law of the country where the award was made; or

(b) The party against whom the award is invoked was not given proper notice of the appointment of the arbitrator or of the arbitration proceedings or was otherwise unable to present his case; or

(c) The award deals with a difference not contemplated by or not falling within the terms of the submission to arbitration, or it contains decisions on matters beyond the scope of the submission to arbitration, provided that, if the decisions on matters submitted to arbitration can be separated from those not so submitted, that part of the award which contains decisions on matters submitted to arbitration may be recognized and enforced; or

(d) The composition of the arbitral authority or the arbitral procedure was not in accordance with the agreement of the parties, or, failing such agreement, was not in accordance with the law of the country where the arbitration took place; or

(e) The award has not yet become binding on the parties, or has been set aside or suspended by a competent authority of the country in which, or under the law of which, that award was made.

Furthermore, Article V(2) of the Convention provides the Court with two additional grounds for denying recognition of an arbitral award:

(a) The subject matter of the difference is not capable of settlement by arbitration under [United States] law ... or

(b) The recognition or enforcement of the award would be contrary to the public policy of [the United States].

As one federal circuit court has observed, "[t]here is now considerable case law holding that... the grounds for relief enumerated in Article V of the Convention are the only grounds available for [denying recognition or enforcement] of a [foreign] arbitral award". Yusuf Ahmed Alghanim & Sons v. Toys "R" Us, Inc., 126 F.3d 15, 20 (2d Cir.1997) (emphasis added) [citing M & C Corp. v. Erwin Behr GmbH & Co., KG, 87 F.3d 844, 851 (6th Cir.1996); Int'l Standard Elec. Corp. v. Bridas Sociedad Anonima Petrolera, Industrial Y Comercial, 745 F.Supp. 172, 181–82 (S.D.N.Y.1990); Brandeis Intsel Ltd. v. Calabrian Chems. Corp., 656 F.Supp. 160, 167 (S.D.N.Y.1987); and Albert Jan van den Berg, The New York Arbitration Convention of 1958: Towards a Uniform Judicial Interpretation 265 (1981)]; see also TermoRio S.A. E.S.P. v. Electranta S.P., 487 F.3d 928, 935 (D.C.Cir.2007) (quoting Yusuf, 126 F.3d at 23) (concluding that where an enforcement action is brought in a jurisdiction outside of where the arbitral award was rendered, "the state may refuse to enforce the award only on the grounds explicitly set forth in Article V of the Convention"). Given that the New York Convention provides only several narrow circumstances when a court may deny confirmation of an arbitral award, confirmation proceedings are generally summary in nature. See, e.g., Zeiler v. Deitsch, 500 F.3d 157, 169 (2d Cir.2007) ("Confirmation under the Convention is a summary proceeding in nature, which is not intended to involve complex factual determinations, other than a determination of the limited statutory conditions for confirmation or grounds for refusal to confirm."). "[T]he showing required to avoid summary confirmation is high," Ottley v. Schwartzberg, 819 F.2d 373, 376 (2d Cir.1987), and the burden of establishing the requisite factual predicate to deny confirmation of an arbitral award rests with the party resisting confirmation, Imperial Ethiopian Gov't v. Baruch–Foster Corp., 535 F.2d 334, 336 (5th Cir.1976); see also New York Convention, art. V ["Recognition and enforcement of the award may be refused, at the request of the party against whom it is invoked, only if that party furnishes (proof) to the competent authority where the recognition and enforcement is sought...."].

The Court also must remain mindful of the principle that "judicial review of arbitral awards is extremely limited," and that this Court "do[es] not sit to hear claims of factual or legal error by an arbitrator" in the same manner that an appeals court would review the decision of a lower court. Teamsters Local Union No. 61 v. United Parcel Serv., Inc., 272 F.3d 600, 604 (D.C.Cir.2001) [quoting Kanuth v. Prescott, Ball & Turben, Inc., 949 F.2d 1175, 1178 (D.C.Cir.1991)]. In fact, careful scrutiny of an arbitrator's decision would frustrate the FAA's "emphatic federal policy in favor of arbitral dispute resolution," Mitsubishi Motors Corp. v. Soler Chrysler–Plymouth, Inc., 473 U.S. 614, 631, 105 S.Ct. 3346, 87 L.Ed.2d 444 (1985) (internal citation omitted)—a policy that "applies with special force in the field of international commerce," id.—by "undermining the goals of arbitration, namely, settling disputes efficiently and avoiding lengthy and expensive litigation," LaPrade v. Kidder, Peabody & Co., 94 F.Supp.2d 2, 4–5 (D.D.C.2000) (Sullivan, J.), aff'd 246 F.3d 702 (D.C.Cir.2001). Instead, "a court must confirm an arbitration award where some colorable support for the award can be gleaned from the record." Id. at 4.

III. Legal Analysis

The overarching issue before the Court is whether the Award should be confirmed under 9 U.S.C. § 207 and Article IV of the New York Convention. By the Court's assessment, DynCorp's arguments in support of its cross-motion to deny confirmation of the Award can be distilled into two parts; first, that the Award should not be confirmed by the Court because the Qatari Court of Cassation set aside the Award, and International Trading is estopped from challenging the competency of that court "to set aside the Award within the meaning of Article V(1)(e) of the New York Convention," Resp'ts' Opp'n at 14, and second, the Court should deny recognition of the Award because the arbitrator acted with manifest disregard of the law, id. at 17. The Court addresses each of these contentions below.

1. Competency of Qatari Court of Cassation to Set Aside the Award

DynCorp argues that the Court should refuse to recognize the Award under Article V(1)(e) of the New York Convention, which states that an arbitral award need not be confirmed if, inter alia,"[t]he award ... has been set aside or suspended by a competent authority of the country in which, or under the law of which, that award was made." DynCorp acknowledges in its opposition memorandum that, as a general matter, a "competent authority," as that term is used under Article V(1)(e), is one located within the country where the arbitration commenced, Resp'ts' Opp'n at 13, and thus had the present case been "a typical enforcement action, the decision of the Qatari Court of Cassation to set aside the Award would not restrict this Court's ability to enforce the Award," id. at 14, because the seat of the arbitration was Paris, France, id. at 13. DynCorp argues, however, that the amended petition now before the Court does not involve a "typical enforcement action," because International Trading assented to judicial review by the Qatari courts. In support of its position, DynCorp argues that International Trading, in "draft [ing] the controlling Arabic version of the arbitration clause[,] .... failed to specify ... that the Award was to be final and binding," and thereby understood that the non-prevailing party (in this case, DynCorp) could "appeal the merits of the Award to the Qatari courts under Qatari law." Id. at 14. DynCorp further asserts that International Trading "consented to the jurisdiction of the Qatari courts", by "voluntarily participat[ing] in the proceedings before those courts without ever objecting", id. at 15 [citing Karaha Bodas Co. v. Perusahaan Pertambangan Minyak Dan Gas, 364 F.3d 274 (5th Cir.2004)], and is now "estopped from contesting that the Qatari Court of Cassation became a ... competent authority to set aside the Award within the meaning of Article V(1)(e) of the New York Convention," id. at 15–16. DynCorp contends that because International Trading's actions have rendered the Qatari Court of Cassation a "competent authority" under Article V(1)(e), the principle of international comity "requires this Court to respect the Qatari Court of Cassation's conclusions regarding the proper application of Qatari law to the underlying dispute." Id. at 16.

To be sure, the Court agrees with DynCorp's acknowledgement that in a "typical enforcement action," the Qatari Court of Cassation's ruling would have no impact on this Court's analysis of whether confirmation of the Award should be denied in this instance. For the Court to deny confirmation of the Award under Article V(1)(e), it would have to find not only that the Award was set aside by a "competent authority," but also that the "competent authority" was located in "the country in which, or under the [arbitral] law of which, that award was made."New York Convention, art. V(1)(e). Neither party disputes that the seat of the arbitration was Paris, France, or that the arbitration was governed by the ICC Rules. See Am. Pet. ¶ 35 [quoting Pet'r's Mem., Ex. W (Terms of Reference) at 6] (agreement by the parties that Qatari law governs questions of substantive law, while the ICC Rules "shall apply to the [a]rbitration procedure"). Thus, the only competent tribunals empowered under the New York Convention to set aside the Award are those located in France, not Qatar.

DynCorp's efforts to distinguish this case from a standard confirmation proceeding is unavailing. First, the terms of the Agreement belie any suggestion that the Award issued by the arbitrator was non-binding. The arbitration clause contained in both the English and Arabic versions of the Agreement provide that "any dispute arising in connection with this agreement" is to be resolved "under the rules ... of the [ICC]."Resp'ts' Opp'n at 6 [quoting Am. Pet, Ex. 2 (the 1998 Agreement) ¶ 13.1]. Furthermore, the ICC rules that were in effect at the time the parties entered into the Agreement stated that "[e]very Award shall be binding on the parties," and that "the parties ... shall be deemed to have waived their right to any form of recourse insofar as such waiver can validly be made." Pet'r's Reply, Ex. KK [ICC Rules, effective January 1, 2008 (the "ICC Rules")], art. 28(6); see also id., Ex. KK (ICC Rules), art. 24(1) {"The time limit within which the Arbitral Tribunal must render its final [a]ward is six months." (emphasis added)}. Thus, even assuming that Qatari law provides for judicial review of arbitration awards that are non-binding, that law has no application here because the parties, by agreeing to be governed by the ICC rules, intended the Award to be final and binding.

Second, DynCorp's contention that International Trading consented to the Qatari courts to serve as "competent authorit[ies]" under Article V(1)(e) of the New York Convention, Resp'ts' Opp'n at 15–16, does nothing to influence the Court's construction of that provision. Whether a tribunal is "competent" under Article V(1)(e) to entertain an action to set aside an arbitral award is an inquiry that goes to that forum's subject-matter jurisdiction to hear a case. See Wachovia Bank v. Schmidt, 546 U.S. 303, 316, 126 S.Ct. 941, 163 L.Ed.2d 797 (2006) ("Subject-matter jurisdiction ... concerns a court's competence to adjudicate a particular category of cases...."); Gulf Petro Trading Co. v. Nigerian Nat'l Petroleum Corp., 512 F.3d 742, 747 (5th Cir.2008) (holding that courts sitting in a country outside the seat of the arbitration "lack subject[-]matter jurisdiction over claims seeking to vacate, set aside, or modify a foreign arbitral award"). And, it is axiomatic that parties cannot confer subject-matter jurisdiction on a tribunal by way of consent. See, e.g., Gosa v. Mayden, 413 U.S. 665, 707, 93 S.Ct. 2926, 37 L.Ed.2d 873 (1973) (Marshall, J., dissenting) ("One of the most basic principles of our jurisprudence is that subject-matter jurisdiction cannot be conferred upon a court by consent of the parties."); American Fire & Cas. Co. v. Finn, 341 U.S. 6, 17–18, 71 S.Ct. 534, 95 L.Ed. 702 (1951) ("The jurisdiction of the federal courts is carefully guarded against expansion by ... prior action or consent of the parties."). Even assuming that International Trading agreed to the jurisdiction of the Qatari courts by voluntarily participating in the proceedings before those tribunals, that consent has no binding effect on this Court; rather, it is this Court's duty to determine whether the Qatari courts are "competent authorit[ies]" within the meaning of Article V(1)(e) Cf. Sabre Technologies, L.P. v. TSM Skyline Exhibits, Inc., Civil Action No. H–08–1815, 2008 WL 4330897, at *4 n. 21 (S.D.Tex. Sept. 18, 2008) [citing Gasch v. Hartford Accident & Ind. Co., 491 F.3d 278, 281 (5th Cir.2007), and Overton v. City of Austin, 748 F.2d 941, 957 n. 19 (5th Cir.1984)] {"Subject[-]matter jurisdiction is an issue of law, and a court is not bound to accept stipulations of law by parties to litigation." (internal citation and quotation marks omitted)}. As discussed above, the plain language of Article V(1)(e), as applied to the facts of this case, provides the courts of France, and not Qatar, with the authority to set aside the Award under the New York Convention.

DynCorp's reliance on Karaha Bodas to support its estoppel argument is misplaced. The main issue confronting the Fifth Circuit in Karaha Bodas was whether a Swiss court or an Indonesian tribunal had jurisdiction to vacate an arbitral award under Article V(1)(e). Karaha Bodas, 364 F.3d at 289–90. The appellee in Karaha Bodas had taken the position in the arbitration proceeding that Swiss arbitral law applied to the dispute, id. at 293, but "[f]or the first time ... in the district court," the appellee argued "that Indonesian, not Swiss, procedural law had applied to the arbitration," id. at 289, because the contracts at issue "refer[red] to certain Indonesian Civil Procedure Rules," id. at 290. The Fifth Circuit rejected this argument, however, reasoning that the appellee's "previous arguments that Swiss arbitral law applied" to the dispute was "strong[ ] evidence [of] the parties' contractual intent," id. at 293 (emphasis added), and thus the appellee was estopped from asserting that Indonesian arbitral law governed the dispute, id. at 294.

And therein lies the distinction between Karaha Bodas and this case. The issue of whether the parties intended for Swiss or Indonesian arbitral law to govern the dispute at issue in that case was a matter of contract interpretation, which raised a factual question. See, e.g., Flynn v. Dick Corp., 481 F.3d 824, 831 (D.C.Cir.2007) ("[T]he interpretation of ambiguous contract language ... is a question of fact...."). In this case, however, the parties both agree that (1) the seat of the arbitration was Paris, France; and (2) that the arbitration was governed by the ICC rules. Thus, even assuming that International Trading consented to the jurisdiction of the Qatari courts by voluntary participating in the judicial proceedings there, the question remains whether the Qatari courts, under the facts of this case, were "competent authorit[ies]" as that phrase is used in Article V(1)(e) of the New York Convention, which raises a pure question of law that is within the province of this Court to decide, without fidelity to any consent or stipulations by the parties. See supra pp. 22-23. Karaha Bodas, therefore, is inapposite.

As for DynCorp's invocation of comity principles, that argument has been effectively rendered moot by the Court's conclusions. It is true that "res judicata effect has ... traditionally been afforded foreign country judgments entitled to recognition consistently with principles of comity." Guinness PLC v. Ward, 955 F.2d 875, 893 n. 14 (4th Cir.1992). But affording comity to foreign judgments is not mandatory, see Paramedics Electromedicina Comercial, Ltda. v. GE Med. Sys. Info. Tech., 369 F.3d 645, 654 (2d Cir.2004) ["United States courts may choose to give res judicata effect to foreign judgments on the basis of comity, but are not obliged to do so" (internal quotation marks omitted)]; rather, "[c]omity will be granted to the decision or judgment of a foreign court if it is shown that the foreign court is a court of competent jurisdiction, and that the laws and public policy of the forum state ... will not be violated." Cunard S.S. Co. v. Salen Reefer Serv. AB, 773 F.2d 452, 457 (2d Cir.1985). Here, the Qatari Court of Cassation was not a "court of competent jurisdiction" because it lacked the authority under the New York Convention to set aside the Award. See supra at 10–11. Thus, the decision rendered by that tribunal is not entitled to deference under principles of comity.

In sum, DynCorp's efforts to distinguish this case from a "typical enforcement proceeding" falls flat. The terms of the Agreement demonstrate a clear and unambiguous intention by the parties to have all disputes arising from the Agreement resolved by binding arbitration and without resort to appeals before the Qatari courts. And, despite International Trading's voluntary participation in the proceedings before the Qatari courts, the Court is obligated to confirm the Award under Article V(1)(e) unless it can be shown that "[t]he award ... has been set aside ... by a competent authority of the country in which, or under the law of which, [an arbitral] award is made." New York Convention, art. V(1)(e). No such showing has been made by DynCorp, given that the Award was issued in France, and the Paris Court of Appeal rejected DynCorp's efforts to set aside the Award on November 4, 2010. Pet'r's Supp. Mem. at 1. The Court, therefore, is without authority to deny confirmation of the Award under Article V(1)(e).

2. Manifest Disregard of the Law

Next, DynCorp argues that "[t]he Qatari Court of Cassation has already determined, albeit in language that may not mimic the phraseology employed by [United States] courts, that the sole arbitrator acted in manifest disregard of Qatari law," thereby allowing this Court to deny confirmation of the Award on that ground. Resp'ts' Opp'n at 20. Specifically, DynCorp asserts that "when a contractual obligation is subject to competing interpretations," Qatari law requires a jurist to "search for the shared intention of the parties 'without pausing at the literal meaning of the words.' " Id. And DynCorp's position is that while "[t]he sole arbitrator acknowledged that he was obligated to interpret ... the 1998 Agreement in light of the shared intention of the parties," id., "the Court of Cassation expressly stated that the sole arbitrator's construction of [the Agreement] 'goes against the apparent meaning of the contract conditions' because of a 'misrepresentation of facts' that resulted in an 'error in the implementation of the law,' " id. at 21 [quoting id., Ex. E (Judgment of the Qatari Court of Cassation) at 3], and thus "the sole arbitrator knew what Qatari law required of him but ... declined to follow that mandate," id. As a consequence, posits DynCorp, this Court is authorized to deny confirmation of the Award either under Article V(1)(c) of the New York Convention, id. at 22, or as an independent ground "[i]n addition to the bases ... listed in Article V of the New York Convention," id. at 18.

The Court harbors a heavy dose of skepticism towards DynCorp's proposition that the Award can be refused confirmation under the New York Convention due to an arbitrator's alleged "manifest disregard of the law." Indeed, it would be a stretch to apply the "manifest disregard of the law" standard to awards falling within the province of the Convention, as the roots of that standard have no grounding in the treaty. Rather, the origin of this standard dates back to the Supreme Court's decision in Wilko v. Swan, 346 U.S. 427, 74 S.Ct. 182, 98 L.Ed. 168 (1953), a decision that predates the enactment of the New York Convention in 1958.8 At issue in Wilko was a court's "[p]ower to vacate an [arbitration] award" under Section 10(a) of the FAA,9 id. at 436, 74 S.Ct. 182 (emphasis added), which states that:

[i]n any of the following cases the United States court in and for the district wherein the award was made may make an order vacating the award upon the application of any party to the arbitration—

(1) where the award was procured by corruption, fraud, or undue means;

(2) where there was evident partiality or corruption in the arbitrators, or either of them;

(3) where the arbitrators were guilty of misconduct in refusing to postpone the hearing, upon sufficient cause shown, or in refusing to hear evidence pertinent and material to the controversy; or of any other misbehavior by which the rights of any party have been prejudiced; or

(4) where the arbitrators exceeded their powers, or so imperfectly executed them that a mutual, final, and definite award upon the subject matter submitted was not made,9 U.S.C. § 10(a). In describing that power, the Supreme Court noted that "interpretations of the law by ... arbitrators in contrast to manifest disregard [of the law] are not subject, in the federal courts, to judicial review for error in interpretation". Wilko, 346 U.S. at 436–37, 74 S.Ct. 182. The Supreme Court was not clear as to which provision of Section 10(a), if any, it relied upon in reaching its conclusion; in fact, the Supreme Court recently acknowledged in Hall Street Associates, LLC v. Mattel, Inc., 552 U.S. 576, 585, 128 S.Ct. 1396, 170 L.Ed.2d 254 (2008), that the "vagueness of [this] phrasing" in Wilko has led to different viewpoints amongst the circuit courts as to how the "manifest disregard of the law" standard fits within the scheme of Section 10(a), with some circuit courts reading this standard to "refer to the § 10 grounds collectively, rather than adding to them," id. [citing Mitsubishi Motors Corp. v. Soler Chrysler–Plymouth, Inc., 473 U.S. 614, 656, 105 S.Ct. 3346, 87 L.Ed.2d 444 (1985) (Stevens, J., dissenting) and I/S Stavborg v. Nat'l Metal Converters, Inc., 500 F.2d 424, 432 (2d Cir. 1974)], with other courts construing the standard to be "shorthand for § 10(a)(3) or § 10(a)(4), the paragraphs authorizing vacatur when the arbitrators were 'guilty of misconduct' or 'exceeded their powers,' " id. [citing Kyocera Corp. v. Prudential–Bache Trade Serv., Inc., 341 F.3d 987, 997 (9th Cir.2003)]. The District of Columbia Circuit, along with several other Circuits, has interpreted this standard to be an additional ground for vacatur outside of those listed under Section 10. See Lessin v. Merrill Lynch, Pierce, Fenner & Smith, Inc., 481 F.3d 813, 816 (D.C.Cir.2007) ("In addition to the grounds under the [FAA] ... on which an arbitration award may be vacated, an award may be vacated only if it is 'in manifest disregard

of the law....' "); Citigroup Global Mkts., Inc. v. Bacon, 562 F.3d 349, 353–54 (5th Cir.2009) ("[T] his circuit, like most other circuits, ultimately came to recognize manifest disregard of the law as a nonstatutory basis for vacatur."); McCarthy v. Citigroup Global Mkts., Inc., 463 F.3d 87, 91 (1st Cir.2006) (referring to the "manifest disregard of the law" standard as a "non-statutory standard of review"); Scott v. Prudential Sec., Inc., 141 F.3d 1007, 1017 (11th Cir.1998) (citing "manifest disregard of the law" as a "non-statutory ground ... to vacate an arbitration award"). But while the circuit courts may differ on the foundational underpinnings of the "manifest disregard of the law" standard,10 one common theme emerges from their decisions: the standard *27 is one that historically has been applied to actions to vacate an arbitral award under Section 10(a) of the FAA, and not proceedings to confirm arbitral awards under the New York Convention.

Moreover, the Court is not persuaded by DynCorp's logic that because Article V(1)(c) of the New York Convention, "like Section 10(a)(4) [of the FAA], ... addresses situations where the arbitrators have exceeded their powers," Article V(1)(c) therefore authorizes the Court to refuse recognition of the Award on the basis of an arbitrator's "manifest disregard of the law," since some courts have "held that arbitrators exceed their powers when they act in manifest disregard of the law." Resp'ts' Opp'n at 22. "In interpreting an international treaty," the Court must remain "mindful that it is in the nature of a contract between nations to which [g]eneral rules of construction apply." Societe Nationale Industrielle Aerospatiale v. U.S. Dist. Court for the S. Dist. of Iowa, 482 U.S. 522, 533, 107 S.Ct. 2542, 96 L.Ed.2d 461 (1987) (internal citation omitted and alteration in original). The starting point for interpreting a treaty provision, therefore, is to look at "the text of the treaty and the context in which the written words are used." Air France v. Saks, 470 U.S. 392, 397, 105 S.Ct. 1338, 84 L.Ed.2d 289 (1985). Here, the plain language of Article V(1)(c) hardly suggests that confirmation of an arbitral award can be denied in every instance where an arbitrator's powers are exceeded. As this Court recently addressed in Republic of Argentina, 764 F.Supp.2d at 30, 2011 WL 182138 at *6:

Unlike Section 10(a)(4) of the FAA, which states that an award may be vacated "where the arbitrators exceeded their powers," Article V(1)(c) is not so broad; rather, Article V(1)(c) authorizes the Court to deny confirmation of an award if "[t]he award deals with a difference not contemplated by or not falling within the terms of the submission to arbitration, or it contains decisions on matters beyond the scope of the submission to arbitration." See also Parsons & Whittemore Overseas Co. v. Societe Generale de L'Industrie du Papier, 508 F.2d 969, 976 (2d Cir. 1974) [recognizing that Article V(1)(c) "tracks in more detailed form [Section] 10(d) of the Federal Arbitration Act ... which authorizes vacating an award 'where the arbitrators exceeded their powers' " (emphasis added)]; 11 Mgmt. & Technical Consultants S.A. v. Parsons–Jurden Int'l Corp.,

820 F.2d 1531, 1534 (9th Cir.1987) ["[I]t is generally recognized that the [New York] Convention tracks the Federal Arbitration Act." (internal citation omitted)]. Put differently, a situation where an arbitrator "deals with a difference not contemplated by or not falling within the terms of the submission to arbitration," New York Convention, art. V(1)(c), is just one "detailed" example of a broader category of acts that can be considered an excessive use of power by an arbitrator under Section 10(a)(4) of the FAA. But arguably, it is only that specific scenario, not other actions that would be encompassed under Section 10(a)(4), that is covered under the New York Convention.

Furthermore, at least one federal circuit court has concluded that Article V does not provide a tribunal with a basis for denying confirmation of an arbitral award where an arbitrator has manifestly disregarded the law. M & C Corp. v. Erwin Behr GmbH & Co., 87 F.3d 844, 851 (6th Cir.1996) [concluding that "Article V of the (New York) Convention lists the exclusive grounds justifying refusal to recognize an arbitral award," and that "[t]hose grounds ... do not include ... manifest disregard of the law"]; see also Yusuf, 126 F.3d at 20 {"[T]o the extent that the Convention prescribes the exclusive grounds for relief from an award under the Convention ... application of the FAA's implied grounds would be in conflict, and is thus precluded."}. "Thus, the plain language of Article V(1)(c) does not appear to have the far reach that [DynCorp] desires." Republic of Argentina, 764 F.Supp.2d at 30, 2011 WL 182138 at *6.

Nor does the text of the Convention suggest that an arbitrator's "manifest disregard of the law" can serve as an independent and additional ground for denying confirmation of an arbitral award. Under Article V of the Convention, the Court's refusal to confirm an arbitral award is limited to "only" those situations where a "party furnishes ... proof that" one of the enumerated provisions applies. Nowhere in the seven enumerated provisions listed under Article V is an arbitrator's "manifest disregard of the law" a ground upon which the Court may deny confirmation of the Award; by negative implication, that basis, along with any other potential grounds for refusing confirmation of an arbitral award, are excluded. See, e.g., United States v. Vonn, 535 U.S. 55, 65, 122 S.Ct. 1043, 152 L.Ed.2d 90 (2002) (recognizing expressio unius est exclusio alterius—"that expressing one item of a commonly associated group or series excludes another left unmentioned"—as a guide for interpreting statutes). Such a narrow reading of the New York Convention comports with the context in which the Convention was enacted, as a broad construction of the Convention would do nothing more than erect additional hurdles to confirmation of arbitral awards, which in turn would contravene the "principal purpose" of the Convention, i.e., "to encourage the recognition and enforcement of commercial arbitration agreements in international contracts." Scherk v. Alberto–Culver Co., 417 U.S. 506, 520 n. 15, 94 S.Ct. 2449, 41 L.Ed.2d 270 (1974). Thus, the Court cannot envision how an arbitrator's "manifest disregard of the law" can serve as an independent ground to deny confirmation of the Award in the face of the Convention's plain language.

It should be no surprise, then, that DynCorp has failed to cite any case law where the "manifest disregard of the law" standard has been considered an express or implied basis for denying recognition of an arbitral award under the New York Convention. Instead, the cases that DynCorp cites (with the exception of one) all involve arbitral awards that had been rendered in the United States, thereby allowing the non-prevailing parties in those cases to seek vacatur of the award under Article V(1)(e) of the Convention. See Int'l Thunderbird Gaming Corp. v. United Mexican States, 473 F.Supp.2d 80, 82 (D.D.C.2007) (Kennedy, J.), aff'd 255 Fed.Appx. 531, 532–33 (D.C.Cir.2007) (denying petition to vacate arbitral award issued in Washington, D.C.); Esso Exploration and Prod. Chad, Inc. v. Taylors Int'l Servs., Ltd., 293 Fed.Appx. 34, 36 (2d Cir.2008) (affirming district court's rejection of petition to vacate arbitral award issued in New York); Jacada (Europe), Ltd. v. Int'l Mktg., Inc., 401 F.3d 701, 703 (6th Cir.2005) (affirming district court's rejection of petition to vacate arbitral award issued in Michigan). This fact is significant because in an action brought under Article V(1)(e) to set aside an arbitral award, "[t]he Convention specifically contemplates that the state in which, or under the law of which, the award is made will be free to set aside ... an award in accordance with its domestic arbitral law and its full panoply of express and implied grounds for relief." Yusuf, 126 F.3d at 23. The applicable "domestic arbitral law [s]" in the United States to vacate an arbitral award, of course, are Section 10(a) of the FAA and any implied grounds recognized by the various federal courts. See id. Thus, these cases do not advance DynCorp's position that the "manifest disregard of the law" standard can be employed by the Court to deny confirmation of an arbitral award under the New York Convention; instead, these cases confirm the Court's observations above that the "manifest disregard of the law" standard has been applied by other courts only when faced with the issue of whether vacatur of an arbitral award is appropriate under Section 10(a) of the FAA.

The one case cited by DynCorp that did not involve a petition to set aside an arbitral award under the FAA and the Convention, In re Chromalloy Aeroservices, 939 F.Supp. 907 (D.D.C.1996) (Green, J.), is also distinguishable from this case but requires further explanation. There, a former member of this Court concluded that an arbitration prevailing party was not entitled to confirmation of the award under the Convention because the "award was made in Egypt, under the laws of Egypt, and ha[d] been nullified by [a] court designated by Egypt to review arbitral awards." Id. at 909. Judge Green, however, concluded that Article VII of the Convention allowed the prevailing party to "avail himself of an arbitral award in the manner and to the extent allowed by the law ... of the count[r]y where such award is sought to be relied upon." Id. (emphasis added). As a result, Judge Green concluded that the prevailing party also could seek confirmation of the arbitral award under Section 9 of the FAA rather than Article IV for the Convention, see id. (citing 9 U.S.C. §§ 1–14), "unless the award is vacated, modified, or corrected as prescribed in [S] ections 10 and 11 of [the FAA]," 9 U.S.C. § 9, or "if the award was made in 'manifest disregard of the law,' " Chromalloy, 939 F.Supp. at 910.

But that line of reasoning has no application here. Judge Green's recognition of the applicability of the "manifest disregard of the law" standard in Chromalloy hinged on the prevailing party's invocation of Section 9 of the FAA through Article VII of the Convention. Here, however, DynCorp does not, and cannot, invoke Article VII because it is not attempting to "avail" itself of an arbitral award; rather, it is only seeking to "avail" itself of the defenses recognized under Section 10 of the FAA. See New York Convention, art. VII ["The provisions of the present Convention shall not ... deprive any interested party of any right he may have to avail himself of an arbitral award in the manner and to the extent allowed by the law ... where such award is sought to be relied upon." (emphasis added)]. Those defenses, as noted above, are not otherwise available to a party petitioning a court to deny confirmation of an arbitral award. See TermoRio, 487 F.3d at 935 (quoting Yusuf, 126 F.3d at 23). Thus, Chromalloy does not support DynCorp's position that an arbitrator's "manifest disregard of the law" is a basis upon which the Court may refuse recognition of the Award.

As shown above, there is simply no support in either the text of the New York Convention or case law for DynCorp's position that an arbitrator's "manifest disregard of the law" is a valid basis upon which the Court can deny confirmation of an arbitral award. But notwithstanding the Court's analysis in this regard, DynCorp's efforts to prevent confirmation of the Award fail for yet another reason: the record is devoid of any evidence that the arbitrator in this case actually disregarded Qatari law. To establish that the arbitrator acted with "manifest disregard of the law", DynCorp has the burden of proving that "(1) the arbitrator knew of a governing legal principle[,] yet refused to apply it or ignored it altogether[,] and (2) the law ignored by the arbitrator[ ] was well[-]defined, explicit, and clearly applicable to the case". LaPrade v. Kidder, Peabody & Co., 94 F.Supp.2d 2, 4–5 (D.D.C.2000) (Sullivan, J.), aff'd 246 F.3d 702 (D.C.Cir.2001). Here, there is no evidence as DynCorp contends that the arbitrator failed to "search for the shared intention of the parties [by] pausing at the literal meaning of the [contractual terms]". Resp'ts' Opp'n at 20. In fact, not only does DynCorp concede that the arbitrator acknowledged his "obligat[ion] to interpret ... the 1998 Agreement in light of the shared intention of the parties," id., but the arbitrator's decision itself reflects his efforts to glean the parties' shared intent from the Agreement. According to the Award, the arbitrator found that Section 9.1 required the Agreement to remain in effect "for a period of sixty months from the date of signature ..., unless and until terminated" by one of the parties thereafter, Pet'r's Mem., Ex. A (Award) at 23. Although the arbitrator acknowledged that Section 9.1 contained an "apparent inconsistency", id.—that the Agreement shall continue "unless terminated by ... giving ... 90 (Ninety) days prior notice expiring on or at any time after the first anniversary of the date" the Agreement was signed, Resp'ts' Opp'n, Ex. A (the 1998 Agreement) at 12—the arbitrator concluded that the two clauses "can be applied in [a] way ... without resulting in any direct contradiction" because any notice given "after 60 months is also necessarily after the first 12 months of the contract," Pet'r's Mem., Ex. A (Award) at 24. The arbitrator also noted that "[i]f the intention of ... the parties was" for the Agreement to be voidable after one year rather than sixty months, then "the Agreement would have been drafted and signed initially for a period of one year," with an option of an annual renewal, Pet'r's Mem., Ex. A (Award) at 24 (emphasis added). Thus, the arbitrator's analysis hardly suggests that he "paus[ed] at the literal meaning of the" contractual terms, as alleged by DynCorp, Resp'ts' Opp'n at 20; rather, the Award reflects an attempt by the arbitrator to reconcile the literal meaning of two clauses that appeared to be directly contradictory in order to discern the parties' shared contractual intent.

DynCorp also asserts that the Qatari Court of Cassation found the sole arbitrator to have acted with manifest disregard of Qatari law, Resp'ts' Opp'n at 20, but the record suggests otherwise. Nowhere in the Qatari Court of Cassation's decision did the tribunal conclude that the arbitrator "refused to apply" or "ignored" Qatari law, LaPrade, 94 F.Supp.2d at 4–5; to the contrary, the Qatari Court of Cassation found that the arbitrator "implement [ed]" Qatari law (albeit erroneously in that court's view) in reaching his decision. See Resp'ts' Mem., Ex. E (Decision of Qatari Court of Cassation) at 4 [concluding that the arbitrator's construction of the 1998 agreement was "error[oneous] in the implementation of the law" (emphasis added)]. DynCorp's position collapses even further when taking into account the decision of the Qatari Court of Appeal, which held that the arbitrator's decision "was resolved on correct, suitable, and accepted... law." Id., Ex. D (Decision of Qatari Court of Appeal) at 12–13. If it were truly the case that the Qatari Court of Cassation found that the arbitrator acted with "manifest disregard of the law," then the necessary implication from that conclusion is that the Qatari Court of Appeal—which this Court can safely assume is composed of jurists well-learned in Qatari jurisprudence—also "refused to apply" or "ignored" Qatari law. The Court finds such a circumstance untenable. What the Qatari Court of Appeal's affirmation of the arbitrator's decision does signify, however, is that the arbitrator's conclusions, at a minimum, were a "colorable" interpretation of the Agreement, and because the arbitrator "was arguably construing or applying the contract, [the C]ourt must defer to the arbitrator's judgment." Madison Hotel v. Hotel & Rest. Emps., Local 25, 144 F.3d 855,

859 (D.C.Cir.1998) (citation and internal quotation marks omitted).

Accordingly, the Court rejects DynCorp's arguments that confirmation of the Award should be denied as a result of the arbitrator's purported "manifest disregard of the law." The New York Convention does not contain any provision that authorizes the Court to deny confirmation of an arbitral award due to an arbitrator's manifest disregard of the law. In any event, even if the Court were empowered to refuse recognition of the Award on this basis, DynCorp has failed to establish any ignorance of Qatari law, let alone a "manifest disregard of the law," by the arbitrator in rendering his decision. DynCorp's arguments are thus entirely without merit.

IV. Conclusion

For all the reasons discussed above, DynCorp's efforts to prevent confirmation of the Award must be rejected. Despite the Qatari Court of Cassation's conclusion that the arbitrator's construction of the 1998 Agreement contravened Qatari law, this Court is without authority to refuse recognition of the Award under Article V(1)(e) based on that ruling. Moreover, notwithstanding the distinct unlikelihood that the Court can deny confirmation of the Award where an arbitrator acts with "manifest disregard of the law," the record does not reveal any evidence suggesting that the arbitrator either "refused to apply" or "ignored" a clear principle of law. LaPrade, 94 F.Supp.2d at 4–5. Having failed to meet "the showing required to avoid summary confirmation," Ottley, 819 F.2d at 376, the Court concludes that the Award must be confirmed, and that International Trading is entitled to damages in the amount of $1,107,764.95, along with $40,000 for costs, and interest of 5% per annum.

SO ORDERED this 21st day of January, 2011.15

【本案评析】

本案涉及国际商事仲裁实务中撤销国际商事仲裁裁决和不予执行仲裁裁决的问题。1998 年 7 月，DynCorp 和国际贸易与工业投资公司签订合同，在卡塔尔建立一个分支机构。2001 年，双方发生争议。本案为国际商会仲裁，仲裁地在巴黎。裁决作出之后，DynCorp 在卡塔尔对裁决提出异议，法院以未能遵守卡塔尔法律为由撤销了裁决。国际贸易与工业投资公司申请美国哥伦比亚地区法院根据《联邦仲裁法》和《纽约公约》确认仲裁裁决。DynCorp 则申请拒绝执行仲裁裁决，理由是卡塔尔法院已经撤销裁决，因此不能执行，并且仲裁员的组成“显然漠视法律”。

美国哥伦比亚地区法院驳回 DynCorp 的主张。法院认为，根据《纽约公约》

的规定，卡塔尔法院不具有撤销仲裁裁决的管辖权，只有仲裁地法院才可以撤销仲裁裁决。此种属物管辖权依《纽约公约》不得由当事人通过合意创设，国际贸易与工业投资公司参与卡塔尔的程序不能认为是同意卡塔尔法院具有撤销仲裁裁决的权力。因此，卡塔尔法院撤销仲裁裁决对于地区法院并无影响，其无权基于仲裁员“显然漠视法律”来拒绝承认仲裁裁决。《纽约公约》并未将其作为一项拒绝执行仲裁裁决的理由。

二、撤销国际商事仲裁裁决和不予执行仲裁裁决案例①

In the Matter of the Arbitration of Certain Controversies Between CHROMALLOY AEROSERVICES, A DIVISION OF CHROMALLOY GAS TURBINE CORPORATION, Petitioner,

and

The ARAB REPUBLIC OF EGYPT, Respondent.

Civil No. 94-2339 (JLG).

July 31, 1996.

JUNE L. GREEN, District Judge.

I. Introduction

This matter is before the Court on the Petition of Chromalloy Aeroservices, Inc., ("CAS") to Confirm an Arbitral Award, and a Motion to Dismiss that Petition filed by the Arab Republic of Egypt ("Egypt"), the defendant in the arbitration. This is a case of first impression. The Court GRANTS Chromalloy Aeroservices' Petition to Recognize and Enforce the Arbitral Award, and DENIES Egypt's Motion to Dismiss, because the arbitral award in question is valid, and because Egypt's arguments against enforcement are insufficient to allow this Court to disturb the award.

II. Background

This case involves a military procurement contract between a U.S. corporation, Chromalloy Aeroservices, Inc., and the Air Force of the Arab Republic of Egypt.

On June 16, 1988, Egypt and CAS entered into a contract under which CAS agreed to provide parts, maintenance, and repair for helicopters belonging to the Egyptian Air Force. [Arbitration Award ("Award") at 3.] On December 2, 1991, Egypt terminated the contract by notifying CAS

① Matter of Arbitration Between Chromalloy Aeroservices, a Div. of Chromalloy GaTurbine Corp. and Arab Republic of Egypt.United States District Court, District of Columbia.July 31, 1996939 F.Supp. 907 (Approx. 12 pages).

representatives in Egypt. (Award at 5.) On December 4, 1991, Egypt notified CAS headquarters in Texas of the termination. (Id.) On December 15, 1991, CAS notified Egypt that it rejected the cancellation of the contract "and commenced arbitration proceedings on the basis of the arbitration clause contained in Article XII and Appendix E of the Contract". (Id.) Egypt then drew down CAS' letters of guarantee in an amount totaling some $11,475,968. (Id.)

On February 23, 1992, the parties began appointing arbitrators, and shortly thereafter, commenced a lengthy arbitration. (Id.) On August 24, 1994, the arbitral panel ordered Egypt to pay to CAS the sums of $272,900 plus 5 percent interest from July 15, 1991, (interest accruing until the date of payment), and $16,940,958 plus 5 percent interest from December 15, 1991, (interest accruing until the date of payment). (Id. at 65-66.) The panel also ordered CAS to pay to Egypt the sum of 606,920 pounds sterling, plus 5 percent interest from December 15, 1991, (interest accruing until the date of payment). (Id.)

On October 28, 1994, CAS applied to this Court for enforcement of the award. On November 13, 1994, Egypt filed an appeal with the Egyptian Court of Appeal, seeking nullification of the award. On March 1, 1995, Egypt filed a motion with this Court to adjourn CAS's Petition to enforce the award. On April 4, 1995, the Egyptian Court of Appeal suspended the award, and on May 5, 1995, Egypt filed a Motion in this Court to Dismiss CAS's petition to enforce the award. On December 5, 1995, Egypt's Court of Appeal at Cairo issued an order nullifying the award. [Decision of Egyptian Court of Appeal ("Egypt Ct.") at 11.] This Court held a hearing in the matter on December 12, 1995.

Egypt argues that this Court should deny CAS' Petition to Recognize and Enforce the Arbitral Award out of deference to its court. (Response to Petitioner's Post-Hearing Brief at 2.) CAS argues that this Court should confirm the award because Egypt "does not present any serious argument that its court's nullification decision is consistent with the New York Convention or United States arbitration law." (Petitioner's Rejoinder at 1.)

III. Discussion

A. Jurisdiction

This Court has original jurisdiction under the Foreign Sovereign Immunities Act, 28 U.S.C. § 1330, et. seq. (1976), which provides in relevant part that:

The district courts shall have original jurisdiction without regard to amount in controversy of any non-jury civil action against a foreign state as defined in section 1603(a) of this title as to any claim for relief in personam with respect to which the foreign state is not entitled to immunity ... under sections 1605-1607 of this title.

28 U.S.C. § 1330(a). Both the Arab Republic of Egypt and the Egyptian Air Force are foreign

states under 28 U.S.C. § 1603(a) & (b). See *909 Republic of Argentina v. Weltover, 504 U.S. 607, 612, n. 1, 112 S.Ct. 2160, 2164-65, n. 1, 119 L.Ed.2d 394 (1992).

(a) A foreign state shall not be immune from the jurisdiction of courts of the United States ... in any case-

* * * * * *

in which the action is brought, either to enforce an agreement made by the foreign state with or for the benefit of a private party to submit to arbitration all or any differences which have arisen or which may arise between the parties with respect to a defined legal relationship, whether contractual or not, concerning a subject matter capable of settlement by arbitration under the laws of the United States, or to confirm an award made pursuant to such an agreement, if

* * * * * *

(b) the agreement or award is ... governed by a treaty or other international agreement in force for the United States calling for the recognition and enforcement of arbitral awards.

28 U.S.C. § 1605(a) & (a)(6) & (a)(6)(b) (emphasis added).

CAS brings this action to confirm an arbitral award made pursuant to an agreement to arbitrate any and all disputes arising under a contract between itself and Egypt, a foreign state, concerning a subject matter capable of settlement by arbitration under U.S. law. See U.S.C. §§ 1-14. Enforcement of the award falls under the Convention on Recognition and Enforcement of Foreign Arbitral Awards, ("Convention"), 9 U.S.C. § 202, which grants "[t]he district courts of the United States ... original jurisdiction over such an action or proceeding, regardless of the amount in controversy." 9 U.S.C. § 203.1

B. Chromalloy's Petition for Enforcement

A party seeking enforcement of a foreign arbitral award must apply for an order confirming the award within three years after the award is made. 9 U.S.C. § 207. The award in question was made on August 14, 1994. CAS filed a Petition to confirm the award with this Court on October 28, 1994, less than three months after the arbitral panel made the award. CAS's Petition includes a "duly certified copy" of the original award as required by Article IV(1)(a) of the Convention, translated by a duly sworn translator, as required by Article IV(2) of the Convention, as well as a duly certified copy of the original contract and arbitration clause, as required by Article IV(1)(b) of the Convention. 9 U.S.C. § 201 note. CAS's Petition is properly before this Court.

1. The Standard under the Convention

This Court must grant CAS's Petition to Recognize and Enforce the arbitral "award unless it finds one of the grounds for refusal ... of recognition or enforcement of the award specified in the ... Convention." 9 U.S.C. § 207. Under the Convention, "Recognition and enforcement of the award may be refused" if Egypt furnishes to this Court "proof that ... [t]he award has ... been set aside ... by a competent authority of the country in which, or under the law of which, that award was made." Convention, Article V(1) & V(1)(e) (emphasis added), 9 U.S.C. § 201 note. In the present case, the award was made in Egypt, under the laws of Egypt, and has been nullified by the court designated by Egypt to review arbitral awards. Thus, the Court may, at its discretion, decline to enforce the award.

While Article V provides a discretionary standard, Article VII of the Convention requires that, "The provisions of the present Convention shall not ... deprive any interested party of any right he may have to avail himself of an arbitral award in the manner and to the extent allowed by the law ... of the count[r]y where such award is sought to be relied upon." 9 U.S.C. § 201 note (emphasis added). In other words, under the Convention, CAS maintains all rights to the enforcement of this Arbitral Award that it would have in the absence of the Convention. Accordingly, the Court finds that, if the Convention did not exist, the Federal Arbitration Act ("FAA") would provide CAS with a legitimate claim to enforcement of this arbitral award. See 9 U.S.C. §§ 1-14. Jurisdiction over Egypt in such a suit would be available under 28 U.S.C. §§ 1330 (granting jurisdiction over foreign states "as to any claim for relief in personam with respect to which the foreign state is not entitled to immunity ... under sections 1605-1607 of this title") and 1605(a)(2) (withholding immunity of foreign states for "an act outside ... the United States in connection with a commercial activity of the foreign state elsewhere and that act causes a direct effect in the United States"). See Weltover, 504 U.S. at 607, 112 S.Ct. at 2160. Venue for the action would lie with this Court under 28 U.S.C. § 1391(f) & (f)(4) (granting venue in civil cases against foreign governments to the United States District Court for the District of Columbia).

2. Examination of the Award under 9 U.S.C. § 10

Under the laws of the United States, arbitration awards are presumed to be binding, and may only be vacated by a court under very limited circumstances:

(a) In any of the following cases the United States court in and for the district wherein the award was made may make an order vacating the award upon the application of any party to the arbitration-

(1) Where the award was procured by corruption, fraud, or undue means.

(2) Where there was evident partiality or corruption in the arbitrators, or either of them.

(3) Where the arbitrators were guilty of misconduct in refusing to postpone the hearing, upon sufficient cause shown, or in refusing to hear evidence pertinent and material to the controversy; or of any other misbehavior by which the rights of any party have been prejudiced.

(4) Where the arbitrators exceeded their powers, or so imperfectly executed them that a

mutual, final, and definite award upon the subject matter submitted was not made.

9 U.S.C. § 10.3

An arbitral award will also be set aside if the award was made in " 'manifest disregard' of the law." First Options of Chicago v. Kaplan, 514 U.S. 938,----, 115 S.Ct. 1920, 1923, 131 L.Ed.2d 985 (1995). "Manifest disregard of the law may be found if [the] arbitrator[s] understood and correctly stated the law but proceeded to ignore it." Kanuth v. Prescott, Ball, & Turben, Inc., 949 F.2d 1175, 1179 (D.C.Cir.1991).

Plainly, this non-statutory theory of vacatur cannot empower a District Court to conduct the same de novo review of questions of law that an appellate court exercises over lower court decisions. Indeed, we have in the past held that it is clear that [manifest disregard] means more than error or misunderstanding with respect to the law.

Al-Harbi v. Citibank, 85 F.3d 680, 683 (D.C.Cir.1996) (internal citations omitted).

In Al-Harbi, "The submission agreement under which the arbitrator decided the controversy mandated that the arbitrator apply 'the procedural and substantive laws of the Southern District of New York, U.S.A.' " Id. at 684. The arbitrator in Al-Harbi ruled that a court applying the laws of New York would dismiss the case on forum non conveniens grounds. Id. Appellant argued on appeal that the arbitrator had manifestly disregarded the substantive laws of New York by disposing of the case on procedural grounds. Id. The D.C. Circuit emphatically rejected this argument, stating that:

Appellant's argument then depends upon the proposition that where a tribunal is to render [a] decision based on procedural and substantive law that tribunal has not only erred, but acted in manifest disregard of the law if it finds that procedural factors are dispositive of the case without then going on to consider substantive law rendered apparently moot by that procedural decision. To state that proposition is to reject it. We find no basis for vacatur.

Id.

In the present case, the language of the arbitral award that Egypt complains of reads:

The Arbitral tribunal considers that it does not need to decide the legal nature of the contract. It appears that the Parties rely principally for their claims and defences, on the interpretation of the contract itself and on the facts presented. Furthermore, the Arbitral tribunal holds that the legal issues in dispute are not affected by the characterization of the contract.

(Award at 30.)

Like the arbitrator in Al-Harbi, the arbitrators in the present case made a procedural decision that allegedly led to a misapplication of substantive law. After considering Egypt's arguments that Egyptian administrative law should govern the contract, the majority of the arbitral panel held that it did not matter which substantive law they applied-civil or administrative. Id. At worst, this decision constitutes a mistake of law, and thus is not subject to review by this Court. See Al-Harbi, 85 F.3d at 684.

In the United States, "[W]e are well past the time when judicial suspicion of the desirability of arbitration and of the competence of arbitral tribunals inhibited the development of arbitration as an alternative means of dispute resolution." Mitsubishi Motors Corp. v. Soler Chrysler-Plymouth, Inc., 473 U.S. 614, 626-27, 105 S.Ct. 3346, 3354, 87 L.Ed.2d 444 (1985). In Egypt, however, "[I]t is established that arbitration is an exceptional means for resolving disputes, requiring departure from the normal means of litigation before the courts, and the guarantees they afford." (Nullification Decision at 8.) Egypt's complaint that, "[T]he Arbitral Award is null under Arbitration Law ... because it is not properly 'grounded' under Egyptian law," reflects this suspicious view of arbitration, and is precisely the type of technical argument that U.S. courts are not to entertain when reviewing an arbitral award. See Montana Power Company v. Federal Power Commission, 445 F.2d 739, 755 (D.C.Cir.1970) [cert. den. 400 U.S. 1013, 91 S.Ct. 566, 27 L.Ed.2d 627 (1971)] (holding that, "Arbitrators do not have to give reasons") [citing United Steelworkers v. Enterprise Wheel & Car Corp., 363 U.S. 593, 598, 80 S.Ct. 1358, 1361-62, 4 L.Ed.2d 1424 (1960)].

The Court's analysis thus far has addressed the arbitral award, and, as a matter of U.S. law, the award is proper. See Sanders v. Washington Metro. Area Transit Auth., 819 F.2d 1151, 1157 (D.C.Cir.1987) (holding that, "When the parties have had a full and fair opportunity to present their evidence, the decisions of the arbitrator should be viewed as conclusive as to subsequent proceedings, absent some abuse of discretion by the arbitrator") [citing the Restatement (Second) of Judgments § 84(3) (1982), Greenblatt v. Drexel Burnham Lambert, Inc., 763 F.2d 1352 (11th Cir.1985)]. The Court now considers the question of whether the decision of the Egyptian court should be recognized as a valid foreign judgment.

As the Court stated earlier, this is a case of first impression. There are no reported cases in which a court of the United States has faced a situation, under the Convention, in which the court of a foreign nation has nullified an otherwise valid arbitral award. This does not mean, however, that the Court is without guidance in this case. To the contrary, more than twenty years ago, in a case involving the enforcement of an arbitration clause under the FAA, the Supreme Court held that:

An agreement to arbitrate before a specified tribunal is, in effect, a specialized kind of forum-selection clause.... The invalidation of such an agreement ... would not only allow the respondent to repudiate its solemn promise but would, as well, reflect a parochial concept that all disputes must be resolved under our laws and in our courts.

Scherk v. Alberto-Culver Co., 417 U.S. 506, 519, 94 S.Ct. 2449, 2457, 41 L.Ed.2d 270 (1974) [reh. den., 419 U.S. 885, 95 S.Ct. 157, 42 L.Ed.2d 129 (1974)] (citations omitted).

In Scherk, the Court forced a U.S. corporation to arbitrate a dispute arising under an international contract containing an arbitration clause. Id. 417 U.S. at 518, 94 S.Ct. at 2456-57. In so doing, the Court relied upon the FAA, but took the opportunity to comment upon the purposes of the newly acceded-to Convention:

The delegates to the Convention voiced frequent concern that courts of signatory countries in which an agreement to arbitrate is sought to be enforced should not be permitted to decline enforcement of such agreements on the basis of parochial views of their desirability or in a manner that would diminish the mutually binding nature of the agreements.... [W]e think that this country's adoption and ratification of the Convention and the passage of Chapter 2 of the United States Arbitration Act provide strongly persuasive evidence of congressional policy consistent with the decision we reach today.

Id. at n. 15. The Court finds this argument equally persuasive in the present case, where Egypt seeks to repudiate its solemn promise to abide by the results of the arbitration.4

C. The Decision of Egypt's Court of Appeal

1. The Contract

"The arbitration agreement is a contract and the court will not rewrite it for the parties." Williams v. E.F. Hutton & Co., Inc., 753 F.2d 117, 119 (D.C.Cir.1985) [citing Davis v. Chevy Chase Financial Ltd., 667 F.2d 160, 167 (D.C.Cir.1981)]. The Court "begin[s] with the 'cardinal principle of contract construction: that a document should be read to give effect to all its provisions and to render them consistent with each other.' " United States v. Insurance Co. of North America, 83 F.3d 1507, 1511 (D.C.Cir.1996) [quoting Mastrobuono v. Shearson Lehman Hutton, Inc., 514 U.S. 52, 115 S.Ct. 1212, 1219, 131 L.Ed.2d 76 (1995)]. Article XII of the contract requires that the parties arbitrate all disputes that arise between them under the contract. Appendix E, which defines the terms of any arbitration, forms an integral part of the contract. The contract is unitary. Appendix E to the contract defines the "Applicable Law Court of Arbitration." The clause reads, in relevant part:

It is ... understood that both parties have irrevocably agreed to apply Egypt (sic) Laws and to choose Cairo as seat of the court of arbitration.

* * * * * *

The decision of the said court shall be final and binding and cannot be made subject to any appeal or other recourse.

[Appendix E ("Appendix") to the Contract.]

This Court may not assume that the parties intended these two sentences to contradict one another, and must preserve the meaning of both if possible. Insurance Co., 83 F.3d 1507, 1511

(D.C.Cir.1996). Egypt argues that the first quoted sentence supersedes the second, and allows an appeal to an Egyptian court. Such an interpretation, however, would vitiate the second sentence, and would ignore the plain language on the face of the contract. The Court concludes that the first sentence defines choice of law and choice of forum for the hearings of the arbitral panel. The Court further concludes that the second quoted sentence indicates the clear intent of the parties that any arbitration of a dispute arising under the contract is not to be appealed to any court. This interpretation, unlike that offered by Egypt, preserves the meaning of both sentences in a manner that is consistent with the plain language of the contract. The position of the latter sentence as the seventh and final paragraph, just before the signatures, lends credence to the view that this sentence is the final word on the arbitration question. In other words, the parties agreed to apply Egyptian Law to the arbitration, but, more important, they agreed that the arbitration ends with the decision of the arbitral panel.

2. The Decision of the Egyptian Court of Appeal

The Court has already found that the arbitral award is proper as a matter of U.S. law, and that the arbitration agreement between Egypt and CAS precluded an appeal in Egyptian courts. The Egyptian court has acted, however, and Egypt asks this Court to grant res judicata effect to that action.

The "requirements for enforcement of a foreign judgment ... are that there be 'due citation' [i.e., proper service of process] and that the original claim not violate U.S. public policy." Tahan v. Hodgson, 662 F.2d 862, 864 (D.C.Cir.1981) [citing Hilton v. Guyot, 159 U.S. 113, 202, 16 S.Ct. 139, 158, 40 L.Ed. 95 (1895)]. The Court uses the term "public policy" advisedly, with a full understanding that, "[J]udges have no license to impose their own brand of justice in determining applicable public policy." Northwest Airlines Inc. v. Air Line Pilots Association, Int'l, 808 F.2d 76, 78 (D.C.Cir.1987). Correctly understood, "[P]ublic policy emanates [only] from clear statutory or case law, 'not from general considerations of supposed public interest.' " Id. [quoting American Postal Workers Union v. United States Postal Service, 789 F.2d 1 (D.C.Cir.1986)].

The U.S. public policy in favor of final and binding arbitration of commercial disputes is unmistakable, and supported by treaty, by statute, and by case law. The Federal Arbitration Act "and the implementation of the Convention in the same year by amendment of the Federal Arbitration Act," demonstrate that there is an "emphatic federal policy in favor of arbitral dispute resolution," particularly "in the field of international commerce." Mitsubishi v. Soler Chrysler-Plymouth, 473 U.S. 614, 631, 105 S.Ct. 3346, 3356, 87 L.Ed.2d 444 (1985) (internal citation omitted); cf. Revere Copper & Brass Inc., v. Overseas Private Investment Corporation, 628 F.2d 81, 82 (D.C.Cir.1980) (holding that, "There is a strong public policy behind judicial enforcement of binding arbitration clauses"). A decision by this Court to recognize the decision of the Egyptian court would violate this clear U.S. public policy.

3. International Comity

"No nation is under an unremitting obligation to enforce foreign interests which are fundamentally prejudicial to those of the domestic forum." Laker Airways Ltd. v. Sabena, Belgian World Airlines, 731 F.2d 909, 937 (D.C.Cir.1984). "[C]omity never obligates a national forum to ignore 'the rights of its own citizens or of other persons who are under the protection of its laws.' " Id. at 942 (emphasis added) [quoting Hilton v. Guyot, 159 U.S. 113, 164, 16 S.Ct. 139, 143-44, 40 L.Ed. 95 (1895)]. Egypt alleges that, "Comity is the chief doctrine of international law requiring U.S. courts to respect the decisions of competent foreign tribunals." However, comity does not and may not have the preclusive effect upon U.S. law that Egypt wishes this Court to create for it.

The Supreme Court's unanimous opinion in W.S. Kirkpatrick & Co., Inc. v. Environmental Tectonics Corp., Int'l, 493 U.S. 400, 408, 110 S.Ct. 701, 706, 107 L.Ed.2d 816 (1990), defines the proper limitations of the "act of state doctrine"and, by implication, judicial comity as well. Kirkpatrick arose out of a dispute between two U.S. companies over a government construction project in Nigeria. Kirkpatrick, the losing bidder, sued Environmental Techtonics, ("ETC"), the winning bidder, alleging that ETC acquired the contract by bribing Nigerian officials in violation of U.S. law. Id. ETC argued that the act of state doctrine precluded U.S. courts from hearing the case because to do so "would impugn or question the nobility of a foreign nation's motivations," and would "result in embarrassment to the sovereign or constitute interference in the conduct of [the] foreign policy of the United States." Id. at 408, 110 S.Ct. at 706. The Supreme Court rejected this argument:

The short of the matter is this: Courts in the United States have the power, and ordinarily the obligation, to decide cases and controversies properly presented to them. The act of state doctrine does not establish an exception for cases and controversies that may embarrass foreign governments, but merely requires that, in the process of deciding, the acts of foreign sovereigns taken within their own jurisdictions shall be deemed valid. That doctrine has no application to the present case because the validity of no foreign sovereign act is at issue.

Id. at 409, 110 S.Ct. at 707 (emphasis added). Similarly, in the present case, the question is whether this Court should give res judicata effect to the decision of the Egyptian Court of Appeal, not whether that court properly decided the matter under Egyptian law.Since the "act of state doctrine," as a whole, does not require U.S. courts to defer to a foreign sovereign on these facts, comity, which is but one of several "policies" that underlie the act of state "doctrine," id. at 409, 110 S.Ct. at 706-07, does not require such deference either.

4. Choice of Law

Egypt argues that by choosing Egyptian law, and by choosing Cairo as the sight of the arbitration, CAS has for all time signed away its rights under the Convention and U.S. law. This argument is specious. When CAS agreed to the choice of law and choice of forum provisions, it waived its right to sue Egypt for breach of contract in the courts of the United States in favor of final and binding arbitration of such a dispute under the Convention. Having prevailed in the chosen forum, under the chosen law, CAS comes to this Court seeking recognition and enforcement of the award. The Convention was created for just this purpose. It is untenable to argue that by choosing arbitration under the Convention, CAS has waived rights specifically guaranteed by that same Convention.

5. Conflict between the Convention & the FAA

As a final matter, Egypt argues that, "Chromalloy's use of [A]rticle VII [to invoke the Federal Arbitration Act] contradicts the clear language of the Convention and would create an impermissible conflict under 9 U.S.C. § 208," by eliminating all consideration of Article V of the Convention. See Vimar Seguros y Reaseguros, S.A. v. M/V Sky Reefer, 515 U.S. 528,----, 115 S.Ct. 2322, 2325, 132 L.Ed.2d 462 (1995) {holding that, "[W]hen two statutes are capable of coexistence ... it is the duty of the courts, absent a clearly expressed congressional intention to the contrary, to regard each as effective"}. As the Court has explained, however, Article V provides a permissive standard, under which this Court may refuse to enforce an award. Article VII, on the other hand, mandates that this Court must consider CAS' claims under applicable U.S. law.

Article VII of the Convention provides that:

The provisions of the present Convention shall not ... deprive any interested party of any right he may have to avail himself of an arbitral award in the manner and to the extent allowed by the law ... of the count[r]y where such award is sought to be relied upon.

9 U.S.C. § 201 note. Article VII does not eliminate all consideration of Article V; it merely requires that this Court protect any rights that CAS has under the domestic laws of the United States. There is no conflict between CAS' use of Article VII to invoke the FAA and the language of the Convention.

IV. Conclusion

The Court concludes that the award of the arbitral panel is valid as a matter of U.S. law. The Court further concludes that it need not grant res judicata effect to the decision of the Egyptian Court of Appeal at Cairo. Accordingly, the Court GRANTS Chromalloy Aeroservices' Petition to Recognize and Enforce the Arbitral Award, and DENIES Egypt's Motion to Dismiss that Petition.

【本案评析】

本案涉及国际商事仲裁实务中的撤销国际商事仲裁裁决和不予执行仲裁裁决的法律问题。在案件中，国防项目承包商根据与埃及空军签订的合同提起诉讼以申请执行仲裁裁决。关于承包商申请承认和执行埃及仲裁裁决以及埃及政府驳回申请的动议，美国地区法院法官 June.L. Green, J. 认为法院的结论是，根据美国法律，仲裁裁决是有效的，其进一步得出结论认为，它不需要对埃及上诉法院决定给予既判力。 因此，法院授予 Chromalloy Aeroservices 申请承认和执行仲裁裁决，并拒绝埃及驳回该申请的动议。

三、国际商事仲裁裁决的承认与执行、撤销仲裁裁决案例①

HASBRO, INC., Plaintiff-Appellant,

v.

CATALYST USA, INC., Defendant-Appellee.

No. 02-4301.

Argued May 27, 2003.Decided May 10, 2004.

Rehearing and Rehearing En Banc Denied June 3, 2004.

DIANE P. WOOD, Circuit Judge.

Although companies often choose arbitration with the hope of avoiding the (presumed) greater time and expense of litigating in court, that was not the fate of the parties in this case.

Hasbro, Inc. and Catalyst USA, Inc. waited more than two years for a final award from an arbitration panel that was adjudicating a dispute between them about a software license. After the award was finally issued, the losing party, Catalyst, asked the district court to vacate the arbitral award. The court agreed that this was appropriate on the ground that the arbitrators had exceeded their authority by waiting too long to issue their decision. While we appreciate the frustration caused by the delay, a closer look at the proceedings shows that no one objected at the crucial time to the panel's conduct of the proceedings. Whatever errors with respect to deadlines may have been committed were either waived or harmless. We therefore reverse and remand for entry of an order enforcing the award.

① Hasbro,Inc. v. Catalyst USA,Inc. United States Court of Appeals, Seventh Circuit.May 10, 2004367 F.3d 689 (Approx. 7 pages).

I

In 1993, Hasbro and Catalyst entered into a software licensing contract, in which they agreed to arbitrate any disputes that arose that could not be resolved amicably. Any such dispute was to be submitted to arbitration pursuant to the Federal Arbitration Act (FAA) and the rules of the American Arbitration Association (AAA).

Six years later, dissatisfied with the performance of Catalyst's software, Hasbro filed a demand for arbitration on October 8, 1999. A hearing was conducted in Milwaukee between October 2000 and March 2001 before a panel of arbitrators from the Commercial Arbitration Tribunal of the AAA. On March 9, 2001, the panel issued an interim scheduling order, providing for briefing to conclude on June 8, 2001, and for oral argument to be held on June 28, 2001. After oral argument, the panel directed additional briefing to be completed by July 10, 2001. In addition, the parties agreed at oral argument to amend their arbitration agreement to permit the panel to award attorneys' fees to the prevailing party. No formal declaration that the hearing was closed was made at this time. Hasbro now claims that it believed that the hearing had not been closed, because evidence about attorneys' fees had not been requested and had not otherwise been deemed necessary.

The parties did not hear again from the AAA or the panel until October 2, 2001, when the AAA sent a bill to the parties seeking compensation for the arbitrators' "post-hearing time" from July to September 2001. In response, Catalyst requested an explanation of the bill. On October 10, 2001, the AAA sent the parties an itemization of charges-a communication that raised red flags for Catalyst. Catalyst found questionable the hours and increased rate charged by the panel chair, Alan Wernick. The itemization of the charges also brought to light other key information. Among the many entries were ones that stated "review and revise damage calculations to provide interest" and "extended conferences with panel regarding damage calculations and award". Because only Hasbro had requested damages, Hasbro alleges that these references to damage calculations should have signaled to Catalyst that Hasbro was the prevailing party.

On October 26, 2001, Catalyst wrote to the AAA challenging the propriety of Wernick's charges. In that letter, it also asserted for the first time that under Rule 37 of the AAA rules, the hearing had been closed on July 10, 2001, "as of the final date set by the arbitrator for the receipt of briefs," and that under Rule 43, the arbitrator had until August 11, 2001, "30 days from the date of closing the hearing," to make the award. The panel's failure to issue the award by August 11, 2001, Catalyst charged, raised "serious questions about the validity of the entire process".

On November 8, 2001, Catalyst received additional information concerning the Wernick bills. Again it wrote to the AAA requesting further information that would help it to analyze the propriety of the charges. It also, at that point, inquired specifically about the status of the overdue award. Not receiving word from the AAA, on November 13, 2001, Catalyst formally objected to the untimeliness of the award. Perhaps prompted by this inquiry, or perhaps for their own reasons, the arbitrators declared the hearing closed on December 5, 2001, and issued their award on January 2, 2002.

The panel awarded Hasbro $799,839.93, plus interest; denied Catalyst's counterclaims; and divided arbitration fees, expenses, and compensation equally between the two parties, requiring Hasbro to pay the remaining $2,083.63 and Catalyst the remaining $22,083.63 outstanding. It declined to award attorneys' fees to either side.

Catalyst moved in district court to vacate the arbitration award on the ground that the arbitrators exceeded their power by issuing an untimely award. The district court agreed, and this appeal followed.

II

Generally, a court will set aside an arbitration award only in "very unusual circumstances," First Options of Chicago, Inc. v. Kaplan, 514 U.S. 938, 942, 115 S.Ct. 1920, 131 L.Ed.2d 985 (1995). Judicial review of arbitration awards is "tightly limited," Baravati v. Josephthal, Lyon & Ross, Inc., 28 F.3d 704, 706 (7th Cir.1994), and confirmation is "usually routine or summary," Riccard v. Prudential Ins. Co., 307 F.3d 1277, 1288 (11th Cir.2002). "With few exceptions, as long as the arbitrator does not exceed [her] delegated authority, her award will be enforced." Butler Mfg. Co. v. United Steelworkers of Am., 336 F.3d 629, 632 (7th Cir.2003). This is so even if the arbitrator's award contains a serious error of law or fact. Major League Baseball Players Assoc. v. Garvey, 532 U.S. 504, 509, 121 S.Ct. 1724, 149 L.Ed.2d 740 (2001) (per curiam); Nat'l Wrecking Co. v. Int'l Bhd. of Teamsters, Local 731, 990 F.2d 957, 960 (7th Cir.1993). We review the district court's decision to vacate the arbitration award de novo, Indep. Employees' Union of Hillshire Farm Co., Inc. v. Hillshire Farm Co., Inc., 826 F.2d 530, 532 (7th Cir.1987), accepting findings of fact that are not clearly erroneous, Slaney v. The Int'l Amateur Athletic Fed'n, 244 F.3d 580, 592 (7th Cir.2001).

The FAA makes arbitration agreements enforceable "to the same extent as other contracts, so courts must 'enforce privately negotiated agreements to arbitrate, like other contracts, in accordance with their terms.' " Sphere Drake Ins. Ltd. v. All American Life Ins. Co., 307 F.3d 617, 620 (7th Cir.2002) [quoting Volt Info. Scis, Inc. v. Stanford Univ., 489 U.S. 468, 478, 109 S.Ct. 1248, 103 L.Ed.2d 488 (1989)]. Under Wisconsin law, which applies to this diversity action, see First Bank Southeast, N.A. v. Predco, Inc., 951 F.2d 842, 846 (7th Cir.1992), untimely performance of a contractual obligation does not result in the harsh penalty of forfeiture or rescission, unless the parties agree that "time is of the essence." Appleton State Bank v. Lee,33 Wis.2d 690, 148 N.W.2d

1, 3 (1967); see also Employers Ins. of Wausau v. Jackson, 190 Wis.2d 597, 527 N.W.2d 681, 688-89 (1995) (applying "time is of the essence" standard to arbitration agreements). Thus, even assuming that the panel's performance was untimely, whether the arbitration agreement was thereby rendered unenforceable depends on whether the parties agreed that time would be of the essence.

Whether this was indeed the parties' agreement is generally a question of fact that, if there was some sign of a material dispute, we would need to remand to the district court as fact-finder. See Employers Ins. of Wausau, 527 N.W.2d at 688. In this case, however, the evidence is entirely documentary and the parties have thoroughly briefed the issue. A remand, in our opinion, is therefore unnecessary and would only prolong this already-too-long proceeding.

Under Wisconsin law, time is generally not of the essence, "unless it is expressly made so by the terms of the contract, or by the conduct of the parties." Stork v. Felper, 85 Wis.2d 406, 270 N.W.2d 586, 589 (1978). In this case, nowhere either in the arbitration agreement or in the AAA rules does it expressly say that time was of the essence. Wisconsin law further indicates that the fact that the AAA rules specify a 30-day deadline is not enough to support the inference that time is of the essence. Zuelke v. Gergo, 258 Wis. 267, 45 N.W.2d 690, 693 (1951) ("The fact that a contract sets a date for the closing of a transaction does not of itself make time of the essence of the contract.").

The absorption of equitable principles by the law has modified the severity of the rule giving undue importance to mere dates .... [U]nless the nature of the contract is such as to make performance on an exact day vital or the contract in terms so provides, the failure by a party to perform on the particular day does not discharge the other party.

Id.

Nor does the conduct of the parties in this case support a finding that time was of *693 the essence. Stork, 270 N.W.2d at 589.

Although Catalyst asserts that the hearing should have been declared closed on July 10, 2001, and an award should have been issued by August 11, 2001, Catalyst itself waited until October 26, 2001, before raising the issue of untimely performance, and until November 13, 2001, before formally objecting to the arbitrators' delay.

Indeed, all indications suggest that Catalyst, the party now complaining of untimely performance, benefited from the delay, given the fact that it was able to hold off payment to Hasbro for several months at no cost (apart from the questionable arbitrators' fees, which we discuss in a moment). A conclusion that time was not of the essence under these circumstances comports with Wisconsin's additional consideration of equity in construing the parties' agreement, by allowing Hasbro to avoid the harsh penalty of forfeiture when the delay caused no prejudice to Catalyst.

There is also a rule which is entitled to serious consideration that when the terms of a contract are, or, by any act of parties under the contract, become indefinite, uncertain and susceptible of two constructions, and by giving them one construction one of the parties would be subject to forfeiture, and by giving them the other no such forfeiture would be incurred and no injustice would be done to the other party, the contract should be construed as not creating a forfeiture.

Zuelke, 45 N.W.2d at 693 [citing Jacobs v. Spalding, 71 Wis. 177, 36 N.W. 608, 614 (1888)].

For these reasons, we find that time was not of the essence under this arbitration agreement. Therefore, the arbitrators did not exceed their authority by issuing an untimely award to the extent that the harsh penalty of forfeiture or rescission was warranted. In a final effort to avoid this outcome, Catalyst has also suggested before this court that an alternate reason to find that the panel exceeded the scope of its powers is that its delay was for the impermissible reason of awarding the panel chair excessive compensation. Because Catalyst did not properly raise this argument before the district court, however, we decline to reach it here. (If this was indeed a problem, it is something the AAA itself can and should investigate and address.)

This is not to say, obviously, that arbitrators may indefinitely delay issuance of an award, in open violation of the AAA rules, without the parties' consent. Under Wisconsin law, "time may be made of the essence after breach of the contract by reasonable notice to the person in default to perform." Ochiltree v. Kaiser, 20 Wis.2d 191, 121 N.W.2d 890, 893 (1963). But the prejudiced party must make its objection known, which Catalyst failed to do here. This entire problem stemmed from the panel's original failure to declare the hearing closed in accordance with Rule 37. Such a declaration would have triggered the 30-day deadline under Rule 43.

From the time Catalyst gave notice of its position that the panel had breached Rule 37, however, there was no further delay or failure to perform to which Catalyst can point. Cf. id. (finding against a party in default that did nothing, even after notified of untimely performance and specifically warned that failure to perform within 30 days would terminate the contract). Upon receiving notice from Catalyst, the panel promptly invited Hasbro to respond. Soon after, it declared the hearing closed and issued an award within 30 days thereafter.

Notwithstanding our enforcement of the arbitral award, we do not condone the panel's substandard performance. The AAA (and judicial tribunals) have good reasons for rules that clarify when a proceeding is concluded. These rules allow *694 all parties to know whether there is still time remaining to raise points with the original tribunal, whether the time has come to appeal, and how much time exists for all such steps. Just as Federal Rule of Civil Procedure 58, which requires a specific document memorializing a final judgment, avoids countless problems with the appellate process that arise when a separate final judgment is missing, the AAA's rules also structure the process so that parties will know at all times where they stand.

III

We therefore VACATE the judgment of the district court and REMAND for enforcement of the arbitral award.

【本案评析】

本案涉及国际商事仲裁实务中的撤销仲裁裁决、承认和执行仲裁裁决的法律问题。案件涉及仲裁庭迟延作出裁决的情况。Hasbro，Inc. 和 Catalyst USA，Inc. 等待两年多的时间从仲裁庭获得最终裁决，裁决事项为软件许可证争议。裁决最终作出后，败诉方要求地区法院撤销仲裁裁决。法院最终同意该申请，理由是仲裁庭迟延作出仲裁裁决的时间超出了时间界限。依照美国仲裁协会规则，仲裁庭从结束庭审开始有 30 日的时间作出仲裁裁决。在上诉中，第七巡回上诉法院审判法官 Diane P. Wood 认为，仲裁员违反《商事争议解决程序（包括仲裁与调节规则）》AAA 规则规定的作出仲裁裁决的时间，不能成为撤销仲裁裁决的正当理由，因此仲裁员没有越权。

【延伸阅读】

一、相关典型案例

1.Wes Johnson v. Wells Fargo Home Mortgage Inc.

2. Citibank,N.A. v. Stork & Associates,P.A.

3. Alfred Janiga v. Quertar Capital Corporation & Weislaw Hessek & Hessek Financial.

4. 德国旭普林国际有限责任公司诉中国无锡沃可通用工程橡胶有限公司案

5. Juan Pedro v. Metrovacesa S.A. AS

6. Rent-A-Center West,Inc.v. Antonio Jackson

7. Popack & Others v. Moshe Lipszyc & Sara Lipszyc

8. Concordia Trading B.V. 申请承认和执行外国仲裁裁决案

9. Resin Systems Inc. V. Industrial Service & Machine Inc.

10. Leonnard Bosack and Sandy Lerner v. David C. Soward

11. ProdOpt v. First

12. Wires Jolley LLP v. Perter Wong

13. China National Chartering Corp. V. Pactrans Air & Sea,Inc.

14. AIG Baker Sterling Heights v. American Multi-Cinema

15. S & Z Consultores Asociados S.A. v. Electric Power Development Co.Ltd.

二、相关学术论著

1. Gary B. Born. *International Arbitration Cases and Materials.* Wolters Kluwer Law & Business, 2001.

2. 许杰:《国际商事仲裁实务》,法律出版社 2017 年版。

3. 林一飞:《最新商事仲裁与司法实务专题案例》(第 1 卷 ~ 第 12 卷),对外经济贸易大学出版社 2008~2013 年版。

4. Steven P.Finizio and Duncan Spell Wilmer Cutler Pickering Hale and Dorr LLP. *A Practical Guide to International Commercial Arbitration: Assessment, Planning and Strategy.* City & Financial Publishing, 2012.

5. 石现明、吕涛:《简明国际商事仲裁法律与实践英文教程》,法律出版社 2016 年版。

三、相关网络资源

1. http://www.uncitral.org.

2. http://www.china-arbitration.com.

3.https://1.next.westlaw.com/Browse/Home/Cases?transitionType=Default&contextData=(sc.Default).

四、相关学术知识点

[内地和香港特区仲裁裁决承认和执行问题介绍]改革开放以后,特别是 1997 年香港回归以来,内地和香港特区之间的经济交往和人员往来日益频繁。随着两地经济合作交流的不断融合,经济和贸易纠纷也随之增多。仲裁制度对于解决商业纠纷相比诉讼而言具有高效、便捷的巨大优势,虽然诉讼和仲裁目前都是解决商事争议的有效手段,但仲裁凭借其优势越来越成为商事争议和纠纷中人们优先选择的方

式。对于跨法域仲裁来说，最关键的步骤是对于仲裁裁决的承认和执行。

根据《中华人民共和国民事诉讼法》第269条规定，外国仲裁裁决需要人民法院承认和执行的，应由当事人直接向有管辖权的中级人民法院申请，法院依照中华人民共和国缔结或参加的国际条约或者互惠原则办理。中华人民共和国缔结或参加的关于承认与执行外国仲裁裁决最重要的条约是1958年《承认及执行外国仲裁裁决公约》（即《纽约公约》）。

1997年前在香港有关仲裁裁决的承认和执行的法律渊源是《仲裁条例》和《纽约公约》。按照2011年6月1日生效的香港特区《仲裁条例》外国裁决的执行与本地裁决并无两样。依该条例外国裁决至少可视情况选择下列方式之一申请执行：

1. 在高等法院原讼法庭提起诉讼，如该庭许可，则仲裁裁决如同该庭所作判决一样予以执行。

2. 按执行“公约裁决”的程序申请执行。所谓“公约裁决”是指在香港特区以外的国家或地区依当事人之间达成的仲裁协议所作出的裁决，且作出该裁决的国家或地区系《纽约公约》成员。

根据《纽约公约》第1条第1款规定，公约不适用于在裁决执行地/国作出的仲裁裁决。根据此规定，所以1997年香港回归中国后，香港作为中国领土主权的一部分，《纽约公约》不再适用于内地与香港特区之间相互执行仲裁裁决。但《纽约公约》仍然继续适用于香港特区，目前仅对于除中国内地之外的其他缔约国适用。为填补由于《纽约公约》不适用与内地和香港特区之间的仲裁裁决的承认和执行的空白，1999年6月内地与香港特区达成了一项《关于内地与香港特别行政区相互执行仲裁裁决的安排》（以下简称《安排》）。《安排》分别从执行法院、申请程序、拒绝执行的条件、执行费用及期限等方面予以了规范，为两地仲裁裁决的自由流动扫清了障碍、铺平了道路。为此，内地最高人民法院在年年初以司法解释的形式将《安排》予以公告。

《安排》的主要内容尽可能地保留了《纽约公约》内容中有关相互执行仲裁裁决的规定。其首段就确认了双方相互执行仲裁裁决，并按照“一国两制”和《基本法》的有关原则，要求分别按照执行地的有关司法程序予以执行。

但《安排》未解决两地的历史遗留问题：首先，《安排》没有解决两地在商事问题保留上的差异；其次，两地在可仲裁性事宜的规定上存在分歧；第三，内地与香港特区对仲裁裁决的时效问题方面存在着不统一；第四，《安排》在两地对公共秩序有着不同的理解。

第四章

国际民事诉讼法律实务

【内容摘要】

本章主要讲述有关国际民事诉讼的理论与实务，具体内容包括：国际民事诉讼基本理论、国际民事诉讼管辖权、国际民事诉讼司法协助、外国法院判决的承认与执行。本章采取理论与实务相结合的方式，确保读者深入了解国际民事诉讼规则的具体应用，充分激发学习兴趣。同时也希望通过对国际民事诉讼法律实务的系统介绍，对“一带一路”国际民事纠纷的解决提供方向引导。

第一节　国际民事诉讼概述

【知识背景/学习要点】

一、国际民事诉讼与国际民事诉讼法

国际民事诉讼又称国际民事诉讼程序，是指一国法院在审理国际民事纠纷案件、当事人和其他诉讼参与人在法院提起诉讼之时所应遵循的程序。国际民事诉讼法不同于国际民事诉讼，分为广义与狭义两种解释，国际民事诉讼法从广义来讲，是指规范国际民事诉讼程序的各种法律总和。狭义的国际民事诉讼法是规范国际民事诉讼专用程序的各种法律规则的总和。[①] 本章采取狭义国际

① 屈广清、欧永福:《国际民商事诉讼程序导论》,武汉大学出版社 2016 年版,第 3 页。

民事诉讼法的概念。

国际民事诉讼审理案件与国内民事诉讼不同，主要审理涉外民事案件[①]，因而具有涉外性的特点，其涉外性主要表现为：诉讼主体涉外；诉讼争议是国际民事法律关系；民事法律关系的产生、变更及消灭的事实发生在国外；诉讼中的证据具有涉外性，在具体案件审判中以外国法作为案件的准据法等。本章节将对国际民事诉讼需要解决的国际民事诉讼管辖权问题、国际民事司法协助问题、外国法院判决承认与执行问题进行系统的分析。

二、国际民事诉讼法的渊源

国际民事诉讼法的渊源具有双重性的特点，除了包括民事诉讼法中所有的国内立法和国内判例这两个主要渊源外，国际条约亦是国际民事诉讼法的重要渊源。

（一）国际条约

国际条约是国际民事诉讼法最为重要的国际渊源。有关国际民事诉讼的国际条约主要分为多边条约和双边条约两个方面的内容。多边条约又包括区域性多边条约与全球性多边条约。区域性多边条约签署最为繁荣的区域为美洲与欧洲区域，该些区域内所签署的关于国际民事诉讼领域的公约种类齐全、数量繁多。例如，1972 年《关于国家豁免的欧洲公约》，1988 年欧盟签订的《关于民商事判决承认与执行的卢加诺公约》，1975 年的《美洲国家间关于国外调取证据公约》，1979 年《美洲国家间关于外国判决与仲裁裁决域外效力的公约》等等。全球性多边条约大多是在海牙国际私法会议之上制定的。主要涉及法院的选择、司法协助、判决承认与执行等方面。[②]除区域性多边条约与全球性多边条

① 参照最高人民法院《关于适用〈中华人民共和国民事诉讼法〉若干问题的意见》第 304 条规定："当事人一方或双方是外国人、无国籍人、外国企业或组织，或者当事人之间民事法律关系的设立、变更、终止的法律事实发生在外国，或者诉讼标的物在外国的民事案件，为涉外民事案件。"

② 海牙国际私法会议上制定的国际民事诉讼公约主要有：1954 年海牙《民事诉讼程序公约》、1958 年海牙《关于国际有机体动产买卖协议公约》、1958 年海牙《抚养儿童义务判决的承认与执行公约》、1965 年《协议选择法院公约》、1965 年《关于向国外送达民事或商事私法文书和司法外文书公约》、1970 年《关于从国外盗取民事或商事证据公约》、1971 年海牙《民事案件外国判决的承认与执行公约》、1973 年《抚养义务判决的承认和执行公约》、1980 年海牙《国际司法救助公约》。

约外，国际双边条约的签署在国际民事诉讼中亦是不胜枚举，且在国际民事诉讼领域占有及其重要的地位。我国现今已与29个国家签订了双边民事司法协助条约，[①]并已加入了海牙《关于向国外送达民事或商事私法文书和司法外文书公约》与《关于从国外盗取民事或商事证据公约》。除此之外，我国《民事诉讼法》中进一步确保了必须信守条约的国际法原则与国际条约优先原则。[②]综上所述，国际条约是国际民事诉讼的重要渊源之一。

（二）国内立法

国内立法是国际民事诉讼法的主要渊源，纵观国际上各国相关法律，国际民事诉讼程序规范在国内立法中有以下几种表现形式：

1. 在相关实体法或者程序法中设置专章规定国际民事诉讼程序

国际民事诉讼程序主要设置在国际私法、民法、民事诉讼法之中。如1979年的《匈牙利关于国际私法的第13号法令》自第9章至第11章分别规定了管辖权、诉讼程序以及外国法院的判决与执行问题；1992年的《罗马尼亚关于调整国际私法法律关系的第105号法》第12章专门规定了国际民事诉讼程序问题；《中华人民共和国民事诉讼法（2017修订）》第259条至第283条就涉外民事诉讼程序中的一般原则、管辖权问题、国际司法协助、外国法院判决的承认与执行问题作了特别规定。

2. 制定单行法规规范国际民事诉讼程序

制定单行法规范是国际上关于国际民事诉讼程序在国内立法中较通行的做法。美国1976年的《美国外国主权豁免法》、日本1938年的《日本外国法院司法协助法》、中国1986年颁布的《外交特权与豁免条例》和1990年的《领事特权与豁免条例》、中国最高人民法院《关于适用〈中华人民共和国民事诉讼法〉若

---

① 该29个国家分别是：法国、波兰、蒙古、比利时、罗马尼亚、意大利、西班牙、俄罗斯、土耳其、古巴、泰国、埃及、保加利亚、哈萨克斯坦、白俄罗斯、乌克兰、匈牙利、希腊、塞浦路斯、摩洛哥、吉尔吉斯斯坦、塔吉克斯坦、新加坡、乌兹别克斯坦、越南、老挝、突尼斯、立陶宛、阿根廷等。

② 我国《民事诉讼法》第260条规定："中华人民共和国缔结或者参加的国际条约同本法有不同规定的，适用该国际条约的规定，但中华人民共和国声明保留的除外。"

干问题的意见》涉外民事诉讼程序的特别规定等，均是国际民事诉讼法的渊源。

3. 将国际民事诉讼程序与国际私法结合制定法典

1964 年《捷克斯洛伐克国际私法及国际民事诉讼法》与 1982 年《土耳其国际私法和国际诉讼程序法》均是国际民事诉讼与国际私法结合规定国际民事诉讼法的典型法规。

（三）国内判例

判例是指可被法院援引，并作为审理同类案件的法律依据的判决和裁定。在国际上，普通法系国家与大陆法系国家关于一国法院的判例能否成为国际民事诉讼法的渊源观点不同。在大陆法系国家，审判的过程中几乎不会使用判例作为审理同类案件的法律依据，但也有例外，譬如：日本在 1967 年出版的《涉外判例百选》之中记载了许多国际民事诉讼法的判例，作为审理相关民事诉讼案件的依据。而在英美法系国家，判例则是国际民事诉讼法的主要渊源。中国目前并不承认判例可以作为国际民事诉讼法的法律渊源。

三、国际民事诉讼基本原则

（一）主权原则

主权原则又称为国家主权原则，是国际民事诉讼领域最为重要的基本原则。国际民事诉讼的国际性，使其会涉及世界上不同区域与国家的司法管辖权，主权原则即指主权国家对于其境内的人和物以及在其境内发生的事件不受外国干预，具有排他的管辖权。

主权原则表明国家享有独立而完整的司法管辖权，并且各个国家可以在国际民事诉讼中保持司法独立与中立。而若是一个国家的司法主权不独立，不能充分和完整地享有管辖权，就表明这个国家不具有完全的主权。以我国为例，自 1840 年鸦片战争后《南京条约》的签订，外国列强纷纷在我国建立了领事裁判权，在当时的民事案件中，凡涉及外国公民的，当时所谓的中国法院均无权过问，全部交由外国法院判定，司法主权被破坏殆尽，这种情况表明旧中国的国家主权亦遭到了严重的破坏。

司法主权原则是国家主权原则在诉讼中的具体化，主要表现在以下几个方面：

第一，国家的国际民事司法管辖权不容侵犯。根据司法主权原则，除依国际法享有管辖豁免者外，一国法院对位于该国境内的一切人和物，无论本国人还是外国人均享有管辖权，在不妨碍有关国家对该人行使属地优先管辖权的情况下，即使本国人在境外，该国依旧可以对其在境外的民事行为行使管辖权。

第二，法院在审理国际民事案件之时，均只能使用内国通用的语言、文字进行诉讼活动。外国法院请求内国法院进行司法协助时，除条约另有规定，有关文件需附有内国通用的语言文字的文本。相反，内国法院也应使用内国的语言文字来进行司法协助。

第三，关于国家法院在审理国际民事案件的诉讼程序法律适用，由该国的冲突法决定，国际条约另有规定的除外。在司法实践上，各国法院审理涉外民事案件基本上均适用法院地的程序法。我国《民事诉讼法》第 259 条也明确规定："在中华人民共和国领域内进行涉外民事诉讼，适用本编规定。本编没有规定的，适用本法其他有关规定。"

第四，关于外国法院判决的承认与执行问题，非经内国法院承认，外国法院的判决不能在内国生效与强制执行，若内国法院认为外国法院的判决侵犯了内国的国家主权或公共秩序，可拒绝承认与执行，我国《民事诉讼法》第 282 条对此作了明确的规定。①

（二）平等互惠原则

平等互惠原则又称国民待遇原则，即在国际民事诉讼中，外国人与本国人

① 我国《民事诉讼法》第 282 条规定："人民法院对申请或者请求承认和执行的外国法院作出的发生法律效力的判决、裁定，依照中华人民共和国缔结或者参加的国际条约，或者按照互惠原则进行审查后，认为不违反中华人民共和国法律的基本原则或者国家主权、安全、社会公共利益的，裁定承认其效力，需要执行的，发出执行令，依照本法的有关规定执行。违反中华人民共和国法律的基本原则或者国家主权、安全、社会公共利益的，不予承认和执行。"

具有平等的诉讼地位，具有相同的诉讼权利与诉讼义务。我国《民事诉讼法》第5条第1款规定:“外国人、无国籍人、外国企业和组织在人民法院起诉、应诉，同中华人民共和国公民、法人和其他组织有同等的诉讼权利与义务。”

现今在国际民事诉讼领域，各国之间一般通过国内立法和国家间签署条约的方式对国民待遇进行相应的规定。而对等原则是保障该平等诉讼地位的基础，对等原则是指一国对另一国当事人的诉讼权利加以限制，另一国有权对该国当事人的诉讼权利作出同样的限制。我国《民事诉讼法》第 5 条第 2 款对对等原则作了明确的规定:“外国法院对中华人民共和国公民、法人和其他组织的民事诉讼权利加以限制的，中华人民共和国人民法院对该国公民、企业和组织的民事诉讼权利、实行对等原则。”由此可见，对等原则是平等互惠原则的前提与基础。

(三)遵守国际条约与国际惯例原则

为了国际民事诉讼程序得以顺利实施，国家间缔结了许多国际条约。根据国际法中的条约必信守原则，一般来说，国家是通过以下两种方式确保条约有效，一是通过国内立法程序把该国际条约转化为国内立法，二是在国内法中承认国际条约的效力，并在二者发生冲突之时，规定国际条约优先适用。我国采用后一种做法。我国《民事诉讼法》第 260 条规定:“中华人民共和国缔结或者参加的国际条约同本法有不同规定的，适用该国际条约的规定，但中华人民共和国声明保留的条款除外。”

(四)便利当事人诉讼和便利法院司法原则

便利当事人诉讼与便利法院司法作为国际民事诉讼的基本原则，要求在国际司法管辖权、国际司法协助等方面充分考虑当事人利益，外国法院判决和执行过程中充分考虑程序便利程度。例如，我国《民事诉讼法》第 268 条与第 269 条所规定的在中华人民共和国领域内没有住所的被告的答辩期间、当事人上诉期间以及被上诉人提出答辩期间比国内民事诉讼程序相应的规定多了 15 日。可以为当事人在国际民事诉讼程序中搜集证据以及准备诉讼提供相应的时间，维护当事人的利益。

四、国际民事诉讼的法律选择

在国际民事争端之中，当争议双方当事人没有选择争端适用的法律之时，由法院直接决定适用的法律或者依据有关法律选择的条约来解决法律选择问题，[①] 而国际民事诉讼的法律选择路径主要分为以下几种：

（一）依据法律性质进行法律选择

来源于巴托鲁斯的法则两分说，他从法则的性质入手将法则区分为“人法”与“物法”两类，并分别规定“人法”与“物法”适用的范围。

（二）法律关系的性质决定法律选择

该说法来源于萨维尼的法律关系本座说，法律关系本座说是指任何一个法律关系总要与某一特定的地域相联系，该特定联系的地域就是该法律关系的“本座”，一个法律关系的本座在什么地方，就应该适用什么地方的法律。[②]

（三）根据最密切联系原则进行法律选择

最密切联系原则是在法律关系本座说的基础上新发展的原则。法院在处理国际民事关系争议之时，要从案件的实际出发，适用与该国际民事关系有密切联系的国家或者地区的法律，且在案件审理过程中，要适当地限制法官的自由裁量权。

（四）根据“利益分析”决定法律选择

该观点由美国的柯里提出，柯里认为：不同国家之间的法律冲突归根结底是不同国家利益之间的冲突，解决法律冲突的方式是由对“政府利益”的分析结论来确定国际民事关系应当适用的法律。

（五）依“结果选择”方法决定法律选择

“结果选择”方法由美国学者卡弗斯提出，他主张法院在选择应适用的法律

---

① Daniel C.K. Chow, International Business Transactions Problems, Cases, and Materials, Wolters Kluwer, 2015, p.633.

② 刘想树：《国际私法》，法律出版社 2009 年版，第 33 页。

时，应考虑法律适用的结果。他为适用法律的结果提供了两个标准：一是要对当事人公正；二是要符合一定的社会目的。为了符合这两项标准，在法院决定适用何国法律之时，应审查以下几个方面：在进行法律选择的过程中，首先，要审查诉讼案件和当事人之间的法律关系；其次，要仔细比较适用不同法律可能导致的结果；最后，衡量这种结果对当事人是否公正以及是否符合社会公共政策。通过以上顺位来决定法律的选择。

（六）依“意思自治”原则自由决定法律选择

该观点由法国杜摩兰提出，主要适用于合同领域的法律选择方法。现今，在该原则实施的过程之中，一些国家在立法、司法实践和签署的国际公约中滥用此种法律选择的方式，造成现今在婚姻家庭领域和继承领域限制使用意思自治原则，意思自治原则在如今的国际社会已经得到很大程度的规制，是现今国际民事诉讼法律选择应用最为广泛的原则之一。

【案例摘录与评析】

国际民事诉讼法律选择案例[①]

ELI LILLY DO BRASIL,LTDA v. FEDERAL EXPRESS CORP
U.S Court of Appeals for the Second Circuit,2007
502F.3d 78

Synopsis

Background: Brazilian shipper of pharmaceuticals from Brazil to Japan brought action against carrier after shipment was stolen in Brazil. The United States District Court for the Southern District of New York, Gerald Lynch, J., 2005 WL 2312547, found that federal common law applied and enforced damage limitation clause in waybill governing transportation of cargo. Shipper appealed.

① United States Court of Appeals, Second Circuit. September 11, 2007 502 F.3d 78 2007 WL 2593831.

Opinion

Judge MESKILL dissents in a separate opinion.

B.D. Parker, Jr., Circuit Judge:

Eli Lilly do Brasil ("Lilly") contracted with Federal Express ("FedEx") to ship drums of pharmaceuticals from Brazil to Japan. While being trucked in Brazil, the shipment was stolen. This appeal considers whether the limitation on liability in FedEx's waybill is enforceable and the answer depends on whether federal common law or Brazilian law applies.

The United States District Court for the Southern District of New York (Lynch, J.) agreed with FedEx that federal common law applied, under which the limitation was enforceable. The District Court declined Lilly's invitation to apply Brazilian law, under which Lilly contended the clause would have been invalid if gross negligence were shown. The District Court concluded that to do so would serve "to invalidate the liability limitations to which the parties voluntarily bound themselves" and would disturb the parties' justified expectation that their contract was enforceable. We agree and we affirm.

I. BACKGROUND

In October 2002, Lilly contracted with Nippon Express do Brasil, who, in turn, subcontracted with FedEx to transport fourteen drums of Cephalexin from Lilly's factory in Guarulhos, Brazil to Narita, Japan, through FedEx's hub in Memphis. FedEx received the cargo and consigned it to Jumbo Jet Transportes Internacionais Ltda. for transportation by truck to Viracopos, Brazil. The truck was hijacked en route and the cargo, worth approximately $800,000, was stolen.

The waybill for the shipment limited FedEx's liability for stolen goods to $20 per kilogram. If a customer, such as Lilly, was dissatisfied with the limitation, it was given the option of securing additional coverage by declaring a higher value and paying additional charges.

The limitation of liability on the face of the waybill was conspicuous.2 Lilly did not elect to declare a higher value or to pay for additional coverage. The record is silent as to the circumstances of the theft. It is not disputed that, if the limitation *80 applied, FedEx's exposure for the loss was approximately $28,000.

Lilly, a Brazilian firm, chose not to sue FedEx in Brazil but instead sued in the Southern District of New York. The parties cross-moved for partial summary judgment. FedEx sought to limit its liability in accordance with the waybill and Lilly sought to have Brazilian law applied, believing that the limitation might not be enforceable if it could prove that the trucking company acted with gross negligence. Both parties assumed that federal common law choice-of-law analysis applied but they disagreed as to the results of that analysis.

The District Court granted FedEx's motion, ruling that substantive federal common law, not

Brazilian law, applied and, as a result, the limitation was valid. The court's choice-of-law analysis, relying on the Restatement (Second) of Conflict of Laws (the "Restatement"), determined that Brazil had an interest in "regulating the liability of—and corollary standards of care to be exercised by—carriers transporting goods within its borders". The court then reasoned that because of Brazil's numerous contacts with the transaction, it undoubtedly had a significant interest in regulating the transaction, while the United States had only a "general policy interest in limiting the liability of FedEx as a federally-certified air carrier."

1. After considering all the Restatement factors, however, including several that favored Lilly, the court concluded that federal common law, which accords primacy to vindicating the parties' justified expectations, trumped Brazilian law. Specifically, Judge Lynch found that because United States law would enforce the contract as written and Brazilian law might permit the contract to be disregarded, "Brazil's interests in defining the liability of carriers operating within its borders, even taking into account its considerable contacts with the transaction, are not so strong here as to occasion unsettling the private agreement of these particular parties, who, to the extent they were aware of Brazilian law, opted to contract around it." Heavily weighting this factor, the court concluded that the United States is "the jurisdiction with the most significant relationship to the transaction and the parties." After the parties stipulated the amount of damages, the court entered a judgment for Lilly in accordance with the limitation in the waybill. This appeal followed.

II. DISCUSSION

A. Standard of Review

We review de novo the district court's determination that federal law applies, Curley v. AMR Corp., 153 F.3d 5, 11 (2d Cir.1998); the district court's determinations regarding questions of Brazilian law, id.; Fed.R.Civ.P. 44.1; as well as the district court's resolution of the cross-motions for summary judgment, Terwilliger v. Terwilliger, 206 F.3d 240, 244 (2d Cir.2000).

B. Choice of Law Analysis

2. Although the Supreme Court has cautioned that it is appropriate for courts to apply federal common law in only a "few and restricted" instances, O'Melveny & Myers v. FDIC, 512 U.S. 79, 87, 114 S.Ct. 2048, 129 L.Ed.2d 67 (1994) (internal quotation marks omitted), this Court has recognized that cases involving the liability of air carriers for lost or damaged freight are controlled by federal common law, see Nippon Fire & Marine Ins. Co., Ltd. v. Skyway Freight Sys., Inc., 235 F.3d 53, 59 (2d Cir.2000). Because this appeal requires us to consider FedEx's liability for lost shipment of freight, and since the parties have conceded the issue, a federal *81 common law choice-of-law analysis is appropriate.

3. As our prior cases indicate, when conducting a federal common law choice-of-law analysis,

absent guidance from Congress, we may consult the Restatement (Second) of Conflict of Laws. See Pescatore v. Pan Am. World Airways, Inc., 97 F.3d 1, 12 (2d Cir.1996); see also DaimlerChrysler Corp. Healthcare Benefits Plan v. Durden, 448 F.3d 918, 923 (6th Cir.2006) (turning to the Restatement where prior caselaw did not address the choice-of-law question at issue); Huynh v. Chase Manhattan Bank, 465 F.3d 992, 997 (9th Cir.2006) ["Federal common law follows the approach outlined in the Restatement (Second) of Conflict of Laws."].

4. In general, "[t]he federal common law choice-of-law rule is to apply the law of the jurisdiction having the greatest interest in the litigation." In re Koreag, Controle et Revision S.A., 961 F.2d 341, 350 (2d Cir.1992). As to the transportation of goods, § 197 of the Restatement provides:

The validity of a contract for the transportation of passengers or goods and the rights created thereby are determined, in the absence of an effective choice of law by the parties, by the local law of the state from which the passenger departs or the goods are dispatched, unless, with respect to the particular issue, some other state has a more significant relationship under the principles stated in § 6 to the contract and to the parties, in which event the local law of the other state will be applied.

Restatement (Second) of Conflict of Laws § 197 (emphasis added).

Section 6 identifies a number of factors relevant to determining which state has the more significant relationship with the parties and the contract:

the needs of the interstate and international systems,

the relevant policies of the forum,

the relevant policies of other interested states and the relative interests of those states in the determination of the particular issue,

the protection of justified expectations,

the basic policies underlying the particular field of law, certainty, predictability and uniformity of result, and ease in the determination and application of the law to be applied.

Restatement (Second) of Conflict of Laws § 6(2).

Brazil's interests in the contract and the parties are by no means insignificant. The contract was negotiated and executed in Brazil, between a Brazilian company and a United States company that regularly transacts business in Brazil. The purpose of the contract was to ship goods located in Brazil, out of Brazil to Japan. The goods did not enter the United States and would have done so only because Memphis is the FedEx transship center. These considerations are important ones to the § 6 analysis. See id. § 188(2) (stating that the principles of § 6 should be analyzed taking into account, among other things, the place of negotiation of the contract, the place of performance, and the place of business of the parties). As explained in the Restatement, the § 188 contacts serve to identify "[t]he states which are most likely to be interested", namely those states "which have one or more of the [section 188] contacts with the transaction or the parties". Id. § 188 cmt. e (emphasis added). Section 188, like § 197, thus establishes something akin to a default rule based on a non-exhaustive list of contacts. In moving beyond the default rule to a determination of what rule of law applies in a particular *82 circumstance, the contacts are "to be taken into account in applying the principles of § 6". Id. § 188(2). However, they do not subsume those principles and are not determinative in themselves. To hold otherwise would render § 6 superfluous.

Thus, our recognition that Brazil's interest, based only on § 188 contacts, is greater than the United States' cannot be the end of our inquiry or determinative of its conclusion. The United States also has some interest in this transaction and the parties, being FedEx's domicile. See id. § 188(2)(e). Which state is most interested under § 188 is a different question from which state has the more significant relationship with the parties and the contract for purposes of § 197.

5. In this case, even taking account of Brazil's superior § 188 contacts, two of the § 6 factors emerge as determinative of United States venue: (1) the relevant policies of other interested states and the relative interest of those states in the determination of the particular issue in dispute, § 6(2)(c), and (2) protection of the parties' justified expectations, § 6(2)(d). Once Lilly—for whatever reason—asked a United States court to consider its contract, it invited application of the well-settled "presumption in favor of applying that law tending toward the validation of the alleged contract." Kossick v. United Fruit Co., 365 U.S. 731, 741, 81 S. Ct. 886, 6 L.Ed.2d 56 (1961); see also Pritchard v. Norton, 106 U.S. 124, 137, 1 S. Ct. 102, 27 L. Ed. 104 (1882) ["The parties cannot be presumed to have contemplated a law which would defeat their engagements." (internal quotation marks omitted)]. This presumption is consistent with the general rule of contract construction that "presumes the legality and enforceability of contracts". Walsh v. Schlecht, 429 U.S. 401, 408, 97 S. Ct. 679, 50 L.Ed.2d 641 (1977); see Nat'l Labor Relations Bd. v. Local 32B–32J Serv. Employees Int'l Union, AFL–CIO, 353 F.3d 197, 202 (2d Cir.2003) (acknowledging the presumption that an ambiguous contract should not be interpreted so that it is rendered invalid and unenforceable); Restatement (Second) of Contracts § 203(a) {"[A]n interpretation which gives a reasonable, lawful, and effective meaning to all the terms is preferred to an interpretation which leaves a part unreasonable, unlawful, or of no effect."}; cf. Kipin Indus., Inc. v. Van Deilen Int'l, Inc., 182 F.3d 490, 495–96 (6th Cir.1999) (observing that under the Restatement, even an explicit choice of law provision is to be considered a mistake if the chosen law would invalidate an express portion of the contract).

The paramount importance of enforcing freely undertaken contractual obligations, especially in commercial litigation involving sophisticated parties, was obvious to the District Court and is obvious to us. The Restatement expressly provides that the justified expectation of enforceability generally predominates over other factors tending to point to the application of a foreign law inconsistent with such expectation. Comment b of § 188 of the Restatement provides:

Parties entering a contract will expect at the very least, subject perhaps to rare exceptions, that the provisions of the contract will be binding upon them. Their expectations should not be disappointed by application of the local law rule of a state which would strike down the contract or a provision thereof unless the value of protecting the expectations of the parties is substantially outweighed in the particular case by the interest of the state with the invalidating rule in having this rule applied. Id. § 188 , cmt. b (emphasis added). Likewise, the comments to § 197 note that the default rule favoring the local law of the *83 state of dispatch may not apply when the contract would be invalid under such law "but valid under the local law of another state with a close relationship to the transaction and the parties."3 Id. § 197 cmt . c. In such a situation, the default shifts to favor the validating law "unless the value of protecting the expectations of the parties by upholding the contract is outweighed in the particular case by the interest of the state of departure or dispatch in having its invalidating rule applied." Id.

6. Under federal common law, the limitation in the waybill is valid. The "release value" doctrine recognizes the validity of provisions limiting the liability of carriers for lost or damaged cargo. See Nippon Fire, 235 F.3d at 59–60(validating such provisions where they are "set forth in a 'reasonably communicative' form so as to result in a 'fair, open, just and reasonable agreement' between carrier and shipper" and "offer the shipper a possibility of higher recovery by paying the carrier a higher rate"); accord Shippers Nat'l Freight Claim Council, Inc. v. Interstate Commerce Comm'n, 712 F.2d 740, 746 (2d Cir.1983); Hill Constr. Corp. v. Am. Airlines, Inc., 996 F.2d 1315, 1317 (1st Cir.1993).

We have little difficulty concluding that this case does not present a rare exception and that the parties reasonably expected—or certainly should have expected—that their contract would be enforceable. As we noted, the contract contained not only a loss limitation clause, but offered Lilly the option of securing more insurance if it paid a higher premium—an option Lilly did not avail itself of. Lilly has offered no satisfactory justification for expecting that it would be permitted to finesse this commitment.

Lilly's principal contention is that the District Court erred in attaching a presumption of validity to the contract because it is commonplace in the sphere of international common carriage, including in Brazil, that a carrier who acts with gross negligence will be precluded from relying on a contractual liability limitation. While acknowledging that the contractual limitation provision controls for simple negligence, Lilly, relying on § 6(2)(c) of the Restatement, contends that under the laws of Brazil—the other interested state—the limitation provision is void if FedEx acted with willful misconduct or gross negligence.

Lilly has not convinced us that this contention is correct. Lilly relies on a declaration by Brazilian transportation attorney, Paulo de C. Machado, which Lilly submitted in support of its motion for summary judgement. The declaration initially states that "there is NO legal limitation for carriers in road or railroad transportation." As the sole authority for this proposition, the declaration refers to a Brazilian legislative decree which states that "[t]he railroads are responsible for the total or partial loss, pilferage or damage to the merchandises which they received to transport". According to the declaration, this decree has been applied to transportation by truck. With regards to air transportation, both domestic and international, the declaration asserts that "[t]here is limitation of liability only in air carriage, but it does not apply in case of gross negligence". The following Brazilian law provisions are offered as support for this proposition:

Decree No. 20.704/31, art. 25:

The carrier has no right to benefit of the dispositions of the [Warsaw] Convention, which exclude or limit their liability, if the loss is consequence of their malice or of their fault, when according to the law of the court analyzing the case fault is equivalent to malice.

Law No. 7.565/86:

The limits of the indemnity, stated in this Chapter, are not applicable if it is proved that the loss resulted from malice or gross fault of the carrier or of their employees.

Lilly's statements of Brazilian law prove too much. Brazilian law does not provide for any specific limitations on liability for losses occurring during truck carriage. Limitations of liability, under Brazilian law, are only expressly allowed in air carriage and are then subject to an exception for gross negligence. Given no real support in the record for Lilly's contention that Brazil's gross negligence exception even applies during ground carriage—let alone support for the proposition that Brazil's interest in applying such an exception outweighs the value of upholding the contract, cf. Restatement § 197 cmt. c.—we are hard-pressed to see how the parties could have had a justified expectation to that effect. In the absence of such support, we are comfortable concluding that our own firmly grounded policy of enforcing contractual obligations assumed by sophisticated commercial entities should apply.

III. CONCLUSION

The judgment of the District Court is affirmed.

MESKILL, Circuit Judge, dissenting:

I agree that we should apply the federal common law's choice of law rules to determine whether this contract is governed by Brazilian law or federal common law and that we may look to the Restatement (Second) of Conflict of Laws (1971) (the Restatement) for guidance. However, I disagree with the majority's conclusion that *85 under federal common law and the Restatement the United States has a greater interest in this litigation than does Brazil. I believe that Brazil's strong interest in regulating commerce within its borders trumps any interest of the United States in enforcing this contract. Therefore, I respectfully dissent.

The Restatement (Second) of Conflict of Laws

The Restatement has four provisions that offer guidance as to how we should resolve this conflict between Brazilian law and federal common law. See Restatement §§ 6, 188, 197 and 207. My analysis begins with the Restatement provisions that specifically apply to conflicts in contract law because "a specific statute controls over a general one". Bulova Watch Co. v. United States, 365 U.S. 753, 758, 81 S. Ct. 864, 6 L.Ed.2d 72 (1961); see also United States v. Torres–Echavarria, 129 F.3d 692, 699–700 n. 3 (2d Cir.1997) ("The operative principle of statutory construction is that a specific provision takes precedence over a more general provision.").

Section 197 of the Restatement Sets Brazil as the Default Jurisdiction Because the Goods Were Dispatched From Brazil.

The FedEx Air Waybill called for the transportation of Lilly's goods from Brazil to Japan. The Waybill contained no choice of law provision. Under Restatement § 197 contracts for the transportation of goods are governed "by the local law of the state from which ... the goods are dispatched." Section 197 sets Brazil as the default jurisdiction because the state of dispatch "will naturally loom large in the minds of the parties" and it "has a natural interest in the contract of transportation and in many instances has a greater interest in the contract than the state of destination, if for no other reason than that there can be no absolute certainty at the time of the departure that ... the goods will reach the latter state." Restatement § 197 cmt. b.

However, while § 197 sets Brazil as the default jurisdiction, it also provides for the possibility that another state may have "a more significant relationship under the principles stated in § 6 to the contract and to the parties." Furthermore, "[o]n occasion" the law of a state other than the state of dispatch might apply. Restatement § 197 cmt. c. This may occur if the contract is invalid under the law of the state of dispatch but valid under the law of a state with "a close relationship to the transaction and the parties." Id. Thus, Brazil's laws will govern this contract unless the United States has either a "more significant relationship" to the contract and to the parties than does Brazil, Restatement § 197 (emphasis added), or the contract is invalid under Brazilian law and the United States has a "close relationship" to the contract and to the parties, Restatement

§ 197 cmt. c (emphasis added). Leaving aside for the moment the issue of whether the FedEx Air Waybill is valid under Brazilian law, I turn to Restatement § 188 for guidance in determining whether the United States has a significant or close relationship to the contract or to the parties.

Under § 188 of the Restatement Brazil Has the Most Substantial Contacts With the Contract and With the Parties

Section 188 of the Restatement is designed to help courts resolve a conflict of laws that involves "an issue in contract." Restatement § 188(1). To determine which state has "the most significant relationship to the transaction and the parties," *86 id., the court evaluates the following five contacts: the place of contracting, the place of negotiation of the contract, the place of performance, the location of the subject matter of the contract, and the domicil, residence, nationality, place of incorporation and place of business of the parties. Id. § 188(2)(a)-(e). Once these contacts are known, the court takes them "into account" by "applying the[m to] the principles of § 6." Id. at § 188(2). The § 6 principles are those general considerations that "underlie all rules of choice of law", id. at § 188(1) cmt. b.: the needs of the interstate and international systems, the relevant policies of the forum, the relevant policies of other interested states and the relative interests of those states in the determination of the particular issue, the protection of justified expectations, the basic policies underlying the particular field of law, certainty, predictability and uniformity of result, and ease in the determination and application of the law to be applied. Id. at § 6(1). Thus, to determine whether the United States has a "significant" or "close" relationship to the contract and to the parties, the Court must first evaluate each state's § 188(2) contacts with the FedEx Air Waybill.

The Place of Negotiation Was Brazil

The FedEx Air Waybill was negotiated between FedEx and Lilly's Brazilian freight forwarder Nippon Express do Brasil, Ltda (Nippon Express) in Brazil. The contract between FedEx and Jumbo Jet Transportes Internacionais, Ltda (Jumbo Jet), and the contract between Lilly and Nippon Express, also were negotiated in Brazil.

The Place of Contracting Was Brazil

The FedEx Air Waybill was issued to Nippon Express in Brazil by the FedEx office in São Paolo. In addition, the following contracts were executed in Brazil: (1) Lilly's contract with Nippon Express, (2) Nippon Express' subcontract with FedEx, and (3) FedEx's subcontract with Jumbo Jet.

Performance Under the Contract Occurred Only In Brazil

Lilly contracted with Nippon Express to transport the fourteen drums of Cephalexin from Lilly's factory in Cosmopolis, São Paolo, Brazil to Lilly's customer in Iwate, Japan. Nippon Express picked up the pharmaceuticals from Lilly's factory in São Paolo and transported them to the

Nippon Express freight forwarding facility at Cumbica Airport in Guarulhos, Brazil. Nippon Express then subcontracted with FedEx to deliver the shipment to Narita International Airport in Chiba, Japan.

FedEx picked up and accepted the pharmaceutical cargo at the Nippon Express freight forwarding facility in Guarulhos, Brazil and subcontracted with Jumbo Jet to transport the cargo locally from Guarulhos to an airport FedEx uses for international shipments located in Viracopos, Brazil. While the goods were on a Jumbo Jet truck on route to Viracopos the truck was hijacked and the pharmaceuticals were stolen. Had the pharmaceuticals made it to Viracopos, FedEx would have transported them to Chiba, Japan via São Paolo and Memphis, Tennessee. However, because the Jumbo Jet truck was hijacked the only *87 performance that ever took place under the contract occurred in Brazil.

Admittedly, performance under the contract also would have taken place in the United States had the shipment not been hijacked.1 However, the goods were only to enter the United States briefly so that FedEx could route them through its hub in Memphis before sending them on to Japan. The United States was neither the final destination state nor the state of dispatch. The cargo's planned brief stopover in Memphis is an insignificant contact when compared with the performance that actually took place in Brazil, especially considering that the performance that is the subject of this contract dispute—the ground transportation between Guarulhos to the airport located in Viracopos—occurred only in Brazil. Therefore, while the contract called for performance in both the United States and Brazil, because the shipment originated in Brazil, the little performance that occurred under the contract occurred in Brazil. The goods never left Brazil. Thus the § 188(2)(c) contact weighs heavily in favor of Brazil.

The Subject Matter of the Contract Was Located in Brazil

The pharmaceutical cargo was in Brazil at the time of contracting and FedEx never transported the cargo out of Brazil.

The Parties Involved Are Either Brazilian Companies Or Companies That Regularly Conduct Business in Brazil

Lilly, Nippon Express and Jumbo Jet are all Brazilian companies domiciled in Brazil. FedEx is not a Brazilian company. Nevertheless, FedEx regularly conducts business in Brazil and the Air Waybill here was issued by the FedEx office in São Paolo.

When the § 188(2) Factors Are Taken Into Account and Applied to the § 6 Principles Brazil Emerges as the State With the Most Significant Relationship to the Transaction and to the Parties

"The states which are most likely to be interested [in the contract] are those which have one or more of the [§ 188(2)] contacts." Restatement § 188 cmt . e. Brazil has the most substantial

§ 188(2) contacts with the FedEx Air Waybill and with the parties. While the majority admits that Brazil's § 188(2) contacts are "important ones," they never proceed to the next step and take those contacts into account and apply them to the principles of § 6. Instead, the majority concludes that two of the § 6 principles—(1) the relevant policies of other interested states and the relative interests of those states in the determination of the particular issue, and (2) the justified expectations of the parties—"emerge as determinative" in favor of applying federal common law.

The majority concludes that federal common law applies over Brazilian law without pointing to a single § 188(2) contact that the United States has with either the FedEx Air Waybill or with the parties. In addition, the majority never acknowledges that under § 197 Brazil is the default jurisdiction whose laws govern this contract unless the United States has a *88 "significant " or "close " relationship to the contract. In my view, §§ 188 and 197 are specific provisions addressing conflicts in contract law that should take precedence over the more general § 6 principles. See Bulova, 365 U.S. at 758, 81 S. Ct. 864. Therefore, I would follow the Restatement and take each states' § 188(2) contacts into account and apply them to the § 6 principles. When this is done, Brazil emerges as the only state with a "significant" or "close" relationship to the contract and to the parties.

I agree with the majority that the most important § 6 principles implicated by this conflict of laws are (1) the relevant policies of the forum, (2) the relevant policies of other interested states and the relevant interests of those states in the determination of the particular issue, and (3) the protection of justified expectations. See Restatement § 6(b),(c) & (d). I also agree with the majority's conclusion that under our federal common law choice of law rules there is "some presumption in favor of applying that law tending toward the validation of [an] alleged contract." Kossick v. United Fruit Co., 365 U.S. 731, 741, 81 S.Ct. 886, 6 L.Ed.2d 56 (1961).

The presumption in favor of applying the law that tends to validate a contract is important where the alternative is no contract at all. This was the conflict of laws choice presented in Kossick, but it is not the conflict of laws choice presented here. In this case application of Brazilian law may invalidate one provision in the FedEx Air Waybill and then only under limited circumstances. However, in Kossick the Court was faced with a much more drastic choice: (1) apply the New York Statute of Frauds, which would render the alleged oral contract wholly invalid, or (2) apply federal maritime law, which generally upholds oral contracts. 365 U.S. at 733–34, 81 S.Ct. 886. Even though the application of New York law would have completely invalidated the contract, the Kossick Court did not treat that factor as dispositive, but instead analyzed whether the contract was "sufficiently related to peculiarly maritime concerns" and whether the contract "though maritime" was "maritime and local." Id. at 738, 81 S. Ct. 886 (internal quotation marks omitted).

The Kossick Court never treated the presumption in favor of applying the law that would validate the contract as dispositive, and under circumstances that presented a much more compelling case for adherence to the presumption than those presently before the Court. Instead, the presumption was just one of "several considerations" the Kossick Court discussed in its choice of law analysis. Id. at 741, 81 S. Ct. 886.

I find no support in Kossick for the majority's conclusion that we must ignore all other traditional choice of law factors and instead apply federal common law because it validates this contract, particularly when it is Brazil that has the dominant interest in this litigation and applying Brazilian law could only affect the amount of damages in a limited situation. Even if the presumption in favor of applying the law that tends to validate contracts applies here, with all of the § 188(2) contacts, Brazil has easily rebutted the presumption.

Furthermore, while the federal common law's presumption in favor of applying the law that tends to validate contracts might mean that the United States has a general interest in validating contracts, the United States still does not have a "significant " or "close " relationship with this contract. Therefore, under § 197 Brazil remains as the default jurisdiction whose laws govern this contract of transportation regardless of whether the liability limitation is valid under Brazilian law. The Restatement does not elevate the forum state's interests above any other state's, nor should we.

I also disagree with the majority's conclusion that the protection of the justified expectations of the parties mandates application of federal common law. First, because choice of law is not expressed in the Waybill the justified expectations of the parties, like the other § 6 principles, must be analyzed in accordance with each state's § 188 contacts. The United States does not have any significant § 188 contacts with this contract. However, Brazil served as the place of negotiation and execution of the contract, the majority of the companies are domiciled in Brazil, and the contract called for the transportation of goods located in Brazil out of Brazil. Under these circumstances, I believe that the parties would be wholly justified in expecting that their contract was governed by Brazilian law.

Second, there has been no allegation by either party that the contract would be rendered completely invalid under Brazilian law. We are only concerned with the validity of the limitation of liability provision and then only under certain conditions. I agree with the Restatement commentary that while "the expectations of at least one of the parties would presumably be disappointed if the [damages] provision is found to be invalid[,][o]n the other hand, a rule declaring such a provision invalid is likely to represent a strongly-felt policy which the forum would be hesitant to override if the state with the invalidating rule was the state with the dominant interest in the issue to be decided." Restatement § 207 cmt. c.4 Regardless of what the parties expectations were, Brazil is the state with the dominant interest in this litigation and by applying federal common law we are overriding Brazil's "strongly-felt policy" regarding the validity of the damages provision.

Third, while I agree with the majority that in many cases "the protection of the justified expectations of the parties is of considerable importance in contracts," Restatement § 188 cmt. b, I do not agree that to protect the justified expectations of the parties we should enforce blindly the contract as written where no choice of law is expressed and that choice might determine the damages allowed. If the majority's interpretation of the Restatement is correct, then §§ 188, 197 and 207 serve no purpose, and we need never consider whether the United States or any other interested state has any contacts with a contract. I do not believe that the presumption in favor of applying the law that tends toward the validation of the contract has supplanted the traditional choice of law analysis embodied in the Restatement.

Of course, where two states have significant interests in the contract the common law presumption in favor of applying the law of the state that tends to validate the contract might prove dispositive. However, this is not such a case. Brazil's interest in regulating commerce within its own borders heavily outweighs any interest the United States has in enforcing this contract. The Supreme Court has instructed courts to "construe[ ] ambiguous statutes to avoid unreasonable interference with the sovereign authority of other nations." F. Hoffmann–La Roche Ltd. v. Empagran S.A., 542 U.S. 155, 164, 124 S.Ct. 2359, 159 L.Ed.2d 226 (2004); see also Murray v. The Schooner Charming Betsy, 6 U.S. (2 Cranch) 64, 118, 2 L.Ed. 208 (1804) ("[A]n act of congress ought never to be construed to violate the law of nations if any other possible construction remains."). Here we are dealing only with a judicially created common law presumption and not an act of Congress, yet the majority somehow concludes that this presumption is an interest that trumps Brazil's sovereign authority.

Lilly's Evidence of Brazilian Law

Finally, the majority faults Lilly for failing to provide sufficient evidence that Brazilian law does not allow common carriers to limit their damages when they are grossly negligent. However, the issue before the Court is whether Brazilian law applies—not what Brazilian law is. I do not see why we need to consider the particulars of Brazilian law at this stage of the proceedings.

But even assuming arguendo that the content of Brazilian law should play a role in resolving this conflict of laws, Lilly has supplied sufficient evidence that Brazil treats limitation of liability provisions differently than does the United States. The majority dismisses the Machado declaration as offering "no real support" for Lilly's assertion that Brazilian law does not allow FedEx to limit its liability for acts of gross negligence. However, the Machado declaration plainly states that "a common carrier is not entitled to limit its liability if found to be grossly negligent in the care of the cargo while said cargo was in its custody, control and possession or in the custody, control and possession of its duly appointed agent or subcontractor." Under the Federal Rules of Civil Procedure, district courts are allowed to make determinations regarding foreign law by considering "any relevant material or source, including testimony, whether or not submitted by a party or admissible under the Federal Rules of Evidence." Fed. R. Civ. P. 44.1. We have "urge[d] district courts to invoke the flexible provisions of Rule 44.1 to determine issues relating to the law of foreign nations" because "such issues can be expected to come to the federal courts with increasing frequency as the global economy expands and cross-border transactions increase." Curley v. AMR Corp., 153 F.3d 5, 13 (2d Cir.1998). Nevertheless, the majority finds the Machado declaration insufficient despite the Federal Rules of Civil Procedure and our case law that would allow the district court to rely on it. This is an odd conclusion because FedEx never challenged Lilly's characterization of Brazilian law.

In the district court proceedings FedEx decided not to submit proof of Brazilian law because "such is premature at this point," and in its brief to this Court FedEx mistakenly informs us that "the parties did not offer factual proof of the substance of Brazilian law." However, only FedEx failed to provide proof of Brazilian law. Lilly's characterization of Brazilian law and the Machado declaration are unchallenged.

I also disagree with the majority's conclusion that Lilly failed to address whether the parties could contract around Brazilian law. The Machado declaration states that "a common carrier is not entitled to limit its liability if found to be grossly negligent." The plain meaning of this sentence is that common carriers in Brazil cannot limit their liability for grossly negligent acts even if they try.

For the foregoing reasons, I respectfully dissent from the majority opinion. I would vacate the district court's judgment and remand this case to allow the district court to determine whether the limitation of liability provision in the FedEx Air Waybill is valid and enforceable under Brazilian law.

All Citations

【本案评析】

以上案例，主要讲述的是依照意思自治原则如何进行法律选择的问题，而国际货物买卖合同中的法律选择，从各国的冲突法和相关国际条约来看，主要有以下两个原则：

1. 意思自治原则，依据国际上各个国家立法规定以及相关的国际条约，国际货物买卖合同首先应当适用当事人明示或默示选择的法律。1985 年海牙《国际货物买卖合同法律适用公约》第 7 条第 1 项规定："货物买卖合同依双方当事人所选择的法律，当事人选择的法律的协议必须是明示的，或者为合同条款和具体案情总的情况所显示……"而在有些国家虽然没有对国际货物买卖合同的法律选择作出专门的规定，但是在一般合同法律选择的过程中确立了意思自治原则，因此该原则可以同样适用于国际货物买卖合同。该案便是适用了该项原则。

2. 最密切联系原则，当事人未选择合同适用的法律之时，应按照最密切联系原则确定国际货物买卖合同的准据法。1985 年的《国际货物买卖合同法律适用公约》第 8 条规定，当事人未选择法律时，合同依缔结时卖方设有其营业所的国家的法律，但如有下列情形之一时，依合同缔结时买方设有其营业所的国家的法律：(1)合同在买方营业所所在国谈判并签订；(2)合同明确规定卖方须在买方营业所所在国履行其交货义务；(3)合同主要依买方确定的条件并应买方发出的招标而订立。此外，如果从总的情况来看，合同若与上述法律以外的另一法律有更密切的联系，则合同依该另一法律。

综上所述，该案件是美国与巴西在国际商事货物买卖合同之中关于法律冲突解决的案件，而在司法实务之中，可以适用以上两个原则进行法律选择，以期解决相应的法律选择问题。

【延伸阅读】

一、相关学术论著

1. 杜新丽：《国际民事诉讼与商事仲裁》，中国政法大学出版社 2009 年版。

2. 李双元、欧福永：《国际民商事诉讼程序研究》，武汉大学出版社 2016 年版。

3. 刘想树：《国际私法》，法律出版社 2011 年版。

4. 李旺：《国际民事诉讼法》，清华大学出版社 2011 年版。

5.Aaron Xavier Fellmeth, T*he Law of International Business Transaction,* Second

Edition. Thomson Reuters Business. 2011.

二、相关网络资源

1.http://www.hcch.net（海牙国际私法会议）

2.http://www.uncitral.org/en-index.htm（联合国贸易法委员会）

3.http://www.translaw.whu.edu.cn（武汉大学国际法研究所）

第二节　国际民事诉讼管辖权

【知识背景 / 学习要点】

一、国际民事诉讼管辖权的概念

国际民事诉讼管辖权是指一国法院根据本国缔结的或参加的国际条约或依照国内法的规定对特定的国际民事案件行使审判权。国际民事诉讼管辖权主要解决两个方面的问题：一是国家间管辖权争议问题；二是国内法院管辖权级别问题。而本节主要涉及的是国家间管辖权争议的确定问题。

二、管辖权的冲突和解决

（一）管辖权的冲突

国际民事诉讼管辖权冲突分为两种情况：一是积极冲突，二是消极冲突。前者是指两个以上国家的法院对同一国际民事案件交叉或重复行使管辖权，后者是指对同一国际民事案件各国均无管辖权或均不行使管辖权。在国际民事诉讼中，管辖权冲突往往表现为积极冲突，至于管辖权的消极冲突，各国通常是在国内立法中赋予法院一定的自由裁量权，法院在方便当事人诉讼的情况下，受理该类案件。

（二）管辖权冲突的解决

1. 当事人协议选择解决法院

诉讼是解决国际民事争端的传统方式，在当今的国际民事诉讼中，法院管辖权的确定较为不易，极易发生冲突，当发生国际民事活动纠纷之时，若当事人之间选择诉讼方式解决问题，但没有确定争端解决的法院，这对于当事人争端的解决是极其不利的，这是因为，多个有管辖权的法院之间，一个对该争端有管辖权的国家法院相较于同样的具有管辖权的其他国家法院在国际民事争端解决方面或多或少会具有更多的优势，如何选择法院成为当事人之间的又一个待解决的争端，这就掩盖了固有的国际民事争端。① 因而，当事人通过协议选择相应的法院，可充分尊重当事人的意志自由，更好地保证国际民事诉讼程序的实施与进行。

2. 签署国际条约或者制定国内法

签署国际条约是解决国际民事管辖权冲突的最重要的途径之一，国际条约主要通过以下两种方式对国际民事管辖权冲突进行解决：一是统一的国际民事诉讼管辖原则和标准；二是要求有关缔约国在一定条件下放弃管辖权。自 20 世纪以来，国际社会已经制定了一系列关于国际民事诉讼管辖权的国际条约，如 1965 年的《协议选择法院公约》②、1968 年的《关于民商事件管辖权及判决执行的公约》③ 等等，这些公约的签署在一定程度上解决了国际民事管辖权的冲突问题。

解决国际民事案件管辖权冲突的另一个有效的路径是制定国内法，由于管辖权冲突分为积极冲突与消极冲突两个方面，各国解决积极冲突的方法主要有以下几种：（1）对特定类型的案件拒绝管辖。（2）确立不方便管辖原则，即指对某一国际民事案件具有管辖权的法院，根据案件的具体情况，认为自己不方便受理该案件，而认为另一个国家的法院对该案件行使管辖权更方便，从而不对

① Aaron Xavier Fellmeth, *The Law of International Business Transactions*. Second edtion, Thomson Reuters business, 2011, p.833.

② 《协议选择法院公约》于 2005 年 6 月 30 日在海牙国际私法会议第 20 届会议上获得通过，该公约适用于民商事项的国际性案件中所签订的排他选择法院协议。

③ 《民商案件管辖权及判决执行公约》是欧洲共同体所设立的为解决国际民商事案件管辖权和判决的承认和执行问题的统一规则。1968 年订于布鲁塞尔，已经生效。

该案件行使管辖权。(3)确定一事不再理原则，即是指同一当事人就同一国际民事案件以相同诉求在不同国家提起诉讼之时，如已有法院受诉在先，则后面的接受案件的法院应解除其本国诉讼程序。为了避免消极冲突，现今国际上各个国家均在尽可能地扩大国内管辖权的范围。目前，国内法院往往设立必要的管辖权来解决管辖权的消极冲突，即某一案件是在外国法院进行起诉，且若不行使管辖权，当事人就无法获得司法救济之时，即使内国法院并非拥有管辖权，内国法院也应行使管辖权。

三、国际民事诉讼管辖权限制

(一)国家豁免

1. 国家豁免的概念与内容

国家豁免亦称国家及其财产豁免，它是指一个国家及其财产未经该国同意不得在另一个国家法院被诉，其财产也不得被另一个国家扣押或强制执行。国家豁免权是国家固有的权利，其来源于国家主权原则，同时又可以维护国家主权原则。[①] 国家豁免的内容一般包括以下四个方面：

(1)司法管辖豁免，即未经一国明确同意，任何其他国家的法院都不得受理以该国国家为被告或者以该外国国家的财产为诉讼标的的案件。

(2)诉讼程序豁免，是指未经一国明确同意，不得强迫其出庭作证或提供证据，不得对该外国财产采取诉讼保全等强制措施。

(3)强制执行豁免，非经该外国国家明确同意，受诉法院不得依据有关判决对该外国国家的财产强制执行。

(4)国家主管机构豁免，国际上大部分国家认为，国家及财产豁免不仅适用于国家及其财产，也适用于政府的部门与机构，在美国也适用于国有企业。由于该类的主管机构是政府，因而其为了国家利益而作出的政府行为，亦是国家管辖权豁免的对象。

---

① 黄进等：《国际私法》，法律出版社 1999 年版，第 196~198 页。

2. 豁免放弃

国家及财产的豁免权，国家均可自愿放弃。豁免放弃主要发生在以下两种情况之中，首先，坚持绝对豁免原则的一些国家，出于政治与经济的考量而自愿放弃豁免权。其次，坚持限制豁免原则的国家，当其认为在某些案件中不应给予豁免，也会提出外国国家自愿放弃豁免的问题。放弃豁免，可以通过明示或者默示的方式进行：明示方式主要通过条约、契约中的有关条款，或者通过协议等方式进行；默示方式主要有主动向他国法院起诉、应诉或提出反诉等方式进行。

3. 国家行为原则

国家行为原则是指对一国制定的法令或在其领土内实施的官方行为，外国法院不得就其有效性进行审判。国家行为原则在国际上许多国家得以适用，例如美国、英国、法国等，但这些国家奉行的该项原则理论不尽相同。国家行为原则与国家主权豁免原则之间相辅相成，既有联系也有区别，二者的联系在于，它们都产生于国际法上的主权平等观念；而区别在于，国家主权豁免是一种对管辖权的抗辩，只能由外国提出此类抗辩，而国家行为原则之中，一国法院对他国行为进行审判过程中所提出的抗辩，可以由外国国家提出，也可以由当事人提出。

（二）外交豁免与国际组织豁免

1. 外交豁免

外交豁免是外交代表机关及其人员在接受国所享有的特殊权利和优惠待遇的总称，即在国家互惠的基础上，依据国际惯例或者相关协议，为使一国外交代表、外交代表机关和外交人员在驻在国能够有效地执行任务，而由驻在国给予的特别权利和优遇。外交特权与豁免本质上属于其所代表的国家，不属于外交代表个人，个人无权自行放弃。

2. 国际组织豁免

国际组织豁免中的国际组织是指在国际范围内从事活动的由若干国家或政

府通过条约设立并取得国际法人格的团体。《联合国特权及豁免公约》规定的相关组织的资产或财产，享有绝对豁免权，但其也可以放弃豁免权。

【案例摘录与评析】

一、国际民事诉讼法院选择案例[①]

PAPER EXPRESS,LIMITED, an Illinois corporation, Plaintiff-Appellant,
v.
PFANKUCH MASCHINEN GmbH, a German corporation, Defendant Appellee.
No.90-3589.
United States Court of Appeals,
Seventh Circuit.(1992)

Illinois corporation brought breach of warranty action against German corporation. The United States District Court for the Northern District of Illinois, Brian Barnett Duff,J., dismissed for want of proper venue, and appeal was taken. The Court of Appeals, Cudahy, Circuit Judge, held that contract clause reading "Warranty: six months according to the rules of 'VDMA' was valid forum-selection clause providing for exclusive venue in Germany."

Before CUDAHY,COFFEY and MANION, Circuit Judges.

CUDAHY, Circuit Judge.

Paper Express, Ltd. ,an Illinois company, appeals from the dismissal for want of proper venue of a breach of warranty action brought in the district court. The principal issue on appeal is whether the parties' contract included a valid forum-selection clause providing for exclusive venue in Germany. We affirm.

In late 1987, An employee of Paper Express traveled to Canada to discuss the possibility of purchasing copying equipment manufactured by Pfankuch Maschnen, a German company, with systems, Inc., a Pfankuch agent. In March 1988, paper Express negotiated to purchase.

A collating machine from Pfankuch for approximately 8200, 000. There was nothing exceptional about the negotiation process : pfankuch prepared several price quotation; and

① Paper Exp., Ltd. v. Pfankuch Maschinen GmbH,United States Court of Appeals, Seventh Circuit. August 11, 1992972 F.2d 753.

on March 21 issued its final quotation on March 31, Paper Express responded by sending a purchase order to Pfankuch along with a check for $75, 000 whieh Pfankuch promptly cashed. Pfankuch later sent an acknowledgment of the order to Paper Express. In November 1988, the collating equipment was delivered and installed at Paper Express' plant in Des Plaines, Illinois. The equipment never worked as promised and Paper Express commenced thig action in the district court seeking damages in an amount in excess of $872000.

Pfankuch filed a counterclaim for the balance of the purchase price Paper Express had refused to pay.2 At the same time it moved to dismiss the complaint for improper venue pursuant to Fed.R.Civ.P.12(6)(3)relying on a clause asserted to be a forum-selection clause contained in all of the relevant documents—the price quotations , the purchase order issued by Paper Express and the acknowledgment issued by Pfankuch. The clause reads: "Warranty:6 months according to the rules of VDMA and ZVEI. The warranty includes six months parts and three months labor from the time the machine is erected in Paper Express' factory." The VDMA, or the Verband Deutscher Maschinen-und Anlagenbau e.V., is an association of German machine manufacturers that promulgates a set of standard commercial terms. According to the rules of the VDMA, the supplier's principal place of business is the forum for resolving all contractual disputes; in this case that would be Ahrensburg. The town in northern Germany where Pfankuch is located. The district court granted the motion to dismiss, finding that the clause incorporated the VDMA venue rule.

Before examining the validity of the purported forum-selection clause, we must consider whether the clause is indeed a forum-selection clause. Paper Express contends that the clause, which on its face does not refer to venue, is nothing more than a warranty provision and that the words "according to the rules of VDMA" relate only to the length of the warranty.

But surely this cannot be correct. In construing contracts, every provision should be given effect and the words should be read with their ordinary meaning. First Commodity Traders, Inc v.Heinold Com-modities, Inc..766 F.2d 1007,1014 (7thCir.1985); Hanley v. James McHughConstr Co.444 F.2d 1006,1009(7th Cir.1971).The clause in this case specifically details the length of the warranty ("War-ranty:6 months".) so Paper Express' reading would render the additional words "according to the rules of VDMA" surplusage. Nor is warranty so narrow a term as to be incompatible with the concept of venue. Indeed, frequently warranty provisions do include terms that specify how anywhere warranty claims are to be resolved See, e.g., Wick u Atlantic Marine,Inc.,605 F.2d 166,167(5th Cir.1979); Martin Maoietta iAluminum, Irnacl u General Plec Co,,586 F.2d 143,145(9th Cir 1978). The word "according to the rules of 'INAMA' add something to this provision in addition to the length of the warranty. According to" is commonly defined as "agreeing with, consistent with. or answering to" "I Oxford English Dictionary 83(2d ed.1989).

Thus, the parties agreed that the warranty is to be read in a manner consistent with the rules of VDMA." It is apparent from this language and the use of the plural "rules" that the parties agreed to incorporate more than just the VDMA rule regarding the length of the warranty. The only meaningful reason for including the provision in question was to incorporate the VDMA rules, including the VDMA venue provision.

Having established that there is a forum-selection clause, we now consider its specific requirements. The VDMA venue provision states: In all disputes arising out of the contractual relationship, the action shall be filed in the court which has jurisdiction for the principle place of business of the supplier, or its branch office which is carrying out the delivery, if the purchaser is a qualified businessman, a legal entity created by law, or a fund created by public law. The supplier also has the right to commence an action against the purchaser at the purchaser's principal place of business.

The central issue is whether the clause is permissive or mandatory. Paper Express argues that the language is permissive, being only a consent to litigate in Germany, and thus may be read to permit venue in Illinois. Pfankuch contends that the clause is mandatory, vesting jurisdiction and venue exclusively in Germany.

We note first that Paper Express did not argue in the district court that the VDMA provision is permissive but only that it was not part of the panties' contract While that might ordinary result in a waiver of the argument, Pfankuch has not argued: that the issue has been waived, and we proceed to consider it on the merits.

Paper Express relies on several cases that have interpreted similar clauses as permissive. In All-Tech Industries, Inc. v. Freitag Elec.,GmbH,No.87 C 10690,1988 WL 84719,at*2,1988 U.S.Dist. LEXIS8856,at*5(N.D.Ill.Aug.5,1988),the court considered a clause that read "Place of jurisdiction is Bad Segeberg, F.R.G." and held it permissive, noting that the clause" does not state that West Germany is the exclusive jurisdiction for adjudicating disputes arising under the contract; it merely declares a consent to the venue and juris-diction of a West German court if either party is sued there." In Pioneer Life Ins.Co.v.Anderson,No.88 C 20249,1988 WL143726,at "1,1988 U.S. Dist. LEXIS 15820, at"5(N.D.Ill.Dec.21,1988),the court held the clause "Winnebago County, Illinois shall be the place of jurisdiction for service and legal purposes" permissive, noting that "the clause does not state that Illinois is the exclusive' place to bring a suit under the contract."

The forum-selection clauses in All-Tech Industries and Anderson are distinguish-able from the forum-selection clause presently under scrutiny because of the additional sentence in the present provision stating that "[t]he supplier also has the right to commence an action against the purchaser at the purchaser's principal place of business." This language supports a finding that the clause confers exclusive jurisdiction because the sentence in question would be appropriate and meaning full only if the clause were in fact mandatory. Thus ,if the clause were permissive, the additional sentence would be redundant. The specific reservation of the supplier's right to file suit at the purchaser's place of business demonstrates that the clause was in all other respects mandatory and exclusive.

The very language of the VDMA venue provision further supports a finding that the clause is mandatory. The language is obligatory. The phrase "shall be filed". coupled with the phrase "all disputes," clearly manifests an intent to make venue compulsory and exclusive. In Docksider, Ltd .v. Sea Technology,Ltd.,875 F.2d 762,763-64(9th Cir.1989), the court construed the language "venue...shall be deemed to be in Gloucester County, Virginia" as mandatory and exclusive. In Sterling Forest Assoc., Ltd. v. Barnett-Range Corp., 840 F.2d 249,250(4th Cir.1988), the court held the following provision mandatory: "This Agreement shall be construed and enforced in accordance with the laws of the State of California and the parties agree that in any dispute jurisdiction and venue shall be in California." Numerous other courts have construed similar language as conferring exclusive jurisdiction.

[3]The law is clear: where venue is specified with mandatory or obligatory language, the clause will be enforced; where only jurisdiction is specified, the clause will generally not be enforced unless there is some further language indicating the parties "intent to make venue exclusive". Docksider, Ltd., 875 F.2d at 764. We conclude that the language of the VDMA venue provision clearly and unmistakably designates the supplier's principal place of business as the exclusive forum.

Next, Paper Express argues that the VDMA venue rule does not apply to this contract because Paper Express is not a qualified businessman under the VDMA. The German Commercial Code ("Handels-gesetzbuch,"or HGB) broadly defines a qualified merchant as one who engages in the processing of merchandise. The German Commercial Code S 1(2) (2)(Goren& Forrester trans.). We think that Paper Express clearly fits the HGB definition, and therefore falls within the scope of the VDMA venue provision. Paper Express also argues that the VDMA rules apply only to domestic transactions. This point, however, is raised for the first time in there reply brief and is therefore waived. See Circuit Rule 28(f); Egert u. Connecticut Gen. L fe Ins,Co., 900 F.2d 1032,1035 (7thir.1990). Moreover, even if the VDMA rules do not apply by their own force to the transaction at issue here, the parties could still choose to incorporate them into their contract.

[4] Like any contract: provision, a forum-selection clause will be enforced unless enforcement would be unreasonable or un-just or the provision was procured by fraud The Bremen v. Zapata or overreaching. Off-Shore Co.,407 U.S..1,10,92 S.Ct.1907,1913,32 L.Ed.2d 513(1972);North-western

Nat!Ins.Co.v.Donovan916 F.2d 372,375 (7th Cir.1990).Paper Express claims that the clause is invalid for all of these reasons.

[5,6] First, Paper Express asserts fraud in that it was unlikely that anyone at Paper Express read the VDMA since the rules are in "extremely fine print" and are in German. An inference of fraud may arise if a clause is actually buried in illegible fine print, and fraud, of course, is a defense to a contract. Donovan,916 F.2dat 377. But it is a fundamental principle of contract law that a person who signs the contract is presumed to know its terms and consents to be bound by them. 3 Arthur L. Corbin, Corbin on Contracts 607(1989);13 Samuel Williston, Williston on Con-tracts 1577(1988).Nothing excuses Paper Express for its failure to read its own purchase order which in eorporated the rules of the VDMA by reference. Ncrdoes the fact that the rules were in German preclude enforcement of the contract. In fact, a blind or illiterate party(or simply one unfamiliar with the contract language) who signs the contract without learning of its contents would be bound. Mere ignorance will not relieve a party of her obligations and she will be bound by the terms of the agreement, Samson Plastic Con-duit &Pipe Corp .v .Battenfeld Eatru. sionstechnik GmbH,718 F.Supp.886,890-91(M. D.Ala.1989);Gaskin u. Stumm Han-del Gmbl,390 F. Supp. 361,866-67(S.D.N.Y.1975);John D, Calamari, Duty to Read Changing Concept 43 Fordham L. ReN, 341,346-47(1974), We live in a global economy and contracts between par-He8s of different nationalities, and speaking different languages, are common place. Butla party who agrees to terms in writing without understanding or investigating those terms does so at his own perill. United States v. Stump Home Specialties Mfg., Inc.,905 F.2d 1117,1120(7th Cir.1990).In the instant case, although the print is not large ,it is legible; and even though Paper Express may not be fluent in German, we are confident that with the aid of a German-English dictionary, or, even better, a translator ,Paper Express could have mastered the rules of the VDMA, which are only two pages long.

[7] Second, Paper Express contends that Pfankuch made misrepresentations to the effect that "VDMA" referred only to the length of the warranty and to the fact that all the parts used in manufacturing the machinery would be "U.L. listed". But reliance on such representations is subject to a rule of reasonableness. Heller Fin., Inc. w. Midwhey Powder Co,883 F.2d 1286,1291(7th Cir.1989).As the district court found, if Paper Express relied on Pfankuch's alleged statements about the VDMA, such reliance was unreasonable since Paper Express had an opportunity to read the VDMA for itself. The parties to this contract are both sophisticated businesses engaged in international commerce, and Paper Express' purported reliance on an oral explanation contrary to the ordinary meaning of its own purchase order and of the rules to which its order referred would be unreasonable.

[8]Third, Paper Express contends that the forum-selection clause is invalid because the

parties did not expressly bargain for the provision, In Carnival Cruise Lines, Inc. v. Shute,-U.S.-,--111S.Ct 1522,1524-27,113 L.Ed.2d622(1991),addressing the validity of a forum selection clause, the Supreme Court enforced the clause even as part of a forum contract and even though not the subject of negotiation As we noted in Donovan. "Ours is not a bazaar economy in which the terms of every transaction, or even most transactions, are individually dickered." 916 F.2d at 87T. Again, the parties to this contract are two sophisticated businesses and nothing in the record indicates that Paper Express was vulnerable or disadvantaged in the negotiations. Hence, Paper Express' contention based on the absence of negotiation must be rejected.

[9] Finally, Paper Express argues that the forum-selection clause is unreasonable and unenforceable because as a practical matter it would be inconvenient and costly to litigate in Germany. In addition, Paper Express contends that it would be nearly impossible to proceed with its suit in Germany because the witnesses and physical evidence are located in Illinois. The Bremen Court held that an otherwise valid forum-selection clause may be unreasonable and unenforceable if the chosen forum is significantly inconvenient for trial.Brelmen,407 U.S.at 16 92 S .Ct. at 1916. However, the Bremen Court also held that the party seeking to escape the contract must demonstrate that "the forum will be so gravely difficult and inconvenient that he will for all practical purposes be deprived of his day in court". Id.at 18,92S.Ct.at 1917.But additional expense does not necessarily invalidate a forum-selection clause since Paper Express was presumably compensated for this burden by way of the consideration it received under the contract .Donotan,916 F.2d at 378;Gor-donsville Industries,549 F.Supp.at 205.In any event, Paper Express simply has not made a showing, in the district court or in this court, that enforcement of the forum-selection clause would be unjust.

For these reasons, the judgment of the district court dismissing the case for improper venue is affirmed.

【本案评析】

以上案例是关于是美德之间国际商事合同诉讼纠纷中关于协议选择管辖法院的案例，法院系统分析了在"VDMA"规则下美德之间关于法院选择条款无效的原因。从该案中可得出经验，在国际民事诉讼中协议选择法院，应注意以下几点：第一，选择法院的协议必须以书面形式或以文件证明形式证明。第二，当事人在协议选择法院的过程中要明示约定该选择法院协议具有排他性，即受某法院的专有司法管辖。第三，确保管辖协议本身有效。海牙《选择法院协议公约》规定："选择法院协议的有效性依据被选择法院国内法进行判断，当该项协议被确定无效和不能生效时，被选择法院有权不行使管辖权，而其他缔约国法院因此获得管辖权。”最后，依据该公约的规定，虽然公约未对选择的法院范围作出规定，但是，每一个缔约国均可声明协议选择的法院的范围，如若超出选择法院的受理范围，被选择的法院可以拒绝受理。

二、国际民事诉讼国家行为原则适用案例①

OPTOPICS LABORATORIES CORPORATION,

a Delaware corporation, as Assignee of Ashford Laboratories, Inc., Plaintiff,

v.

SAVANNAH BANK OF NIGERIA, LTD., Defendant.

No. 91 Civ. 0312 (LBS).

March 22, 1993.

OPINION

SAND, District Judge.

This case is brought by Optopics Laboratories Corporation, a Delaware corporation, as assignee of Ashford Laboratories, Inc., against Savannah Bank of Nigeria, Ltd. For nonpayment on a letter of credit issued by defendant. Jurisdiction is found under 28 U.S.C. § 1330, which provides that district courts shall have original jurisdiction over non-jury civil actions against a foreign state, and also under the Foreign Sovereign Immunities Act. Currently before the Court are cross-motions for summary judgment. Because we find that no genuine issues of material fact are in dispute and that plaintiff is 901 entitled to payment on the Letter of Credit as a matter of law, plaintiff's motion for summary judgment is granted. Defendant's motion for summary judgment is denied.

The material facts surrounding the transaction at issue in this lawsuit are undisputed. In October 1982, Ashford Laboratories, Inc. (“Ashford”), a New Jersey corporation, contracted to sell to a Nigerian importer, Mabson Pharmaceuticals, Ltd. (“Mabson”), cold capsules for $32,265. In order to effect payment, Mabson applied for an irrevocable letter of credit with defendant, a government owned bank, Savannah Bank of Nigeria (the “Bank”). On the reverse side of the Application are printed certain “General Terms & Conditions”, including one which will be discussed in further detail below, which reads: “This Letter of Credit is subject to the usual terms

① Optopics Laboratories Corp.v. Savannah Bank of Nigeria, Ltd. United States District Court, S.D. New York. March 22, 1993816 F.Supp. 89820 UCC Rep. Serv. 2d 1021.

and conditions operating in the center where the Credit be established."

Subsequent to the submission of the Application to the Bank by Mabson, Bank America International ("Bank America") advised Ashford that a letter of credit known as L–82493 in the amount of $32,265, payable in New York, in United States dollars, had been established by the defendant in Ashford's favor. (Exh. A to Aff. of Frank Nicholas, Sept. 24, 1992). The Letter of Credit is a two-page document, and is dated November 1, 1982. (Exh. B to Aff. of Frank Nicholas, Sept. 24, 1992). The Letter of Credit provides that it is subject to the Uniform Customs and Practice for Documentary Credits, 1974 Revision, International Chamber of Commerce Publication No. 290 (the "UCP").

After the Letter of Credit was established and in reliance thereon, Ashford shipped the pharmaceuticals to Mabson. Ashford presented conforming documents in strict compliance with the Letter of Credit on or about November 30, 1982. Each document specifically identified in the Letter of Credit was submitted by Ashford.

The Bank approved the Letter of Credit for payment on December 20, 1982. Both the Application and the Letter of Credit made clear that due to Nigeria's foreign exchange controls, a Form M would have to be filed by the importer, Mabson, through the defendant. A Form M is an application directed to the Central Bank to purchase foreign exchange. Defendant complied with this requirement on January 20, 1983, with the request that "the Foreign Currency should be paid to Bank of America, New York". The record suggests that Mabson also complied with related procedures regarding the Form M.

The Bank failed to pay on the Letter of Credit, claiming that it was unable to remit United States dollars to Bank America due to the failure of the Central Bank of Nigeria to provide foreign exchange. A June 8, 1983 cable from the Bank advised Bank America that it could negotiate the documents for the Letter of Credit but that Bank America would not be reimbursed by defendant until foreign exchange cover was made available. Similar cables were sent by defendant to Bank America on February 21, 1984, and January 15, 1985. Bank America, justifiably, has not negotiated the payment of the Letter of Credit. Significantly, the defendant has admitted that it would like to pay the Letter of Credit, and has offered to do so in Naira, the Nigerian currency. Plaintiff has rejected that offer.

Sometime subsequent to defendant's acceptance of the Letter of Credit, the Government of Nigeria engaged in a program to reschedule the payment of foreign debt, referred to as the "refinancing exercise". Defendant contends that as part of that refinancing exercise, Nigeria required, as a condition to payment on the Letter of Credit, that Ashford submit a claim form to Chase Manhattan Bank. Defendant further avers that at least as early as April 15, 1985, Ashford received a document entitled "The Central Bank of Nigeria—Circular dated 18th April, 1984", which gave notice that creditors must lodge claims with Chase Manhattan Bank to have debts paid by the Central Bank. Ashford never submitted any such claim form. Defendant asserts that due to Ashford's failure to submit the required document, the conditions of the Letter of Credit were not strictly complied with and the Bank is not required to honor the Letter of Credit.

Two other sets of facts should be noted at this point. In a letter to Mabson dated October 5, 1990, defendant acknowledged receipt of payment from Mabson for the Letter of Credit, and stated that "[w]e have not been able to remit same to the exporters [i.e. Ashford] due to a non-provision of the required foreign exchange cover by the Central Bank of Nigeria." (Exh. H to Aff. of Frank Nicholas, August, 1992). This indicates both that refusal to release funds is not due to any withholding of the money by the bank's customer, and furthermore, that the reason for the refusal is non-provision of foreign exchange, as stated in the cables to Bank America, and not any failure on Ashford's part to strictly comply with the terms of the Letter of Credit.

Act of State:

Defendant argues that the Nigerian exchange controls are governmental policy, and that any adjudication by this Court would be an interference with a sovereign act of state. Although we find that the act of state doctrine is not implicated, it is a claim which is of the utmost seriousness and will be addressed fully.

The act of state doctrine recognizes both that the laws of nations as applied within their own borders are sovereign and should not be passed upon by our courts, and that the judiciary must be restrained from rendering decisions which will affect the United States' foreign policy, a sphere of power constitutionally assigned to the executive and legislative branches. "The act of state doctrine declares that a United States court will not adjudicate a politically sensitive dispute which would require the court to judge the legality of the sovereign act of a foreign state." *International Ass'n of Machinists v. OPEC,* 649 F.2d 1354, 1358 (9th Cir.1981), *cert. denied,* 454 U.S. 1163, 102 S.Ct. 1036, 71 L.Ed.2d 319 (1982). A prerequisite for the application of the act of state doctrine is that the act in question is one which takes effect entirely within the boundaries of the sovereign nation. Where this is not the case, our courts will give extraterritorial effect to the law of another nation, based on comity, only where it does not conflict with the laws and policies of the United States.

Defendant ignores a number of Second Circuit cases which indicate the nature of the pertinent inquiry in determining whether the application of Nigeria's exchange control regulations to the Letter of Credit takes place entirely within the boundaries of Nigeria.

In *Allied Bank Int'l v. Banco Credito Agricola,* 757 F.2d 516 (2d Cir.1985), the plaintiff brought an action to recover on promissory notes issued by three Costa Rican banks wholly owned by the Government of Costa Rica, which were payable in United States dollars, in New York. The banks defaulted on the notes solely due to the Costa Rican government's suspending all external debt payments. The court explained that the primary concern in applying the act of state doctrine is whether "adjudication would embarrass or hinder the executive in the realm of foreign relations", and that the rule is to be applied flexibly on a case by case basis.

The Second Circuit in *Allied* held that the applicability of the act of state doctrine depends on the situs of the debt, defined as the right to receive repayment from the banks in accordance with the loan agreements. The court viewed the Costa Rican government's actions in extinguishing plaintiff's right to receive payment as a "taking", and reasoned that if the taking occurred within the foreign sovereign's territory, then the act of state doctrine would prohibit the courts of this country from adjudicating the matter. The court said that locating the debt "depends in large part on whether the purported taking can be said to have 'come to complete fruition within the dominion of the [foreign] government' ".

In applying that standard, the *Allied* court held that "Costa Rica could not wholly extinguish the Costa Rican banks' obligation to timely pay United States dollars to Allied in New York. Thus the situs of the debt was not Costa Rica." 757 F.2d at 521. The court proceeded to state that Costa Rica's interest in the contracts at issue is essentially limited to the extent to which it can unilaterally alter the payment terms. Costa Rica's potential jurisdiction over the debt is not sufficient to locate the debt there for the purposes of the act of state doctrine analysis.

The *Allied* court further stated that "acts of foreign governments purporting to have extraterritorial effect ... should be recognized by the courts only if they are consistent with the law and policy of the United States." Because the United States would not condone the Costa Rican government's attempt to change unilaterally the terms of the contracts, the court did not give effect to the Costa Rican directives.

Two other Second Circuit cases employ the same analysis and reach the same result. In *Braka v. Bancomber,* 762 F.2d 222 (2d Cir.1985), a case decided after *Allied,* the plaintiffs, United States citizens, purchased peso and dollar certificates of deposits from a Mexican bank, with the principal and interest payable in Mexico. Subsequently, the Mexican government decreed that all domestic obligations would be paid in pesoes and at a devalued exchange rate. Plaintiffs then filed suit in federal district court in New York. The court held that the situs of the debt was Mexico, since the Mexican decree could wholly extinguish the plaintiffs' rights within the dominion of the foreign government. The act of state doctrine therefore barred plaintiffs' recovery.

In *Garcia v. Chase Manhattan Bank, N.A.,* 735 F.2d 645 (2d Cir.1984), plaintiffs sued over the proceeds of two certificates of deposit which were issued by Chase's Cuba branch prior to the time Cuba seized the assets of the bank. The CDs provided that they were redeemable at any Chase branch worldwide. The Court found that the situs of the debt was wherever it could be collected, and therefore the acts of the Cuban government could not wholly extinguish the plaintiffs' rights. The act of state doctrine was therefore inapplicable.

The application of *Allied, Braka,* and *Garcia* to the case before this Court is clear. The "taking" is plaintiff's right to receive the proceeds of the Letter of Credit in United States dollars at a bank in New York. The act of the Nigerian government in refusing to provide the foreign exchange to defendant is not enough to wholly extinguish the Nigerian bank's obligation to pay on the Letter of Credit in New York. Therefore, the situs of the debt is not Nigeria, and the act of state doctrine is not implicated. Furthermore, because the Nigerian government's attempt to unilaterally modify a private letter of credit contract is against the law and policy of the United States, this Court will not enforce the Nigerian policy extraterritorially.

In response to this caselaw, defendant appears to place reliance on last year's Supreme Court decision in *Republic of Argentina and Banco Central de la Republica Argentina v. Weltover, et al.,* 504 U.S. 607, 112 S.Ct. 2160, 119 L.Ed.2d 394 (1992). That case however did not address the act of state doctrine at all, but instead dealt with the Foreign Sovereign Immunities Act ("FSIA"), the application of which has not been seriously challenged in this action. *Weltover* makes clear that the FSIA would not bar plaintiff here, as the acts of the defendant clearly fall within the commercial activity exception in the statute and have a direct effect in the United States. For the foregoing reasons, we find that the act of state doctrine is inapplicable and does not bar plaintiff's suit against the bank.

Turing to the letter of credit issues, the court held that Ashford had strictly complied with the terms of the letter of credit and was entitled to payment from Savannah Bank and entered judgment in favor of the plaintiff.

【本案评析】

以上案例核心争议点就在于“国家行为原则”的适用例外。被告以国家行为为由拒绝本案原告的指控是不成立的。“国家行为原则”是指对一国制定的法令或在其领土内实施的官方行为，外国法院不得就其有效性进行审判。但在实践中“国家行为原则”在适用过程中会有一些例外规定，该案就是以商业行为例外排除了国家行为原则的适用。美国最高法院于“登希路案”中认为，国家行为原则不适用于主权者的商业行为。同一法院在后来的“麦克唐奈尔案”中也明确声明，主权者纯粹的商业行为一般不要求司法限制。但若涉及国家对外关系，则在一定程度上国家的商业行为也适用于“国家行为原则”。

【延伸阅读】

一、相关学术论著

（一）著作类

1. Richard Fentiman, *International Commercial Litigation*, second edtion. Oxford. 2010.

2.Chow Schenbaum, *International Business Transactions*. Third Edition, Wolters Kluwer. 2012.

3. 李双元、欧永福：《国际私法教学案例》，北京大学出版社 2007 年版。

（二）论文类

1. 任明艳：《美国国家行为原则评析》，载《法学》2006 年第 7 期。

2. 孙劼：《论国家主权豁免与我国民事诉讼管辖制度的衔接》，载《武大国际法评论》2018 年第 4 期。

3. 李双元：《再论起草我国涉外民事关系法律适用法的几个问题》，载《时代法学》2010 年第 8 期。

二、相关网络资源

1.http://www.court.gov.cn/zgcpwsw/（裁判文书网）

2. http://www.court.gov.cn/（最高人民法院网）

第三节　国际司法协助

【知识背景 / 学习要点】

一、国际司法协助概述

（一）国际司法协助的内涵

国际司法协助是指一个国家或地区的司法机关依据另一个国家或地区的司法机关或相关当事人的请求，代为履行司法行为或在司法方面提供其他方面的协助。关于国际司法协助的内涵，在国际上主要有广义和狭义两种观点。狭义的观点认为，国际司法协助仅仅包括司法协助中的文书送达与调查取证。而广义的司法协助的观点认为，除了包括文书送达、调查取证之外还包括外国法院判决的承认与执行问题，在本节中，采用司法协助的狭义内涵观点。

（二）司法协助的主体

1. 中央机关

中央机关是一国依据本国缔结与参与的国际条约和国内法规定指定或建立的机关，并在国际民事司法协助中主要担任联系，传递作用。对于各国中央机关的指定，国际上没有统一规定，一般情况下由各国依据本国的法律和国情自主决定。除此之外，中央机关的职能并不限于司法协助，其具体职能取决于相关国际条约和国内法的规定。

2. 外交部门

外交部门在司法协助中的作用主要包括：首先，作为国际司法协助的联系机关，在司法协助过程中，若两国没有缔结相关的司法协助条约，两国之间的司法协助一般通过外交部门进行。其次，解决司法协助过程中所引发的争议。最后，在法院审理过程中，查明外国法。除此之外，外交部门亦包括领事机构，领事机构在国际司法协助过程中的流程如下：请求国的司法机关可以依照内国规定的途径，将请求书传递给该国在被请求国的领事机构，然后由领事机构传递给被请求国的司法机关。

3. 司法机关及其他主管机构

在大多数国家之中，司法机关是司法协助的主体，在国际上，司法机关主要包括法院以及有权提出司法协助请求和执行该请求的机关。但在实践中，除了司法机关以外，也存在指定司法机关以外的机关或个人提出或者执行司法协助请求的情况。①

---

① 譬如在波兰，公证处有时也接受国际上其他国家有关遗嘱有效性和遗嘱保护方面的司法协助请求。

二、域外文书送达

(一)域外文书送达的含义

域外文书送达是国际司法协助的重要内容之一。域外文书送达是指一国法院根据国际条约或内国法的规定,按照互惠原则将司法(外)文书送达给居住在国外的诉讼当事人或诉讼参与人的行为。

(二)域外文书送达的方式

1. 直接送达

(1)外交代表送达

外交代表送达也称领事送达,是指内国法院将需要在国外送达的法律文书交给本国驻送达人所在国家的外交代表或领事,由领事交予受送达人。这是国际社会所普通承认和采用的一种方式。外交代表送达的方式的前提是两国已签署双边司法协助协定或共同参加了双边条约,如果两国均不符合上述两个条件,但若二者已建立外交关系且存在送达互惠关系,亦可采用该种方式进行送达。一般来说,采用这种方式进行域外送达的对象只能是所属国国民,并且不能采取强制措施。许多国家的国内立法和有关国际条约都对这种方式的送达作了明确的规定。1963 年《维也纳领事关系公约》第 5 条[①]、我国《民事诉讼法》第 267 条[②] 均规定了外交送达的方式。

(2)邮寄送达

邮寄送达是指内国法院通过邮寄的方式直接将法律文书寄给国外的诉讼当事人或其他诉讼参与人,各国对于这种方式的送达所持的态度不同。如 1954

① 《维也纳领事关系公约》第 5 条第 10 款规定:“领事职务……依现行国际协定之规定或于无此种国际协定时,以符合接受国法律规章之任何其他方式,转送司法书状与司法以外文件或执行嘱托调查书或代派遣国法院调查证据之委托书……”

② 《民事诉讼法》第 267 条规定:“人民法院对在中华人民共和国领域内没有住所的当事人送达诉讼文书,可以采用下列方式:(一)依照受送达人所在国与中华人民共和国缔结或者共同参加的国际条约中规定的方式送达;(二)通过外交途径送达;(三)对具有中华人民共和国国籍的受送达人,可以委托中华人民共和国驻受送达人所在国的使领馆代为送达;(四)向受送达人委托的有权代其接受送达的诉讼代理人送达;(五)向受送达人在中华人民共和国领域内设立的代表机构或者有权接受送达的分支机构、业务代办人送达……”

年《民事诉讼程序公约》第 6 条[①]和 1965 年《海牙送达公约》第 10 条[②]均规定内国法院有权通过邮局直接将法律文书寄给在外国的有关人员。但也有一些国家如德国、瑞士、土耳其等国家明确表示反对，中国在加入《海牙送达公约》之时也对此提出了保留，反对采用邮寄的方式在我国境内送达文书。

（3）个人送达

个人送达是指内国法院将文书委托给具有一定身份的个人代为送达。拥有一定身份的人可能是有关当事人的诉讼代理人、当事人选定的人或与当事人关系密切的人。个人送达方式一般为普通法系各国所承认和采用，大陆法系大多不采用此种送达方式。

（4）公告送达

公告送达是指将文书的内容用张贴公告或登报的方法告知有关的当事人或其他诉讼参与人，自公告之日起经过一定的时间之后即视为送达。世界上大多数国家均承认了公告送达的方式，中国也规定在一定条件下可采用公告送达，但对该种送达方式具有严格的限制，通常规定是在其他方式无法送达之时，采用该种方式送达。

（5）按当事人协商的方式送达

这是普通法系国家所采用的一种送达方式。如依美国法规定，对外国国家的代理人或代理处，对外国国家或外国的政治实体的送达，可依诉讼双方当事人间特别协商的办法进行送达[③]。

① 民事诉讼程序公约第 6 条规定："……（一）有权将文书直接邮寄给居住在外国的利害关系人……"

② 原文如下：Provided the State of destination does not object, the present Convention shall not interfere with: a) the freedom to send judicial documents, by postal channels, directly to persons abroad, b) the freedom of judicial officers, officials or other competent persons of the State of origin to effect service of judicial documents directly through the judicial officers, officials or other competent persons of the State of destination, c)the freedom of any person interested in a judicial proceeding to effect service of judicial documents directly through the judicial officers, officials or other competent persons o the State of destination.

③ 宋渝玲：《涉外民事诉讼法律实务》，厦门大学出版社 2017 年版，第 277 页。

2. 间接送达

间接送达应依照双方共同缔结参加的条约的有关规定，通过缔约国的中央机关依照特定的程序来进行。间接送达的条件包括：

（1）请求主体，依照 1965 年《海牙送达公约》的规定，提出请求的主体应该是依照请求国的法律规定的主管当局或者司法助理人员。

（2）法律依据，提出请求应按照相关国际条约的规定进行，如果没有相关条约关系，可以通过外交途径进行。

（3）送达方式，一国执行外国提出的送达请求，主要有三种方式：第一，是由被请求国中央机关予以送达的正式送达。第二，按照请求方要求采用的特定方式进行送达，但此种方式不得与被请求国的法律相抵触。第三，非正式递交。未严格遵守相关公约中的形式要求而在被送达人自愿接受时向其送达文书，在被送达人拒绝之时，再来采用正式送达方式。最后采用送达回证或由有关机构出具送达证明书的方式，通知执行结果。

（4）送达文书有具体格式要求，要严格依照国家间公约进行文书撰写。如果送达文书中被请求国的中央机关认为请求书不符合要求、地址不详或者执行该请求将有损被请求国的公共秩序，可以拒绝送达。

三、域外调查取证

（一）域外调查取证的概念与方式

域外调查取证是指一国司法机关请求境外主管机关代为收集该国境内的与案件有关的证据，或者受诉法院国有关机关直接提取有关案件所需的证据。域外调查取证分为直接取证和间接取证两种方式，直接取证不涉及取证地国家主管机关的司法行为，其主要包括外交和领事人员取证、特派员取证、当事人或诉讼代理人自行取证三个方面的内容。而间接取证是大多数国家采取的主要取证方式，一般是通过外国主管机关的负责机构代为收集取证。

（二）国际民事域外调查取证的法律冲突与协调

1. 域外取证的冲突

国际民事诉讼域外调查取证冲突主要表现为大陆法系与英美法系的冲突，其具体冲突表现在于：

（1）取证主体差异

英美法系国家，收集证据的主体在当事人和律师的手中。但大陆法系国家法官在案件审判中掌控证据收集的程序，所有的证据收集方法都要求有一个正式的法庭程序。

（2）取证范围不同

在英美法系国家，取证的范围不做限定，开展取证行为时，尤其是美国，只要律师认为材料可能与诉讼有关，就可以取证。而在大陆法系国家，证据收集大多有着明确的规定。

（3）取证程序不同

以英美法系的代表美国为例，当事人在证据收集中占主导地位，证据的收集主要由当事人的律师发起，司法机关一般不会参与。而在大陆法系国家，证据的搜集工作都必须向法院提出申请。

2. 国际民事域外调查取证法律的协调

国际民事域外调查取证的协调主要通过国际公约进行协调。现行的关于国际民事域外调查取证的国际公约主要有 1970 年的《域外取证公约》、《欧盟域外取证规则》、《美洲取证公约》几个公约。

【案例摘录与评析】

国际民事诉讼司法协助案例[①]

Tulip Computer int' l B.V.

v.

Dell computer Corp.

United States District Court

District of Delaware,2003 254 F.supp.2d 469

Synopsis

Dutch computer manufacturer sued American competitor for patent infringement. On defendant's motion for international judicial assistance with discovery, the District Court, Jordan, J., held that issuance of letters rogatory was warranted.

JORDAN, District Judge.

I. INTRODUCTION

Presently before the Court are two motions (D.I.458, D.I.459) by defendant Dell Computer Corporation ("Dell"). One of the motion requests international judicial assistance to take evidence from Mr. Gerardus Franciscus Duynisveld (D.I.458) and the other motion requests international judicial assistance to take evidence from Mr. Frans Dietz (D.I.459). Both Mr. Duynisveld and Mr. Dietz are citizens of the Netherlands. (D.I. 458 at 2; D.I. 459 at 2.) Dell has filed these motions pursuant to 28 U.S.C. § 1781, Federal Rule of Civil Procedure 28(b)(2), and the Hague Convention on the Taking of Evidence Abroad in Civil or Commercial Matters ("Hague Evidence Convention" or "Convention"), 23 U.S.T. 2555; T.I.A.S. No. 7444; 847 U.N.T.S. 231, reproduced in 28 U.S.C.A. following § 1781. (D.I. 458 at 1; D.I. 459 at 1.) Plaintiff Tulip Computers International B.V. ("Tulip") opposes the motions. (D.I. 468; D.I. 469.)

II. DISCUSSION

A. The Hague Evidence Convention

The Hague Evidence Convention serves as an alternative or "permissive" route to the Federal Rules of Civil Procedure for the taking of evidence abroad from litigants and third parties alike. See Societe Nationale Industrielle Aerospatiale v. United States District Court for the Southern District of Iowa, 482 U.S. 522, 538, 107 S. Ct. 2542, 96 L.Ed.2d 461 (1987). The Convention allows judicial

① Tulip Computers Intern. B.V. v. Dell Computer Corp. United States District Court, D. Delaware. February 4, 2003 Not Reported in F.Supp.2d2003 WL 1606081.

authorities in one signatory country to obtain evidence located in another signatory country "for use in judicial proceedings, commenced or contemplated." Hague Evidence Convention, Art. 1. The United States and the Netherlands are contracting states under the Hague Evidence Convention. 23 U.S.T. 2555; T.I.A.S. No. 7444; 847 U.N.T.S. 231, reproduced in 28 U.S.C.A. following § 1781.

1.There are three available methods of taking evidence pursuant to the Convention:

(1) by a Letter of Request or "letter rogatory" from a U.S. judicial authority to the competent authority in the foreign state ..., (2) by an American or foreign diplomatic or consular officer or agent after permission is obtained from the foreign state, and (3) by a private commissioner duly appointed by the foreign state.

Newman & Zaslowsky, LITIGATING INTERNATIONAL COMMERCIAL DISPUTES 139 n. 3 (1996).

Dell has opted to employ the first mechanism list, supra, Letters of Requests. (See D.I. 458; D.I. 459.) Pursuant to the Convention, a Letter of Request must provide the contracting state with specific information regarding the lawsuit and the information sought. Hague Evidence Convention, Art. 3. The signatory state, upon receipt and consideration, "shall [then] apply the appropriate measure of compulsion" as is customary "for the execution of orders issued by the authorities of its own country." Hague Evidence Convention, Art. 10. Signatory states may refuse to execute a Letter of Request if the request "does not fall within the function of the judiciary" or if the "sovereignty or security" of the contracting state would be prejudiced but, execution "may not be refused solely on the ground that under its internal law the State of execution claims exclusive jurisdiction over the subject-matter of the action or that its internal law would not admit a right of action on it." Hague Evidence Convention, Art. 12.

The person to whom the discovery requests in a Letter of Request are directed has the right to "refuse to give evidence" to the extent that the person has a privilege under the law of the State of execution or the State of origin. Hague Evidence Convention, Art. 11. However, the Netherlands has stated that "[o]nly the court which is responsible for executing the Letter of Request shall be competent to decide whether any person concerned by the execution has a privilege or duty to refuse to give evidence under the law of a State other than the State of origin; no such privilege or duty exists under Dutch law." Hague Evidence Convention, Netherlands 2i, Art. 11.

The Netherlands has also adopted reservations to the Hague Evidence Convention pursuant to Article 23 of the Convention, which provides that "[a] Contracting State may at the time of signature, ratification or accession, declare that it will not execute *473 Letters of Request issued for the purpose of obtaining pretrial discovery of documents as known in Common Law countries." Hague Evidence Convention, Netherlands 2i. Thus, as implemented by the Netherlands, Letters of Request may not be acted upon if "issued for the purpose of obtaining pre-trial discovery of documents as known in Common Law countries." Hague Evidence Convention, Netherlands 2i, Art. 23. The Netherlands, therefore, may choose not to enforce Letters of Request for pre-trial discovery of documents which require a person to state the relevancy of the documents to the proceedings for which the documents are sought or Letters of Request that ask a person "to produce any document other than particular documents specified in the Letter of Request as being documents which the court which is conducting the proceedings believe to be in his possession, custody or power." Id.

B. The Parties' Arguments

1. Dell's Position

Dell asserts that "[w]hile in the employment of Tulip, Mr. Duynisveld had knowledge of and participated in R & D activities that may be directly relevant to Dell's defenses in this case." (D.I. 458 at 2.) Similarly, Dell maintains that "[w]hile engaged by Tulip, Mr. Frans Dietz had knowledge of and participated in patent procurement activities that may be directly relevant to Dell's defenses in this case." (D.I. 459 at 2.) In particular, Dell contends that Mr. Duynisveld [and Mr. Dietz] may be able to provide information relating to "the validity of the '621 patent; the enforceability of the '621 patent; and the alleged infringement by Dell of the '621 patent." (D.I. 458 at 2–3; D.I. 459 at 2–3.) Dell contends, therefore, that since Mr. Duynisveld and Mr. Dietz are foreign nationals residing in the Netherlands and are not parties to the present litigation, discovery pursuant to the Hague Evidence Convention is proper. (D.I. 458 at 3–4; D.I. 459 at 3–4.)

Dell further asserts that the taking of evidence from these individuals compels proceeding under the Convention since all alternative efforts to obtain the evidence have failed. (D.I. 473 at 1–3.) Dell contends that the Netherlands' reservations pursuant to Article 23 of the Convention do not weigh against its requests. (Id. at 3–4.) In addition, notes Dell, the parties have, during the course of this case, proceeded pursuant to the Convention to obtain evidence from other individuals. (Id. at 4–5.) Moreover, argues Dell, Tulip's opposition is not well founded since the Dutch authorities will weigh the breadth of the evidence sought to assure compliance with the Convention and Netherlands judicial procedure. (Id. at 5–9) Dell contends that the documents and testimony sought are not privileged as Tulip maintains and, even if the evidence were privileged, it would first be returned to this Court, thus placing the Court in a position "to determine whether any applicable privilege prohibits the production of certain documents to Dell." (Id. at 7.)

2. Tulip's Position

Tulip contends that the Court must apply a much higher standard then is applied in this country when ordering discovery, if the Court authorizes Dell's request to proceed pursuant to the

Hague Evidence Convention, since use of the Convention raises issues of territoriality and comity. (D.I. 468 at 3–5; D.I. 469 at 3–5.)

In particular, Tulip argues that Article 23 of the Convention prohibits the broad document inquiry sought by Dell because Dell's requests do not conform to the Netherlands' reservations with regard to Article 23, which may be characterized as prohibiting American-style discovery "fishing expeditions." (D.I. *474 468 at 5–7; D.I. 469 at 5–7.) In addition, asserts Tulip, the Court should deny Dell's requests because much of the evidence Dell seeks is privileged information. (D.I. 468 at 7–12; D.I. 469 at 7–11.) Moreover, maintains Tulip, the evidence sought is either irrelevant to the proceedings or constitutes inadmissible hearsay. (D.I. 468 at 12–13; D.I. 469 at 9–11.)

C. Analysis

2.3 "A party which seeks the application of the Hague [Evidence] Convention procedures rather than the Federal Rules [of Civil Procedure] bears the burden of persuading the trial court[ ]" of the necessity of proceeding pursuant to the Hague Evidence Convention. Valois of Am., Inc. v. Risdon Corp., 183 F.R.D. 344, 346 (D.Conn.1997) (citations omitted). That burden is not great, however, since the "Convention procedures are available whenever they will facilitate the gathering of evidence by the means authorized in the Convention." Aerospatiale, 482 U.S. at 541, 107 S. Ct. 2542. Factors relevant to the Court's decision include "considerations of comity, the relative interests of the parties including the interest in avoiding abusive discovery, and the ease and efficiency of alternative formats for discovery." Madanes v. Madanes, 199 F.R.D. 135, 141 (S.D.N.Y.2001) (citations omitted).

4.Resort to the Hague Evidence Convention in this instance is appropriate since both Mr. Duynisveld and Mr. Dietz are not parties to the lawsuit, have not voluntarily subjected themselves to discovery, are citizens of the Netherlands, and are not otherwise subject to the jurisdiction of the Court. Those factors restricting the availability of the evidence Dell seeks weigh in favor of proceeding under the Hague Evidence Convention. See Orlich v. Helm Brothers, Inc., 160 A.D.2d 135, 143, 560 N.Y.S.2d 10 (N.Y.A.D.1990) {"When discovery is sought from a non-party in a foreign jurisdiction, application of the Hague [Evidence] Convention, which encompasses principles of international comity, is virtually compulsory."}; Aerospatiale, 482 U.S. at 546, 107 S.Ct. 2542 ("The exact line between reasonableness and unreasonableness in each case must be drawn by the trial court, based on its knowledge of the case and of the claims and interests of the parties and the governments whose statutes and policies they invoke.").

Tulip's arguments go more particularly to the scope of the discovery Dell seeks pursuant to the Hague Evidence Convention. (See D.I. 468 at 3–11; D.I. 469 at 3–13.) The arguments do not justify wholly precluding Dell's efforts to acquire the evidence it seeks. Tulip's primary argument is that the evidence sought is privileged and Mr. Duynisveld and Mr. Dietz, therefore, should not be placed in a position to determine for themselves what information is or is not privileged in the case. (D.I. 468 at 9–11; D.I. 469 at 10–13.) Tulip contends, therefore, that in order to prevent an abuse of privilege the Court should deny Dell's requests in toto. (Id.) The Court disagrees. Mr. Duynisveld and Mr. Dietz may avail themselves of the privilege provided in this country and in the executing country under Article 11 of the Convention. Presumably, they may also obtain counsel, if they wish, and Tulip will be free to express its own views on privilege and, if necessary, to seek this Court's opinion with respect to those views.

The Court is also not persuaded by Tulip's assertions with regard to the Netherlands reservations pursuant to Article 23 of the Convention as applied to Dell's proposed document requests. "[T]he emerging view of this exception to discovery is that it applies only to 'requests that lack sufficient specificity or that have not been reviewed for relevancy by the requesting *475 court.' " Aerospatiale, 482 U.S. at 564, 107 S. Ct. 2542 (Blackmun, J., concurring in part, dissenting in part) (citations omitted). "Thus, in practice, a reservation is not the significant obstacle to discovery under the Convention that the broad wording of Article 23 would suggest." Id. If Dell's document requests are overly broad under the law of the Netherlands, as Tulip maintains, then the requests will presumably be narrowed by the appropriate judicial authorities in the Netherlands before any documents are produced. [D.I. 469 at 4 (citing Ex. A, Ebbink Aff. ¶¶ 4–5).] The Court is content that such officials will make the appropriate determination under their own law. See Aerospatiale, 482 U.S. at 542, 107 S. Ct. 2542 ("It is well known that the scope of American discovery is often significantly broader than is permitted in other jurisdictions, and we are satisfied that foreign tribunals will recognize that the final decision on the evidence to be used in litigation conducted in American courts must be made by those courts.").

Accordingly, IT IS HEREBY ORDERED

That Dell's motions (D.I. 458; D.I. 459) to approve requests for international judicial assistance, pursuant to the Hague Evidence Convention of 18 March 1970 on the taking of evidence in civil or commercial matters, to take evidence from Mr. Duynisveld (D.I.458) and Mr. Dietz (D.I.459) are GRANTED. Dell shall prepare final versions of its letters of requests, which shall contain limiting language to clarify that it will not inquire into matters which are subject to the attorney-client or any other applicable privilege, and, in taking any evidence which the Netherlands' authorities may permit it take, Dell shall take the most restrictive view of privilege applicable, whether it be under United States or Netherlands' law.

All Citations

【本案评析】

以上案例讲述的是荷兰郁金香电脑公司与美国戴尔电脑公司专利纠纷案。在此案中被告美国戴尔电脑请求国际司法协助。荷兰与美国均是《海牙证据公约》的缔约国，在该案中两国均依照《海牙证据公约》的规定进行了相关的证据搜集。在本案之中，当事人是通过请求书的方式进行取证的，无论是请求的提出与接受，还是请求书的形式与内容均符合《海牙证据公约》的规定，综上所述，该案的司法取证过程合法合理。

【延伸阅读】

一、相关典型案例

Giant Light Metal Technology(Kunshan)Co. Ltd . v. Aksa Far East Pte Ltd.

二、相关学术论著

（一）经典文献

1. 宋渝玲：《涉外民事诉讼法律实务》，厦门大学出版社 2017 年版。

2. 斯蒂文·苏本、玛格瑞特·伍：《美国民事诉讼的真谛》，蔡彦敏、徐卉译，法律出版社 2002 年版。

3. 李玉泉：《国际民事诉讼与商事仲裁》，武汉大学出版社 1994 年版。

（二）期刊类

1. 何其生：《我国域外送达机制的困境与选择》，载《法学研究》2005 年第 2 期。

2. 董丽萍、刘国明：《我国国际司法协助的发展和问题》，载《人民司法》1998 年第 10 期。

三、相关网络资源

https://www.hcch.net/（海牙国际私法会议）

第四节　外国法院判决的承认与执行

【知识背景 / 学习要点】

一、外国法院判决承认与执行的内涵

（一）外国法院判决承认与执行的含义

外国法院判决的承认与执行指一国法院依据其国内立法或有关的国际条约承认相关外国法院的民事判决在国内的效力，并在必要时依法强制执行。依据国家主权原则，一国法院对国际民事案件所作出的判决，只能在该国领域内有效，而在该国领域之外并不当然具有法律效力。然而，应保护和发展国际民事关系发展之需，国家之间也往往在互惠的前提下互相承认和执行对方国家法院的判决。

（二）外国法院判决承认与执行的关系

外国法院判决的承认与执行包括承认和执行外国法院的判决两个方面的内容，而这两个方面的内容是既有联系又有区别的两个不同的法律问题。第一，承认是执行的前提，未经承认的外国法院判决，也就不能执行。第二，执行是承认的结果，虽经承认但未必会被执行，例如在司法实践中，针对个人身份和能力方面的确认判决就仅仅需要承认而并不需要执行。第三，承认是对外国法院判决自身权利的确认，法律效果较为抽象，而执行的法律效果则是具体的，表现为将外国法院判决不断地从书面领域转化到实际过程之中。

二、外国法院判决承认与执行的条件

（一）判决作出国法院的管辖权适格

判决作出国法院具有合格的管辖权是内国法院承认与执行外国法院判决的首要条件，而该合格的管辖权仅关注判决作出国管辖权是否适格，并不关注判

决作出国国内法院管辖体制等国内法问题。在审查外国法院是否具有管辖权时，国际上主要有以下几种做法：第一，依承认和执行判决国家的内国法律来确定原判决国法院的管辖权，德国、英国、东欧等国家依照此种方法确定管辖权。第二，依判决作出国法律来判定其管辖权，欧盟多实行此种方法。第三，管辖权确定方法较为灵活，并不强制要求按照第一种方法确定管辖权，可依照有关外国法院相关规定确定管辖权，日本、匈牙利、西班牙等国均实行此种方式。第四，依照多数国际条约的规定，只要求原判决国法院依有关条约的规定具有管辖权，其他缔约国便应承认其具有管辖权。[①] 如 1971 年缔结的《关于承认与执行外国民事和商事判决的公约》第 4 条就对此作出规定。[②]

（二）国家间存在互惠关系

在当今国际社会关于外国法院判决承认与执行的实践之中，除了允许内国法院对外国法院判决进行实质性审查的国家和只允许内国法院基于国际条约承认和执行外国法院判决的国家以外，其他国家一般都只规定内国法院基于互惠原则承认与执行外国法院的判决。[③] 而互惠关系的确认，国际上通常通过签署双边判决承认条约的形式进行，一旦签署相关条约，则不存在拒绝承认与执行判决的情况。

（三）不违背内国的公共秩序

在国际民商事判决中，不违背公共秩序是一条底线，也是国际社会公认的条件，各国法律、双边司法协助条约和国际公约均对公共秩序的内容作了系统的规定。公共秩序从其内容来看是关系到一国基本法律原则、道德规则、政治经济秩序等内容的；从价值上看，它是一国所认定的正义、公平等价值。因此，一国判决在被认定违背被请求国和执行国的公共秩序时，可以对其拒绝承认和执行。

---

① 屈广清、欧永福：《国际民商事诉讼程序导论》，武汉大学出版社 2016 年版，第 554 页。

② 《关于承认与执行外国民事和商事判决的公约》第 4 条原文如下："a decision rendered in one of the Contracting States shall be entitled to recognition and enforcement… 1) if the decision was given by a court considered to have jurisdiction within the meaning of this convention and…"

③ 李双元、谢石松：《国际民商事诉讼程序概论》，武汉大学出版社 2001 年版，第 465~468 页。

（四）判决作出国法院的诉讼程序公正

诉讼程序公正是判决作出后请求承认和执行过程中的必备要件。从国际实践上来看，各国对判决实体问题的审查较为宽松，除非涉及如损害判决承认与执行国家的公共秩序等，损害一国根本利益的实体性问题。但在程序问题上，各国立法和有关国际条约均规定，内国法院在承认或执行外国法院判决时，要求在判决作出的程序中，对败诉一方当事人的诉讼权利给予充分的保护。① 否则，便可以认定有关的诉讼因缺乏公正性而可以拒绝承认或执行其判决。1971 年的《关于承认和执行外国民商事判决的海牙公约》是国际层面较为广泛接受的统一行动规则，该公约第 5 条明确体现了程序公正的要求。② 现今，各国在审查判决的承认与执行时，都将判决国法院的诉讼程序公正列为必备的条件。

（五）判决已经生效且具有执行力

诉讼判决的执行通常需要参考一国是否承认和执行外国判决的相关法规，各国立法普遍规定了此点，例如依照 1979 年的《日本民事执行法》第 24 条第 3 款的规定，在没有证明外国法院是“已经确定的判决时”可以驳回执行请求。③ 但在实践中，如何判定判决为生效判决成为当今国际民事诉讼中的难点问题，国际民事诉讼案件在程序上存在着一审终审、两审终审、三审终审等多种形式，国际上公认终审判决一旦生效便立即具有执行力，非终审判决的执行力要看案件是否上诉，且为了防止滥诉，各国通常对非终审判决的上诉规定一定期限的上诉期，在上诉期内判决未生效，不具有执行力，若当事人不提起上诉，在上诉期过后，该判决即为终审判决，立即生效。而在一国承认和执行外国法院判决时，判决效力应依照何国法律判断是其中的难点问题，因为对同一类案件均具有管辖权的国家法院，各国诉讼程序不同，而从当今国际实践来看，大多数国家

① 作为败诉方而言，其诉讼权利可能因以下两种情况而受到损害，其一是未经合法传唤，其二是在无诉讼行为能力时未得到适当的代理。

② 1971 年《关于承认和执行外国民商事判决的海牙公约》第 5 条规定：“在未给予任何一方当事人充分机会陈述其意见的情况下作出的判决，缔约国可拒绝承认与执行。”

③ 白绿铉：《日本新民事诉讼法》，中国法制出版社 2000 年版。

采取依照判决作出国法律来判定判决的具体性质。中国与外国缔结相关的双边司法协助条约时均将依判决作出国判决已生效作为具有执行力或者作为承认与执行的必要条件之一。[①]

三、法院判决承认与执行的具体程序

外国法院判决的承认与执行的具体程序在国际具体实践中有多种类型，本章将对其中较为重要的三种程序作出介绍。

（一）执行令程序

执行令程序是大陆法系国家主要采用的程序，是指有关的内国法院在受理当事人或其他利害关系人提出的承认与执行某一外国法院判决的请求后，先对该外国法院判决进行审查，认为如果符合内国法所规定的有关条件，即由该法院作出裁定，并发给执行令。从而赋予该外国法院判决与内国法院判决同等的效力，并按照与执行本国法院判决的同样程序执行。法国、日本、德国就是应用此种程序的典型代表。

（二）登记程序

登记程序是普通法系国家主要采用的承认外国法院判决与执行的程序，是指被请求国法院在收到当事人的执行申请后，只要查明外国法院判决符合被请求国法律规定的条件，就予以登记，经过登记的外国法院判决就可以得到执行。英国法院目前是应用该种程序的典型代表，根据原判决法院所属国的不同，分别采用登记程序来决定是否承认与执行外国法院判决。

（三）重新审理程序

重新审理程序是普通法系常采用的承认与执行外国法院判决的重要程序之一，即被请求国法院不直接承认与执行外国法院的判决，而是要求申请承认和执行的当事人以该外国法院判决为依据，在被请求国法院重新提起诉讼，由被请求国法院进行审查，如果被申请执行人提出异议则还要进行审理。被请求国

① 如1987年《中法司法协助协定》第22条、1987年《中波（兰）司法协助协定》第20条、1989年《中蒙司法协助条约》第18条、1991《中意司法协助条约》第21条，等。

法院如果认为该外国法院判决与本国法律并无抵触，作出一个与外国法院判决内容相同的判决，并按照本国的执行程序予以执行。这种程序在性质上已经不再是外国法院判决的承认和执行程序。这种做法与英美法系国家在传统上不承认外国法的法律相同，即仅承认被转化成内国法院判决的外国判决。

【案例摘录与评析】

国际民事诉讼法院判决的承认与执行案例[①]

SOCIETY OF LLOYD'S v. SIEMON–NETTO
United States Court of Appeals, District of Columbia Circuit, 2006
457 F.3d 94

Background: Overseer of English insurance syndicates brought action against American syndicate member to enforce money judgments obtained in England. Member asserted counterclaims. The United States District Court for the District of Columbia granted summary judgment for plaintiff. Member appealed.

Opinion for the court filed by Circuit Judge GARLAND.

Defendants Gillian and Uwe Siemon–Netto are two among the hundreds of "Names" whom the Society of Lloyd's has sued for nonpayment of reinsurance premiums. The English High Court of Justice, Queen's Bench Division, entered money judgments in favor of Lloyd's against the Siemon–Nettos. Lloyd's then sued to enforce those judgments in the United States District Court for the District of Columbia. The district court granted summary judgment in favor of Lloyd's ,and we now affirm.

I

A

The Parliament of the United Kingdom authorized the Society of Lloyd's to regulate a London insurance market through a series of Parliamentary Acts, known as the "Lloyd's Acts," passed between 1871 and 1982. In worth, the Fifth Circuit explained the structure of the Lloyd's market Lloyd's is a 300–year–old market in which individual and corporate underwriters known as "Names"

① Society of Lloyd's v. Siemon-Netto United States Court of Appeals, District of Columbia Circuit. August 8, 2006457 F.3d 94372 U.S.App.D.C. 448.

underwrite insurance. The Corporation of Lloyd's, which is also known as the Society of Lloyd's, provides the building and personnel necessary to the market's administrative operations. The Corporation is run by the Council of Lloyd's, which promulgates "Byelaws", regulates the market, and generally controls Lloyd's administrative functions. Lloyd's does not underwrite insurance; the Names do so by forming groups known as syndicates. Within each syndicate, participating Names underwrite for their own accounts and at neither own risk...... Each syndicate is managed and operated by a Managing Agent, who owes the Names a contractual duty to conduct the syndicate's affairs with reasonable care...

Names must become members of Lloyd's in order to participate in the market. Prospective members are solicited and assisted in the process of joining by Member's Agents, whose duties to the Names are fiduciary in nature.

Names must pass a means test to ensure their ability to meet their underwriting obligations, post security (typically, a letter of credit), and personally appear in London before a representative of the Council of Lloyd's to acknowledge their awareness of the various risks and requirements of membership, and in particular the fact that underwriting in the Lloyd's market subjects them to unlimited personal liability.

Haynsworth, 121 F.3d at 958–59.

B

Gillian and Uwe Siemon-Netto were among the Names who neither accepted their settlement offers nor paid the reinsurance premium for their outstanding underwriting liabilities. Nor did they take the opportunity afforded by the English courts to pursue separate fraud claims against Lloyd's .

On March 24, 1997, Lloyd's sued the Siemon–Nettos in England for breach of their contractual obligations to pay the reinsurance premiums. The Siemon–Nettos' counsel entered an appearance on their behalf. The English courts granted summary judgment against the Siemon Nettos in the Fraser case, see Society of Lloyd's v. Fraser, [1998] EWCA (Civ)1378, and on December 21, 1998, entered individual money judgments against Gillian Siemon–Netto for £280,055.72 and against Uwe Siemon–Netto for £87,109.97, On July 15, 2003, Lloyd's filed suit against the Siemon–Nettos in the United States District Court for the District of Columbia, seeking recognition and enforcement of the English judgments under the District's Uniform Foreign Money Judgments Recognition Act of 1995 ("Recognition Act"), D. C. Code § 15–381 et seq. Venue was based on the Siemon Nettos' status as District residents and jurisdiction on diversity of citizenship.

II

Section 15–382 of the Recognition Act provides, in pertinent part, that "except as provided in section 15–383," a "foreign-money judgment is enforceable in the same manner as the judgment of a sister jurisdiction which is entitled to full faith and credit." D. C. Code § 15–382. 3 Section 15–383 contains a list of specific exceptions, only one of which the Siemon–Nettos claim here:

A foreign-money judgment need not be recognized if: TTT (3)[t]he cause of action on which the judgment is based is repugnant to the public policy of the District of Columbia.

D.C.Code § 15–383(b)(3). Concluding that none of the Siemon–Nettos' four affirmative defenses came within that exception, the district court struck them all as legally insufficient to bar enforcement of the English judgments. We consider the first defense in subpart A, and the remaining defenses in subpart B.

As their first affirmative defense, the Siemon–Nettos' contend that "the foreign-money judgment[s] obtained by Lloyd's in the courts of the United Kingdom [are] repugnant to the public policy of the District of Columbia and should not be recognized because the cause of action on which [they were] based conflicts with the public policy of the District of Columbia." Am. Answer ¶ 69. The defendants list three grounds for finding repugnancy: (1) "a contract cannot be enforced against the party who did not knowingly assent to its terms"; (2) "the legislation on which the foreign cause of action was based (Lloyd's Act 1982) and [the] Reconstruction and Renewal Byelaw were unenforceable and voidable as a result of Lloyd's failure to satisfy the conditions imposed on it by the in exchange for the legislation"; and (3) "the Lloyd's Act 1982 constituted an unlawful delegation of legislative and governmental power to Lloyd's, a private business entity".

1. As their first ground, the defendants contend that the English judgments are repugnant to District public policy because they enforce a contract to which they did not assent. The contract at issue, they argue, is the Equitas reinsurance contract. That contract was not signed by them, butrather by the substitute agent appointed by Lloyd's to negotiate and sign for all Names who rejected the Reconstruction and Renewal (R & R) Plan. Recognition of such a contract, they insist, is repugnant to the general contract law principle that a contract requires mutual assent.

Section 15–383(b)(3) of the Recognition Act permits non recognition of a foreign judgment only if "the cause of action on which [it] is based" is repugnant to public policy. D. C.Code § 15–383(b)(3) (emphasis added). A cause of action is the legal authority (here, English contract law) that permits a court to provide redress for a particular kind of claim (here, Lloyd's contention that the defendants breached their obligations to pay the reinsurance premiums). See Trudeau v. FTC, 456 F.3d 178, 188 n. 15 (D. C. Cir. July 28, 2006). Accordingly, the dispositive question is whether the core principles of English contract law are repugnant to the public policy of the District of Columbia, not whether any particular application of that cause of action is repugnant.

That question is easily answered. As the district court noted, the Siemon–Nettos "have not suggested that English contract law principles differ substantively from those in the District of Columbia." Mem. Op. at 7 (Aug. 20, 2004). Indeed, District of Columbia contract law, like American contract law in general, is historically derived from (and similar to) the English common law of contract. That being the case, it would be hard to regard the latter as repugnant to the former, and no federal court has done so.

The defendants do not suggest, for example, that English contract law principles permit parties to be bound to a contract without their consent. Rather, they contend only that this is the "practical effect" of the English judgments holding them responsible for a reinsurance contract they refused to sign. Appellant's Br. But even if we were to consider repugnancy on such an "as applied" basis, we still could not find the judgments repugnant to public policy, because the English court did not bind the Siemon–Nettos to a contract to which they did not assent. To the contrary, it held them to a contract to which they did assent: the General Undertaking.

When the Siemon–Nettos became Names, they (not their agents) personally signed a "standardized contract between Lloyd's and the individual Names" known as the General Undertaking. Hayns-worth, 121 F.3d at 959; see J.A. 25–26(showing the signature of Gillian Siemon–Netto on a copy of the General Undertaking dated Sept. 9, 1986); J.A. 28–29 (showing the signature of Uwe Siemon-Netto on a copy of the General Undertaking dated Jan. 1, 1988). Under the General Under-taking, the Siemon–Nettos agreed to be bound by the Lloyd's Acts 1871–1982, as well as by current and future Lloyd's Bye-laws. See General Undertaking ¶ 1; Oral Arg. Tr. at 11–12. The Lloyd's Act 1982 specifically authorized Lloyd's to make Byelaws for the purpose of appointing substitute agents to bind Names, see Lloyd's Act, 1982, Sched. 2, § 18(b), and such a "Substitute Agents Byelaw" was in existence when the defendants signed the General Undertaking, see J.A. 32–33.Thereafter, Lloyd's issued another series of Byelaws that authorized the appointment of "substitute agent[s] on behalf of Names specifically 'to execute the Reinsurance Contract for itself and on behalf of the Members.' " Turner, 303 F.3d at 328 n. 3 (citing Lloyd's Byelaw No. 20 of 1983; Byelaw No. 82 of 1995; AUA9 Resolution of 1996).

It was no doubt risky for the defendants to agree to be bound by future Byelaws in this way. But the General Undertaking was no contract of adhesion. The Siemon–Nettos were investors who qualified for status as Lloyd's Names under a set of stringent criteria, and who presumably thought the upside potential was worth the downside risk (including the express risk of unlimited personal liability). Regardless of whether we would reach the same disposition under District of Columbia contract law, we cannot say that the English courts' decision to bind the defendants under these circumstances is repugnant to the public policy of this jurisdiction.

The defendants' second ground for claiming that the English judgments are repugnant to District policy begins with their contention that the legislation (the Lloyd's Act 1982) that permitted Lloyd's to promulgate Byelaws—particularly the Byelaws that authorized Lloyd's to appoint substitute agents to execute the reinsurance contract on behalf of the Names—also imposed certain conditions on Lloyd's (i.e., the provision of better quality information to Names about the status of the Lloyd's market). See Am. Answer 40–43. The defendants argue that, because Lloyd's assertedly failed to satisfy those conditions, the Byelaws assed pursuant to that legislation "were unenforceable and voidable." Id. ¶ 69. But the question of whether the Lloyd's Byelaws were valid under English law is itself a question of English—not District of Columbia—law. And it is a question that the English courts have already answered, concluding that the pertinent Byelaws are indeed valid. See Society of Lloyd's v. Leighs, [1997] C.L.C. 759 (Q.B.). We cannot reconsider that decision here. See Medellin v. Dretke, 544 U.S. 660, 670, 125mS.Ct. 2088, 161 L.Ed.2d 982 (2005) {"[W]here 'comity of this nation' calls for recognition of a judgment rendered abroad, 'the merits of the case should not be tried afresh upon the mere assertion that the judgment was erroneous in law or in fact.' "} [quoting Hilton v. Guyot, 159 U.S. 113, 202–03, 16 S.Ct.139, 40 L. Ed. 95 (1895)]. Certainly the defendants have pointed to nothing about the principles applied by the English courts in reaching that decision that would render repugnant the contractual cause of action on which Lloyd's judgments are based.

The third ground advanced by the defendants is their claim that "the Lloyd's Act 1982 [itself] constituted an unlawful delegation of legislative and governmental power to Lloyd's, a private business entity". Am. Answer 69. But whether the Lloyd's Act constituted an "unlawful delegation" under English law is again a question that only the English courts can answer; in fact, it is a question hat the act of state doctrine bars us from even asking. See World Wide Minerals, Ltd. v. Republic of Kazakhstan, 296 F.3d 1154, 1164 (D.C.Cir.2002) (noting that the "act of state doctrine 'precludes the courts of this country from inquiring into the validity of the public acts a recognized foreign sovereign power committed within its own territory' ") [quoting Banco Nacional de Cuba v. Sabbatino, 376 U.S. 398,401, 84 S. Ct. 923, 11 L.Ed.2d 804 (1964)]. Moreover, there is once again nothing in the defendants' argument to support the only ground the defendants advance for non-recognition of Lloyd's English judgments: that the contractual cause of action on which those judgments are based is repugnant to District policy.

In sum, we conclude that the district court committed no error in striking any of the Siemon–Nettos' affirmative defenses under Federal Rule of Civil Procedure.

At oral argument, counsel for the defendants made clear that the underlying basis of their defense is their belief that the English courts are biased in favor of Lloyd's: that is, that those courts have a "bias and prejudice in favor of Lloyd's under circumstances which make it impossible for a Name to win." Oral Arg. Tr. at. The Recognition Act includes an exception for this kind of defense to a foreign judgment, but it requires proof that the "judgment was rendered under a system that does not provide impartial tribunals or procedures compatible with the requirements of due process of law." D.C. Code§ 15–383(a)(1).

The defendants do not assert that English courts fall within that category and could not prove it if they did. Indeed, the Siemon–Nettos' only evidence of the English courts' asserted "bias and prejudice" is that other Names in their position—whose arguments they believe had merit—lost their cases in those courts. But the fact that the Names' arguments did not prevail hardly establishes the partiality of the courts that heard them. Indeed, if it did, the fact that Names have lost similar (albeit not identical) cases in eight United States Courts of Appeals, see supra note , would require us to reach the same conclusion regarding American courts.

【本案评析】

在上述案例中，美国法院以作出该判决的诉讼不符合被请求国的基本程序为由拒绝承认与执行。在司法实践中，美国对于判决的承认与执行的问题，一般是区分金钱判决和非金钱判决两种。对于金钱判决，大多数州的立法与司法实践都遵循英国法中的重新审理程序，要求利害关系人在美国法院提起一个新的诉讼，由有关的美国法院作出一个新的判决，之后才可以进行执行。请求承认与执行外国法院判决的当事人或其他利害关系人既可以以有关的外国法院判决为依据重新提起一个诉讼，也可以以原来的诉讼为依据重新提起诉讼。在前一种情况下，请求人应向法院提供所有能证实有关判决的文件，美国法院在审查了所有文件及有关的情况以后，认为不违反美国现行法律规定的，即作出一个判决，并交付执行。在后一种情况下，美国法院将重新审理有关案件，并作出判决，交付执行。

【延伸阅读】

一、相关学术论著

（一）著作类

1. 黄进：《国际商事争议解决机制研究》，武汉大学出版社 2010 年版。

2. 王吉文：《外国判决承认与执行制度研究》，中国政法大学出版社 2003 年版。

3. 宣增益:《国家间判决承认与执行问题研究》,中国政法大学出版社 2009 年版。

4. 屈广清、欧永福:《国际民商事诉讼程序导论》,武汉大学出版社 2016 年版。

5. 李双元、谢石松:《国际民商事诉讼程序概论》,武汉大学出版社 2001 年版。

(二)期刊类

1. 郭玉军、向在胜:《欧盟〈民商事管辖权及判决的承认与执行条例〉》,载《法学评论》2001 年第 2 期。

2. 杜涛:《互惠原则与外国法院判决的承认与执行》,载《环球法律评论》2007 年第 1 期。

二、相关网络资源

1. http//www.ccmt.org.cn/(中国涉外商事海事审判网)

2. http//www.chinacourt.org/index.shtml(中国法院网)

三、相关学术知识点

在中国香港,民事诉讼作为传统的争议解决方式,是指将争议提交给法院,由法院审理民事案件并解决民事纠纷的公权力法律行动。随着香港与内地日益密切的联系,两地之间的商事纠纷解决机制的沟通和合作变得非常重要,例如两地生效判决的互相承认和执行问题。以香港单边为例,根据 2008 年 8 月 1 日《最高人民法院关于内地与香港特别行政区法院相互认可和执行当事人协议管辖的民商事案件判决的安排》(简称《安排》)规定,允许在中国内地执行香港的区域法院或以上法院作出的判决。其中,以下与强制执行相关事宜需要关注:(1)《安排》仅适用于商业合同,不包括消费者合同、雇佣关系等;(2)合同须受香港法院的专有司法管辖,即如果合同载有仲裁条款或香港法院无专有司法管辖权,《安排》则不可被援引,判决也不得在中国内地强制执行;(3)强制执行不得违背中国内地的公共政策和利益。

第五章

反倾销争端解决程序实务

【内容摘要】

反倾销争端解决，包括国内反倾销调查及WTO多边反倾销争端解决，是一种典型的国际商事争端解决程序。作为一种特殊的贸易救济争端，反倾销争端解决与后两章介绍的反补贴争端解决及保障措施争端解决存在一定的联系和区别。因此，本章从反倾销争端解决的国内和多边两个层面入手，重点介绍国内反倾销的主要程序，包括反倾销争端调查的启动、反倾销争端调查的进行、反倾销措施的实施程序以及WTO多边反倾销争端程序中的评审标准与特殊或附加程序规则等争端解决程序实务问题。鉴于GATT1994第6条和乌拉圭回合达成的《关于实施1994年关税与贸易总协定第6条的协定》（以下简称《反倾销协定》）已经成为世界各国反倾销立法和执法的重要指引，本章在介绍反倾销争端解决程序实务过程中也将其作为主要的参考依据，并广泛结合涉及《反倾销协定》的WTO争端解决案例原文进行讲解，以全面反映反倾销争端解决程序中的基本和特殊问题。

第一节　反倾销争端调查的启动

【知识背景/学习要点】

一、申请的条件

反倾销通常是由国内产业或企业向进口成员方主管机关提起，其同时需要提交一份正式的书面申请，说明发生损害性倾销的相关情况。对申请书内容的要求，WTO《反倾销协定》第 5.2 款进行了详细的规定，其必须包括倾销、损害以及两者之间具有因果关系的证据。具体而言，申请应包括申请人可合理获得的关于下列内容的信息：

（1）申请人的身份和申请人提供的对国内同类产品生产的数量和价值的说明。如代表国内产业提出书面申请，则申请应通过一份列出同类产品的所有已知国内生产者的清单（或同类产品的国内生产者协会），确认其代表提出申请的产业，并在可能的限度内，提供此类生产者所占国内同类产品生产的数量和价值的说明。

（2）对被指控的倾销产品的完整说明、所涉一个或多个原产国或出口国名称、每一已知出口商或国外生产者的身份以及已知的进口所涉产品的人员名单。

（3）所涉产品销售供一个或多个原产国或出口国国内市场消费时的价格信息（或在适当时，关于该产品自一个或多个原产国或出口国向一个或多个第三国销售价格的信息，或关于该产品推定价格的信息），出口价格信息，或在适当时该产品首次转售给进口成员领土内一独立购买者的价格信息。

（4）被指控的补贴进口产品数量变化的信息，这些进口产品对国内市场同类产品价格的影响，以及由影响国内产业状况的有关因素和指标所证明的这些产品对国内产业造成的影响，例如第 3 条第 2 款和第 4 款中所列的因素和指标。

从第 5.2 款的规定来看，申请书必须载有根据该款向申请人“可合理获得”的资料，其并不要求申请书包含任何对指控申请的分析，而只需要其包含证据意义上的支持指控的相关信息。因此，没有相关证据证明的简单判断并不是充分的，不能被认为符合这一条款的要求。

二、证据的审查

《反倾销协定》第 5.3 款的规定，进口成员主管机关应审查申请中提供的证据的准确性和充分性，以确定是否有足够的证据证明发起调查是正当的。因此，未经任何证据证实的陈述和判断不能构成《反倾销协定》第 5.3 款所指的充分证据。但是须注意，第 5.3 款本身并没有关于此项审查的特点，包括证据审查的范围以及审查的程度的任何细节规定。

（一）证据的范围

根据《反倾销协定》第 5.3 款的规定，没有经任何证据证实的陈述和判断不能构成充分的证据。但该条款并未明确规定哪些陈述和判断是需要用证据证明的，也就是说，条款中的证据涉及的范围，是否包括调查启动之后同倾销、损害及因果关系相同的证据仍不明确。然而，这却是启动调查的重要依据，因此很多专家组都通过个案解释来进行判断。

（二）审查的程度

《反倾销协定》第 5.3 款并没有要求调查主管机关有义务在作出调查决定时就对其考虑的所有潜在问题提出解决办法。[①] 专家组曾经指出，反倾销调查启动时所需的证据在数量和质量上低于调查之后对倾销、损害和因果关系初步或最终确定所需的证据。不过，在决定是否有足够证据展开调查时，调查当局并不局限于申请书内所载的资料。另外，根据《反倾销协定》第 5.6 款的规定，在特殊情况下，如有关主管机关在未收到国内产业或代表国内产业提出的发起调查的书面申请的情况下决定发起调查，则只有在具备第 5.2 款所述关于倾销、损害和因果关系的充分证据证明发起调查是正当的情况下，才可以发起调查。

三、代表性审查

反倾销调查通常根据《反倾销协定》第 4 条所界定的“由国内产业或其代表”提交的书面申请进行。[②] 主管机关一般都会对国内同类产品生产者对反倾

---

① 参 见 Panel Report, Mexico–Anti-Dumping Investigation of High Fructose Corn Syrup (HFCS) from the United States, WT/DS132/R, 28 January 2000 , paras. 7.94 and 7.102.

② 根据《反倾销协定》第 4 条“国内产业的定义”第 1 款的规定，就本协定而言，“国内产业”一词应解释为指同类产品的国内生产者全体，或指总产量构成同类产品国内总产量主要部分的国内生产者。

销调查申请表示的支持或反对的程度进行审查，从而确定申请是否是由国内产业或代表国内产业提出的，否则不得发起调查。因此，为保证反倾销调查程序的顺利启动，国内同类产品的生产商必须对申请给予足够的支持。根据《反倾销协定》第5.4款的规定，如申请达到总产量构成国内产业中表示支持或反对申请的国内同类产品生产者生产的同类产品总产量的50%以上，则该申请应被视为"由国内产业或代表国内产业提出"。但如表示支持申请的国内生产者的产量不足国内产业生产的同类产品总产量的25%，则不得发起调查。

四、启动前公告通知

进行反倾销调查的主管机关在调查开始前应对调查申请进行保密处理。《反倾销协定》第5.5款要求调查主管机关"除非已作出启动调查的决定，否则应避免公布启动调查的申请"。虽然不予公告但是进口主管机关在调查启动前应当通知出口方的政府。根据第5.5款的规定，在收到一份附有适当证明文件的申请书后，主管机关应在着手展开调查之前，通知有关出口成员的政府。对于此种通知形式，《反倾销协定》并没有进行规定，但是对于通知的时限反倾销委员会有相关建议。[①]《反倾销协定》第12.1款也有关于展开调查的公告要求。[②]

五、调查的终止

对启动反倾销调查的申请，经调查机关认定没有足够的倾销或者损害证据的，应当予以驳回，并迅速终止调查。[③] 此外，为了避免进行不必要的调查，第5.8款规定了两种立即终止调查的情况，即（1）倾销幅度属微量（即倾销幅度按出口价格的百分比表示小于2%）；（2）特定国家的进口产品的数量可忽略不计（通常不到进口成员中同类产品进口额的3%，除非这些国家合计超过该进口成

---

① 参见 *Recommendation Concerning the Timing of the Notification under Article 5.5*, adopted by the Committee on Anti-Dumping Practices on 29 October 1998, G/ADP/5, 3 November 1998.

② 参见《反倾销协定》第5.5款。另参见 *Recommendation Concerning the Timing of the Notification under Article 5.5*, adopted by the Committee on Anti-Dumping Practices on 29 October 1998, G/ADP/5, 3 November 1998.

③ 参见《反倾销协定》第5.8款。

员中同类产品进口的 7%)。[①]

从第 5.8 款规定的表述来看，两句采用了“迅速”(promptly)和“立即”(immediate)的不同措辞，反映出此条强调，微量倾销和可忽略不计损害的调查结果往往只能在调查提前进行的情况下作出。另外，与 WTO《补贴和反补贴措施协定》和《保障措施协定》不同，《反倾销协定》没有对发展中国家提出更高的要求。

【案例摘录与评析】

一、2000 年美国诉墨西哥对高果糖谷物糖浆的反倾销调查争端案[②]

MEXICO – ANTI-DUMPING INVESTIGATION OF HIGH FRUCTOSE CORN SYRUP (HFCS) FROM THE UNITED STATES
(WT/DS132/R)

7.70 In addressing this issue we must consider first, what information Article 5.2 requires to be in an application, and second, whether SECOFI's conclusion that the Sugar Chamber's application contained the information reasonably available to the Sugar Chamber on those elements was consistent with the AD Agreement. The main issue in dispute between the parties is, in a case where threat of injury is alleged, what is the information concerning the factors set forth in Article 3.4 of the AD Agreement, and what is the information regarding the existence of a causal link, that must be provided in the application, pursuant to Article 5.2(iv).

6.71 We turn first to the text of Article 5.2, which provides in pertinent part:

"An application under paragraph 1 shall include evidence of (a) dumping, (b) injury within the meaning of Article VI of GATT 1994 as interpreted by this Agreement and (c) a causal link between the dumped imports and the alleged injury. Simple assertion, unsubstantiated by relevant evidence, cannot be considered sufficient to meet the

① 参见 Appellate Body Report, Mexico-Definitive Anti-Dumping Measures on Beef and Rice, WT/DS295/AB/R, 29 November 2005, paras. 217 and 305.

② Panel Report, Mexico–Anti-Dumping Investigation of High Fructose Corn Syrup (HFCS) from the United States, WT/DS132/R, 28 January 2000, paras.7.70-7.78.

requirements of this paragraph. The application shall contain such information as is reasonably available to the applicant on the following: ...

(iv)information on the evolution of the volume of the allegedly dumped imports, the effect of these imports on prices of the like product in the domestic market and the consequent impact of the imports on the domestic industry, as demonstrated by relevant factors and indices having a bearing on the state of the domestic industry, such as those listed in paragraphs 2 and 4 of Article 3".

7.72 It is clear from the text of the provision that an application must contain "information", in the sense of evidence, regarding the consequent impact of the (allegedly dumped) imports on the domestic industry. It is also clear from the text that this "information" must "demonstrate" the consequent impact of the imports on the domestic industry.①

7.73 However, the inclusion in Article 5.2(iv) of the word "relevant" and the phrase "such as" in the reference to the factors and indices in Articles 3.2 and 3.4 in our view makes it clear that an application is not required to contain information on all the factors and indices set forth in Articles 3.2 and 3.4. Rather, Article 5.2(iv) requires that the application contain information on factors and indices relating to the impact of imports on the domestic industry, and refers to Articles 3.2 and 3.4 as illustrative of factors which may be relevant.② Which factors and indices are relevant to demonstrate the consequent impact of imports on the domestic industry will vary depending on the nature of the allegations made by the industry, and the nature of the industry itself. If the industry provides information reasonably available to it concerning factors which are relevant to the allegation of injury (or threat of injury) it makes in the application, and the information concerning those factors demonstrates, that is, "shows evidence of", the consequent impact of dumped imports on the domestic industry, we believe that Article 5.2(iv) is satisfied.③

7.74 Obviously, the quantity and quality of the information provided by the applicant need not be such as would be required in order to make a preliminary or final determination of injury. Moreover, the applicant need only provide such information as is "reasonably available" to it with respect to the relevant factors. Since information regarding the factors and indices set out in Article 3.4 concerns the state of the domestic industry and its operations, such information would generally be available to applicants. Nevertheless, we note that an application which is consistent

---

① We do not understand "demonstrate" in this context to mean "prove", but rather to mean "show evidence of; describe or explain by help of specimens...". Concise Oxford Dictionary, 1976.

② However, as discussed in section VII.D.1. below, the requirements of Article 3.4 are not merely illustrative in the context of final determinations.

③ This does not mean that such an application is or would necessarily be sufficient for purposes of initiation. That is a separate issue, which is addressed further below.

with the requirements of Article 5.2 will not necessarily contain sufficient evidence to justify initiation under Article 5.3.①

7.75 The application submitted by the Sugar Chamber on its face contains information on relevant Article 3.4 factors, and that information shows evidence of the allegations of threat of injury and causal link in the application. Some of this information is contained in confidential Annexes to the application. Some of this information is requested in sections of the SECOFI application form to which the Sugar Chamber responded "N/A".② However, we do not consider that whether the Sugar Chamber filled out the application form provided by SECOFI in the clearest and best manner is in any way dispositive of whether the application satisfied the requirements of Article 5.2. Rather, we look to whether the necessary information was actually provided.

7.76 The Sugar Chamber alleged that dumped imports of HFCS threatened the domestic industry with material injury. The application contained information showing increases in imports, and information showing that market prices for sugar did not reach the maximum price level, while HFCS was priced below sugar, HFCS substitutes for sugar, and producers in the United States could reduce their prices. The application also contained information, *inter alia*, on the Mexican sugar producers' production, sales, exports, imports, consumption, inventories and employment③; cash flow, financial situation, income, production costs and financial ratios④; installed capacity⑤; and investment projects in the sugar industry⑥. The United States argues that an application

① *Guatemala-Cement Panel Report*, para. 7.49-7.51. As the Panel noted in that case, the investigating authority may, but is not required to, obtain additional information which, together with that provided in the application, constitutes sufficient evidence to justify initiation under Article 5.3. *Id.* para. 7.53.

② We note in this regard that SECOFI's application form instructs applicants, in para. 4.4 "It is important to mention that an anti-dumping investigation cannot be initiated for injury and threat of injury simultaneously, given that the two concepts are mutually exclusive". US-5 (a) & (b) . This instruction may be the reason the Sugar Chamber responded "N/A" to section 4.2 of the application form, which sets out the information SECOFI requires for applications alleging injury, but provided information in response to section 4.3 of the application, which sets out the information SECOFI requires for applications alleging threat of injury. Section 4.3 of the application form requests information on the Article 3.7 factors, and on expected return on investments, but does not specifically mention information concerning consequent impact on the domestic industry, or refer to the Article 3.2 and 3.4 factors. The Sugar Chamber's application includes information on these latter as annexes to its response under section 4.3 of the application.

③ See Application, MEXICO-16 and Annex 6-A to Application, and the national balance for sugar, MEXICO-17.

④ See Application, MEXICO-16 and Annexes 4.19, 4.20 and 4.21 to Application, MEXICO-33.

⑤ See Application, MEXICO-16 and Annex 4.22 to Application, MEXICO-30.

⑥ See Application, MEXICO-16 and Annex 4.24 to Application, MEXICO-32.

alleging only threat of material injury must contain some "meaningful analysis" of the likely impact of allegedly dumped imports on the domestic industry, and that the Sugar Chamber's application in this case did not. However, Article 5.2 does not require an application to contain analysis, but rather to contain information, in the sense of evidence, in support of allegations. While we recognize that some analysis linking the information and the allegations would be helpful in assessing the merits of an application, we cannot read the text of Article 5.2 as requiring such an analysis in the application itself.①

7.77 This information, if read in the light of the allegations, provides evidence in support of the allegation that dumped imports of HFCS from the United States threatened material injury to the Mexican sugar industry. The United States has concentrated much of its argument on the proposition that the application should have contained information concerning "potential negative effects" on various of the Article 3.4 factors. In this regard, we note that information, in the sense of evidence, concerning the future is at best a calculated estimate based on past experience. While we agree that specific projections concerning a domestic industry's sales, output, profits, market share, employment, etc., would certainly be relevant in an application alleging threat of material injury, we cannot conclude that the absence of such projections constitutes a fatal flaw which demands rejection of the application.

7.78 We therefore conclude that the Sugar Chamber's application was consistent with the requirements of Article 5.2(iv) of the AD Agreement.

【本案评析】

以上案例节选自2000年美国诉墨西哥对高果糖谷物糖浆的反倾销调查争端案专家组报告。在审理根据《反倾销协定》第5.2款第（4）项提出的申请中必须提供的资料的性质和范围时，该案专家组指出，申请人提供信息的数量和质量显然不需要达到初步或最后确定损害的要求。此外，申请人只需就有关因素提供"合理可获得"的信息。关于第3.4款所列因素和指数的资料涉及国内工业及其运作的状况，申请人一般可以获得这些资料。然而，符合第5.2款要求的申请并不一定包含足够的证据来证明根据第5.3款启动程序是正当的。

① Of course, the investigating authority must examine the accuracy and adequacy of the information in the application to determine whether there is sufficient evidence to justify initiation, pursuant to Article 5.3, a question which is addressed further below. However, this obligation falls on the investigating authority, and does not imply a requirement for analysis resting on the applicant.

二、2007 年危地马拉诉墨西哥对危地马拉钢管和管材产品反倾销措施案①

Mexico - Anti-dumping Duties on Steel Pipes and
Tubes from Guatemala
(WT/DS331/R)

7.15 In respect of Economía's initiation of the investigation, Guatemala has made claims of violation of three provisions: Articles 5.2, 5.3 and 5.8 of the *Anti-Dumping Agreement*.② At the heart of all of these claims is Guatemala's allegation that the evidence pertaining to dumping and to injury on which Economía based its initiation decision was "insufficient" in the sense of Article 5.3, in a number of respects, such that Economía's evaluation of that evidence was inadequate for the purposes of Article 5.3. This central question thus is the main focus of our analysis. In order to structure this analysis, we first cite the text of these provisions and consider the nature of, and relationship among, the obligations that they contain.

...

7.19 Article 5.2 refers to the contents of the application by the domestic industry requesting the initiation of an investigation. It requires that the application shall include, *inter alia*, information on certain specific areas to the extent that it is "reasonably available" to the applicant. In this regard, Article 5.2 states that "[s]imple assertion, unsubstantiated by relevant evidence, cannot be considered sufficient to meet the requirements of this paragraph". Article 5.3 makes it clear that the investigating authority has to examine the accuracy and adequacy of the evidence provided in the application to determine whether there is sufficient evidence to justify the initiation of the investigation. In any case where the investigating authority judges the evidence in the application not to be a sufficient basis for initiating an investigation, Article 5.8 requires the authority to reject the application and terminate the investigation.

---

① Panel Report, Mexico-Anti-dumping Duties on Steel Pipes and Tubes from Guatemala, WT/DS331/R, adopted 24 July 2007, paras.7.15-7.25.

② We address below, paras. 7.346-7.347, Guatemala's claim under Article 5.4–that Economía should have, but did not, reassess "standing" during the course of the investigation as the covered product scope was enlarged–in the context of Guatemala's other claims and arguments concerning those changes in the product scope.

7.20 Mexico suggests that where the evidence in the application is sufficient to initiate an investigation, the mere fact that an investigating authority initiated the investigation indicates that it examined the evidence in the application and determined that it was sufficient to justify initiation for the purposes of Article 5.3. Mexico cites the *EC-Bed Linen* panel report in support of this proposition[①]. We note that the facts and legal issues in that case were different from the case before us. In particular, in contrast to Guatemala's claim before us, India's claim in that case was purely process-related; that is, India claimed that the European Communities failed *to examine* the accuracy and adequacy of the evidence before initiating the investigation, but made no claim in respect of the *sufficiency* of that evidence.[②] Although the *EC-Bed Linen* panel found that Article 5.3 does not address the *nature* of the examination to be carried out, and does not require the investigating authority to explain how it performed its examination[③], we do not read that case as standing for the proposition implied by Mexico[④], namely that Article 5.3 imposes *no substantive* obligation upon an investigating authority in respect of its assessment of the *sufficiency* of the evidence before it. Thus, in our view, the findings of the *EC-Bed Linen* panel are not germane to the substantive issue before us, which concerns Economía's assessment of the sufficiency of the evidence before it at the time of initiation.

7.21 Although there is no express reference to evidence of "dumping" or "injury" or "causation" in Article 5.3, evidence on the three elements necessary for the imposition of an anti-dumping measure may be inferred into Article 5.3 by way of Article 5.2. In particular, Article 5.2 requires that the application contain evidence on dumping, injury and causation, and Article 5.3 requires the investigating authority to satisfy itself as to the accuracy and adequacy of "the evidence provided in the application" to determine that that evidence is sufficient to justify initiation. Thus, reading Article 5.3 in the context of Article 5.2 makes clear that the evidence to which Article 5.3 refers is the evidence in the application concerning dumping, injury and causation. We note, as have past panels in this context, that the meanings of the concepts of "dumping", "injury" and "causation" in Article 5 are the same as those in the relevant substantive provisions of the Agreement (i.e., Article 2 for dumping and Article 3 for

① Panel Report, *EC-Bed Linen*, paras. 6.199-6.201.

② See Panel Report, *EC-Bed Linen*, para. 6.200.

③ We note that the panel in *Mexico-Corn Syrup* (para. 7.102) similarly concluded that Article 5.3 did not itself establish any obligation to make, or to make known, a determination concerning issues underlying the decision to initiate.

④ Mexico's response to question 137 from the Panel.

injury and causation).[①]

7.22 We must emphasize, however, that while the concepts are the same, we agree with Mexico[②] that it is not necessary for an investigating authority to have irrefutable proof of dumping or injury prior to initiating an anti-dumping investigation.[③] We note in this respect that Article 5.1 refers to the initiation of an investigation "to determine the existence, degree and effect of any *alleged dumping*" (emphasis added), and that Article 5.2 refers to "alleged injury", the "allegedly dumped product" and "allegedly dumped imports". We also are mindful that an anti-dumping investigation is a process where certainty on the existence of all of the elements necessary in order to adopt a measure is reached gradually as the investigation moves forward.[④] While we disagree with Mexico that the information contained in a request for initiation does not have to be more than a "mere indication" ("*mero indicio*")[⑤], we note that Mexico nevertheless acknowledges that the investigating authority must verify that the evidence presented constitutes "reasonable indications" (*indicios razonables*) in order to initiate.[⑥]

7.23 Turning now in more detail to the provisions cited by Guatemala, we first consider Article 5.2. Here, a claim under Article 5.2 may focus on whether an application contains information "reasonably available" to the applicant, but the textual differences between Articles 5.2 and 5.3 lead us to observe that the "reasonable availability" of the evidence to the applicant is not determinative as to the "sufficiency", in the sense of Article 5.3, of that evidence as the basis for an investigating authority's decision to initiate. By the same token, in examining whether there is sufficient evidence to justify initiation, an investigating authority is not precluded from gathering information additional to that in the application so as to corroborate and verify the contents of the application.[⑦]

7.24 That said, the chapeau of Article 5.2 makes clear that in an application, "[s]imple assertion, unsubstantiated by relevant evidence, cannot be considered sufficient to meet the

---

① Panel Report, *Guatemala-Cement II*, para. 8.35; Panel Report, Argentina–Poultry Anti-Dumping Duties, paras. 7.61, 7.62.

② "... it is clear that such evidence does not necessarily have to be of the quality that would be necessary to support a preliminary or final determination" (emphasis in original). First written submission of Mexico, para. 9.

③ Panel Report, Guatemala-Cement II, para. 8.35.

④ Panel Report, Guatemala-Cement II, paras. 8.35, 8.36; *Argentina–Poultry Anti-Dumping Duties*, paras. 7.61, 7.62.

⑤ Second oral submission of Mexico, para. 5(i).

⑥ See Mexico's response to question 136 from the Panel.

⑦ Panel Report, *Guatemala–Cement II*, para. 8.62; Panel Report, *US–Softwood Lumber* V, para. 7.75 (point not appealed).

requirements of this paragraph." Therefore, for the purpose of Article 5.2, the applicant must submit a degree of actual evidence of alleged dumping allegedly causing injury, and for the purpose of Article 5.3, that evidence must constitute an objectively *sufficient* factual basis to initiate an investigation. While the absolute threshold of sufficiency will depend upon the circumstances of a given case, Article 5.3 makes clear that the determination of sufficiency must be based on an assessment of the "accuracy" and "adequacy" of the information. In this context, we are mindful that a piece of evidence that on its own might appear to be of little or no probative value *could*, when placed beside other evidence of the same nature, form part of a body of evidence that, in totality, was "sufficient". We are, furthermore, aware that it is appropriate for a panel to examine the evidence before the investigating authority at the time of the decision in the light of the investigating authority's own methodology and to review the decision on its own terms. As we have already mentioned, we are not entitled to conduct a *de novo* review of the investigating authority's determinations.①

7.25 Turning to Article 5.8, this provision requires the rejection of an application and prompt termination of the investigation as soon as the authorities concerned are satisfied that there is not sufficient evidence of either dumping or injury to justify proceeding with the case. The portion of Article 5.8 that applies to the pre-initiation phase of an anti-dumping investigation ("an application ... shall be rejected ...") does not impose additional substantive obligations beyond those in Article 5.3 on the authority in connection with the initiation of an investigation.② That is, if there is sufficient evidence to justify initiation under Article 5.3, there can be no violation of Article 5.8 in not rejecting the application at that point.③

【本案评析】

以上案例节选自2007年危地马拉诉墨西哥对危地马拉钢管和管材产品反倾销措施案专家组报告。该案专家组指出，虽然《反倾销协定》第5.3款没有明确提及“倾销”或“损害”或“因果关系”的证据，但是如果将第5.3款置于5.2款的上下文中进行解释，就可以明确地知道，第5.3款所指的证据是在涉及申请书中“倾销”或“损害”或“因果关系”的证据。

① See e.g. Appellate Body Report, *US–Countervailing Duty Investigation on DRAMS*, paras. 141-152.

② We find support in Panel Report, *Guatemala–Cement II*, paras. 8.72-8.75.

③ In response to questioning, Guatemala confirmed that its Article 5.8 claim flows from its claims under Article 5.2 and/or Article 5.3, both jointly and independently. See Guatemala's response to question 3 from the Panel.

三、2000年危地马拉对来自墨西哥的灰波特兰水泥采取最终反倾销措施争端案①

GUATEMALA- DEFINITIVE ANTI-DUMPING MEASURES ON GREY PORTLAND CEMENT FROM MEXICO
(WT/DS156/R)

8.34 Guatemala argues that the evidence of normal value and export price before its investigating authority was sufficient to justify the initiation of an investigation. Guatemala asserts that the AD Agreement does not require that an application contain information on prices for a particular number of transactions or a particular minimum value or volume of sales, and that there is no requirement to provide evidence on possible adjustments, since the relevant information is not available to applicants. In Guatemala's view, Articles 2.1 (defining dumping), 2.4 (requirement of a fair comparison), and 5.8 (rejection of application and termination of investigation for lack of sufficient evidence) are not applicable to the decision to initiate. Guatemala asserts that it complied with Articles 5.1, (written application), 5.2 (requirement of evidence in application), and 5.3 (examination of accuracy and adequacy of evidence in application to determine sufficiency to initiate), which in its view are the only provisions of the AD Agreement which apply at the initiation stage.

8.35 In light of Guatemala's arguments, we need to examine the relationship between the requirements of Article 5.3 regarding sufficiency of evidence to justify the initiation of an investigation and the substantive provisions in Article 2 regarding dumping. In this respect, we first observe that, although there is no express reference to evidence of dumping in Article 5.3, evidence on the three elements necessary for the imposition of an anti-dumping measure may be inferred into Article 5.3 by way of Article 5.2. In other words, Article 5.2 requires that the application contain sufficient evidence on dumping, injury and causation, while Article 5.3 requires the investigating authority to satisfy itself as to the accuracy and adequacy of the evidence to determine that it is sufficient to justify initiation. Thus, reading Article 5.3 in the context of Article 5.2, the evidence mentioned in Article 5.3 must be evidence of dumping, injury and causation. We further observe that the only clarification of the term "dumping" in the AD Agreement is that

① Panel Report, Guatemala–Definitive Anti-Dumping Measures on Grey Portland Cement from Mexico , WT/DS156/R, adopted 17 November 2000, paras.8.34-8.35 and 8.59-8.62.

contained in Article 2. In consequence, in order to determine that there is sufficient evidence of dumping, the investigating authority cannot entirely disregard the elements that configure the existence of this practice as outlined in Article 2. This analysis is done not with a view to making a determination that Article 2 has been violated through the initiation of an investigation, but rather to provide guidance in our review of the Ministry's determination that there was sufficient evidence of dumping to warrant an investigation. We do not of course mean to suggest that an investigating authority must have before it at the time it initiates an investigation evidence of dumping within the meaning of Article 2 of the quantity and quality that would be necessary to support a preliminary or final determination. An anti-dumping investigation is a process where certainty on the existence of all the elements necessary in order to adopt a measure is reached gradually as the investigation moves forward. However, the evidence must be such that an unbiased and objective investigating authority could determine that there was sufficient evidence of dumping within the meaning of Article 2 to justify initiation of an investigation. ①

...

2. Sufficiency of the application – Article 5.2

8.59 In light of our finding that the Ministry's determination that it had sufficient evidence to justify the initiation of an investigation was inconsistent with Article 5.3, we do not consider it necessary to rule on Mexico's Article 5.2 claims regarding the sufficiency of Cementos Progreso's application.

8.60 We would note, however, that for the purposes of our analysis of claims under Article 5.3, we assumed that information in the application was, in fact, all that was reasonably available to the applicant. We would like to make clear that this assumption has been made purely for the purpose of analysis, and we are not at all convinced that the information presented in the application was all that was reasonably available to the applicant, especially with regard to evidence of threat of injury.

8.61 Article 5.2(iv) of the AD Agreement provides that an application "shall contain such information as is reasonably available to the applicant on ... the effect of the allegedly dumped

① On this question we concur fully with the reasoning of the Guatemala-Cement I panel when they state that: "In our view, the reference in Article 5.2 to 'dumping' must be read as a reference to dumping as it is defined in Article 2. This does not, of course, mean that the evidence provided in the application must be of the quantity and quality that would be necessary to make a preliminary or final determination of dumping. However, evidence of the relevant type is, in our view, required in a case such as this one where it is obvious on the face of the application that the normal value and export price alleged in the application will require adjustments in order to effectuate a fair comparison. At a minimum, there should be some recognition that a fair comparison will require such adjustments. " Guatemala-Cement I, WT/DS60/R, para. 7.64.

imports on prices of the like product in the domestic market, and the consequent impact of allegedly dumped imports on the domestic industry". Such information would normally be in the hands of the domestic industry filing an application for anti-dumping relief. This is even more likely to be the case when the company bringing the application is the sole producer of the domestic product, as in this investigation. Of the specific elements for which information is required in Article 5.2(iv), Cementos Progresos's application contained little evidence on the evolution of the volume of the allegedly dumped imports. It might have been reasonable for the investigating authority not to expect the applicant to provide information on the evolution of the volume of the imports, as a private company might not have easy access to the import statistics kept by the national customs authority. However, regarding the other factors in Article 5.2(iv), concerning information on the effect of the allegedly dumped imports on prices of the domestic like product in the domestic market and consequent impact of the imports on the domestic industry, Cementos Progreso merely makes some allegations. These allegations are not supported by evidence, and in most cases are not quantified. Given that this information should be readily available to the sole domestic producer composing the domestic industry producing cement in Guatemala, this information should have been included in the application.

8.62 It is evident to us that the Guatemalan authorities relied on the same evidence that was presented in the application for purposes of the initiation. We have expressed the view that Articles 5.2 and 5.3 contain different obligations. One of the consequences of this difference in obligations is that investigating authorities need not content themselves with the information provided in the application but may gather information on their own in order to meet the standard of sufficient evidence for initiation in Article 5.3. On this issue we are in full agreement with the reasoning and findings expressed in by the *Guatemala-Cement I* panel which made the following comments:

> "7.53 We have concluded that the question whether there is 'sufficient evidence' to justify initiation is not answered by a determination that the application contains all the information 'reasonably available' to the applicant on the factors specified in Article 5.2 (i)- (iv). This does not, however, mean that investigations may not be initiated in cases where 'sufficient evidence' is not 'reasonably available' to the applicant. In particular, there is nothing in the Agreement to prevent an investigating authority from seeking evidence and information on its own, that would allow any gaps in the evidence set forth in the application to be filled. We do not suggest that such action by the investigating authority is in any case required by the ADP Agreement. However, if, as in this case, an authority chooses to refrain from such action, the 'reasonably available'

language in Article 5.2 does not permit the initiation of an investigation based on evidence and information which, while all that is 'reasonably available' to the applicant is not, objectively judged, sufficient to justify initiation. Indeed, in this case the applicant requested that the Ministry obtain certain information on import volumes which it was unable to obtain itself. This the Ministry did not do, however, until **after** it had initiated the investigation based on the information in the application."[①]

【本案评析】

以上案例选自2000年危地马拉对来自墨西哥的灰波特兰水泥采取最终反倾销措施争端案专家组报告。该案专家组在开展反倾销[②]调查所需证据的性质和范围时指出，他们并不打算建议调查主管机关在提出第2条所指的倾销调查证据时，必须具备支持初步或最终裁定所必需的数量和质量的证据。反倾销调查是随着调查的进行，对采取措施所必需的所有要素的确定逐步达到的一个过程。然而，证据必须使无偏见和客观的调查主管机关能够用来确定，在第2条含义范围内有足够的倾销证据来证明发起调查是正当的。该案专家组也认为，《反倾销协定》第5.2款和第5.3款所规定的义务不同。这种差异导致，调查当局不必满足于申请书中提供的信息，而是可以自行收集信息，以符合第5.3款中关于启动程序的充分证据标准。

四、2000年日本诉美国《1916年反倾销法》争端案[③]

United States – Anti-Dumping Act of 1916, Complaint by Japan
(WT/DS162/R)

(d)Violation of Articles 4 and 5 of the Anti-Dumping Agreement

6.255 Japan claims that Articles 4 and 5 of the Anti-Dumping Agreement set forth requirements limiting the party or parties that may properly pursue an anti-dumping claim. Article 5.1 requires that a request for initiation of an anti-dumping investigation be made by or

① *Guatemala–Cement I*, WT/DS60/R, para. 7.53.

② 关于对国内工业造成损害的证据以及倾销进口品与损害之间的因果关系也是如此。

③ Panel Report, United States–Anti-Dumping Act of 1916, Complaint by Japan, WT/DS162/R , 29 May 2000.

on behalf of the domestic industry. Article 4.1 defines "domestic industry" for the purpose of the Anti-Dumping Agreement. Article 5.4 requires the investigating authorities to determine that an application is supported by "those producers which collective output constitutes more than 50 per cent of the total production of the like product" of those producers supporting or opposing the application. Moreover, under no circumstances can an investigation be initiated if those supporting the application account for less than 25 per cent of total domestic production of the like product. In contrast, as evidenced by the most recent cases initiated under the 1916 Act, a complaint under the 1916 Act can be initiated by a single United States producer. Article 5 also requires that applications contain evidence of the three elements of dumping, injury and causation, and sets a de minimis threshold applicable to the dumping element. The 1916 Act contains none of these elements. On the contrary, Japan argues that, under the US Federal Rules of Civil Procedure 8(a)(2), a complainant under the 1916 Act needs only to present a short and plain statement of its claims. Finally, Article 5.10 of the Anti-Dumping Agreement requires Members to complete their investigations and decide whether or not to impose duties within 18 months. The 1916 Act contains no such deadline.

6.256 We note that Japan's claims under Article 4 and 5 of the Anti-Dumping Agreement are closely linked because one of the conditions for the initiation of an investigation under Article 5.1 is that the application be made on behalf of the domestic industry, which is defined in Article 4.1.

6.257 We recall that civil proceedings under the 1916 Act are available to "any person injured in his business or property"① by reason of a violation of the 1916 Act. This term is nowhere qualified by a statement that this person should be sufficiently representative of an industry of the United States, within the meaning of Article 4 of the Anti-Dumping Agreement. We note that the 1916 Act refers to the intent of destroying or injuring an industry in the United States, or of preventing the establishment of an industry in the United States. However, we have no evidence that a minimum representation level for a given industry must be established by the complainant before filing a case before a federal court. On the contrary, we note that all cases so far have, in fact, been initiated by individual companies under their own responsibility. The fact that, in certain cases, these companies may have represented a very large portion of the US industry in the economic sector concerned does not seem to be linked to any legal requirement of representation under the 1916 Act and is most probably fortuitous. We have not been referred to any provisions of the US Federal Rules of Civil Procedure which would qualify the terms of the 1916 Act in line with the terms of Article 4 and 5 of the Anti-Dumping Agreement. In light of the terms of the 1916 Act, especially the term "any person injured in his business or property"

① Emphasis added.

which is clear, we have no reason to believe that US federal courts will be in a position to interpret that provision—which conflicts with the terms of the Anti-Dumping Agreement—to meet the requirements of Articles 4 and 5 of the Anti-Dumping Agreement in terms of representation of the complainants.

6.258 Regarding the requirement of Article 5.2 that applications contain evidence of the three elements of dumping, injury and causation, we note that Japan referred to the provisions of the US Federal Rules of Civil Procedure to support its argument that no such requirement applies to complainants under the 1916 Act. We note that the United States did not contest, as a matter of fact, the applicability to the 1916 Act of the provisions of the US Federal Rules of Civil Procedure cited by Japan. We also recall that the 1916 Act does not require the establishment of injury within the meaning of Article VI of the GATT 1994. We therefore conclude that there is no obligation for a complainant under the 1916 Act to respect the obligations of Article 5.2 of the Anti-Dumping Agreement in terms of the type of evidence to be included in an application.

6.259 Finally, Japan argues that Article 5.10 of the Anti-Dumping Agreement requires Members to complete their investigations and decide whether or not to impose duties within 18 months. Japan claims that the 1916 Act contains no such deadline.

6.260 As we noted in a similar situation for certain claims of Japan under Article 2 of the Anti-Dumping Agreement, the fact that the 1916 Act does not include a deadline for the completion of proceedings is not as such sufficient to establish a violation. We do not consider it a priori impossible that US courts, in the absence of a conflict, read that deadline into the text of the 1916 Act in application of the Charming Betsy doctrine. Japan did not submit evidence that the absence in the 1916 Act of an express deadline compatible with the provisions of Article 5.10 of the Anti-Dumping Agreement was a violation of the WTO Agreement. Even though we are not sure that the 18-month deadline could always be imposed by the judge on the parties to a 1916 Act case, we consider that Japan, as a complainant, did not establish a prima facie case in that respect and we refrain from making a finding under Article 5.10 on the 1916 Act.

6.261 We therefore find that the 1916 Act, because it does not require a minimum representation of a US industry in applications for the initiation of proceedings under the 1916 Act, violates Article 4.1 and Article 5.1, 5.2 and 5.4 of the Anti-Dumping Agreement.

【本案评析】

以上案例节选自2000年日本诉美国《1916年反倾销法》争端案专家组报告。在该案中，专家组裁定，美国违反了《反倾销协定》第4条和第5条的规定，因为美国的《1916年反倾销法》并不要求美国产业界在根据《1916年反倾销法》提起诉讼的申请中有最低限度的代表权。

五、2001 年泰国对波兰进口铁、非合金钢的角材、型材和异型材以及工字钢征收反倾销税案[①]

THAILAND – ANTI-DUMPING DUTIES ON ANGLES, SHAPES AND SECTIONS OF IRON OR NON-ALLOY STEEL AND H-BEAMS FROM POLAND
(WT/DS122/R)

(b) Article 5.5: alleged insufficiency of notification
(i)Arguments of the parties

Poland

7.80 Poland argues that, in violation of Thailand's obligations under Article 5.5 AD read in conjunction with Article 12.1 AD, Thailand did not provide proper or timely notification to Poland regarding the filing of the application for initiation of the Thai anti-dumping investigation. Poland recognizes that this claim is based on a disagreement with Thailand as to the content of a discussion held on 17 July 1996 between government officials from Thailand and Poland. Poland believes that, due to the difficulty for a panel to rule on something that was communicated orally, Article 5.5 should be read to require written notice. Poland submits that no such written notice was provided in this case.

Thailand

7.81 Thailand argues that the meeting on 17 July 1996 between government officials from Thailand and Poland complied with the requirements of Article 5.5 AD with respect to the timing, form, and content of the notification. With respect to timing, Thailand submits that it notified Poland less than one month after the receipt of the application and six weeks before the decision to initiate the investigation. In Thailand's view, this satisfies Article 5.5 AD and falls within the "window" contemplated by the relevant Recommendation adopted by the WTO Anti-Dumping Committee.[②] With respect to form, Thailand submits that the text of Article 5.5 AD does not

① Panel Report, Thailand-Anti-Dumping Duties on Angels, Shapes and Sections of Iron or Non-Alloy Steel and H-Beams from Poland, WT/DS122/R, adopted 5 April 2001.

② Thailand refers to the "Recommendation concerning the timing of the notification under Article 5.5", adopted by the ADP Committee on 29 October 1998, G/ADP/5, 3 November 1998.

specify whether notification should be written or oral.[①] For Thailand, discussions on this issue in the Anti-Dumping Committee's Ad Hoc Group on Implementation also do not specify whether notice should be written or oral.[②] Thailand argues that its interpretation that notification under Article 5.5 AD may be written or oral is a permissible interpretation that the Panel should accept in accordance with Article 17.6(ii) of the AD Agreement. With respect to content, Thailand considers that the language of Article 5.5 AD is vague and gives no indication of what should be notified. Referring to the Thai government note summarizing the 17 July 1996 meeting[③], Thailand states that Thailand indicated to Poland during the meeting that an application had been received and that the authorities were considering whether it contained sufficient information to justify initiation. In Thailand's view, the Panel should ignore Poland's reference to Article 12 of the AD Agreement in this context, as Article 12 is not within the Panel's terms of reference.

(ii) Evaluation by the Panel

7.82 Article 5.5 AD states:

i. "The authorities shall avoid, unless a decision has been made to initiate an investigation, any publicizing of the application for the initiation of an investigation. However, after receipt of a properly documented application and before proceeding to initiate an investigation, the authorities shall notify the government of the exporting Member concerned."

7.83 In this case, the parties agree that there was a meeting in Bangkok between government officials of Thailand and Poland on 17 July 1996, and that the issues arising in this dispute under Article 5.5 AD are due to a difference of views between the parties as to the nature of the obligations imposed by Article 5.5 AD with respect to the timing, form and content of the notification.

---

① In their responses to Panel Question 3 (Annexes 3-7, 3-8 and 3-9), the third parties offered their views on the form of the notification required under Article 5.5. The European Communities was of the view that while the term "notify" "implies some degree of formality", this "did not necessarily exclude that a notification can be made orally in the course of an official meeting…". Japan noted that although the text of the provision does not specify that the notification should be in writing, other considerations "suggest that Article 5.5 requires written notification". The United States submitted that Article 5.5 is silent on this issue and that a meeting of government officials could satisfy this requirement, "provided that the objective of the meeting is specific and sufficiently documented to support a review on the record by a panel".

② The Ad Hoc Group is a subsidiary body of the ADP Committee established by decision of that Committee on 29 April 1996 to prepare recommendations on issues where agreement seems possible, and report to the Committee. In addition, the Ad Hoc Group could consider other issues regarding implementation on which Members believe discussion would be helpful. See G/ADP/M/7, paras. 53-54.

③ Exhibit Thailand-56.

7.84 Based on evidence on the Panel record submitted by Thailand that Poland has not specifically contested[①], the Panel's understanding of the factual situation underlying this claim is as follows. On 21 June 1996, Thailand received an anti-dumping application from SYS. Some time prior to 17 July 1996, the Polish Commercial Counsellor in Bangkok, Mr. Byckowski, telephoned Ms. Chutima Bunyapraphasara (Director of the Multilateral Trade Division) to seek clarification regarding an article in a publication called "Metal Bulletin". The article apparently reported that SYS had requested the Thai government to investigate dumped steel products from Poland. A meeting was scheduled for 17 July 1996 between Mr. Byckowski and officials from DBE. Thailand submits that the meeting is summarized in an internal Thai government note written by Ms. Chutima to the Director-General of DBE dated 18 July 1996.[②] According to this note, DBE officials indicated in the course of the 17 July 1996 meeting "that the company had filed an application requesting the Thai Government to investigate the dumped steel products from Poland..." and that "the matter was under consideration whether the company had enough information for the Committee to initiate the investigation."[③] On 30 August 1996, Thailand initiated the anti-dumping investigation.

7.85 We turn to a consideration of whether this meeting that both parties agree occurred between their government officials on 17 July 1996 satisfied the notification requirements of Article 5.5 of the AD Agreement with respect to its timing, form and content.

7.86 With respect to the timing of the notification required under Article 5.5, the second sentence of Article 5.5 provides that "after receipt of a properly documented application and before proceeding to initiate an investigation, the authorities shall notify the government of the exporting Member concerned." Footnote 1 of the AD Agreement defines the term "initiated" as follows: "The term 'initiated' as used in this Agreement means the procedural action by which a Member formally commences an investigation as provided in Article 5." Together, these provisions make it clear that at a point in time between two specified events, the authorities of the importing Member must notify the exporting Member.

7.87 In the present case, the application was filed on 21 June 1996.[④] The investigation was initiated on 30 August 1996. Therefore, the 17 July 1996 meeting occurred (approximately one

---

① See, *inter alia*, response by Thailand to Question 18 by the Panel, Annex 2-6.

② Exhibit Thailand-56.

③ Exhibit Thailand-56.

④ The Thai investigating authorities subsequently requested, and received, certain additional information from SYS. See Exhibits Thailand-1, Thailand-53.

month) following receipt of the initial application[①] and (approximately six weeks) prior to the initiation of the investigation. We find that the 17 July 1996 meeting fell within the "window" of time envisaged by Article 5.5 and therefore satisfied the timing requirements imposed by Article 5.5.[②]

7.88 We next turn to consider whether the 17 July 1996 meeting satisfied the requirements as to form under Article 5.5 of the AD Agreement.

7.89 Article 5.5 AD does not specify the form that the notification must take. The *Concise Oxford Dictionary* defines the term "notify" as: "inform or give notice to (a person)"; "make known, announce or report (a thing)". We consider that the form of the notification under Article 5.5 must be sufficient for the importing Member to "inform" or "make known" to the exporting Member certain facts. While a written notification might arguably best serve this goal and the promotion of transparency and certainty among Members, and might also provide a written record upon which an importing Member could rely in the event of a subsequent claim of inconsistency with Article 5.5 of the AD Agreement, the text of Article 5.5 does not expressly require that the notification be in writing.[③]

7.90 We consider that a formal meeting between government officials could satisfy the notification requirement of Article 5.5, provided that the meeting is sufficiently documented to support meaningful review by a panel. For these reasons, we find that the fact that Thailand notified Poland under Article 5.5 orally in the course of a meeting between government officials, rather than in written form, does not render the notification inconsistent with Article 5.5.

7.91 We turn to a consideration of whether the 17 July 1996 meeting satisfied the

① Thailand submits that at this meeting, the DBE notified Mr. Byckowski that a properly documented anti-dumping application had been received. Thailand's first written submission, Annex 2-1, para. 120.

② We note that a recommendation adopted by the WTO Committee on Anti-Dumping Practices states: "...the Committee recommends that the notification required by the second sentence of Article 5.5 should be made as soon as possible after the receipt by the investigating authorities of a properly documented application, and as early as possible before the decision is taken regarding the initiation of an investigation on the basis of that properly documented application". "Recommendation concerning the timing of the notification under Article 5.5", adopted by the Committee on 29 October 1998, G/ADP/5, 3 November 1998. We consider that this decision is a relevant but non-binding indication of the understanding of Members as to appropriate implementation practice regarding the obligations under Article 5.5 AD with respect to the timing of the notification. Moreover, we note that the language of the recommendation ("should...") is hortatory.

③ While there have been discussions in the Ad Hoc Group on the issue of the form of the notification (See G/ADP/AHG/R/4, para. 19 (Exhibit Thailand-61); G/ADP/AHG/R/5, paras. 18-19 (Exhibit Thailand-59); G/ADP/AHG/R/2, para. 5 (Exhibit Thailand-60), there has been no recommendation adopted by the ADP Committee on this issue.

requirements of Article 5.5 with respect to the content of the notification. The text of Article 5.5 does not specify the contents of the notification. It provides: "after receipt of a properly documented application and before proceeding to initiate an investigation, the authorities shall notify the government of the exporting Member concerned."[①] Because the text of the provision specifies that notification necessarily follows the receipt of a properly documented application, we consider that the fact of the receipt of a properly documented application would be an essential element of the contents of the notification.

7.92 We note that any notification provided in this case was provided orally in the course of a meeting between government officials. The only written evidence on the Panel record relating to the content of any such notification is an internal Thai government note[②] summarizing the meeting and several subsequent communications from the Thai government to the Polish government.[③] The internal Thai government note states, *inter alia*, that the Thai government indicated in the course of the 17 July 1996 meeting "that the company had filed an application requesting the Thai Government to investigate the dumped steel products from Poland..." and that "the matter was under consideration whether the company had enough information for the Committee to initiate the investigation."[④] Poland has not explicitly contested in these proceedings that this internal Thai government note accurately reflects the content of the oral communication between the parties' government officials at the meeting. We therefore consider that the meeting of 17 July 1996 was sufficient with respect to its content in that it served to inform the Polish government of the fact that the Thai government had received the SYS application and therefore constitutes sufficient notice under Article 5.5.

7.93 Poland has invoked Article 12 of the AD Agreement as "useful context" in connection with its Article 5.5 AD claim, but has not made a claim under Article 12 of the AD Agreement. We note that both Articles 5.5 and 12.1 contain a requirement to notify the government of the exporting Member concerned of certain events connected with the initiation of an investigation at a certain point in time. However, it is clear that the requirements as to the timing, form and content of these notifications is different. Article 5.5 makes it clear that the notification referred to in that provision must take place "after receipt of a properly documented application and before proceeding to initiate an investigation". By contrast, Article 12.1 of the AD Agreement

① While there have been discussions in the Ad Hoc Group on the elements that certain Members consider relevant in this context (G/ADP/AHG/R/4, para. 18 (Exhibit Thailand-61), G/ADP/AHG/R/5, para. 17 (Exhibit Thailand-59) there has been no recommendation adopted by the ADP Committee on this issue.

② Exhibit Thailand-56.

③ Exhibit Thailand-14/Poland-4 and Thailand-57.

④ Exhibit Thailand-56.

concerns notification of initiation, as it requires notification to "the Member or Members the products of which are subject to such investigation...", "[w]hen the authorities are satisfied that there is sufficient evidence to justify the initiation of an anti-dumping investigation pursuant to Article 5 ..." and requires "public notice" of initiation. As Article 12.1 provides that such "public notice" must "contain, or otherwise make available through a separate report, adequate information ..." the notice must presumably be in writing. Furthermore, Article 12 involves the notification of a decision to initiate, which a Member may not yet have taken at the time of an Article 5.5 notification. That Article 12 specifically enumerates certain requirements with respect to the contents and form of the notice it requires, and Article 5.5 does not, strongly suggests to us that the requirements of Article 12 do not apply to notification under Article 5.5, and in no way changes our interpretation of the requirements concerning the timing, form and content of the notification to be given under Article 5.5.

7.94 For these reasons, we find that Thailand did not act inconsistently with the respect to the timing, form and content of the notification under Article 5.5 of the AD Agreement in informing Poland orally in the course of the 17 July 1996 meeting between government officials of Thailand and Poland that Thailand had received an application from SYS for initiation of an anti-dumping investigation with respect to imports of H-beams from Poland. As Poland has not made any arguments concerning an independent violation of Article VI of the GATT 1994 in this context, we also find that Poland has not established a violation of that provision.

【本案评析】

以上案例节选自2001年泰国对波兰进口铁、非合金钢的角材、型材和异型材以及工字钢征收反倾销税案专家组报告。专家组指出，尽管书面通知可以说是最有利于实现向出口成员方通知某些事实的目标，以及促进成员之间的透明度和确定性，而且当被声称与《反倾销协定》第5.5款不符后，进口成员也可以依靠这种其已经提供书面记录作为依据，但第5.5款的条文并未明确要求通知是以书面形式发出的。专家组认为，政府官员之间的正式会议可以满足第5.5款的通知要求，条件是会议有充分的文件记录，足以支持由专家组进行有意义的审查。因此该案专家组认定，泰国在政府官员会晤过程中根据第5.5款口头通知波兰，而非以书面形式通知波兰，并不违反第5.5款的规定。

六、2005年墨西哥大米和牛肉的最终反倾销措施案[①]

Mexico -Definitive Anti-Dumping Measures on Beef and Rice
(WT/DS295/R)

(a)Arguments of the Parties

(i)United States

7.243 The United States argues that Article 68 of the Act requires the investigating authority to conduct reviews of final anti-dumping and countervailing measures with respect to companies that were found not to have been dumping or not to have received countervailable subsidies during the original period of investigation. The United States submits that this is clearly inconsistent with the explicit requirement of Article 5.8 of the AD Agreement and 11.9 of the SCM Agreement to terminate the investigation immediately in case no margin of dumping or countervailable subsidy was found to exist.

7.244 In addition, the United States argues that Article 68 of the Act is inconsistent with the AD and SCM Agreement as it requires exporters or producers requesting a review to demonstrate that the sales during the review period were "representative", while no such additional requirement for obtaining a review exists in Articles 9.3 and 11.2 of the AD Agreement and 21.2 of the SCM Agreement. In the view of the United States, these provisions do not permit the introduction of such an additional requirement. The United States therefore submits that by requiring the authority to deny a review unless a party demonstrates that its exports were "representative", Article 68 of the Act is inconsistent as such with the AD Agreement and the SCM Agreement.

(ii)Mexico

7.245 Mexico rejects the US allegations of inconsistency of Article 68 of the Act with Articles 5.8, 9.3 and 11.2 of the AD Agreement and Articles 11.9 and 21.2 of the SCM Agreement. First, Mexico argues that Article 5.8 of the AD Agreement and 11.9 of the SCM Agreement do not apply to reviews but only to original investigations. Mexico therefore considers that the US argument that Article 68 of the Act violates Articles 5.8 of the AD Agreement and 11.9 of the SCM Agreement in subjecting to administrative reviews exporters for whom no margin of dumping or subsidization was determined is without merit since the allegedly infringed Articles do not even apply in the case of reviews. Furthermore, Mexico is of the view that Article 5.8 of the AD

① Panel Report and Appellate Body Report, Mexico-Definitive Anti-Dumping Measures on Beef and Rice, WT/DS295/R, 6 June 2005, WT/DS295/AB/R, 29 November 2005.

Agreement and Article 11.9 of the SCM Agreement do not require the exclusion of an exporter from the measure and therefore from being subjected to reviews simply because no margin of dumping was established in the original investigation. According to Mexico, Article 3.3 of the AD Agreement and 15.3 of the SCM Agreement clearly show that an investigation is only to be terminated in case the margin of dumping calculated on a country-wide basis rather than a firm-specific basis is below *de minimis*. In any case, Mexico is of the view that a review does not imply the imposition of a duty and thus does not negatively affect the exporters concerned. Such reviews are thus similar to those provided in Article 9.3.1 of the AD Agreement concerning the determination of final liability for payment of anti-dumping duties.

7.246 Mexico further submits that Article 68 of the Act does not impose a "representativeness" requirement as a condition for the investigating authority to conduct reviews such as those provided for in Article 21.2 of the SCM Agreement and Articles 9.3 and 11.2 of the AD Agreement. According to Mexico, there are no clear provisions in the AD Agreement or SCM Agreement as to the procedures for conducting administrative reviews and new exporter reviews, and the "representativeness" requirement of Article 68 of the Act is merely a means of ascertaining that the export volumes reported in administrative review or new shipper reviews reflect normal volumes that are representative of the sales policies of exporters seeking such reviews. Mexico asserts that an exporter is not required to show "representative volume of sales" in order to obtain the initiation of a review, but that an interested party will need to demonstrate such representativeness in order to be able to determine a margin of dumping for that party.① In any case, according to Mexico, the United States fails to demonstrate that such a requirement is a sine qua non requirement for the initiation of such reviews.②

7.247 Finally, Mexico submits that, in any case, by virtue of Article 133 of its Constitution, treaties such as the WTO Agreements are self-executing and automatically applicable in Mexican law, and as Article 2 of the Act makes clear, the Act will be implemented in a manner which is congruent with the provisions of the WTO Agreements. According to Mexico, the Act thus does not mandate any WTO inconsistent action.

(b)Analysis

7.248 The United States makes two claims concerning Article 68 of the Act. First, the United States argues that by subjecting exporters for which the original investigation showed a margin of dumping or subsidization below *de minimis* to administrative reviews, Article 68 of the Act is

① Mexico First Answers to Questions, question 31.

② Mexico asserts that this is clear from a recent review on imports of dessert apples from the United States (Exhibit MEX-13).

inconsistent with Article 5.8 of the AD Agreement and 11.9 of the SCM Agreement. Second, the United States submits that by requiring exporters requesting a review to show that their volume of sales during the review period was representative, Article 68 of the Act is in breach of Articles 9.3 and 11.2 of the AD Agreement and Article 21.2 of the SCM Agreement.

7.249 We will first examine the US claim of violation of Article 5.8 of the AD Agreement and Article 11.9 of the SCM Agreement. Article 5.8 of the AD Agreement provides as follows[①]:

...

7.251 Article 68 of the Act thus requires the review of producers for which during the original investigation it was determined that they had not been engaged in dumping practices or had not received any subsidies. In our view, and for the reasons set forth above when discussing the US claims concerning the inclusion in the Anti-dumping measures on rice of the two exporters found not to have been dumping during the period of investigation, we find that Article 5.8 of the AD Agreement requires the termination of the investigation with regard to such exporters found not to have been dumping above *de minimis* levels, and requires that such exporters be excluded from the measures imposed. The logical consequence of such an exclusion of producers found not to have been dumping is that they can not subsequently be subjected to administrative or changed circumstances reviews. While we agree with Mexico that the specific requirements concerning *de minimis* do not apply in the case of reviews of the duties imposed, this does not imply that Article 68 of the Act dealing with reviews cannot be inconsistent with Article 5.8 of the AD Agreement insofar as it imposes the review of measures with regard to producers to which such measures should not have been applied in the first place. The possibility of reviewing the zero per cent duty margin imposed on such non-dumping exporters also reveals the important meaning of the imposition of such a zero per cent duty which, in spite of its appearance, does not equal the termination of the investigation as required by Article 5.8 of the AD Agreement. We therefore find that Article 68 of the Act is as such inconsistent with Article 5.8 of the AD Agreement. For the same reasons, *mutatis mutandis*, Article 68 of the Act is in breach of Article 11.9 of the SCM Agreement.

---

① Article 11.9 of the SCM Agreement provides as follows: An application under paragraph 1 shall be rejected and an investigation shall be terminated promptly as soon as the authorities concerned are satisfied that there is not sufficient evidence of either subsidization or of injury to justify proceeding with the case. There shall be immediate termination in cases where the amount of a subsidy *is de minimis*, or where the volume of subsidized imports, actual or potential, or the injury, is negligible. For the purpose of this paragraph, the amount of the subsidy shall be considered to be *de minimis* if the subsidy is less than 1 per cent ad *valorem*.

Mexico -Definitive Anti-Dumping Measures on Beef and Rice (WT/DS295/AB/R)

301 The United States argued before the Panel that Article 68 is inconsistent with Article 5.8 of the *Anti-Dumping Agreement* and Article 11.9 of the *SCM Agreement*. The Panel confirmed its finding, made in the context of evaluating the United States' "as applied" claims①, that Article 5.8 of the *Anti-Dumping Agreement* requires an investigating authority to exclude, from the definitive anti-dumping measure, exporters found not to have been dumping above *de minimis* levels. The Panel further observed that the "logical consequence" of such exclusion is that those exporters may not be subjected to administrative reviews or changed circumstances reviews.② As Article 68 requires that such exporters be subject to such reviews upon request of an interested party, the Panel found Article 68 to be inconsistent with Article 5.8 of the *Anti-Dumping Agreement* and, *mutatis mutandis*, Article 11.9 of the *SCM Agreement*.③

302 Mexico alleges on appeal that the Panel erred in interpreting Article 5.8 of the *Anti-Dumping Agreement* and Article 11.9 of the *SCM Agreement*. According to Mexico, by finding that Article 68—which deals exclusively with reviews—is inconsistent with these provisions, the Panel failed to recognize that the obligations contained in these provisions are limited to original investigations.④ Mexico contends that Article 5.8 and Article 11.9 do not apply to events subsequent to the original investigation, including reviews.⑤ Even if those provisions did apply, Mexico argues, they require only that the investigating authority not *levy duties* on the relevant respondents; these provisions do not address the question whether those respondents may be included in the *definitive measure* at the end of an investigation.⑥ Thus, according to Mexico, because Article 68 does not require that duties be imposed on such respondents, this basis for the Panel's finding of inconsistency is erroneous.

303 We begin with the relevant provisions of the *Anti-Dumping Agreement* and the *SCM Agreement*. Article 5 of the *Anti-Dumping Agreement* is titled "Initiation and Subsequent

① See Panel Report, para. 7.166.

② *Ibid*., para. 7.251.

③ The Panel provided no further reasoning as to why its analysis under Article 5.8 of the *Anti-Dumping Agreement* applies equally to Article 11.9 of the *SCM Agreement*.

④ Mexico's appellant's submission, para. 259(b)

⑤ *Ibid*., para. 259(c).

⑥ *Ibid*., para. 259(d)-(g). Mexico explains that inclusion of an exporter in the measure does not necessarily mean a duty will be levied on that particular respondent; this is because such a respondent may be assigned a duty of zero.

Investigation". Paragraph 8 of Article 5 provides:

...

305 We have already indicated that the Panel was correct in finding that Article 5.8 of the *Anti-Dumping Agreement* requires an investigating authority to terminate the investigation "in respect of" an exporter found not to have a margin above *de minimis*, and that the exporter consequently must be excluded from the definitive anti-dumping measure.① An investigating authority does not, of course, impose duties—including duties at zero per cent—on exporters excluded from the definitive anti-dumping measure. We therefore agree with the Panel that the "logical consequence"② of this approach is that such exporters cannot be subject to administrative and changed circumstances reviews, because such reviews examine, respectively, the "duty *paid*"③ and "the need for the *continued imposition* of the duty".④ Were an investigating authority to undertake a review of exporters that were excluded from the anti-dumping measure by virtue of their *de minimis* margins, those exporters effectively would be made subject to the anti-dumping measure, inconsistent with Article 5.8. The same may be said with respect to Article 11.9 of the *SCM Agreement*.

306 We now consider whether Article 68 of the FTA is consistent with these treaty provisions. The Panel found that Article 68 requires Economía to "review ... producers for which during the original investigation it was determined that they had not been engaged in dumping practices or had not received any subsidies".⑤ As we have stated, such exporters were to have been excluded from the anti-dumping measure, by virtue of Article 5.8 of the *Anti-Dumping Agreement*, and from the countervailing duty measure, by virtue of Article 11.9 of the *SCM Agreement*. Excluding these exporters from anti-dumping or countervailing duty measures necessarily implies that they must also be excluded from administrative and changed circumstances reviews. By requiring Economía to conduct a review for exporters with no margins and, by extension, *de minimis* margins, Article 68 is inconsistent with Article 5.8 of the *Anti-Dumping Agreement* and Article 11.9 of the *SCM Agreement*.

307 We therefore *uphold* the Panel's findings, in paragraphs 7.251 and 8.5(c) of the Panel Report, that Article 68 of the FTA is inconsistent, as such, with Article 5.8 of the *Anti-Dumping Agreement* and Article 11.9 of the *SCM Agreement*.

---

① *Supra*, paras. 216-218.

② Panel Report, para. 7.251.

③ Article 9.3.2 of the *Anti-Dumping Agreement*. (emphasis added)

④ Article 11.2 of the *Anti-Dumping Agreement*; Article 21.2 of the *SCM Agreement*. (emphasis added)

⑤ Panel Report, para. 7.251.

【本案评析】

以上案例节选自2005年墨西哥大米和牛肉的最终反倾销措施案专家组和上诉机构报告。该案专家组指出,《反倾销协定》第5.8款要求对未达到反倾销最低限度的出口商立即终止调查,并要求将这些出口商排除在所采取的措施之外,这一规定的逻辑后果是,这些出口商随后也无须接受行政或情势变更的复审。虽然关于微量倾销的具体要求不适用于对已经征收关税的情况进行审查,但是这并不意味着涉及审查的相关法律规定不可以与《反倾销协定》第5.8款相抵触,因为该条规定了对本来不应对生产者适用的这种措施进行审查。对那些没有倾销的出口商征收零税率进行审查的可能性也揭示了征收零税率的重要意义,虽然表面上是零税率,但是这并不等同于对《反倾销协定》第5.8款所要求调查的终止。因此,该案专家组裁定,墨西哥对于原调查期间认定未进行倾销的两个美国出口商不终止调查且不排除对这两个出口商适用最终反倾销措施的行为不符合《反倾销协定》第5.8款的规定。对专家组的这一结论上诉机构予以同意并且指出,第5.8款"合乎逻辑的后果"是,这类出口商不能接受"已缴税款"和"继续征收税款必要性"的审查,如果调查主管机关对因微量倾销而被排除在反倾销措施之外的出口商进行审查,那么这些出口商实际上将受到反倾销措施的约束,而这不符合第5.8款的要求。

【延伸阅读】

一、相关典型案例

1.Argentina—Definitive Anti-Dumping Duties on Poultry from Brazil(WT/DS241)

2.European Communities—Anti-Dumping Duties on Imports of Cotton-type Bed Linen from India(WT/DS141)

3.European Communities—Anti-Dumping Duties on Malleable Cast Iron Tube or Pipe Fittings from Brazil(WT/DS219)

4.European Communities—Anti-Dumping Measure on Farmed Salmon from Norway(WT/DS337)

5.United States—Anti-Dumping Measures on Stainless Steel Plate in Coils and Stainless Steel Sheet and Strip from Korea（WT/DS179）

6.United States—Anti-Dumping Measures on Certain Hot-Rolled Steel Products from Japan(WT/DS184)

二、相关学术论著

1. 赵维田:《世界贸易组织（WTO）的法律制度》，吉林人民出版社 2000 年版。

2. Andreas F. Lowenfeld, *International Economic Law*, Oxford University Press, 2008.

3. Andrew T. Guzman and Joost H.B. Pauwelyn, *International Trade Law,* Aspen Publishers, 2009.

三、相关网络资源

1. https://www.wto.org/english/docs_e/legal_e/19-adp_01_e.htm.

2.http://ec.europa.eu/trade/policy/accessing-markets/trade-defence/actions-against-imports-into-the-eu/anti-dumping/.

3. https://tdi.mofcom.gov.cn/.

4. http://cacs.mofcom.gov.cn/.

5. https://enforcement.trade.gov/petitioncounseling/index.html.

第二节　反倾销争端调查的进行

【知识背景 / 学习要点】

《反倾销协定》是关于进行反倾销调查的详细程序规则，第 6 条和第 12 条确立了反倾销调查中有关各方的证据、信息和程序等方面的正当程序性权利。第 6.2 款要求被调查的当事方“应有为其利益进行辩护的充分机会”。第 6.9 款要求，在作出最后决定之前，当局应“将构成裁定基础的所审议的基本事实通知所有利害关系方”。

一、证据规则

（一）征询书面证据的通知

出于正当程序的考虑，通常反倾销调查机关不应仅凭借申请人的一面之词即开始调查，一般也需要综合考虑相关利害方的证据和材料，这就需要向相关当事人征询相关资料，而采取的方式就是对所需证据信息进行通知。《反倾销协定》第 6.1 款要求主管机关向反倾销调查的所有利害关系方发出通知，告知所要提供的资料，并提供其充分机会以书面形式提出认为与所涉调查有关的所有证据。上诉机构曾强调，"无视被申诉方的证据，不符合被申诉方根据第 6.1 款提交其认为与日落复审有关证据的权利"。①

由于反倾销调查是由进口国的国内生产者提出申请才启动的，因此国内生产者可以更好地控制和利用其提交启动反倾销调查申请书的时间，也有机会收集到必要的证据以支持其申诉。而在调查开始之前，答复方通常不会收到通知。在实践中，调查主管机关通常会向感兴趣的当事方发出"调查问卷"，说明其为开展调查而需要的信息。《反倾销协定》第 6.1.1 项所指的"调查问卷"是一种特殊类型的文件，其中载有在调查初期分发的大量要求提供资料的请求，调查机关通过该文件征求大量关于将由主管机关进行的调查的包括倾销、损害和因果关系等在内的主要方面的信息。②

为保护出口商和外国生产商，《反倾销协定》第 6.1.1 项要求调查机关应至少给予他们 30 日的调查问卷答复时间，并允许在可行的情况下，根据其提出的理由给予延期。③ 这条明确规定了出口商和外国生产商有充分机会作出答复的

① 参见 Appellate Body Report, United States–Sunset Reviews of Anti-Dumping Measures on Oil Country Tubular Goods from Argentina, WT/DS268/AB/R, adopted 17 December 2004, para. 246.

② 参见 Appellate Body Report, European Communities-Definitive Anti-Dumping Measures on Certain Iron or Steel Fasteners from China, WT/DS397/AB/R, 15 July 2011, paras. 612-613.

③ 根据第 6.1.1 项，调查主管机关可以对调查问卷的答复规定提交时限，但这些时限不一定是绝对和不变的，在适当情况下这些时限必须延长。上诉机构曾指出，第 6.1 款为所有利害关系方提交和答复调查问卷规定了"灵活"的 30 日最低时限。参见 Appellate Body Report, United States–Anti-Dumping Measures on Certain Hot-Rolled Steel Products from Japan, WT/DS184/AB/R, adopted 23 August 2001, paras. 73-75.

具体正当程序利益。[①]第6.1.2项要求调查机关将利害关系方以书面形式提出的证据迅速提供给参与调查的其他利害关系方，但须遵守机密信息保护的要求。[②]同时，第6.1.1项的适用也必须考虑到调查机关在控制反倾销调查过程和在规定时间内完成调查方面的利益。[③]此外，所有感兴趣的当事方都享有参加反倾销调查程序和发言的相关权利。根据第6.12款的规定，主管机关应向被调查产品的工业用户，或在该产品通常为零售的情况下，向具有代表性的消费者组织提供机会，使其能够提供与关于倾销、损害和因果关系的调查有关的信息。第6.13款也规定，主管机关应适当考虑利害关系方、特别是小公司在提供所要求的信息方面遇到的任何困难，并应提供帮助。

（二）提供利益辩解的机会

在整个反倾销调查期间，所有利害关系方均有为其利益进行辩护的充分机会。《反倾销协定》第6.2款要求调查机关给予利害关系方“为其利益进行辩护的充分机会”。该款规定，经请求，主管机关应向所有利害关系方提供与具有相反利益的当事方会面的机会，以便陈述对立的观点和提出反驳的论据。提供此类机会必须考虑保护机密和方便有关当事方的需要。任何一方均无必须出席会议的义务，未能出席会议不得对该方的案件产生不利。利害关系方还有权在说明正当理由后口头提出其他信息。

（三）披露相关信息的义务

为确保反倾销调查和程序的透明度，调查机关必须及时提供机会，让所有

① 上诉机构曾表示，第6.1款和第6.2款分别提供的“广泛的”和“充分的”机会不能无限期地延长而且必须在某一时刻合法地停止存在……如果继续给予提交证据和参加听证的机会，将会影响调查主管机关“控制其调查的进行”和及时完成日落复审所要求的“执行多项步骤”的能力，则此时被申诉方已经达到第6.1款和第6.2款所规定的“广泛的”和“充分的”机会的极限。参见 Appellate Body Report, *United States–Sunset Reviews of Anti-Dumping Measures on Oil Country Tubular Goods from Argentina*, WT/DS268/AB/R, adopted 17 December 2004, para. 242.

② 参见 Appellate Body Report, European Communities–Definitive Anti-Dumping Measures on Certain Iron or Steel Fasteners from China–Recourse to Article 21.5 of the DSU by China ,WT/DS397/AB/RW, 18 JANUARY 2016, para. 5.153.

③ 参见 Appellate Body Report, European Communities-Definitive Anti-Dumping Measures on Certain Iron or Steel Fasteners from China, WT/DS397/AB/R, 15 July 2011, paras. 610-611.

利害关系方了解与其案件的陈述有关并由调查当局使用的所有非机密信息。[①]《反倾销协定》第6.4款要求调查主管机关及时为利害关系方提供机会，以查看与其案件陈述有关的、非第6.5款所界定的，并且主管机关在反倾销调查中使用的机密信息。[②]第6.4款的规定使得利害关系方，可以获取调查机关在执行反倾销调查过程中所需使用的范围广泛的信息。这里受第6.4款约束的“广泛的信息”可以采取各种形式，包括利害关系方提交的数据，以及调查主管机关处理、汇总或概括的信息。

需注意的是，第6.4款规定的信息披露的目的，也包括允许利害关系方可以此信息为基础准备陈述。与第6.2款合并解读，可以发现利害关系方获得所有这些信息是非常重要的，因为没有这些信息，相关利害关系方可能没有为他们的利益进行辩护的机会。但是，调查机关的法律推理或内部审议不受第6.4款规定的约束。[③]

同样涉及信息披露的还有包括价格比较中的信息披露要求以及涉及裁决作出前“基本事实”的披露。为了确保出口价格与正常价值之间的公平比较，《反倾销协定》第2.4款最后一句规定，主管机关应向所涉各方指明为保证进行公平比较所必需的信息，并不得对这些当事方强加不合理的举证责任。涉及裁决作出前“基本事实”披露的，主要是《反倾销协定》第6.9款的规定。[④]2011年中国诉欧盟紧固件反倾销案的上诉机构指出，与利害关系方案件陈述有关的“信息”可能是比调查主管机关所依赖的第6.9款意义上的“基本事实”更广泛

① 参见《反倾销协定》第6.4款的规定。

② 参见 Appellate Body Report, European Communities–Definitive Anti-Dumping Measures on Certain Iron or Steel Fasteners from China–Recourse to Article 21.5 of the DSU by China, WT/DS397/AB/RW, 18 January 2016, paras. 5.107-5.109.

③ 参见 Appellate Body Report, European Communities-Definitive Anti-Dumping Measures on Certain Iron or Steel Fasteners from China, WT/DS397/AB/R, 15 July 2011, para. 480.

④ 虽然根据第2.4款、第6.2款和第6.4款的披露义务适用于整个调查过程，但上诉机构强调，根据第6.9款的披露只是在调查结束前进行。参见 Appellate Body Report, European Communities–Definitive Anti-Dumping Measures on Certain Iron or Steel Fasteners from China–Recourse to Article 21.5 of the DSU by China ,WT/DS397/AB/RW, 18 January 2016, para. 5.191.

的概念，或者它们可能是重叠的。[①]

（四）机密信息保护要求

反倾销调查涉及大量机密和敏感的商业信息，因为这些信息要求公司向进口成员主管机关提交各个市场的详细价格和成本信息。一旦这些信息披露，竞争者将获得重大的竞争优势，或对提供信息的人产生重大的不利影响。为了进行最佳的法律辩护，感兴趣的当事方一般情况下也需要获取对方提交的机密信息，同时其也极不愿意向竞争对手提供自己的保密信息。因此，为了确保公平竞争和平等，必须在这些相互竞争的利益之间进行平衡，而且必须给予对方平等的获取信息的机会。

因此，出于信息披露义务的平衡，反倾销调查也需要对机密信息予以保护。《反倾销协定》第 6.5 款规定了对具有机密性质的信息或调查当事方在保密基础上提供的信息的保密原则。[②] 因此，当有关各方向进口成员主管机关提交书面资料时，它们一般应同时编写保密版本和非保密版本。机密版本将仅供进口成员调查机关查阅，而非机密版本将放在非机密文件档案中，可供调查中的所有有关各方查阅。

根据第 6.5 款的规定，无论保密信息的类型如何，都必须证明有“正当理由”才能获得保密待遇。[③] 根据该款的规定，调查主管机关必须对要求机密信息保护处理的一方所提出的“正当理由”进行审查。保密处理的“正当理由”要求既适用于“本质上”保密的信息，也适用于“在保密的基础上”提供给调查机

① 参见 Appellate Body Report, European Communities-Definitive Anti-Dumping Measures on Certain Iron or Steel Fasteners from China, WT/DS397/AB/R, 15 July 2011, para. 483.

② 《反倾销协定》第 6.5 款第 17 个脚注指出，在某些成员的领土上，可能需要根据狭义的保护性命令进行披露。除其他外，美国和加拿大就是这种情况。

③ 上诉机构指出，《反倾销协定》第 6.5 款保护本质上是保密的信息（即披露将使得竞争者获得重大竞争优势或对提供信息的人产生重大不利影响的信息），或由接受调查的各方以保密方式提供的信息。然而，无论机密信息的类型如何，必须显示出其有资格获得保密待遇的正当理由。参见 Appellate Body Reports, United States–Anti-Dumping Measures on Certain Hot-Rolled Steel Products from Japan, WT/DS184/AB/R, adopted 23 August 2001, para. 536.

关的信息。[①] 当然，可以证明信息需要机密处理的“正当理由”很多，比如使得竞争对手获得了优势，或者对提交方或可以获得该信息的当事方产生不利的影响。因此，当事方必须证明潜在结果的风险，证明避免这些风险足够重要到需要确保信息不披露。从实际案例来看，如果向公众和对调查感兴趣的其他当事方隐瞒信息没有充分“正当理由”，则这些当事方将有权查看这些信息。[②] 在调查机关给予保密处理时，应要求有关各方提供足够详细的非机密摘要，以便能够合理地理解保密提交资料的实质内容。[③] 但是，在特殊情况下，当事方也可以表示此类信息不可能进行摘要，但必须说明理由。[④]

（五）“可获得事实”规则

依据《反倾销协定》，通过信息征询或者利害关系方提交，调查主管机关一般获得的都是第一手的资料。但是，出于保密或者无法获取等情况，也会出现利害关系方不提交或者拖延提交被征询信息的情况，这样就会直接导致调查机构无法获取相关证据信息，导致调查停滞或者程序拖延。对此，《反倾销协定》的规定解决了调查机关可在何种情况下利用在其他方面掌握的可获得事实（facts available），即“最佳可获得信息”，从而克服有关各方在答复中信息缺失的问题。第 6.8 款规定，如任何利害关系方不允许使用或未在合理时间内提供必要的信息，或严重妨碍调查，则初步和最终裁定，无论是肯定的还是否定的，均可在可获得的事实基础上作出。第 6.8 款还规定，《反倾销协定》在适用本款时应遵守附件 2 的规定。

根据第 6.8 款的规定，对缺乏“合作”的利害关系方而言，可能是会因为

---

① 参见 Appellate Body Reports, European Communities–Definitive Anti-Dumping Measures on Certain Iron or Steel Fasteners from China–Recourse to Article 21.5 of the DSU by China, WT/DS397/AB/RW , 18 January 2016, paras. 5.36-5.40.

② 参见 Appellate Body Report, European Communities-Definitive Anti-Dumping Measures on Certain Iron or Steel Fasteners from China, WT/DS397/AB/R, 15 July 2011, paras. 537-540.

③ 参见《反倾销协定》第 6.5.1 项。

④ 参见 Appellate Body Report, European Communities-Definitive Anti-Dumping Measures on Certain Iron or Steel Fasteners from China, WT/DS397/AB/R, 15 July 2011, paras. 535 and 543-544.

只能利用现有可获得的事实而导致对其“不利”的结果。《反倾销协定》附件2“按照第6条第8款可获得的最佳信息”第7段指出，“如主管机关的调查结果，包括对正常价值的调查结果，只能依据第二来源的信息，包括在发起调查的申请中提供的信息，则应特别慎重。但是很显然，如一利害关系方不予合作，而使调查机关不能获得有关信息，则此情况可导致比该方进行合作时更为不利的结果”。根据第6.8款的规定，如果利害关系方不“严重阻碍”调查，那么只有在利害关系方“在合理期限内”未提交必要资料的情况下，才可求助于现有事实。因此，如果“在合理期限内”提供信息，调查机关就不能利用“可获得事实”规则，而必须利用利害关系方提交的信息。

二、调查的期限

各国反倾销调查机关通常使用在调查开始日期之前的固定“调查期”的数据进行反倾销调查。《反倾销协定》提及了“调查期”（period of investigation）的概念，第5.10款规定，这种调查必须在一年内完成，而且在任何情况下都不得超过18个月，即在启动之后18个月之内必须完成。而《反倾销协定》相关条款也有类似期限的规定，如第2.2.1款规定，“同类产品以低于单位（固定和可变）生产成本加管理、销售和一般费用的价格在出口国国内市场的销售或对第三国的销售，只有在主管机关确定此类销售属在持续时间内以实质数量且以不能在一段合理时间内收回成本的价格进行时，方可以价格原因将其视为未在正常贸易过程中进行的销售，且可在确定正常价值时不予考虑。如在进行销售时低于单位成本的价格高于调查期间的加权平均单位成本，则此类价格应被视为能在一段合理时间内收回成本”。该款还对“持续时间”进行注释，称该持续时间通常应为1年，但决不能少于6个月。

2000年，WTO反倾销措施委员会通过了一项《关于反倾销调查数据收集期的建议》。[①] 根据这项建议，用于倾销调查的数据收集期通常不应超过12个月，而且无论如何不应少于6个月，在可行的情况下，截止日期应尽可能接近启动日期。此外，损害调查的数据收集期通常至少应为3年，除非所收集的数据所针对的当事方存在的时间较短，并应包括倾销调查的整个数据收集期。

【案例摘录与评析】

一、2011年中国诉欧盟紧固件反倾销案[②]

EUROPEAN COMMUNITIES – DEFINITIVE ANTI-DUMPING MEASURES ON CERTAIN IRON OR STEEL FASTENERS FROM CHINA
(WT/DS397/AB/R)

VII Appeal of the Panel's Findings Regarding Aspects of the Dumping Determination in the Fasteners Investigation under Articles 6.4, 6.2, and 2.4 of the Anti-Dumping Agreement

A.Introduction

469 We turn now to address the European Union's and China's appeals of the Panel's findings regarding certain aspects of the Commission's dumping determination in the fasteners investigation. Specifically, the European Union appeals the Panel's finding that it acted inconsistently with Articles 6.4 and 6.2 of the *Anti-Dumping Agreement* by not providing a timely opportunity for Chinese interested parties to see the product types used by the Commission for purposes of comparing export price and normal value in the dumping determination. China appeals the Panel's finding that the European Union did not act inconsistently with Article 2.4 of the *Anti-Dumping Agreement* by failing to make a "fair comparison" between the export price and the normal value in the dumping determination. We begin our analysis with a description of the relevant factual background underlying both the European Union's and China's claims. We then

① 参见 G/ADP/6, adopted by the Committee on Anti-Dumping Practices on 5 May 2000. 虽然这项建议反映了成员方的共同实践，但是其本身作为一项建议没有约束力。参见 E. Vermulst, *The WTO Anti-Dumping Agreement: A Commentary*, Oxford University Press, 2006, pp.82~83.

② Appellate Body Reports, European Communities-Definitive Anti-Dumping Measures on Certain Iron or Steel Fasteners from China, WT/DS397/AB/R, 15 July 2011.

discuss the relevant interpretation of the provisions of the *Anti-Dumping Agreement* under which the European Union's and China's claims are raised. Next, we address the specific claims and arguments raised on appeal.

B. The Relevant Factual Background

470. The Panel found that, in the questionnaires sent to the producer in India①, Pooja Forge, and to the Chinese producers, the Commission requested that information on the investigated products be reported on the basis of categories defined by Product Control Numbers ("PCNs").② The Panel noted that the following six elements made up the PCNs identified by the Commission: type of fasteners (by CN code); strength/hardness; coating; presence of chrome on coating; diameter; and length/thickness. All but two of these elements, in turn, are further divided into subcategories, each of which is assigned a code in the form of a number or a letter. The elements contained in the PCNs thus represent 38 narrowly defined specifications of fasteners. The questionnaire provided, as an example, a product having the following characteristics: "selftapping screw, case hardening, not coated, diameter 4,2 millimeters, length 13 millimeters." On the basis of the corresponding numbers and letters assigned to each of the characteristics, this product would have a PCN of 2XNR042013.③

471. The questionnaire sent to Pooja Forge also requested that information be provided on the basis of the same PCNs. However, Pooja Forge did not provide information categorized on the basis of the PCNs as requested. Because the normal value in the fasteners investigation was established on the basis of the information provided by Pooja Forge, the Commission could not base its comparison between the normal value and export price on full PCNs.④ Therefore, it resorted to the use of "product types" defined by two factors, strength class and the distinction between standard and special fasteners, in the price comparisons for the dumping determination.⑤

472. The Panel found that the Chinese producers were informed very late in the proceedings

① We recall that, due to the European Union's designation of China as an NME, and the fact that MET was not granted to the Chinese producers in the fasteners investigation, the Commission established the normal value on the basis of the prices of fasteners sold in the analogue country, India. The Commission identified two Indian companies that produced the fasteners that were the subject of the investigation, and one of them, Pooja Forge, cooperated with the investigation. (See Definitive Regulation, supra, footnote 4, recitals 38 and 92)

② See Panel Report, para. 7.292 (referring to European Commission, Anti-Dumping Questionnaire for Chinese Exporters/Producers (Panel Exhibit CHN-51), pp. 11~13).

③ See Panel Exhibit CHN 51, *supra*, footnote 666, pp. 11~13.

④ See Panel Report, para. 7.293 [referring to European Union's response to Panel Question 43(b)].

⑤ See Panel Report, para. 7.293 (referring to Definitive Regulation, *supra*, footnote 4, recital 102; and Panel Exhibit CHN 31, *supra*, footnote 310, p. 2).

of the product types that formed the basis of the comparisons underlying the Commission's dumping determinations. Specifically, the General Disclosure Document, issued towards the end of the investigation on 3 November 2008, indicated that the Commission based its normal value determination on product types, but did not specify the number of, or relevant characteristics of, the product types or how they were determined.①

473. On 8 November 2008, two Chinese producers sought clarification from the Commission regarding the product types used, and specifically asked for a linkage between the PCNs on which the Chinese producers based their questionnaire submissions and the product types eventually used by the Commission. According to the Panel, this letter "clearly convey[ed] these two Chinese producers' request to see information regarding the product types that established the basis of the Commission's normal value determination and the relationship between these product types and the PCNs pertaining to the Chinese producers' products".② The Commission replied on 13 November 2008, stating that, "beside[s] product characteristics as specified in the PCN, a distinction was introduced between standard and special products since this was found to have a significant impact on prices".③ It went on to say that, for these two Chinese producers, "their entire export volume was considered as being standard products".④ The Panel found that this response did "not explain how the product types were established in the determination of normal value, or the relevant characteristics of those product types".⑤

474. On 17 November 2008, the Chinese producers again sought clarification. They noted that the nonconfidential version of Pooja Forge's questionnaire response contained no indication that Pooja Forge reported sales on the basis of PCNs. Thus, the Chinese producers asked:

> In abstract terms, was normal value established on a PCN basis, or were more general types of [the Indian producer's] fasteners matched with groups of PCNs from our clients? In that context, it would still be very useful for us if we could have a listing simply of which type of fastener or which PCNs of [the Indian producer] were matched

① See Panel Report, para. 7.485. In addition, under the heading "Comparison", the General Disclosure Document stated that the price comparison between the fasteners from China and those sold by Pooja Forge on the Indian market was "made by distinguishing between standard and special fastener types". (General Disclosure Document, supra, footnote 73, para. 93) The same statement is also contained in recital 102 of the Definitive Regulation.

② Panel Report, para. 7.486.

③ Panel Report, para. 7.487 [quoting Email Message dated 13 November 2008 from the European Commission to Van Bael & Bellis (Panel Exhibit CHN 29), p. 1].

④ Panel Report, para. 7.487 (quoting Panel Exhibit CHN 29, supra, footnote 672, p. 1).

⑤ Panel Report, para. 7.487.

with the PCNs of our clients.①

The Panel described this letter as "clearly repeat[ing] these Chinese producers' request to see information on the basis of which product types for the Indian producer were established".②

475. The Commission replied in a letter dated 21 November 2008 that the comparison "was not made on the basis of the full PCN, but on part [*sic*] of the characteristics of the product, namely the strength class as well as the abovementioned distinction between special and standard products".③ The Panel found that this was the first time the Commission clearly informed the Chinese producers that it did not make its findings based on PCNs, but on the characteristics of strength class and the distinction between standard and special fasteners. The letter came one working day before the deadline to make comments on the General Disclosure Document.④

476. The Panel record indicates that, on 24 November 2008, two days after the deadline for comments, one Chinese producer sent another letter to the Commission, expressing the view that it was not possible for it to comment on the Commission's dumping determination without knowing what types or groups of products of Pooja Forge were actually matched with the Chinese products.⑤

477. Thus, the Panel's factual findings, as well as the Panel record, indicate the following timeline relating to the relevant events that occurred in the context of the Commission's dumping determination:

...

C.The Relevant Interpretation of Articles 6.4 and 2.4 of the Anti-Dumping Agreement

478. Article 6.4 of the *Anti-Dumping Agreement* provides:

The authorities shall whenever practicable provide timely opportunities for all interested parties to see all information that is relevant to the presentation of their cases, that is not confidential as defined in paragraph 5, and that is used by the authorities in an anti-dumping investigation, and to prepare presentations on the basis of this information.

---

① Panel Report, para. 7.488 (quoting Letter dated 17 November 2008 from Van Bael & Bellis to the European Commission concerning the Definitive Disclosure Document: Request for Information II on behalf of Kunshan Chenghe Standard Component Co. Ltd and Ningbo Jinding Fastening Piece Co. Ltd. (Panel Exhibit CHN 30), p. 2). (emphasis omitted)

② Panel Report, para. 7.488.

③ Panel Report, para. 7.489 (quoting Panel Exhibit CHN 31, supra, footnote 310, p. 2).

④ Panel Report, para. 7.489.

⑤ Letter dated 24 November 2008 from Van Bael & Bellis on behalf of Kunshan Chenghe Standard Component Co. Ltd. to the European Commission, Comments on the Definitive Disclosure Document (Panel Exhibit CHN 59), p. 4.

479. The Appellate Body has found that Article 6.4 refers to "provid[ing] timely opportunities for all interested parties to see all information that is relevant to the presentation of *their* cases", and that the possessive pronoun "their" "clearly refers to the earlier reference in that sentence to 'interested parties'".[①] Therefore, it is the interested parties, rather than the authority, who determine whether the information is in fact "relevant" for the purposes of Article 6.4.[②] Moreover, according to the Appellate Body, whether the information was "used" by the authority does not depend on whether the authority specifically relied on that information. Rather, it depends on whether the information is related to "a required step in the anti-dumping investigation".[③] Thus, Article 6.4 concerns information relating to "issues which the investigating authority is required to consider under the [*Anti-Dumping Agreement*], or which it does, in fact, consider, in the exercise of its discretion, during the course of an anti-dumping investigation."[④]

480. The interested parties' right under Article 6.4, therefore, is to see *all* nonconfidential information relevant to the presentation of their cases and used by the investigating authority. Article 6.4 thus applies to a broad range of information that is used by an investigating authority for purposes of carrying out a required step in an anti-dumping investigation. We note the European Union's view that the term "information" in Article 6.4 "concerns facts and raw data rather than factual determinations and conclusions by the investigating authorities".[⑤] In our view, there is no textual basis in Article 6.4 for limiting information "relevant to the presentation of [parties'] cases" and "used by the authorities" to facts or raw data unprocessed by the authorities. Indeed, the broad range of information subject to the obligation under Article 6.4 may take various forms, including data submitted by the interested parties, and information that has been processed, organized, or summarized by the authority. We do not see why only facts and raw data would be relevant to the parties' presentation of their cases. A proper interpretation of Article 6.4 does not mean, however, that an investigating authority's reasoning or internal deliberation in reaching its final determination is also subject to the obligation under Article 6.4. Article 6.4 concerns the information that is used by an authority, rather than an authority's detailed analysis of the information, or the determination it reaches based on such information.

481. The European Union also argues that the context of Article 6.4, as provided by the other paragraphs of Article 6, confirms that the obligation under Article 6.4 only concerns facts and raw data submitted by interested parties. The European Union submits that Articles 6.1 to

① Appellate Body Report, *EC–Tube or Pipe Fittings*, para. 145. (original emphasis)

② See Appellate Body Report, *EC–Tube or Pipe Fittings*, para. 145.

③ Appellate Body Report, *EC–Tube or Pipe Fittings*, para. 147.

④ Panel Report, *EC–Salmon (Norway)*, para. 7.769. (footnotes omitted)

⑤ European Union's appellant's submission, para. 253.

6.3 provide parties the right to submit their *own* information, and Articles 6.6 and 6.7 impose an obligation on investigating authorities to verify the information submitted by the parties. Article 6.8, in turn, allows the use of "facts available" when an interested party does not provide necessary information.① Thus, the European Union asserts, Article 6.4 is limited to addressing "the parties' right to know what *other interested parties have submitted* in terms of evidence and information".② In our view, however, the European Union's recourse to the other paragraphs under Article 6 is unavailing. The only qualification on the term "information" under Article 6.4 is that it is "relevant to the presentation of their cases", "not confidential as defined in paragraph 5", and "used by the authorities in an anti-dumping investigation". Article 6.2 further confirms that access to all such information is important because, without such information, the interested parties may not have "a full opportunity for the defence of their interests". Moreover, where the term "information" is to be specifically qualified, the relevant paragraphs under Article 6 clearly provide so. For example, Article 6.3 refers to "oral information", Article 6.5 applies to information that is "by nature confidential", and Article 6.6 concerns information "supplied by interested parties". Without such qualifications, we see no textual basis in Article 6.4, or contextual basis under Article 6, for limiting the term "information" in Article 6.4 to only that provided by other interested parties.

482. The European Union further argues that, pursuant to Article 6.9, the authorities must inform all interested parties of "the essential facts under consideration which form the basis for the decision" before a final determination is made. In the European Union's view, the use of the phrase "essential facts" rather than the word "information" in Article 6.9 indicates that Articles 6.1 to 6.8 concern the information gathering process. The European Union also argues that Article 6.9 marks the end of the process and requires a disclosure of the authority's essential factual conclusions③, and that the "product types" used to compare export price and normal value fall into the category of essential facts.④ The European Union further contends that the differences between the obligations under Articles 6.4 and 6.9 are "well established in WTO jurisprudence". For example, the European Union argues that in *Guatemala – Cement II* the panel found that Article 6.4 generally provided an "access to the file"⑤ right, whereas Article 6.9 required more and could not be satisfied "simply by offering to provide interested parties with copies of all

① European Union's appellant's submission, paras. 258, 259, 262, and 263.

② European Union's appellant's submission, para. 260. (original emphasis).

③ European Union's appellant's submission, paras. 264 and 265.

④ European Union's responses to questioning at the oral hearing.

⑤ European Union's appellant's submission, para. 261 (quoting Panel Report, *Guatemala–Cement II*, para. 8.133).

information in the file".[①]

483. The differences alleged by the European Union between Article 6.9 and the other paragraphs of Article 6 do not, in our view, restrict the meaning of the word "information" in Article 6.4 to the narrow scope the European Union attributes to it. As discussed above, Article 6.4 refers broadly to "*all* information that is relevant to the presentation of [the interested parties'] cases". Such information may come in different forms, including not only "facts or raw data" submitted by the other parties, but also information that an investigating authority organizes, processes, or summarizes at each stage of an anti-dumping investigation. Although Article 6.9 refers to "the essential facts under consideration which form the basis" for the authority's final determination, we do not consider that what the terms "information" and "essential facts" refer to must be mutually exclusive. Depending on the specific circumstances of a case, the "information" relevant to the presentation of an interested party's case can be a broader concept than the essential facts relied on by the authority, or it may overlap with such "essential facts". The "essential facts" under Article 6.9, which form the basis for a final determination, are those that are material for the authority's decision, whereas "information" that is relevant to the presentation of a party's case, and used by the authority, is not necessarily what the authority relies on in reaching its final determination. Moreover, information within the meaning of Article 6.4 has to be provided to interested parties in a timely fashion throughout the investigation. It is not sufficient to provide such information only "before a final determination is made" within the meaning of Article 6.9. In sum, we consider that the European Union's reliance on the context of Article 6.4 is unavailing to its position.

484. The European Union refers to the panel's finding in *Korea – Certain Paper* to point out that what had to be disclosed upon request in that dispute were the actual figures for cost of manufacture, expenses or profits used in the calculation of the constructed normal value.[②] The European Union further submits that the Appellate Body's finding in *EC – Tube or Pipe Fittings*, that the European Communities was required to disclose a document containing a summary of the "raw data"[③] on some of the injury factors under Article 3.4 of the *Anti-Dumping Agreement*, also supports its understanding of the term "information" in Article 6.4. However, the fact that the findings in prior disputes under Article 6.4 may have concerned such "raw data" only shows that that was the "information" at issue in those disputes. The particular "information" found

① Panel Report, *Guatemala–Cement II*, para. 8.230.

② European Union's appellant's submission, para. 253 (referring to Panel Report, *Korea–Certain Paper*, para. 7.199).

③ European Union's appellant's submission, para. 254 (referring to Appellate Body Report, *EC–Tube or Pipe Fittings*, paras. 138-141).

to be subject to Article 6.4 in specific disputes, however, does not limit the scope of the term in Article 6.4 in all disputes arising under that provision. Moreover, with regard to the Appellate Body's finding in *EC – Tube or Pipe Fittings*, to the extent that the European Union uses the term "raw data"① to mean information submitted by the parties and not processed by the investigating authority, we note that this view is contradicted by the facts at issue in that dispute. Rather, the "information" relevant to the Appellate Body's finding under Article 6.4 in that case consisted of data that had been aggregated and summarized by the Commission as well as the Commission's evaluation of this data. More specifically, the "information" contained worksheets prepared by the European investigating authority regarding the injury factors listed in Article 3.4 on the basis of evidence submitted by the interested parties.②

485. In sum, under Article 6.4 of the *Anti-Dumping Agreement*, what information is considered "relevant to the presentation of [the interested parties'] cases" and "used by the authorities" would depend on the specific "step" of the anti-dumping investigation and the particular issue before the investigating authority. We recall that, in this dispute, China claims that the Commission failed to provide timely opportunities for the Chinese producers to see certain information relevant to the comparison between the export price and normal value for purposes of the dumping determination in the fasteners investigation. We therefore focus our analysis on the type of "information" covered under Article 6.4 and when it has to be disclosed, in the context of the comparison between the export price and normal value within the meaning of Article 2.4 of the *Anti-Dumping Agreement*.

...

495. With respect to the first ground of appeal, as discussed above, we disagree with the European Union's view that the term "information" in Article 6.4 only "concerns facts and raw data rather than factual determinations and conclusions by the investigating authorities".③ Rather, Article 6.4 applies to a broad range of information that is relevant to the presentation of the interested parties' cases and is used by an investigating authority for purposes of carrying out a required step in an anti-dumping investigation. Such information includes evidence submitted by the interested parties, as well as data processed, organized, or summarized by the authority. An authority's reasoning or internal deliberation in reaching a determination, however, does not constitute "information" subject to the obligation under Article 6.4.

---

① European Union's appellant's submission, para. 254.

② Panel Report, *EC–Tube or Pipe Fittings*, para. 7.307 and footnote 256 thereto. See also China's appellee's submission, para. 397.

③ European Union's appellant's submission, para. 253.

496. In this dispute, the product types used by the Commission concerned "a required step"① in an anti-dumping investigation, namely, the comparison between export price and normal value for purposes of the dumping determination. The product types used by the Commission for purposes of the dumping determination were particularly relevant to the interested parties' cases, given the factual background of this case. We recall that the questionnaire sent to the Chinese producers and the Indian producer requested that products be identified on the basis of PCNs, thus leaving at least two Chinese exporters② with the impression that such PCNs would be used for purposes of the comparison between export price and normal value. As the Panel noted, "it appears from the structure of the questionnaires that [requests for adjustments to ensure a fair comparison] will not be necessary because of the categorization of the product according to PCN groups".③ Indeed, by using the PCNs as the organizing principle when gathering product information from the interested parties, the Commission's approach created a reasonable expectation that price comparisons would be conducted on a very particular basis. Moreover, in the light of the very precise nature of the physical characteristics listed under the PCNs, it was also reasonable to assume that few adjustments would be necessary, as prices of narrowly defined products by the Chinese producers would have been compared to prices of equally narrowly defined products in the analogue country, India.

497. Nonetheless, although the Chinese producers provided information on the basis of PCNs, the Indian producer, Pooja Forge, did not provide information on that basis. Consequently, the Commission decided to use a different method of product grouping to conduct the comparison, namely, what it called "product types", which it defined on the basis of two factors: strength class and the distinction between standard and special fasteners. The product types used by the Commission were thus a critical piece of information relating to a required step in the investigation, and these product types were in turn established on the basis of the product information provided by the Indian producer. They were not simply the Commission's reasoning in reaching its final determination.

498. Moreover, we recall that the PCNs include six elements further divided into 38 specifications, which could have resulted in hundreds of different combinations. Yet, the PCN characteristics and the product types overlap only with regard to one element, namely, the strength class. Thus, the differences between the PCNs and the product types used by the

① Appellate Body Report, *EC–Tube or Pipe Fittings*, para. 147.

② These two producers later requested the Commission to clarify the meaning of "product types" used in the dumping determination.

③ Panel Report, para. 7.491.

Commission could have prompted the Chinese producers to request that adjustments be made for any differences that might have affected price comparability between the Chinese and Indian fasteners, within the meaning of Article 2.4 of the *Anti-Dumping Agreement*. Indeed, without knowing what constituted "product types", "it would be difficult if not impossible, for foreign producers to request adjustments that they consider necessary in order to ensure a fair comparison."[①] Thus, the information concerning the product types, including their characteristics and how they were determined, constituted "information" within the meaning of Article 6.4 of the *Anti-Dumping Agreement*, because they were used in the dumping determination made by the Commission[②], and were indispensible to the parties' presentation of their cases concerning the dumping determination.

499. Turning to the European Union's claim that the Panel violated Article 11 of the DSU, we recall that, as discussed above in section VI.E, not every error allegedly committed by a panel amounts to a violation of Article 11 of the DSU. Rather, a participant claiming that a panel ignored certain evidence, and hence acted inconsistently with Article 11, must explain why the evidence is so material to its case that the panel's failure to address such evidence has a bearing on the objectivity of the panel's factual assessment.

500. In this regard, we note the European Union's assertion that "[o]ne *might* wrongly conclude from the Panel's findings" that the Chinese producers requesting to see the product types were unable to make any presentations due to time constraints.[③] According to the European Union, one Chinese producer "did submit comments" on the requested information in a letter dated 24 November 2008[④] and, in that letter, it did not request an extension of the time for making presentations.[⑤] The European Union argues that this letter shows that "timing was *not* the problem for the interested parties", but the letter was not mentioned by the Panel in its reasoning.[⑥] In our view, the assertion that the Panel's findings "might" give a certain impression does not explain why the Panel's alleged "disregard" of a piece of evidence calls into question the objectivity of the Panel's factual assessment. On its face, such a claim simply does not rise to the

① Panel Report, para. 7.491.

② See Panel Report, EC–Salmon (Norway), para. 7.769.

③ European Union's appellant's submission, para. 291. (emphasis added)

④ European Union's appellant's submission, para. 291. (emphasis omitted)

⑤ European Union's appellant's submission, para. 292.

⑥ European Union's appellant's submission, para. 294. (original emphasis)

level of egregiousness that a violation of Article 11 of the DSU requires.[①]

501. The European Union further submits that the Panel disregarded the Information Document, which "signall[ed] the use of 'product types'" three months prior to the issuance of the General Disclosure Document.[②] Thus, in the European Union's view, any "problem with the timing of the disclosure" regarding product types "was in large part due to the fact that the Chinese interested parties never requested to see the basis for the product type groupings until very late in the proceedings."[③]

502. Although the European Union's argument suggests that the Information Document was an important piece of evidence supporting its position, a review of the relevant evidence indicates the contrary. The Information Document, like the General Disclosure Document, stated that the Commission based its normal value determination on product types, but did not specify the relevant characteristics of the product types or how they were determined.[④] Moreover, as the Panel properly found, the correspondence between the Commission and the two Chinese producers requesting clarification regarding the product types showed that "until the receipt of the General Disclosure Document, the Chinese producers were under the impression that the Commission would make its dumping determinations on the basis of PCNs, as requested in the questionnaires sent to the Chinese and the Indian producers".[⑤] It should also be recalled that the "information" sought by the Chinese producers was a clarification of what constituted "product types" as referenced in the General Disclosure Document. Thus, the fact that the Information Document referred to the concept of product types does not alter the Panel's ultimate finding that the Commission did not disclose the requested clarification until one working day before the deadline for comments. We therefore do not agree with the European Union's assertion that the Panel erroneously ignored the evidence contained in the Information Document in reaching its finding.

503. The European Union also claims that, because some Chinese producers submitted

① In any event, we note that, in the letter referred to by the European Union, the Chinese producer expressed the view that it was not possible to comment on the Commission's dumping determination without knowing what types or groups of products of Pooja Forge were actually matched with the Chinese products. The letter thus shows that the Chinese producers still considered the information provided by the Commission insufficient for them to comment properly on the dumping determination. This letter, therefore, does not lend support to the European Union's position, and the Panel acted properly in not relying on this evidence for reaching its finding.

② European Union's appellant's submission, para. 284.

③ European Union's appellant's submission, para. 286.

④ Information Document, supra, footnote 81, p. 12.

⑤ Panel Report, para. 7.490.

information describing certain characteristics that, they believed, distinguished different types of fasteners, and because the product types used for purposes of the dumping determination reflected the same characteristics, the Chinese producers "clearly were able to make presentations based on this 'information'".[①] Specifically, the European Union refers to a submission made on 22 February 2008 by Jiaxing Association of Fastener Import & Export Companies ("Jiaxing Association") describing the difference between fasteners produced by Chinese producers and those produced by EU producers. Jiaxing Association argued that the Chinese companies mostly produced standard fasteners in lower strength classes, while EU producers mostly produced nonstandard fasteners in higher strength classes,[②] and that fasteners by Chinese and EU producers were not competitive with each other. The European Union asserts that "the Panel's conclusion that Chinese producers were not given a timely opportunity to 'see information relevant to the presentation of their cases' is flawed as the alleged 'information' was no other than what the Chinese interested parties had been presenting as being the main characteristics for distinguishing between product types throughout the investigation."[③]

504. However, the evidence that the European Union claimed the Panel "disregarded" was not apposite to the issue examined by the Panel under Article 6.4 of the *Anti-Dumping Agreement*. As discussed, what information may be considered "relevant for the presentation" of the interested parties' cases under Article 6.4 depends on the particular stage of the anti-dumping investigation and the specific issue before the investigating authority. China's claim and the Panel's finding under Article 6.4 concern the information on product types that the Commission used for purposes of price comparisons between fasteners produced by the Indian producer (rather than EU producers) and by the Chinese producers in its dumping determination. Thus, the information contained in Jiaxing Association's submission, which was made in a context unrelated to the issue of price comparisons between the Indian and Chinese fasteners, cannot be considered as information that the two Chinese producers requested as relevant to the presentation of their cases regarding the dumping determination. Therefore, we do not consider that the Panel erred in not relying on the evidence concerning Jiaxing Association's submission in making its finding under Article 6.4.

505. In sum, we consider that the product types used by the Commission for purposes of comparing the export price and normal value in the fasteners investigation constituted

① European Union's appellant's submission, para. 288.

② Jiaxing Association of Fasteners Import & Export Companies, Submission of 22 February 2008 (Panel Exhibit EU 13), p. 4. The two Chinese producers requesting clarification regarding product types were not part of this association.

③ European Union's appellant's submission, para. 288 (referring to Panel Report, para. 7.492).

"information relevant to the presentation" of the Chinese parties' case. This is because, without such information, "it would be difficult if not impossible, for foreign producers to request adjustments that they consider necessary in order to ensure a fair comparison."[①] We further consider that the Panel correctly found that the European Union violated Article 6.4 of the *Anti-Dumping Agreement* "by not providing a timely opportunity for Chinese producers to see information regarding the product types on the basis of which normal value was established".[②] We therefore decline to accept the European Union's appeal of these findings.

With regard to the Panel's finding under Article 6.2 of the *Anti-Dumping Agreement*, the European Union maintains that, because it has demonstrated that the Panel's finding under Article 6.4 was flawed, the Panel's "purely consequential" finding under Article 6.2 was also in error.[③] In the light of our finding that the Panel did not err in reaching its finding under Article 6.4, we also disagree with the European Union's assertion that the Panel's finding under Article 6.2 was in error.

【本案评析】

以上案例节选自2011年中国诉欧盟紧固件反倾销案上诉机构报告。对于第6.4款的规定，即利害关系方有权了解与其案件陈述有关的且主管机关在反倾销调查中使用的所有信息，该案上诉机构驳回了欧共体的意见，即“信息”一词“涉及的是事实和原始数据，而不是调查机关的事实认定和结论”。但上诉机构也进一步指出，对第6.4款的适当解释并不意味着调查机关在作出最后认定时的推理或内部审议也须遵守第6.4款的规定。上诉机构强调，第6.4款中规定的哪些信息被认为是与有关各方的“案件陈述有关的”和“主管机关使用的”，将取决于反倾销调查的具体步骤和调查机关要处理的具体问题。关于“信息”一词是否包括将产品分成不同类型的问题，该案上诉机构不同意欧共体的观点，即“信息”一词仅限于事实和原始数据，而不包括事实认定。上诉机构指出，第6.4款适用于范围广泛的信息，包括“有关各方提交的证据以及主管机关处理、整理或汇总的数据”，因此该案上诉机构不同意欧盟的意见，即专家组在得出调查结果时错误地忽略了资料文件中所载的证据，也不认为专家组在根据第6.4款作出调查结果时不依赖嘉兴协会提交的证据是错误的。在此基础上，上诉机构得出结论认为，欧盟

① Panel Report , para. 7.491.

② Panel Report, para. 7.494.

③ European Union's appellant's submission, para. 275.

委员会为比较紧固件调查中的出口价格和正常价值而使用的产品类型构成了向当事方中国的“陈述有关的信息”；本案专家组正确地认定了欧共体对第6.4款的违反，因为其没有为中国生产者提供及时的机会，使后者能够了解确定正常价值所依据的产品类型的信息。

二、2016年中国诉欧盟紧固件反倾销（DSU第21.5条）争端案①

EUROPEAN COMMUNITIES – DEFINITIVE ANTI-DUMPING MEASURES ON CERTAIN IRON OR STEEL FASTENERS FROM CHINA RECOURSE TO ARTICLE 21.5 OF THE DSU BY CHINA (WT/DS397/AB/RW)

5.163. Article 2.4 requires investigating authorities to ensure a fair comparison between the export price and the normal value and, to this end, to make due allowance, or adjustments, for differences affecting price comparability. The obligation to ensure a fair comparison “lies on the investigating authorities”.② As part of their investigation, they “are charged with comparing normal value and export price and determining whether there is dumping of imports.”③ However, as the Appellate Body has explained, this does not mean that interested parties do not have a role to play in the process of ensuring a fair comparison.④ Rather, “exporters bear the burden of substantiating, ‘as constructively as possible’, their requests for adjustments reflecting the ‘due allowance’ within the meaning of Article 2.4.”⑤ As such, “[i]f it is not demonstrated to the authorities that there is a difference affecting price comparability, there is no obligation to make an adjustment.”⑥ However, the authorities “must take steps to achieve clarity as to the adjustment

① Appellate Body Reports, European Communities–Definitive Anti-Dumping Measures on Certain Iron or Steel Fasteners from China–Recourse to Article 21.5 of the DSU by China ,WT/DS397/AB/RW, 18 JANUARY 2016.

② Appellate Body Report, *EC–Fasteners (China),* para. 487 (quoting Appellate Body Report, *US Hot Rolled Steel*, para. 178).

③ Appellate Body Report, *EC–Fasteners (China)*, para. 487 (quoting Appellate Body Report, *US Hot Rolled Steel*, para. 178).

④ Appellate Body Report, *EC–Fasteners (China)*, para. 488.

⑤ Appellate Body Report, *EC–Fasteners (China)*, para. 488 (quoting Panel Report, *EC–Tube or Pipe Fittings*, para. 7.158).

⑥ Appellate Body Report, *EC–Fasteners (China)*, para. 488 (referring to Panel Report, *Korea–Certain Paper*, para. 7.147).

claimed and then determine whether and to what extent that adjustment is merited."①

5.164. The last sentence of Article 2.4, in turn, imposes an obligation on investigating authorities to "indicate to the parties in question what information is necessary to ensure a fair comparison" and "not [to] impose an unreasonable burden of proof on those parties". This provision thus adds a "procedural requirement" to the general obligation to ensure a fair comparison.②

5.165. As the Appellate Body explained in the original proceedings:

> [W]hereas the exporters may be required to "substantiate their assertions concerning adjustments", the last sentence of Article 2.4 requires the investigating authorities to "indicate to the parties" what information these requests should contain, so that the interested parties will be in a position to make a request for adjustments. This process has been described as a "dialogue" between the authority and the interested parties. ③

5.166. The Appellate Body further found that, "as a starting point for the dialogue between the investigating authority and the interested parties to ensure a fair comparison, the authority must, at a minimum, inform the parties of the product groups with regard to which it will conduct the price comparisons."④

5.167. In addition, the Appellate Body explained the particular relevance of the procedural requirement under Article 2.4 in the context of an investigation where the normal value is

---

① Appellate Body Report, *EC–Fasteners (China)*, paras. 488 and 519 (quoting Panel Report, *EC Tube or Pipe Fittings*, para. 7.158).

② Appellate Body Report, *EC–Fasteners (China)*, para. 489.

③ Appellate Body Report, *EC–Fasteners (China)*, para. 489 (quoting, respectively, Panel Reports, *EC–Tube or Pipe Fittings*, para. 7.158; and *Egypt–Steel Rebar*, para. 7.352). As the panel in *Egypt–Steel Rebar* explained: Finally, we note the affirmative information gathering burden on the investigating authority in this context, that it "shall indicate to the parties in question what information is necessary to ensure a fair comparison and shall not impose an unreasonable burden of proof on those parties" (emphasis added). In short, where it is demonstrated by one or another party in a particular case, or by the data itself that a given difference affects price comparability, an adjustment must be made. In identifying to the parties the data that it considers would be necessary to make such a demonstration, the investigating authority is not to impose an unreasonable burden of proof on the parties. Thus, the process of determining what kind or types of adjustments need to be made to one or both sides of the dumping margin equation to ensure a fair comparison, is something of a dialogue between interested parties and the investigating authority, and must be done on a case by case basis, grounded in factual evidence.

④ Appellate Body Report, *EC–Fasteners (China)*, para. 490.

established on the basis of data provided by an analogue country producer, rather than the exporter under investigation, by stating that:

> [W]here the normal value is not established on the basis of the foreign producers' domestic sales, but is established on the basis of the domestic sales in an analogue country, the investigating authority's obligation to inform the interested parties of the basis of the price comparison is even more pertinent for ensuring a fair comparison. This is because foreign producers are unlikely to have knowledge of the specific products and pricing practices of the producer in an analogue country. Unless the foreign producers under investigation are informed of the specific products with regard to which the normal value is determined, they will not be in a position to request adjustments they deem necessary.①

5.168. With this understanding in mind, we examine below the European Union's claims of error in respect of the Panel's interpretation and application of the last sentence of Article 2.4 of the Anti-Dumping Agreement.

...

5.172. We agree that the fact that normal value is determined based on a methodology involving data of an analogue country producer does not affect the legal obligation imposed on investigating authorities under the last sentence of Article 2.4. In all anti-dumping investigations, "[t]he authorities shall indicate to the parties in question what information is necessary to ensure a fair comparison and shall not impose an unreasonable burden of proof on those parties".② As explained, this provision requires investigating authorities to indicate to the parties what information requests for adjustments should contain, so that the interested parties will be in a position to make such requests.③ Depending on the factual circumstances at hand, this provision may require investigating authorities to provide certain information to parties requesting adjustments, in particular where the exporter under investigation is missing information pertaining to the normal value determined by the investigating authority because it is based on the domestic sales of an analogue country producer, rather than the exporter's own domestic sales. Therefore, as we have set out above, the procedural requirement under Article 2.4 is necessarily even more pertinent in the context of an investigation involving information

---

① Appellate Body Report, *EC–Fasteners (China)*, para. 491.

② Article 2.4, last sentence of the Anti-Dumping Agreement.

③ Body Report, *EC–Fasteners (China)*, para. 489.

from an analogue country producer. This, however, does not mean that the legal obligation under the last sentence of Article 2.4 is more far reaching when the analogue country methodology is used. Rather, this issue relates to the application of this provision to a particular factual background.

【本案评析】

以上案例节选自2016年中国诉欧盟紧固件反倾销(DSU第21.5条)争端案上诉机构报告。《反倾销协定》第2.4款要求调查当局对所调查的出口产品的价格与正常价值进行公平比较,并适当考虑到影响价格可比性的差异。该款最后一句规定,调查机关有义务“向有关当事方表明为确保公平比较所需的信息”。也就是说,对于价格公平比较,虽然出口商应当证实其调整请求,但调查机关必须首先向当事各方通报其为确保公平比较将需要何种信息。本案上诉机构认为,这一条款在确保公平比较的一般义务中增加了一项“程序要求”。上述机构指出,这一条款要求调查机构向要求价格调整的当事方提供某些信息,特别是在调查机构采用替代国(analogue country)制度,而不是出口商自己的国内销售价格时,受调查的出口商缺少对调查机构确定正常价值所需有关的信息了解。上诉机构也强调,虽然第2.4款下的程序要求在涉及替代国生产者提供的资料的调查中必然更为恰当,但是这并不意味着在使用替代国方法时,第2.4款最后一句所规定的法律义务的作用会更大,因为这涉及适用条款到特定事实背景的问题。

而在之前的专家组报告之中,明确指出中欧双方在替代国企业产品清单和特征的保密处理、替代国产品特征信息披露等方面存在分歧,专家组对其进行了系统判定。针对替代国企业产品清单和特征的保密处理,专家组认为应当由提出保密处理的一方说明正当理由,调查机关在客观分析保密理由是否正当后才能决定是否进行保密处理。根据中欧双方提交的证据,专家组认为欧委会没有客观分析替代国生产企业提出的保密理由是否正当,所以欧委会对替代国生产企业产品特征进行保密处理的做法,违反了《反倾销协定》第6.5条。针对替代国产品特征信息披露,专家组认为替代国生产企业产品特征的信息关系到中国出口商的正常价值和倾销幅度的认定,又是调查机关在反倾销调查中使用的信息。虽然欧盟辩称欧委会已根据第6.9条在最终披露中将该信息作为定案的基本信息提供给中国出口商，但专家组认为欧委会对于替代国产品特征直到调查结束前才做披露，这一做法不符合第 6.4 条关于“迅速提供机会了解案情”的要求，中国生产商无法以此信息为基础准备抗辩。

三、2015 年欧盟和日本诉中国对进口的高性能不锈钢无缝钢管（HP–SSST）征收反倾销税措施案①

China - Measures Imposing Anti-Dumping Duties on High-Performance Stainless Steel Seamless Tubes (“HP-SSST”) from the European Union and Japan
(WT/DS454/AB/R, WT/DS460/AB/R)

5.3.2 Assessment of the Panel’s analysis

5.92. On appeal, China argues that the Panel erred in construing Article 6.5 of the Anti-Dumping Agreement as imposing an obligation on an investigating authority to explain why it considers that confidential treatment is warranted.241 China refers to the panel report in Mexico–Steel Pipes and Tubes and the Appellate Body report in EC Fasteners (China) to argue that, while an investigating authority must review and decide whether “good cause” was shown, there is no obligation for an investigating authority to provide any explanation regarding its assessment and scrutiny of the alleged showing of “good cause”.

5.93. Japan and the European Union observe that, contrary to what China suggests, the Panel did not find that Article 6.5 of the Anti-Dumping Agreement contains an obligation for the investigating authority to “provide an explanation” for its reasons for granting confidentiality. Rather, the Panel’s finding was that, in the absence of any explanation by MOFCOM, the Panel had no basis to conclude that MOFCOM undertook an objective assessment and properly determined that the petitioners had shown “good cause” for their requests for confidential treatment with respect to the full text of the four reports at issue. 243 At the oral hearing, Japan and the European Union agreed that the degree of substantiation required from an investigating authority depends on the nature of the information for which confidential treatment is sought, noting however that, in the absence of any evidence that MOFCOM had objectively assessed the “good cause” alleged for confidential treatment, the Panel correctly concluded that China had acted

① Appellate Body Report, China-Measures Imposing Anti-Dumping Duties on High-Performance Stainless Steel Seamless Tubes (HP-SSST) from the European Union and Japan,WT/DS454/AB/R,WT/DS460/AB/R,14 October 2015. 原文脚注省略。

inconsistently with Article 6.5.

5.94. We begin our analysis by examining the text of Article 6.5 of the Anti-Dumping Agreement, which provides:

...

5.95. In EC – Fasteners (China), the Appellate Body explained that Article 6.5 covers information that is "by nature confidential", as well as information that is "provided on a confidential basis", and that a "good cause" showing by the party seeking confidential treatment is required for both of these categories of information.245 The Appellate Body added that "[t]he 'good cause' alleged must constitute a reason sufficient to justify the withholding of information from both the public and from the other parties interested in the investigation."246 According to the Appellate Body, "'[g]ood cause' must be assessed and determined objectively by the investigating authority, and cannot be determined merely based on the subjective concerns of the submitting party." The Appellate Body further stated:

In practice, a party seeking confidential treatment for information must make its "good cause" showing to the investigating authority upon submission of the information. The authority must objectively assess the "good cause" alleged for confidential treatment, and scrutinize the party's showing in order to determine whether the submitting party has sufficiently substantiated its request. In making its assessment, the investigating authority must seek to balance the submitting party's interest in protecting its confidential information with the prejudicial effect that the non-disclosure of the information may have on the transparency and due process interests of other parties involved in the investigation to present their cases and defend their interests. The type of evidence and the extent of substantiation an authority must require will depend on the nature of the information at issue and the particular "good cause" alleged. The obligation remains with the investigating authority to examine objectively the justification given for the need for confidential treatment. If information is treated as confidential by an authority without such a "good cause" showing having been made, the authority would be acting inconsistently with its obligations under Article 6.5 to grant such treatment only "upon good cause shown".

5.96. The Appellate Body further noted that, "[w]henever information is treated as confidential, transparency and due process concerns will necessarily arise because such treatment entails the withholding of information from other parties to an investigation." The Appellate Body stated that "Articles 6.5 and 6.5.1 accommodate the concerns of confidentiality, transparency, and due process by protecting information that is by nature confidential or is submitted on a confidential basis and upon 'good cause' shown, but establishing an alternative method for communicating its content so as to satisfy the right of other parties to the investigation to obtain a reasonable understanding of the substance of the confidential information, and to defend their interests."

5.97. The Appellate Body added that an investigating authority "must objectively assess the 'good cause' alleged for confidential treatment, and scrutinize the party's showing in order to determine whether the submitting party has sufficiently substantiated its request".251 However, the Appellate Body did not further say how the sufficiency of a showing of "good cause" is to be assessed by an investigating authority, or how it is to be assessed by a reviewing panel. As we see it, a panel tasked with reviewing whether an investigating authority has objectively assessed the "good cause" alleged by a party must examine this issue on the basis of the investigating authority's published report and its related supporting documents, and in the light of the nature of the information at issue and the reasons given by the submitting party for its request for confidential treatment. The type of evidence and the extent of substantiation the investigating authority must require will depend on the nature of the information at issue and the particular "good cause" alleged.254 In reviewing whether an investigating authority has assessed and determined objectively that "good cause" for confidential treatment has been shown to exist, it is not for a panel to engage in a de novo review of the record of the investigation and determine for itself whether the existence of "good cause" has been sufficiently substantiated by the submitting party.

5.98. Turning to the present case, we note that, in finding that there was no evidence that MOFCOM objectively assessed the "good cause" alleged for confidential treatment, the Panel stressed that it was not concluding that MOFCOM could not have treated the full text of the reports contained in appendix V and the appendix to the petitioners' supplemental evidence of 29 March 2012 as confidential. Rather, the Panel found that there was "no evidence that MOFCOM ever considered whether good cause had been shown for such treatment", and thus no evidence of an objective assessment.

5.99. Pursuant to Article 6.5 of the Anti-Dumping Agreement, it is for the investigating authority to require a party that seeks confidential treatment of information to explain and provide reasons as to why the information at issue should be treated as confidential. The investigating authority, in turn, is under an obligation to assess objectively the "good cause" alleged by the submitting party for confidential treatment, and to "scrutinize the party's showing in order to determine whether the submitting party has sufficiently substantiated its request". As the Appellate Body has explained, "'[g]ood cause' must be assessed and determined objectively by the investigating authority, and cannot be determined merely based on the subjective concerns of the submitting party."258 In the present case, however, MOFCOM merely summarized the reasons provided by the petitioners for confidential treatment of the full text of two of the four reports at issue.259

5.100. Therefore, we see no error in the Panel's finding that, in the absence of any evidence that MOFCOM objectively assessed the "good cause" alleged, it had no basis to conclude that MOFCOM undertook an objective assessment and properly determined that the petitioners had shown "good cause" for their requests for confidential treatment.260 In these circumstances, we also see no error in the Panel's conclusion that there was no basis for it to find that "MOFCOM properly determined that the petitioners had shown 'good cause' for their requests for confidential treatment from the fact that MOFCOM ultimately granted their request for confidential treatment."

【本案评析】

以上案例节选自 2015 年欧盟和日本诉中国对进口的高性能不锈钢无缝钢管(HP-SSST)征收反倾销税措施案上诉机构报告。该案上诉机构认为，专家组在审查调查机关是否客观评估了当事方所称的"正当理由"时，必须根据调查机关已经公布的报告及其相关支撑文件，并依据所涉信息的性质和请求方所提出的保密理由。调查机关所必需的证据类型和证实程度的要求将取决于所涉信息的性质和所指称的特定"正当理由"。在评审调查机关是否对保密处理的"正当理由"进行了客观的评估和确定时，不应由专家组对调查记录进行新的审查，并自行确定请求方是否充分证实了"正当理由"的存在。上诉机构也指出，"正当理由"必须由调查机关客观地评估和确定，而不能仅仅根据请求方的主观关切来确定。值得注意的是，此案上诉机构在审查第 5.6 款法律问题时也援引了 2011 年中国诉欧盟紧固件案上诉机构报告。在紧固件案中，上诉机构提出，在作出评估时，调查当局必须设法平衡请求人保护其机密信息的利益与不披露这些信息可能对参与调查的其他各方在澄清其案件和捍卫其权利方面的透明度和正当程序利益所产生的损害。客观审查需要保密待遇理由的义务仍然是调查机关的。如果一个主管机关在没有提出这种"正当理由"的情况下将资料视为机密，则主管当局将不能按照第 6.5 款规定的义务采取行动，其只有"在提出正当理由的情况下"才给予这种待遇。

四、2001 年美国对日本热轧钢产品的反倾销措施案①

UNITED STATES – ANTI-DUMPING MEASURES ON CERTAIN HOT-ROLLED STEEL PRODUCTS FROM JAPAN
(WT/DS184/AB/R)

77. Article 6.8 identifies the circumstances in which investigating authorities may overcome a lack of information, in the responses of the interested parties, by using "facts" which are otherwise "available" to the investigating authorities. According to Article 6.8, where the interested parties do not "significantly impede" the investigation, recourse may be had to facts available only if an interested party fails to submit necessary information "within a reasonable period". Thus, if information is, in fact, supplied "within a reasonable period", the investigating authorities cannot use facts available, but must use the information submitted by the interested party.

...

99. Paragraph 7 of Annex II indicates that a lack of "cooperation" by an interested party may, by virtue of the use made of facts available, lead to a result that is "less favourable" to the interested party than would have been the case had that interested party cooperated. We note that the Panel referred to the following dictionary meaning of "cooperate": to "work together for the same purpose or in the same task." 65 This meaning suggests that cooperation is a process, involving joint effort, whereby parties work together towards a common goal. In that respect, we note that parties may very well "cooperate" to a high degree, even though the requested information is, ultimately, not obtained. This is because the fact of "cooperating" is in itself not determinative of the end result of the cooperation. Thus, investigating authorities should not arrive at a "less favourable" outcome simply because an interested party fails to furnish requested information if, in fact, the interested party has "cooperated" with the investigating authorities, within the meaning of paragraph 7 of Annex II of the Anti-Dumping Agreement.

100. Paragraph 7 of Annex II does not indicate what degree of "cooperation" investigating authorities are entitled to expect from an interested party in order to preclude the possibility of such a "less favourable" outcome. To resolve this question we scrutinize the context found in Annex II. In this regard, we consider it relevant that paragraph 5 of Annex II prohibits investigating

① Appellate Body Report, United States–Anti-Dumping Measures on Certain Hot-Rolled Steel Products from Japan, WT/DS184/AB/R, adopted 23 August 2001. 原文脚注省略。

authorities from discarding information that is "not ideal in all respects" if the interested party that supplied the information has, nevertheless, acted "to the best of its ability". (emphasis added) This provision suggests to us that the level of cooperation required of interested parties is a high one – interested parties must act to the "best" of their abilities.

101. We note, however, that paragraph 2 of Annex II authorizes investigating authorities to request responses to questionnaires in a particular medium (for example, computer tape) but, at the same time, states that such a request should not be "maintained" if complying with that request would impose an "unreasonable extra burden" on the interested party, that is, would "entail unreasonable additional cost and trouble". (emphasis added) This provision requires investigating authorities to strike a balance between the effort that they can expect interested parties to make in responding to questionnaires, and the practical ability of those interested parties to comply fully with all demands made of them by the investigating authorities. We see this provision as another detailed expression of the principle of good faith, which is, at once, a general principle of law and a principle of general international law, that informs the provisions of the Anti-Dumping Agreement, as well as the other covered agreements. 66 This organic principle of good faith, in this particular context, restrains investigating authorities from imposing on exporters burdens which, in the circumstances, are not reasonable.

102. We, therefore, see paragraphs 2 and 5 of Annex II of the Anti-Dumping Agreement as reflecting a careful balance between the interests of investigating authorities and exporters. In order to complete their investigations, investigating authorities are entitled to expect a very significant degree of effort – to the "best of their abilities" – from investigated exporters. At the same time, however, the investigating authorities are not entitled to insist upon absolute standards or impose unreasonable burdens upon those exporters.

【本案评析】

以上案例节选自 2001 年美国对日本热轧钢产品的反倾销措施案上诉机构报告。该案上诉机构强调，合作是一个涉及共同努力的过程，各方为此共同努力。在这方面，即使最终没有获得所要求的信息，缔约方也可能在很大程度上"合作"了。这是因为"合作"的事实本身并不决定合作的最终结果。因此，调查机关不应仅仅因为利害关系方没有提供所要求的信息而得出"不利的"结果，而事实上，利害关系方已与"反倾销协定"附件 2 第 7 段所指的调查机关进行了"合作"。上诉机构也进一步指出,《反倾销协定》附件 2 第 2 和第 5 段反映了调查机关与出口商之间的谨慎平衡。为了完成调查，调查机关有权期望被调查的出口商作出非常大的努力“尽其所能”。但同时，调查机关无权坚持绝对标准或对这些出口商施加不合理的负担。

五、2003年巴西诉欧共体管道配件反倾销案①

European Communities – Anti-Dumping Duties on Malleable Cast Iron Tube or Pipe Fittings from Brazil
(WT/DS219/AB/R)

78. We also consider that certain anomalous results would flow from Brazil's assertion that when a major change, such as in this case a steep and lasting devaluation, occurs at a late stage of the POI, the dumping determination should be confined to and based on the data following that major change. If such a change were to take place at the very end of the POI, Brazil's approach would imply that the determination would have to be based on the data of a very short period.71 By the same logic, if the major change were to occur after the end of the POI, but before the provisional determination of the investigating authority (in this case, for example, after 1 April 1999 but before 28 February 2000), the investigating authority, under Brazil's approach, should ignore the analysis based on the data of the entire POI and review or reassess the determination on the basis of post-POI data. Indeed, this could imply an obligation on the investigating authority to select a new POI starting from the time of the major change.72

79. We can also foresee the opposite situation. Suppose, for example, that the major change is not devaluation, but revaluation or appreciation of the currency of the exporting country. Suppose further that the investigating authority finds no dumping on the basis of the data pertaining to the first three quarters of the POI, but the revaluation in the last quarter has resulted in a situation where only sales in that last quarter were made at less than normal value. Brazil's assertion in this case could open up the possibility of the investigating authority making an affirmative dumping determination based solely on the data of the last quarter of the POI.

80. Permitting such discretionary selection of data from a period of time within the POI would defeat the objectives underlying investigating authorities' reliance on a POI for the purposes of a dumping determination. As the Panel correctly noted, the POI "form[s] the basis for an objective and unbiased determination by the investigating authority." Like the Panel and

① Appellate Body Report, European Communities–Anti-Dumping Duties on Malleable Cast Iron Tube or Pipe Fittings from Brazil, WT/DS219/AB/R, adopted 18 August 2003. 原文脚注省略。

the parties to this dispute, we understand a POI to provide data collected over a sustained period of time, which period can allow the investigating authority to make a dumping determination that is less likely to be subject to market fluctuations or other vagaries that may distort a proper evaluation. We agree with the Panel that the standardized reliance on a POI, although not fixed in duration by the Anti-Dumping Agreement, assures the investigating authority and exporters of "a consistent and reasonable methodology for determining present dumping", which anti-dumping duties are intended to offset. In contrast to this consistency and reliability, Brazil's approach would introduce a significant level of subjectivity on the part of the investigating authority to determine when data from a subset of the POI may be a reliable indicator of an exporter's future pricing behaviour. As the European Communities points out, the "broad judgmental role" accorded investigating authorities by Brazil's approach is not consistent with the detailed nature of the rules and obligations of the Anti-Dumping Agreement governing various aspects of the dumping determination.

81. In our view, the Anti-Dumping Agreement takes into account the possibility of such major changes occurring at a late stage of the POI, or even after the POI, not by allowing investigating authorities to pick and choose a subset of data or sub-periods of a POI according to their subjective considerations, but by review mechanisms. Article 11.1 of the Anti-Dumping Agreement is categorical that "[a]n anti-dumping duty shall remain in force only as long as and to the extent necessary to counteract dumping which is causing injury." In furtherance of this general rule, Article 11.2 requires investigating authorities in certain circumstances, including at the request of an interested party after a reasonable period of time, to "review the need for the continued imposition of the duty". The Anti-Dumping Agreement, in sub-paragraphs 1 through 3 of Article 9.3, also lays down that the anti-dumping duty collected shall at no point in time exceed the dumping margin and that any such excess shall be refunded. Therefore, if a major change that occurs during or after the POI has reduced the margin of dumping or eliminated the dumping altogether, these provisions of the Anti-Dumping Agreement ensure that the exporter's legitimate interests are safeguarded.

【本案评析】

以上案例节选自2003年巴西诉欧共体管道配件反倾销案上诉机构报告。该上诉机构同意专家组的意见，即在一个调查期内酌情选择一段时间内的数据会使调查机关对这一期间的依赖程度低于目标，调查期间构成调查机关客观和无偏见的确定的基础。上诉机构进一步指出，调查期提供持续一段时间内收集的数据，这段时间可以让调查机关作出不太可能受到市场波动或可能扭曲适当评估的其他反复无常的倾销决定。《反倾销协定》虽然没有规定调查期的期限，但是对调查期的标准依赖，保证调查机关和出口商采取“一贯和合理的方法来确定目前的倾销”，而反倾销税的目的是抵消这种方法。

【延伸阅读】

一、相关典型案例

1.European Communities—Anti-Dumping Measure on Farmed Salmon from Norway(WT/DS337)

2.Guatemala—Definitive Anti-Dumping Measures on Grey Portland Cement from Mexico (WT/DS156)

3.Mexico—Anti-Dumping Investigation of High Fructose Corn Syrup (HFCS) from the United States(WT/DS132)

4.Mexico—Definitive Anti-Dumping Measures on Beef and Rice(WT/DS295)

5.Thailand—Anti-Dumping Duties on Angels, Shapes and Sections of Iron or Non-Alloy Steel and H-Beams from Poland(WT/DS122)

6.United States—Anti-Dumping Measures on Stainless Steel Plate in Coils and Stainless Steel Sheet and Strip from Korea（WT/DS179）

7.United States—Anti-Dumping Act of 1916, Complaint by Japan(WT/DS162)

二、相关学术论著

1. 高永富、张玉卿:《国际反倾销法》,复旦大学出版社 2001 年版。

2.Edwin Vermulst, *The WTO Anti-Dumping Agreement: A Commentary,* Oxford University Press, 2006.

3.Petros C. Mavroidis, George A. Bermann and Mark Wu, *The Law of the World Trade Organization (WTO): Documents, Cases & Analysis,* Thomas Reuters, 2010.

三、相关网络资源

1.https://www.wto.org/english/docs_e/legal_e/19-adp_01_e.htm.

2.http://ec.europa.eu/trade/policy/accessing-markets/trade-defence/actions-against-imports-into-the-eu/anti-dumping/.

3. https://tdi.mofcom.gov.cn/.

4. http://cacs.mofcom.gov.cn/.

5. https://enforcement.trade.gov/links.html.

第三节　反倾销措施的实施程序

【知识背景 / 学习要点】

世界各国的反倾销立法中都基本上规定了三种可以实施的反倾销措施，即临时反倾销措施、价格承诺和最终反倾销税。为了保证反倾销措施的实施不影响国际贸易自由化带来的成果，WTO《反倾销协定》也从反倾销措施的实施程序，包括反倾销措施实施所需进行的公告程序角度，对成员方实施三种不同类型的反倾销措施规定了必须遵守的纪律要求。

一、临时反倾销措施

由于反倾销调查期限较长，故主管机关一般会在调查期间采取临时措施，一方面促进反倾销调查的顺利开展，另一方面也防止调查期间损害的继续扩大。《反倾销协定》第 7 条是关于实施临时措施的规则。在实施临时反倾销措施之前，调查机关必须对倾销、损害和因果关系作出初步肯定性的裁定。此外，调查机关必须判断，这种措施是必要的，以防止在调查期间造成损害。临时措施可采取征收临时税的形式，或更可取的是，采取现金保证金或保函等担保形式，其数额应等于初步确定的倾销幅度。

关于临时措施的适用期限，临时措施不得在调查开始后 60 日内采取，同时

《反倾销协定》第 7.4 款规定，适用期限应尽可能短，最长不超过 4 个月，或应有关主管机关的决定，在所涉贸易中占很大比例的出口商的请求下，适用期限不超过 6 个月。在调查过程中，如该成员调查机关在执行反倾销税时适用“较低征税规则”（即审查低于倾销幅度的反倾销税是否足以消除损害），则临时措施实施期限一般为 6 个月，如出口商提出要求，可延长至 9 个月。

需要注意的是，《反倾销协定》第 7 条使用了“措施”一词，而不是“征税”。根据《反倾销协定》的规定，当进口成员裁定征收最终反倾销税时，它还必须裁定是否追溯征收临时反倾销税。

二、价格承诺

若出口商承诺按倾销价格调整价格或停止向有关地区出口产品，使主管机关确信倾销的损害性影响已消除，则可中止或终止反倾销调查，而不征收反倾销税，这被称为“价格承诺”。《反倾销协定》第 8 条规定了提供和接受价格承诺作为征收反倾销税的替代选择办法。只有在调查机关对倾销、损害和因果关系作出肯定的初步裁定后，才能作出按倾销价格调整或停止出口的价格承诺。价格承诺是出口商和调查主管机关双方在自愿基础上达成的，即使有国内产业提出反对，出口商也可要求在接受承诺后继续调查。在对倾销、损害或因果关系作出否定性的最终裁定时，价格承诺将自动失效。[①]

价格承诺往往是出口商首选的解决办法。但事实上，有些主管机关在政策上不愿意接受价格承诺。在涉及发展中国家的案件中，接受价格承诺可被视为一种建设性的补救办法。

三、最终反倾销税

一旦确认符合反倾销的构成要件，主管机关即可根据本国的反倾销相关规则，对进口产品实施最终反倾销税措施。不过，WTO 的许多成员方在其国内立法中列入一项公共利益条款，使其即便认定有害的倾销也能够避免征收反倾

① 对于违反价格承诺的规定，参见《反倾销协定》第 8.6 款。

销税。《反倾销协定》第 9 条规定了反倾销税的征收纪律。这一条款确立的一项基本原则是，即使已经满足所有征税要求，反倾销税的征收仍然是可选择的。第 9 条还规定了所谓的“较低征税规则”，根据该规则，如果较少的征税足以消除对国内产业的损害，那么所征收的反倾销税低于倾销幅度应是“可取的”。[①]

（一）非歧视基础上征收

反倾销税应在非歧视的基础上对从所有来源[②]进口的产品征收。《反倾销协定》第 9.2 款要求各成员对从所有来源发现的倾销和造成损害的进口产品不加歧视地征收反倾销税。[③] 因此，最惠国待遇（MFN）的原则适用于反倾销税的征收，而且国家主管机关应列出有关产品供应商的名称。但是，若涉及来自同一国家的多个供应商，且不能列出所有供应商的名称，则主管机关可列出相关供应国的名称。若涉及来自一个以上国家的多个供应商，则主管机关可列出所有供应商的名称，如果这样做不可行，也可列出所有涉及的供应国的名称。[④]

根据《反倾销协定》第 9.3 款的规定，征收的反倾销税不得超过第 2 条规定的倾销幅度。该款规定了将“倾销幅度”作为征收反倾销税的上限，无论这些征税是“追溯性”的还是“预期性”的。[⑤]如果超出上限，调查机关有退款的义务。例如 2007 年美国与归零和日落复审有关的措施争端案上诉机构裁定，在任何征税制度下，根据第 2 条确定的倾销幅度是出口商销售所征反倾销税的最高限额。如进口商已缴付税款，该进口商可在超出上限时要求退款。同样，在追溯

① 欧盟一般使用“较低征税规则”，美国并不采用。参见 P. F. J. Macrory, The Anti-Dumping Agreement, in P. Macrory, A. Appleton and M. Plummer (eds.), The World Trade Organization: Legal, Economic and Political Analysis ,Springer, 2005, p. 519.

② 上诉机构曾指出，《反倾销协定》第 9.2 款中使用的“所有来源”，是指单独的出口商或生产商，而不是指整个国家。参见 Appellate Body Report, European Communities-Definitive Anti-Dumping Measures on Certain Iron or Steel Fasteners from China, WT/DS397/AB/R, 15 July 2011, para. 338.

③ 反倾销税不会适用于正在实施有效价格承诺的进口商品。

④ 参见《反倾销协定》第 9.2 款。

⑤ 预期基础上征收反倾销税和回溯性基础上征收反倾销税，参见《反倾销协定》第 9.3.1 和 9.3.2 项。上诉机构指出，《反倾销协定》在征收反倾销税的不同制度上是中立的，参见 Appellate Body Report, United States–Measures Relating to Zeroing and Sunset Reviews, WT/DS322/AB/R, adopted 23 January 2007, para. 156.

征税制度下，美国有权在特定交易的基础上自由评估关税，但征收的反倾销税总额不准超过出口商或外国生产者的倾销幅度。[①]

（二）单独倾销幅度与抽样计算

在征收反倾销税时，根据《反倾销协定》第6.10款的规定，调查机关"作为一项规则"（as a rule）应当计算所调查产品的每一已知出口商或生产者的各自倾销幅度。然而，第6.10款承认，这并非总是可能的，[②]如该款第2句所述，在出口商、生产者、进口商的数量或所涉及的产品种类特别多而使得作出此种确定不实际的情况下，不可能确定单独倾销幅度。在这种情况下，主管机关可通过在作出选择时可获得的信息基础上使用统计上有效的抽样方法，将其审查限制在合理数量的利害关系方或产品上，或限制在可进行合理调查的来自所涉国家出口量的最大百分比上。这种限制性的检查通常被称为"抽样方法"。[③]

在使用"抽样方法"时，根据《反倾销协定》第9.4款第1句的规定，对未接受单独审查的出口商或生产商征收的反倾销税（"其他税率"）是根据为个别受调查出口商或生产商实际确定的加权平均倾销幅度计算的。然而，调查机关在加权平均计算中，不得包括任何零幅度、微量幅度或基于可获得事实的倾销幅度，同时其也必须为在调查期间已经提供必要信息的任何出口商或生产者的

---

① 参见 Appellate Body Report, United States–Measures Relating to Zeroing and Sunset Reviews, WT/DS322/AB/R, adopted 23 January 2007, paras. 162-163.

② 一般地，当出口商、生产者、进口商或产品种类数量较多时，就会产生这种情况。2011年中国诉欧盟紧固件案上诉机构指出，第6.10款中的义务（使用"应当"一词）通过"作为一项规则"短语来限定。这个短语的使用表明，第6.10款中的义务不是绝对的，预示了例外的可能性。然而，上诉机构也补充说，虽然"作为一项规则"短语应被理解为修改了确定单独倾销幅度的义务，但并没有导致其变成唯一的选择。否则，第一句中使用的"应该"一词将被剥夺其通常含义。参见 Appellate Body Report, European Communities-Definitive Anti-Dumping Measures on Certain Iron or Steel Fasteners from China, WT/DS397/AB/R, 15 July 2011, para. 317.

③ 即使没有使用统计上有效的样本，但也可以实施用于限定审查的第二种替代方案，这种审查通常被称为"抽样"。"抽样"是确定第6.10款明确规定的单独倾销幅度的唯一例外。See Appellate Body Report, European Communities-Definitive Anti-Dumping Measures on Certain Iron or Steel Fasteners from China, WT/DS397/AB/R, 15 July 2011, para. 318.

进口产品计算单独倾销幅度。[①]关于对未单独审查的来源所适用的“其他税率”，上诉机构在2001年美国对日本热轧钢产品的反倾销措施案中指出，第9.4款没有规定WTO成员为确定实际适用于未接受调查的出口商或生产者的“其他税率”而应当采用的任何方法。相反，第9.4款只是确定了调查机关在确定“其他税率”时“不应超过的最高限额或上限”。[②]

关于在调查期间通常存在的不属于进口来源的“新的货主”计算单独倾销幅度的问题，《反倾销协定》第9.5款规定，主管机关应迅速进行审查，以确定单独的倾销幅度。因此，调查机关应再迅速进行一次审查，以确定这类“新的货主”的出口产品的特定倾销幅度。同时，在审查进行期间，不得对来自这类出口商或生产商的进口产品征收反倾销税。[③]

（三）禁止追溯性征收及例外

原则上反倾销税是禁止追溯性征收的。《反倾销协定》第10条确立了一项原则，即只有在对倾销、损害和因果关系作出初步或最终裁定生效之后，才能征收临时或最终反倾销税。[④]然而，第10条对特定情况下反倾销税的追溯征收也进行了规定。根据第10.2款的规定，如作出损害的最终裁定（而非损害威胁或实质性阻碍的最终裁定），或在虽已作出损害威胁的最终裁定，但如无临时措

---

① 参见《反倾销协定》第9.4款。若在《反倾销协定》第6.8款规定的“可获得事实”基础计算的倾销幅度，此倾销幅度也不得用于计算“其他”税率。参见 Appellate Body Report, United States–Anti-Dumping Measures on Certain Hot-Rolled Steel Products from Japan, WT/DS184/AB/R, adopted 23 August 2001, paras. 122-123.

② 在2001年美国对日本热轧钢产品的反倾销措施案中，上诉机构证实了专家小组的结论，即经修正的1930年“美国关税法”的一项规定，要求在计算合作/未抽样生产商的税率时，部分依据“可获得事实”规定计算的倾销幅度不符合“反倾销协定”第9.4款。但上诉机构也指出，《反倾销协定》第9.4款具有防止未被要求在调查中合作的出口商因被调查出口商提供的信息中的差距或缺陷而受到损害的目的。第9.4款的漏洞在于，尽管第9.4款禁止在计算“其他税率”的上限时使用某些倾销幅度，但其没有明确说明，当所有倾销幅度根据第9.4款被禁止的情况排除在计算之外，则“其他税率”的上限如何计算的问题。参见 Appellate Body Report, United States–Anti-Dumping Measures on Certain Hot-Rolled Steel Products from Japan, WT/DS184/AB/R, adopted 23 August 2001, paras. 116,123-126.

③ 但是，主管机关可预扣估算和/或要求作出担保，以保证在该审查确定此类出口商或生产者存在倾销时，能够自该审查开始之日起追溯征收反倾销税。参见《反倾销协定》第9.5款。

④ 参见《反倾销协定》第10.1款。

施，将会导致对倾销进口产品的影响作出损害的裁定的情况下，则反倾销税可对已经实施临时措施（如有）的期间追溯征收。[①]

禁止追溯性征税还涉及对于在临时反倾销措施中已经支付或预估的相关金额的处理，因为这些金额有可能与最终反倾销税之间有差额，这就涉及是否需要继续支付或者退款的问题。一般而言，如最终反倾销税高于已付或应付的临时税或为担保目的而估计的金额，则差额部分不得收取。但是，若最终税低于已付或应付临时税或为担保目的而估计的金额，则差额部分应根据具体情况予以退还，或重新计算税额。[②]

但是在特殊情况下，作为一种例外，也允许追溯实施最终反倾销税。《反倾销协定》第 10.6 款规定了这种例外情况的条件是，存在造成损害的倾销的历史记录，或进口商已经知道或理应知道出口商实行倾销，且此类倾销会造成损害；并且损害是由在相对较短时期内倾销产品的大量进口造成的，（例如进口产品的库存快速增加），该倾销产品可能会严重破坏即将实施的最终反倾销税的补救效果。[③] 在这种情况下，第 10.6 款允许最终反倾销税可对在实施临时措施之日前 90 日内进口供消费的产品追溯征收。

四、反倾销措施的公告程序

《反倾销协定》第 6.9 款和第 12 条都涉及反倾销调查和裁定的透明度。这两项规定都要求向有关各方和一般公众作出通知。

（一）裁决前基本事实披露

第 6.9 款要求调查机关在作出最终裁定之前，向所有利害关系方通知“正在审查中的基本事实”，这是决定是否采取最终反倾销措施的依据。这种披露应在足够的时间内进行，以使当事各方能有充分的时间为其利益进行辩护。

上诉机构曾强调，第 6.9 款并不要求披露主管机关收集的所有事实，而只是

① 参见《反倾销协定》第 10.2 款。

② 参见《反倾销协定》第 10.3 款。

③ 此情况的前提是只要已经给予有关进口商发表意见的机会。

“基本”事实，即重要的、关键的或突出的事实，这些是调查主管机关在作出是否征收最终反倾销税的裁定时可以加以考虑的记录在案的事实。虽然第 6.4 款和第 2.4 款适用于整个国内程序，但是第 6.9 款指向调查结束前的那段时间，此时调查机关正在对最终裁定所依据的重要事实进行考量。“基本事实”是指在那些在决定是否采取最终反倾销措施方面具有重要性的事实。主管机关应以一致的方式披露这些事实，以便让有关各方了解作出是否采取最终措施决定的依据。因此，必须基于根据《反倾销协定》能够满足实施最终措施相关实体性义务所需的裁定内容以及每个争端案件的实际情况，来理解什么是“基本事实”。正如上诉机构所述，根据第 6.9 款披露正在审查的基本事实，对于确保有关各方有能力维护其利益是至关重要的，因此，这种披露应在各方有足够时间处理的情况才下进行。①

在 2015 年欧盟和日本诉中国对进口的高性能不锈钢无缝钢管（HP-SSST）征收反倾销税措施案中，上诉机构进一步澄清说，某一特定事实“在作出决定的过程中”是基本的还是重大的，取决于特定实质性义务的性质和范围、满足相关实质性义务所需的特殊裁决的内容，以及每个案件的实际情况，包括有关各方提交的论点和证据。如果调查机关援引了利害关系一方所掌握的数据，上诉机构并不认为仅此事实即可说明，调查机关是以一致的方式披露了事实，以便让有关各方能够了解中间或最终结论作出的依据，从而确保其适当地维护了利益。②

（二）公告与裁定说明

《反倾销协定》第 12 条涉及调查机关应当进行公告的详细要求，包括（1）展

① 参见 Appellate Body Report, China-Countervailing and Anti-Dumping Duties on Grain Oriented Flat-rolled Electrical Steel from the United States, adopted on 18 October 2012, WT/DS414/AB/R, para. 240.

② 参见 Appellate Body Reports, China-Measures Imposing Anti-Dumping Duties on High-Performance Stainless Steel Seamless Tubes (HP-SSST) from the European Union and Japan, WT/DS454/AB/R,WT/DS460/AB/R,14 October 2015, paras. 5.130-5.131.

开调查[①],(2)初步裁定[②],(3)最终裁定[③]和(4)价格承诺[④]。前述第6.9款规定的“基本事实的披露”要求在最终裁定作出之前进行，但是第12条的公告则必须在决定或裁定作出之后进行。比如对第12.2.2项意义上的调查结论公告，一旦调查机关对实施最终反倾销税作出肯定性裁定，才需要进行公告。

《反倾销协定》第12条规定“公告”纪律的目的是，提高调查机关所作决定的透明度，并鼓励为这类裁定提供可靠和透彻的推理。例如，关于最终裁定的公告必须充分详细地列出或通过单独报告详细提供调查主管机关就其认为重要的所有事实问题和法律问题所得出的调查结果和结论。例如在2003年巴西诉欧共体管道配件反倾销案中，专家组裁定，欧共体的行为与《反倾销协定》第12.2款和第12.2.2项不一致，因为欧共体虽然按照第3.4款处理或解释了某些该款所列因素缺乏重要性的问题，但是从已公布的临时或最终裁定意见中并不能直接看出来。[⑤]

关于相关信息必须披露的形式，第12.2.2项允许主管机关自主决定是将这些信息纳入公告本身，还是通过这些信息的单独报告提供。然而，对于公告和报告必须包括的内容有:(1)供应商的名称，或在不可行的情况下，所涉供应国的名称;(2)符合海关要求的产品说明;(3)确定的倾销幅度并充分说明第2条规定的确定和比较出口价格和正常价值所采用的方法的理由;(4)与第3条所规定的损害确定有关的考虑因素;(5)裁定基于的主要理由的情况，第12.2.2项也要求适当注意机密信息的保护。

---

① 参见《反倾销协定》第12.1.1项。

② 参见《反倾销协定》第12.2.1项。

③ 参见《反倾销协定》第12.2.2项。

④ 参见《反倾销协定》第12.2.2项。

⑤ 参见 Panel Report, European Communities–Anti-Dumping Duties on Malleable Cast Iron Tube or Pipe Fittings from Brazil, WT/DS219/ R, para. 7.435.

【案例摘录与评析】

一、2016 年欧盟对阿根廷生物柴油反倾销措施案[①]

European Union—Anti-dumping Measures on Biodiesel from Argentina (WT/DS473/AB/R)

6.1.2 Imposition of anti-dumping duties: Article 9.3 of the Anti-Dumping Agreement and Article VI:2 of the GATT 1994

6.90. The European Union requests us to reverse the Panel's finding that "[t]he European Union acted inconsistently with Article 9.3 of the Anti-Dumping Agreement and Article VI:2 of the GATT 1994 by imposing anti-dumping duties in excess of the margins of dumping that should have been established under Article 2 of the Anti-Dumping Agreement and Article VI:1 of the GATT 1994, respectively". The European Union contends that the Panel erred in its interpretation and application of Article 9.3 of the Anti-Dumping Agreement by: (i) considering that Article 9.3 of the Anti-Dumping Agreement calls for a comparison between the amount of duties and the dumping margins that should have been calculated consistently with Article 2 of that Agreement, and that a violation of Article 2 automatically results in a violation of Article 9.3; and (ii) relying on the margins of dumping calculated in the Provisional Regulation in applying Article 9.3 to the facts of this dispute. Argentina maintains that the European Union's appeal of the Panel's findings under Article 9.3 of the Anti-Dumping Agreement and Article VI:2 of the GATT 1994 is without merit and should be dismissed.

6.91. We begin with a brief overview of the relevant Panel findings before considering the interpretation of Article 9.3 of the Anti-Dumping Agreement and whether the Panel erred in reaching its findings.

6.1.2.1 The Panel's findings

6.92. Argentina alleged before the Panel that, as a result of its erroneous construction of the normal value and the consequent unduly high margin of dumping, the European Union imposed and levied anti-dumping duties in excess of the margin of dumping that should have been established in accordance with Article 2 of the Anti-Dumping Agreement, and thereby acted inconsistently with Article 9.3 of the Anti-Dumping Agreement and Article VI:2 of the GATT 1994.

---

① Appellate Body Report, European Union-Anti-dumping Measures on Biodiesel from Argentina, WT/DS473/AB/R , adopted October 2016, paras. 6.90-6.97, 6.104. 原文脚注省略。

6.93. In addressing Argentina's claim, the Panel considered that the question before it was whether the phrase "margin of dumping as established under Article 2" in Article 9.3 of the Anti-Dumping Agreement "refers to the margin of dumping that an investigating authority would have established in the absence of any errors or inconsistencies with [Article 2]". Analysing the text of Article 9.3, the Panel considered that the term "margin of dumping" in Article 9.3 "relates to a margin that is established in a manner subject to the disciplines of Article 2 and which is therefore consistent with those disciplines". The Panel added that an error or inconsistency under Article 2 "does not necessarily or automatically mean that the anti-dumping duty actually applied will exceed the correct margin of dumping", and hence be inconsistent with Article 9.3. This is because, even in situations in which the dumping margin is not determined consistently with Article 2, the actual anti-dumping duty rate could still be lower than the correct margin of dumping, for example, due to the application of the lesser duty rule.

6.94. The Panel recalled its finding that the European Union acted inconsistently with Articles 2.2.1.1 and 2.2 of the Anti-Dumping Agreement and with Article VI:1(b)(ii) of the GATT 1994 in establishing the dumping margins in the Definitive Regulation due to the "use of surrogate input prices in the construction of each investigated Argentine producer's normal value". The Panel contrasted this with the EU authorities' use of actual input prices when constructing the normal value and calculating dumping margins at the provisional stage. The Panel also noted that Argentina highlighted that the duties imposed in the Definitive Regulation are "two to three times higher" than the dumping margins calculated in the Provisional Regulation. While acknowledging that it could not "infer the exact dumping margins that would have been established had the determinations been done in accordance with Article 2", the Panel nevertheless expressed the view that "the dumping margins established in the Provisional Regulation provide a reasonable approximation of what margins calculated in accordance with Article 2 of the Anti-Dumping Agreement might have been." To the Panel, the fact that the anti-dumping duties imposed in the Definitive Regulation were substantially higher than the dumping margins calculated in the Provisional Regulation suggested that the definitive anti-dumping duties "exceeded what the dumping margins could have been had they been established in accordance with Article 2".

6.95. The Panel therefore concluded that Argentina had made a prima facie case that the European Union had acted inconsistently with Article 9.3 of the Anti-Dumping Agreement. Applying its reasoning under Article 9.3 of the Anti-Dumping Agreement, mutatis mutandis, to Argentina's claim under Article VI:2 of the GATT 1994, the Panel found that the European Union also acted inconsistently with the latter provision. On the basis of the foregoing, the Panel found that the European Union acted inconsistently with Article 9.3 of the Anti-Dumping Agreement and

Article VI:2 of the GATT 1994 by imposing anti-dumping duties in excess of the margin of dumping that should have been established under Article 2 of the Anti-Dumping Agreement.

6.1.2.2 Whether the Panel erred in its interpretation of Article 9.3 of the Anti-Dumping Agreement

6.96. Article 9 of the Anti-Dumping Agreement contains several provisions relating to the imposition and collection of anti-dumping duties. Article 9.3, in particular, provides that "[t]he amount of the anti-dumping duty shall not exceed the margin of dumping as established under Article 2." The words "shall not exceed" indicate that Article 9.3 sets a ceiling for the maximum amount of the anti-dumping duty that may be imposed and collected. This maximum level is "the margin of dumping as established under Article 2". The phrase "as established under" is immediately followed by the reference to "Article 2". Article 2, in turn, sets out detailed rules that govern various aspects of a dumping determination, including the determination of the normal value and the export price and their comparison, for purposes of calculating the margin of dumping. Read in light of the detailed rules on dumping determinations set out in Article 2, the phrase "as established under Article 2" indicates that the "margin of dumping" in Article 9.3 is a margin that is established in a manner consistent with these rules. We therefore share the Panel's understanding that the "'margin of dumping' referred to in Article 9.3 relates to a margin that is established in a manner subject to the disciplines of Article 2 and which is therefore consistent with those disciplines".

6.97. Furthermore, we note that Article 9.3 is the chapeau to three provisions concerning the assessment and collection of anti-dumping duties.All three provisions are "subject to the overarching requirement in Article 9.3 that the amount of anti-dumping duty 'shall not exceed the margin of dumping as established under Article 2'" of the Anti-Dumping Agreement. The "margin of dumping" referred to in Article 9.3 thus provides the benchmark against which the consistency of the amount of the anti-dumping duty with Article 9.3 must be examined under any of the duty assessment systems envisaged in Articles 9.3.1 to 9.3.3. In our view, it would frustrate the benchmark function of Article 9.3 if the margin of dumping were itself inconsistent with the Anti-Dumping Agreement. We also note that, pursuant to Article 9.2 of the Anti-Dumping Agreement, "[w]hen an anti-dumping duty is imposed in respect of any product, such anti-dumping duty shall be collected in the appropriate amounts in each case". Read in light of Article 9.2, the benchmark provided by Article 9.3 is one specific demarcation of when the amounts of anti-dumping duties will be appropriate.

6.98. Our understanding of the phrase "margin of dumping as established under Article 2" is supported by the context provided by Article VI:2 of the GATT 1994. This Article provides that a WTO Member "may levy on any dumped product an anti-dumping duty not greater in amount than the margin of dumping in respect of such product". It further states that, "[f]or the purposes of this Article, the margin of dumping is the price difference determined in accordance with [Article VI:1]."As the Panel correctly pointed out, the term "in accordance with" in the second sentence of this provision "makes it clear ... that Article VI:2 prohibits the levying of anti-dumping duties in excess of the dumping margin determined consistently with Article VI:1 of the GATT 1994 in the same way as the phrase 'as established under Article 2' does in Article 9.3."

6.99. The Appellate Body's findings in past disputes under Article 9.3 of the Anti-Dumping Agreement further support the interpretation above. In US — Zeroing (EC), the Appellate Body took note of the reference in Article 9.3 to Article 2. The Appellate Body considered that it followed from this reference that, under Article 9.3, the amount of the assessed anti-dumping duties may not exceed the relevant margin of dumping, namely, a margin that has been established consistently with Article 2.

6.100. Similarly, in US – Zeroing (Japan), having found that margins of dumping calculated using zeroing in original investigations are margins of dumping inconsistent with Article 2 of the Anti-Dumping Agreement, the Appellate Body disagreed with that panel's view that the term "margins of dumping" can have different meanings under different provisions of the Anti-Dumping Agreement. That panel had relied, in support of its view, on the differences between the retrospective and prospective duty assessment systems referred to under Article 9.3. The Appellate Body, however, noted that "the introductory clause of Article 9.3 applies equally to prospective and retroactive duty assessment systems." The Appellate Body emphasized that, under either system, "the authority is required to ensure that the total amount of anti-dumping duties collected ... does not exceed the total amount of dumping ... calculated according to the margin of dumping established for that exporter or foreign producer without zeroing" and that, "[u]nder any system of duty collection, the margin of dumping established in accordance with Article 2 operates as a ceiling for the amount of anti-dumping duties that could be collected in respect of the sales made by an exporter."

6.101. In our view, therefore, the Panel properly considered that the Appellate Body's findings in US – Zeroing (EC) and US – Zeroing (Japan) confirm that Article 9.3 prohibits the amount of the anti-dumping duties from exceeding a dumping margin that is determined consistently with Article 2 of the Anti-Dumping Agreement.

6.102. The European Union acknowledges that "[i]t is undisputed that the ordinary meaning of the phrase 'the margin of dumping as established under Article 2' is that of a margin of dumping established in accordance with the provisions of Article 2." The European Union nonetheless asserts that, contrary to the Panel's interpretation, "what the text of Article 9.3 requires is merely a comparison between the anti-dumping duties actually imposed and the dumping margin actually calculated by the investigating authority, irrespective of the investigating authority's possible errors when calculating the dumping margin." We have difficulty reconciling these two statements of the European Union. We fail to see how a dumping margin "actually calculated" by the investigating authority, which nonetheless contains "errors" in light of the requirements of Article 2, could at the same time be a margin "established in accordance with the provisions of Article 2".

6.103. The European Union contends that the WTO-consistency of the calculation of the margin of dumping under Article 2, on the one hand, and the comparison called for in Article 9.3, on the other hand, are "two different stages in the analysis", and the finding of a WTO-inconsistency in one stage should not automatically lead to a finding of WTO-inconsistency in the other stage. At the oral hearing, the European Union further clarified that it takes issue with the Panel's understanding that an inconsistency with Article 2 automatically leads to an inconsistency with Article 9.3. The Panel, however, did not interpret Article 9.3 in this way. To the contrary, the Panel explicitly made clear that "[a]n error or inconsistency under Article 2 does not necessarily or automatically mean that the anti-dumping duty actually applied will exceed the correct margin of dumping." According to the Panel, "it is possible that an anti-dumping duty could be applied at a rate that is lower than the WTO-inconsistent dumping margin." The Panel referred, by way of example, to the lesser duty rule under Article 9.1 of the Anti-Dumping Agreement. According to the Panel, where the lesser duty rule is applied, it is conceivable that the final duties imposed will "not only be lower than the WTO-inconsistent dumping margin, but also lower than the dumping margin that would have been established in accordance with Article 2", and hence not inconsistent with Article 9.3 of the Anti-Dumping Agreement.

6.104. We agree with the above analysis of the Panel. Indeed, understanding the "margin of dumping" referred to in Article 9.3 as one established consistently with Article 2 of the Anti-Dumping Agreement does not mean that any error in the calculation of the dumping margin will necessarily lead to a violation of Article 9.3. The application of the lesser duty rule provides one example of when this may not be the case. Moreover, because Article 9.3 is concerned with the maximum amount of anti-dumping duties that may be collected, the errors under Article 2 that matter for purposes of Article 9.3 are those that result in a higher dumping margin than the one that would have been calculated had the authority acted consistently with Article 2. Not all breaches of Article 2 will invariably or predictably entail such a result. In this respect, we also share the European Union's understanding that a complainant "must show something more than a simple erroneous calculation of normal value" in order to succeed with a claim under Article 9.3.In our view, the complainant must show that anti-dumping duties are imposed at a rate that is higher than the dumping margin that would have been established had the authority acted consistently with Article 2.

【本案评析】

以上案例节选自2016年欧盟对阿根廷生物柴油反倾销措施案上诉机构报告。该案上诉机构支持专家组的结论，即欧盟的行为与第9.3款不符，征收的反倾销税超过了第2条本应规定的倾销幅度。上诉机构同意专家组的意见，认为第9.3款中援引的"倾销幅度"是与按照第2条确定的倾销幅度一致的。然而，上诉机构也指出，这一解释并不意味着在计算倾销幅度方面的任何错误将必然导致违反第9.3款，因为第9.3款涉及的是可能征收的最高额反倾销税，因此为第9.3款的目的，根据第2条所犯的错误是导致倾销幅度高于如果主管机关按照第2条行事本可计算出的幅度，并非所有违反第2条的行为都必然或有可能导致这种结果。上诉机构认为，申诉方必须证明，征收反倾销税的税率高于如果主管当局按照第2条行事本可确定的倾销幅度。

二、2012年中国对美国取向电工钢征收反倾销税和反补贴税案①

China-Countervailing and Anti-Dumping Duties on Grain
Oriented Flat-rolled Electrical Steel
from the United States
(WT/DS414/AB/R)

255. Article 12.2.2 of the Anti-Dumping Agreement and Article 22.5 of the SCM Agreement provide in relevant part:

A public notice of conclusion or suspension of an investigation in the case of an affirmative determination providing for the imposition of a definitive duty ... shall contain, or otherwise make available through a separate report, all relevant information on the matters of fact and law and reasons which have led to the imposition of final measures ... due regard being paid to the

① Appellate Body Report, China-Countervailing and Anti-Dumping Duties on Grain Oriented Flat-rolled Electrical Steel from the United States , adopted on 18 October 2012, WT/DS414/AB/R. 原文脚注省略。

requirement for the protection of confidential information. In particular, the notice or report shall contain the information described in [Article 12.2.1 of the Anti-Dumping Agreement/Article 22.4 of the SCM Agreement].

256. Relevant to this dispute is the requirement in Articles 12.2.2 and 22.5 that a public notice contain "all relevant information" on "matters of fact" "which have led to the imposition of final measures". With regard to "matters of fact", these provisions do not require authorities to disclose all the factual information that is before them, but rather those facts that allow an understanding of the factual basis that led to the imposition of final measures. The inclusion of this information should therefore give a reasoned account of the factual support for an authority's decision to impose final measures. Moreover, we note that the obligations under Articles 12.2.2 and 22.5 come at a later stage in the process than the requirement to disclose the essential facts pursuant to Articles 6.9 and 12.8. While the disclosure of essential facts must take place "before a final determination is made", the obligation to give public notice of the conclusion of an investigation within the meaning of Articles 12.2.2 and 22.5 is triggered once there is an affirmative determination providing for the imposition of definitive duties.

257. As noted in our examination of Articles 6.9 and 12.8, the imposition of final anti-dumping or countervailing duties requires that an authority finds dumping or subsidization, injury, and a causal link between the dumping or subsidization and the injury to the domestic industry. What constitutes "relevant information on the matters of fact" is therefore to be understood in the light of the content of the findings needed to satisfy the substantive requirements with respect to the imposition of final measures under the Anti-Dumping Agreement and the SCM Agreement, as well as the factual circumstances of each case. These findings each rest on an analysis of various elements that an authority is required to examine, which, in the context of an injury analysis, are set out in, inter alia, Articles 3.1, 3.2, 3.4, and 3.5 of the Anti-Dumping Agreement and Articles 15.1, 15.2, 15.4, and 15.5 of the SCM Agreement. Articles 3.2 and 15.2 require, inter alia, an investigating authority to consider the effect of the subject imports on prices by considering whether there has been significant price undercutting, or whether the effect of such imports is otherwise to depress prices to a significant degree or prevent price increases, which otherwise would have occurred, to a significant degree. We note that Articles 12.2.2 and 22.5 further underscore the requirement of public notice of these elements by cross-referencing, respectively, to Articles 12.2.1 of the Anti-Dumping Agreement and 22.4 of the SCM Agreement, which require that the public notice or report contain considerations relevant to the injury determination as set out in Articles 3 and 15.

258. Articles 12.2.2 and 22.5 are both situated in the context of provisions that concern

the public notice and explanation of determinations in anti-dumping and countervailing duty investigations. In the case of an affirmative determination providing for the imposition of a definitive duty, Articles 12.2.2 and 22.5 provide that such notice shall contain all relevant information on the matters of fact and law and reasons which have led to the imposition of final measures. Articles 12.2.2 and 22.5 capture the principle that those parties whose interests are affected by the imposition of final anti-dumping and countervailing duties are entitled to know, as a matter of fairness and due process, the facts, law and reasons that have led to the imposition of such duties. The obligation of disclosure under Articles 12.2.2 and 22.5 is framed by the requirement of "relevance", which entails the disclosure of the matrix of facts, law and reasons that logically fit together to render the decision to impose final measures. By requiring the disclosure of "all relevant information" regarding these categories of information, Articles 12.2.2 and 22.5 seek to guarantee that interested parties are able to pursue judicial review of a final determination as provided in Article 13 of the Anti-Dumping Agreement and Article 23 of the SCM Agreement.

259. With respect to the form in which the relevant information must be disclosed, Articles 12.2.2 and 22.5 allow authorities to decide whether to include the information in the public notice itself "or otherwise make [it] available through a separate report". We note that Articles 12.2.2 and 22.5 also provide that the notice or report shall pay "due regard ... to the requirement for the protection of confidential information". When confidential information is part of the relevant information on the matters of fact within the meaning of Articles 12.2.2 and 22.5, the disclosure obligations under these provisions should be met by disclosing non-confidential summaries of that information.

260. In sum, in the context of the second sentence of Articles 3.2 and 15.2, we consider that "all relevant information on the matters of fact" consists of those facts that are required to understand an investigating authority's price effects examination leading to the imposition of final measures. We now turn to assess the Panel's analysis under Articles 12.2.2 and 22.5.

C. Assessment of the Panel's Analysis under Article 12.2.2 of the Anti-Dumping Agreement and Article 22.5 of the SCM Agreement

261. China challenges the Panel's finding that MOFCOM failed adequately to disclose "all relevant information on the matters of fact" underlying MOFCOM's conclusion regarding the "low price" of subject imports, as required by Article 12.2.2 of the Anti-Dumping Agreement and Article 22.5 of the SCM Agreement. China argues that MOFCOM adequately provided public notice of its finding of significant price depression and suppression, which, contrary to the Panel's view, does not require a causal relationship between subject imports and these adverse price effects.426

China highlights that the Panel did not examine this finding and, rather, focused on the existence and magnitude of price undercutting, thereby making a comparison of subject import prices to domestic prices "essential elements" and "an important aspect" of MOFCOM's price effects examination.

262. We recall our finding that the Panel was correct to conclude that, although MOFCOM did not make a finding of significant price undercutting, MOFCOM's finding as to the "low price" of subject imports referred to the existence of price undercutting between 2006 and 2008, and that MOFCOM relied on this factor to support its finding of significant price depression and suppression. Accordingly, in the context of this aspect of MOFCOM's reasoning, the "relevant information on the matters of fact" included those facts underlying the existence of price undercutting that would have allowed for an understanding of this element of MOFCOM's finding of significant price depression and suppression.

263. Against this background, we note that the Final Determination contains weighted average prices for subject imports for the years 2006, 2007, 2008, and the first quarter of 2009, as well as the percentages reflecting the changes in these prices during these periods. With respect to the price of the like domestic products, the Final Determination only contains percentages reflecting price variations for the years 2006, 2007, 2008, and the first quarter of 2009, without including the prices of domestic products. Regarding the impact of subject import prices on the prices of like domestic products, the Final Determination states that, "[b]ecause the sale of the product concerned was kept at a low price, and the import volume of the product concerned increased greatly beginning from 2008, under this impact, domestic producers lowered their price to keep the market share." As noted in the context of our examination of Articles 6.9 and 12.8, China argued before the Panel that the existence of price undercutting supported MOFCOM's finding that subject imports were at a "low price", and, for this purpose, submitted to the Panel data regarding AUVs of subject imports and domestic products between 2006 and 2008. As found by the Panel, MOFCOM's Final Determination does not, however, include this AUV data.

264. On appeal, China argues that MOFCOM adequately provided public notice of its finding regarding the existence of significant price depression and suppression in the Final Determination by stating, respectively, that "average prices dropped", and that the "price-cost differential" dropped. China further argues that the Panel erred by "focus[ing] entirely on the degree of public notice not just about the existence of price undercutting ... but also the specific magnitude of the price undercutting." In China's view, given that the Panel determined that MOFCOM made a finding of price depression and suppression, and not of price undercutting, the evidence about price undercutting during the 2006-2008 period is the type of "supporting record evidence"

that the Appellate Body considered would not need to be disclosed under Article 22.5 of the SCM Agreement. We disagree with this argument for the following reasons. As found above, the Panel was correct to conclude that MOFCOM's Final Determination relied on evidence of price undercutting to establish that the effects of subject imports were to depress and suppress prices to a significant degree. Notably, as found by the Panel, MOFCOM did not disclose information relating to the price comparisons between subject imports and domestic products. Thus, MOFCOM's disclosure that "average domestic prices dropped" and that the "price-cost differential dropped" is insufficient to convey all the relevant information on the matters of fact relating to MOFCOM's finding that subject imports were at a "low price".

265. China further argues that the Panel erred in three respects in considering a comparison of subject import prices to domestic prices "essential elements" and "an important aspect" of MOFCOM's Final Determination. First, China submits that the Panel erred in faulting MOFCOM for not disclosing the margin by which the prices of subject imports were below the prices of domestic producers. China highlights that this fact—or any facts about such relative prices—was never a "matter of fact" on which MOFCOM actually based its decision to impose final measures. Second, China argues that, pursuant to Articles 12.2 of the Anti-Dumping Agreement and 22.3 of the SCM Agreement, the public notice requirement only extends to those facts "considered material" by the investigating authority. China adds that, given that the Final Determination does not contain any finding of price undercutting, such facts were not material to MOFCOM's Final Determination. Consequently, argues China, these facts need not have been disclosed in the Final Determination. At the outset, we note that the facts that an investigating authority may consider material to its determinations are circumscribed by the framework of the substantive provisions of the Anti-Dumping Agreement and the SCM Agreement. Moreover, we recall our finding, in the context of Articles 3.2 and 15.2, that the Panel was correct to conclude that MOFCOM's finding as to the "low price" of subject imports referred to the existence of price undercutting between 2006 and 2008, and that MOFCOM relied on this factor to support its finding of significant price depression and suppression. Accordingly, we disagree with China's arguments, as they are premised on its contention that MOFCOM did not rely on the existence of price undercutting for its finding of significant price depression and suppression.

266. Finally, China asserts that the Panel ignored MOFCOM's finding on the pricing policy of producers of the product concerned, even though MOFCOM disclosed the basic facts underlying this finding, namely, the existence of such a policy, its analytic relevance, and the fact that the "contracts and records of price setting" were collected during an onsite verification. China further contends that the Panel did not take into consideration MOFCOM's disclosure of the other two

elements discussed in the Final Determination, namely, decreasing import prices and increasing import volume. We fail to see how asserting that the Panel ignored MOFCOM's finding on the pricing policy and "the significance of decreasing import prices and increasing import volume" demonstrates that MOFCOM included in the Final Determination "all relevant information on the matters of fact" with respect to the "low price" of subject imports. We are therefore not persuaded by China's argument.

267. In sum, MOFCOM was required to disclose "all relevant information on the matters of fact" relating to the "low price" of subject imports on which it relied for its finding of significant price depression and suppression. Consequently, in addition to the finding in its Final Determination that subject imports were at a "low price", MOFCOM was also required to disclose the facts of price undercutting that were required to understand that finding. As the Panel found, the Final Determination only states that subject imports were at a "low price", without providing any facts relating to the price comparisons of subject imports and domestic products. We consider that these facts constituted "relevant information on the matters of fact" within the meaning of Articles 12.2.2 and 22.5, which should have been included in MOFCOM's Final Determination. Consequently, we uphold the Panel's finding in paragraphs 7.592 and 8.1(f) of the Panel Report that China acted inconsistently with Article 12.2.2 of the Anti-Dumping Agreement and Article 22.5 of the SCM Agreement.

【本案评析】

以上案例节选自 2012 年中国对美国取向电工钢征收反倾销税和反补贴税案上诉机构报告。对于什么是第 12.2.2 项"关于事实问题的相关信息"，上诉机构认为，必须基于能够根据《反倾销协定》满足实施最终措施有关实体性义务所需的裁定内容，以及每个争端案件的实际情况来理解。对此，上诉机构进一步指出，第 12.2.2 项并不要求主管机关披露其获得的所有事实信息，而只要求披露能够理解实施最终措施所依据的那些相关事实依据资料。因此，此种信息列入的同时应对主管机关决定采取最终措施的事实依据给出合理的说明。此外，公告或报告必须列出接受或拒绝出口商和进口商所提的有关论据或请求事项的各项理由。上诉机构强调，第 12.2 款规定了一项原则，即对其利益受到最终反倾销税影响的当事方而言，按照公平和正当程序的要求，其有权了解导致征收反倾销税的事实、法律和理由。第 12.2 款规定的披露义务是以"相关性"的要求为依据的，这就需要披露与采取最终反倾销措施决定具有逻辑合理性的事实、法律和理由矩阵

(matrix)。该条款要求披露涉及这些种类信息的“所有相关信息”，旨在确保利害关系方能够按照《反倾销协定》第13条的规定对最终裁定进行司法审查。

三、济南玫德集团有限公司玛钢管件案欧盟上诉案

2012年2月16日，欧盟委员会对来自中国、泰国和印度尼西亚的玛钢管件发起反倾销调查。2013年5月13日，欧委会发布终裁，裁定中国三家抽样企业的税率分别为24.6%、40.8%和57.8%，非抽样企业平均税率为41.1%，全国统一税为57.8%。其中，济南玫德集团有限公司(下称济南玫德)产品的反倾销税率为40.8%。企业受损严重。2013年8月7日，济南玫德向欧盟初等法院提起上诉。

(一)济南玫德起诉欧洲初等法院的主要诉点

1.欧委会没有披露完整的倾销幅度计算

替代国生产商Jaisons Industries于2013年3月18日致函欧委会，明确授权欧委会向济南玫德的代理律师披露其保密版的答卷及核查附件，并告知欧委会已经将保密答卷和核查附件给了济南玫德。由于替代国生产商Jaisons Industries的数据已经不再是保密数据，2013年3月18日和19日，济南玫德请求欧委会披露完整的倾销幅度计算过程，包括正常价值的计算。但是，欧委会于2013年3月21日回复邮件予以拒绝，理由是如果披露，将对于其他出口商产生构成歧视。

2.欧委会没有基于所有出口计算倾销幅度

济南玫德的产品规格众多，而替代国生产商生产的规格很少，导致欧委会无法获得数量占40%出口规格的正常价值。在以往案件中，欧委会都不再计算不可比的产品规格的正常价值，而将这部分产品排除在倾销幅度计算之外。但是，由于WTO紧固件案件的裁决，欧委会知道，如果将部分产品排除在倾销幅度计算之外违法风险太大，因此采取了特殊的方法。欧委会认为，不可比的产

品规格与可比的产品规格的差异的市场价值反映到了出口价格中，因此按照出口价格之间的比例关系，折算了不可比的产品规格的正常价值。欧委会的这一做法，表面上将所有产品规格考虑在内计算倾销幅度，实际上推定了不可比产品规格的倾销幅度和可比产品规格的倾销幅度一致，在实质上仍然没有基于所有出口计算倾销幅度。

3. 欧委会拒绝价格比较的成本差异调整

替代国生产商与中国生产商在生产过程存在巨大差异，生产工艺不同，主原料不同，消耗差异很大，生产效率差异很大。对此，济南玫德提出了具体的调整要求，并且提交了调整计算过程和支持性材料。此外，对于这些差异，替代国生产商明确承认存在，并且影响了定价，并且提供的由此造成的生产成本差异比例和济南玫德提供的调整计算完全吻合，这些在案件材料里都有。这些因素影响价格可比性，应当根据《反倾销协定》第 2.4 条进行调整。

对于济南玫德提出的价格调整要求，欧委会拒绝，具体理由如下：适用替代国的理论依据就是非市场经济国家的成本和价格，甚至生产要素都是非市场力量的结果，所以欧委会采用的是替代国生产商的所有数据，无论生产要素或生产方法是否与中国生产商存在差异。但是，生产工艺差异，并不会受到该国是否为市场经济的影响。济南玫德提出的价格调整要求是基于生产环节的工艺差异、原料不同以及数量耗用不同，而没有要求调整基于市场价格或者成本金额的差异。欧委会在以往的替代国实践中就生产要素的差异曾经做出过调整。

4. 欧委会关于被调查产品进口数量的评估存在瑕疵

欧委会依据欧盟海关数据计算了从中国进口被调查产品的数量，由于同一海关税号下包括了大量其他产品，因此虚夸了中国被调查产品的实际进口数量。在调查过程中，中国五矿商会提交了依据中国海关数据计算的被调查产品出口数量，但被欧委会拒绝，原因是提交时间太晚了。然而，欧委会却接受了进口商提交更晚的一份材料，进而对于进口数量进行了调低，即排除了无螺纹的产品。即使是欧委会排除部分进口商无螺纹产品的做法也存在问题，因为从这些进口商总进口中排除的产品比例很大，欧委会而没有进一步调查其他进口商是否也存在类似的问题。最终，欧委会认定进口数量为 28000 吨左右，而实际从中国进口被调查产品应该在 18000 吨左右。

（二）欧洲初等法院的裁决

关于以上四个诉点，欧洲初等法院只对第一个诉点进行裁决，判定济南玫德胜诉，欧盟理事会对济南玫德征税的最终裁决无效。但是，对于后面三个诉点，欧洲初等法院使用了“司法经济”原则，没有进行裁决。理由是依据第一个诉点终裁已经无效，没有必要再审查后面三个诉点。关于第一个诉点，欧洲初等法院裁定违法的理由如下：

1. 欧委会没有披露正常价值；

2. 正常价值属于披露义务所要求的“基本事实”（essential facts）；

3. 欧委会拒绝披露的理由，即对于其他中国出口商构成歧视性，不成立；

4. 欧委会拒绝披露正常价值，影响了济南玫德的抗辩权利，很可能会影响税率的结果。目前，欧盟理事会已经放弃上诉到欧盟最高法院，即该法院裁决已经生效。

【本案评析】

以上案例节选自欧盟初等法院判决济南玫德集团有限公司玛钢管件反倾销案，判决已具体介绍该案争议点，该案出于“司法经济原则”并未对第二和第三诉点进行系统分析，而关于本案的第二和第三诉点，在事实和法律上和紧固件案非常相似，在紧固件案中 2015 年 4 月欧洲初等法院判中国出口商败诉，2016 年 1 月 WTO 上诉机构裁定中方胜诉，目前关于这两个诉点正在欧洲最高法院上诉。在本案中，欧洲初等法院对于该两个诉点处理难度较大，如果判济南玫德胜诉，则违背欧洲初等法院在紧固件案中的裁决，并且在欧洲最高法院前面裁决；如果判济南玫德败诉，很可能之后被欧洲最高法院推翻，因为欧洲最高法院极有可能会保持和 WTO 上诉机构裁决一致。所以，在本案中，欧洲初等法院回避了对于第二和第三个诉点的裁决。

【延伸阅读】

一、相关典型案例

1. China—Measures Imposing Anti-Dumping Duties on High-Performance Stainless Steel Seamless Tubes (HP-SSST) from the European Union and Japan (WT/DS454,WT/DS460)

2. European Communities—Anti-Dumping Measure on Farmed Salmon from Norway (WT/DS337)

3. European Communities—Definitive Anti-Dumping Measures on Certain Iron or Steel Fasteners from China (WT/DS397)

4. Thailand—Anti-Dumping Duties on Angels, Shapes and Sections of Iron or Non-Alloy Steel and H-Beams from Poland (WT/DS122)

5. United States—Anti-Dumping Act of 1916, Complaint by Japan (WT/DS162)

6. United States—Anti-Dumping Measures on Certain Hot-Rolled Steel Products from Japan (WT/DS184)

7. United States—Anti-Dumping measures on Stainless Steel Plate in Coils and Stainless Steel Sheet and Strip from Korea (WT/DS179)

8. United States—Sunset Reviews of Anti-Dumping Measures on Oil Country Tubular Goods from Argentina (WT/DS268)

二、相关学术论著

1. 王贵国:《世界贸易组织法》,法律出版社 2003 年版。

2. 曹建明、贺小勇:《世界贸易组织》,法律出版社 2011 年版。

3. Xiaochen Wu, *Anti-dumping Law and Practice of China,* Kluwer Law International, 2008.

4. Edwin Vermulst, *The WTO Anti-Dumping Agreement: A Commentary,* Oxford University Press, 2006.

三、相关网络资源

1.https://www.wto.org/english/docs_e/legal_e/19-adp_01_e.htm.

2.http://ec.europa.eu/trade/policy/accessing-markets/trade-defence/actions-against-imports-into-the-eu/anti-dumping/.

3. https://www.usitc.gov/trade_remedy/.

4. http://cacs.mofcom.gov.cn/.

第四节　反倾销措施的复审及司法审查

【知识背景 / 学习要点】

为了回应一些成员对某些国家反倾销税无限期实施的关注，《反倾销协定》第 11 条除了规定有关反倾销税实施期限的规则外，主要针对成员方提出了对持续征收反倾销税必要性进行定期复审的纪律要求。

一、反倾销税的实施期限

对于反倾销税的实施期限，《反倾销协定》第 11.1 款规定，反倾销税应仅在抵消造成损害的倾销所必需的时间和限度内实施。根据第 11.2 款最后一句的规定，如作为根据本款复审的结果，主管机关确定反倾销税已无正当理由，则反倾销税应立即终止。2004 年美国对来自阿根廷的石油工业用管材反倾销措施日落复审案上诉机构指出，"第 11.1 款规定了反倾销税'期限'和'复审'的总体原则……这一原则适用于整个反倾销税的有效期。如果在任何时候可以证实倾销进口产品不会对国内产业造成损害，那么继续征税的理由就会停止"。①

二、"期间复审"

征收反倾销税实施一段时间后，如果利害关系方提出或者调查主管机关发现，无须继续征收反倾销税的正当理由，或者撤销或改变反倾销税足以防止损

① 参见 Appellate Body Report, United States–Sunset Reviews of Anti-Dumping Measures on Oil Country Tubular Goods from Argentina, WT/DS268/AB/R, adopted 17 December 2004, para. 115.

害继续发生或再度发生的情况，则此时调查主管机关应该进行审查继续实施反倾销税的必要性，否则继续实施将会超出抵消倾销的目的与必要限度。这就是反倾销税的期间复审，主要包括两种[①]复审情况：第一种是有无继续实施反倾销税正当理由的审查；第二种是撤销或者改变反倾销税是否足以防止损害继续发生或再度发生的情况审查。《反倾销协定》第 11.2 款要求调查主管机关除其他特殊情况外，在利害关系方请求时执行复审，并在认为"不再有正当理由"的情况下终止反倾销税。第 11.2 款规定这项义务的条件是，最终反倾销税的征收已经过一段合理时间，并且应提交证实复审必要性肯定信息的任何利害关系方请求。2005 年墨西哥大米和牛肉的最终反倾销措施案的上诉机构认为，在特定情况下，如果所提供的信息与出口数量无关，也可满足后一种条件。在符合第 11.2 款条件的情况下，该条款清晰地表明，主管机关没有拒绝执行复审，包括考虑是否应根据复审结果终止征税的自由裁量权。[②]

第 11.2 条第 1 句要求调查机关在有正当理由的情况下，自行复审或在最终反倾销税的征收经过了一段合理时间之后，经提交证实复审必要性肯定信息的任何利害关系方请求，复审继续征税的必要性。[③] 第 11.2 款第 2 句要求调查机关复查是否有必要"继续征收"反倾销税以抵消倾销，以及关于损害方面，"如撤销或改变反倾销税，损害是否有可能继续或再度发生"。

三、"日落复审"

根据《反倾销协定》第 11.3 款（所谓的"日落条款"）的规定，任何最终反

① 当然，也可能同时复审这两种情况。

② 参见 Appellate Body Report, Mexico-Definitive Anti-Dumping Measures on Beef and Rice, WT/DS295/AB/R, 29 November 2005, para. 314.

③ 2003 年巴西诉欧共体管道配件反倾销案专家组指出，对自行启动复审的良好和充分的理由的裁定，必然取决于特定案件中的实际情况并且会因案而异。参见 Panel Report, European Communities–Anti-Dumping Duties on Malleable Cast Iron Tube or Pipe Fittings from Brazil, WT/DS219/ R, para. 7.115. 1999 年美国对韩国出口的 1 兆及 1 兆以上半导体动态随机存储器征收反倾销税争端案专家组指出，利害关系人请求复审的，必须根据所举证据证明继续实施征税的必要性。参见 Panel Report, United States-Anti-Dumping Duty on Dynamic Random Access Memory Semiconductors (DRAMS) of One Megabit or Above from Korea, WT/DS99/R, 29 January 1999, para. 6.42.

倾销税应在征收之日起(或在复审涉及倾销和损害两者的情况下，自根据第2款进行的最近一次复审之日起，或根据本款)5年内终止，除非主管当局在该日之前发起的一项复审中认定，征税期限的届满“可能会导致倾销和损害的继续或再次发生”。这种复审通常被称为“日落复审”，其可因以下情况而启动：(1)由调查机关主动提出或(2)应国内产业或国内产业代表提出的有充分证据的请求。根据《反倾销协定》第11.3款的规定，在日落复审的结果产生之前，可继续实施反倾销税。根据第11.4款的规定，第6条关于证据和程序的规定应适用于根据本条进行的任何复审。任何此种复审应迅速进行，通常应在开始审查之日起12个月内完成。

因此，根据第11.3款的规定，终止征收反倾销税有两种情况。第一种即第11.3款本身的规定，除非主管机关认定5年期限的届满“有可能导致倾销和损害的继续或再次发生”。在确定两者都有可能发生的情况下，征税可能仍然有效，而5年的期限从那时起重新开始。第二种情况即根据第11.2款对倾销和损害进行复审后的5年期限，但这个期限可以在特殊情况下延长，例如在第4年进行这样一次复审，就可以有效地将日落复审延长到从最初确定的时间起9年。然而，在第一种情况下，第11.3款明确规定延长5年期限的条件是认定倾销和损害有可能继续发生或再次发生。而在第二种情况涉及第11.2款所指的复审，该款未有明确的条件作为审查参考标准。对于第二种情况的参考标准，争端案件专家组曾指出，由于两种复审(即期间复审和日落复审)的实际效果都是将反倾销税的适用期限延长到5年以上，因此调查机关有权对第11.2款和第11.3款下倾销继续或再次发生可能性的复审适用同样的检验标准。[①]

此外，对于第11.3款的评审标准，2004年美国对来自阿根廷的石油工业用管材反倾销措施日落复审案上诉机构曾裁定，第11.3款并不要求调查机关确定

① 参见Panel Report, United States-Anti-Dumping Duty on Dynamic Random Access Memory Semiconductors (DRAMS) of One Megabit or Above from Korea, adopted on 29 January 1999, WT/DS99/R, para. 6.48, fn. 494.

可能的倾销与可能的损害之间存在“因果关系”，但是相反的是，根据第 11.3 款其要求调查机关确定征税的到期是否可能导致倾销和损害的继续或再次发生。因此，为了继续征税，在“反倾销征收到期”与“倾销和损害的继续或再次发生”之间必定存在一种联系，从而使前者“有可能导致”后者。这种联系必须清楚地加以证明。①

四、国内司法审查

按照第 13 条“司法审查”的规定，国内立法包含反倾销措施规定的每一成员均应设有司法、仲裁或行政庭或程序，以确保迅速审查与最终裁定有关的行政行为和对裁定的审查。此类法庭或程序应独立于负责所涉裁定或审查的主管机关。

【案例摘录与评析】

一、1999 年美国对韩国出口的 1 兆及 1 兆以上半导体动态随机存储器征收反倾销税争端案②

United States—Anti-Dumping Duty on Dynamic Random Access Memory Semiconductors (DRAMS) of One Megabit or Above from Korea
(WT/DS99/R)

1. Whether Article 11.2 of the AD Agreement precludes an anti-dumping duty being deemed “necessary to offset dumping” where there is no present dumping to offset

6.24 Korea argues that Article 11.2 of the AD Agreement contains procedures to ensure that a duty is not applied when it is no longer “necessary to offset dumping” that is causing injury, e.g.,

① 参见 Appellate Body Report, United States–Sunset Reviews of Anti-Dumping Measures on Oil Country Tubular Goods from Argentina, WT/DS268/AB/R, adopted 17 December 2004, para. 108.

② Report of the Panel, United States-Anti-Dumping Duty on Dynamic Random Access Memory Semiconductors (DRAMS) of One Megabit or Above from Korea, WT/DS99/R, 29 January 1999. 原文脚注省略。

where an exporter is found not to have been dumping. We understand Korea to claim that Article 11.2 of the AD Agreement precludes an anti-dumping duty being deemed "necessary to offset dumping" where there is no present dumping to offset, and that Article 11.2 requires duties to be revoked as soon as there is a finding of "no dumping".

6.25 Having regard to the rules of treaty interpretation contained in Article 31.1 of the Vienna Convention, we consider that the following textual and contextual analysis of Article 11.2 of the AD Agreement is appropriate in resolving this issue.

6.26 First, we note that the second sentence of Article 11.2 refers to an examination of "whether the continued imposition of the duty is necessary to offset dumping". We note further that this sentence is expressed in the present tense. In addition, the second sentence of Article 11.2 does not explicitly include any reference to dumping being "likely" to "recur", as is the case with the injury review envisaged by that sentence.

6.27 However, the second sentence of Article 11.2 requires an investigating authority to examine whether the "continued imposition" of the duty is necessary to offset dumping. The word "continued" covers a temporal relationship between past and future. In our view, the word "continued" would be redundant if the investigating authority were restricted to considering only whether the duty was necessary to offset present dumping. Thus, the inclusion of the word "continued" signifies that the investigating authority is entitled to examine whether imposition of the duty may be applied henceforth to offset dumping.

6.28 Furthermore, with regard to injury, Article 11.2 provides for a review of "whether the injury would be likely to continue or recur if the duty were removed or varied" (emphasis supplied). In conducting an Article 11.2 injury review, an investigating authority may examine the causal link between injury and dumped imports. If, in the context of a review of such a causal link, the only injury under examination is injury that may recur following revocation (i.e., future rather than present injury), an investigating authority must necessarily be examining whether that future injury would be caused by dumping with a commensurately prospective timeframe. To do so, the investigating authority would first need to have established a status regarding the prospects of dumping. For these reasons, we do not agree that Article 11.2 precludes a priori the justification of continued imposition of anti-dumping duties when there is no present dumping.

6.29 In addition, we note that there is nothing in the text of Article 11.2 of the AD Agreement that explicitly limits a Member to a "present" analysis, and forecloses a prospective analysis, when conducting an Article 11.2 review.

6.30 Turning to the context of Article 11.2, we consider that Article 11.3 of the AD Agreement is particularly relevant in giving support for and reinforcing this interpretation. Article 11.3

provides:

> "Notwithstanding the provisions of paragraphs 1 and 2, any definitive anti-dumping duty shall be terminated on a date not later than five years from its imposition (or from the date of the most recent review under paragraph 2 if that review has covered both dumping and injury, or under this paragraph), unless the authorities determine, in a review initiated before that date on their own initiative or upon a duly substantiated request made by or on behalf of the domestic industry within a reasonable period of time prior to that date, that the expiry of the duty would be likely to lead to continuation or recurrence of dumping and injury.* The duty may remain in force pending the outcome of such a review."

6.31 We note that, with regard to dumping, the "sunset provision" in Article 11.3 of the AD Agreement envisages inter alia an examination of whether the expiry of an anti-dumping duty would be likely to lead to "continuation or recurrence"of dumping. If, as argued by Korea, an anti-dumping duty must be revoked as soon as present dumping is found to have ceased, the possibility (explicitly envisaged by Article 11.3) of the expiry of that duty causing dumping to recur could never arise. This is because the reference to "expiry" in Article 11.3 assumes that the duty is still in force, and the reference to "recurrence" of dumping assumes that dumping has ceased, but may "recur" as a result of revocation. Korea's textual interpretation of Article 11.2 would effectively exclude the possibility of an Article 11.3 review in circumstances where dumping has ceased but the duty remains in force. Korea's interpretation therefore renders part of Article 11.3 ineffective. As stated by the Appellate Body in Gasoline, "[a]n interpreter is not free to adopt a reading that would result in reducing whole clauses or paragraphs of a treaty to redundancy or inutility". An interpretation of Article 11.2 which renders part of Article 11.3 meaningless is contrary to the customary or general rules of treaty interpretation, and thus should be rejected.

6.32 Furthermore, Korea's argument that Article 11.2 requires the immediate revocation of an anti-dumping duty in case of a finding of "no dumping" (e.g., when a retrospective assessment finds that no duty is to be levied) is also inconsistent with note 22 of the AD Agreement. Note 22 states that, in cases where anti-dumping duties are levied on a retrospective basis, "a finding in the most recent assessment proceeding ... that no duty is to be levied shall not by itself require the authorities to terminate the definitive duty". If Korea's interpretation of Article 11.2 were accurate, then an investigating authority would be obligated under Article 11.2 to terminate an anti-dumping duty upon making such a finding, and note 22 would be meaningless. In our view, this confirms a finding that the absence of present dumping does not in and of itself require the immediate termination of an anti-dumping duty pursuant to Article 11.2.

6.33 We have also taken into account the basic operation of the AD Agreement more generally. Under the AD Agreement, a Member is entitled to impose anti-dumping duties with prospective effect on the basis of an examination of past dumping during a recent period of investigation, provided that it creates a duty assessment mechanism under Article 9.3 to ensure that the amount of the anti-dumping duty does not exceed the margin of dumping. As the basic operation of the AD Agreement is intrinsically prospective, it appears to us that any departure from this approach would be explicitly provided for, which, as noted in para. 6.29 above, is manifestly not the case. Thus, the Panel finds that, absent any such explicit provision, the AD Agreement does not require the automatic revocation of anti-dumping duties as soon as dumping ceases after the date of imposition of the duties.

6.34 In light of the above, the Panel rejects the claim that Article 11.2 of the AD Agreement requires revocation as soon as an exporter is found to have ceased dumping, and that the continuation of an anti-dumping duty is precluded a priori in any circumstances other than where there is present dumping.

...

6.41 We agree with the parties that, by virtue of Article 11.1 of the AD Agreement, an anti-dumping duty may only continue to be imposed if it remains "necessary" to offset injurious dumping. We are of the view that Article 11.1 contains a general necessity requirement, whereby anti-dumping duties "shall remain in force only as long as and to the extent necessary" to counteract injurious dumping. That anti-dumping duties "shall remain in force only as long as and to the extent necessary" to counteract injurious dumping is therefore an unambiguous requirement of Article 11.1. We also agree with the parties that the application of the general rule in Article 11.1 is specified in Article 11.2, which provides generally that "authorities shall review the need for the continued imposition of the duty", and requires authorities "to examine whether the continued imposition of the duty is necessary to offset dumping" in the context of Article 11.2 dumping reviews.

6.42 Accordingly, we must assess the essential character of the necessity involved in cases of continued imposition of an anti-dumping duty. We note that the necessity of the measure is a function of certain objective conditions being in place, i.e. whether circumstances require continued imposition of the anti-dumping duty. That being so, such continued imposition must, in our view, be essentially dependent on, and therefore assignable to, a foundation of positive evidence that circumstances demand it. In other words, the need for the continued imposition of the duty must be demonstrable on the basis of the evidence adduced.

6.43 The necessity of the continued imposition of the anti-dumping duty can only arise in a defined situation pursuant to Article 11.2: viz to offset dumping. Absent the prescribed situation, there is no basis for continued imposition of the duty: the duty cannot be "necessary" in the sense of being demonstrable on the basis of the evidence adduced because it has been deprived of its essential foundation. In this context, we recall our finding that Article 11.2 does not preclude a priori continued imposition of anti-dumping duties in the absence of present dumping. However, it is also clear from the plain meaning of the text of Article 11.2 that the continued imposition must still satisfy the "necessity" standard, even where the need for the continued imposition of an anti-dumping duty is tied to the "recurrence" of dumping. We recognize that the certainty inherent to such a prospective analysis could be conceivably somewhat less than that attached to purely retrospective analysis, reflecting the simple fact that analysis involving prediction can scarcely aspire to a standard of inevitability. This is, in our view, a discernable distinction in the degree of certainty, but not one which would be sufficient to preclude that the standard of necessity could be met. In our view, this reflects the fact that the necessity involved in Article 11.2 is not to be construed in some absolute and abstract sense, but as that appropriate to circumstances of practical reasoning intrinsic to a review process. Mathematical certainty is not required, but the conclusions should be demonstrable on the basis of the evidence adduced. This is as much applicable to a case relating to the prospect of recurrence of dumping as to one of present dumping.

...

1. Is an ex officio Article 11.2 injury review warranted after three years and six months' no dumping?

6.57 Korea argues that the United States violated Article 11.2 of the AD Agreement because, "after concluding for three years that no injury was occurring as a result of dumping, the authorities had an obligation on their own initiative ('it was warranted') to investigate whether injury as well as dumping would be likely to resume if the order were revoked". Korea is effectively claiming that Article 11.2 necessarily requires an investigating authority to self-initiate an Article 11.2 injury review solely on the basis of three years and six months' no dumping, because any injury found to exist will not be caused by dumped imports due to the absence of dumping.

6.58 The issue before us is whether Article 11.2 necessarily requires an investigating authority, following three years and six months' findings of no dumping, to find that an ex officio Article 11.2 review of "whether the injury would be likely to continue or recur if the duty were removed or varied" is "warranted".

6.59 A review of "whether the injury would be likely to continue or recur if the duty were removed or varied" could include a review of whether (1) injury that is (2) caused by dumped imports would be likely to continue or recur if the duty were removed or varied. With regard to injury, we believe that an absence of dumping during the preceding three years and six months is not in and of itself indicative of the likely state of the relevant domestic industry if the duty were removed or varied. With regard to causality, an absence of dumping during the preceding three years and six months is not in and of itself indicative of causal factors other than the absence of dumping. If the only causal factor under consideration is three years and six months' no dumping, the issue of causality becomes whether injury caused by dumped imports will recur. This necessarily requires a determination of whether dumping will recur. Thus, the "injury" review that Korea believes is "warranted" on the basis of three years and six months' no dumping would be entirely dependent upon a determination of whether dumping will recur. This is precisely the type of determination that the United States sought to make in the present case. The mere fact of three years and six months' findings of no dumping does not require the investigating authority to, in addition, self-initiate a review of "whether the injury would be likely to continue or recur if the duty were removed or varied".

6.60 We therefore reject Korea's claim that the United States violated Article 11.2 of the AD Agreement by failing to initiate, solely on the basis of three years and six months' no dumping, an ex officio Article 11.2 review of "whether the injury would be likely to continue or recur if the duty were removed or varied".

【本案评析】

以上案例节选自1999年美国对韩国出口的1兆及1兆以上半导体动态随机存储器征收反倾销税争端案专家组报告。该案专家组解释第11.2款第2句时认为,"继续"这个词涵盖了过去和未来之间的时间关系,如果调查机关考虑的只是征税对抵消现在的倾销是否必要,则"继续"一词便属多余。因此,"继续"一词的加入意味着调查机关有权审查反倾销税的征收可否抵消以后的倾销。专家组指出,对于调查机关按照第11.2款进行的损害与倾销进口间因果关系的复审,如果审查中的唯一损害是在撤销后可能再次发生的损害(即未来的而不是现在的损害),则调查机关必须审查在相应的预期时间框架内,倾销是否会造成未来的损害。要做到这一点,调查机关首先需要确定倾销预期状况。基于这些理由,该案专家组不认为,第11.2款预先排除了在目前没有倾销的情况下,继续征收反倾销税的正当理由。专家组指出,《反倾销协定》第 11.2 款的文本并没有明确将 WTO 成员执行第 11.2 款下的复审,限制在只能进行“现在”分析,并排除进行预期性分析的可能性。因此该案专家组裁定,关于损害,过去 3 年零 6 个月中没有倾销本身并不代表如果反倾销税被取消或改变,相关国内产业的可能状态。同样,在因果关系方面,过去 3 年零 6 个月内没有倾销本身并不代表排除没有倾销以外的其他原因因素。然而专家组也认为,从第 11.2 款条文的简单含义可以看出,即使继续征收反倾销税的必要性与倾销的再次发生是有关联性的,继续征收反倾销税仍然必须符合“必要性”标准。

二、2004 年美国对日本耐腐蚀扁平碳钢产品征收反倾销税的日落复审案[①]

United States – Sunset Review of Anti-Dumping Duties on Corrosion-Resistant Carbon Steel Flat Products from Japan (WT/DS244/AB/R)

VI. Japan's Specific Claims under Article 11.3 of the Anti-Dumping Agreement

A. Overview

102. Japan's appeal raises a number of specific issues concerning whether the Panel properly applied Article 11.3 of the Anti-Dumping Agreement. These issues relate to: (i) the dumping margins used by USDOC in the CRS sunset review; (ii) USDOC's making of determinations in sunset reviews on an order-wide basis; and (iii) the factors considered by USDOC in making a determination in a sunset review. Before turning to these issues, it is worth considering briefly Article 11.3 as a whole.

103. Article 11.3 of the Anti-Dumping Agreement governs sunset reviews of anti-dumping duties. It provides:

...

104. Article 11.3 imposes a temporal limitation on the maintenance of anti-dumping duties. It lays down a mandatory rule with an exception. Specifically, Members are required to terminate an anti-dumping duty within five years of its imposition "unless" the following conditions are satisfied: first, that a review be initiated before the expiry of five years from the date of the

① Appellate Body Report, United States–Sunset Review of Anti-Dumping Duties on Corrosion-Resistant Carbon Steel Flat Products from Japan, WT/DS244/AB/R, adopted 9 January 2004. 原文脚注省略。

imposition of the duty; second, that in the review the authorities determine that the expiry of the duty would be likely to lead to continuation or recurrence of dumping; and third, that in the review the authorities determine that the expiry of the duty would be likely to lead to continuation or recurrence of injury. If any one of these conditions is not satisfied, the duty must be terminated.

105. This appeal concerns the obligations that apply to investigating authorities with respect to the second of these conditions. It focuses on the particular disciplines with which authorities must comply in determining, in accordance with Article 11.3, "that the expiry of the duty would be likely to lead to continuation or recurrence of dumping". In this Report, we refer to this determination as the "likelihood determination". The likelihood determination is a prospective determination. In other words, the authorities must undertake a forward-looking analysis and seek to resolve the issue of what would be likely to occur if the duty were terminated.

106. In considering the nature of a likelihood determination in a sunset review under Article 11.3, we recall our statement in US – Carbon Steel, in the context of the SCM Agreement, that:

... original investigations and sunset reviews are distinct processes with different purposes. The nature of the determination to be made in a sunset review differs in certain essential respects from the nature of the determination to be made in an original investigation.

107. This observation applies also to original investigations and sunset reviews under the Anti-Dumping Agreement. In an original anti-dumping investigation, investigating authorities must determine whether dumping exists during the period of investigation. In contrast, in a sunset review of an anti-dumping duty, investigating authorities must determine whether the expiry of the duty that was imposed at the conclusion of an original investigation would be likely to lead to continuation or recurrence of dumping.

108. An examination of the language in Article 11.3 sheds light on the obligations of investigating authorities in conducting a sunset review. Article 11.3 refers to, but does not define, the word "dumping". Article VI:1 of the GATT 1994 provides that dumping occurs where "products of one country are introduced into the commerce of another country at less than the normal value of the products". Article 2.1 of the Anti-Dumping Agreement confirms this definition in the following terms:

Determination of Dumping

2.1 For the purpose of this Agreement, a product is to be considered as being dumped, i.e. introduced into the commerce of another country at less than its normal value, if the export price of the product exported from one country to another is less than the comparable price, in the ordinary course of trade, for the like product when destined for consumption in the exporting country. (emphasis added)

109. We agree with Japan that the words "[f]or the purpose of this Agreement" in Article 2.1 indicate that this provision describes the circumstances in which a product is to be considered as being dumped for purposes of the entire Anti-Dumping Agreement, including Article 11.3. This interpretation is supported by the fact that Article 11.3 does not indicate, either expressly or by implication, that "dumping" has a different meaning in the context of sunset reviews than in the rest of the Anti-Dumping Agreement. Therefore, Article 2.1 of the Anti-Dumping Agreement and Article VI:1 of the GATT 1994 suggest that the question for investigating authorities, in making a likelihood determination in a sunset review pursuant to Article 11.3, is whether the expiry of the duty would be likely to lead to continuation or recurrence of dumping of the product subject to the duty (that is, to the introduction of that product into the commerce of the importing country at less than its normal value). The Panel also appeared to reach a similar conclusion.

110. Turning to the word "determine" in Article 11.3, we note that the dictionary definitions of this verb include "[c]onclude from reasoning or investigation, deduce" as well as "[s]ettle or decide (a dispute, controversy, etc., or a sentence, conclusion, issue, etc.) as a judge or arbiter". As for "review", definitions of this noun include "[a]n inspection, an examination" and a "general survey or reconsideration of some subject". Finally, the adjective "likely" is defined as "[h]aving an appearance of truth or fact; that looks as if it would happen, be realized, or prove to be what is alleged or suggested; probable; to be reasonably expected".

111. This language in Article 11.3 makes clear that it envisages a process combining both investigatory and adjudicatory aspects. In other words, Article 11.3 assigns an active rather than a passive decision-making role to the authorities. The words "review" and "determine" in Article 11.3 suggest that authorities conducting a sunset review must act with an appropriate degree of diligence and arrive at a reasoned conclusion on the basis of information gathered as part of a process of reconsideration and examination. In view of the use of the word "likely" in Article 11.3, an affirmative likelihood determination may be made only if the evidence demonstrates that dumping would be probable if the duty were terminated—and not simply if the evidence suggests that such a result might be possible or plausible.

112. In addition to the text of Article 11.3, certain other provisions of the Anti-Dumping Agreement confirm that sunset reviews must conform to the principles outlined above. Article 11.4 applies the provisions of Article 6 regarding "evidence and procedure" to reviews, and Article 12.3 applies the provisions of Article 12 on "Public Notice and Explanation of Determinations" to reviews. Thus, even though the rules applicable to sunset reviews may not be identical in all respects to those applicable to original investigations, it is clear that the drafters of the Anti-

Dumping Agreement intended a sunset review to include both full opportunity for all interested parties to defend their interests, and the right to receive notice of the process and reasons for the determination.

113. Article 11.3 states that, notwithstanding the provisions of Articles 11.1 and 11.2, Members "shall" terminate an anti-dumping duty "unless" the authorities make an affirmative likelihood determination in a sunset review. This confirms that the mandatory rule in Article 11.3 applies in addition to, and irrespective of, the obligations set out in the first two paragraphs of Article 11. This also suggests to us that authorities must conduct a rigorous examination in a sunset review before the exception (namely, the continuation of the duty) can apply. In addition, our view of the exacting nature of the obligations imposed on authorities under Article 11.3 is supported by a consideration of the implications of initiating a sunset review. The last sentence of Article 11.3 allows the relevant duty to continue while the review is underway, and Article 11.4 contemplates that the review process may take up to one year. These provisions create an additional exception to the requirement that anti-dumping duties will be terminated after five years, permitting a Member to maintain the duty for the period during which the review is ongoing, regardless of the outcome of that review. This, too, suggests that the drafters of the Anti-Dumping Agreement saw the sunset review as a rigorous process that can take up to one year, involving a number of procedural steps, and requiring an appropriate degree of diligence on the part of the national authorities.

114. The Panel described Article 11.3 as imposing the following obligations on investigating authorities in a sunset review:

The text of Article 11.3 contains an obligation "to determine" likelihood of continuation or recurrence of dumping and injury. The text of Article 11.3 does not, however, provide explicit guidance regarding the meaning of the term "determine". The ordinary meaning of the word "determine" is to "find out or establish precisely" or to "decide or settle". The requirement to make a "determination" concerning likelihood therefore precludes an investigating authority from simply assuming that likelihood exists. In order to continue the imposition of the measure after the expiry of the five-year application period, it is clear that the investigating authority has to determine, on the basis of positive evidence, that termination of the duty is likely to lead to continuation or recurrence of dumping and injury. An investigating authority must have a sufficient factual basis to allow it to draw reasoned and adequate conclusions concerning the likelihood of such continuation or recurrence. (footnotes omitted)

115. The Panel's description of the obligations of investigating authorities in conducting a sunset review closely resembles our own, and we agree with it.

【本案评析】

以上案例节选自2004年美国对日本耐腐蚀扁平碳钢产品征收反倾销税的日落复审案上诉机构报告。对于日落复审条款的结构和内容，该案上诉机构认为，第11.3款对维持反倾销税规定了时间限制。它制定了一条有例外的强制性规则。具体而言，WTO成员方被要求在征收反倾销税之日起5年内终止反倾销税，“除非”符合以下条件：第一，在征收反倾销税之日起5年届满前启动了复审；第二，主管机关在复审中确定，反倾销征税到期，可能会导致倾销的继续或再次发生；第三，主管机关在复审中确定，反倾销征税到期很可能会导致损害的继续或再次发生。如果其中任何一个条件不满足，则必须终止征税。上诉机构强调，不终止反倾销税的决定必须基于倾销是否有可能继续或再次发生，以及损害是否有可能继续或再次发生的作出。但对于日落复审的具体方法要求，上诉机构同意专家组的意见，即第11.3款没有明确规定调查机关在日落复审中作出可能的决定时可以使用的任何具体方法。第11.3款也不确定调查主管机关在作出这样的决定时必须考虑的任何具体因素。因此，第11.3款既没有明确要求日落复审调查机关计算新的倾销幅度，也没有明确禁止它们依赖过去计算的倾销幅度。第11.3款条文中的这种沉默表明，调查机关没有义务计算或依赖日落复审中的倾销幅度。

对于评估日落复审所适用的审查标准，该案上诉机构指出，原先调查和日落复审之间的区别在于，在原先的反倾销调查中，调查主管机关必须确定倾销是否在调查期间存在。与此相反，在反倾销税日落复审中，调查当局必须确定在原先调查结束时所征收的反倾销税在到期之后是否有可能导致倾销的继续或再次发生。该案上诉机构认为，第11.3款中的这一措辞清楚地表明，它设想了一个将调查和裁定两个方面结合起来的过程。换言之，第11.3款赋予主管机关一项主动的而非被动的决策职能。第11.3款中所用的“复审”和“决定”两个词表明，进行日落复审的主管机关必须适度的谨慎，并根据重新考虑和审查程序过程中收集的资料得出合理的结论。考虑到第11.3款中使用的“可能”一词，只有在证据表明如果终止反倾销税则倾销有可能性，而不是仅仅如果证据表明这种结果可能或有可能是的情况下，才可作出对可能性的肯定裁定。上诉机构强调，日落复审的裁定必须在“严格审查”的基础上作出，从而得出“合理和充分的结论”，并且必须得到“积极证据”和“充分的事实依据”的支持。

【延伸阅读】

一、相关典型案例

1. United States—Anti-Dumping Measures on Certain Hot-Rolled Steel Products from Japan（DS184）

2. European Communities—Anti-Dumping Measure on Farmed Salmon from Norway（DS337）

3. EC—Anti-Dumping Duties on Imports of Cotton-type Bed Linen from India（DS141）

4. United States—Anti-Dumping measures on Stainless Steel Plate in Coils and Stainless Steel Sheet and Strip from Korea（DS179)

5. United States—Final Dumping Determination on Softwood Lumber from Canada（DS264）

6. United States—Sunset Reviews of Anti-Dumping Measures on Oil Country Tubular Goods from Argentina(WT/DS268)

二、相关学术论著

1. 胡晓红:《中国反倾销法理论与实践》,中国社会科学出版社 2001 年版。

2. 高永富、张玉卿:《国际反倾销法》,复旦大学出版社 2001 年版。

3. Andrew T. Guzman and Joost H.B. Pauwelyn, *International Trade Law,* Aspen Publishers, 2009.

4. Petros C. Mavroidis, George A. Bermann and Mark Wu, *The Law of the World Trade Organization (WTO): Documents, Cases & Analysis,* Thomas Reuters, 2010.

三、相关网络资源

1.https://www.wto.org/english/docs_e/legal_e/19-adp_01_e.htm.

2.http://ec.europa.eu/trade/policy/accessing-markets/trade-defence/actions-against-imports-into-the-eu/anti-dumping/.

3. http://cacs.mofcom.gov.cn/.

4. https://pubapps2.usitc.gov/sunset/.

第五节　WTO 多边反倾销争端解决程序

【知识背景 / 学习要点】

《反倾销协定》规定了成员方主管机关实施反倾销的权利和义务，但这也引起发了大量的争端。根据《反倾销协定》第 17.1 款的规定，除另有规定外，成员之间关于反倾销措施与《反倾销协定》规定的义务相一致的争端，须遵守《关于争端解决规则和程序的谅解》（DSU）所载的规制进行解决。本部分主要介绍《反倾销协定》第 17 条规定的其他特殊或附加争端解决规则和程序，包括：（1）第 17.6 款规定的评审标准；（2）第 17.4 款、第 17.5 款和第 17.7 款规定的其他特别或补充规则和程序。

一、评审标准

WTO 争端解决机构对于反倾销措施多边争端解决的处理过程，不同于国内反倾销争端调查和裁决程序，涉及对一成员方其主管机关是否正当履行了《反倾销协定》权利与义务进行的审查，处理与考量的对象既包括国内反倾销调查中涉及的相关事实和证据，也包括主管机关其调查程序和裁决结果本身。因此，在 WTO 多边反倾销争端解决实务中最为重要的问题涉及争端解决机构采用何种标准审视当事成员的反倾销调查结果及其程序的实施，这就是所谓的“评审标准”问题。

对于评审标准，可以发现，DSU 第 11 条规定了专家组可以适用的一种审查标准，即“客观评审”标准。然而，《反倾销协定》第 17.6 款又另外专门规定了适用于专家组处理 WTO 反倾销措施争端解决的两项特别评审标准规则。以下主要围绕这两项评审标准进行分析。

（一）对事实问题的评审标准

对实施问题的评审标准，来自《反倾销协定》第 17.6 款第（i）项的特别规定，即专家组在评审事实问题事项时，应确定主管机关对事实的认定是否适当，以及对事实的评审是否公正和客观。如事实的认定是适当的，且评审是公正和客观的，那么即使专家组可能得出不同的结论，该项评估也不得被推翻。

在这方面，2001 年美国对日本热轧钢产品的反倾销措施案上诉机构强调，必须牢记专家组和调查主管机关的不同职能。调查主管机关的职责是对与倾销和损害总体裁定有关的事实作出认定，而专家组的任务只是去评审调查机关对事实的“确认”和“评审”。[①]《反倾销协定》第 17.6 款第（i）项要求专家组不能进行“新的和独立的事实调查”，或对调查机关的证据进行重新审查。相应的，专家组的任务仅限于评审当事成员方的调查机关对于证据的评估是否是“公正和客观”的。因此，专家组应评审调查机关收到的所有机密和非机密资料。[②]

2015 年欧盟和日本诉中国对进口的高性能不锈钢无缝钢管（HP-SSST）征收反倾销税措施案上诉机构指出，注意到 WTO 专家组的任务是审查调查机关是否充分履行了其调查职能，并充分解释了证据对其结论的支持，这项任务来自对调查机关的要求，即调查机关必须对其结论提供“合理和充分的”解释，并且调查机关的整个认定理由必须在其裁定报告书中列出。这并不是说一项认定的含义不能通过记录在案（on the record）的证据来进行解释或支持。然而，在所有情况下，调查机关的书面报告（和佐证文件）中所作的解释都应予以评估，以确定这一裁定是否得到充分的解释和说明。[③]

① 参见 Appellate Body Report,United States-Anti-Dumping Measures on Certain Hot-Rolled Steel Products from Japan, WT/DS184/AB/R, adopted 23 August 2001, para. 55.

② 参见 Appellate Body Report, Thailand-Anti-Dumping Duties on Angels, Shapes and Sections of Iron or Non-Alloy Steel and H-Beams from Poland, WT/DS122/AB/R, paras.113-120.

③ 参见 Appellate Body Report, China-Measures Imposing Anti-Dumping Duties on High-Performance Stainless Steel Seamless Tubes (HP-SSST) from the European Union and Japan,WT/DS454/AB/R,WT/DS460/AB/R,14 October 2015, para. 5.255.

与 DSU 第 11 条一并解读，按照《反倾销协定》第 17.6 款第(i)项的授权，专家组应对调查机关就事实的确认和评估作出客观的评审。在解释第 17.6 款第(i)项时，上诉机构基本上将这些特别条款所规定的评审标准与 DSU 第 11 条规定的评审标准等同视之。在 2001 年美国对日本热轧钢产品的反倾销措施案中，上诉机构指出，第 17.6 款第(i)项反映了 DSU 第 11 条规定的专家组“对事实作出客观评估”的义务要求。如果第 17.6 款第(i)项要求专家组作出客观的“争端事实评估”以外的任何其他要求，这是不可想象的。我们认为《反倾销协定》第 17.6 款第(i)项与 DSU 第 11 条并无“冲突”。①

(二)对法律问题的评审标准

评审标准的第 2 项特别规则是《反倾销协定》的第 17.6 款第(ii)项，其涉及对争端案件法律问题的评审标准。该条款的第 1 句明确要求专家组应按照“国际公法有关解释的习惯规则解释协定的有关条款”。然而，第 17.6 款第(ii)项的第 2 句的规定“如果专家组认为一项相关条款允许不止一种可允许的解释，则如果主管机关的措施符合其中一种允许的解释，专家组应认定该措施符合本协定”则成为《反倾销协定》中最具争议的规则之一。

对于“国际公法有关解释的习惯规则”，在 2001 年美国对日本热轧钢产品的反倾销措施案中上诉机构承认，第 17.6 款第(ii)项第 2 句的前提是适用《维也纳条约法公约》第 31 条和第 32 条有关条约的解释规则，至少可引起对《反倾销协定》某些条款的两种解释，根据该公约，这样的两种解释都是“被允许的解释”。②

二、其他特殊或附加程序规则

如上所述，第 17.4 款，第 17.5 款和第 17.7 款规定的其他特殊和附加规则

---

① 参见 Appellate Body Report,United States–Anti-Dumping Measures on Certain Hot-Rolled Steel Products from Japan, WT/DS184/AB/R, adopted 23 August 2001, para. 55.

② 参见 Appellate Body Report,United States–Anti-Dumping Measures on Certain Hot-Rolled Steel Products from Japan, WT/DS184/AB/R, adopted 23 August 2001, para. 59.

与程序也适用于《反倾销协定》下的争端。如果磋商未能达成双方同意的解决办法，而且反倾销调查机关根据第17.4款采取了最终措施，则该事项可以提交争端解决机构（DSB）处理。如果一项临时措施具有重大的影响，并且被指控违反了第7条与临时措施有关的规定要求，那么这种措施也可提交给DSB。

应申诉方的请求，DSB应按照第17.5款的规定设立一个专家组来审查这一事项，条件包括：（1）提出请求成员的书面陈述，其中表明该成员在本协定项下直接或间接获得的利益如何丧失或减损，或本协定目标的实现如何受到阻碍，及（2）根据适当国内程序的使进口国的主管机关可获得的事实。第17.7款还进一步规定，未经提供此类信息的个人、机构或主管机关正式授权，向专家组提供的机密信息不得披露。如果该信息为专家组要求提供，但未授权专家组公布该信息，那么经提供该信息的个人、机构或主管机关授权，应提供该信息的非机密摘要。

【案例摘录与评析】

2009年美国归零方法的持续存在与适用争端案[①]

United States – Continued Existence and Application of Zeroing Methodology (WT/DS350/AB/R)

1. Article 17.6 of the Anti-Dumping Agreement

265. On appeal, the United States argues that the Panel misapplied the standard of review set out under Article 17.6(ii) of the Anti-Dumping Agreement. According to the United States, the Panel viewed the Anti-Dumping Agreement "as admitting of more than one permissible interpretation" and considered that the use of zeroing in periodic reviews rests "on one of those interpretations". On this basis, the United States argues that the Panel should have found that the application of simple zeroing in the 29 periodic reviews at issue was permissible under the

① Appellate Body Report, United States–Continued Existence and Application of Zeroing Methodology, WT/DS350/AB/R, adopted 19 February 2009. 原文脚注省略。

Anti-Dumping Agreement. The United States suggests that the Panel's departure from Article 17.6(ii) appears to rely on Articles 3.2 and 3.3 of the DSU, but notes that Article 1.2 specifies that the provisions of the DSU are "'subject to' the special or additional rules listed in Appendix 2 to the DSU", which includes Article 17.6(ii) of the Anti-Dumping Agreement. The United States adds that Article 17.6(ii) was negotiated "as a recognition that some provisions of the [Anti-Dumping Agreement] would be susceptible to multiple permissible interpretations". As we see it, the United States' appeal in this regard is predicated on the existence of two permissible interpretations.

266. The European Communities contends that the United States' interpretation cannot be "permissible" within the meaning of Article 17.6(ii) of the Anti-Dumping Agreement "[i]f all of the interpretative elements in the Vienna Convention support the position of the European Communities, and disprove the position of the United States." According to the European Communities, 15 past Appellate Body and panel reports have confirmed the correct legal interpretations of the GATT 1994 and the Anti-Dumping Agreement with respect to this matter. Further, the European Communities disagrees with the United States' proposition that Article 17.6(ii) of the Anti-Dumping Agreement "overrides" or "replaces" the provisions of the DSU; rather, the European Communities agrees with the Appellate Body that Article 17.6 "supplements" the provisions of the DSU. The European Communities adds that the Panel followed previous Appellate Body findings and thus complied with its obligations under Article 11 of the DSU in this case. In the European Communities' view, "it is for the Appellate Body to change its own mind; not for a panel to do it on the Appellate Body's behalf."

267. Article 17.6(ii) consists of two sentences. The first sentence clarifies that panels are charged with the obligation to interpret the provisions of the Anti-Dumping Agreement "in accordance with customary rules of interpretation of public international law". The same language is found in Article 3.2 of the DSU. Panels examining claims under the Anti-Dumping Agreement are therefore required to apply the customary rules of treaty interpretation codified in Articles 31 and 32 of the Vienna Convention. Article 31(1) of the Vienna Convention provides that a "treaty shall be interpreted in good faith in accordance with the ordinary meaning to be given to the terms of the treaty in their context and in the light of its object and purpose."Article 32 further stipulates that "recourse may be had to supplementary means of interpretation, including the preparatory work of the treaty and the circumstances of its conclusion, in order to confirm the meaning resulting from the application of [A]rticle 31 or to determine the meaning". The latter applies when interpretation according to Article 31 leaves the meaning ambiguous or obscure, or leads to a result that is manifestly absurd or unreasonable. The customary rules of

treaty interpretation apply to any treaty, in any field of public international law, and not just to the WTO agreements. As the Appellate Body has said, they "impose certain common disciplines upon treaty interpreters, irrespective of the content of the treaty provision being examined and irrespective of the field of international law concerned."

268. The principles of interpretation that are set out in Articles 31 and 32 are to be followed in a holistic fashion. The interpretative exercise is engaged so as to yield an interpretation that is harmonious and coherent and fits comfortably in the treaty as a whole so as to render the treaty provision legally effective. A word or term may have more than one meaning or shade of meaning, but the identification of such meanings in isolation only commences the process of interpretation, it does not conclude it. Nor do multiple meanings of a word or term automatically constitute "permissible" interpretations within the meaning of Article 17.6(ii). Instead, a treaty interpreter is required to have recourse to context and object and purpose to elucidate the relevant meaning of the word or term. This logical progression provides a framework for proper interpretative analysis. At the same time, it should be kept in mind that treaty interpretation is an integrated operation, where interpretative rules or principles must be understood and applied as connected and mutually reinforcing components of a holistic exercise.

269. The second sentence of Article 17.6(ii) imposes an obligation on panels that is not found elsewhere in the covered agreements. It stipulates that:

Where the panel finds that a relevant provision of the Agreement admits of more than one permissible interpretation, the panel shall find the authorities' measure to be in conformity with the Agreement if it rests upon one of those permissible interpretations.

270. The Appellate Body has reasoned that the second sentence of Article 17.6(ii) presupposes "that application of the rules of treaty interpretation in Articles 31 and 32 of the Vienna Convention could give rise to, at least, two interpretations of some provisions of the Anti-Dumping Agreement, which, under that Convention, would both be 'permissible interpretations'." Where that is the case, a measure is deemed to be in conformity with the Anti-Dumping Agreement "if it rests upon one of those permissible interpretations." As the Appellate Body has said, "[i]t follows that, under Article 17.6(ii) of the Anti-Dumping Agreement, panels are obliged to determine whether a measure rests upon an interpretation of the relevant provisions of the Anti-Dumping Agreement which is permissible under the rules of treaty interpretation in Articles 31 and 32 of the Vienna Convention."

271. The second sentence of Article 17.6(ii) must therefore be read and applied in the light of the first sentence. We wish to make a number of general observations about the second sentence. First, Article 17.6(ii) contemplates a sequential analysis. The first step requires a

panel to apply the customary rules of interpretation to the treaty to see what is yielded by a conscientious application of such rules including those codified in the Vienna Convention. Only after engaging this exercise will a panel be able to determine whether the second sentence of Article 17.6(ii) applies. The structure and logic of Article 17.6(ii) therefore do not permit a panel to determine first whether an interpretation is permissible under the second sentence and then to seek validation of that permissibility by recourse to the first sentence.

272. Secondly, the proper interpretation of the second sentence of Article 17.6(ii) must itself be consistent with the rules and principles set out in the Vienna Convention. This means that it cannot be interpreted in a way that would render it redundant, or that derogates from the customary rules of interpretation of public international law. However, the second sentence allows for the possibility that the application of the rules of the Vienna Convention may give rise to an interpretative range and, if it does, an interpretation falling within that range is permissible and must be given effect by holding the measure to be in conformity with the covered agreement. The function of the second sentence is thus to give effect to the interpretative range rather than to require the interpreter to pursue further the interpretative exercise to the point where only one interpretation within that range may prevail.

273. We further note that the rules and principles of the Vienna Convention cannot contemplate interpretations with mutually contradictory results. Instead, the enterprise of interpretation is intended to ascertain the proper meaning of a provision; one that fits harmoniously with the terms, context, and object and purpose of the treaty. The purpose of such an exercise is therefore to narrow the range of interpretations, not to generate conflicting, competing interpretations. Interpretative tools cannot be applied selectively or in isolation from one another. It would be a subversion of the interpretative disciplines of the Vienna Convention if application of those disciplines yielded contradiction instead of coherence and harmony among, and effect to, all relevant treaty provisions. Moreover, a permissible interpretation for purposes of the second sentence of Article 17.6(ii) is not the result of an inquiry that asks whether a provision of domestic law is "necessarily excluded" by the application of the Vienna Convention. Such an approach subverts the hierarchy between the treaty and municipal law. It is the proper interpretation of a covered agreement that is the enterprise with which Article 17.6(ii) is engaged, not whether the treaty can be interpreted consistently with a particular Member's municipal law or with municipal laws of Members as they existed at the time of the conclusion of the relevant treaty.

274. In the present case, the United States argues that the Panel viewed the Anti-Dumping Agreement "as admitting of more than one permissible interpretation" and considered that the use of zeroing in periodic reviews rests "on one of those interpretations". By contrast,

the European Communities and Brazil emphasize that, whilst the Panel may have made an intermediate statement to the effect that the United States' interpretation was permissible, this was not the Panel's ultimate finding.

275. We are not required in this case to determine whether the Panel considered the use of zeroing in periodic reviews to rest on a permissible interpretation of the relevant provisions of the covered agreements because, now that the matter is before us on appeal, we must decide whether the Panel erred in finding that the United States acted inconsistently with Article 9.3 of the Anti-Dumping Agreement and Article VI:2 of the GATT 1994. In so doing, we must determine whether the second sentence of Article 17.6(ii) is of application. It is to this issue that we now turn.

【本案评析】

以上案例节选自2009年美国归零方法的持续存在与适用争端案上诉机构报告。该案产生了一个问题，即反倾销争端解决程序中根据第17.6款第（ii）项第2句，是否可以认定在计算倾销幅度时的归零是一种可以被允许的对《反倾销协定》有关实质性规定的解释。该案上诉机构最终认定，美国的“归零”做法并非基于对《反倾销协定》任何条款的“允许的解释”。

对于第17.6款第（ii）项的适用，该案上诉机构指出，第17.6款第（ii）项设定了一种有顺序的分析。第一步要求专家组适用条约解释的习惯规则，以确定通过认真的适用包括《维也纳条约法公约》订立的规则在内的这些规则，可以产生的效果。只有在这之后，专家组才能认定第17.6款第（ii）项第2句是否适用。因此，第17.6款第（ii）项的结构和逻辑并不允许专家组首先确定一项解释根据第2句的规定是不是被允许的，然后再通过援用第1句寻求对这种允许的验证。上诉机构进一步指出，第17.6款第（ii）项第2句不能以使其成为多余的方式或减损国际公法有关解释的习惯规则的方式加以解释……第2句允许适用《维也纳条约法公约》的规则可能性会产生一个解释的范围，如果是这样，那么在该范围内的解释是被允许的，而且必须通过保持与涵盖协定相符的措施的方式来使其有效。同时，上诉机构也提出，《维也纳条约法公约》的规则和原则不能包括结果相互矛盾的解释，因为解释的目的是确定一项条款的适当的含义——一项与条约的术语、背景、目标和宗旨相符的解释。因此，这样做的目的是缩小解释的范围，而不是产生相互冲突、相互竞争的解释。上诉机构指出，如果适用那些纪律产生了冲突而不是所有相关条款之间的协调一致，那么这将是对《维也纳条约法公约》的解释性纪律的破坏。此外，该案上诉机构强调，符合第17.6款第（ii）项第2句目的而被允许的解释，并不是一项咨询的结果，即通过适用《维也纳条约法公约》询问是否一项国内法条款是"必然排除"的。这种做法破坏了条约和国内法之间的层级关系。这是对与第17.6款第（ii）项运用相关的涵盖协定的适当解释，而不是条约能否与特定成员的国内法或成员在缔结有关条约时所存在的国内法一致性地加以解释。

【延伸阅读】

一、相关典型案例

1. China—Countervailing and Anti-Dumping Duties on Grain Oriented Flat-rolled Electrical Steel from the United States（WT/DS414）

2. China—Measures Imposing Anti-Dumping Duties on High-Performance Stainless Steel Seamless Tubes (HP-SSST) from the European Union and Japan（WT/DS454,WT/DS460）

3. European Communities—Definitive Anti-Dumping Measures on Certain Iron or Steel Fasteners from China(WT/DS397）

4. United States—Laws, Regulations and Methodology for Calculating Dumping Margins（DS294）

5. Argentina—Definitive Anti-Dumping Duties on Poultry from Brazil（DS241）

6. Thailand—Anti-Dumping Duties on Angles, Shapes and Sections of Iron or Non-Alloy Steel and H Beams from Poland（DS122）

二、相关学术论著

1. 王贵国:《世界贸易组织法》，法律出版社2003年版。

2. Peter Van den Bossche, *The Law and Policy of the WTO: Text, Cases and Materials,* Cambridge University Press, 2017.

3. Edwin Vermulst, *The WTO Anti-Dumping Agreement: A Commentary,* Oxford University Press, 2006.

4. Xiaochen Wu, *Anti-Dumping Law and Practice of China,* Kluwer Law International, 2008.

三、相关网络资源

1. https://www.wto.org/english/docs_e/legal_e/19-adp_01_e.htm.

2. http://ec.europa.eu/trade/policy/accessing-markets/trade-defence/actions-against-imports-into-the-eu/anti-dumping/.

3. http://cacs.mofcom.gov.cn/.

4. https://enforcement.trade.gov/tlei/index.html.

第六章

反补贴争端解决程序实务

【内容摘要】

与反倾销程序类似，反补贴程序也是一种针对产业损害性的国际贸易，由当事国主管机关通过行政手段实施的救济方式。从全球反补贴规则立法来看，处理反补贴的程序主要有两种，即国内反补贴争端调查程序和WTO多边反补贴争端解决程序。国内反补贴争端调查程序是通过反补贴调查和征收反补贴税抵消外国出口商因补贴而获得的不公平优势，从而为面临来自进口补贴竞争的国内产业重建公平的国内竞争环境，因此主要包括反补贴争端调查的启动、反补贴争端调查的进行以及反补贴措施的实施三个重要环节。WTO多边反补贴争端解决程序主要是根据乌拉圭回合达成的《补贴与反补贴措施协定》(本章以下简称《SCM协定》)规范调查损害性补贴的国内主管机关在反补贴调查程序中必须遵守的各种实体和程序义务以及处理其对前述义务纪律可能的违反。因此本章重点对于这样两种程序中的相关实践和争端实务进行了系统介绍和解释。鉴于反补贴与反倾销争端解决程序的类似，本章在某些部分中，对反补贴争端解决中的特殊程序性问题进行了重点介绍。

第一节　反补贴争端调查的启动

【知识背景 / 学习要点】

反补贴争端调查的启动通常有两种方式：一是由当事方申请并经主管机关审查决定，二是调查主管机关自行决定。但是在实践中，除非是非常特殊的情况，反补贴争端调查程序一般都是经当事人申请启动的。而且，无论是当事方申请还是主管机关自行决定发起，都需要进行类似的举证证明[①]，因此以下主要从当事方申请的角度来介绍反补贴争端调查的启动程序。

一、申请启动的条件

（一）书面申请

反补贴争端调查的启动通常从当事方申请开始，即利害关系方向调查主管机关提交存在损害性补贴的书面申请。提交申请书的当事方，一般是据称因进口补贴而受到损害的国内产业或国内产业的代表。[②]《SCM 协定》第 11.1 款规定，在第 6 款中有规定者除外，为裁定任何据称的补贴之存在、程度和影响而进行的调查，应根据国内产业提出的或代表其提出的书面请求发起。

（二）证据提交

在实践中，能否启动调查，申请当事方不仅仅需要提交申请书，还需要列举相关的证据，缺乏相关证据而仅仅作出简单的判断是不能视为足以满足发起反补贴调查程序要求的。根据《SCM 协定》第 11.2 款的规定，申请应包括充足证据以证明存在（1）补贴及其金额；（2）属于由协定所解释的 GATT1994 第 6

---

① 在特殊情况下，调查主管机关也可以自行决定启动反补贴调查。然而，只有在有充分证据证明存在补贴、损害和因果关系的，且发起调查是正当的情况下才可以这样做。参见《SCM 协定》第 11.6 款。

② 参见《SCM 协定》第 11.1 款。

条范围内的损害；以及（3）补贴进口产品与被指控损害之间存在因果关系。[①]

二、证据的审查

对于当事方提交的申请材料，调查主管机关应审查申请中所提出的证据是否准确与充分，以判定证据是否足以证明发起调查具有正当性，因此在某种程度上，能否发起调查的关键取决于调查机关对申请的初步审查和评估过程。[②]值得注意的是，《SCM 协定》第 11.3 款只规定了需要进行审查这项程序，没有具体规定如何进行这项审查的方式和要求，因此这就留待各国的主管机关自由裁量了。

当然，从实践来看，提交申请的同时所举证据毕竟与在经过调查后裁定当事方补贴成立，在认定的要求和标准上存在不同，所以调查发起前审查相关证据是否“准确与充分”、足以证明调查正当性，就需要与作出反补贴裁定时的证据要求有所区分。2012 年中国对美国取向电工钢征收反倾销税和反补贴税案专家组曾指出，虽然没有必要根据第 11.3 款就补贴、损害和因果关系的存在和性质提供确切的证据，但是提交充分证据以说明这些要素的存在仍属必要。在确定是否有足够的证据启动调查时，调查主管机关应平衡两种相互竞争的利益，即国内产业“确保调查的启动”的利益和被申诉方确保“调查不是基于草率或毫无根据”的利益。[③]

① 《SCM 协定》第 11.2 款详细规定了申请书必须包含的信息。申请书还应包括申请人理应可以得到的关于下述方面的资料：⑴申请人身份及由申请人对国内同类产品生产的产量和产值的说明，如果申请是由国内产业代表代为提出的，则申请书应用一份国内同类产品所有已知生产者（或国内同类产品生产者协会）的名单并在可能的范围内用一份对由这些生产者所占国内同类产品产量及产值的说明来确认申请书所代的产业。⑵对据称的受补贴产品所做的完整说明，有关出口或原产国国名，每个已知出口商或外国生产者的身份，以及已知的有关产品的进口者名单。⑶关于有关补贴存在、数量和性质的证据。⑷由受补贴进口通过补贴的作用而引起据称的对国内产业损害的证据。这些证据包括关于据称的受补贴出口数量演变。这些进口对国内市场同类产品价格影响以及对国内该产业造成冲击的资料，如第 15 条第 2 款和第 4 款所列那些对国内产业状况有影响的有关因素和指数所表示。

② 参见《SCM 协定》第 11.3 款。值得注意，《SCM 协定》第 11.3 款没有具体规定如何进行这项审查，当然这里的“充分的证据”所要求的标准与“完全的证明”是不同的。

③ 参见 Panel Report, China-Countervailing and Anti-Dumping Duties on Grain Oriented Flat-rolled Electrical Steel from the United States , WT/DS414/R, paras. 7.54-7.55.

三、代表性审查

如上所述，启动反补贴调查的申请是由据称因补贴进口而受到了损害的国内产业提出的或国内产业的代表提出的。因此，国内反补贴的申请者还需要具备一定的代表性，才有资格启动审查，当然这种资格也是与产业有关的，因为作为贸易救济措施，反补贴针对的是具有国内产业损害性的补贴做法。根据《SCM 协定》第 11.4 款的规定，如果受到其合计产量占表示支持或反对该申请的国内产业所生产同类产品总产量 50% 以上的那些国内生产者的支持，则该申请应被视为“由国内产业或国内产业代表提出”。但是，如表示支持申请的国内生产者的产量不足国内产业生产的同类产品总产量的 25%，则不得发起调查。

在实践中，对于申请者的产业代表性，调查主管机关也需要按照相关立法进行审查，但可以发现，《SCM 协定》第 11.4 款虽然对代表性问题进行了客观的定量规定，但是对于如何判断相关国内产业或国内生产者是否支持调查申请，以及主管机关审查支持的程度或方式的相关要求，没有进行具体的规定。正如在 2003 年美国《2000 年持续倾销和补贴抵消法》争端案中上诉机构所指出的，“表示支持”和“明确支持”这两个术语的使用表明，第 11.4 款只要求主管机关“确定”足够数量的国内生产者“表示”了支持。因此……“审查”支持的“程度”，而不是支持的“性质”是必需的。换言之，问题在于支持的“数量”而非“质量”。①

四、调查的终止

除代表性外，作为一种贸易救济行政性程序，反补贴调查的启动也会对当事方和国家之间的贸易往来产生直接的影响，因此主管机关在调查开始前对于补贴构成要件的审查也必须非常审慎，特别是如果出现不能进行调查的情形必须立即终止。比如，虽然有一定的证据可以支持启动调查的申请，但是经调查

① 参见 Appellate Body Report, United States–Continued Dumping and Subsidy Offset Act of 2000, WT/DS217/AB/R , WT/DS234/AB/R, para. 283.

主管机关的初步确定，这些证据对于补贴和损害没有充分的证明力或者证据显示损害的结果对于产业影响不大，则调查应立即终止。

在实务中，调查主管机关发现没有关于补贴或损害的充分证据可以证明继续该案反补贴调查的行为正当时，即应驳回发起调查的申请，并应迅速终止调查。此外，在调查阶段，如果调查主管机关发现，补贴金额属于微量，或受补贴进口产品实际或潜在的数量或损害可以忽略不计的情况，一般也应立即终止调查。根据《SCM 协定》第 11.9 款的规定，补贴金额如果少于商品价值的 1%，那么其数量就应被视为是微量的。[①]

在 2005 年墨西哥大米和牛肉的最终反倾销措施案中，上诉机构进一步指出，如果在最初的调查期间发现一家公司未获得超出微量的可抵消补贴，那么根据《SCM 协定》第 11.9 款的规定，对此类公司不能再进行行政和改变情况的审查。[②]

五、启动前磋商

与启动反倾销调查不同的是，在实际调查开始之前，反补贴调查主管机关应邀请补贴成员进行磋商，而且这种磋商将在整个调查期间持续进行。[③]《SCM 协定》第 13 条要求进口成员方应在第 11 条中所规定的调查申请被接受后，并在调查开始前，尽快邀请其产品可能成为调查对象的成员方参加磋商，以澄清上述第 11.2 款所述及的情况，并达成彼此同意的解决方案。

美国和欧盟等国家或地区的反补贴法律实践表明，这种调查前的磋商往往是防止反补贴争端调查启动的一项重要手段。国内产业提交启动调查申请书时往往也会列出补贴做法的细目清单，在调查启动前进行双边的磋商可能会剔除那些表面上没有反补贴价值的补贴做法（例如非专向性的或其没有被相关出口商使用）。

① 参见《SCM 协定》第 11.9 款的规定。

② 参见 Appellate Body Report, Mexico-Definitive Anti-Dumping Measures on Beef and Rice, WT/DS295/AB/R, 29 November 2005, January 16, 2003 , para. 305.

③ 参见《SCM 协定》第 13.1 和 13.2 款。

【案例摘录与评析】

2002年美国对来自德国的部分防腐蚀平板碳钢产品的反补贴措施争端案[①]

United States – Countervailing Duties on Certain Corrosion- Resistant Carbon Steel Flat Products from Germany
(WT/DS213/AB/R)

75. This brings us to an examination of the reasoning used by the Panel to find that the *de minimis* standard of Article 11.9 "must be applicable to sunset reviews as it is to investigations".[②] The Panel was of the view that "the sole or principal rationale for the de minimis standard set out in Article 11.9 is that a de minimis subsidy is considered to be non-injurious".[③]

76. Using this rationale, the Panel reasoned that it would be "difficult to see how de minimis rate of likely subsidisation could be considered injurious at the stage of sunset review and continuation of a CVD, when the same rate is considered non-injurious at the stage of investigation and imposition of a CVD".[④] The Panel summarized its reasoning as follows:

> ... the rationale for the de minimis standard set out in Article 11.9 is clearly that CVDs are to be used to counter injurious subsidisation, and the threshold set out in this provision demarcates the level below which subsidisation is deemed to be so small as to be non-injurious for purposes of the imposition of CVDs. Having found this to be the case, and having established that one of the objects and purposes of the SCM Agreement is to regulate the imposition of CVDs and to create a disciplinary framework therefor, we are of the view that the de minimis standard must be applicable to sunset reviews as it is to investigations. Finding otherwise would compromise the very object and purpose of the SCM Agreement and the disciplinary framework that the drafters sought to create through the Agreement.[⑤]

---

① 参见 Appellate Body Report, United States–Countervailing Duties on Certain Corrosion-Resistant Carbon Steel Flat Products from Germany, WT/DS213/AB/R, 19 December 2002.

② *Ibid.*, para. 8.79.

③ *Ibid.*, para. 8.61.

④ *Ibid.*, para. 8.65.

⑤ Panel Report, para. 8.79.

77. The Panel's approach was centered on the premise that the de minimis standard set forth in Article 11.9 represents a threshold below which subsidization is always *non-injurious*. The Panel formed this opinion after examining a 1987 Note prepared by the Secretariat for the Uruguay Round Negotiating Group on Subsidies and Countervailing Measures①, which was brought to the Panel's attention by the European Communities.② The Panel cited part of the Note which recognized that there are two alternative (but not mutually exclusive) theoretical justifications for a de minimis rule.③ The Panel continued:

> [w]hile it is not known which of the two rationales, if not both ("not mutually exclusive"), served as a basis for Article 11.9, the language of that provision suggests to us that it was the first rationale that was the basis for, or was at least paramount in, the drafting of that provision.④

78. We observe, first, that in taking this approach, the Panel did not explain why it thought that it was appropriate to rely on the 1987 Note, but simply stated that "it is useful to consider the rationale for the application of a de minimis standard to investigations, as reflected in a Note by the Secretariat prepared in April 1987".⑤ In any event, it seems to us that the 1987 Note does not support the Panel's conclusion that the "rationale" for the de minimis standard in Article 11.9 is that a *de minimis* subsidy is considered to be non-injurious. As the Panel itself recognized, the 1987 Note sets forth *two* rationales for de minimis standards, but does not suggest which of them is more compelling or preferable. Nor was any evidence adduced before the Panel suggesting that the negotiators of the *SCM Agreement* considered these or other rationales and

① *Ibid*., para. 8.60, referring in footnote 296 to MTN.GNG/NG10/W/4, 28 April 1987.

② The 1987 Note was first referred to by the European Communities in its comments on the responses of the United States to questions from the Panel following the first meeting of the Panel with the parties. (Panel Report, para. 5.320.) For further discussion of the Note by the parties, see also, Panel Report, paras. 5.464-5.466, 5.501-5.504 and 5.530-5.536. The 1987 Note was submitted by the United States to the Panel as Exhibit US-7.

③ The first view that "no action should be taken … 'where the effect of the subsidy on the industry in the importing country is not such as to cause material injury' ". The second was that " 'de minimis non curat lex': the law does not take notice of minimal matters". (original underlining) (Panel Report, para. 8.60, quoting from the 1987 Note, MTN.GNG/NG10/W/4, p. 2)

④ Panel Report, para. 8.60.

⑤ *Ibid*., para. 8.60. It is, for example, unclear to us whether the Panel considered the Note to form part of the preparatory work of the treaty and intended to use it as a supplementary means of treaty interpretation within the meaning of Article 32 of the *Vienna Convention*.

expressed a preference for any of them. The Panel chose to base its interpretation of Article 11.9 on only one of these rationales. Even if it were appropriate to rely on the 1987 Note in interpreting the *SCM Agreement* in accordance with the rules of interpretation set forth in the *Vienna Convention*, selective reliance on such a document does not provide a proper basis for the conclusion reached by the Panel in this regard.

79. More importantly, leaving aside the 1987 Note, the *SCM Agreement* does not, in our view, support the "rationale" attributed by the Panel to the *de minimis* standard in Article 11.9. Article 15 of the *SCM Agreement*, which deals with injury and how it is to be determined, refers, in its paragraph 3, to the *de minimis* standard in Article 11.9 only for the purpose of cumulation of imports. Moreover, footnote 45 to Article 15 indicates that, in the SCM *Agreement*, the term "injury" is, "unless otherwise specified", to:

> ... be taken to mean material injury to a domestic industry, threat of material injury to a domestic industry or material retardation of the establishment of such an industry and shall be interpreted in accordance with the provisions of [Article 15].

In defining the concept of injury, footnote 45 does not make any reference to the amount of subsidy involved.

80. Similarly, Article 1 of the *SCM Agreement* sets out a definition of "subsidy" that applies to the whole of that Agreement. This definition includes *all* such subsidies, regardless of their amount. None of the provisions in the *SCM Agreement* that uses the term "subsidization" confines the meaning of "subsidization" to subsidization at a rate equal to or in excess of 1 percent *ad valorem*, or to any other *de minimis* threshold.① It is also worth noting that, under Part II of the *SCM Agreement*, prohibited subsidies are prohibited regardless of the amount of the subsidy.

81. Thus, in our view, the terms "subsidization" and "injury" each have an independent meaning in the *SCM Agreement* which is not derived by reference to the other. It is *unlikely* that very low levels of subsidization could be demonstrated to *cause* "material" injury. Yet such a possibility is not, *per se*, precluded by the Agreement itself, as injury is not defined in the *SCM Agreement* in relation to any specific level of subsidization.

82. We note, too, that Articles 27.10 and 27.11 of the *SCM Agreement* require termination of a countervailing duty *investigation* with respect to a developing country Member whenever "the overall level of subsidies granted does not exceed" 2 or 3 percent, depending on the circumstances.

① The term "subsidization" is used in the following Articles of the *SCM Agreement*: 6.1(a); 8.3; 11.9; 12.10; 15.3; 17.2; 18.2; 18.4; 19.4; 21.1; 21.2; 21.3; as well as in Annex IV.

These provisions require authorities, in a countervailing duty investigation, to apply a higher *de minimis* subsidization threshold to imports from developing country Members. To accept the Panel's reasoning—that *de minimis* subsidization is non-injurious subsidization—would imply that, for the same product, imported into the same country, and affecting the same domestic industry, the *SCM Agreement* establishes different thresholds at which the same industry can be said to suffer injury, depending on the origin of the product. This unreasonable implication casts further doubt on the "rationale" attributed by the Panel to Article 11.9 's *de minimis* standard.

83. To us, there is nothing in Article 11.9 to suggest that its *de minimis* standard was intended to create a special category of *"non-injurious"* subsidization, or that it reflects a concept that subsidization at less than a *de minimis*threshold *can never* cause injury. For us, the *de minimis* standard in Article 11.9 does no more than lay down an agreed rule that if *de minimis* subsidization is found to exist in an original investigation, authorities are obliged to terminate their investigation, with the result that no countervailing duty can be imposed in such cases.

84. Accordingly, we do not believe that there is a clear "rationale" behind the 1 percent *de minimis* rule of Article 11.9 that must also apply in the context of reviews carried out under Article 21.3. However, the Panel reasoned that it would be "difficult to see how de minimis rate of likely subsidisation could be considered injurious at the stage of sunset review and continuation of a CVD, when the same rate is considered non-injurious at the stage of investigation and imposition of a CVD."① The Panel added that "[s]uch an interpretation would also yield irrational results".② For the reasons that follow, we are not persuaded that this is so.

85. Under the *SCM Agreement,* it is the *countervailing duty* that comes up for a review under Article 21.3. Once the Agreement has been in operation for a sufficient number of years, a countervailing duty subject to such a review will typically be a duty that was imposed after the entry into force of the *SCM Agreement.*③ For this reason the underlying subsidy will have been

① Panel Report, para. 8.65.

② *Ibid*., para. 8.69.

③ Articles 32.3 and 32.4 of the *SCM Agreement* provide:

Subject to paragraph 4, the provisions of this Agreement shall apply to investigations, andreviews of existing measures, initiated pursuant to applications which have been made on or after the date of entry into force for a Member of the WTO Agreement. For the purposes of paragraph 3 of Article 21, existing countervailing measures shall be deemed to be imposed on a date not later than the date of entry into force for a Member of the WTO Agreement, except in cases in which the domestic legislation of a Member in force at that date already included a clause of the type provided for in that paragraph. By virtue these provisions, even countervailing duties imposed as a result of investigations initiated prior to the date of entry into force of the *WTO Agreement* are subjected to sunset review in accordance with the requirements of Article 21.3. With the passage of time, however, countervailing duties reviewed under Article 21.3 will increasingly be countervailing duties that were imposed as a result of an investigation initiated *after* the date of entry into force of the *WTO Agreement.*

found, in a proper investigation conducted in accordance with the requirements of the *SCM Agreement*, to be a subsidy that was in excess of the *de minimis* standard of Article 11.9 (or Article 27.10 or Article 27.11 as the case may be) at the time of imposition of the countervailing duty. There would be no countervailing duty to be reviewed where, in the original investigation, the amount of subsidy was found to be less than the *de minimis* standard. In that case, the investigation itself would have been terminated and no duty could have been imposed.①

86. We believe that the relevant question to be addressed is, therefore, what obligations the negotiators intended to apply in the case of a review of a countervailing duty where the underlying subsidy has fallen below the *de minimis* standard of Article 11.9 subsequent to the original investigation. It is not inconceivable that the negotiators of the *SCM Agreement* took the view that when a subsidy, originally found to be in excess of the *de minimis* level and to be causing injury, has fallen below the *de minimis* level subsequent to the investigation stage, authorities conducting a sunset review should nevertheless determine whether revocation of the duty is still likely to lead to continuation or recurrence of the injury to the domestic industry. The automatic termination of the countervailing duty may not have been considered desirable in such a situation.

【本案评析】

以上案例节选自2002年美国对来自德国的部分防腐蚀平板碳钢产品的反补贴措施争端案上诉机构报告。该案上诉机构探讨了《SCM协定》第11.9款规定的微量补贴规则的性质。上诉机构提出，对我们来说，《SCM协定》第11.9款没有任何内容表明，其微量标准意在设立一个“非损害性”补贴的特殊类别，或者它反映出低于微量的补贴不可能造成损害的理念。《SCM协定》第11.9款中的微量标准只不过是规定了一条被同意的规则，即如果在最初的调查中发现存在微量补贴，主管机关有义务终止调查该案且不能课征任何反补贴税。

① We note that in the instant case of carbon steel, the original countervailing duty was imposed in 1993, before the *SCM Agreement* came into force. Had this been a case where the original subsidy was the subject of an investigation under the *SCM Agreement*, the investigation would have been terminated under Article 11.9 as the original subsidy was below the 1 percent *de minimis* standard.

【延伸阅读】

一、相关典型案例

1. Brazil—Export Financing Programme for Aircraft(WT/DS46)

2. China—Countervailing and Anti-Dumping Duties on Grain Oriented Flat-rolled Electrical Steel from the United States（WT/DS414）

3. Canada—Measures Affecting the Export of Civilian Aircraft（WT/DS70）

4. United States—Measures Treating Export Restraints as Subsidies(WT/DS194)

5. United States—Continued Dumping and Subsidy Offset Act of 2000（WT/DS217, WT/DS234）

6. United States—Final Countervailing Duty Determination with respect to certain Softwood Lumber from Canada（WT/DS257）

二、相关学术论著

1. 赵维田:《世界贸易组织（WTO）的法律制度》, 吉林人民出版社 2000 年版。

2. 杨荣珍:《国外对华反补贴案例研究》, 对外经济贸易大学出版社 2015 年版。

3. Konstantinos Adamantopoulos & Maria J Pereyra-frierichsen, *EU Anti-subsidy Law and Practice,* Sweet & Maxwell, 2007.

三、相关网络资源

1. https://www.wto.org/english/tratop_e/scm_e/scm_e.htm.

2. http://ec.europa.eu/trade/policy/accessing-markets/trade-defence/actions-against-imports-into-the-eu/anti-subsidy/.

3. https://www.usitc.gov/trade_remedy/731_ad_701_cvd/investigations/active/index.htm.

4. http://cacs.mofcom.gov.cn/.

第二节　反补贴争端调查的进行

【知识背景 / 学习要点】

在调查机关决定启动调查后，无论是应国内产业的请求还是主动进行的，都必须遵守若干程序义务，以便对可能受到调查影响的当事人提供充分的保护。反补贴调查通常应在开始后的 1 年内完成，在任何情况下不得超过 18 个月[①]。即对调查机关而言，这 18 个月的最长期限是绝对的。

一、公告与通知

在对申请初步调查的基础上，若主管机关确信有充分证据证明发起的调查是正当的，则应通知其产品将接受该调查的一个或多个成员，以及调查主管机关已知的与该调查有利害关系的其他利害关系方，并应发布公告。因此，调查的启动必须进行通知并发布公告。[②]《SCM 协定》第 22.2 款规定了调查发起公告应当包括或者通过单独的报告应提供的信息资料，包括：(1) 出口国和所涉及产品名称；(2) 调查发起的日期；(3) 对受调查补贴行为的说明；(4) 于损害的指控所依据因素的摘要；(5) 各利害关系成员和各利害关系方送交陈述书的地址；(6) 允许各利害关系成员和各利害关系方陈述意见的时限。

此外，经过磋商一旦启动调查，主管机关应立即将其收到的申请书的全文向已知出口商和出口成员的主管机关提供，并应请求也要向其他涉及的利害关系方提供。[③] 根据《SCM 协定》第 12.1.3 项中的脚注规定，若所涉及的出口商的数量特别多，则申请书的全文应改为只向出口成员的主管机关或向有关贸易协会提供，贸易协会随后应向有关出口商转交副本。

① 参见《SCM 协定》第 11.11 款。
② 参见《SCM 协定》第 22.1 款。
③ 根据《SCM 协定》第 12.1.3 项，应适当注意按第 4 款规定的保护机密信息的要求。

二、提交证据信息

调查主管机关应将其要求提供的资料通知在调查中有利害关系的成员和所有利害关系方，并给予其以书面形式提出其认为与该调查有关的一切证据的充分机会。[①] 根据《SCM 协定》第 12.9 款的规定，利害关系方应包括：(1)受调查产品的出口商或外国生产者或进口商，或其多数成员为该产品的生产者或出口商或进口商的贸易或商业协会；和(2)进口成员方同类产品的生产者或在进口成员方境内其多数成员为同类产品生产者的贸易或商业协会。并且此名单不应阻止成员方允许将上述未被提及的国内或国外各方包括到利益方之列。

为便于调查主管可以在调查中开展听证，因此对于证据信息的提交方式一般是采用书面的形式，但是在特殊的情况下，若利害关系成员和利害关系方说明正当理由后，也可以口头提供相关信息但对于此类口头提供的信息，利害关系成员和利害关系方随后需要将此类提交的信息转为书面形式。[②]《SCM 协定》第 12.2 款进一步规定，调查主管机关的任何决定只能根据主管机关书面记录的此类信息和论据作出，且该书面记录应已经使参与调查的利害关系成员和利害关系方可获得，同时考虑保护机密信息的需要。

此外，除给予利害关系方提交证据信息的机会，为调查的顺利进行，调查主管机关也应向被调查产品的工业用户，或在该产品通常为零售的情况下，向具有代表性的消费者组织提供机会，使其能够提供与关于补贴、损害和因果关系的调查有关的信息。[③]

三、答复调查问卷

在实践中，反补贴调查常采用问卷调查方式进行，但是由于问卷调查涉及传递、翻译、核查、填写、提交等诸多环节，因此较短的期限对于被调查方而言显然不利。因此一般而言，调查主管机关应至少给予当事方和利害关系成员方

① 参见《SCM 协定》第 12.1 款。
② 参见《SCM 协定》第 12.2 款。
③ 参见《SCM 协定》第 12.10 款。

30 日的时间答复调查机关的调查问卷时间，而且对于 30 日期限延长的任何请求也应给予适当的考虑，并根据所陈述的原因，只要可行，调查机关即应予以延长。[①]

对于答复问卷期限的起算，根据《SCM 协定》第 12.1.1 项中的脚注，作为一般规则，出口商的时限应自收到问卷之日起计算，为此，该问卷应被视为在送往答卷或转交出口成员的适当外交代表之日起一周内已经收到，若为 WTO 单独关税区成员，则为出口领土的官方代表。例如，在 2005 年墨西哥大米和牛肉的最终反倾销措施案中，上诉机构明确指出，从收到调查问卷之日起，必须给予收到此问卷的所有出口商和外国生产商 30 日的时间。上诉机构强调必须严格地解释 30 日的期限，因此裁定，启动调查公告之日起的 28 个工作日的期限是不够的。

四、核实调查信息[②]

除非有特殊情况，在调查过程中，调查主管机关应设法使自己确定利害关系成员或利害关系方提供的、其调查结果所依据的信息的准确性。[③]根据《SCM 协定》第 12.5 款的规定，这种特殊情况指的是第 12.7 款的规定，亦即任何利害关系成员或利害关系方不允许使用或未在合理时间内提供必要的信息或严重妨碍调查。根据各国反补贴实践，这种确定准确性的方法就是对信息的核实调查。

一般而言，调查主管机关可根据相关协定，按需要在其他国家领土内进行调查，只要它们已经及时通知所涉国家，除非该国家反对该核实调查。此外，如某一公司同意并且也已经获得所涉国家的接受，则调查主管机关可在该公司所在地进行调查且可审查该公司的记录。[④]《SCM 协定》附件 6 规定了适用于在

---

① 参见《SCM 协定》第 12.1.1 款。

② 参见 Appellate Body Report, Mexico-Definitive Anti-Dumping Measures on Beef and Rice, WT/DS295/AB/R, 29 November 2005, paras.280-283.

③ 参见《SCM 协定》第 12.5 款。

④ 参见《SCM 协定》第 12.6 款。

企业所在地点进行核查的程序。在遵守保护机密信息要求的前提下，主管机关应使任何此类调查的结果可获得，或应根据第 8 款向与调查结果有关的公司披露，并使申请人可获得此类结果。

五、非机密信息披露

调查主管机关在可行的情况下，应向所有感兴趣的成员方和利害关系方提供机会，使其了解与其案件陈述有关的，且主管机关在反补贴调查中使用的所有非机密信息，并应根据此信息准备陈述。[①] 此外，在遵守保护机密信息要求的前提下，调查主管机关也应提供机会，使得某一利害关系成员或几个利害关系方提出的书面证据迅速使参与调查的其他利害关系成员和利害关系方可获得。[②]

然而，如果披露的任何信息使竞争对手获得重大竞争优势，或对提供信息（即在保密基础上提供的任何机密信息或其他信息）的当事方会产生重大的不利影响，那么调查主管机关必须根据申请方所提出的正当理由，将其视为机密信息。只有在提交方的专门许可下，调查主管机关才能将此类机密信息披露给相关当事方。

六、机密信息保护

任何原属机密性质的信息（如由于信息披露会给竞争对手带来巨大的竞争优势，或由于信息的披露会给信息提供者或给向信息获得者提供信息的人带来严重的不利影响），或由调查参加方在保密基础上提供的信息，调查主管机关应在对方说明正当原因后，应按照机密信息予以保护处理。此类信息未经提供方特别允许不得披露。因此，调查当事国一般国内立法都会有涉及信息保护或者保密的相关法律法规，这些保护性制度就是机密信息保护的依据，也是各国如果需要在反补贴中进行信息保护而必须考虑首先严格制定的。[③]

① 参见《SCM 协定》第 12.1.2 款。

② 参见《SCM 协定》第 12.4 款。

③ 《SCM 协定》第 12.4 款脚注称，各成员意识到，在某些成员领土内，可能需要根据严格制定的保护性法令披露信息。

对于按照机密信息保护的材料，调查主管机关应要求提供机密信息的利害关系成员或利害关系方提供此类信息的非机密摘要。根据《SCM 协定》第 12.4 款的规定，这些摘要应足够详细，以便能够合理了解以机密形式提交的信息的实质内容。在特殊情况下，此类成员或各方可表明此类信息无法进行摘要。在此类特殊情况下，必须提供一份关于为何不能进行摘要的原因的说明。

但是，如果调查主管机关认为关于保密的请求缺乏正当理由，且如果信息提供者不愿披露信息，或不愿授权以概括或摘要的形式披露信息，那么主管机关可忽略此类信息，除非主管机关可从适当的来源满意地证明此类信息是正确的。[①]

七、“可获得事实”

在调查主管机关尽管尽了最大努力，仍未能获得所有相关信息时，他们可基于“可获得的事实”作出决定。《SCM 协定》第 12.7 款规定，如果任何利害关系成员方或利害关系方拒绝在合理的期限内让主管机关使用或向其提供必要的情报资料，或严重地妨碍调查，那么肯定或否定的初步或最终的裁定均可在可获得事实的基础上作出。

虽然对调查主管机关而言，其利用“可获得事实”很重要，可以避免调查工作因缺乏持有相关信息的当事方的配合而受挫和陷入僵局，但是这显然也有可能引起调查主管机关的权力滥用。为确保反补贴调查的正当程序，《SCM 协定》第 12.8 款要求主管机关在作出最终裁定之前，应将考虑中的、构成是否实施最终措施决定依据的基本事实通知所有利害关系成员和利害关系方。此披露应使各方有充分的时间为其利益进行辩护。至于必须披露的信息类型，该条款包括了“主管机关在作出是否实施裁定时其可以考虑的那些记录在案的事实”。

与第 22.5 款规定在反补贴调查结束时披露相关事实、法律和理由不同，第

① 参见《SCM 协定》第 12.4.2 项。

12.8 款的披露义务只涉及“在作出最终裁定之前”的调查过程中的“基本事实”披露。2012 年中国对美国取向电工钢征收反倾销税和反补贴税案上诉机构认为，第 12.8 款不要求披露主管机关获得的“所有”事实，而是“必要的”，亦即有意义的、重要的或有显著含义的事实。在考虑哪些事实是“必要的”时，首先应考虑的是那些构成“是否采取最终措施的依据”的事实，其次是确保有关利害方能为其利益进行辩护的事实。上诉机构强调，调查机关必须“以连贯一致的方式披露这些事实，以便让利害方能够了解作出最终措施决定的依据”，因为根据第 12.8 款披露正在考虑的基本事实“对于有关各方当事人确保维护其利益的能力至关重要”。①

【案例摘录与评析】

一、2005 年墨西哥大米和牛肉的最终反倾销措施案②

Mexico -Definitive Anti-Dumping Measures on Beef and Rice
(WT/DS295/AB/R)

290. We turn now to Article 12.7 of the SCM Agreement. The Panel based its finding of inconsistency with that provision on the reasoning it had developed with respect to the obligations in Article 6.8 of the Anti-Dumping Agreement and paragraphs 1, 3, 5, and 7 of Annex II thereto. We observe, however, that there are important textual differences between the relevant provisions of the Anti-Dumping Agreement and the SCM Agreement—namely, the absence in the SCM Agreement of an equivalent to Annex II to the Anti-Dumping Agreement.

291. Article 12.7 of the SCM Agreement provides:

In cases in which any interested Member or interested party refuses access to, or otherwise does not provide, necessary information within a reasonable period or significantly impedes the

① 参见 Appellate Body Report, China-Countervailing and Anti-Dumping Duties on Grain Oriented Flat-rolled Electrical Steel from the United States. , WT/DS414/AB/R, para. 240.

② Appellate Body Report, Mexico-Definitive Anti-Dumping Measures on Beef and Rice , WT/DS295/AB/R, 29 November 2005 . 原文脚注省略。

investigation, preliminary and final determinations, affirmative or negative, may be made on the basis of the facts available.

Like Article 6.8 of the Anti-Dumping Agreement, Article 12.7 of the SCM Agreement permits an investigating authority, under certain circumstances, to fill in gaps in the information necessary to arrive at a conclusion as to subsidization (or dumping) and injury. As in the Anti-Dumping Agreement, Article 12.7 prescribes the information that may be used for such purposes as the "facts available". Unlike the Anti-Dumping Agreement, the SCM Agreement does not expressly set out in an annex the conditions for determining precisely which "facts" might be "available" for an agency to use when a respondent fails to provide necessary information. This does not mean, however, that no such conditions exist in the SCM Agreement.

292. Turning to the context of Article 12.7, we are of the view that, like Article 6 of the Anti-Dumping Agreement, Article 12 of the SCM Agreement as a whole "set[s] out evidentiary rules that apply throughout the course of the ... investigation, and provide[s] also for due process rights that are enjoyed by 'interested parties' throughout ... an investigation". In this respect, Article 12.1 provides:

Interested Members and all interested parties in a countervailing duty investigation shall be given notice of the information which the authorities require and ample opportunity to present in writing all evidence which they consider relevant in respect of the investigation in question.

This due process obligation—that an interested party be permitted to present all the evidence it considers relevant—concomitantly requires the investigating authority, where appropriate, to take into account the information submitted by an interested party.

293. Moreover, we note that Article 12.7 is intended to ensure that the failure of an interested party to provide necessary information does not hinder an agency's investigation. Thus, the provision permits the use of facts on record solely for the purpose of replacing information that may be missing, in order to arrive at an accurate subsidization or injury determination.

294. In view of the above, we understand that recourse to facts available does not permit an investigating authority to use any information in whatever way it chooses. First, such recourse is not a licence to rely on only part of the evidence provided. To the extent possible, an investigating authority using the "facts available" in a countervailing duty investigation must take into account all the substantiated facts provided by an interested party, even if those facts may not constitute the complete information requested of that party. Secondly, the "facts available" to the agency are generally limited to those that may reasonably replace the information that an interested party failed to provide. In certain circumstances, this may include information from secondary sources.

295. This understanding of the limitations on an investigating authority's use of "facts available" in countervailing duty investigations is further supported by the similar, limited recourse to "facts available" permitted under Annex II to the Anti-Dumping Agreement. Indeed, in our view, it would be anomalous if Article 12.7 of the SCM Agreement were to permit the use of "facts available" in countervailing duty investigations in a manner markedly different from that in anti-dumping investigations.

296. We now consider the consistency of the challenged provision of the FTA with the above provisions of the Anti-Dumping Agreement and the SCM Agreement. The Panel understood Article 64 to mandate Economía to calculate the highest possible margin on the basis of the facts available and apply that margin to, inter alia, foreign producers that do not appear in the investigation and to those that did not export the subject merchandise during the period of investigation. In other words, Article 64 appears to require the agency to apply indiscriminately such a margin—the highest that could be calculated on the basis of the facts available—to certain foreign producers or exporters. The provision so requires even in instances—such as the case of foreign producers that do not appear in an investigation—where the producer is not sent a questionnaire and thus may not be informed of the consequences for its failure to provide requested information.

297. Article 64 also does not on its face permit the agency to use any information that might be provided by a foreign producer or exporter, even if incomplete, where the use of such information would result in a margin lower than the highest facts available margin. Nor does it allow the agency to engage in the "evaluative, comparative assessment" necessary in order to determine which facts are "best" to fill in the missing information. Furthermore, Article 64 requires Economía to use those facts necessary to arrive at the highest margin that can be calculated, even if those facts, although "substantiated", might be deemed unreliable by the agency after exercising "special circumspection".Thus, in all situations of incomplete information—including those of producers not appearing in the investigation and producers not exporting the subject merchandise during the period of investigation—we read Article 64 as preventing Economía from engaging in the reasoned and selective use of the facts available directed by Article 6.8 of the Anti-Dumping Agreement, Annex II thereto, and Article 12.7 of the SCM Agreement.

298. In the light of the above, we uphold the Panel's findings, in paragraphs 7.242 and 8.5(b) of the Panel Report, that Article 64 of the FTA is inconsistent, as such, with Article 6.8 of the Anti-Dumping Agreement, paragraphs 1, 3, 5, and 7 of Annex II thereto, and Article 12.7 of the SCM Agreement.

【本案评析】

以上案例节选自2005年墨西哥大米和牛肉的最终反倾销措施案上诉机构报告。对于反补贴中的"可获得事实"规则，该案上诉机构指出，第12.7款旨在确保利害关系方不提供必要的信息并不会妨碍主管机关的调查。因此，该条款允许使用记录在案事实的目的，仅仅是为了替换可能缺少的信息，以便准确地确定补贴或损害。由于《SCM协定》第12.7款的规定和《反倾销协定》第6.8款类似，上诉机构在进行比较后认为，该款还"允许调查机关为就倾销和损害得出结论，而在某些情况下填补必要的信息空白"。

上诉机构指出，援引"可获得事实"规则，不允许调查主管机关以其选择的任何方式来使用任何信息。首先，这种援引并不是许可仅依靠所提供的部分证据进行裁定。在可能的情况下，反补贴调查中使用"可获得事实"的调查主管机关必须考虑利害关系方提供的所有经证实的事实，即使这些事实可能并不构成该方被要求提供的全部资料。其次，主管机关"可获得的事实"一般仅限于那些可以合理地替代利害关系方未能提供的那些信息。在某些情况下，这也可能包括来自二手的信息。

上诉机构承认，《反倾销协定》第6.8款关于调查主管机关使用"可获得事实"的规则更为详细，但其也认为，如果《SCM协定》第12.7款允许在反补贴调查中以与反倾销调查明显不同的方式使用"可获得事实"，这将是不正常的。

二、2014年美国对印度特定热轧碳钢板产品的反补贴措施案[①]

United States – Countervailing Measures on Certain Hot-Rolled Carbon Steel Flat Products from India
(WT/DS436/AB/R)

4.415. Our analysis commences with the text of Article 12.7 of the SCM Agreement, construed within its immediate context and in the light of the object and purpose of the SCM Agreement. Thereafter, we turn to the further context of the other covered agreements, in

① Appellate Body Report, United States–Countervailing Measures on Certain Hot-Rolled Carbon Steel Flat Products from India, WT/DS436/AB/R, 8 December 2014. 原文脚注省略。

particular Annex II to the Anti-Dumping Agreement.Article 12.7 of the SCM Agreement states:

...

4.416. First, we note that Article 12.7 of the SCM Agreement limits use of the "facts available" to instances where an interested Member or interested party "refuses access to, or otherwise does not provide, necessary information within a reasonable period or significantly impedes the investigation". This sets the parameters within which an investigating authority makes a determination on the basis of the "facts available", namely, in a context of missing "necessary information". It is the absence of this particular information that the use of the "facts available" is designed to mitigate.This suggests that the process of identifying the "facts available" should be limited to identifying replacements for the "necessary information" that is missing from the record. In this regard, the use of the term "necessary" to qualify the term "information" carries significance. It is meant to ensure that Article 12.7 is not directed at mitigating the absence of "any" or "unnecessary" information, but is rather concerned with overcoming the absence of information required to complete a determination. In that vein, the Appellate Body has held that Article 12.7 "permits the use of facts on record solely for the purpose of replacing information that may be missing, in order to arrive at an accurate subsidization or injury determination". Accordingly, there has to be a connection between the "necessary information" that is missing and the particular "facts available" on which a determination under Article 12.7 is based. For this reason, the Appellate Body in Mexico – Anti-Dumping Measures on Rice stated that an investigating authority must use those "facts available" that "reasonably replace the information that an interested party failed to provide", with a view to arriving at an accurate determination.

4.417. It is also clear from the text of the provision that determinations made under Article 12.7 must be based on available "facts". "The" facts "available" refers to those facts that are in the possession of the investigating authority and on its written record. This may include, for instance, facts contained in the application of the domestic industry that led to the initiation of the investigation, or facts contained in information requested by, and submitted to, the investigating authority by other interested parties or interested Members. Thus, "the facts available" in Article 12.7 refers to pieces of information that can be used as evidence and that are on the written record of the investigating authority. As determinations made under Article 12.7 are to be made on the basis of the "facts available", they cannot be made on the basis of non-factual assumptions or speculation.

4.418. In our view, this understanding is confirmed by the immediate context of Article 12.7. First, we consider that the title of Article 12, namely, "Evidence", situates recourse to the "facts available" under Article 12.7 within a broader process of identifying and gathering evidence for the countervailing duty investigation. In Article 11.2 of the SCM Agreement, the term "sufficient evidence" is juxtaposed against the phrase "[s]imple assertion, unsubstantiated by relevant evidence". This indicates that the function of "evidence" is to substantiate assertions by interested parties. Article 12.5 of the SCM Agreement, which provides that "the authorities shall during the course of an investigation satisfy themselves as to the accuracy of the information supplied by interested Members or interested parties upon which their findings are based", gives a similar indication on the process of identifying and gathering evidence. In the light of this context, we consider that the task of ascertaining which "facts available" reasonably replace the missing "necessary information" under Article 12.7 calls for a process of reasoning and evaluation. In our view, it would not be possible to identify whether replacements for the missing "necessary information" are "reasonable", and thus constitute the "evidence" on which to ground a determination, without engaging in such a process.

4.419. We further consider that, as part of the process of reasoning and evaluating which "facts available" reasonably replace the missing information, all substantiated facts on the record must be taken into account. It would frustrate the function of Article 12.7, namely, to "replac[e] information that may be missing, in order to arrive at an accurate subsidization or injury determination", if certain substantiated facts were arbitrarily excluded from consideration. In addition, we note that the participants agree that Article 12.7 should not be used to punish non-cooperating parties by choosing adverse facts for that purpose. Rather, the participants agreed at the oral hearing that the function of Article 12.7 is to replace the missing "necessary information" with a view to arriving at an accurate determination.

4.420. In the process of reasoning and evaluating which "facts available" constitute reasonable replacements for the missing "necessary information", an investigating authority may be called upon to draw inferences from the evidence before it in order to reach a conclusion. As the Appellate Body has recognized, albeit in another – yet similar – context, the drawing of an inference to reach a conclusion on the veracity of evidence, including from the refusal to provide information, is "an ordinary aspect of the task of all panels to determine the relevant facts of any dispute involving any covered agreement".

4.421. Further, we note that the extent of the evaluation of the "facts available" that is required, and the form it may take, depend on the particular circumstances of a given case, including the nature, quality, and amount of the evidence on the record, and the particular determinations to be made in the course of an investigation. Similarly, whereas the explanation and analysis provided in a published report must be sufficient to allow a panel to assess whether the "facts available" employed by the investigating authority are reasonable replacements for the missing "necessary information", their nature and extent will necessarily vary from determination to determination.

4.422. We also consider that Articles 12.4 and 12.11 shed light on the meaning of Article 12.7. This is because these provisions recognize some potential reasons why the "necessary information" referred to in Article 12.7 may not be provided, namely, confidentiality and resource constraints. This is implicit in the requirement for investigating authorities to protect confidentiality and to provide any assistance practicable, in particular to small companies, in the provision of information. In our view, the context provided by these provisions suggests that the manner or procedural circumstances in which information is missing can be relevant to an investigating authority's use of "facts available" under Article 12.7. In particular, Article 12.11 requires an investigating authority to take "due account of any difficulties experienced by interested parties", which includes interested parties that have not provided the "necessary information" referred to in Article 12.7. The kinds of "difficulties", or lack thereof, experienced by interested parties to be taken into account by an investigating authority in having recourse to Article 12.7 could relate, inter alia, to the nature and availability of the evidence being sought, the adequacy of protection accorded by an investigating authority to the confidentiality of information, the time period provided in which to respond, and the extent or number of opportunities to respond, including in relation to the essential facts under consideration as provided in Article 12.8. Whether and how such procedural circumstances should be taken into account by an investigating authority, and any appropriate inferences that may be drawn, will necessarily depend on the particularities of a given investigation. We recall, however, that determinations under Article 12.7 must be made on the basis of "facts" that reasonably replace the "necessary information" that is missing, and thus cannot be made on the basis of procedural circumstances alone.

4.423. Additional context for the interpretation of Article 12.7 of the SCM Agreement is provided by Article 6.8 of the Anti-Dumping Agreement and its associated Annex II. The Appellate Body noted in Mexico – Anti-Dumping Measures on Rice both textual similarities and differences between Article 12.7 of the SCM Agreement and Article 6.8 of the Anti-Dumping Agreement. On the one hand, as a difference, the Appellate Body noted the absence of an equivalent, in the SCM Agreement, to Annex II to the Anti-Dumping Agreement. On the other hand, as similarities, the Appellate Body noted first that both provisions "permit[] an investigating authority, under certain circumstances, to fill in gaps in the information necessary to arrive at a conclusion as to subsidization (or dumping) and injury". Further, the Appellate Body noted that both provisions use the term "facts available" to denote what may replace the missing "necessary information", and both provisions appear within the context of disciplines on the identification and collection of evidence. Thus, while Annex II to the Anti-Dumping Agreement does not form part of the SCM Agreement, it has been found by the Appellate Body to be relevant context for the interpretation of Article 12.7, which is almost identically worded to Article 6.8 of the Anti-Dumping Agreement. In particular, the similarities between these provisions led the Appellate Body to state that its understanding of the limitations of an investigating authority's use of "facts available" in Article 12.7:

... is further supported by the similar, limited recourse to "facts available" permitted under Annex II to the Anti-Dumping Agreement. Indeed, in our view, it would be anomalous if Article 12.7 of the SCM Agreement were to permit the use of "facts available" in countervailing duty investigations in a manner markedly different from that in anti-dumping investigations.

4.424. As regards the nature of the "facts available" that may form the basis of determinations under Article 12.7, the title of Annex II, "Best Information Available in Terms of Paragraph 8 of Article 6", supports our understanding that these facts must be limited to those that reasonably replace the missing "necessary information". In respect of the process for ascertaining which "facts available" to use, we note that the Appellate Body in Mexico – Anti-Dumping Measures on Rice quoted from and agreed with the panel's explanation in respect of Article 6.8 of the Anti-Dumping Agreement that "[d]etermining that something is 'best' inevitably requires ... an evaluative, comparative assessment", and that the nature of this standard depends on the "particular circumstances" of a given case. This supports our understanding of Article 12.7, namely, that ascertaining the reasonable replacements for the missing "necessary information" involves a process of reasoning and evaluation. As with Article 6.8 of the Anti-Dumping Agreement, this in turn calls for a consideration of all substantiated facts on the record.

4.425. We find further support for this understanding in the references in paragraph 7 of Annex II to exercising "special circumspection" when relying on information from secondary sources, and to, where practicable, "check[ing] the information from other independent sources", both of which are indicative of a process of reasoning and evaluation. The final sentence of paragraph 7 of Annex II to the Anti-Dumping Agreement is also relevant to the interpretation of Article 12.7 of the SCM Agreement, particularly in respect of the measure at issue. It states that:

It is clear, however, that if an interested party does not cooperate and thus relevant information is being withheld from the authorities, this situation could lead to a result which is less favourable to the party than if the party did cooperate.

4.426. This clause acknowledges that non-cooperation could lead to an outcome that is less favourable for the non-cooperating party. It describes what could occur as a result of a non-cooperating party's failure to supply or otherwise withhold relevant information and the investigating authority's use of the "facts available" on the record. The juxtaposition between the "result" and the "situation" of non-cooperation in this clause confirms our understanding that the non-cooperation of a party is not itself the "basis" for replacing the "necessary information". Rather, non-cooperation creates a situation in which a less favourable result becomes possible due to the selection of a replacement for an unknown fact. Annex II to the Anti-Dumping Agreement thus provides contextual support for our understanding that the procedural circumstances in which information is missing are relevant to an investigating authority's use of "facts available" under Article 12.7 of the SCM Agreement. In this regard, we note that paragraph 1 of Annex II makes a connection between the "awareness" of an interested party, and the ability for an investigating authority to have recourse to the "facts available". This suggests that the knowledge of a non-cooperating party of the consequences of failing to provide information can be taken into account by an investigating authority, along with other procedural circumstances in which information is missing, in ascertaining those "facts available" on which to base a determination and in explaining the selection of facts. Having said that, where there are several "facts available" from which to choose, an investigating authority must nevertheless evaluate and reason which of the "facts available" reasonably replace the missing "necessary information", with a view to arriving at an accurate determination.

4.6.1.3 Evaluation of India's claim of error

4.427. With these considerations in mind, we turn to assess India's claim on appeal that the Panel erred in its interpretation of Article 12.7 of the SCM Agreement. We recall that India takes issue with the Panel's statement that investigating authorities are not required under Article 12.7 to engage in a comparative evaluation of all available evidence with a view to selecting the best information, or in other words, the most fitting or most appropriate information available.

4.428. We begin with an assessment, in general terms, of whether the Panel's approach to Article 12.7 of the SCM Agreement comports with the Appellate Body's findings in Mexico – Anti-Dumping Measures on Rice as discussed above, before turning to India's specific allegation of error. The Panel first noted that Article 12.7 refers to the available "facts", and thus determinations made under its auspices must have a factual foundation. We find this statement to be unobjectionable. In particular, we have found that, as determinations made under Article 12.7 are to be on the basis of the "facts available", they may not be made on the basis of non-factual assumptions or speculation.

4.429. Second, the Panel noted the Appellate Body's consideration in Mexico – Anti-Dumping Measures on Rice of the due process context of Article 12, before citing the Appellate Body's finding in that case that an investigating authority having recourse to Article 12.7 must take into account all the substantiated facts provided by an interested party, and that it must generally limit itself to those facts that reasonably replace the information that an interested party failed to provide. In the light of these considerations, the Panel articulated its understanding of Article 12.7 in the following terms:

[T]he standard in Article 12.7 of the SCM Agreement requires that all substantiated facts on the record be taken into account, that "facts available" determinations have a factual foundation, and that "facts available" be generally limited to those facts that may reasonably replace the missing information.4.430. In our view, this articulation comports with the interpretation of Article 12.7 by the Appellate Body in Mexico – Anti-Dumping Measures on Rice and as set out above. However, we note further that the Appellate Body in that case enunciated the standard for Article 12.7 in the light of its function, namely, to facilitate "arriv[ing] at an accurate ... determination". It is in view of this function that an investigating authority is generally limited to those facts that may reasonably replace the missing information under Article 12.7.4.431. We note that the Panel referenced this function of Article 12.7. However, the Panel appears to have misunderstood this function in rejecting, without further clarification, India's proposition that Article 12.7 requires a comparative evaluation of all available evidence with a view to identifying the best information, or in other words, the most fitting or appropriate information on the record. Rather, as we explain above, we would expect that a process of reasoning and evaluation in respect of the "facts available" on the record flows from the legal standard for Article 12.7, although the degree and nature of the reasoning and evaluation required will depend on the circumstances of a particular case. Where there are several "facts available" from which to choose, it would seem to follow naturally that the process of reasoning and evaluation would involve a degree of comparison.

...

4.432. The Panel's reasoning for rejecting India's proposition is founded on the role of Annex II to the Anti-Dumping Agreement in the interpretation of Article 12.7 of the SCM Agreement. In our view, the Panel correctly considered that Annex II to the Anti-Dumping Agreement should not be "imported" into the SCM Agreement, of which it is not a part. The Panel also correctly noted the Appellate Body's statement in Mexico – Anti-Dumping Measures on Rice that the lack of an equivalent, in the SCM Agreement, to Annex II to the Anti-Dumping Agreement gives rise to "important textual differences". However, the Panel appears to have misread the significance of such "differences" to the interpretation of Article 12.7 of the SCM Agreement. It relied on the lack of an equivalent, in the SCM Agreement, to Annex II to the Anti-Dumping Agreement for differentiating between the legal standards under Article 12.7 of the SCM Agreement and Article 6.8 of the Anti-Dumping Agreement. The Appellate Body, however, clarified in Mexico – Anti-

Dumping Measures on Rice that the absence of an equivalent, in the SCM Agreement, to Annex II to the Anti-Dumping Agreement does not mean that "no such conditions exist in the SCM Agreement". Instead, the Appellate Body used Article 6.8 of the Anti-Dumping Agreement and its Annex II as context to inform the meaning of Article 12.7 of the SCM Agreement. It found that it would be "anomalous if Article 12.7 of the SCM Agreement were to permit the use of 'facts available' in countervailing duty investigations in a manner markedly different from that in anti-dumping investigations".

4.433. In the light of these general observations regarding the Panel's interpretation of Article 12.7, we now turn to India's specific allegation of error. India alleges that the Panel erred in rejecting its proposition that "the findings of the panel in Mexico – Anti-Dumping Measures on Rice establish that Article 12.7 of the SCM Agreement requires that investigating authorities engage in a comparative evaluation of all available evidence with a view to selecting the best information, i.e. the most fitting or most appropriate information available." According to India, Article 12.7 includes "an 'obligation of conduct' to engage in a comparative evaluation of all the available evidence, prior to making this determination". As we understand it, India argues that Article 12.7 requires a comparative evaluation of all available evidence as a necessary pre-requisite to the making of a determination under Article 12.7.

4.434. We consider India's conception of the evaluation that flows from the legal standard for Article 12.7 to be too rigid. Rather, as we have set out above, the extent to which an "evaluation" of the "facts available" is required under Article 12.7, and the form it should take, depend on the particular circumstances of a given case, including the quantity and quality of the available facts on the record, and the types of determinations to be made in a given investigation. In this regard, we recall that the Appellate Body expressed agreement with the standard articulated by the panel in Mexico – Anti-Dumping Measures on Rice, including the proposition that "for the conditions of Article 6.8 of the [Anti-Dumping] Agreement and Annex II to be complied with, there can be no better information available to be used in the particular circumstances." Thus, we do not agree with India that the Appellate Body's finding in Mexico – Anti-Dumping Measures on Rice stands for the proposition that a "comparative evaluation" is a necessary pre-requisite to making a determination in every instance in which an investigating authority has recourse to the "facts available". Conceivably, there may be circumstances where the kind of "comparative evaluation" envisaged by India is not practicable. For instance, a comparative approach to the evaluation required would not be feasible where there is only one set of reliable information on the record that is relevant to a particular issue and may thus serve as a factual basis for a determination. Thus, we do not accept India's argument that Article 12.7 of the SCM Agreement requires a comparative evaluation of the "facts available" in every case.

4.435. Turning to the specific statement of the Panel articulating the legal standard of Article 12.7 that is appealed by India, we observe that it is somewhat ambiguous and open to different readings. On the one hand, it could be read to reject the proposition that Article 12.7 requires, in every case, the kind of "comparative evaluation" referred to in Mexico – Anti-Dumping Measures on Rice. When read in this way, we would agree with the statement of the Panel, because, as we have explained above, the extent and nature of the evaluation required will depend on the particular circumstances of a given case. On the other hand, the Panel's statement could be read to expressly exclude, in all instances, a "comparative evaluation" and the use of the "best information" from the legal standard for Article 12.7 of the SCM Agreement. When read in this way, we would disagree with the statement. This is because, as we have explained above, an investigating authority would generally be expected to engage in a process of reasoning and evaluation with regard to the facts on the record as an incident of conforming to the legal standard for Article 12.7, i.e. to ascertain those "facts available" that reasonably replace the missing "necessary information", with a view to arriving at an accurate determination. Where there are several "facts available" from which to choose, it would seem to follow naturally that the process of reasoning and evaluation would involve a degree of comparison. Thus, to the extent that the Panel Report can be read to exclude, in all instances, a comparative evaluation of all available evidence with a view to selecting the best information from the legal standard for Article 12.7 of the SCM Agreement, we **modify** the Panel's finding. We instead **find** that Article 12.7 requires an investigating authority to use "facts available" that reasonably replace the missing "necessary information", with a view to arriving at an accurate determination, which calls for a process of evaluation of available evidence, the extent and nature of which depends on the particular circumstances of a given case.

【本案评析】

以上案例节选自2014年美国对印度特定热轧碳钢板产品的反补贴措施案上诉机构报告。该案进一步澄清了采用“可获得事实”的相关要求，上诉机构注意到，“可获得事实”是指调查主管机关掌握并在其书面记录中的事实，其中可能包括，例如，在国内产业启动调查申请书中所载的事实，或其他向利害关系方或有关成员要求后提交给调查主管机关的资料中所载的事实。上诉机构认为，查明“可获得事实”的过程应限于查明那些在记录中缺少的“必要信息”的替代者。相应地，其在推理和评估哪一“可获得的事实”可以合理地取代缺失信息的过程中，必须考虑记录在案的所有已证实的事实。对所要求的“可获得事实”的评估程度及其可能采取的形式，取决于特定案件的具体情况，包括记录在案的证据的性质、质量和数量，以及在调查过程中作出的具体认定。信息缺失的方式或程序情况可能与调查主管机关对“可获得事实”使用有关。

该案专家组裁定，排除对所有可获得证据进行一种“比较评估”，理由是出于根据第 12.7 款的法律标准而选择最佳信息，但是上诉机构修改了这项裁定。上诉机构指出，第 12.7 款要求调查主管机关使用“可获得事实”合理地取代缺失的“必要信息”，是出于作出准确裁定的考量，这就要求基于具体案件的特定情况对可获得的证据及其程度和性质，进行一项评估程序。

三、2007 年日本对韩国进口动态随机存取存储器反补贴税案①

Japan – Countervailing Duties on Dynamic Random Access Memories from Korea (WT/DS336/AB/R)

236. Article 12.9 of the SCM Agreement provides that:

For the purposes of this Agreement, “interested parties” shall include:

(i) an exporter or foreign producer or the importer of a product subject to investigation, or a trade or business association a majority of the members of which are producers, exporters or importers of such product; and

(ii) a producer of the like product in the importing Member or a trade and business association a majority of the members of which produce the like product in the territory of the importing Member.

This list shall not preclude Members from allowing domestic or foreign parties other than those mentioned above to be included as interested parties.

237. As noted above, Korea's contention is that the JIA erred by designating certain financial institutions as interested parties although they had no “interest in the outcome of the proceeding”. We observe that Article 12.9 of the SCM Agreement does not, by its explicit terms, require that an investigating authority must establish that a party has “an interest in the outcome of [a] proceeding”. Nor do we see any provision of the SCM Agreement that defines the nature

① Appellate Body Report, Japan–Countervailing Duties on Dynamic Random Access Memories from Korea, WT/DS336/AB/R, 28 November 2007. 原文脚注省略。

of the interest required for an entity to be included as an interested party.

238. Korea argues that the parties listed in subparagraphs (i) and (ii) of Article 12.9, which are required to be included by an investigating authority as interested parties–that is, exporters, importers, foreign producers, domestic producers, and their associations–all have a clear and direct interest in the outcome of a countervailing duty investigation. For Korea, the types of entities included in the list provide a "strong indication" that an entity cannot be an interested party if it does not have such an interest. We agree that the entities specified in subparagraphs (i) and (ii)—which are all involved in the production, export, or import of the product under investigation, or in the production of the like product in the importing country–are likely to "have an interest in the outcome of the proceeding", but we find nothing in Article 12.9 to suggest that interested parties are restricted to entities of this kind under the residual clause of Article 12.9. Although the term "interested party" by definition suggests that the party must have an interest related to the investigation, the mere fact that the lists in subparagraphs (i) and (ii) comprise entities that may be directly interested in the outcome of the investigation does not imply that parties that may have other forms of interest pertinent to the investigation are excluded.

239. The last sentence of Article 12.9 provides that Members are not precluded from allowing domestic or foreign parties other than those listed in subparagraphs (i) and (ii) to be included as interested parties. Korea takes issue with the Panel's interpretation of the term "allowing" in that sentence. Korea claimed before the Panel that the term "allowing" had the meaning of "granting permission". The Panel found that, while the term could refer to an investigating authority allowing an entity to be designated as an interested party following a request, it could also refer to a Member "allowing, through national legislation or implementing regulations, certain parties to participate in investigations as interested parties." The Panel further explained that, since there are a number of provisions of the SCM Agreement, for instance Article 21.2, that provide specifically for the term "upon request" where such a requirement is contemplated, the absence of this phrase in Article 12.9 supports the interpretation that the inclusion of a party as an interested party is not predicated on a request.

240. We agree with the Panel's interpretation of the term "allowing" in Article 12.9. While a response to a request is certainly one way by which an investigating authority may allow an entity to be recognized as an interested party, we do not believe this is the only way for a party to be included. In our view, the term "allowing" in the residual clause connotes the power or authority given to a Member to include other parties as interested parties, rather than a restriction on such power of inclusion to those parties that make a request.

【本案评析】

以上案例节选自2007年日本对韩进口动态随机存取存储器反补贴税案上诉机构报告。该案专家组和上诉机构讨论了是否需要事先确定某一当事方对调查结果有利害关系，才能将其列为利害关系方当事人的问题。申诉方韩国认为，这一要求在第12.9款的措辞中有所暗示。然而，该案专家组不同意这一看法，认为第12.9款并没有提供详尽的清单说明哪些缔约方可被视为“利害关系方”。该案上诉机构指出，虽然其同意韩国的意见，但是也认为，第12.9款没有任何规定表明，利害关系方应仅限于第12.9款中的这类实体。上诉机构指出，虽然“利害关系人”一词的定义表明，当事方必须与调查有利害关系，但是第（i）项和第（ii）项中的清单仅包括对调查结果可能有直接利害的实体，并不意味着可能与调查有其他形式利害关系的当事方被排除了。第12.9款最后一句规定，此名单不应阻止成员方允许将上述未被提及的国内或国外各方包括到利害关系方之列。然而，这并不意味着调查主管机关在指定实体为利害关系方时享有不受限制的自由裁量权，可以不考虑这些实体与进行客观调查的相关性如何。同时，调查主管机关需要有一定的自由裁量权，为进行客观调查而获取与手头调查资料或证据相关的实体作为利害关系方加入进来。此外，上诉机构也强调，在指定实体为利害关系方时，调查主管机关必须考虑到这种指定可能给其他利害关系方带来的负担。

【延伸阅读】

一、相关典型案例

1.Brazil—Export Financing Programme for Aircraft(WT/DS46)

2.China—Countervailing and Anti-Dumping Duties on Grain Oriented Flat-rolled Electrical Steel from the United States（WT/DS414）

3.Canada—Measures Affecting the Export of Civilian Aircraft（WT/DS70）

4.United States—Countervailing Duties on Certain Corrosion-Resistant Carbon Steel Flat Products from Germany（WT/DS213）

5.United States—Continued Dumping and Subsidy Offset Act of 2000（WT/DS217

, WT/DS234）

6.United States—Final Countervailing Duty Determination with respect to certain Softwood Lumber from Canada（WT/DS257）

7.United States—Subsidies on Upland Cotton（WT/DS267）

8. United States—Countervailing Duty Investigation on Dynamic Random Access Memory Semiconductors (DRAMS) from Korea(WT/DS296)

二、相关学术论著

1. 曹建明、贺小勇:《世界贸易组织》,法律出版社 2012 年版。

2.Andrew T. Guzman and Joost H.B. Pauwelyn, *International Trade Law,* Aspen Publishers, 2009.

3. Andreas F. Lowenfeld, *International Economic Law,* Oxford University Press, 2008.

4.Themistoklis K. Giannakopoulos, *A Concise Guide to the EU Anti-dumping/Anti-Subsidies Procedures,* Kluwer Law International, 2006.

三、相关网络资源

1.https://www.wto.org/english/tratop_e/scm_e/scm_e.htm.

2.http://ec.europa.eu/trade/policy/accessing-markets/trade-defence/actions-against-imports-into-the-eu/anti-subsidy/.

3. https://www.usitc.gov/trade_remedy/731_ad_701_cvd/investigations/active/index.htm.

4. http://cacs.mofcom.gov.cn/.

第三节　反补贴措施的实施程序

【知识背景 / 学习要点】

一、反补贴措施的种类

一般而言，各国的反补贴措施包括国内措施和根据 DSU 采取的多边制裁措施，其中的国内反补贴措施又进一步划分为临时措施、价格承诺、最终反补贴税。这些反补贴措施的实施根据都是GATT1994和《SCM协定》。此外，《SCM协定》本身没有排除在WTO多边争端解决程序中对禁止性或可诉性补贴提出申诉，因为争端解决机制本身就是一种和其他措施一样被GATT1994和《SCM协定》允许的补贴应对方式。但是，除上述措施以外，WTO成员方不允许采取其他形式的反补贴措施。

《SCM协定》第32.1款特别规定，除非依照由本协定解释的GATT1994条款的规定外，不得针对另一成员方的补贴采取任何特别行动。2003年的美国《2000年持续倾销和补贴抵消法》争端案上诉机构指出，根据第32.1款的规定，针对可抵消补贴实施的措施必须是GATT1994或《SCM协定》中规定的四种形式之一。[①] 例如2005年墨西哥大米和牛肉的最终反倾销措施案专家组裁定，墨西哥对受反补贴调查的进口产品的进口商处以罚款的规定，是一种针对补贴的"特别行动"，GATT1994或《SCM协定》没有规定这样的罚款，因此相关罚款不符合《SCM协定》第32.1款。[②] 又如，2005年欧共体影响商船贸易措施案专家组裁定，欧洲造船条例构成一种形式的"特别行动"，但由于该法规不是"针对"补贴的，因此没有违反《SCM协定》第32.1款。[③]

本节以下重点介绍《SCM协定》规定的三种国内反补贴措施，以及反补贴措施的复审与终止、反补贴程序的公告要求与司法审查等相关制度和实践做法。

二、临时反补贴措施

在初步确定补贴对国内产业造成损害或有损害威胁之后，进口成员可对补

① 参见 Appellate Body Report, United States-Continued Dumping and Subsidy Offset Act of 2000, WT/DS217/AB/R and WT/DS234/AB/R , January 16, 2003, para. 269.

② 参见 Panel Report, Mexico-Definitive Anti-Dumping Measures on Beef and Rice , WT/DS295/R, para. 7.278.

③ 参见Panel Report, European Communities–Measures Affecting Trade in Commercial Vessels, WT/DS301/R, para. 7.143.

贴进口产品实施临时反补贴措施，条件是如果主管机关判断这种措施对防止调查期间造成的损害是必需的。临时措施可采取临时计算的、与补贴数额相等的现金存款或债券作担保的临时反补贴税形式。[①]然而，临时措施不得早于发起调查之日起60日实施。此外，临时措施的实施应限制在尽可能短的时间内，不超过4个月。[②]例如，在2002年美国涉加拿大某种软木反补贴初裁案中，专家组认定，美国违反了《SCM协定》第17.3款和第17.4款，因为美国在发起日期后的60日期限届满之前即对进口软木实施了临时反补贴措施，并且超过了4个月的最长期限3个多月。[③]

三、自愿承诺

若收到符合条件的自愿承诺，则调查程序可以中止或终止，而不采取临时措施或征收反补贴税。这些自愿承诺包括，出口成员政府同意取消或限制补贴，或采取其他与此影响有关的措施；或者出口商同意修改价格，从而使调查主管确信补贴的损害影响已经消除。根据此类承诺的价格提升不得超过消除补贴金额所必需的限度。如提价幅度小于补贴金额即足以消除对国内产业的损害，则该提价幅度是可取的。[④]

根据《SCM协定》第18.2款的规定，除非进口成员的主管机关已就补贴和补贴所造成的损害作出初步肯定性裁定，否则不得寻求或接受承诺。在出口商作出承诺的情况下，必须已获得出口成员方的同意。《SCM协定》第18.4款规定，在一项承诺已被接受的条件下，如果出口成员方希望或者进口成员方决定，那么对补贴和损害的调查仍应予以完成。[⑤]

① 参见《SCM协定》第17.2款。

② 参见《SCM协定》第17.3款和第17.4款。

③ 参见Panel Report, United States-Preliminary Determinations With Respect To Certain Softwood Lumber From Canada, WT/DS236/R, 1 November 2002, para. 7.101.

④ 参见《SCM协定》第18.1款。

⑤ 《SCM协定》第18.6款规定了违反自愿承诺的相关结果。

四、征收反补贴税

成员方只有在最终确定存在可抵消的补贴和补贴进口对国内产业造成或可能造成损害之后，才能实施最终反补贴征税。[①]

（一）限制性征税与关联分析

主管机关征收的最终反补贴税是有一定限制的。对于所征收的反补贴税数额，《SCM 协定》第 19.4 款规定，对任何进口产品征收的反补贴税均不得超过被认定存在的，接受补贴出口产品单位补贴额计算的补贴数额。这通常被称为“较少征税”规则。因此，虽然成员方在决定补贴量的计算方法时，有一定的自由裁量权，但是第 19.4 款对反补贴税的征收数额设定了上限，即不得超过补贴量的额度。此外，如果所造成的损害金额低于补贴金额，那么最终反补贴税应限于抵消所造成的损害所必需的数额范围。[②] 2004 年美国对加拿大某种软木实施最终反补贴税裁定争端案上诉机构指出，根据第 19.4 款对于单位补贴额计算的提及，支持了允许调查主管机关以合计方式计算补贴金额和补贴率的解释。[③]

由于《SCM 协定》第 19.4 款和 GATT1994 第 6.3 款要求成员方调查主管机关不得对补贴产品征收超过所认定的补贴额的反补贴税。因此，在实践中调查主管机关会采用“关联分析”的方法，来确定调查中的某一特定产品是否接受了补贴。对此 WTO 上诉机构指出，如果补贴的给予与有关产品的生产或销售有关，或以该产品的生产或销售为条件，那么补贴是与特定产品“有关联的”。这种联系或条件关系是否存在的评估将不可避免地取决于每个案件的具体情况。在进行“关联分析”时，调查主管机关应审查所涉补贴措施的设计、结构和运作，并考虑有关给予补贴的所有相关事实。例如，2016 年美国对韩国

① 参见《SCM 协定》第 19.1 款。

② 反补贴税是按补贴全额还是按少于全额来征收，要由进口成员方调查机关作出决定。因此，成员甚至可能决定放弃征收反补贴税。参见《SCM 协定》第 19.2 款。

③ 参见 Appellate Body Report, United States–Final Countervailing Duty Determination with Respect to Certain Softwood Lumber in Canada, WT/ DS57/AB/R, para. 153.

进口家用大型洗衣机双反措施案上诉机构认为，专家组不恰当支持了美国商务部在洗衣机反补贴调查中采用的一种有缺陷的关联性测试，即只有在批准机关知道补贴的用途并在授予补贴之前或在授予补贴的同时予以承认的情况下，才认为补贴与特定产品挂钩。该案上诉机构还指出，专家组在审查国内主管机关“关联分析”的调查结果时，错误地将《SCM 协定》第 1.1(b)条下的“利益接受者”概念与《SCM 协定》第 19.4 款和 GATT1994 年第 6.3 款下的“补贴产品”概念混为一谈。[①]

(二)非歧视性征税原则

和反倾销税征收类似，反补贴税必须在非歧视的基础上征收。《SCM 协定》第 19.3 款规定，若对任何产品征收反补贴税，则应对已被认定接受补贴和造成损害的所有来源的此种进口产品根据每一案件的情况在非歧视基础上收取适当金额的反补贴税，除非任何所涉补贴已经放弃，或者按本协定条件做出的承诺已被接受的那些渠道的进口。

虽然征收反补贴税的成员方须“在非歧视的基础上”征收反补贴税，但是这并不意味着对每一个出口商来说，所征收的反补贴税的“适当”金额必定是相同的。出口商或生产商如曾接受个别审查并曾在调查中给予合作，通常会被主管机关征收单独的反补贴税。《SCM 协定》第 19.3 款规定，如果出口须缴纳最终反补贴税，但未受到实际调查的任何出口商，有权进行快速审查，以便调查主管机关能够迅速确定该出口商的单独的反补贴税税率。[②]

此外，WTO 上诉机构曾强调，只有在调查主管机关确定补贴存在，对国内产业的损害以及两者之间的因果关系之后，才能根据《SCM 协定》第五部分规定征收全国范围或特定公司的反补贴税率。换言之，第 19 条允许对未经单独调查的生产商或出口商征收反补贴税的事实，并不能免除成员方按照《SCM 协

① 参见Appellate Body Report, United States–Anti-Dumping and Countervailing Measures on Large Residential Washers from Korea, WT/DS464/AB/R, para. 5.274. and para. 5.305.

② 请注意，这不适用于那些因为拒绝与调查机关进行合作，从而没有为其确定单独的反补贴税的出口商。参见《SCM 协定》第 19.3 款。

定》和 GATT1994 第 6 条的规定确定补贴总额和反补贴税率的义务。[①]

（三）不得追溯征收

根据《SCM 协定》第 20.1 款的规定，反补贴税原则上不得追溯适用，即它们只能适用于实施反补贴税的裁定生效后进口的产品。[②]《SCM 协定》第 20.5 款规定，若最终裁定是否定性的，则在实施临时性措施期间所交纳的任何现金应迅速予以退还，任何担保应迅速予以解除。[③]

五、反补贴征税的复审与终止

和反倾销类似，反补贴税措施的实施，也应考虑该措施本身的特性及其无期限实施会带来的不利效果。《SCM 协定》第 21.1 款规定，反补贴税应仅在抵消造成损害的补贴所必需的时间和限度内实施。WTO 上诉机构曾指出，《SCM 协定》第 21.1 款是总体性的规则，即在征收反补贴税后，继续适用该税须遵守的某些纪律。这些纪律涉及反补贴税的期限（“只有……有必要”）、幅度（“只有……在必要时”）及目的（“为抵消造成损害的补贴”）。因此，第 21.1 款的总体规则强调了反补贴税复审的相关要求，以及这种复审中的须知因素。[④] 与反倾销类似，征收反补贴税的复审，也包括期间复审与日落复审两种。

（一）期间复审

主管机关在有正当理由的情况下，自行复审或在最终反补贴税的征收已经过一段合理时间后，应提交证实复审必要性的肯定信息的任何利害关系方请求，复审继续征税的必要性。利害关系方有权请求主管机关复审是否需要继续征收反补贴税以抵消补贴，若取消或改变反补贴税，则损害是否有可能继续或

---

① 参见 Appellate Body Report, United States–Final Countervailing Duty Determination with Respect to Certain Softwood Lumber in Canada, WT/ DS257/AB/R, para. 154.

② 但是，在特定情况下，反补贴税的追溯适用是允许的。参见《SCM 协定》第 20.2 款和第 20.6 款的规定。

③ 如果最终反补贴税高于现金存款或债券担保的数额，其差额不得再行征收。参见《SCM 协定》第 20.3 款。

④ 参见 Appellate Body Report, United States–Countervailing Duties on Certain Corrosion Resistant Carbon Steel Flat Products from Germany, WT/DS213/AB/R, 19 December 2002, para. 70.

再度发生，或同时复审两者。[①] 利害关系方可在最终反补贴税实施后的一段合理时间内，要求进行此种复审，但必须主动提交材料，证明进行复审有必要。[②] 调查主管机关应利害关系人的请求，应按照与原调查同样的程序规则进行复审，审查的内容应限于：(1)是否有必要继续征税以抵销补贴和(2)若征税被撤销或更改，则就损害是否可能继续或再次发生。[③] 如果调查主管机关在复审后得出结论，认为不再需要继续征收反补贴税，那么就应立即终止。[④] 如果调查主管机关认定反补贴税征收仍有正当理由，那么尽管可能会降低税率水平，但反补贴税也将继续适用。

在 2000 年美国对英国热卷铅条和铋碳钢产品的反补贴税案中，上诉机构指出，调查主管机关在第 21.2 款复审中作出的裁定，必须依据利害关系方向其提交的信息以及它所收到的与复审期有关的其他证据进行评估，调查机关必须确定继续适用反补贴税是否有必要。调查主管机关不能随意忽略这类信息。如果其忽略了这些信息，第 21.2 款项下的复审机制将没有任何意义。关于第 21.2 款复审中是否存在“利益”的问题，该案上诉机构裁定，其不同意专家组暗示的意见，即根据第 21.2 款进行的行政复审，调查主管机关必须始终确认在复审期间是否存在和调查主管机关必须在原调查中确定的“利益”一样的“利益”……在原调查中，调查主管机关必须确认，为征收反补贴税，《SCM 协定》中规定的所有条件都已得到满足。然而，在行政复审中，调查主管机关必须处理利害关系方向其提出的问题，或在自行进行调查的情况下，处理那些需要复

① 参见《SCM 协定》第 21.2 款。See also Appellate Body Report, United States–Imposition of Countervailing Duties on Certain Hot-Rolled Lead and Bismuth Carbon Steel Products Originating in the United Kingdom, WT/DS138/AB/R, 10 May 2000, para. 53. See also Panel Report, US–Softwood Lumber III (2002), para. 7.151.

② 参见《SCM 协定》第 21.2 款。

③ 参见《SCM 协定》第 21.2 和 21.4 款。2005 年墨西哥对大米的反倾销措施案上诉机构裁定，成员方不得将在《SCM 协定》第 21.2 款规定以外的要求作为利害关系方复审权的条件。参见 Appellate Body Report, Mexico-Definitive Anti-Dumping Measures on Beef and Rice , WT/DS295/AB/R, 29 November 2005, para. 314.

④ 参见《SCM 协定》第 21.2 款。

审的问题。因此，该案上诉机构将最初的调查与第 21.2 款的复审程序进行了区别。[①]

（二）日落复审

《SCM 协定》第 21.3 款规定了一个所谓的“日落”条款，根据该条款，所有最终反补贴税必须在实施或最近一次复审之后的最长 5 年内终止。然而，如果调查主管机关确定反补贴税的到期可能导致补贴和损害的继续或再次发生，那么该征税将不会被终止。[②]调查主管机关按照第 21.3 款进行的审查通常被称为“日落复审”。

主管机关可主动或应国内产业或国内产业代表经适当证明的请求，启动“日落复审”。但是，“日落复审”的请求必须在反补贴征税到期之前的合理时间内提出，调查机关也必须在反补贴税到期之前开始复审。此外，与第 11.9 款不同的是，第 21.3 款没有规定“日落复审”的最低限度标准。[③]

2002 年美国对来自德国的部分防腐蚀平板碳钢产品实施反补贴措施争端案上诉机构认为，第 11.9 款规定的微量要求在第 21.3 款中也没有暗示。对于由调查机关主动发起的“日落复审”，该案上诉机构裁定，第 21.3 款没有规定有关主动发起“日落复审”的证据标准。此外，该案上诉机构解释了第 21.3 款与第 21.2 款之间的区别，即第 21.2 款确定了调查主管机关有义务复审（“应当复审”）是否有必要继续征收反补贴税的某些情况，相反，在第 21.3 款中规定的主要义务本身并不是进行复审，而是终止一项反补贴税，除非在复审中特别裁定继续征收是必要的。[④]

此外，对于原调查中的证据收集、透明度、正当程序的认定也适用“日落复

① Appellate Body Report, United States–Imposition of Countervailing Duties on Certain Hot-Rolled Lead and Bismuth Carbon Steel Products Originating in the United Kingdom, WT/DS138/AB/R, 10 May 2000, paras. 61-63.

② 参见《SCM 协定》第 21.3 款。

③ 参见《SCM 协定》第 21 条。

④ 参见 Appellate Body Report, United States–Countervailing Duties on Certain Corrosion Resistant Carbon Steel Flat Products from Germany, WT/DS213/AB/R, 19 December 2002, paras.92, 108 and 112.

审”规则。[①]《SCM 协定》第 21.4 款规定，关于证据和程序的第 12 条规定应适用于按本条所进行的任何复审。“日落复审”应迅速进行，复审应在启动后的 12 个月内完成。[②]

六、反补贴程序的公告要求

为了提高调查机关反补贴程序和裁定的透明度，《SCM 协定》第 22 条对于调查主管机关启动调查、临时反补贴措施、自愿承诺或最终反补贴税裁定的作出，规定了详细的公告要求。

例如，根据《SCM 协定》第 22.5 款的规定，在调查主管机关决定征收最终反补贴税或接受承诺的肯定裁定的情况下，关于终止或中止调查的公告应包含或通过一份单独报告提供，导致实施最终措施或接受承诺的所有有关的事实问题和法律问题及理由。[③] 具体而言，公告或报告必须包括：(1)供应商名称，如不可行，则为所涉及的供应国名称；(2)足以符合报关目的的产品描述；(3)确定的补贴金额和确定补贴存在的依据；(4)按第 15 条所列与损害裁定有关的考虑；(5)导致作出裁定的主要理由。[④] 此外，公告或报告必须列出接受或拒绝利害关系成员及进口商和出口商所提有关论据或请求事项的理由。[⑤]

2012 年中国对美国取向电工钢征收反倾销税和反补贴税案上诉机构认定，第 22.5 款要求披露“有关事实问题的相关信息”，并不要求主管机关披露其所获得的所有事实信息，而是要求主管机关披露能够足以理解导致最终措施实施的事实依据的那些事实信息。[⑥] 上诉机构认为，“有关事实问题的相关信息”的构成应根据裁定的内容来理解，满足根据《SCM 协定》采取最终反补贴措施的实质性要求，并考虑到每个案件的实际情况。上诉机构就《SCM 协定》第 22.5

① 参见《SCM 协定》第 21.4 款。

② 在此种复审的结果产生之前，可继续征税。参见《SCM 协定》第 21.3 款。

③ 参见《SCM 协定》第 22.5 款。然而 Article 22.5 同时要求应适当考虑保护机密信息。

④ 参见《SCM 协定》第 22.4 款。

⑤ 参见《SCM 协定》第 22.5 款。

⑥ 列入这一信息应合理说明调查机关决定采取明确措施的事实依据。

款规定的“公告”要求指出，该款规定的披露义务是以“相关性”的要求为基础的，这就需要披露导致征收反补贴税决定的整个事实、法律和理由的逻辑体系……第 22.5 款设法保证有关各方能够按照第 23 条的规定对最终裁定进行司法审查。①

七、反补贴的国内司法审查

按照《SCM 协定》第 23 条的要求，国内立法包含反补贴税措施规定的每一成员均应设有司法、仲裁或行政庭或程序，其目的特别包括迅速审查与最终裁定的行政行为有关，且属《SCM 协定》第 21 条范围内的对裁定的审查，即“司法审查”。此类法庭或程序应独立于负责所涉裁定或审查的主管机关，且应向参与行政程序及直接和间接受行政行为影响的所有利害关系方提供了解审查情况的机会。②

【案例摘录与评析】

一、2003 年美国《2000 年持续倾销和补贴抵消法》争端案③

United States - Continued Dumping and Subsidy Offset Act of 2000
(WT/DS217/AB/R and WT/DS234/AB/R)

II. Factual Background

11. The CDSOA was enacted on 28 October 2000 as part of the Agriculture, Rural Development, Food and Drug Administration and Related Agencies Appropriations Act, 2001. The CDSOA amended Title VII of the Tariff Act of 1930 (the “Tariff Act”), entitled “Countervailing and Anti-dumping Duties”, by adding a new Section 754 entitled “Continued Dumping and Subsidy

① 参见 Appellate Body Report, China-Countervailing and Anti-Dumping Duties on Grain Oriented Flat-rolled Electrical Steel from the United States, WT/DS414/AB/R, paras.256-258.

② 参见《SCM 协定》第 23 条。

③ Appellate Body Report, United States-Continued Dumping and Subsidy Offset Act of 2000, WT/DS217/AB/R and WT/DS234/AB/R , January 16, 2003. 原文脚注省略。

Offset”.

12. The CDSOA provides that the United States Commissioner of Customs (“Customs”) shall distribute, on an annual basis, duties assessed pursuant to a countervailing duty order, an anti-dumping duty order, or a finding under the United States Anti-dumping Act of 1921, to “affected domestic producers” for “qualifying expenditures”.An “affected domestic producer” is defined as a domestic producer that: (a) was a petitioner or interested party in support of the petition with respect to which an anti-dumping duty order, a finding under the Anti-dumping Act of 1921, or a countervailing duty order has been entered; and (b) remains in operation. The term “qualifying expenditures” refers to expenditures on specific items identified in the CDSOA, which were incurred after the issuance of the anti-dumping duty finding, or order or countervailing duty order. Those expenditures must relate to the production of the same product that is subject to the anti-dumping or countervailing duty order, with the exception of expenses incurred by associations which must relate to the same case.

13. The CDSOA, together with its implementing regulations issued by Customs, provides that Customs shall establish a special account and a clearing account with respect to each countervailing duty order, anti-dumping duty order, or a finding under the Anti-dumping Act of 1921. All anti-dumping and countervailing duties assessed under such orders or findings are first deposited into a “clearing account”. Transfers from “clearing accounts” to “special accounts” are made by Customs throughout the fiscal year. Such transfers are made only after the entries in question that are subject to a countervailing duty order or an anti-dumping order or finding have been properly “liquidated”. Thus, when, and only when, the entries have been liquidated, will the proceeds be transferred to a special account. Only once there are funds in a special account (not a clearing account), can distributions to domestic producers under the CDSOA be made. Therefore, if liquidation of entries has been enjoined, for instance, by a court—perhaps pending judicial review of the determination of dumping or countervailable subsidization—or if liquidation of entries has been suspended due to an administrative review of those entries, the relevant special account will be empty and no distribution can be made to domestic producers under the CDSOA.

14. Pursuant to the CDSOA, Customs shall distribute all funds (including all interest earned on the funds) from the assessed duties received in the preceding fiscal year (and contained in the special accounts) to each affected domestic producer based on a certification by the affected domestic producer that it is eligible to receive the distribution and desires to receive a distribution for qualifying expenditures incurred since the issuance of the order or finding. Funds deposited in each special account during each fiscal year are to be distributed no later than 60 days after the

beginning of the following fiscal year. There is no statutory or regulatory requirement as to how a disbursement is to be spent. The Panel found that CDSOA distributions to "affected domestic producers" made as of December 2001 totalled over $206 million.

...

A. The Term "Specific" in the Phrase "Specific Action Against" Dumping or a Subsidy

237. We observe that Article 18.1 of the Anti-Dumping Agreement is identical in language, terminology and structure to Article 32.1 of the SCM Agreement, except for the reference to dumping instead of subsidy. The Panel analyzed the terms "specific" and "against" in Article 18.1 in the same manner as it did with respect to their use in Article 32.1. We agree with the Panel's approach. We also note that the United States does not challenge such approach and that, at the oral hearing, none of the appellees or third participants expressed the view that the terms, as used in Article 18.1 should have a different meaning as used in Article 32.1.

238. As mentioned above, in US – 1916 Act, we interpreted the phrase "specific action against dumping" in Article 18.1 of the Anti-Dumping Agreement. We said:In our view, the ordinary meaning of the phrase "specific action against dumping" of exports within the meaning of Article 18.1 is action that is taken in response to situations presenting the constituent elements of "dumping". "Specific action against dumping" of exports must, at a minimum, encompass action that may be taken only when the constituent elements of "dumping" are present.①

239. We recall that, in US – 1916 Act, the United States argued that the 1916 Act did not fall within the scope of Article VI of the GATT 1994 because it targeted predatory pricing, as opposed to dumping. We disagreed, and determined that the 1916 Act was a "specific action against dumping" because the constituent elements of dumping were "built into" the essential elements of civil and criminal liability under the 1916 Act. We also found that the "wording of the 1916 Act ... makes clear that these actions can be taken only with respect to conduct which presents the constituent elements of 'dumping' ". Accordingly, a measure that may be taken only when the constituent elements of dumping or a subsidy are present, is a "specific action" in response to dumping within the meaning of Article 18.1 of the Anti-Dumping Agreement or a "specific action" in response to subsidization within the meaning of Article 32.1 of the SCM Agreement. In other words, the measure must be inextricably linked to, or have a strong correlation with, the constituent elements of dumping or of a subsidy. Such link or correlation may, as in the 1916 Act,

① We do not find it necessary, in the present cases, to decide whether the concept of "specific action against dumping" may be broader.

Given that Article 18.1 of the Anti-Dumping Agreement and 32.1 of the SCM Agreement are identical except for the reference in the former to dumping, and in the latter to a subsidy, we are of the view that this finding is pertinent for both provisions.

be derived from the text of the measure itself.

240. This leads to the question of how to determine what are the constituent elements of dumping or a subsidy. We recall that, in US – 1916 Act, we said the constituent elements of dumping are found in the definition of dumping in Article VI:1 of the GATT 1994, as elaborated in Article 2 of the Anti-Dumping Agreement. As regards the constituent elements of a subsidy, we are of the view that they are set out in the definition of a subsidy found in Article 1 of the SCM Agreement.

241. We turn now to determine whether the CDSOA is a "specific action" against dumping or subsidization within the meaning of Article 18.1 of the Anti-Dumping Agreement or Article 32.1 of the SCM Agreement.

242. In our view, the Panel was correct in finding that the CDSOA is a specific action related to dumping or a subsidy within the meaning of Article 18.1 of the Anti-Dumping Agreement and Article 32.1 of the SCM Agreement. It is clear from the text of the CDSOA, in particular from Section 754(a) of the Tariff Act, that the CDSOA offset payments are inextricably linked to, and strongly correlated with, a determination of dumping, as defined in Article VI:1 of the GATT 1994 and in the Anti-Dumping Agreement, or a determination of a subsidy, as defined in the SCM Agreement. The language of the CDSOA is unequivocal. First, CDSOA offset payments can be made only if anti-dumping duties or countervailing duties have been collected. Second, such duties can be collected only pursuant to an anti-dumping duty order or countervailing duty order. Third, an anti-dumping duty order can be imposed only following a determination of dumping, as defined in Article VI:1 of the GATT 1994 and in the Anti-Dumping Agreement. Fourth, a countervailing duty order can be imposed only following a determination that exports have been subsidized, according to the definition of a subsidy in the SCM Agreement. In the light of the above elements, we agree with the Panel that "there is a clear, direct and unavoidable connection between the determination of dumping and CDSOA offset payments" , and we believe the same to be true for subsidization. In other words, it seems to us unassailable that CDSOA offset payments can be made only following a determination that the constituent elements of dumping or subsidization are present. Therefore, consistent with the test established in US – 1916 Act, we find that the CDSOA is "specific action"

...

252. Turning to considerations of object and purpose, we do not consider that the object and purpose of the Anti-Dumping Agreement and of the SCM Agreement, as reflected in Article 18.1 of the Anti-Dumping Agreement and in Article 32.1 of the SCM Agreement, support the incorporation into these provisions, through the term "against", of a requirement that the

measure must come into direct contact with the imported good, or the entity responsible for it. Both provisions fulfil a function of limiting the range of actions that a Member may take unilaterally to counter dumping or subsidization. Excluding from Article 18.1 of the Anti-Dumping Agreement and Article 32.1 of the SCM Agreement actions that do not come into direct contact with the imported good or the entity responsible for the dumped or subsidized good, would undermine that function.

253. We, therefore, agree with the Panel that in Article 18.1 of the Anti-Dumping Agreement and Article 32.1 of the SCM Agreement, there is no requirement that the measure must come into direct contact with the imported product, or entities connected to, or responsible for, the imported good such as the importer, exporter, or foreign producer. We also agree with the Panel that the test should focus on dumping or subsidization as practices. Article 18.1 refers only to measures that act against "dumping"; there is no express requirement that the measure must act against the imported dumped product, or entities responsible for that product. Likewise, Article 32.1 of the SCM Agreement refers to specific action against "a subsidy", not to action against the imported subsidized product or a responsible entity.

254. Recalling the other two elements of the definition of "against" from the New Shorter Oxford Dictionary relied upon by the United States, namely "of motion or action in opposition" and "in hostility or active opposition to", to determine whether a measure is "against" dumping or a subsidy, we believe it is necessary to assess whether the design and structure of a measure is such that the measure is "opposed to", has an adverse bearing on, or, more specifically, has the effect of dissuading the practice of dumping or the practice of subsidization, or creates an incentive to terminate such practices. In our view, the CDSOA has exactly those effects because of its design and structure.

255. The CDSOA effects a transfer of financial resources from the producers/exporters of dumped or subsidized goods to their domestic competitors. This is demonstrated by the following elements of the CDSOA regime. First, the CDSOA offset payments are financed from the anti-dumping or countervailing duties paid by the foreign producers/exporters. Second, the CDSOA offset payments are made to an "affected domestic producer", defined in Section 754(b) of the Tariff Act as "a petitioner or interested party in support of the petition with respect to which an anti-dumping duty order, a finding under the Anti-dumping Act of 1921, or a countervailing duty order has been entered" and that "remains in operation". In response to our questioning at the oral hearing, the United States confirmed that the "affected domestic producers" which are eligible to receive payments under the CDSOA, are necessarily competitors of the foreign producers/exporters subject to an anti-dumping or countervail order. Third, under the

implementing regulations issued by the United States Commissioner of Customs ("Customs") on 21 September 2001, the "qualifying expenditures" of the affected domestic producers, for which the CDSOA offset payments are made, "must be related to the production of the same product that is the subject of the related order or finding, with the exception of expenses incurred by associations which must relate to a specific case". Fourth, Customs has confirmed that there is no statutory or regulatory requirement as to how a CDSOA offset payment to an affected domestic producer is to be spent , thus indicating that the recipients of CDSOA offset payments are entitled to use this money to bolster their competitive position vis-à-vis their competitors, including the foreign competitors subject to anti-dumping or countervailing duties.

256. All these elements lead us to conclude that the CDSOA has an adverse bearing on the foreign producers/exporters in that the imports into the United States of the dumped or subsidized products (besides being subject to anti-dumping or countervailing duties) result in the financing of United States competitors—producers of like products—through the transfer to the latter of the duties collected on those exports. Thus, foreign producers/exporters have an incentive not to engage in the practice of exporting dumped or subsidized products or to terminate such practices. Because the CDSOA has an adverse bearing on, and, more specifically, is designed and structured so that it dissuades the practice of dumping or the practice of subsidization, and because it creates an incentive to terminate such practices, the CDSOA is undoubtedly an action "against" dumping or a subsidy, within the meaning of Article 18.1 of the Anti-Dumping Agreement and of Article 32.1 of the SCM Agreement.

257. We note that the United States challenges what it views as the Panel's incorporation of a "conditions of competition test" in Article 18.1 of the Anti-Dumping Agreement and in Article 32.1 of the SCM Agreement. In our view, in order to determine whether the CDSOA is "against" dumping or subsidization, it was not necessary, nor relevant, for the Panel to examine the conditions of competition under which domestic products and dumped/subsidized imports compete, and to assess the impact of the measure on the competitive relationship between them. An analysis of the term "against", in our view, is more appropriately centred on the design and structure of the measure; such an analysis does not mandate an economic assessment of the implications of the measure on the conditions of competition under which domestic product and dumped/subsidized imports compete.

258. As mentioned above , the finding of the Panel that the CDSOA is a measure against dumping or a subsidy is also based on the view that the CDSOA provides a financial incentive for domestic producers to file or support applications for the initiation of anti-dumping and countervailing duty investigations, and that such an incentive will likely result in a greater number

of applications, investigations and orders. We agree with the United States that this consideration is not a proper basis for a finding that the CDSOA is "against" dumping or a subsidy; a measure cannot be against dumping or a subsidy simply because it facilitates or induces the exercise of rights that are WTO consistent. The Panel's reasoning would give Article 18.1 of the Anti-Dumping Agreement and Article 32.1 of the SCM Agreement a scope of application that is overly broad. For example, the Panel's reasoning would imply that a legal aid program destined to support domestic small-size producers in anti-dumping or countervailing duty investigations should be considered a measure against dumping or a subsidy within the meaning of Article 18.1 of the Anti-Dumping Agreement and of Article 32.1 of the SCM Agreement, because it could be argued that such legal aid is a financial incentive likely to result in a greater number or applications, investigations and orders.

259. The United States also argues that the Panel erred in relying on the stated purpose of the CDSOA, as expressed in the "Findings of Congress" set forth in Section 1002 of the CDSOA, to support its finding that the CDSOA is a measure against dumping or a subsidy. We note that the Panel referred to the "Findings of Congress", not as a basis for its conclusion that the CDSOA constitutes a specific action against dumping or subsidies, but rather as a consideration confirming that conclusion. We agree with the Panel that the intent, stated or otherwise, of the legislators is not conclusive as to whether a measure is "against" dumping or subsidies under Article 18.1 of the Anti-Dumping Agreement or Article 32.1 of the SCM Agreement. Thus, it was not necessary for the Panel to inquire into the intent pursued by United States legislators in enacting the CDSOA and to take this into account in the analysis. The text of the CDSOA provides sufficient information on the structure and design of the CDSOA, that is to say, on the manner in which it operates, to permit an analysis whether the measure is "against" dumping or a subsidy. Specifically, the text of the CDSOA establishes clearly that, by virtue of that statute, a transfer of financial resources is effected from the producers/exporters of dumped or subsidized goods to their domestic competitors. This essential feature of the CDSOA constitutes, in itself, the decisive basis for concluding that the CDSOA is "against" dumping or a subsidy—because it creates the "opposition" to dumping or subsidization, such that it dissuades such practices, or creates an incentive to terminate them. Therefore, there was no need to examine the intent pursued by the legislators in enacting the CDSOA. In our view, however, the Panel did not err in simply noting that the stated legislative intent, which appears in the statute itself, confirms the conclusion it had reached as to the scope of the measure.

...

266. As regards subsidization, the United States argues that Article VI:3 of the GATT 1994,

read in conjunction with Article 10 of the SCM Agreement, does not limit the permissible remedies for subsidies to duties. The United States submits that the legal regime governing permissible responses to dumping is different from that governing the permissible responses to subsidization. Therefore, it is inappropriate to rely on the reasoning from US – 1916 Act to determine what is meant by "in accordance with the provisions of the GATT 1994" as that phrase relates to permissible responses to subsidies.

267. The United States also submits that the CDSOA is in accordance with Article VI:3 of the GATT 1994 and the provisions of Part V of the SCM Agreement, because those provisions do not encompass all measures taken against subsidization; they contemplate only countervailing duties (and by implication, provisional measures and price undertakings). Thus, it cannot properly be concluded that the CDSOA violates Article VI:3 of the GATT 1994 or the provisions of Part V of the SCM Agreement, because the CDSOA offset payments are not countervailing duties (or provisional measures or price undertakings), and, therefore, do not constitute an action covered by these provisions. In support of its submissions, the United States contrasts the language of Article VI:2 of the GATT 1994 and Article 1 of the Anti-Dumping Agreement with Article VI:3 of the GATT 1994 and Article 10 of the SCM Agreement. The United States argues, on the basis of textual differences, that the conclusion we reached in US – 1916 Act that Article VI of the GATT 1994 encompasses all measures taken against dumping, was based on the specific language of Article VI:2 of the GATT 1994 and Article 1 of the Anti-Dumping Agreement. Therefore, according to the United States, such a conclusion should not be extended to the textually different subsidy provisions of Article VI of the GATT 1994 and of Part V of the SCM Agreement, which are limited to the imposition of countervailing duties (and by implication, provisional duties and price undertakings). In particular, the United States argues that the permissible responses to dumping are limited to definitive anti-dumping duties, provisional measures and price undertakings, because Article 1 of the Anti-Dumping Agreement refers to anti-dumping measures, a generic expression that encompasses all measures taken against dumping, and not only duties. Article 10 of the SCM Agreement, by contrast, refers to countervailing duties, and thus only countervailing duties (and, by implication, provisional duties and price undertakings) are governed by Article VI:3 of the GATT 1994 and Part V of the SCM Agreement.

268. We disagree with these submissions for the following reasons. As the Panel noted, our analysis in US – 1916 Act "was not based on any particular AD provision in isolation, but on the AD Agreement as a whole". We agree with the Panel that:

Since the Appellate Body's analysis [in US – 1916 Act] was not based exclusively on AD Article 1, we fail to see why a different approach should apply in respect of the permissible responses to subsidization, simply because of a difference between the text of AD Article 1 and SCM Article 10. In identifying the permissible responses to subsidization, we consider it important to have regard to the type of remedies foreseen by the SCM Agreement. (emphasis added)

As pointed out above, Article 32.1 of the SCM Agreement is identical in terminology and structure to Article 18.1 of the Anti-Dumping Agreement, except for the reference to subsidy instead of dumping. We endorse Canada's contention that "[t]his identical wording gives rise to a strong interpretative presumption that the two provisions set out the same obligation or prohibition."

269. Article VI of the GATT 1994 and the Anti-Dumping Agreement identify three responses to dumping, namely, definitive anti-dumping duties, provisional measures and price undertakings. No other response is envisaged in the text of Article VI of the GATT 1994, or the text of the Anti-Dumping Agreement. Therefore, to be in accordance with Article VI of the GATT 1994, as interpreted by the Anti-Dumping Agreement, a response to dumping must be in one of these three forms. We confirmed this in US – 1916 Act. We fail to see why similar reasoning should not apply to subsidization. The GATT 1994 and the SCM Agreement provide four responses to a countervailable subsidy: (i) definitive countervailing duties; (ii) provisional measures; (iii) price undertakings; and (iv) multilaterally-sanctioned countermeasures under the dispute settlement system. No other response to subsidization is envisaged in the text of the GATT 1994, or in the text of the SCM Agreement. Therefore, to be "in accordance with the GATT 1994, as interpreted by" the SCM Agreement, a response to subsidization must be in one of those four forms.

270. We note that interpreting these provisions as limiting the permissible responses to a countervailable subsidy to the four remedies envisaged in the SCM Agreement and the GATT 1994 is consistent with footnote 35 to Article 10 of the SCM Agreement, and with the function of Article 32.1 of the SCM Agreement. Footnote 35 reads as follows:

The provisions of Part II or III may be invoked in parallel with the provisions of Part V; however, with regard to the effects of a particular subsidy in the domestic market of the importing Member, only one form of relief (either a countervailing duty, if the requirements of Part V are met, or a countermeasure under Articles 4 or 7) shall be available. The provisions of Parts III and V shall not be invoked regarding measures considered non-actionable in accordance with the provisions of Part IV. However, measures referred to in paragraph 1(a) of Article 8 may be investigated in order to determine whether or not they are specific within the meaning of Article 2. In addition, in the case of a subsidy referred to in paragraph 2 of Article 8 conferred pursuant to a programme which has not been notified in accordance with paragraph 3 of Article 8, the provisions of Part III or V may be invoked, but such subsidy shall be treated as non-actionable if it is found to conform to the standards set forth in paragraph 2 of Article 8. (emphasis added)

It is appropriate to emphasize the phrase "only one form of relief (either a countervailing duty, if the requirements of Part V are met, or a countermeasure under Articles 4 or 7) shall be available". It expressly sets out two forms of specific action, and provides that WTO Members may choose to apply one or the other against a subsidy. The assumption underlying the requirements of footnote 35 is that remedies under the SCM Agreement are limited to countervailing duties (and, by implication, provisional measures and price undertakings), explicitly envisaged in Part V of the SCM Agreement, and to countermeasures under Articles 4 and 7 of the SCM Agreement. Footnote 35 requires WTO Members to choose between two forms of remedy; such a requirement would be meaningless if responses to a countervailable subsidy, other than definitive countervailing duties, provisional measures, price undertakings and multilaterally-sanctioned countermeasures, were permitted under the GATT 1994 and the SCM Agreement.

271. Moreover, Article 32.1 of the SCM Agreement limits the range of actions a WTO Member may take unilaterally to counter subsidization. Restricting available unilateral actions against subsidization to those expressly provided for in the GATT 1994 and in the SCM Agreement is consistent with this function. The United States' reasoning would deprive Article 32.1 of the SCM Agreement of effectiveness. As we have stated on many occasions, the internationally recognized interpretive principle of effectiveness should guide the interpretation of the WTO Agreement , and, under this principle, provisions of the WTO Agreement should not be interpreted in such a manner that whole clauses or paragraphs of a treaty would be reduced to redundancy or inutility. Accepting the United States' contention that Article VI:3 of the GATT 1994 and Part V of the SCM Agreement cover only countervailing duties would render Article 32.1 of the SCM Agreement redundant or inutile, because, under the United States' approach, Article 32.1 of the SCM Agreement would not provide additional discipline. Thus, a violation of Article 32.1 would flow only from a violation of another provision; violating Article 32.1 would be only a mechanical consequence of a violation of another provision.

272. Furthermore, Article 32.1 of the SCM Agreement would be inutile with respect to "specific action[s] against a subsidy" other than countervailing duties, as it would be impossible, in such case, to find a violation of Article 32.1. Given that Article VI:3 of the GATT 1994 and Part V of the SCM Agreement would, under the United States' reasoning, be limited to countervailing duties, such specific actions would always be in accordance with Article VI:3 of the GATT 1994 and Part V of the SCM Agreement and, therefore, consistent with Article 32.1. Consequently, we reject the United States' contention that Article VI:3 of the GATT 1994 and Part V of the SCM Agreement encompass only countervailing duties.

273. In our view, Article VI:3 of the GATT 1994 and Part V of the SCM Agreement encompass all measures taken against subsidization. To be in accordance with the GATT 1994, as interpreted by the SCM Agreement, a response to subsidization must be either in the form of definitive countervailing duties, provisional measures or price undertakings, or in the form of multilaterally sanctioned countermeasures resulting from resort to the dispute settlement system. As the CDSOA does not correspond to any of the responses to subsidization envisaged by the GATT 1994 and the SCM Agreement, we conclude that it is not in accordance with the provisions of the GATT 1994, as interpreted by the SCM Agreement, and that, therefore, the CDSOA is inconsistent with Article 32.1 of the SCM Agreement.

274. Accordingly, we uphold, albeit for different reasons, the finding of the Panel that the CDSOA is a non-permissible specific action against dumping or a subsidy, contrary to Article 18.1 of the Anti-Dumping Agreement and Article 32.1 of the SCM Agreement.

【本案评析】

以上案例节选自2003年美国《2000年持续倾销和补贴抵消法》争端案上诉机构报告。本案的争议措施是美国《2000年持续倾销和补贴抵消法》。根据该法案，美国海关应向“受影响的国内生产者”支付根据反补贴税执行令评估得出的反补贴税，以弥补其“合格的开支”。上诉机构认为，在本案中将《SCM协定》第32.1款适用于所涉措施时，有必要评估某项措施的设计及结构，是否足以令该措施对补贴做法是“反对的”，有不利影响的，或更具体地说是有阻碍作用的，或足以创造出一种终止该补贴做法的激励机制。

对于一项措施是否构成第32.1款中的“特别行动”，该案上诉机构设定了如下的标准，只有当补贴构成要素存在时才可以实施的一项措施，才是符合《SCM协定》第32.1款所指补贴的“特别行动”。即该措施必须与倾销或补贴的构成要素不可分割地联系在一起，或与之密切相关。这种联系或关联可能是从措施本身的文本中产生出来的。基于该标准，该上诉机构指出，《2000年持续倾销和补贴抵消法》正是因为其设计和结构而产生了这些效果。而且上诉机构进一步解释说，为了确定该法案是否“反对”……补贴，专家组没有必要也没有意义去审查国内产品和补贴进口产品竞争之间的竞争条件，并评估措施对其间竞争关系的影响。

然而，上诉机构也提出，一项措施不能仅仅因为其有利于或会产生与WTO相一致的权利的实施，就是“反对”一项补贴的。最终，上诉机构裁定，由于《2000

年持续倾销和补贴抵消法》不符合 GATT1994 和《SCM 协定》设定的对补贴的任何针对性措施，因此不符合《SCM 协定》所解释的 GATT1994 条款，也不符合《SCM 协定》第 32.1 款。

二、2007 年日本对韩国进口动态随机存取存储器反补贴税案[①]

Japan – Countervailing Duties on Dynamic Random Access Memories from Korea (WT/DS336/R)

7.351 Regarding Article 19.4 of the SCM Agreement, there is no disagreement between the parties that an investigating authority must establish the existence of subsidization before levying any countervailing duties. This is because Article 19.4 refers explicitly to a subsidy having been "found to exist". The question is whether subsidization must be "found to exist" at the time of imposition, or whether a determination that a subsidy was "found to exist" during some prior period suffices. In our view, the ordinary meaning of the phrase "found to exist" does not resolve this issue. We therefore turn to relevant context for guidance.

7.352 We consider that Article 19.1 provides relevant context for resolving this issue, since it provides that countervailing duties may be imposed once it is established that "subsidized imports are causing injury". In light of the present tense used in this provision, we understand this to mean that countervailing duties may be imposed if subsidized imports, i.e., imports that are presently subsidized, are presently causing injury. This interpretation is entirely consistent with the purpose of countervailing duties, which is to "offset[] any subsidy bestowed directly or indirectly upon the manufacture, production or export of any merchandise". There would be no subsidy to offset, and therefore no basis for imposing countervailing duties, if the imports at the time of duty imposition were not found to be subsidized.

7.353 Japan asserts that a finding of subsidization in respect of a past period of investigation suffices for the imposition of countervailing duties. Japan refers in this regard to Article VI:3 of the GATT 1994, which refers to the subsidy "determined to have been granted, directly or indirectly, on the manufacture, production or export of [the imported] product" (emphasis supplied). Japan also refers to a statement by the panel in US – Lead and Bismuth II that "a countervailing duty may

① Panel Report and Appellate Body Report, Japan–Countervailing Duties on Dynamic Random Access Memories from Korea, WT/DS336 /R, 13 July 2007 and WT/DS336/AB/R, 28 November 2007. 原文脚注省略。

only be imposed on an imported product if it is demonstrated that a (countervailable) subsidy was bestowed directly or indirectly on the manufacture, production or export of that merchandise" (emphasis supplied). While Japan relies on these sources because of their use of the past tense, we do not consider that the use of the past tense is necessarily at odds with a finding that countervailing duties are imposed to offset the injurious effects of present subsidization. This is because the fact that a nonrecurring subsidy was formally bestowed in the past does not necessarily mean that that subsidy does not continue to confer a benefit in the present.

7.354 We note that Article VI of the GATT 1994 was referred to by the panel in EC – Tube or Pipe Fittings when it found, in the context of anti-dumping, that "the point [of anti-dumping duties] is to offset present dumping." Likewise, the Appellate Body found in Mexico – Anti-Dumping Measures on Rice that "the conditions to impose [an anti-dumping duty] are to be assessed with respect to the current situation". In light of the Declaration On Dispute Settlement Pursuant to the Agreement On Implementation of Article VI of the General Agreement on Tariffs and Trade 1994 or Part V of the Agreement on Subsidies and Countervailing Measures, which provides for "the consistent resolution of disputes arising from anti-dumping and countervailing duty measures", it is entirely reasonable and appropriate to interpret Article VI:3 of the GATT 1994, and the provisions of the SCM Agreement, in a way that recognizes that the point of countervailing duties is to offset present subsidization.

7.355 In light of these contextual considerations, we conclude that Article 19.4 of the SCM Agreement provides that countervailing duties may only be imposed if there is present subsidization at the time of duty imposition.

7.356 The obligation to establish present subsidization does not mean that investigating authorities are prevented from establishing the existence of subsidization (and injury and causing) by reference to data taken from a past period of investigation. To the contrary, given the need for investigating authorities to issue questionnaires, collect reliable and verifiable data, process and verify that data, and safeguard the due process rights of interested parties, investigating authorities have no choice but to establish the existence of subsidization (and injury) on the basis of past periods of investigation. Thus, countervailing duties may be imposed on the basis of the investigating authority's review of a past period of investigation. We are not suggesting that an investigating authority is somehow required to conduct a new investigation at the time of imposition, in order to confirm the continued existence of the subsidization found to exist during the period of investigation. That would defeat the very purpose of using periods of investigation in the first place.

7.357 However, the use of a past period of investigation does not negate the need for an investigating authority to be satisfied that there is present subsidization. Rather, the historical data from the period of investigation "is being used to draw conclusions about the current situation," "[b]ecause the conditions to impose [a duty] are to be assessed with respect to the current situation". In this sense, the situation during the period of investigation is used as a proxy for the situation pertaining "current[ly]", at the time of imposition. In the case of non-recurring subsidies, if the review of the period of investigation indicates that the subsidy will no longer exist at the time of imposition, the existence of subsidization during the period of investigation will not suffice to demonstrate "current" subsidization at the time of imposition.

7.358 In the present case, the JIA used a past period of investigation to establish the existence of subsidization. That period of investigation covered the year 2003. The JIA's determination of subsidization in 2003 was made based on an allocation of the benefit conferred by certain of the nonrecurring subsidies provided by the October 2001 restructuring from 2001 to 2005. If the JIA had imposed countervailing duties in 2004, or 2005, its determination in respect of the period of investigation would have established that there was "current[ly]" subsidization in either of those two years, as benefit from those subsidies was still being conferred in those years. This is because, in investigating the period of investigation, the JIA had allocated the benefit of 2001 subsidies over the period 2001 to 2005. Once the JIA sought to impose countervailing duties in 2006, however, its finding of subsidization in respect of those subsidies for the period of investigation no longer demonstrated that there was "current[ly]" subsidization. This is because one important element of the JIA's determination in respect of the period of investigation was that certain of the 2001 subsidies needed to be allocated, and would no longer confer any benefit in 2006.

7.359 Japan denies that, in analyzing the period of investigation, the JIA made any finding regarding the existence of subsidization in 2006. In particular, Japan denies that the JIA had fully allocated the benefit from certain non-recurring subsidies over the period 2001 to 2005. Japan asserts that the JIA determined that the amount of the October 2001 subsidy to be allocated to the period of investigation was one-fifth of the originally granted amount of the non-recurring subsidy, and nothing more.

7.360 On our review of the JIA's determination, we do not think that it is correct to say that the JIA did not find that the subsidy would be of a certain amount, each year, for five years. We note that the JIA allocated the benefit conferred by certain of the non-recurring subsidies provided by the October 2001 restructuring using the formula set forth in section 2.3.2.2.2 of Annex 1 (Essential Facts). One of the integers in that formula is "n", which corresponds to "the useful life" of the subsidized production facilities. The JIA had determined that the duration of "n" should be five years, in accordance with certain provisions of Korean tax law. In our view, the use of a five-year allocation period is a finding (even if only implicit) that the benefit will expire after a period of five years. The JIA's determination does not suggest that there might continue to be a subsidy after the period over which the benefit conferred by that (non-recurring) subsidy has expired.

4. Conclusion

7.361 In light of the above considerations, and having regard to the JIA's decision to allocate the benefit conferred by certain of the non-recurring subsidies resulting from the October 2001 restructuring from 2001 to 2005, we find that Japan imposed countervailing duties in 2006 on imports which the JIA itself had found were not subsidized at the time of imposition. Accordingly, in respect of those non-recurring subsidies whose benefit was allocated using the abovementioned Formula 2, we conclude that Japan levied countervailing duties "in excess of the amount of the subsidy found to exist", contrary to Article 19.4 of the SCM Agreement.

Japan – Countervailing Duties on Dynamic Random Access Memories from Korea (WT/DS336/AB/R)

205. Japan asserts that the Panel's interpretation of Article 19.4 effectively requires that an investigating authority update its finding of subsidization at the time of imposition of the duty. In Japan's view, a finding of subsidization in respect of a past period of investigation suffices for the imposition of countervailing duties.

206. Korea insists that it "never claimed that the JIA was required to update its decision based on more recent information." Instead, Korea argues that, by allocating benefit conferred by the October 2001 Restructuring to the years 2001 through 2005, the JIA itself had found that no benefit would be conferred in 2006, because that year "would be outside the five-year life of the subsidy". Korea suggests that duties could not be imposed after that time since, by the JIA's own logic, there would no longer be any subsidy left to countervail.

207. As we see it, this issue relates to the question of whether countervailing duties can be imposed, in the case of non-recurring subsidies, when the determination made by the investigating authority indicates that the subsidy will no longer exist at the time of imposition.

208. We begin our analysis by considering the text of Article 19.4 of the SCM Agreement:

...

209. In our view, Japan misreads the Panel Report when it alleges that the Panel interpreted Article 19.4 to require that an investigating authority update its finding of subsidization and show that there is subsidization at the time of imposition of the countervailing duty. On the contrary, the Panel explicitly said that it was "not suggesting that an investigating authority [was] somehow

required to conduct a new investigation at the time of imposition, in order to confirm the continued existence of the subsidization found to exist during the period of investigation. That will defeat the very purpose of using periods of investigation in the first place."

210. By its terms, Article 19.4 refers to a subsidy "found to exist". We see no requirement in Article 19.4 for an investigating authority to conduct a new investigation or to "update" the determination at the time of imposition of a countervailing duty in order to confirm the continued existence of the subsidy. However, in the case of a non-recurring subsidy, a countervailing duty cannot be imposed if the investigating authority has made a finding in the course of its investigation as to the duration of the subsidy and, according to that finding, the subsidy is no longer in existence at the time that the Member makes a final determination to impose a countervailing duty. This is because, in such a situation, the countervailing duty, if imposed, would be in excess of the amount of subsidy found to exist, contrary to the provisions of Article 19.4.

211. In the light of the above, we do not find fault with the Panel's interpretation of Article 19.4 of the SCM Agreement.

【本案评析】

以上案例节选自2007年日本对韩国进口动态随机存取存储器反补贴税案专家组和上诉机构报告。该案在适用《SCM协定》第19.4款时涉及的一个问题是，补贴是否必须如第19.4款所述在征收补贴税时"被认定存在"，还是在之前就已经"被认定存在"就足够了。该案专家组根据上下文解释认为，只有在征税时有补贴存在的情况下，才可征收反补贴税。但该案专家组也指出，这样的解释并不排除调查主管机关依赖之前数据的可能性。专家组提出，调查期间的情况可以作为征收时主要情况的代表。然而，就非经常性补贴而言，如果对调查期限的复审表明在征税时补贴将不再存在，则调查期间存在补贴这一事实将不足以证明在征收反补贴税时"正在"补贴。

该案上诉机构同意专家组对第19.4款的解释，同时也指出，第19.4款没有要求调查主管机关在征收反补贴税时去执行新的调查或"更新"裁定，以确认补贴的持续存在。然而，对于非经常性的补贴，如调查主管机关在调查期间就补贴是否持续已经作出裁定，并且根据该裁定，该成员方在作出征收反补贴税最终裁定时补贴已不复存在，则反补贴税不应被征收。这是因为，如果在这种情况下征收反补贴税，将超出"被认定存在"的补贴的数额，从而违反了第19.4款的规定。

三、2011 年美国对中国某些进口产品实施“双反”措施争端案①

United States – Definitive Anti-Dumping and Countervailing Duties on Certain Products from China
(WT/DS379/AB/R)

541. Before turning to the specific issues on appeal, we consider it useful to outline the concept of “double remedies” at issue in this dispute. In essence, “double remedies” may arise when both countervailing duties and anti-dumping duties are imposed on the same imported products. The term “double remedies” does not, however, refer simply to the fact that both an anti-dumping and a countervailing duty are imposed on the same product. Rather, as explained below, “double remedies”, also referred to as “double counting”, refers to circumstances in which the simultaneous application of anti-dumping and countervailing duties on the same imported products results, at least to some extent, in the offsetting of the same subsidization twice. “Double remedies” are “likely” to occur in cases where an NME methodology is used to calculate the margin of dumping.

542. A more detailed explanation of how and why double remedies may occur is set out in paragraphs 14.67 through 14.75 of the Panel Report. We recap the main points here. When investigating authorities calculate a dumping margin in an anti-dumping investigation involving a product from an NME, they compare the export price to a normal value that is calculated based on surrogate costs or prices from a third country. Because prices and costs in the NME are considered unreliable, prices, or, more commonly, costs of production, in a market economy are used as the basis for calculating normal value. In the dumping margin calculation, investigating authorities compare the product’s constructed normal value (not reflecting the amount of any subsidy received by the producer) with the product’s actual export price (which, when subsidies have been received by the producer, is presumably lower than it would otherwise have been). The resulting dumping margin is thus based on an asymmetric comparison and is generally higher than would otherwise be the case.

543. As the Panel explained, the dumping margin calculated under an NME methodology “reflects not only price discrimination by the investigated producer between the domestic and

① Appellate Body Report, United States–Definitive Anti-Dumping and Countervailing Duties on Certain Products from China, WT/DS379/AB/R, 11 March 2011 . 原文脚注省略。

export markets ('dumping')", but also "economic distortions that affect the producer's costs of production", including specific subsidies to the investigated producer of the relevant product in respect of that product. An anti-dumping duty calculated based on an NME methodology may, therefore, "remedy" or "offset" a domestic subsidy, to the extent that such subsidy has contributed to a lowering of the export price. Put differently, the subsidization is "counted" within the overall dumping margin. When a countervailing duty is levied against the same imports, the same domestic subsidy is also "counted" in the calculation of the rate of subsidization and, therefore, the resulting countervailing duty offsets the same subsidy a second time. Accordingly, the concurrent imposition of an anti-dumping duty calculated based on an NME methodology, and a countervailing duty may result in a subsidy being offset more than once, that is, in a double remedy. Double remedies may also arise in the context of domestic subsidies granted within market economies when anti-dumping and countervailing duties are concurrently imposed on the same products and an unsubsidized, constructed, or third country normal value is used in the anti-dumping investigation.

544. The Panel understood the United States to have accepted the principle that double remedies may result from the concurrent imposition, on the same product, of countervailing duties and anti-dumping duties calculated using an NME methodology. The United States nevertheless argued that the existence of a double remedy depends on whether the subsidy leads to a reduction in the export price in any given instance, and contended that it cannot be presumed that domestic subsidies lower export prices pro rata, or one-for-one. The Panel was of the view that it would "be a rare case in which a subsidy ... has no effect at all on either the producer's costs of production or ... export prices." In any event, the Panel considered that the answer to the question of "whether a complete double remedy necessarily results from all instances of concurrent imposition of anti-dumping duties calculated under an NME methodology and of countervailing duties" would not "invalidate the general proposition that at least some double remedy will likely arise from the concurrent imposition of countervailing duties and anti-dumping duties calculated under an NME methodology."

...

554. We continue our consideration of the meaning of the term "appropriate amounts" in its context, by turning to other paragraphs of Article 19 of the SCM Agreement. We observe, in this regard, that in interpreting "appropriate amounts" in Article 19.3, the Panel appears to have ascribed great significance to Article 19.4 of the SCM Agreement, which provides that "[n]o countervailing duty shall be levied on any imported product in excess of the amount of the subsidy found to exist, calculated in terms of subsidization per unit of the subsidized and exported

product." Article 19.4 thus places a quantitative ceiling on the amount of a countervailing duty, which may not exceed the amount of the subsidization.

555. The Panel's finding that countervailing duties are collected "in the appropriate amounts insofar as the amount collected does not exceed the amount of subsidy found to exist" points to Article 19.4 as the key determinant of what is an "appropriate" amount, for purposes of Article 19.3. We share the Panel's view that Article 19.4 provides context relevant to the interpretation of Article 19.3. Yet, we are not persuaded, as the Panel seems to have been, that Article 19.4, alone, defines when the amount of duty is "appropriate". Indeed, if any amount of countervailing duty that does not exceed the amount of the subsidy is an "appropriate" amount within the meaning of Article 19.3, then the requirement in Article 19.3 would be rendered redundant, as Article 19.4 already prescribes that duties not be levied in excess of the amount of the subsidy found to exist.

556. Thus, while we agree that Article 19.4 informs Article 19.3, we do not see any indication that Article 19.4 exhausts the universe according to which "appropriateness" is to be gauged. Article 19.4 makes clear that the amount that could be "appropriate" cannot be more than the amount of the subsidy. However, Article 19.4 neither requires that the amount of countervailing duties equal the full amount of the subsidy found to exist, nor bears upon the question of whether there may be circumstances in which the "appropriate amount" of a countervailing duty will be an amount less than the full amount of the subsidy found to exist.

557. It is, rather, Article 19.2 of the SCM Agreement that appears more relevant to this question. While expressly leaving to the importing Member's investigating authorities the decision as to whether the amount of the countervailing duty to be imposed shall be the full amount of the subsidy or less, Article 19.2 nevertheless states that it is "desirable" that "the duty should be less than the total amount of the subsidy if such lesser duty would be adequate to remove the injury". Article 19.2 thus encourages such authorities to link the actual amount of the countervailing duty to the injury to be removed.

558. Moreover, once a causal link between the subsidized imports and injury has been demonstrated, the imposition and levying of countervailing duties are not hermetically isolated from any consideration related to injury. In addition to Article 19.2, a link between the amount of the countervailing duty and the injury that the subsidized imports are found to be causing is reflected in Article 19.3 itself, which provides that a "countervailing duty shall be levied, in the appropriate amounts in each case ... on imports of such product ... found to be subsidized and causing injury" (emphasis added). Other provisions of the SCM Agreement also link the countervailing duty to the injury that the subsidized imports are found to be causing. Article 19.1 allows for the imposition of countervailing duties when subsidized imports "are causing injury".

The use of the present tense in this provision suggests that injury is a continuing prerequisite for the imposition and levying of countervailing duties. This is confirmed by Article 21.1 that states that "[a] countervailing duty shall remain in force only as long as and to the extent necessary to counteract subsidization which is causing injury."

...

580. In the present dispute, having reviewed Article 19.3 of the SCM Agreement and its relevant context559, we do not consider it necessary to confirm the interpretation of Article 19.3 of the SCM Agreement by relying on supplementary means of interpretation, such as the circumstances of conclusion of the treaty. In any event, we are not persuaded that a provision that explicitly addressed the issue of the concurrent imposition of anti-dumping and countervailing duties in respect of imports from NMEs, clearly supports an interpretation of Articles 19.3 and 19.4 of the SCM Agreement "as not addressing or encompassing the question of the permissibility of double remedies".

581. In particular, we are not persuaded that the existence in a predecessor agreement of a provision prohibiting the concurrent imposition of anti-dumping and countervailing duties to imports from NMEs allows an interpreter to conclude, a contrario, that, in the SCM Agreement, Members intended to allow double remedies. We have already cautioned, in respect of Article VI:5 of the GATT 1994, against mechanistic a contrario reasoning, and recalled that "omissions in different contexts may have different meanings, and omission, in and of itself, is not necessarily dispositive". Article 15 of the Tokyo Round Subsidies Code does more than merely prohibit double remedies, in that it prohibits the concurrent application of anti-dumping and countervailing duties, regardless of whether they offset the same situation of subsidization. In the light of this, the absence of a provision like Article 15 of the Tokyo Round Subsidies Code in the SCM Agreement cannot be interpreted as indicating that Members intended to exclude from the scope of the SCM Agreement a different and narrower obligation, such as a prohibition on double remedies.

582. In sum, based on all of the above, we consider that the Panel erred in its interpretation of Article 19.3 of the SCM Agreement and failed to give meaning and effect to all the terms of that provision. Under Article 19.3 of the SCM Agreement, the appropriateness of the amount of countervailing duties cannot be determined without having regard to anti-dumping duties imposed on the same product to offset the same subsidization. The amount of a countervailing duty cannot be "appropriate" in situations where that duty represents the full amount of the subsidy and where anti-dumping duties, calculated at least to some extent on the basis of the same subsidization, are imposed concurrently to remove the same injury to the domestic industry. Dumping margins calculated based on an NME methodology are, for the reasons explained above,

likely to include some component that is attributable to subsidization.

583. We, therefore, reverse the Panel's interpretation of Article 19.3 and, in particular, its findings that "the imposition of anti-dumping duties calculated under an NME methodology has no impact on whether the amount of the concurrent countervailing duty collected is 'appropriate' or not", and that Article 19.3 of the SCM Agreement does not address the issue of double remedies. We find instead that the imposition of double remedies, that is, the offsetting of the same subsidization twice by the concurrent imposition of anti-dumping duties calculated on the basis of an NME methodology and countervailing duties, is inconsistent with Article 19.3 of the SCM Agreement.

【本案评析】

以上案例节选自2011年美国对中国某些进口产品实施“双反”措施争端案。该案涉及“双反”实施的“双重计算”或“双重补救”问题，即对来自非市场经济国家的同一进口产品，因其被指控同一损害，而根据《反倾销协定》和《SCM协定》同时征税的情况。该案上诉机构认为《SCM协定》第19.3款与“双重补救”问题有关，因为根据第19.3款的规定，在不考虑对同一产品征收反倾销税以抵消同一补贴的情况下，不能确定反补贴税额的适当性。上诉机构指出，如果反补贴税代表的是全部补贴量，并且至少在一定程度上基于同一补贴计算的反倾销税也被同时征收来消除对国内产业的相同损害，则此种情况下所征收的反补贴税额将是不“适当的”。因此，采用非市场经济方法基础上计算出来的倾销幅度，可能也会包括可以归因于补贴的那一部分。上诉机构最后裁定，双重补救的做法，即以基于非市场经济方法计算的反倾销税和反补贴税的同时征收，两次抵消同一补贴，不符合《SCM协定》第19.3款的规定。

四、中国光伏企业反补贴调查案

（一）案例回顾

2011年应美国光伏企业Solar World申请，美国商务部对中国光伏企业发起了反倾销和反补贴调查。2012年10月，美国商务部公布终裁结果，决定对中国输美太阳能电池征收14.78%至15.97%的反补贴税和18.32%至249.96%

的反倾销税。2018 年，美国国际贸易法院（以下简称“美国法院”）作出中国光伏企业阿特斯和天合光能起诉美国商务部关于光伏产品反补贴第三轮行政复审终裁的判决。美国法院在买方信贷、低价提供铝边框项目的专项性、低价提供铝边框和光伏玻璃项目的外部基准选择、低价提供多晶硅料项目的外部基准选择和低价提供电力专项性的 5 个诉点上支持了原告阿特斯和天合光能，判决美国商务部重新做出反补贴第三轮复审终裁。本次美国法院判决中，中国光伏企业起诉针对的是美国商务部对中国光伏电池反补贴调查第三轮年度复审终裁。该案第三轮年度复审于 2016 年 2 月发起，阿特斯和天合光能是两家全球领先的光伏产品制造企业，被选为强制应诉企业。2017 年 7 月，美国商务部公布终裁结果，中国企业的税率为 17.14% 至 18.16%。此后，阿特斯与天合光能分别于 2017 年 8 月 3 日和 8 月 5 日向美国法院起诉，将反补贴第三轮复审终裁中美国商务部在买方信贷、原材料外部基准、原材料项目的专项性等 8 个补贴认定问题上存在违规告到美国法院。随后，上海比亚迪和 SolarWorld 也分别起诉。2017 年 9 月，美国法院决定合并审理上述诉讼案件。最终，经过一年零四个月的审理，美国法院在 5 个关键争议问题上判决中国企业胜诉，

（二）本案争议点

本案争议点之一“买方信贷”项目，该项目是美国对华反补贴调查的传统老项目，仅此一项在本案中占到的所谓补贴率就高达 5.46%。而中国企业在买方信贷上并未接受政府补贴。在光伏案中，起诉方指控中国进出口银行对中国出口企业提供买方信贷。中国应诉企业向美国商务部提交了其美国客户的声明，证明未享受买方信贷项目。但是，美国商务部在要求中国政府提交进出口银行内部文件未果的情况下，无视已经获得的证据，以中国政府不配合为理由对该项目适用了不利可得事实。《美国关税法》第 776 节（d）规定，在适用不利可得事实规则时，美国商务部可以适用之前涉及相同国家的反补贴调查当中类似补贴项目所裁定的补贴率，该项目下 5.46% 的税率是来源于光伏第一轮年度复审中河北光为绿色新能源股份有限公司在政策性贷款项目下被认定的补贴率。

美国法院在判决中认为，美国商务部需要解释中国政府没有配合提供信息的种类才导致适用不利可获得事实，以及什么事实或信息让美国商务部作出不利推定认为应诉企业享受买方信贷项目。此外，美国商务部需要解释为什么应诉企业提供的其美国客户未使用该项目的声明不可以进行核查，如果美国商务部重审认为美国客户声明可以进行核查，那么其必须在这样做之后才能作出终裁认定。尽管美国法院给了美国商务部在重新裁定中对该问题进行解释的机会，但是还是对美国商务部在终裁中的分析方法进行了直接的批驳。也就是说，美国商务部需要在重新终裁中做更充分的分析，而不是简单地重复其在对中国的反补贴调查中关于该项目一贯采用的理由。

另外，本案的争议点之二是在原材料采购的专项性以及电力采购的专项性问题。在反补贴调查中，调查机关有义务证明某项获益是否属对授予机关管辖范围内的企业或产业的专项性补贴。美国商务部在其终裁中认为，根据中国政府的答卷共有六个行业使用了铝边框，即（1）建筑制造业；（2）运输业；（3）电气行业；（4）机器设备行业；（5）耐用消费品行业；及（6）其他行业，因此以接受补贴的行业只有六个而认为该项目具有专项性。美国法院判决认为，DOC需要解释为什么对范围如此广泛的行业进行补贴能得出是具有专项性的结论，而不是普遍性的获益。美国法院将该问题发回美国商务部重审，要求严格分析认定专项性的方法问题。在对电力采购项目的专项性问题上，美国商务部又以中国政府拒绝提供部分信息为由适用不利可获得事实，而裁定该项目具有专项性。美国法院在裁决中写道："不利可获得事实并不是美国商务部可以跳过对案卷资料的分析而直接得到不利结果的魔术字眼。"美国法院判决要求，美国商务部必须严格分析案卷资料，并解释如何通过不利事实得到电力采购项目具有专项性的结论。

【本案评析】

以上案例涉及在年度复审调查期内中国对美光伏产品18亿美元出口问题，如果美国商务部按照法院判决执行，中国光伏企业将获得巨额退税。不仅如此，

此次判决否定了美国商务部对中国反补贴实践中的一些普遍的违规做法，因此不仅是对光伏产品反补贴调查个案取得的突破性胜利，并且对美国目前对中国产品反补贴调查的普遍实践具有重要的积极影响。本案最大的胜诉点在于美国国商务部在对华反补贴实践中惯用的政策性做法受到了的美国司法审查的制约。美国商务部为了提高中国企业的反补贴税率，政策性地以中国某些部门不提供信息为理由，适用不利可获得事实，人为地大幅提高中国企业的反补贴率。虽然光伏产品双反案在反倾销税率上曾获突破，但是反补贴税率水平一直处于较高水平，根本原因是美国商务部政策性地基于不利可获得事实，通过买方信贷和低价提供生产要素项目虚增了反补贴税率。可以说，在行政调查程序中，中国光伏企业已经穷尽了所有的抗辩努力，而寻求美国国内司法救济，将美国商务部的不公正裁决结果告到美国法院是美国国内法上的最终手段。

【延伸阅读】

一、相关典型案例

1.China—Countervailing and Anti-Dumping Duties on Grain Oriented Flat-rolled Electrical Steel from the United States（WT/DS414）

2.United States—Preliminary Determinations with Respect to Certain Softwood Lumber from Canada（WT/DS236）

3.United States—Final Countervailing Duty Determination with respect to certain Softwood Lumber from Canada（WT/DS257）

4.United States—Subsidies on Upland Cotton（WT/DS267）

5.United States—Countervailing Duty Investigation on Dynamic Random Access Memory Semiconductors (DRAMS) from Korea(WT/DS296)

6.United States—Countervailing Measures on Certain Hot-Rolled Carbon Steel Flat Products from India(WT/DS436)

7.United States—Imposition of Countervailing Duties on Certain Hot-Rolled Lead and Bismuth Carbon Steel Products Originating in the United Kingdom(WT/DS138)

8.European Communities—Measures Affecting Trade in Commercial Vessels(WT/DS301)

二、相关学术论著

1. 王贵国:《世界贸易组织法》,法律出版社 2003 年版。

2.Kostantinos Adamantopoulos, *EU Anti-subsidy Law and Practice,* Sweet & Maxwell, 2007.

3. International Trade Centre, *Business Guide to Trade Remedies in the European Community: Anti-dumping, Anti-subsidy and Safeguards Legislation, Practices and Procedures,* International Trade Centre UNCTAD/WTO,2005.

三、相关网络资源

1. https://www.wto.org/english/tratop_e/scm_e/scm_e.htm.

2. http://ec.europa.eu/trade/policy/accessing-markets/trade-defence/actions-against-imports-into-the-eu/anti-subsidy/.

3. https://www.usitc.gov/trade_remedy/731_ad_701_cvd/investigations/active/index.htm.

4. http://cacs.mofcom.gov.cn/.

5. https://enforcement.trade.gov/sunset/index.html.

第四节　WTO 多边反补贴争端解决程序

【知识背景 / 学习要点】

虽然如前所述，WTO 多边争端解决机制（DSU）的相关规定，也适用于与补贴和反补贴措施有关的磋商和争端解决，但是《SCM 协定》第 4 条和第 7 条也对禁止性补贴和可诉性补贴分别规定了加速和特定救济程序，而且相较于 DSU 规定的程序,《SCM 协定》的反补贴程序期限规定更短。

一、禁止性补贴的多边争端解决程序

《SCM 协定》第 4 条规定了禁止性补贴，包括出口补贴和进口替代补贴的多边补救程序规则。根据第 4.1 款的规定，只要一成员有理由认为另一成员正在给予或维持一项禁止性补贴，该成员即可请求与该另一成员进行磋商。这种措施请求应包括“列出有关所涉补贴的存在和性质的可获得的证据”。[①] 若磋商未能解决争端，则可将争端提交争端解决专家组，然后再提交上诉机构进行裁决。[②]

《SCM 协定》第 4 条规定的若干“特别或附加规则和程序”与 DSU 规则和程序之间最显著的区别在于时间要求的不同，例如一般的争端专家组程序的时限是从专家组成立之日起 6 个月，[③] 而根据《SCM 协定》第 4 条的规定，涉及禁止性补贴的专家组程序期限为 3 个月。对比可知，《SCM 协定》第 4 条规定的时限是 DSU 规定的一半，[④] 而且在发生冲突时优先于 DSU 规则适用。另外，《SCM 协定》第 4 条还规定，专家组设立后可就所涉措施是否属禁止性补贴请求“常设专家小组”（《SCM 协定》中称“PGE”）予以协助，[⑤]PGE 的确定对专家组具有约束力。[⑥]

如果专家组认定一项措施为禁止性补贴，《SCM 协定》第 4.7 款规定，专家组应建议补贴成员毫不迟延地撤销其补贴。而且，专家组应在其建议中规定撤销的期限。专家组和上诉机构曾多次强调，在其具体规定的撤销期限内，必须毫不迟延地撤销禁止性补贴。[⑦] 正如在 2000 年加拿大诉巴西航空器出口融资

① 参见《SCM 协定》第 4.2 款。

② 包括磋商和裁决的主要规则适用 DSU 的规定。

③ 参见 DSU 第 12.8 款。

④ 但是成员方可以且一般也会同意延长这些特殊时间安排。但是，如果当申请方提出的主张既包括在《SCM 协定》也涉及其他 WTO 协定的，则《SCM 协定》中规定的较短时限不予适用。参见《SCM 协定》第 4.12 款。

⑤ “常设专家小组”根据《SCM 协定》第 24 条的规定设立。

⑥ 参见《SCM 协定》第 4.5 款。

⑦ 参见Appellate Body Report, United States-Tax Treatment for “Foreign Sales Corporations”-Second Recourse to Article 21.5 of the DSU by the European Communities, WT/DS108/AB/RW2, 14 March 2006, para. 82.

项目 DSU 第 21.5 条争端案上诉机构澄清的那样，撤销禁止性补贴涉及对补贴的撤销。①

一般情况下，对违反 WTO 法律行为的救济只是针对以后是否会发生的情况，但是 2000 年美国诉澳大利亚汽车皮革生产和出口补贴 DSU 第 21.5 条争端案中，原申诉方美国并没有提出偿还出口补贴的请求，但是该案专家组认为，第 4.7 款规定的撤销禁止性补贴的义务要求已经获得非经常性禁止性补贴的公司要将补贴再次偿还给提供补贴的成员方。专家组最终裁定，只有偿还所收到的补贴，才能满足撤销禁止性补贴的义务。其理由是认为，专家组有责任解释“撤销补贴”，使之具有实际意义。如果裁定“撤销补贴”一词不包括偿还，将引起涉及救济效力的严重问题，即在过去涉及一次性支付补贴的禁止性补贴案例中，这些补贴的保留并不取决于未来的出口业绩。②该专家组的这一裁决因其追溯性而受到 WTO 成员的强烈批评。③迄今为止，没有其他的专家组作出类似的裁决。④

在禁止性补贴的争端解决程序中，对于专家组指定了禁止性补贴撤销期限的，成员方应按照《SCM 协定》第 4.7 款的要求“毫不迟延地撤销”。例如，专家组在 2005 年欧盟诉韩国造船业补贴争端案中提出，一方面考虑到为执行我们的建议可能需要的程序，另一方面又考虑到韩国“毫不迟延地”撤销补贴的要求，因此建议韩国在90日内撤销其单独的APRG和PSL补贴。⑤到目前为止，

① 参见Appellate Body Report, Brazil–Export Financing Programme for Aircraft–Recourse by Canada to Article 21.5 of the DSU, WT/DS46/AB/R, 20 August 1999, para. 45.

② 参见Panel Report, Australia–Subsidies Provided to Producers and Exporters of Automotive Leather–Recourse to Article 21.5 of the DSU by the United States, WT/DS126/R, 25 May 1999,para. 6.35.

③ 参见 Dispute Settlement Body, *Minutes of the DSB Meeting of 11 February 2000*, WT/DSB/M/75.

④ 2000 年巴西诉加拿大影响民用飞机出口措施 DSU 第 21.5 条争端案和 2000 年加拿大诉巴西航空器出口融资项目 DSU 第 21.5 条争端案中，都没有对补贴的偿还问题作出裁决，因为申诉方没有要求偿还补贴，专家组也认为其调查结果应限于当事方之间分歧的范围。参见 Panel Report, Canada-Measures Affecting the Export of Civilian Aircraft–Recourse by Brazil to Article 21.5 of the DSU, WT/DS70/R, para. 5.48 和 Panel Report, Brazil–Export Financing Programme for Aircraft–Recourse by Canada to Article 21.5 of the DSU, WT/DS46/RW.

⑤ 参见 Panel Report, Korea–Measures Affecting Trade in Commercial Vessels, WT/DS273/R, 11 April 2005, para. 8.5.

专家组指定的撤销禁止性补贴的期限一般为3个月时间。但在2000年欧盟诉美国外国销售公司的税收待遇争端案专家组指定了1年以上的期限，目的是以便美国能够通过必要的财政立法。[①]

对于禁止性补贴指定的撤销期限是否可以延长，或者有无例外，很多争端案例表明，一般是不可以的。在2000年巴西航空器出口融资项目DSU第21.5条争端案中，上诉机构指出，“毫不迟延撤销禁止性补贴的义务”不受成员方其本身根据国内法可能承担的合同义务的影响。[②]同样，在2002年欧盟诉美国外国销售公司的税收待遇DSU第21.5条争端案中，上诉机构也裁定，为保护私人当事方的合同利益或者为确保向新措施制度有序地过渡，延长第4.7款规定的撤销期限“没有依据”。上诉机构指出，如果在DSU第21.5条程序中，为遵守原程序中的《SCM协定》第4.7款建议而采取的措施，因为保留了原来禁止性补贴的全部或部分或者因为其用另一种禁止性补贴取代了这种补贴，没有实现完全撤销禁止性补贴，那么执行成员方对完全撤销禁止性补贴仍有义务。[③]

如果在专家组规定的期限内没有按照建议撤销禁止性补贴，DSB必须应原申诉人的请求，并以反向协商一致，可以根据《SCM协定》第4.10款的规定，授权原申诉人采取“适当的反措施”。在禁止性补贴争端中，这些“适当的反措施”取代了DSU规定的中止减让或其他义务，即报复措施，后者主要是应对除《SCM协定》外的其他协定在WTO争端中未予执行的情况。值得注意的是“适当的反措施”与“报复措施”实施效果不同，“适当的反措施”的水平可以是禁止性补贴数额，而不是任何贸易效果或由其带来的利益丧失或者减损的水平。

---

① 参见 Panel Report, United States–Tax Treatment for ‘Foreign Sales Corporations’, WT/DS108/RW, para. 8.8.

② Appellate Body Report, Brazil–Export Financing Programme for Aircraft–Recourse by Canada to Article 21.5 of the DSU, WT/DS46/AB/RW, paras. 45-46.

③ 参见 Appellate Body Report, United States–Tax Treatment for ‘Foreign Sales Corporations’–Recourse to Article 21.5 of the DSU by the European Communities, WT/DS108/AB/RW, 29 January 2002, paras. 82 and 229-230.

二、可诉性补贴的多边争端解决程序

如果专家组认定补贴对另一成员的利益造成不利影响（无论是国内产业损害、利益丧失或减损，还是严重侵害利益），那么给予或维持该补贴的成员应采取适当步骤以消除不利影响或撤销该补贴。[①]《SCM 协定》第 7 条规定了可诉性补贴的多边争端解决程序。与禁止性补贴一样，可诉性补贴的多边争端解决程序也不同于 DSU 中的规定，相关时间规定比 DSU 的短。例如，专家组程序的时限为 4 个月。[②] 但是，相较于禁止性补贴，可诉性补贴的多边争端解决程序时限较长且没有“常设专家小组”（PGE）。

在 2005 年巴西诉美国陆地棉花补贴案中，上诉机构指出，《SCM 协定》第 7.8 款规定，如果已确定“任何补贴对另一成员的利益产生了不利影响”，那么补贴成员必须“采取适当步骤消除不利影响或撤销补贴”。使用“产生”（resulted in）一词表明，在支付补贴与任何相应的不利影响之间可能存在时间上的滞后。如果在 WTO 争端解决程序中不能对过去支出所依据的已经失效的措施提出挑战，就很难寻求对这种不利影响的救济办法。此外，与 DSU 第 3.7 款和第 19.1 款[③] 相反，《SCM 协定》第 7.8 款对补贴不利影响规定的救济办法是撤销补贴或消除不利影响。如果一项到期的措施将自动排除在专家组的职权范围之外，就不可能通过撤销补贴以外的行动消除不利影响。[④]

补贴成员必须在 DSB 通过报告后的 6 个月内撤销补贴或消除不利影响。如不撤销有争议的补贴或消除其不利影响，补贴成员也可以与申诉成员就赔偿问题达成协议。[⑤] 如果 DSU 第 21.5 条合规程序在报告通过后 6 个月内发现补

---

① 参见《SCM 协定》第 7.8 款。

② 参见《SCM 协定》第 7.5 款。

③ DSB 一旦通过专家组或上诉机构报告，就会“建议和裁定”败诉方采取措施以遵守 WTO 法。如不存在一项相互满意的解决办法，WTO 争端解决机制的首要目标，通常是保证撤销或纠正已被确认为违反 WTO 协定的有关措施。根据 DSU 第 3 条第 7 款和第 19 条第 1 款，DSB 一般建议败诉方使该项措施与所违反的适用协定保持一致，并且并可以就实施建议的方法提出建议。

④ 参见 Appellate Body Report, United States–Subsidies on Upland Cotton, WT/DS267/AB/R, 21 March 2005, para. 273.

⑤ 在此情况下，补偿是使该措施与 WTO 法保持相符的一种替代办法，但 DSU 下不是这样的情况。

贴未被撤销或其不利影响没有消除，或未能就赔偿问题达成协议，那么DSB必须应申诉成员的请求并以反向协商一致意见授权申诉成员采取反措施。这些反措施必须与被给予的补贴的不利影响程度和性质相称。[①]

【案例摘录与评析】

2008年巴西诉美国陆地棉花补贴DSU第21.5条争端案[②]

United States – Subsidies on Upland Cotton – Recourse to Article 21.5 of the DSU by Brazil (WT/DS267/AB/RW)

E. *Whether Marketing Loan and Counter-cyclical Payments Made After 21 September 2005 are Properly within the Scope of These Article 21.5 Proceedings*

233. Brazil and the United States disagree on whether the original panel's findings extend to the marketing loan and counter-cyclical payments programmes, or are limited to the payments made under the programmes. The Panel in these Article 21.5 proceedings concluded that the original panel's findings were addressed to the payments, and not to the programmes themselves. Brazil conditionally appeals this finding, but requests that we address its claim only if we reverse the Panel's finding on the admissibility of Brazil's claim against marketing loan and counter-cyclical payments made after 21 September 2005.

234. We have some difficulty accepting the notion that a subsidy programme and the payments provided under that programme can be assessed separately. While the payments may cause adverse effects, the amount of the payments, beneficiaries, and the terms and conditions of eligibility will be provided in the subsidy programme or legislation authorizing those payments. However, because Brazil has made it clear that its appeal is conditional upon our reversal of the Panel's findings concerning the payments, we begin our analysis by considering the United States' claim that the Panel erred in finding that marketing loan and counter-cyclical payments made after 21 September 2005 are properly within the scope of these Article 21.5 proceedings.

235. In cases like this one, involving a determination that subsidies have resulted in adverse

① 参见《SCM协定》第7.9款。

② Appellate Body Report, United States–Subsidies on Upland Cotton–Recourse to Article 21.5 of the DSU by Brazil, WT/DS267/AB/RW, 2 June 2008. 原文脚注省略。

effects to the interests of another WTO Member, Article 7.8 of the SCM Agreement provides that "the Member granting or maintaining" the subsidy "shall take appropriate steps to remove the adverse effects or shall withdraw the subsidy". Article 7.8 is one of the "special or additional rules and procedures on dispute settlement contained in the covered agreements" that are identified in Article 1.2 and Appendix 2 of the DSU, which prevail over the general DSU rules and procedures to the extent that there is a difference between them. As we see it, Article 7.8 specifies the actions that the respondent Member must take when a subsidy granted or maintained by that Member is found to have resulted in adverse effects to the interests of another Member. This means that, in order to determine whether there is compliance with the DSB's recommendations and rulings in a case involving such actionable subsidies, a panel would have to assess whether the Member concerned has taken one of the actions foreseen in Article 7.8 of the SCM Agreement. We agree, therefore, with the Panel that we must also take into account Article 7.8 of the SCM Agreement in order to determine the proper scope of these Article 21.5 proceedings.

236. Pursuant to Article 7.8, the implementing Member has two options to come into compliance. The implementing Member: (i) shall take appropriate steps to remove the adverse effects; or (ii) shall withdraw the subsidy. The use of the terms "shall take" and "shall withdraw" indicate that compliance with Article 7.8 of the SCM Agreement will usually involve some action by the respondent Member. This affirmative action would be directed at effecting the withdrawal of the subsidy or the removal of its adverse effects. A Member would normally not be able to abstain from taking any action on the assumption that the subsidy will expire or that the adverse effects of the subsidy will dissipate on their own.

237. The question then becomes: With respect to which subsidies must the implementing Member take such action? Such action would certainly be expected with respect to subsidies granted in the past and which may have formed the basis of a panel's determination of present serious prejudice and adverse effects. However, we do not see the obligation in Article 7.8 as being limited to subsidies granted in the past. Article 7.8 expressly refers to a Member "granting or maintaining such subsidy". The verb "maintain" suggests, to us, that the obligation set forth in Article 7.8 is of a continuous nature, extending beyond subsidies granted in the past. This means that, in the case of recurring annual payments, the obligation in Article 7.8 would extend to payments "maintained" by the respondent Member beyond the time period examined by the panel for purposes of determining the existence of serious prejudice, as long as those payments continue to have adverse effects. Otherwise, the adverse effects of subsequent payments would simply replace the adverse effects that the implementing Member was under an obligation to remove. Such a reading of Article 7.8 would not give meaning and effect to the term "maintain",

which is distinct from the term "grant", and has also been included in that Article. Indeed, it would render the term "maintain" redundant. In addition, it would fail to give meaning and effect to the obligation to "take appropriate steps to remove the adverse effects" in Article 7.8, and to the requirement under Article 21.5 to "comply" with the DSB's recommendations and rulings, including the requirement to take the remedial action foreseen in Article 7.8 as a consequence of a finding of adverse effects.

238. Our interpretation of Article 7.8 is consistent with the context provided by Article 4.7 of the SCM Agreement, which applies in cases involving prohibited subsidies. In US – FSC (Article 21.5 – EC II), the Appellate Body stated that, "if, in an Article 21.5 proceeding, a panel finds that the measure taken to comply with the Article 4.7 recommendation made in the original proceedings does not achieve full withdrawal of the prohibited subsidy—either because it leaves the entirety or part of the original prohibited subsidy in place, or because it replaces that subsidy with another subsidy prohibited under the SCM Agreement—the implementing Member continues to be under the obligation to achieve full withdrawal of the subsidy". Similarly, a Member would not comply with the obligation in Article 7.8 to withdraw the subsidy if it leaves an actionable subsidy in place, either entirely or partially, or replaces that subsidy with another actionable subsidy. We recognize that, unlike Article 4.7, Article 7.8 gives Members the option of removing the adverse effects as an alternative to withdrawing the subsidy. The availability of this option is arguably a consequence of the fact that actionable subsidies are not prohibited per se; rather, they are actionable to the extent they cause adverse effects. Nevertheless, the option of removing the adverse effects cannot be read as allowing a Member to continue to cause adverse effects by maintaining the subsidies that were found to have resulted in adverse effects. As observed earlier, if the contrary proposition were accepted, the adverse effects of subsequent subsidies, especially in the case of recurrent subsidies, would simply replace the adverse effects that the implementing Member was required to remove, making the obligation in Article 7.8 to "take appropriate steps to remove the adverse effects" meaningless.

239. Our interpretation of Article 7.8 is also consistent with the approach taken under the SCM Agreement with respect to countervailing duty measures. A determination that the existence of a subsidy causes material injury provides a basis for the prospective application of countervailing duty measures. Thus, even though the basis for a countervailing duty determination is the injury determined to exist in the past, the remedial measures are prospective.

240. The United States submits that "the obligation under Article 7.8 extends only as far as the DSB's recommendations and rulings", and asserts that Article 7.8 cannot modify "the terms of reference or the scope of compliance proceedings under Article 21.5 of the DSU". We

believe the United States misinterprets the relevance of Article 7.8 for interpreting the scope of DSB recommendations and rulings in cases where subsidies are found to cause adverse effects. Article 7.8 informs the meaning and scope of the DSB's recommendations and rulings arising from the original proceedings. In our view, Article 7.8 specifies the actions that the United States had to take in order to comply with the DSB's recommendations and rulings. To the extent a WTO Member fails to comply with the requirement in Article 7.8 that it take steps to remove the adverse effects or withdraw the subsidy, because it maintains the subsidy, it cannot be said to have achieved full compliance with these DSB recommendations and rulings.

241. Brazil and several of the third participants have cautioned that accepting the United States' approach would deny effective relief to WTO Members who successfully demonstrate that subsidies provided by another Member have resulted in adverse effects. The United States, however, rejects the notion that its interpretation would "undermine the effectiveness of Article 7.8" of the SCM Agreement. It asserts that "[d]isallowing Brazil's over-expansive claims in this proceeding would not mean that Members have no remedy to address the adverse effects of a subsidy" because "[n]othing prevents Members from challenging the present adverse effects of past or current payments; the threat of serious prejudice of past, current, or future payments; or present adverse effects or threat of serious prejudice from payment programs 'as such.'"

242. We examine, first, the United States' argument that Brazil could have challenged the programmes "as such". As we indicated above, we have difficulty accepting the notion that payments under a subsidy programme can be assessed separately from the programmes or legislation pursuant to which those payments are made. This is because the terms and conditions, beneficiaries, amounts, and other aspects of a payment will be set in the programme or authorizing legislation, especially in the case of annually recurring payments. The difficulty of divorcing the payments from the programmes, in this case, is evident in the Panel's approach to this issue. Despite finding that only the payments were properly within the scope of the Article 21.5 proceedings, the Panel nevertheless considered that it could not exclude completely from its assessment the programmes under which the payments were provided.

243. Moreover, even if a complainant brings an "as such" challenge to a subsidy programme, it is difficult to see how a panel would assess whether the subsidy has resulted in adverse effects without reviewing the payments actually made under that programme during a past reference period. The United States acknowledges that "serious prejudice, by its nature, is fact-specific and depends on the situation in the market, a situation that may be constantly changing such that the terms and conditions for a subsidy that causes serious prejudice during one time period are not causing serious prejudice for another time period." Thus, we find it difficult to conceive how

an analysis of whether a programme "as such" resulted in adverse effects would differ from an analysis of whether payments under a programme have resulted in such effects.

244. Secondly, the United States asserts that payments made after 21 September 2005 would have been covered by the DSB's recommendations and rulings if Brazil had succeeded in its threat of serious prejudice claim in the original proceedings. The United States notes, in this regard, that the original panel "declined to make any finding of 'threat' of serious prejudice with respect to payments allegedly 'mandated' to be made in MY 2003-2007; and ... declined to make any find[ing] of 'threat' of serious prejudice with respect to the Step 2, marketing loan, and counter-cyclical payment programs themselves (which would have implicated all payments under the programs)." However, a claim of serious prejudice may relate to a different situation than a claim of threat of serious prejudice. A claim of present serious prejudice relates to the existence of prejudice in the past, and present, and that may continue in the future. By contrast, a claim of threat of serious prejudice relates to prejudice that does not yet exist, but is imminent such that it will materialize in the near future. Therefore, a threat of serious prejudice claim does not necessarily capture and provide a remedy with respect to the same scenario as a claim of present serious prejudice. A distinction between injury and threat of injury also exists in the context of countervailing duty measures. Once a determination of present material injury is made, a Member may impose countervailing duties on future imports without any obligation to demonstrate a threat of material injury.

245. Thus, the approach advocated by the United States would have serious implications for a complaining Member's ability to obtain relief against adverse effects of actionable subsidies. Under such an approach, a complaining Member that has demonstrated that subsidies provided by another Member have resulted in adverse effects would obtain relief only with respect to any lingering effects of the subsidies provided during the period examined by the panel. As Australia notes, such panel findings would essentially be declaratory in nature, because there would be no impact on subsidies granted or maintained after the panel made its finding. The complaining Member would have to initiate another dispute to obtain relief with respect to payments made after the period examined by the panel, even if those subsidies are recurring payments or otherwise of the same nature as those found to have resulted in adverse effects. Even if the complaining Member were to succeed in its claims a second time, the subsidizing Member could provide further subsidies after the second panel's ruling, and the complaining Member would have to initiate yet another dispute, and this cycle could continue. As Brazil and several of the third participants have warned, the inability of a complaining Member to obtain relief against subsidies that result in adverse effects to its interests would seriously undermine the disciplines

contained in Articles 5 and 6 of the SCM Agreement.

246. The approach advocated by the United States would not only compromise the effectiveness of the provisions on actionable subsidies in the SCM Agreement, it is also difficult to reconcile with the objectives of the DSU. According to Article 3.3, one of the objectives of the DSU is "the prompt settlement of situations in which a Member considers that any benefits accruing to it directly or indirectly under the covered agreements are being impaired by measures taken by another Member". Article 21.1 further provides that "[p]rompt compliance with recommendations or rulings of the DSB is essential in order to ensure effective resolution of disputes to the benefit of all Members". Requiring a WTO Member to initiate new proceedings to challenge the same type of recurrent subsidies that were found to result in adverse effects, simply because the subsidies were provided subsequent to the original proceedings, does not promote "prompt settlement" nor "prompt compliance". Moreover, the issue before us is one of admissibility. Even if the claim is allowed to proceed in an Article 21.5 proceeding, the complaining Member would still have to establish the existence of adverse effects that allegedly result from the subsidies at issue.

247. It is undisputed that the only action the United States had taken to comply with the DSB's recommendations and rulings concerning serious prejudice, and thereby with its obligations under Article 7.8 of the SCM Agreement, was the repeal of the Step 2 payments programme effective as of 1 August 2006. The United States has not contested that it continues to provide marketing loan and counter-cyclical payments to United States producers of upland cotton and that "the legislative and regulatory provisions governing these ... payments have not been changed". Thus, the question that remained before the Panel was whether the United States had taken "appropriate steps to remove the adverse effects" of the subsidies found to have resulted in adverse effects to the interests of Brazil. In order to respond to that question, it was proper for the Panel to examine the marketing loan and counter-cyclical payments made by the United States after the expiration of the implementation period on 21 September 2005.

248. Accordingly, we agree with the Panel that, "to the extent marketing loan payments and counter-cyclical payments made by the United States after 21 September 2005 are provided under the same conditions and criteria as the marketing loan payments and counter-cyclical payments subject to the original panel's finding of 'present' serious prejudice, they are subject to the obligation of the United States under Article 7.8 of the SCM Agreement to take appropriate steps to remove the adverse effects of the subsidy". We further agree that, as a consequence, Brazil's claim that the United States failed to comply with its obligations under Article 7.8 with respect to those payments was properly within the scope of the Article 21.5 proceedings, because the "claim

pertains to a disagreement between the parties as to the 'existence or consistency with a covered agreement of measures taken to comply' with the recommendations and rulings of the DSB." More precisely, the claim relates to whether the measure taken by the United States achieves full compliance with the DSB's recommendations and rulings as informed by the obligation of the United States under Article 7.8 of the SCM Agreement.

249. For these reasons, we uphold the Panel's finding, in paragraph 9.81 of the Panel Report, that Brazil's claims against marketing loan and counter-cyclical payments made by the United States after 21 September 2005 are properly within the scope of these Article 21.5 proceedings.

【本案评析】

以上案例节选自2008年巴西诉美国陆地棉花补贴DSU第21.5条争端案上诉机构报告。该案上诉机构进一步阐述了根据第7.8款撤销补贴或消除不利影响的相关要求。上诉机构强调,《SCM协定》第7.8款是“在涵盖协定中所载关于争端解决的特殊或附加规则和程序”之一,这一规则和程序与DSU的一般规则和程序的差异是其优先适用。上诉机构指出,根据第7.8款执行成员方有两种选择可供遵守,一是应采取适当步骤消除不利影响,二是应撤销补贴。使用“应采取”和“应撤销”这两个短语表明,遵守《SCM协定》第7.8款通常涉及被诉成员方的一些行动。这一肯定性行动的目的是撤销补贴或消除其不利影响。因此,成员方通常不能在假设补贴到期或补贴的不利影响自行消失的情况下,不采取任何行动。

对于撤销补贴或消除不利影响的具体执行,该案上诉机构裁定,《SCM协定》第7.8款中的义务不限于过去给予的补贴。上诉机构认为,第7.8款明确提及成员方“给予或维持此种补贴”,这就意味着在每年定期支付的情况下,第7.8款中的义务将延伸到被诉成员方在专家组确定是否存在实质性损害的审查以外时间的支付,只要那些支付继续产生不利的影响。否则,后续支付的不利影响只会取代有消除义务的执行成员的不利影响。根据《SCM协定》第7.8款的规定,执行成员方有权选择消除不利影响或者取消补贴。在上诉机构看来,这一选择权可以说是可诉补贴本身不受禁止这一事实的结果。然而,上诉机构也强调,执行成员可以选择消除不利影响而不是撤销补贴,不能被理解为允许成员方通过维持已发现产生不利影响的补贴而继续造成不利影响。

【延伸阅读】

一、相关典型案例

1. Brazil—Export Financing Programme for Aircraft(WT/DS46)

2. China—Countervailing and Anti-Dumping Duties on Grain Oriented Flat-rolled Electrical Steel from the United States（WT/DS414）

3. Canada—Measures Affecting the Export of Civilian Aircraft（WT/DS70）

4. European Communities—Measures Affecting Trade in Commercial Vessels(WT/DS301)

5. United States—Countervailing Duty Investigation on Dynamic Random Access Memory Semiconductors (DRAMS) from Korea(WT/DS296)

6. United States—Countervailing Measures on Certain Hot-Rolled Carbon Steel Flat Products from India (WT/DS436)

7. United States—Imposition of Countervailing Duties on Certain Hot-Rolled Lead and Bismuth Carbon Steel Products Originating in the United Kingdom(WT/DS138)

8. United States—Tax Treatment for "Foreign Sales Corporations" - Second Recourse to Article 21.5 of the DSU by the European Communities(WT/DS108)

二、相关学术论著

1. 赵维田:《世界贸易组织（WTO）的法律制度》,吉林人民出版社 2000 年版。

2. 杨国华:《WTO 的理念》,厦门大学出版社 2012 年版。

3. Peter Van den Bossche, *The Law and Policy of the World Trade Organization: Text, Cases and Materials,* Cambridge University Press, 2017.

4. Andrew T. Guzman and Joost H.B. Pauwelyn, *International Trade Law,* Aspen Publishers, 2009.

三、相关网络资源

1. https://www.wto.org/english/tratop_e/scm_e/scm_e.htm.

2. http://ec.europa.eu/trade/policy/accessing-markets/trade-defence/actions-against-

imports-into-the-eu/anti-subsidy/.

3. https://www.usitc.gov/trade_remedy/731_ad_701_cvd/investigations/active/index.htm .

4. http://cacs.mofcom.gov.cn/.

第七章

保障措施争端解决程序实务

【内容摘要】

保障措施程序是国内主管机关在进口激增造成或可能造成国内产业严重损害的情况下所实施的一种紧急性救济措施。作为一种贸易救济的手段，与反倾销和反补贴争端程序类似，保障措施也是通过国内行政程序实现的，因此保障措施争端解决程序也包括了两个方面，即国内保障措施实施程序和多边保障措施争端解决程序。由于保障措施的特殊性，即实施保障措施不是针对特定外国的倾销和补贴，而是一种经济的特殊紧急情况，目的是通过暂时地限制进口，使国内相关产业有时间根据新的经济情况进行结构调整和恢复，因此从 GATT1994 第 19 条以及 WTO 乌拉圭回合达成的《保障措施协定》来看，相较于反倾销和反补贴调查程序，保障措施实施程序的多边纪律规定较少，主要由各国国内立法予以规定。本章结合相关争端解决案例原文，重点介绍和有选择地分析了国内保障措施实施程序中的程序性和实体性要求，以及 WTO 保障措施多边争端解决程序中的特殊性规则解释问题。

第一节　保障措施的实施程序

【知识背景 / 学习要点】

一、临时保障措施的程序

《保障措施协定》第 6 条允许成员方在“紧急情况”下实施临时保障措施，这种“紧急情况”被定义为“迟延会造成难以弥补的损害”。因此，在采取临时保障措施之前，对于存在明确证据表明进口激增已经或正在造成严重损害或威胁时，国内调查机关应作出初步的认定。临时保障措施只能采取提高关税的形式，且实施期限只有不能延长的 200 日。《保障措施协定》第 6 条进一步规定，这是为了计算第 7 条第 1 款、第 2 款和第 3 款所指的最初适用期及其任何延展期的一部分。[①]

在临时保障措施期限届满前，实施措施的成员方应满足《保障措施协定》第 2 条至第 7 条和第 12 条的有关要求。但是，如果随后进行的调查未能确定进口激增对国内产业已经或正在造成严重损害或威胁则提高的关税应迅速予以退还。[②] 这里提及“随后进行的调查”（即在实施临时措施之后）即表明，在未进行全面调查的情况下就可以实施临时保障措施，但条件是国内调查主管机关经初步认定，有明确证据表明进口激增已经造成或有可能造成严重损害，因而可以推测存在“紧急情况”。这一推测也可以通过相关事实予以证明，即只有在实施临时措施之后，《保障措施协定》第 6 条才要求成员符合第 2 条至第 7 条的条件（包括与调查有关的条件）。

鉴于临时保障措施的最长期限，以及 WTO 争端解决程序的期限要求和救

① 临时保障措施是不可能延期的，因为在计算最终保障措施的期限时，临时保障措施的期限将被计算在内。

② 参见《保障措施协定》第 6 条。

济的预期性质，在争端解决实践中往往对临时措施难以提出有效的挑战。在2012年多米尼加共和国关于聚丙烯包装袋和圆筒织物保障措施案中，专家组认为没有必要对在专家组成立时已经过期且已被最终保障措施所取代的临时措施作出具体的结论，因为申诉方对已过期临时措施提出的请求和对最终措施提出的是相同的。①

二、最终保障措施的实施

《保障措施协定》第5条分两个条款规定了保障措施实施的具体程序规则。不同于反倾销和反补贴，保障措施实施中的大部分自由裁量权留给成员方掌握，因此在程序规则上第5条主要涉及的是保障措施可以采取的形式以及不同形式下保障措施的具体实施要求。

（一）措施实施形式

对于保障措施的实施形式，《保障措施协定》似乎并没有做限制性的规定。第5.1款规定，“一成员应仅在防止或补救严重损害并促进调整的必要限度内实施保障措施。若使用数量限制，则该措施不得把进口量降到最近一段时期的进口水平以下，即统计数据表明有代表性的前3年的平均进口水平，除非有明确的正当理由表明某一不同水平对防止和补救严重损害是必要的。为达到这些目标，各成员应选择最合适的措施。”从条款规定来看，仅在第2句提及了“数量限制”，而在其他语句中均未对保障措施的实施形式有所提及，这就产生了一个问题，即第2句话对数量限制的要求是否也适用于其他保障措施的实施形式。

在1999年韩国对某种奶制品进口实施最终保障措施争端案中，专家组认为，成员方总是需要“在实施一项保障措施的建议或裁定中，他们对获取的事实如何考虑以及在裁定作出时其如何得出措施的实施对救济严重损害和便利

① 参见 Panel Report, Dominican Republic–Safeguard Measures on Imports of Polypropylene Bags and Tubular Fabric, WT/DS415/R, WT/DS416/R, WT/DS417/R, WT/DS418/R,31 January 2012, para. 7.22.

产业调整是必要的，进行解释”。[①]但是在该案中，上诉机构没有接受专家组的观点。上诉机构承认，“采取保障措施的成员方有义务确保措施的实施与防止或救济严重损害或者促进调整的目标是相当的”，这一义务在履行中应不考虑保障措施可能采取的特别形式。但上诉机构也指出，第 5.1 款第 2 句所要求的“正当理由”，仅仅针对的是采取数量限制形式将进口数量降至最近有统计数据的三个代表性年份的进口平均数以下的保障措施，而不涉及其他形式的保障。[②]

（二）数量限制方式

如果采用数量限制方式实施保障措施的，对于在供应国之间需要分配配额的情况，《保障措施协定》第 5.2 款（a）项规定了具体的规则。这些规则与 GATT1994 年关于“数量限制的非歧视管理”第 13 条规定相类似。实施限制的成员可就配额份额的分配问题寻求与在供应有关产品方面具有实质利益的所有其他成员达成协议。在没有达成协议的情况下，有关成员应根据在供应该产品方面具有实质利益的成员在以往一代表期内的供应量占该产品进口总量或进口总值的比例，将配额分配给此类成员，同时适当考虑可能已经或正在影响该产品贸易的任何特殊因素。

根据《保障措施协定》第 5.2 款（b）项的规定，对提出正当理由的进口成员，其配额水平可以不依照过去的市场份额进行调整，即成员可偏离第 5.2 款（b）项的规定，但有三项条件是：其一，只有在措施救济的是严重损害而不只是损害威胁的情况下，才允许偏离第 5 条第 2 款（a）项。其二，必须与供应方成员进行事先磋商。其三，进口成员必须向 WTO 保障措施委员会清楚表明：（1）自某些成员进口增长的百分比与有关产品进口的总增长不成比例；（2）这种偏离有正当的理由；（3）这种偏离的条件对有关产品的所有供应商都是公平的。在

① 参见 Panel Report, Korea–Definitive Safeguard Measure on Imports of Certain Dairy Products, WT/DS98/R, Jun 21, 1999, para.7.109.

② 参见 Appellate Body Report, Korea–Definitive Safeguard Measure on Imports of Certain Dairy Products, WT/DS98/AB/R, Dec 14, 1999, paras.96-98.

此基础上采取的偏离措施的实施期限不能超过 4 年。

（三）关税配额方式

由于有些国家采用关税配额形式实施保障措施，但是关税配额的分配与上述一般性配额的情况不同，因此就产生了一个问题，即采用关税配额分配的形式，是否可以依据《保障措施协定》第 5.2 款。可以发现，《保障措施协定》第 5.2 款在规定上与 GATT1994 年第 13 条第 2 款（d）项是相对应的。① 由于 GATT1994 年第 13 条第 5 款中明确扩大了此类措施的适用范围，② 因此 GATT1994 年第 13 条第 2 款（d）项也适用于数量限制以外的关税配额。但是，《保障措施协定》第 5.1 款第 2 句和第 5.2 款对于关税配额的可适性没有明确的规定。在 2002 年美国对于韩国圆形焊接碳质管道钢管采取的最终保障措施案中，专家组明确提出，在没有明确延伸的情况下，区别于 GATT1994 第 13 条，第 5.1 条第 2 句和第 5.2（a）条不适用于关税配额。③ 因此，为实施保障措施而采取的关税配额分配，只能根据 GATT1994 年第 13 条而不能根据《保障措施协定》第 5.2 款提出。

三、保障措施实施的期限

（一）期限的总体规定

保障措施本质上是一项临时性措施。《保障措施协定》第 7.1 款规定，一成员仅应在防止或补救严重损害和便利调整所必需的期限内实施保障措施。事实上，从最终保障措施实施开始，期限不得超过 4 年，这也包括临时措施实施期限

---

① GATT1994 年第 13 条第 2 款 (d) 项规定，如果配额系在各供应国之间进行分配，实施限制的缔约国可谋求与供应有关产品有实质利害关系的所有缔约国就配额的分配达成协议。如果不能采用这种办法，在考虑了可能已经影响或正在影响有关产品的贸易的特殊因素的情况下，有关缔约国应根据前一代表时期供应产品的缔约国在这一产品进口总量或总值中所占的比例，将份额分配给与供应产品有实质利害关系的国家。除这一份额应予配额所定的限制内进口以外，有关缔约国不得设立任何条件或手续来阻碍任何其他缔约国充分利用其从这一总额或总值中所分得的份额。

② 本条的规定应适用于任何缔约国建立或维持的关税配额，而且本条的原则应尽可能地适用于出口限制。

③ 参见 Panel Report, United States–Definitive Safeguard Measures on Imports of Circular Welded Carbon Quality Line Pipe from Korea, WT/DS202 /R, para. 7.75.

在内。此外,《保障措施协定》第 7.4 款规定,保障措施期限超过 1 年的,应在实施期内按固定时间间隔逐渐放宽该措施。如果措施期限超过 3 年的,则实施该措施的成员方应在不迟于该措施实施期的中期复审有关情况,如应适当撤销该措施或加快放宽速度。①

(二)实施期限的延长

保障措施 4 年的实施期限也可以延长,但延长条件不同于《保障措施协定》第 5.1 款第 1 句规定的提出请求的条件。根据《保障措施协定》第 7.2 款的规定,延长条件是:(1)保障措施仍然是对防止或补救严重损害有必要的;②(2)有证据表明国内产业正在进行调整。③ 由于必须援引相关事实才可以继续实施该措施,因此提出延长要求的当事方必须提交从最初实施保障措施之后的一段时期内相关的经济数据。此外,还必须证明国内产业调整已经开始。但是在任何情况下,保障措施的全部实施期限,包括任何临时措施的实施期、最初实施期及任何延长期限,都不得超过 8 年。④

(三)重复实施期限间隔

保障措施在不同的时间段对同一产品重复实施,这也是在实践中实施保障措施的进口国经常采用的方式。但是,《保障措施协定》不只是规定保障措施的实施期限,还通过期限的规定确保上述同一产品重复被实施保障措施的情况受到限制。《保障措施协定》第 7.5 款规定,保障措施不得再次适用于同一产品,直至相当于先前实施保障措施的期限(或至少 2 年)届满。⑤ 例如,如果成员方

---

① 作为审查结果,成员必须在适当情况下,撤销保障措施或提高贸易自由化率。参见《保障措施协定》第 7.4 款。

② 请注意,如果原措施本身与《保障措施协定》第 2 条、第 3 条、第 4 条或第 5 条不一致,则根据定义,这种措施的任何延长也会受到不一致的影响。参见 Panel Report, Chile–Price Band System and Safeguard Measures Relating to Certain Agricultural Products, WT/DS207/R,23 October 2002, para.7.198.

③ 参见《保障措施协定》第 7.2 款。延长的保障措施可能不应比最初期限结束的时候更具限制性。See Panel Report, Argentina–Safeguard Measures on Imports of Footwear, WT/DS121/ R, paras. 8.303-8.304.

④ 参见《保障措施协定》第 7.3 款。

⑤ 但是保障措施不能再被实施的最短期限为 2 年。参见《保障措施协定》第 7.5 款。

对进口电脑设备实施了为期 8 年的保障措施，在该措施终止后的 8 年内，便不能再对同类进口电脑设备实施任何保障措施。

通过这样的规定，《保障措施协定》可以防止调查主管机关通过一系列独立的保障措施将临时性的进口保护实际上变成一个永久的国内市场封闭，从而规避对于保障措施的临时性措施的定位。允许对同一产品重复实施保障措施，也将规避对先前实施和延长措施规定的 4 年和 8 年的期限。这就是《保障措施协定》第 7 条规定重复实施保障措施期限间隔要求的原因。

虽然有第 7.5 款的规定，但是如果第一次保障措施持续时间不超过 180 日，那么新的保障措施可以再次适用于同一产品，条件包括（1）自实施第一次保障措施以来至少经过 1 年和（2）在紧接实施新措施之前的 5 年期间，同一产品成为保障措施的对象不超过两次。[①] 但须注意，如果保障措施的适用期限被延长，对于延长的保障措施的限制不应超过最初期限结束时的限制。若总期限超过 1 年的，则应继续放宽。

（四）发展中国家特殊期限

《保障措施协定》第 9.2 款允许发展中国家成员作为保障措施的实施者在期限方面有更大的灵活性。根据该款的规定，发展中成员可实施最长为 10 年的保障措施，而不是《保障措施协定》第 7.3 款规定的 8 年。此外发展中国家成员也可比发达国家成员方更早对同一产品实施新的保障措施，这个期限间隔仅为原来实施措施期限的一半（尽管仍然必须保持 2 年的最低间隔）。[②]

① 参见《保障措施协定》第 7.6 款。

② 《保障措施协定》第 9.2 款规定，一发展中国家成员有权将一保障措施的实施期在第 7 条第 3 款规定的最长期限基础上再延长 2 年。尽管有第 7 条第 5 款的规定，但是一发展中国家有权对已经受在《WTO 协定》生效之日后采取的保障措施约束的产品的进口，在等于以往实施该措施期限一半的期限后，再次实施保障措施，但是不适用期至少为 2 年。

【案例摘录与评析】

2002 年美国对于韩国圆形焊接碳质管道钢管采取的最终保障措施案①

United States – Definitive Safeguard Measures on Imports of Circular Welded Carbon Quality *Line Pipe from Korea*
(WT/DS202/AB/R)

231. We then addressed the second sentence of Article 5.1:

This sentence requires a "clear justification" if a Member takes a safeguard measure in the form of a quantitative restriction which reduces the quantity of imports below the average of imports in the last three representative years for which statistics are available. We agree with the Panel that this "clear justification" has to be given by a Member applying a safeguard measure at the time of the decision, in its recommendations or determinations on the application of the safeguard measure. (original emphasis)

232. With respect to the need to provide a "clear justification" for measures other than those specifically described in that second sentence, we stated in the same appeal that:

... we do not see anything in Article 5.1 that establishes such an obligation for a safeguard measure other than a quantitative restriction which reduces the quantity of imports below the average of imports in the last three representative years. In particular, a Member is not obliged to justify in its recommendations or determinations a measure in the form of a quantitative restriction which is consistent with "the average of imports in the last three representative years for which statistics are available". (original emphasis)

233. It is clear, therefore, that, apart from one exception, Article 5.1, including the first sentence, does not oblige a Member to justify, at the time of application, that the safeguard measure at issue is applied "only to the extent necessary". The exception we identified in Korea – Dairy lies in the second sentence of Article 5.1. That exception concerns safeguard measures in the form of quantitative restrictions, which reduce the quantity of imports below the average of imports in the last three representative years. That exception does not apply to the line pipe measure.

234. Thus, our findings in Korea – Dairy establish that Article 5.1 imposes a general

① Appellate Body Report, United States–Definitive Safeguard Measures on Imports of Circular Welded Carbon Quality Line Pipe from Korea, WT/DS202/AB/R, 15 February 2002. 原文脚注省略。

substantive obligation, namely, to apply safeguard measures only to the permissible extent, and also a particular procedural obligation, namely, to provide a clear justification in the specific case of quantitative restrictions reducing the volume of imports below the average of imports in the last three representative years. Article 5.1 does not establish a general procedural obligation to demonstrate compliance with Article 5.1, first sentence, at the time a measure is applied.

235. Accordingly, since the line pipe safeguard measure is not a quantitative restriction, we uphold the Panel's finding in paragraph 7.81 of its Report that "the United States was not required to demonstrate, at the time of imposition, that the line pipe measure was 'necessary to prevent or remedy serious injury and to facilitate adjustment'."

236. This does not imply, as Korea seems to assert, that the measure may be devoid of justification or that the multilateral verification of the consistency of the measure with the Agreement on Safeguards is impeded. The Member imposing a safeguard measure must, in any event, meet several obligations under the Agreement on Safeguards. And, meeting those obligations should have the effect of clearly explaining and "justifying" the extent of the application of the measure. By separating and distinguishing the injurious effects of factors other than increased imports from those caused by increased imports, as required by Article 4.2(b), and by including this detailed analysis in the report that sets forth the findings and reasoned conclusions, as required by Articles 3.1 and 4.2(c), a Member proposing to apply a safeguard measure should provide sufficient motivation for that measure. Compliance with Articles 3.1, 4.2(b) and 4.2(c) of the Agreement on Safeguards should have the incidental effect of providing sufficient "justification" for a measure and, as we will explain, should also provide a benchmark against which the permissible extent of the measure should be determined.

...

244. With this in mind, we look now at the text of Article 5.1, first sentence. We are, as always, guided by Article 31(1) of the Vienna Convention, which codifies the fundamental rule of treaty interpretation, and which provides that a treaty shall be interpreted in good faith in accordance with the ordinary meaning of its terms, in their context and in the light of the object and purpose of the treaty.

245. We observe, first of all, that the words of Article 5.1, first sentence, state that a safeguard measure may be applied "only to the extent necessary to prevent or remedy serious injury and to facilitate adjustment ". (emphasis added) This phrase sets the maximum permissible extent for the application of a safeguard measure under the Agreement on Safeguards. To address this claim by Korea, we must discern the meaning of certain terms found in this phrase.

246. We note the presence of the words "only to the extent necessary". We see these words

as indicating that this provision has a limited objective. We see them also as drawing the outer boundary of that limited objective—the maximum permissible "extent" to which a safeguard measure may be applied. These words instruct WTO Members to focus on what is "necessary" to fulfill that limited objective, which is "to prevent or remedy serious injury and to facilitate adjustment."

247. The limited objective of this provision is founded in the determination of "serious injury" that justifies the application of a safeguard measure. For this reason, a key to understanding the nature of the objective, and thus to determining whether a measure has been applied "only to the extent necessary" to achieve that objective, is the "serious injury" to which this phrase in the first sentence of Article 5.1 refers.

248. To what "serious injury" does this phrase refer? The Panel did not answer this question because the Panel did not reach the substantive issue of the meaning of Article 5.1, first sentence. For the reasons we will set out, we believe that we must do so in order to address the issue raised in this appeal.

249. In our view, the "serious injury" to which Article 5.1, first sentence, refers is, in any particular case, necessarily the same "serious injury" that has been determined to exist by competent authorities of a WTO Member pursuant to Article 4.2. We think it's reasonable to assume that, as the Agreement provides only one definition of "serious injury", and as the Agreement does not distinguish the "serious injury" to which Article 5.1 refers from the "serious injury" to which Article 4.2 refers, the "serious injury" in Article 5.1 and the "serious injury" in Article 4.2 must be considered as one and the same. On this, we agree with the United States. But, contrary to what the United States argues, the fact that these two provisions refer to the same "serious injury" does not necessarily lead to the conclusion that a safeguard measure may address the "entirety" of the "serious injury", including the part of the "serious injury" that is attributable to factors other than increased imports.

250. This is because Article 5.1, first sentence, sets out the maximum permissible extent to which a safeguard measure may be applied. With its emphasis on the "entirety" of the "serious injury", the United States seems to read the word "all" as if it were between the word "remedy" and the words "serious injury" in this provision, so that the phrase would be "remedy all serious injury". But the word "all" is not there. And, as we have said more than once, words must not be read into the Agreement that are not there.

251. We do not see the text of Article 5.1, first sentence, alone, as indicating one certain meaning. Therefore, in keeping with our customary approach, we must seek the meaning of the terms of this provision in their context and in the light of the object and purpose of the

Agreement.

252. We observe here that the non-attribution language of the second sentence of Article 4.2(b) is an important part of the architecture of the Agreement on Safeguards and thus serves as necessary context in which Article 5.1, first sentence, must be interpreted. In our view, the non-attribution language of the second sentence of Article 4.2(b) has two objectives. First, it seeks, in situations where several factors cause injury at the same time, to prevent investigating authorities from inferring the required "causal link" between increased imports and serious injury or threat thereof on the basis of the injurious effects caused by factors other than increased imports. Second, it is a benchmark for ensuring that only an appropriate share of the overall injury is attributed to increased imports. As we read the Agreement, this latter objective, in turn, informs the permissible extent to which the safeguard measure may be applied pursuant to Article 5.1, first sentence. Indeed, as we see it, this is the only possible interpretation of the obligation set out in Article 4.2(b), last sentence, that ensures its consistency with Article 5.1, first sentence. It would be illogical to require an investigating authority to ensure that the "causal link" between increased imports and serious injury not be based on the share of injury attributed to factors other than increased imports while, at the same time, permitting a Member to apply a safeguard measure addressing injury caused by all factors.

253. This interpretation of this important context of Article 5.1 is further reinforced if we look at Article 5.1 from an overall perspective of the WTO Agreement. We found, in United States–Transitional Safeguard Measure on Combed Cotton Yarn from Pakistan ("US – Cotton Yarn "), with respect to Article 6.4, second sentence, of the Agreement on Textiles and Clothing (the "ATC"), that "the part of the total serious damage attributed to an exporting Member must be proportionate to the damage caused by the imports from that Member."

254. In support of this conclusion, we pointed there to Article 22.4 of the DSU, which provides:

The level of the suspension of concessions or other obligations authorized by the DSB shall be equivalent to the level of the nullification or impairment.

255. We noted there that:

... Article 22.4 of the DSU stipulates that the suspension of concessions shall be equivalent to the level of nullification or impairment. This provision of the DSU has been interpreted consistently as not justifying punitive damages. (footnotes omitted)

256. We concluded:

It would be absurd if the breach of an international obligation were sanctioned by proportionate countermeasures, while, in the absence of such breach, a WTO Member would be subject to a disproportionate and, hence, "punitive", attribution of serious damage not wholly caused by its exports. In our view, such an exorbitant derogation from the principle of proportionality in respect of the attribution of serious damage could be justified only if the drafters of the ATC had expressly provided for it, which is not the case. (emphasis added)

257. We think the same reasoning applies here. If the pain inflicted on exporters by a safeguard measure were permitted to have effects beyond the share of injury caused by increased imports, this would imply that an exceptional remedy, which is not meant to protect the industry of the importing country from unfair or illegal trade practices, could be applied in a more trade-restrictive manner than countervailing and anti-dumping duties. On what basis should the WTO Agreement be interpreted to limit a countermeasure to the extent of the injury caused by unfair practices or a violation of the treaty but not so limit a countermeasure when there has not even been an allegation of a violation or an unfair practice?

258. The object and purpose of the Agreement on Safeguards support this reading of the context of Article 5.1, first sentence. The Agreement on Safeguards deals only with imports. It deals only with measures that, under certain conditions, can be applied to imports. The title of Article XIX of the GATT 1994 is "Emergency Action on Imports of Particular Products". (emphasis added) It seems apparent to us that the object and purpose of both Article XIX of the GATT 1994 and the Agreement on Safeguards support the conclusion that safeguard measures should be applied so as to address only the consequences of imports. And, therefore, it seems apparent to us as well that the limited objective of Article 5.1, first sentence, is limited by the consequences of imports.

259. We note as well the customary international law rules on state responsibility, to which we also referred in US – Cotton Yarn. We recalled there that the rules of general international law on state responsibility require that countermeasures in response to breaches by States of their international obligations be proportionate to such breaches. Article 51 of the International Law Commission's Draft Articles on Responsibility of States for Internationally Wrongful Acts provides that "countermeasures must be commensurate with the injury suffered, taking into account the gravity of the internationally wrongful act and the rights in question". Although Article 51 is part of the International Law Commission's Draft Articles, which do not constitute a binding legal instrument as such, this provision sets out a recognized principle of customary international law. We observe also that the United States has acknowledged this principle elsewhere. In its comments on the International Law Commission's Draft Articles, the United States stated that "under customary international law a rule of proportionality applies to the exercise of countermeasures".

260. For all these reasons, we conclude that the phrase “only to the extent necessary to prevent or remedy serious injury and to facilitate adjustment” in Article 5.1, first sentence, must be read as requiring that safeguard measures may be applied only to the extent that they address serious injury attributed to increased imports.

【本案评析】

以上案例节选自2002年美国对于韩国圆形焊接碳质管道钢管采取的最终保障措施案上诉机构报告。该上诉机构认为，第5.1款规定了一项一般性的实体性义务，即只在允许的范围内实施保障措施；也规定了一项特殊的程序性义务，即具体明确说明使进口数量低于最近三年平均进口量的数量限制的实施理由。第5.1款没有规定在实施保障措施时证明遵守第5.1款第1句的一般程序性义务。然而，这并不意味着在第5.1款第2句未包括的情况下，“措施可能没有正当理由，或对该措施是否符合《保障措施协定》的多边审查会受到阻碍”。

上诉机构指出，《保障措施协定》中的项义务，包括那些要求成员分开和区别进口激增以外的其他因素造成的损害影响［第4.2款（b）项］，以及在其裁定和合理的结论的报告中包括一项详细分析［第3条第1款和第4.2款（c）项］，具有为措施提供充分的“理由”的附带效果，也应当是为确定该措施允许的范围提供了一个基准。第4.2款（b）项[①]第2句中的用语“非归因于”支持这一解释，这是为确保在总体损害中只有恰当份额被归因于进口激增提供了的基准。[②]而这反过来又明确了根据第5.1款实施保障措施可以被允许的程度。

上诉机构强调，如果要求成员方调查主管机关确保进口激增与严重损害之间的“因果联系”并不是基于将可归因于进口激增以外因素所导致的那部分损害，而与此同时又允许一个成员方对所有因素造成的损害实施保障措施，这将是不合逻辑的。

---

① 第4.2款(b)项规定，“除非调查根据客观证据证明有关产品增加的进口与严重损害或严重损害威胁之间存在因果关系，否则不得作出(a)项所指的确定。如增加的进口之外的因素正在同时对国内产业造成损害，则此类损害不得归因于增加的进口。”

② 上诉机构注意到，“在若干因素同时造成损害的”情况下，不归因要求旨在防止调查机关基于进口增加以外的因素造成的损害效果，推断进口增加与严重损害或其威胁之间存在必要的“因果关系”。

【延伸阅读】

一、相关典型案例

1. Argentina—Safeguard Measures on Imports of Footwear (WT/DS121)

2.Chile—Price Band System and Safeguard Measures Relating to Certain Agricultural Products(WT/DS207)

3. Dominican Republic—Safeguard Measures on Imports of Polypropylene Bags and Tubular Fabric(WT/DS415, WT/DS416, WT/DS417, WT/DS418)

4. Korea—Definitive Safeguard Measure on Imports of Certain Dairy Products (WT/DS98)

二、相关学术论著

1. [比] 让·弗朗索瓦·百利斯（Jean-Francois Bellis）、[比] 菲利普·得·贝尔（Philippe De Baere）:《欧盟贸易保护商务指南 反倾销、反补贴和保障措施法规、实践与程序》，岳云霞译，社会科学文献出版社 2007 年版。

2. Peter Van den Bossche, *The Law and Policy of the World Trade Organization: Text, Cases and Materials,* Cambridge University Press, 2008.

3. Yong-Shik Lee, *Safeguard Measures in World Trade: The Legal Analysis,* Edward Elgar, 2014.

三、相关网络资源

1.http://www.wto.org/english/tratop_e/dispu_e/dispu_agreements_index_e.htm?id=A18#selected_agreement.

2. http://trb.mofcom.gov.cn/article/cx/.

第二节　实施保障措施的程序性要求

【知识背景 / 学习要点】

《保障措施协定》第 3 条要求一成员方只有在其主管机关依照确定的并按 GATT1994 第 10 条公布的程序进行调查之后，才可以实施保障措施。[①] 因此，主管调查机关实施保障措施前在调查过程中的相关纪律构成了实施保障措施的程序性要求。总的来讲，这包括两个方面的要求，即透明度义务和机密信息保护义务。

一、透明度的义务

保障措施调查中的透明度义务在《保障措施协定》第 3.1 款中作了简要的规定，其中包括：(1) 向所有利害关系方进行调查的合理公告和公布结论的报告；(2) 提供利害关系方能够陈述证据和看法的公开听证会或其他适当方式的权利（包括对其他相关方的陈述作出回答并提出其观点的机会，特别是对保障措施的采用是否考虑公众利益的）。

第 3.1 款将这些权利赋予"所有利害关系方"，即与保障措施调查最为相关的当事方，包括国内生产者、外国生产者（出口商）和国内进口商。事实上，第 3.1 款虽然明确提到了进口商和出口商，但是"利害关系方"一词的含义相当宽泛，可被解释为包括其他 WTO 的出口成员方，也可包括行业协会、行业组织和消费者协会等。在特定情况下，"利害关系方"的认定将由 WTO 成员方根据其国内规则和程序自行决定。

（一）说明措施的实施理由

国内调查主管机关必须公布一份报告，说明其对所有有关事实问题和法律

① 参见《保障措施协定》第 3.1 款。

问题的调查结果和理由充分的结论。《保障措施协定》第 3.1 款最后一句话概括性地规定了说明保障措施实施理由的义务。[①] 如果主管机关不这样做，将导致在实施保障措施之时存在形式上的缺陷。除第 3.1 款规定的一般义务外，《保障措施协定》第 4.2 款（c）项也有类似的规定，即对于严重损害，调查主管机关应按照第 3 条的规定，迅速公布对被调查案件详细分析和对已审查因素相关性的裁定。

但是在实践中，说明实施理由还会涉及上述规定以外的其他内容，如国内调查机关在评估严重损害或严重损害威胁时已经或应该审查的其他因素，或《保障措施协定》中没有具体提及、但国内机关仍认为有相关性的其他信息。同样，如果实际上将额外的或者与已公布报告中最初列出的信息不同的其他信息，保留作为保障措施的依据的，也必须说明这些额外信息和替代的理由。[②] 因此，如果国内调查主管机关在一项保障措施的说明理由或在单独公布的报告中没有澄清某些《保障措施协定》的要求，将不符合保障措施协定的要求。例如，如果主管机关的报告没有涉及第 2 条（进口激增）或第 4 条（严重损害）所引起的问题，就等于没有满足第 2 条或第 4 条的要求，可能导致违反《保障措施协定》第 2 条或第 4 条。此外，当事方提请国内主管机关注意的其他可能的解释，如果是与作为裁定依据的事实或理由相反，那么主管机关也必须进行澄清，并说明这些事实或理由为何不足以得出不同的结论。[③]

需要指出的是，上述规定不仅适用于《保障措施协定》的协定，而且也适用于 GATT1994 第 19 条的规定，因为 GATT1994 第 19 条和《保障措施协定》

---

① 援引不构成“公布的”报告文件中有关信息作为证据审议是不允许的。参见 Panel Report, Chile–Price Band System and Safeguard Measures Relating to Certain Agricultural Products, WT/DS207/R,23 October 2002, para. 7.128.

② 参见 Appellate Body Report, United States-Definitive Safeguard Measures on Imports of Wheat Gluten from the European Communities, WT/DS166/AB/R, adopted 19 January 2001, para. 55.

③ 参见 Appellate Body Report, United States-Safeguard Measures on imports of Fresh, Chilled or Frozen Lamb Meat from New Zealand and Australia, WT/DS177/AB/R, WT/DS178/AB/R, adopted 16 May 2001, paras. 159-161.

是同时适用的。例如，在2001年美国对自新西兰和澳大利亚进口的新鲜、冷冻或冰冻的羔羊肉的保障措施争端案中，上诉机构裁定，根据“未预见的发展”的要求，美国的做法违反了GATT1994第19条第1款，因为相关的调查报告没有讨论、证明或甚至解释这一要求是如何满足的。此外，上诉机构指出，《保障措施协定》第3.1款要求国内调查机关就所有相关事实和法律问题提出调查结果和理由充分的结论，也就要求这些调查机关列入对“未预见的发展”裁定的合理结论。[①]

（二）通知保障措施委员会

保障措施调查的启动，进口激增导致国内产业遭受或可能受到严重损害裁定的作出，以及实施或延长保障措施（包括临时措施）的决定，都有义务立即通知WTO保障措施委员会。[②] 根据《保障措施协定》第12款的规定，各成员有义务将保障措施实施的相关事项立即通知WTO保障措施委员会，并就这些措施与其他成员进行磋商。[③]

《保障措施协定》第12.1款要求各成员在启动调查、对进口增加所造成的严重损害或严重损害威胁作出裁定，或就实施或延长保障措施作出决定时，应“立即”通知WTO保障措施委员会。为便利通知义务的履行，WTO保障措施委员会制定了专门的表格和指引，WTO秘书处还编写了有关通知要求的技术合作手册。[④]

《保障措施协定》第12.2款规定，作出严重损害或损害威胁的裁定，或者决定实施或延长保障措施的成员方在向WTO保障措施委员会通知的同时，如果其建议采取或延长保障措施的，也应向委员会提供所有相关信息，强制性提供的信息包括：进口增加所造成严重损害或严重损害威胁的证据、对所涉及的产

① 参见Appellate Body Report, United States-Safeguard Measures on imports of Fresh, Chilled or Frozen Lamb Meat from New Zealand and Australia (US-Lamb), WT/DS177/AB/R, WT/DS178/AB/R, adopted 16 May 2001, paras.72-76.

② 参见《保障措施协定》第12.1款和第12.4款。

③ 参见《保障措施协定》第12.1款和第12.3款。

④ 参见Docs. G/SG/1, 1 July 1996 and WT/TC/NOTIF/SG/1, 15 October 1996.

品和拟议措施的准确描述、拟议采取措施的日期、预计的期限以及逐步放宽的时间表。[①] 在延长保障措施的情况下，还必须提供国内产业调整的证据。上诉机构曾指出，证明“严重损害的证据”还要符合第 4.2 款（a）项的要求，而非仅仅是实施保障措施的成员方认为足够的证据。[②]

此外，根据《保障措施协定》第 12.5 款的规定，依据第 12 条和第 8 条进行磋商的结果、第 7.4 款中所规定的中期审查结果、第 8.1 款所指的任何形式的补偿以及第 8.2 款所指的拟议减让或其他义务的中止，均应由有关成员方立即通知货物贸易理事会。

（三）提供充分磋商的机会

在实施保障措施前，WTO 成员还必须为出口成员提供充分的磋商机会。《保障措施协定》第 12.3 款规定，建议实施或延长保障措施的成员，应向作为有关产品的出口方并具有实质利益的 WTO 成员提供事先磋商的充分机会，尤其是为了审议根据第 12.2 款提供的信息、就该措施交换意见及就实现上述第 8.1 款所列目标的方式达成谅解。从该款的表述来看，磋商的范围除必须涵盖通知中要处理的所有事项（包括措施建议）外，还涉及第 8.1 款的目标。第 8.1 款规定：“提议实施保障措施或寻求延长保障措施的成员，应依照第 12.3 款的规定，努力在它与可能受该措施影响的出口成员之间维持与在 GATT 1994 项下存在的水平实质相等的减让和其他义务水平。为实现此目标，有关成员可就该措施对其贸易的不利影响议定任何适当的贸易补偿方式。”因此，进口成员保持其与出口成员之间关税减让平衡的可能方式，也属于磋商的内容范围。对于临时保障措施，可按照 GATT1994 年第 19 条第 2 款的规定，在其实施后仍可以立即进行磋商。

① 货物贸易理事会或保障措施委员会可要求提议实施或延长该措施的成员提供其认为必要的额外信息。

② Appellate Body Report, Korea–Definitive Safeguard Measure on Imports of Certain Dairy Products, WT/DS98/AB/R , Dec 14, 1999, paras. 107-108.

二、机密信息保护

在国内保障措施程序中，保护机密信息的条款旨在协调与平衡不同的利益需求。一方面，为满足各方的最终利益需求，对贸易争端事实的彻底调查需要获取这种敏感信息，并且需要与之相关的某种形式的抗辩程序。另一方面，相关的当事方（提起调查的国内生产者和出口商或进口商）不能因为其对保障措施调查的配合，而产生向竞争对手泄露商业秘密或其他敏感商业信息的风险。

对于机密信息的处理，根据《保障措施协定》第 3.2 款的规定，国内主管机关不得披露其性质为保密的信息或未经提交方许可在保密基础上提供的信息，但须符合两个条件。一方面，保密待遇必须是正当的。另一方面，可要求提供机密信息的当事方提供此类信息的非机密摘要，或解释为何不能对这些信息进行摘要。如主管机关认为有关保密的请求缺乏理由，且如果利害关系方不愿披露该信息，或不愿授权以概要形式披露该信息，则主管机关可忽略此类信息，除非它们可从有关来源满意地证明该信息是正确的。

【案例摘录与评析】

2001 年美国对欧盟进口的小麦面筋实施最终保障措施案①

United States - Definitive Safeguard Measures on Imports of Wheat Gluten from the European Communities
(WT/DS166/AB/R)

105. As regards the meaning of the word “immediately” in the chapeau to Article 12.1, we agree with the Panel that the ordinary meaning of the word “implies a certain urgency”.101 The degree of urgency or immediacy required depends on a case-by-case assessment, account being taken of the administrative difficulties involved in preparing the notification, and also of the

① Appellate Body Report, United States-Definitive Safeguard Measures on Imports of Wheat Gluten from the European Communities, WT/DS166/AB/R, adopted 19 January 2001. 原文脚注省略。

character of the information supplied. As previous panels have recognized, relevant factors in this regard may include the complexity of the notification and the need for translation into one of the WTO's official languages. Clearly, however, the amount of time taken to prepare the notification must, in all cases, be kept to a minimum, as the underlying obligation is to notify "immediately".

106. "Immediate" notification is that which allows the Committee on Safeguards, and Members, the fullest possible period to reflect upon and react to an ongoing safeguard investigation. Anything less than "immediate" notification curtails this period. We do not, therefore, agree with the United States that the requirement of "immediate" notification is satisfied as long as the Committee on Safeguards and Members of the WTO have sufficient time to review that notification. In our view, whether a Member has made an "immediate" notification does not depend on evidence as to how the Committee on Safeguards and individual Members of the WTO actually use that notification. Nor can the requirement of "immediate" notification depend on an ex post facto assessment of whether individual Members suffered actual prejudice through an insufficiency in the notification period.

...

3. Notification pursuant to Article 12.1(c)

117. The United States also appeals the Panel's finding that the United States did not notify its decision to apply a safeguard measure "immediately", as required by Article 12.1(c) of the Agreement on Safeguards.

118. The Panel found that, on 30 May 1998, the President of the United States decided to apply, effective 1 June 1998, a safeguard measure on imports of wheat gluten and that, on 4 June 1998 (that is, 5 days after the decision was taken), the United States notified the Committee on Safeguards of the decision to apply a safeguard measure.In assessing the timeliness of this notification, the Panel concluded that:

... the United States notification of this decision after the measure had been implemented, violated the United States obligation under Article 12 SA to make timely notification under Article 12.1 (c) SA of its decision to apply a measure. (emphasis added)

119. The United States appeals this finding on the ground that the Panel erred by interpreting Article 12.1(c) of the Agreement on Safeguards as requiring notification of a "decision to apply or extend a safeguard measure" prior to implementation of that decision.

120. In examining the ordinary meaning of Article 12.1(c), we observe that the relevant triggering event is the "taking" of a decision. To us, Article 12.1(c) is focused upon whether a "decision" has occurred, or has been "taken", and not on whether that decision has been given effect. On the face of the text, the timeliness of a notification under Article 12.1(c) depends only

on whether the notification was immediate.

121. The Panel considered that Article 12.2 of the Agreement on Safeguards, which, in its opening clause, specifically refers to notifications made pursuant to Articles 12.1(b) and 12.1(c), provides relevant context in determining the timeliness of notifications under Article 12.1(c). Article 12.2 provides:

In making the notifications referred to in paragraphs 1(b) and 1(c), the Member proposing to apply or extend a safeguard measure shall provide the Committee on Safeguards with all pertinent information, which shall include evidence of serious injury or threat thereof caused by increased imports, precise description of the product involved and the proposed measure, proposed date of introduction, expected duration and timetable for progressive liberalization. ... (emphasis added)

122. The Panel deduced from this provision that a notification under Article 12.1(c) must be of a "proposed measure" and its "proposed date of introduction", and, on that basis, concluded that a notification under Article 12.1(c) must be made before implementation of the "proposed" safeguard measure.

123. Article 12.2 is related to, and complements, Article 12.1 of the Agreement on Safeguards. Whereas Article 12.1 sets forth when notifications must be made during an investigation, Article 12.2 clarifies what detailed information must be contained in the notifications under Articles 12.1(b) and 12.1(c). We do not, however, see the content requirements of Article 12.2 as prescribing when the notification under 12.1(c) must take place. Rather, in our view, timeliness under 12.1(c) is determined by whether a decision to apply or extend a safeguard measure is notified "immediately". A separate question arises as to whether notifications made by the Member satisfy the content requirements of Article 12.2. Answering this separate question requires examination of whether, in its notifications under either Article 12.1(b) or Article 12.1(c), the Member proposing to apply a safeguard measure has notified "all pertinent information", including the "mandatory components" specifically enumerated in Article 12.2.

124. Thus, the obligations set forth under Articles 12.1(b), 12.1(c) and 12.2 relate to different aspects of the notification process. Although related, these obligations are discrete. A Member could notify "all pertinent information" in its Articles 12.1(b) and 12.1(c) notifications, and thereby satisfy Article 12.2, but still act inconsistently with Article 12.1 because the relevant notifications were not made "immediately". Similarly, a Member could satisfy the Article 12.1 requirement of "immediate" notification, but act inconsistently with Article 12.2 if the content of its notifications was deficient.

125. In our view, in finding that the United States acted inconsistently with Article 12.1(c) solely because the decision to apply a safeguard measure was notified after that decision had been implemented, the Panel confused the separate obligations imposed on Members pursuant to Article 12.1(c) and Article 12.2 and, thereby, added another layer to the timeliness requirements in Article 12.1(c). Instead of insisting on "immediate" notification, as stipulated by Article 12.1(c), the Panel required notification to be made both "immediately" and before implementation of the safeguard measure. We see no basis in Article 12.1(c) for this conclusion.

126. In consequence, we reverse the Panel's finding that:

... the United States notification of this decision after the measure had been implemented, violated the United States obligation under Article 12 SA to make timely notification under Article 12.1 (c) SA of its decision to apply a measure.

127. Although we have reversed the Panel's finding on this issue, we believe that we should complete the legal analysis on the basis of the factual findings of the Panel or the undisputed facts in the Panel record. In examining the timeliness of the United States' notification under Article 12.1(c), we recall that the United States made the notification to the Committee on Safeguards in a communication dated 4 June 1998, or 5 days after the President of the United States had "taken the decision" to apply the safeguard measure. Although the Panel did not reach the issue of whether the 4 June notification had been submitted "immediately", it nevertheless stated:

We note in passing that the delay of 5 days between the decision to apply a safeguard measure and the notification thereof might well satisfy the requirement of immediate notification of Article 12.1 SA.

128. In response to questioning at the oral hearing, the European Communities also accepted that a delay of 5 days "could have been" consistent with the obligation of "immediate" notification under Article 12.1(c).

129. We believe that notification within 5 days was, in this case, consistent with the requirement of "immediacy" contained in Article 12.1(c) of the Agreement on Safeguards. In this regard, we consider it relevant that notification was made the day after the decision of the President of the United States was published in the United States Federal Register , and during the course of the fourth working day following the taking of the decision.

130. In sum, as regards the findings made by the Panel under Article 12.1 of the Agreement on Safeguards, we uphold the Panel's findings, in paragraphs 8.197 and 8.199 of the Panel Report, that the United States did not satisfy the requirements of immediate notification set out in Articles 12.1(a) and 12.1(b); and we reverse the Panel's finding, in paragraph 8.207 of the Panel Report, that the United States failed to make timely notification under Article 12.1(c) of the Agreement

on Safeguards of its decision to apply a safeguard measure.

...

134. The Panel, however, revisited the issue of the adequacy of consultations under Article 12.3 as part of its evaluation of the European Communities' claim under Article 8.1 of the Agreement on Safeguards. The Panel found that:

While the parties have confirmed that consultations did take place on the basis of the United States notifications under Article 12.1(b) concerning the USITC's finding of serious injury and the USITC's recommendations on remedy, no consultations were held on the final proposed measure as approved by the United States President on 30 May 1998. Therefore, the Panel considers that, while consultations may have been held on the basis of the notifications made by the United States under Article 12.1(b) SA, the United States did not provide "an adequate opportunity for prior consultations" on this final proposed measure, within the meaning of Article 12.3 SA.

135. On appeal, the United States argues that it complied with Article 12.3 because, in its notifications under Article 12.1(b) of the Agreement on Safeguards, the United States supplied all the information required by Article 12.2 of that Agreement. As a result, the United States contends that, prior to consultations, the European Communities knew the precise product under consideration, the evidence of serious injury caused by increased imports, and all relevant details relating to the proposed measure. The United States concludes, therefore, that it provided the European Communities with an "adequate opportunity for prior consultations", as required by Article 12.3 of the Agreement on Safeguards.

136. We note, first, that Article 12.3 requires a Member proposing to apply a safeguard measure to provide an "adequate opportunity for prior consultations" with Members with a substantial interest in exporting the product concerned. Article 12.3 states that an "adequate opportunity" for consultations is to be provided "with a view to": reviewing the information furnished pursuant to Article 12.2; exchanging views on the measure; and reaching an understanding with exporting Members on an equivalent level of concessions. In view of these objectives, we consider that Article 12.3 requires a Member proposing to apply a safeguard measure to provide exporting Members with sufficient information and time to allow for the possibility, through consultations, for a meaningful exchange on the issues identified. To us, it follows from the text of Article 12.3 itself that information on the proposed measure must be provided in advance of the consultations, so that the consultations can adequately address that measure. Moreover, the reference, in Article 12.3, to "the information provided under" Article 12.2, indicates that Article 12.2 identifies the information that is needed to enable meaningful consultations to occur under Article 12.3. Among the list of "mandatory components" regarding

information identified in Article 12.2 are: a precise description of the proposed measure, and its proposed date of introduction.

137. Thus, in our view, an exporting Member will not have an "adequate opportunity" under Article 12.3 to negotiate overall equivalent concessions through consultations unless, prior to those consultations, it has obtained, inter alia, sufficiently detailed information on the form of the proposed measure, including the nature of the remedy.

138. With these considerations in mind, we examine whether, in this case, the Panel erred in finding that the United States did not provide the European Communities with an "adequate opportunity for prior consultations" on the proposed safeguard measure, as required by Article 12.3 of the Agreement on Safeguards.

139. The Panel found that the United States and the European Communities held consultations on 24 April 1998 and 22 May 1998 , and that these consultations were held on the basis of the information provided by the United States in its notifications under Article 12.1(b) , that is, on the basis of the information contained in the USITC Report. The Panel also found, as a matter of fact, that no consultations were held on the final measure that was approved by the United States President on 30 May 1998.

140. We note that the USITC Report set out a number of "recommendations" to the President of the United States, including:

> ... that, within the overall quantitative restriction, the President allocate separate quantitative restrictions for the European Union, Australia, and "all other" non-excluded countries, taking into account the disproportional growth and impact of imports of wheat gluten from the European Union ...

141. We note that the recommendations made by the USITC did not include specific numerical quota shares for the individual exporting Members concerned, and the recommendations imply, without providing details, that the individual quota shares could be less favourable to imports from the European Communities.We consider that these "recommendations" did not allow the European Communities to assess accurately the likely impact of the measure being contemplated, nor to consult adequately on overall equivalent concessions with the United States.

142. Accordingly, we see no error in the Panel's conclusion that the United States' notifications under Article 12.1(b) did not provide a description of the measure under consideration sufficiently precise as to allow the European Communities to conduct meaningful consultations with the United States, as required by Article 12.3 of the Agreement on Safeguards.

143. We, therefore, uphold the Panel's finding that the United States did not comply with its obligation under Article 12.3 of the Agreement on Safeguards to provide an adequate opportunity for prior consultations on the proposed safeguard measure.

C. Article 8.1 of the Agreement on Safeguards

144. The United States also appeals the Panel's finding that it acted inconsistently with its obligations under Article 8.1 of the Agreement on Safeguards. Article 8.1 provides:

A Member proposing to apply a safeguard measure or seeking an extension of a safeguard measure shall endeavour to maintain a substantially equivalent level of concessions and other obligations to that existing under GATT 1994 between it and the exporting Members which would be affected by such a measure, in accordance with the provisions of paragraph 3 of Article 12. To achieve this objective, the Members concerned may agree on any adequate means of trade compensation for the adverse effects of the measure on their trade.

145. Article 8.1 imposes an obligation on Members to "endeavour to maintain" equivalent concessions with affected exporting Members. The efforts made by a Member to this end must be "in accordance with the provisions of" Article 12.3 of the Agreement on Safeguards.

146. In view of this explicit link between Articles 8.1 and 12.3 of the Agreement on Safeguards, a Member cannot, in our view, "endeavour to maintain" an adequate balance of concessions unless it has, as a first step, provided an adequate opportunity for prior consultations on a proposed measure. We have upheld the Panel's findings that the United States did not provide an adequate opportunity for consultations, as required by Article 12.3 of the Agreement on Safeguards. For the same reasons, we also uphold the Panel's finding, in paragraph 8.219 of its Report, that the United States acted inconsistently with its obligations under Article 8.1 of the Agreement on Safeguards.

【本案评析】

以上案例节选自 2001 年美国对欧盟进口的小麦面筋实施最终保障措施案上诉机构报告。对于《保障措施协定》第 12.1 款中“立即”一词的解释，上诉机构指出，“立即”一词的使用表明通知具有一定程度的紧迫性。但要求“立即”通知并不意味着“在实际可能的情况下尽快”通知。立即通知的义务所要求的“紧急程度”是根据具体情况进行评定的。这种“紧急程度”将取决于行政困难、信息的性质和翻译文件的需要（若存在）。无论如何，通知所需的时间应保持在最低限度。

对于“决定实施或延长保障措施”的情况下何时发出通知，该案专家组认为，第 12.1 款（c）项规定的通知必须在“已经建议”的保障措施实施之前作出。但是上诉机构否定了专家组的观点，认为这是将成员方在第 12.1 款（c）项和第 12.2 款下的不同义务相混淆。上诉机构指出，第 12.1 款（c）项相关触发的事件是一项决定的“作出”，条款侧重于“决定”已经存在或已经“作出”，而不是决定是否“生效”。因此，需要发出通知只有在作出决定之后，而不是当决定被建议的同时。

对于第 12.3 款的解释，上诉机构指出，“充分的机会”意味着应向出口成员提供足够的信息和时间，以便就所指出的问题进行有意义的交流。上诉机构强调，所实施的最终保障措施应与事先磋商期间所建议的措施大致相同，因为如果……建议的措施与后来实施的措施“有很大不同”的情况下，而不能作为“事先磋商”的结果，那么第 12.3 款所要求的“事先磋商”的意义就没有了。上诉机构还认为，违反第 12.3 款会自动引发《保障措施协定》第 8.1 款的违反，因为《保障措施协定》第 8.1 款和第 12.3 款之间有明确的联系，成员方除非作为第一步已经提供了就建议的措施进行事先磋商的充分机会，否则其不符合“努力维持”充分的减让义务平衡。

【延伸阅读】

一、相关典型案例

1. Korea—Definitive Safeguard Measure on Imports of Certain Dairy Products(WT/DS98)

2. Chile—Price Band System and Safeguard Measures Relating to Certain Agricultural Products (WT/DS207)

3. United States—Safeguard Measures on imports of Fresh, Chilled or Frozen Lamb Meat from New Zealand and Australia (WT/DS177)

4. United States—Definitive Safeguard Measures on Imports of Circular Welded Carbon Quality Line Pipe from Korea (WT/DS202)

二、相关学术论著

1. 王衡：《国际贸易法》，法律出版社 2014 年版。

2. Edwin Vermulst and Folkert Graafsma, *WTO Disputes Anti-Dumping, Subsidies*

and Safeguards, Cameron May, 2002.

3. Fabio Spadi, Discriminatory Safeguards in the Light of the Admission of the People's Republic of China to the World Trade Organization, *Journal of International Economic Law*, 2002 5(2), 421-443.

三、相关网络资源

1. https://www.wto.org/english/tratop_e/safeg_e/safeg_info_e.htm.

2. http://ec.europa.eu/trade/policy/accessing-markets/trade-defence/actions-against-imports-into-the-eu/safeguards/.

第三节　实施保障措施的实体性要求

【知识背景 / 学习要点】

一、非歧视实施原则

（一）基本原则

保障措施应在非歧视的基础上实施，即不在供应国之间加以区分地实施保障措施，是《保障措施协定》引入的一项重要原则。《保障措施协定》第 2.2 款规定，保障措施应针对正在进口的产品实施，且不考虑其来源。

GATT1947 对于是否可以有选择性地适用保障措施，即只仅针对某些特定供应国而不针对其他供应国实施措施存在着很大的分歧。与 GATT 第 19 条相比，《保障措施协定》对非歧视原则的适用有其自身的特点。《保障措施协定》明确要求在非歧视基础上实施保障措施，禁止在出口成员方之间歧视性地选择实施。例如，如果成员甲国的通讯产业因从成员乙国进口的手机突然激增而遭受严重损害，那么甲国有权采取保障措施，如以手机进口配额的形式，但这一措施必须适用于所有“同类或直接竞争”的手机进口，无论是从成员乙国还是从其他成员国的进口。

在一些争端中，出现了与保障措施的非歧视实施原则有关的问题，即 WTO 成员方能否将其在自由贸易区（FTA）或关税同盟 (CU) 的国家所生产的产品排除在保障措施实施对象之外，而对其他 WTO 成员不给予豁免。GATT1994 第 24 条允许在某些条件下偏离最惠国义务和 GATT 的其他条款，以促进自由贸易区或缔约国之间更加深入的经济一体化。但有争议的是，允许贸易自由化只在自由贸易区或关税同盟的成员之间深入展开，而不需要扩展到其他非成员，是否也可以推论允许将 FTA 或 CU 伙伴成员排除在保障措施的实施对象之外。由于第 24 条仅提及 GATT 规则，其原则上不包括对 WTO 其他条款如《保障措施协定》第 2.2 款的援引，因此问题就变得更加复杂。在 2000 年欧共体诉阿根廷鞋类保障措施争端案中，上诉机构裁定，如果一个实施保障措施的 WTO 成员对所有来源的进口进行了调查，那么其同样也要按照《保障措施协定》第 2.2 款的要求对所有来源，包括自由贸易区的其他国家实施这一措施。①

（二）例外规则

《保障措施协定》也规定了禁止“选择性”实施保障措施的两种例外情况。这些例外情况是《保障措施协定》第 5.2 款（b）项和第 9.1 款。

如前所述，第 5.2 款（b）项允许除其他要求之外，如果实施成员方向保障措施委员会作出明确的证明，自某些成员的进口增长的百分比与有关产品进口的总增长不成比例，那么可以以配额的形式在供应国之间采取选择性的保障措施。②

虽然第 2 条规定了非歧视义务，但是根据《保障措施协定》的规定，如果低于某些标准，WTO 成员有义务不对从发展中国家进口的产品实施保障措施。《保障措施协定》第 9.1 款规定了为发展中国家成员利益而禁止“选择性”实施的例外情况。该款规定，对于来自发展中国家成员的产品，只要其有关产品的

① 参见Appellate Body Report, Argentina–Safeguard Measures on Imports of Footwear, WT/DS121/AB/R, 14 Dec. 1999, para. 112.

② 参见本章第一节中第二部分“最终保障措施的实施”（二）有关数量限制方式的相关内容。

进口份额在进口成员中不超过 3%，即不得对该产品实施保障措施，但是进口份额不超过 3% 的发展中国家成员份额总计不得超过有关产品总进口的 9%。

在 2012 年多米尼加共和国关于聚丙烯包装袋和圆筒织物保障措施案中，专家组解释了将符合第 9.1 款规定要求的发展中国家成员的进口产品排除在保障措施实施范围之外的义务。专家组认为，即使这些进口行为造成了实质性的损害和因果关系，发展中国家的进口也应排除在实施范围之外。专家组裁定，多米尼加为确定仅从非排除国家的进口是否存在进口增加、造成严重损害和因果关系，没有进行新的分析就将那些发展中国家的进口排除在根据第 9.1 款保障措施可实施的范围之外，这一做法并不违反《保障措施协定》。①

二、对应性原则

除第 2 条第 2 款中的非歧视原则外，上诉机构对《保障措施协定》第 2.1 款的解释中还提出了所谓"对应性"（parallelism）要求。在 2001 年美国对欧盟进口的小麦面筋实施最终保障措施案中，上诉机构强调，在通常情况下，根据《保障措施协定》第 2.1 款和第 4.2 款作出的裁定中所包括的进口应与根据《保障措施协定》第 2.2 款实施的保障措施中所包括的进口相一致。② 这被称为"对应性"原则。在 2002 年美国对于韩国圆形焊接碳质管道钢管采取的最终保障措施案和 2002 年美国对印度钢板的反倾销反补贴措施案中，上诉机构解释"对应性"原则的依据是《保障措施协定》第 2 条第 1 款和第 2 款。③

根据这一原则，保障措施的范围必须与被调查的且符合实施保障措施要求

① 参见 Panel Report, Dominican Republic–Safeguard Measures on Imports of Polypropylene Bags and Tubular Fabric, WT/DS415/R, WT/DS416/R, WT/DS417/R, WT/DS418/R, 31 January 2012, paras. 7.367-7.392.

② 参见 United States-Definitive Safeguard Measures on Imports of Wheat Gluten from the European Communities, WT/DS166/AB/R, adopted 19 January 2001, para. 96.

③ 参见 Appellate Body Report, United States–Definitive Safeguard Measures on Imports of Circular Welded Carbon Quality Line Pipe from Korea, WT/DS202/AB/R, 15 February 2002; Appellate Body Report, United States–Anti-Dumping and Countervailing Measures on Steel Plate from India, WT/DS206/AB/R.

（“进口增加”“严重损害”或其威胁，以及“因果关系”）的进口范围相一致。[①]比如，在对保障措施实施要求进行评估的同时，也要考虑某些供应成员方的进口情况，若将这些供应成员方的进口排除在保障措施范围之外就是不合适的。因此，对《保障措施协定》第 2.2 款意义上的“来源”的歧视，也可能是由于未能尊重受调查的进口与那些受保障措施制约的进口之间的“对应性”而引发的。例如，上诉机构曾裁定，如果一个实施保障措施的 WTO 成员对所有来源的进口进行了调查，那么其同样也要按照《保障措施协定》第 2.2 款的要求对所有来源进口，包括自由贸易区的国家，实施这一措施。[②]

三、必要性要求

《保障措施协定》第 5.1 款规定，保障措施应仅在防止或补救严重损害并便利调整所必要的限度内实施。对第 5.1 款第 1 句话的解释是，国内主管机关在其实施保障措施时，不要求其在防止或救济严重损害并便利国内产业调整方面提供清晰和特别的证明。[③]然而，如果实施措施时没有满足《保障措施协定》的实质性要求，特别是如果措施所针对的损害或损害威胁不是由进口激增所造成的，该措施就超出了“必要性”的范围。

此外，如果成员方主管机关选择以数量限制的形式实施保障措施，那么根据《保障措施协定》第 5.1 款第 2 句，该措施不得将进口量减少到近期的进口水平（即有统计数据的最近三年进口量的平均值）以下，除非有明确的理由表明，采取不同措施对于防止或补救严重伤害是有必要的。换言之，在规定的这种具

① 参见 Appellate Body Report, United States–Definitive Safeguard Measures on Imports of Circular Welded Carbon Quality Line Pipe from Korea, WT/DS202/AB/R, 15 February 2002, para. 197.

② 参见 Appellate Body Report, Argentina–Safeguard Measures on Imports of Footwear, WT/DS121/AB/R, 14 Dec. 1999, para. 112.

③ 参见 Appellate Body Report, Korea–Definitive Safeguard Measure on Imports of Certain Dairy Products, WT/DS98/AB/R , Dec 14, 1999, para. 99; Appellate Body Report, United States–Definitive Safeguard Measures on Imports of Circular Welded Carbon Quality Line Pipe from Korea, WT/DS202/AB/R, 15 February 2002, paras. 133-134.

体情况下，需要对实施措施时的必要性提出明确的正当理由。[①]

必要性也要求调查主管机关在保障措施实施中不得谋求解决进口激增以外其他因素造成的损害。在2002年美国对于韩国圆形焊接碳质管道钢管采取的最终保障措施案中，美国提出，2001年美国对欧盟进口的小麦面筋实施最终保障措施案的上诉机构裁定，在根据《保障措施协定》第4.2款认定“严重损害”时，不必排除进口增加以外的其他因素造成的损害，因为保障措施可适用于处理严重损害的“整体”。该案上诉机构否定了这个观点并指出，“严重损害”一词在《保障措施协定》第4.2款和第5条中的含义相同，但保障措施只能适用于因进口激增所造成的严重损害（或其威胁）。上诉机构强调，GATT1994年第19条和《保障措施协定》的目的和宗旨都支持这样的结论，即保障措施实施只能处理进口的结果，因此第5.1款第1句的有限目标受到进口结果的限制。[②]

四、补偿方式要求

实施保障措施会扰乱WTO当事成员方之间权利与义务的平衡。因此，《保障措施协定》第8.1款首先要求成员方努力与可能受保障措施影响的成员方维持在GATT1994项下实质相等的减让和其他义务的水平。为实现此目标，有关成员可就该措施对其贸易的不利影响议定任何适当的贸易补偿方式。

为实现适当的贸易补偿，进口成员必须先遵守《保障措施协定》第12.3款的规定，就措施的不利影响与受影响成员进行贸易补偿磋商。若进口成员没有按照第12.3款征求受影响成员的意见，则违反了《保障措施协定》第8.1款的规定。[③]但若在30日内没有达成补偿协议，则根据《保障措施协定》第8.2款的规定，受保障措施影响的国家可对实施保障措施国家中止实施GATT1994

① 参见 Appellate Body Report, Korea–Definitive Safeguard Measure on Imports of Certain Dairy Products, WT/DS98/AB/R, Dec 14, 1999, para. 99.

② 参见 Appellate Body Report, United States–Definitive Safeguard Measures on Imports of Circular Welded Carbon Quality Line Pipe from Korea, WT/DS202/AB/R, 15 February 2002, paras. 242-262.

③ 第8条第1款和第12条第3款都明确相互援引，因此两款在适用中是关联性的。

项下的贸易减让或其他义务，只要货物贸易理事会对此不持异议。[①]同时，获准中止程序应在保障措施实施后的 90 日内完成。[②]

然而，出于权利义务对等性的考虑，受影响的出口成员也不能总是可以行使中止权，《保障措施协定》还对中止权的行使进行了额外的限制。《保障措施协定》第 8.3 款规定，在保障措施生效的前三年，若保障措施是由于进口数量的绝对增加而采取的且这一措施符合协定以及其他规定，则不得授权行使中止权。在 2003 年美国钢铁保障措施争端案中，美国在实施保障措施之前没有就补偿问题进行充分磋商，因为美国在通知措施后仅 15 日就执行保障措施。虽然没有向专家组提出这个问题，但是若干成员国受到影响，包括欧盟、日本、中国、瑞士和挪威，按照《保障措施协定》第 12.5 款的要求，中止对美国同等数量的减让。[③] 2002 年 9 月，美国通报了受其保障措施限制的钢材品种的削减情况。[④]在专家组和上诉机构裁定其钢铁保障措施与 WTO 不符之后，美国撤销了其保障措施，而其他成员方威胁实施的中止措施也没有得到执行。[⑤]

---

① 中止“实质上相等的减让”权利的行使，应将暂时中止措施的建议已经通知货物贸易理事会，且理事会并无表示不同意而定。由于货物贸易理事会以协商一致方式作出决定，不同意的情况事实上较少出现。

② 某些 WTO 成员已经通知特定情况下他们同意推迟 90 日的最后期限。在实践中，这意味着受保障措施影响的成员放弃执行第 8.2 款的授权以及随后权利的行使。虽然从第 8.2 款的条文看不出，这一最后期限可能会被某些或所有保障措施相关成员之间达成的协议减损效力，但很明显的是，这类协议显然不属于 DSU 第 1.1 款所指的“涵盖协定”。因此，如发生违约的情况，不能通过争端解决程序强制执行。

③ 例如，欧共体理事会公告 (OJ 2002,L157,8) 称 ,2002 年 6 月 13 日通过的（EC）1031/2002 号条例，对某些原产于美国的产品设定了进口附加关税。条例裁定，由美国实施的保障措施不针对进口的绝对增长，因此，与进口的绝对增长而实施保障措施相对应的以及代表 3 亿 7900 万欧元可实施征税金额的欧共体部分减让可能会在 2002 年 6 月 18 日起承担额外的义务。然而，欧共体也表示，其也将基于美国对在经济上有意义的产品排除和可以接受的贸易补偿发价的提出，来考虑是否实施这项额外的征税。

④ 参见 G/SG/N/10/USA/6/Suppl.7, G/SG/N/11/USA/5/Suppl.7, September 2002.

⑤ 参见 Appellate Body Report, United States–Definitive Safeguard Measures on Imports of Certain Steel Products, WT/DS248/AB/R, WT/DS249/AB/R, WT/DS251/AB/R, WT/DS252/AB/R, WT/DS253/AB/R, WT/DS254/AB/R, WT/DS258/AB/R, WT/DS259/AB/R, adopted 10 December 2003.

【案例摘录与评析】

2002 年美国对于韩国圆形焊接碳质管道钢管采取的最终保障措施案[①]

United States – Definitive Safeguard Measures on Imports of Circular Welded Carbon Quality Line Pipe from Korea
(WT/DS202/AB/R)

VII. Exclusion of "de minimis" Developing Country Exporters from the Line Pipe Measure

120. Next we turn to Article 9.1 of the Agreement on Safeguards, which states:

...

121. Korea claimed before the Panel that the line pipe measure is inconsistent with Article 9.1 because it treats developing countries the same as all other suppliers and allocates to each of the developing countries, irrespective of their previous import levels, the same quota of 9,000 short tons that has been allocated to all other exporters. Korea argued before the Panel that Article 9.1 of the Agreement on Safeguards requires a Member imposing a safeguard measure to "determine which developing countries were to be exempted from the measure" , and that the United States did not fulfill this requirement.

122. As we have explained, the line pipe measure took the form of a duty increase for three years, effective as of 1 March 2000. The first 9,000 short tons of imports from each country, irrespective of their origin, were excluded each year from the duty increase, with annual reductions in the rate of duty in the second and third years. In the first year, imports above 9,000 short tons were subject to an additional duty of 19 percent ad valorem. The additional duty was reduced to 15 percent in the second year. The additional duty is to be reduced to 11 percent in the third year. Imports from Canada and Mexico have been excluded in their entirety from the measure. The measure has no explicit exclusion for developing countries exporting under the de minimis levels set out in Article 9.1 of the Agreement on Safeguards. Nor does the measure contain an explicit inclusion of developing countries exporting above those de minimis levels.

123. In considering whether this measure complies with Article 9.1, the Panel asked, first, whether it is necessary to make an express exclusion of those developing countries exporting below de minimis levels. The Panel's answer to this question was not conclusive. The Panel said: "[i]n our view, if a measure is not to apply to certain countries, it is reasonable to expect an

① Appellate Body Report, United States–Definitive Safeguard Measures on Imports of Circular Welded Carbon Quality Line Pipe from Korea, WT/DS202/AB/R, 15 February 2002. 原文脚注省略。

express exclusion of those countries from the measure".

124. In an effort to determine whether the line pipe measure contains an express exclusion of those developing countries which fit the description of de minimis importers in Article 9.1, the Panel examined the notification by the United States to the WTO Committee on Safeguards pursuant to footnote 2 to Article 9, as well as three internal United States documents relating to the implementation of the measure. The Panel found that the notification by the United States to the Committee on Safeguards did not specify the developing countries excluded from the measure. Likewise, the Panel found also that none of the internal United States documents—namely, the Presidential Proclamation of the measure, dated 18 February 2000; the President's Memorandum to the Secretary of the Treasury and the United States Trade Representative, dated 18 February 2000; and the Memorandum from the Customs Service Director of Trade Programs to all Port Directors, dated 29 February 2000—contained a list of developing countries excluded from the measure, or any other indication of how the measure would comply with the obligation under Article 9.1.[127] The Panel, therefore, found that these documents "do not contain any express exclusion", and, "[i]n the absence of any other relevant documentation", concluded that the line pipe measure "applies to those developing countries" with de minimis imports. Accordingly, the Panel found that "the United States has not complied with its obligations under Article 9.1".

125. The Panel then went on to ask whether, despite the absence of an express exclusion, the measure was crafted, as the United States asserted, in such a way as to ensure that it would not be "applied against a product originating in a developing country Member" whose share of imports is below the de minimis levels provided in Article 9.1. The United States acknowledged before the Panel that the 9,000 short-ton exemption from the supplemental duty represented only 2.7 percent of total imports in 1998, but argued that, because the total volume of imports would decrease as a result of the measure, any country reaching the 9,000 ton limit of the exemption would in fact account for more than three percent of total imports in 2000 and thereafter. In considering this argument, the Panel noted that the line pipe measure does not set an overall limit on the quantity of imports of line pipe and that, therefore, if importers are willing to pay the duty for over-quota imports, there is no restriction on the total volume of line pipe imports that may enter the United States from any one country. The Panel also noted that, given that Canada and Mexico were completely excluded from the measure, there is no impediment to an increase in imports from those countries. For this reason, the Panel found that there was no assurance in the line pipe measure that the total volume of imports would decrease, or that the three-percent threshold would be exceeded. The Panel concluded that:

Article 9.1 contains an obligation not to apply a measure, and we find that the line pipe measure "applies" to all developing countries in principle, even though it may not have any impact in practice. Therefore, for the reasons described above we find that the United States has not complied with its obligations under Article 9.1 of the Agreement on Safeguards.

126. The United States appeals this finding. The United States argues on appeal that the "most basic flaw in the Panel's reasoning is that Article 9.1 does not obligate Members to provide specifically for 'non-application' of a safeguard measure", and that the "text requires only that the safeguard measure 'not be applied' against a developing country Member having less than three percent of imports". According to the United States, Article 9.1 "is silent as to how a Member may meet this obligation [in Article 9.1], and certainly does not require a list of the developing countries [excluded from the measure]". The United States believes that it met the Article 9.1 requirement by establishing a mechanism—a 9,000 ton exemption for each country—under which the safeguard duty on imports could not possibly apply to any developing country Member accounting for less than three percent of total imports.

127. We agree with the United States that Article 9.1 does not indicate how a Member must comply with this obligation. There is nothing, for example, in the text of Article 9.1 to the effect that countries to which the measure will not apply must be expressly excluded from the measure. Although the Panel may have a point in saying that it is "reasonable to expect" an express exclusion, we see nothing in Article 9.1 that requires one.

128. We agree also with the United States that it is possible to comply with Article 9.1 without providing a specific list of the Members that are either included in, or excluded from, the measure. Although such a list could, and would, be both useful and helpful by providing transparency for the benefit of all Members concerned, we see nothing in Article 9.1 that mandates one.

129. The United States argues as well that special attention should be paid to the word "apply" in Article 9.1. On this point, we start by observing that Article 9.1 obliges Members not to apply a safeguard measure against products originating in developing countries whose individual exports are below a de minimis level of three percent of the imports of that product, provided that the collective import share of such developing countries does not account for more than nine percent of the total imports of that product. We believe the United States is correct insofar as it stresses the significance of the word "applied" in Article 9.1. However, we note that Article 9.1 is concerned with the application of a safeguard measure on a product. And we note, too, that a duty, such as the supplemental duty imposed by the line pipe measure, does not need actually to be enforced and collected to be "applied" to a product. In our view, duties are "applied against a product" when a Member imposes conditions under which that product can enter that Member's market—including when that Member establishes, as the United States did here, a duty to be

imposed on over-quota imports. Thus, in our view, duties are "applied" irrespective of whether they result in making imports more expensive, in discouraging imports because they become more expensive, or in preventing imports altogether.

130. The United States argues in its appellant's submission that it has complied with Article 9.1 by structuring the safeguard duty "so that it automatically would not apply to developing countries accounting for less than three percent of imports". On this basis, the United States argues that the line pipe measure has not been "applied" to those developing countries with de minimis imports in the United States. But, according to the latest data available at the time the line pipe measure took effect—data found in the Panel record and not disputed by the United States—the 9,000 short-ton exemption from the over-quota duty imposed by the line pipe measure did not represent three percent of the total imports. Rather, the exemption represented only 2.7 percent of total imports. According to the evidence in the Panel record, an exemption of approximately 10,000 short tons would have amounted at the time to a three-percent exclusion. The exemption applied by the United States was, on the evidence, too small.

131. As we have already noted, the United States argued before the Panel that it "expected" the measure would result in a decrease from the total volume of imports in 1998 and that, consequently, the general 9,000 short-ton exemption from the supplemental duty would satisfy the requirements of Article 9.1 because "any country reaching the 9000 ton limit of the exemption would account for more than three per cent of total imports." But expectations are not realized "automatically". The facts indicate that, when the measure was adopted, the 9,000 ton exclusion represented less than three percent of total imports into the United States market. The over-quota duty applied to imports that exceeded the 9,000 short-ton exemption, irrespective of their origin.

132. As the Panel emphasized, too, the available documents reveal no effort whatsoever by the United States—apart from the claimed "automatic" structure of the measure itself—to make certain that de minimis imports from developing countries were excluded from the application of the measure. Whatever the "expectations" of the United States, we are not persuaded by the facts before us that the United States took all reasonable steps that it could and, thus, should have taken to exclude developing countries exporting less than the de minimis levels in Article 9.1 from the scope and, therefore, the application of the supplemental duty.

133. For these reasons, we find that the line pipe measure has been applied against products originating in those developing countries whose imports into the United States are below the de minimis levels set out in Article 9.1. And, consequently, we uphold the Panel's findings in paragraphs 7.180 and 7.181 of its Report, that the United States acted inconsistently with its obligations under Article 9.1 of the Agreement on Safeguards.

【本案评析】

以上案例节选自2002年美国对于韩国圆形焊接碳质管道钢管采取的最终保障措施案上诉机构报告。该案被诉方美国为每个国家没有任何区别地规定了9000吨的进口数量配额，免于征收附加关税。这9000吨占其进口总额的2.7%。美国争辩说，由于保障措施将降低进口水平，因此其“预期”任何违反其9000吨免配额进口门槛的国家，同样也将违反《保障措施协定》第9.1款规定的3%的最低水平。上诉机构驳回了其这一论点并指出，第9.1款并没有包含提供一份列入或排除在保障措施之外的发展中国家成员具体名单的义务要求。上诉机构最终裁定，美国没有采取一切合理的步骤，确保将在美国起算点以上但仍低于微量水平的发展中国家成员的进口，排除在保障措施实施范围之外。因此，美国的做法不符合《保障措施协定》第9.1款的规定。

【延伸阅读】

一、相关典型案例

1. Argentina—Safeguard Measures on Imports of Footwear(WT/DS121)

2. Dominican Republic—Safeguard Measures on Imports of Polypropylene Bags and Tubular Fabric(WT/DS415, WT/DS416, WT/DS417, WT/DS418)

3. United States—Definitive Safeguard Measures on Imports of Wheat Gluten from the European Communities(WT/DS166)

4. United States—Safeguard Measures on imports of Fresh, Chilled or Frozen Lamb Meat from New Zealand and Australia (WT/DS177)

5. United States—Definitive Safeguard Measures on Imports of Certain Steel Products, (WT/DS248, WT/DS249, WT/DS251, WT/DS252, WT/DS253, WT/DS254, WT/DS258, WT/DS259)

二、相关学术论著

1. 杨利军:《全球保障措施能否将自贸区协定成员排除在外？》，载《国际贸易》2012年第7期。

2. 余敏友等:《世贸组织保障措施协定解析》,湖南科学技术出版社 2006 年版。

3. Yong-Shik, Lee, Safeguard Measures: Why are They not Applied Consistently with the Rules?: Lessons for Competent National Authorities and Proposal for the Modification of the Rules on Safeguards, *Journal of World Trade*, Vol. 36, no. 4 (August 2002), pp. 641-674.

三、相关网络资源

1. http://trb.mofcom.gov.cn/article/cx/.

2. https://www.wto.org/english/tratop_e/safeg_e/safeg_info_e.htm#definitive.

第四节　WTO 多边保障措施争端解决程序

【知识背景 / 学习要点】

根据《保障措施协定》第 14 条的规定,WTO 成员方有关本协定项下产生的保障措施的磋商和争端解决,适用由 DSU 纳入的 GATT1994 第 22 条和第 23 条(磋商和争端解决)的规定。因此,处理保障措施争端的多边救济程序,主要适用的是包括 DSU 第 4 条和第 6 条在内的一般规定。由于本书其他章节专门介绍 WTO 的争端解决程序,故本节不对相关条款进行展开。以下就保障措施的多边争端解决程序中的一些特殊问题进行介绍。

一、"评审标准"

《保障措施协定》本身的条款对于在多边争端解决中保障措施的评审标准没有进行规定,根据相关实践,DSU 第 11 条中对专家组审理案件的要求规则可以成为保障措施相符性问题审查的适当评审标准,[①] 因而 WTO 专家组对保

① DSU 第 11 条规定,"专家组的职能是协助 DSB 履行本谅解和适用协定项下的职责。因此,专家组应对其审议的事项作出客观评估,包括对该案件事实及有关适用协定的适用性和与有关适用协定的一致性的客观评估,并作出可协助 DSB 提出建议或提出适用协定所规定的裁决的其他调查结果。专家组应定期与争端各方磋商,并给予它们充分的机会以形成双方满意的解决办法。"

障措施的评审适用 DSU 第 11 条的规定。根据 DSU 第 11 条的规定，适当的评审标准既不是“重新审查”（即对事实的彻底审查和重新评价），也不是“完全尊重”，而是“对事实的客观评审”。[①] 因此，专家组对当事成员方提交给其审查的保障措施争端的相关事实应当进行“客观评审”。

但是，专家组按照 DSU 第 11 条要求对保障措施争端进行的“客观评审”也存在一定的问题，因为可以发现除了《反倾销协议》第 17.6 款之外，WTO 法律条文并未明确规定专家组对任何其他措施的审查标准规定。如前所述，《反倾销协议》第 17.6 款规定了适用于专家组处理 WTO 多边反倾销措施争端的两项特别评审标准规则，包括事实和法律评审标准。而处理 WTO 反倾销措施争端的评审标准，肯定在保障措施多边争端解决中是不适用的。故在实践中，保障措施多边争端解决程序中的“客观评审标准”，只能依靠专家组和上诉机构结合 DSU 第 11 条和《保障措施协定》中的某项具体条款进行综合解释。

二、新的解释观点

保障措施多边争端解决中也会涉及，受影响的申诉方在争端解决过程中对保障措施实施成员方提出的解释进行质疑，并且有的情况下甚至会给出新的替代解释。此时 WTO 专家组就要考虑是否接受这些新的解释观点，以及如何处理这些新的解释与被诉保障措施实施成员所作解释之间的关系的问题。

比如在 2001 年美国对自新西兰和澳大利亚进口的新鲜、冷冻或冰冻的羔羊肉的保障措施争端案中，申诉方澳大利亚和新西兰在专家组阶段就提出了新的替代解释观点。但是该案专家组却认为，申诉方的任何替代解释实际上都是对记录在案证据的新的分析，它们是与专家组的评审无关的，并且这些事实和法律观点只有在其是在原调查中提出的，而且专家组需要考虑在该调查中美国

① 上诉机构特别强调，“重新评估”不能被宽泛的解释。参见 Appellate Body Report, United States-Safeguard Measures on imports of Fresh, Chilled or Frozen Lamb Meat from New Zealand and Australia (US-Lamb), WT/DS177/AB/R, WT/DS178/AB/R, adopted 16 May 2001, paras. 102-107.

ITC 是否给出合理和充分解释时，才是与专家组的评审有关的。[①]

值得注意的是，《反倾销协议》第 17.6 款第（ii）项的第 2 句特别规定，“如果专家组认为一项相关条款允许不止一种可允许的解释，则如果主管机关的措施符合其中一种允许的解释，专家组应认定该措施符合本协定”。也就是说，在反倾销多边争端解决中，如果产生多种合理解释的话，WTO 争端审理机构必须尊重国内调查主管机关作出的解释。但是，由于保障措施多边争端解决缺乏类似的规定，因此类似必须尊重国内调查主管机关所作解释的义务，可能对处理保障措施争端的专家组而言并无必要。

三、机密信息处理

在涉及保障措施的争端解决程序中讨论的另一个程序性问题，是向专家组和世贸组织其他成员提供信息的保密问题。如果根据机密信息保护的措施在多边争端解决程序中受到质疑，那么前述 WTO 成员为履行其国内程序而在国内达成的平衡也可能受到影响。特别是，措施受到质疑的 WTO 成员可能面临两难的境地，要么在多边争端解决程序中提供其在国内视为机密的信息，要么无法证明其措施实施的正当性。在这方面，应当指出，DSU 第 13 条为争端当事各方规定了一项特定的义务，从而确保了多边争端解决程序的保密性。[②] 因此，根据该款，专家组可要求争端当事方提供它们认为与对事实评审相关的信息，争端当事方有义务为此进行配合。

在 2001 年的美国对欧盟进口的小麦面筋实施最终保障措施案中，虽然专

① Appellate Body Report, United States-Safeguard Measures on imports of Fresh, Chilled or Frozen Lamb Meat from New Zealand and Australia (US-Lamb), WT/DS177/AB/R, WT/DS178/AB/R, adopted 16 May 2001, para.110-113.

② DSU 第 13 条以“信息寻求权”（Right to Seek Information）为标题作出如下规定，“1. 每一专家组有权向其认为适当的任何个人或机构寻求信息和技术建议。但是，在专家组向一成员管辖范围内的任何个人或机构寻求此类信息或建议之前，应通知该成员主管机关。成员应迅速和全面地答复专家组提出的关于提供其认为必要和适的当信息的任何请求。未经提供信息的个人、机构或成员主管机关正式授权，所提供的机密信息不得披露。2. 专家组可向任何有关来源寻求信息，并与专家进行磋商以获得它们对该事项某些方面的意见。对于一争端方所提科学或其他技术事项的事实性问题，专家组可请求专家审议小组提供书面咨询报告。设立此类咨询小组的规则及其程序列在附录 4 中。”

家组根据 DSU 第 12.1 款愿意提供两套不同的商业机密信息保护程序，但是美国仍然拒绝向专家组和欧共体的代表提供专家组根据 DSU 第 13.1 款向其征询的信息。对此，该案上诉机构指出，美国拒绝提供所要信息的这种做法，不但严重损害了专家组根据 DSU 第 11 条的规定对事实和问题作出客观评估的能力，而且还削弱了世贸组织其他成员根据其讨价还价所达成的 DSU 中的程序，寻求“迅速”和“令人满意”地解决争端的能力。① 不过，2002 年美国对于韩国圆形焊接碳质管道钢管采取的最终保障措施案专家组裁定，以索引、汇总或加权平均（而不是完整的）形式等提供在国内保障措施调查程序中被作为机密的数据，足以对事实作出客观的评估。②

【案例摘录与评析】

2001 年美国对自新西兰和澳大利亚进口的新鲜、冷冻或冰冻的羔羊肉的保障措施争端案③

United States - Safeguard Measures on imports of Fresh, Chilled or Frozen Lamb Meat from New Zealand and Australia
(WT/DS177/AB/R, WT/DS178/AB/R)

A. Standard of Review

97. At the outset of its findings, the Panel considered the standard of review appropriate for examination of the claims made by Australia and New Zealand. After citing our Report in Argentina – Footwear Safeguard, the Panel formulated the standard in the following terms:

① Appellate Body Report, United States-Definitive Safeguard Measures on Imports of Wheat Gluten from the European Communities, WT/DS166/AB/R, adopted 19 January 2001, para. 171.

② 参见 Panel Report, United States-Definitive Safeguard Measures on Imports of Circular Welded Carbon Quality Line Pipe from Korea, WT/DS202/R, WT/DS178/R, adopted 8 March 2002, 以及 Appellate Body Report WT/DS202/AB/R, WT/DS178/AB/R, paras.7.8-7.10.

③ Appellate Body Report, United States-Safeguard Measures on imports of Fresh, Chilled or Frozen Lamb Meat from New Zealand and Australia (US-Lamb), WT/DS177/AB/R, WT/DS178/AB/R, adopted 16 May 2001. 原文脚注省略。

... the standard of review that applies in safeguard disputes, as set out above, requires us to refrain from a de novo review of the evidence reflected in the report published by the competent national authorities. Our task is limited to a review of the determination made by the USITC and to examining whether the published report provides an adequate explanation of how the facts as a whole support the USITC's threat determination.

98. When the Panel came to examine the specific claims of Australia and New Zealand under Article 4.2, the Panel stated:

In examining the USITC's threat of serious injury determination we examine, first, whether the USITC evaluated "all relevant factors of an objective and quantifiable nature having a bearing on the situation of [the] industry", in particular, the factors listed in SG Article 4.2(a), as well as any other relevant factors. Second, we examine whether the approach followed by the USITC consisted of a fact-based, future oriented consideration of increased imports and of the condition of the US domestic industry. (emphasis in original)

99. Australia and New Zealand challenge two aspects of the Panel's standard of review. First, they argue that the Panel erred in its interpretation, and, therefore, formulation, of the legal standard to be used to review the determinations made by competent authorities in safeguard investigations. Second, they assert that, in reviewing the USITC's determination of a threat of serious injury, the Panel erred in its application of the standard of review.

100. As the Panel noted, we had occasion to examine, in Argentina – Footwear Safeguard, the standard of review appropriate to a panel's examination of claims made under the Agreement on Safeguards. In that appeal, we observed that:

[t]he Agreement on Safeguards ... is silent as to the appropriate standard of review. Therefore, Article 11 of the DSU, and, in particular, its requirement that "... a panel should make an objective assessment of the matter before it, including an objective assessment of the facts of the case and the applicability of and conformity with the relevant covered agreements", sets forth the appropriate standard of review for examining the consistency of a safeguard measure with the provisions of the Agreement on Safeguards.

101. As regards the standard of review contained in Article 11 of the DSU, we recall that, in European Communities – Hormones, we stated that "the applicable standard is neither de novo review as such, nor 'total deference', but rather the 'objective assessment of the facts' ".

102. In our Report in Argentina – Footwear Safeguard, we gave certain indications as to the application of the standard of review in Article 11 of the DSU in disputes where claims are made under Article 4 of the Agreement on Safeguards:

> ... with respect to its application of the standard of review, we do not believe that the Panel conducted a de novo review of the evidence, or that it substituted its analysis and judgement for that of the Argentine authorities. Rather, the Panel examined whether, as required by Article 4 of the Agreement on Safeguards, the Argentine authorities had considered all the relevant facts and had adequately explained how the facts supported the determinations that were made. Indeed, far from departing from its responsibility, in our view, the Panel was simply fulfilling its responsibility under Article 11 of the DSU in taking the approach it did. To determine whether the safeguard investigation and the resulting safeguard measure applied by Argentina were consistent with Article 4 of the Agreement on Safeguards, the Panel was obliged, by the very terms of Article 4, to assess whether the Argentine authorities had examined all the relevant facts and had provided a reasoned explanation of how the facts supported their determination. (underlining added)

103. Thus, an "objective assessment" of a claim under Article 4.2(a) of the Agreement on Safeguards has, in principle, two elements. First, a panel must review whether competent authorities have evaluated all relevant factors, and, second, a panel must review whether the authorities have provided a reasoned and adequate explanation of how the facts support their determination. Thus, the panel's objective assessment involves a formal aspect and a substantive aspect. The formal aspect is whether the competent authorities have evaluated "all relevant factors". The substantive aspect is whether the competent authorities have given a reasoned and adequate explanation for their determination.

104. This dual character of a panel's review is mandated by the nature of the specific obligations that Article 4.2 of the Agreement on Safeguards imposes on competent authorities. Under Article 4.2(a), competent authorities must, as a formal matter, evaluate "all relevant factors". However, that evaluation is not simply a matter of form, and the list of relevant factors to be evaluated is not a mere "check list". Under Article 4.2(a), competent authorities must conduct a substantive evaluation of "the 'bearing', or the 'influence' or 'effect' " or "impact" that the relevant factors have on the "situation of [the] domestic industry". (emphasis added) By conducting such a substantive evaluation of the relevant factors, competent authorities are able to make a proper overall determination, inter alia, as to whether the domestic industry is seriously injured or is threatened with such injury as defined in the Agreement.

105. It follows that the precise nature of the examination to be conducted by a panel, in reviewing a claim under Article 4.2 of the Agreement on Safeguards, stems, in part, from the

panel's obligation to make an "objective assessment of the matter" under Article 11 of the DSU and, in part, from the obligations imposed by Article 4.2, to the extent that those obligations are part of the claim. Thus, as with any claim under the provisions of a covered agreement, panels are required to examine, in accordance with Article 11 of the DSU , whether the Member has complied with the obligations imposed by the particular provisions identified in the claim. By examining whether the explanation given by the competent authorities in their published report is reasoned and adequate, panels can determine whether those authorities have acted consistently with the obligations imposed by Article 4.2 of the Agreement on Safeguards.

106. We wish to emphasize that, although panels are not entitled to conduct a de novo review of the evidence, nor to substitute their own conclusions for those of the competent authorities, this does not mean that panels must simply accept the conclusions of the competent authorities. To the contrary, in our view, in examining a claim under Article 4.2(a), a panel can assess whether the competent authorities' explanation for its determination is reasoned and adequate only if the panel critically examines that explanation, in depth, and in the light of the facts before the panel. Panels must, therefore, review whether the competent authorities' explanation fully addresses the nature, and, especially, the complexities, of the data, and responds to other plausible interpretations of that data. A panel must find, in particular, that an explanation is not reasoned, or is not adequate, if some alternative explanation of the facts is plausible, and if the competent authorities' explanation does not seem adequate in the light of that alternative explanation. Thus, in making an "objective assessment" of a claim under Article 4.2(a), panels must be open to the possibility that the explanation given by the competent authorities is not reasoned or adequate.

107. In this respect, the phrase "de novo review" should not be used loosely. If a panel concludes that the competent authorities, in a particular case, have not provided a reasoned or adequate explanation for their determination, that panel has not, thereby, engaged in a de novo review. Nor has that panel substituted its own conclusions for those of the competent authorities. Rather, the panel has, consistent with its obligations under the DSU, simply reached a conclusion that the determination made by the competent authorities is inconsistent with the specific requirements of Article 4.2 of the Agreement on Safeguards.

108. In this case, as we have noted, the Panel formulated the standard of review by reference to our Report in Argentina – Footwear Safeguard, and the Panel also, explicitly, rejected any standard implying a de novo review of the evidence. Indeed, the Panel quoted the passage in our Report in Argentina – Footwear Safeguard to which we have just referred, and specifically drew attention to our statement, in that passage, that panels must examine whether competent

authorities have examined all relevant factors and whether those authorities have provided a reasoned and adequate explanation for their determination. Accordingly, we find that the Panel correctly interpreted the standard of review appropriate to the examination of the claims by Australia and New Zealand.

109. It will be recalled, though, that Australia and New Zealand have also appealed the Panel's application of the standard of review. For the most part, their appeal on the application of the standard of review is related to these participants' respective appeals that the Panel erred in finding that the USITC had acted consistently with Article 4.2 of the Agreement on Safeguards in determining that there existed a threat of serious injury to the United States' domestic lamb meat industry. We will, therefore, examine most of these arguments when we consider the issues relating to the existence of a threat of serious injury.

110. However, one aspect of New Zealand's appeal on the application of the standard of review raises a general procedural question we will address now. This pertains to the arguments that a panel is entitled to consider in reviewing competent authorities' determinations. The Panel said in this regard:

> ... to the extent that any of the alternative explanations put forward by Australia and New Zealand are in effect new analyses of the record evidence, they are not relevant to our review. Rather, these factual and legal arguments would be relevant to our review only to the extent that they were raised in the investigation, in which case we would need to consider whether the USITC gave a reasoned explanation of why the facts supported its conclusions in respect of them, and whether that explanation is persuasive. (emphasis added)

111. Thus, the Panel confined its own review of the competent authorities' determination to an examination of that determination in terms of the factual and legal arguments put forward by the interested parties during the domestic investigation conducted under Article 3.1 of the Agreement on Safeguards.

112. In our report in Thailand – Anti-Dumping Duties on Angles, Shapes and Sections of Iron or Non-Alloy Steel H-Beams from Poland, in the course of our examination of the specificity of Poland's request for the establishment of a panel under Article 6.2 of the DSU, we said:

The Panel's reasoning seems to assume that there is always continuity between claims raised in an underlying anti-dumping investigation and claims raised by a complaining party in a related dispute brought before the WTO. This is not necessarily the case. The parties involved in an underlying anti-dumping investigation are generally exporters, importers and other commercial entities, while those involved in WTO dispute settlement are the Members of the WTO. Therefore, it cannot be assumed that the range of issues raised in an anti-dumping investigation will be the same as the claims that a Member chooses to bring before the WTO in a dispute. (emphasis added)

113. Although the claim under examination in that appeal was different, the same reasoning applies in respect of the relationship between domestic investigations culminating in the imposition of a safeguard measure, and dispute settlement proceedings under the DSU regarding that safeguard measure. In arguing claims in dispute settlement, a WTO Member is not confined merely to rehearsing arguments that were made to the competent authorities by the interested parties during the domestic investigation, even if the WTO Member was itself an interested party in that investigation. Likewise, panels are not obliged to determine, and confirm themselves the nature and character of the arguments made by the interested parties to the competent authorities. Arguments before national competent authorities may be influenced by, and focused on, the requirements of the national laws, regulations and procedures. On the other hand, dispute settlement proceedings brought under the DSU concerning safeguard measures imposed under the Agreement on Safeguards may involve arguments that were not submitted to the competent authorities by the interested parties.

114. Furthermore, we recall that, in United States – Wheat Gluten Safeguard, we reversed a finding by the panel that competent authorities are obliged to evaluate only those other relevant factors, under Article 4.2(a), which were actually raised by the interested parties during the investigation before it. We said there that competent authorities have an independent duty of investigation and that they cannot "remain passive in the face of possible short-comings in the evidence submitted, and views expressed, by the interested parties." (emphasis added) In short, competent authorities are obliged, in some circumstances, to go beyond the arguments that were advanced by the interested parties during the investigation. As competent authorities themselves are obliged, in some circumstances, to go beyond the arguments of the interested parties in reaching their own determinations, so too, we believe, panels are not limited to the arguments submitted by the interested parties to the competent authorities in reviewing those determinations in WTO dispute settlement.

115. We wish to emphasize that the discretion that WTO Members enjoy to argue dispute settlement claims in the manner they deem appropriate does not, of course, detract from their obligation, under Article 3.10 of the DSU, "to engage in dispute settlement procedures 'in good faith in an effort to resolve the dispute'." It follows that WTO Members cannot improperly

withhold arguments from competent authorities with a view to raising those arguments later before a panel. In any event, as a practical matter, we think it unlikely that a Member would do so.

116. At the oral hearing before us, New Zealand indicated that, in its view, the Panel had failed to consider the econometric arguments it had set forth in Exhibit NZ-13 on the ground that these arguments had not been presented to the USITC. In view of our findings below, we do not find it necessary to examine the significance of Exhibit NZ-13.

【本案评析】

以上案例节选自2001年美国对自新西兰和澳大利亚进口的新鲜、冷冻或冰冻的羔羊肉的保障措施争端案上诉机构报告。该案申诉方澳大利亚和新西兰提出两项质疑，即专家组对于保障措施主管机关的裁定在评审法律标准的解释上存在错误，以及专家组在审查美国ITC对损害威胁的裁定时的评审标准适用错误。

对于第一项质疑，上诉机构在考察相关案件的基础上裁定，DSU第11条中对专家组审理案件的要求规则可以成为本案涉及美国实施的保障措施与《保障措施协定》第4条的相符性评审问题的适当标准。基于DSU第11条提出的"对事实的客观评审"和本案涉及的《保障措施协定》第4.2款(a)项，上诉机构认为，本案专家组必须审查国内主管机关是否按照第4条的要求考虑了所有相关的事实，并充分解释了这些事实是如何支持其所作出的裁定的。上诉机构进一步提出，根据《保障措施协定》第4.2款(a)项对申诉进行的"客观评审"有两个要素：一个是形式要素，另一个是实质要素。专家组必须评审的形式要素是指，主管机关是否对所有相关要素进行了评估，而专家组必须评审的实质要素是指，调查主管机关是否就相关事实如何支持其裁定提供了合理和充分的解释。基于这一分析，上诉机构指出，专家组在审查根据第4.2款(a)项提出的申诉时，对于主管机关其裁定的解释是否合理和充分，只有专家组在根据已经获得的事实，对调查主管机关的解释进行了深入的审查后才能评估。专家组必须审查主管机关的解释是否充分澄清了数据的性质，特别是数据的复杂性，并对该数据的其他合理解释作出回应。专家组尤其必须发现，如果对事实的某种替代性解释是可信的，而且若根据这种替代性解释，主管机关的解释看来并不充分，则主管机关的解释是没有理由的，或者是不充分的。总之，在对根据第4.2款(a)项提出的主张进行"客观评审"时，专家组必须对主管机关所作的解释不合理或不充分的可能性持开放的态度。

第二项质疑主要来自该案专家组的裁定，亦即该案专家组将对主管机关裁定的自身评审局限于，采用利害关系方在根据《保障措施协定》第3.1款执行国内调查时所提出的相关事实和法律观点。对此，上诉机构分析了最终实施保障措施的国内调查与DSU关于该保障措施的争端解决程序之间的关系，并否定了专家组的裁定。上诉机构指出，WTO成员方就争端解决中的主张进行辩论时，不仅限于就国内调查期间利害关系方向调查主管机关提交的论点进行辩论，即使WTO成员方本身是调查中的利害关系方。同样，专家组们自身也没有义务去认定和确认利害关系方向主管机关提交的论点的性质与特征。国内调查主管机关的观点可能受到国家法律、法规和程序要求的影响，并侧重于这些要求。另外，与根据《保障措施协定》实施的保障措施有关的依据DSU提起的争端解决程序可能会涉及利害关系方尚未向主管机关提出的观点。

【延伸阅读】

一、相关典型案例

1. Argentina—Safeguard Measures on Imports of Footwear(WT/DS121)

2. Chile—Price Band System and Safeguard Measures Relating to Certain Agricultural Products(WT/DS207)

3. Dominican Republic—Safeguard Measures on Imports of Polypropylene Bags and Tubular Fabric(WT/DS415, WT/DS416, WT/DS417, WT/DS418)

4. Korea—Definitive Safeguard Measure on Imports of Certain Dairy Products(WT/DS98)

5. United States—Definitive Safeguard Measures on Imports of Wheat Gluten from the European Communities(WT/DS166)

6. United States—Definitive Safeguard Measures on Imports of Circular Welded Carbon Quality Line Pipe from Korea(WT/DS202)

7. United States—Definitive Safeguard Measures on Imports of Certain Steel Products, (WT/DS248, WT/DS249, WT/DS251, WT/DS252, WT/DS253, WT/DS254, WT/DS258, WT/DS259)

二、相关学术论著

1. 曹建明、贺小勇:《世界贸易组织》,法律出版社 2012 年版。

2. 杨国华:《WTO 的理念》,厦门大学出版社 2012 年版。

3. Dukgeun Ahn, *"Restructuring the WTO Safeguard System",in Mitsuo Matsushita, Dukgeun Ahn and Tain-Jy Chen,eds.,The WTO Trade Remedy System: East Asian Perspective,* London, Cameron May Publishers, 2006, pp.11~31.

4. Peter Van den Bossche, *The Law and Policy of the World Trade Organization: Text, Cases and Materials,* Cambridge University Press, 2017.

三、相关网络资源

1. http://trb.mofcom.gov.cn/article/cx/.

2. https://www.wto.org/english/tratop_e/safeg_e/safeg_info_e.htm#special.

第八章

WTO 争端解决法律实务

【内容摘要】

在WTO运行的过程中，WTO争端解决机制作为“王冠上的明珠”，为WTO的良好运行打下了坚实的基础。WTO争端解决机制继承与完善了GATT时期争端解决机制。WTO争端解决机制程序主要分为磋商、专家组程序、上诉审议程序和执行程序四个阶段。不过，WTO争端解决机制也仍然存在着一定的缺陷，需要进一步完善。总体而言，WTO争端解决机制较为行之有效，获得了WTO成员方的普遍认可。随着中国逐渐推进“一带一路”建设，与“一带一路”倡议相关的贸易纠纷也将大量出现，WTO争端解决机制也将在争端解决中发挥重要作用。

第一节　WTO 争端解决概述

【知识背景 / 学习要点】

WTO争端解决机制属于WTO组成部分，同样由乌拉圭回合谈判成果发展而来。其继承自运行数十年的GATT争端解决机制，并在此基础上进行了完善。经过乌拉圭回合的漫长谈判，《建立世界贸易组织马拉喀什协议》于1994年4月15日正式签署，同样获得通过的还有其附件《关于争端解决规则和程序的谅解》(*Understanding on Rules and Procedures Governing the Settlement of Disputes, DSU*)。

一、WTO 争端解决机制的规则及其适用范围

WTO 争端解决机制有一整套 WTO 规则体系作为支撑。具体而言，DSU 建立了一套完善的争端解决程序，因而成为 WTO 争端解决机制的核心文件。DSU 具体包括了 27 个条款和 4 个附件。其中，第 1 条至第 3 条为关于 WTO 争端解决机制的总的规定，具体包括了范围和适用、管理和总则等内容。第 4 条至第 22 条则为 WTO 争端解决的程序性规定，具体包括了磋商、斡旋调解和调停、专家组的设立、专家组的职权范围、专家组的组成、多个投诉方的程序、第三方、专家组的职能、专家组的程序、寻求信息的权利、保密性、中期审议阶段、专家组报告的通过、上诉审议、与专家组或上诉机构的联系、专家组和上诉机构的建议、DSB 的时限、监督建议和裁决的执行、补偿和减让的中止等内容。第 23 条至第 27 条则规定了一定的补充规则，对特殊问题进行了补充规定，具体包括多边体制的加强、涉及最不发达成员的特殊程序、仲裁、秘书处的职责等内容。除正文条款外，《本谅解适用的协议》、《适用协议所含特殊或附加规则与程序》、《工作程序》、《专家审议小组》DSU4 个附件，分别对相关议题进行了进一步的补充。其中，专家组和上诉机构工作程序的规定包括 DSU 附件 3《工作程序》和附件 4《专家审议小组》，以及在 WTO 解决争端的实践中 DSB 所制定的大量工作程序，如《上诉机构工作程序》、《DSB 会议议事规则》、《DSB 行为规则》、《关于争端解决程序的工作实践》、《根据〈反补贴措施协定〉第 8 条第 5 款进行仲裁的程序》等等。

除了 DSU 及其有关规则外，GATT1994 第 22 条、第 23 条同样规定了争端解决的核心问题。它们最初可以追溯至 GATT 成立之初的 GATT1947 第 22 条和第 23 条。在随后的实践中，GATT 争端解决机制逐步得到完善。尤其在 GATT 存续期间，有关争端解决机制的大量决议得以通过。这些决议中的绝大部分在乌拉圭回合谈判中被 DSU 所吸收，因而成为 DSU 形成的重要基础。此外，GATS 第 22 条、第 23 条也规定了服务贸易争端解决的相关内容，具体

包括了磋商、争端解决与执行程序等。由于服务贸易与货物贸易在特点、待遇等方面存在区别，故GATS与GATT第22条、第23条在磋商、争端解决机制启动等方面也存在着一定的差异。[①]

根据DSU第1条的规定，WTO争端解决机制的规则和程序应适用于按照DSU附录1所列各项协定(适用协定)的磋商和所提出的争端，并适用于各成员间有关他们在《建立世界贸易组织协定》(《WTO协定》)和DSU规定下的权利义务磋商和争端解决。据此，WTO争端解决机制适用于成员方根据以下协定进行的磋商和提起的争端，它们包括了WTO协定、多边贸易协定，包括了附件1A GATT及其附件、附件1B《服务贸易总协定》(GATS)、附件1C《与贸易有关的知识产权协定》(TRIPs)与附件2 DSU，以及附件4中的《民用航空器贸易协定》与《政府采购协定》等。除此之外，还有其他较为特殊的协定同样属于DSU的适用范围。例如，《中华人民共和国入世议定书》第1.2条的规定，《入世议定书》和《中国加入世界贸易组织工作组报告》第342段所指的承诺，应成为《建立世界贸易组织协定》的组成部分。这意味着《入世议定书》和《中国加入世界贸易组织工作组报告》第342段所指的承诺，也属于WTO争端解决机制的适用范围。上述规定为有关《入世议定书》适用的有关争端能够适用DSU与WTO争端解决机制提供了法律依据。

二、WTO争端解决机制所处理的争端类型

针对WTO争端解决机制所处理的争端类型，GATT1994第23条规定了三种类型：违反之诉、非违反之诉和其他情况之诉。DSU第3条第8款和第26条对此问题又进行了更详细的规定。此外，GATS第23条也规定了服务贸易争端解决的两种类型：违反之诉与非违反之诉——与GATT第23条相比，其并未规定其他情况之诉。

① 李秀香等：《WTO规则解读与运用》，东北财经大学出版社2012年版，第294~295页。

（一）违反之诉

根据 GATT 第 23 条第 1 款（a）的规定，“违反之诉”是指一成员认为其依照协定所享有的直接或间接利益由于另一成员违反协定义务的行为被抵消或减损而提起的诉讼。为了具体界定该问题，在 GATT 实践中发展出了“初步被抵消或减损的情况”（a prima facie case of nullification or impairment）的理论。与之相比，GATS 所规定的违反之诉并不要求结果要件，只要措施构成对 WTO 义务的违反，则申诉方即拥有充分条件发起服务贸易争端解决程序。不过实践中，在 GATT 相关的争端解决案件在审理中，专家组往往采取模式推定的态度，而结果要件存在与否并不影响违反之诉的成立。这一推定也为 DSU 第 3 条第 8 款所确认——根据 DSU 第 3 条第 8 款的规定，只要“被诉方”违反了协定义务，该行动即被视为初步构成利益抵消或减损的情况

（二）非违反之诉（Non-violation Complaints）

根据 GATT 第 23 条第 1 款（b）项提起的申诉，通常被称为非违反之诉。具体来说，一成员在他成员“非违反”的情况下提起“诉讼”，必须首先证明自身的利益被抵消或减损。这种规定不仅在法律上，而且在事实上保障成员方利益，确保成员方获得更广泛的权利义务平衡的各种商业机会。但是，由于理论上并未对非违反之诉的范围进行明确的界定，实践中提起非违反之诉是比较容易的，只需证明自己的利益被抵消或减损即可。这样，稍有不慎就可能出现滥用“非违反之诉”的情况。对此，GATT 时期的“智利诉澳大利亚补贴硫酸铵案”中确立了“合理期望原则”，一旦一成员的措施否定了其贸易成员可以合理期望获得的利润，则该非违反行为所造成的抵消或减损就可成立。合理期望原则应符合以下条件：（1）投诉方原来产生期望时，不可预见这一被控措施的出现；（2）被诉的措施使投诉方根据已达成的协定、被诉方的言辞或行为而产生的对更好的市场准入条件的合理期望落空。与之相比，GATS 的非违反之诉的规定更加具体和严密，体现了对于货物贸易争端解决时间经验的吸收与完善。

WTO 成立之后，DSU 第 26 条第 1 款不仅重申了 GATT 第 23 条第 1 款

（b）项的规定，而且还在此基础之上，要求投诉方在非违反之诉中应当提供详细的理由，证明被诉方的措施虽然不违反协定，但是其根据这些协定应得的利益受到了影响，或者协定目标的实现受到了阻碍，即投诉方负举证责任。被诉方没有义务撤销该措施，专家组或上诉机构应建议有关成员达成一项相互满意的调整方法，补偿可以作为调整的一种方式。经争端一方的要求，可以通过仲裁来决定关于利益被抵消或减损的各项水平，仲裁也可以提出调整方法和手段的建议。

（三）其他情况之诉

迄今为止，GATT/WTO 中没有涉及“其他情况之诉”的案例。投诉方只有在认为不存在上述两种诉由时，才能提起“其他情况之诉”。投诉方应当提供详细的理由，说明不存在违反或不违反的情况而自己的应得利益受到了影响，或者协定目标的实现受到了阻碍。

三、WTO 争端解决机制机构设置与决策方式

（一）WTO 争端解决机构设置

在 WTO 的组织架构中，涉及争端解决程序的机构主要包括了总理事会、争端解决机构、总干事及其领导的秘书处、上诉机构，以及非常设的专家组。其中，专家组也包括了 DSU 第 21 条与第 22 条所分别规定的程序专家组与仲裁程序仲裁人。

争端解决机构主要在于设立专家组，审议专家组或上诉机构报告并决定是否予以通过，确定执行的合理期限并监督裁决执行，以及最终的授权报复并确定报复范围与水平。总干事则有权提供斡旋、调节或调停，也可以应争端方请求决定专家组的组成。秘书处则应当协助专家组，在法律、程序等方面提供支持。对于争端方而言，秘书处也负有提供专家组名单并向争端方提供建议的专家组提名、收取争端方书面陈述以及专家组与其他争端方的程序方面的职责。上诉机构是争端解决机构中的常设机构，负责对被提起上诉的专家组报告中的

法律问题进行审查。上诉机构共 7 名成员，一般由其中 3 人组成审判庭审理专家组报告中的对应内容。上诉机构对于保证 WTO 规则适用的准确性、统一性与一致性具有重要的意义。相较于上诉机构，专家组则是争端解决机构的非常设机构，一般由争端双方成员磋商后从秘书处的专家名单中选择。在双方难以达成合意时，专家组成员由总干事负责任命。专家组主要职责在于对争端的事实问题与法律问题进行审议与认定，以协助争端解决机构作出裁决与建议。而特殊的程序专家组与仲裁程序裁决者，通常均为原专家组。前者主要职责在于裁定被诉一方对于裁决或建议的执行是否与有关协定的要求一致，而后者则负责裁定拟中止减让水平是否等同于利益丧失或受损水平，并确定具体的中止减让额度。

（二）WTO 争端解决的决策方式

在 WTO 之前，GATT 实行协商一致的决策原则，专家组审理案件通常要经过争端当事方的同意，而专家组报告生效也须以缔约方全体通过为前提。这为败诉方阻挠专家组报告通过创造了机会，并严重影响了争端解决机制的正常运转。为解决这一弊病，WTO 对争端解决机制的决策方式进行了变革。根据《建立世界贸易组织协定》和 DSU 的相关规定，WTO 争端解决机制实行“反向协商一致”（negative consensus）的决策方式，即，只要不是全体成员方一致否决，该决策事项就自动获得通过。采用这一决策方式的事项主要包括专家组设立、专家组报告和上诉机构报告的通过、授权报复等争端解决过程中的重要问题。这种“反向协商一致”的决策方式，基本上使 WTO 争端解决机制的裁定自动生效，从而解决了国际法裁决约束力不足的问题，迫使各成员方保证国内法与 WTO 规则的一致性，并使得争端方最终接受并执行争端解决机制的裁决。WTO 自成立以来的实践表明，这种决策方式对于保障争端解决机制的效率起了决定性的作用。

【协定文本摘录】

《关税与贸易总协定》第 22 条和第 23 条

General Agreement on Tariff and Trade

Article XXII

Consultation

Each contracting party shall accord sympathetic consideration to, and shall afford adequate opportunity for consultation regarding, such representations as may be made by another contracting party with respect to any matter affecting the operation of this Agreement.

The CONTRACTING PARTIES may, at the request of a contracting party, consult with any contracting party or parties in respect of any matter for which it has not been possible to find a satisfactory solution through consultation under paragraph 1.

Article XXIII

Nullification or Impairment

1. If any contracting party should consider that any benefit accruing to it directly or indirectly under this Agreement is being nullified or impaired or that the attainment of any objective of the Agreement is being impeded as the result of

(a) the failure of another contracting party to carry out its obligations under this Agreement, or

(b) the application by another contracting party of any measure, whether or not it conflicts with the provisions of this Agreement, or

(c) the existence of any other situation, the contracting party may, with a view to the satisfactory adjustment of the matter, make written representations or proposals to the other contracting party or parties which it considers to be concerned.

Any contracting party thus approached shall give sympathetic consideration to the representations or proposals made to it.

2. If no satisfactory adjustment is effected between the contracting parties concerned within a reasonable time, or if the difficulty is of the type described in paragraph 1 (c) of this Article, the matter may be referred to the CONTRACTING PARTIES. The CONTRACTING PARTIES shall promptly investigate any matter so referred to them and shall make appropriate recommendations to the contracting parties which they consider to be concerned, or give a ruling on the matter, as appropriate. The CONTRACTING PARTIES may consult with contracting parties, with the Economic and Social Council of the United Nations and with any appropriate inter-governmental

organization in cases where they consider such consultation necessary. If the CONTRACTING PARTIES consider that the circumstances are serious enough to justify such action, they may authorize a contracting party or parties to suspend the application to any other contracting party or parties of such concessions or other obligations under this Agreement as they determine to be appropriate in the circumstances. If the application to any contracting party of any concession or other obligation is in fact suspended, that contracting party shall then be free, not later than sixty days after such action is taken, to give written notice to the Executive Secretary① to the Contracting Parties of its intention to withdraw from this Agreement and such withdrawal shall take effect upon the sixtieth day following the day on which such notice is received by him.

【延伸阅读】

一、相关典型案例

1. Brazil—Measures Affecting Desiccated Coconut, (WT/DS22)

2. India—Patent Protection for Pharmaceutical and Agricultural Chemical Products, (WT/DS50)

3. United States—Anti-Dumping Measures on Certain Hot-Rolled Steel Products from Japan, (WT/DS184)

4. Argentina—Definitive Anti-Dumping Duties on Poultry from Brazil, (WT/DS241)

5. Korea—Measures Affecting Trade in Commercial Vessels, (WT/DS273)

6. United States—Certain Measures Affecting Imports of Poultry from China, (WT/DS392)

二、相关学术论著

1. 黄东黎、杨国华:《世界贸易组织法: 理论•条约•中国案例》, 社会科学文献出版社 2013 年版。

2. 曹建明、贺小勇:《世界贸易组织》, 法律出版社 2012 年版。

3. 王传丽:《国际贸易法》, 法律出版社 2012 年版。

4. 韩立余:《既往不咎——WTO 争端解决机制研究》, 北京大学出版社 2009 年版。

① By the Decision of 23 March 1965, the CONTRACTING PARTIES changed the title of the head of the GATT secretariat from “Executive Secretary” to “Director-General”.

5. 李秀香等:《WTO 规则解读与运用》，东北财经大学出版社 2012 年版。

6. 毛燕琼:《WTO 争端解决机制问题与改革》，法律出版社 2010 年版。

7. Abhijit Das, James J. Nedumpara, *WTO Dispute Settlement at Twenty: Insiders' Reflections on India's Participation,* Springer, 2016.

8. Ralph H. Folsom, *Principles of International Litigation and Arbitration,* West Academic Publishers, 2016.

9.Rüdiger Wolfrum, Peter-Tobias Stoll, And Karen Kaiser, *WTO–Institutions And Dispute Settlement,* Martinus Nijhoff Publishers, 2006.

三、相关网络资源

https://www.wto.org/english/res_e/publications_e/ai17_e/dsu_e.htm.

第二节　WTO 争端解决机制的程序要点

【知识背景 / 学习要点】

WTO 争端解决机制的法律程序主要包括了三个阶段，分别为磋商阶段、审理阶段与执行阶段。其中，审理阶段又可以具体分为专家组程序与上诉审查程序这两个部分的内容。因此，本部分内容主要包括了磋商、专家组程序、上诉审查程序与裁决执行程序这四个部分的内容。

一、磋商程序

磋商程序是 WTO 争端解决的必经程序，其目的在于促使成员方之间通过协商，探讨解决争端的可能性。该程序是 WTO 争端解决的第一步，一旦磋商启动，则标志着争议案件进入了争端解决程序。有关磋商的程序由 DSU 第 4 条规定。根据相关规定，一旦成员方接到磋商请求，被请求磋商的成员应该在收到请求的 10 日内就是否磋商进行答复，并且在不超过 30 日内善意地进行磋商。双方也可以另行商定进行磋商的时限，且不受上述期限的约束。此外，第三方若认为磋商问题涉及自身实质性利益，可以在磋商公告后 10 日内通告争端解决机构以及磋商各方，要求参与磋商。若其所声称的实质性利益确实存在，则第三方参与磋商的请求应当被接受。

若磋商中出现以下几种情况，在磋商请求方的请求之下，专家组程序将会启动。其一，如果在上述期限内没有给予答复或者开展磋商，磋商请求方可以直接申请设立专家组，磋商程序就此告一段落。其二，如果在收到磋商请求后 60 日内不能通过磋商解决争端，请求方可以申请设立专家组。其三，若双方一致认为磋商无法解决该争端，请求方可以申请设立专家组。在紧急情况下，应在 10 日内进行磋商，如 20 日内不能通过磋商解决争端，申请方可以要求设立专家组。需要注意的是，上述规定只是为磋商请求方创设了请求设立专家组的权利，在上述相关期限届满之后，如果磋商请求方认为仍有必要继续磋商，仍然可以与被请求方继续磋商。实践中，很多案件的磋商时间都大大超过了上述 60 日的期限。

磋商请求应以书面形式作出，其中需包括请求理由、争端中各项措施的资料以及请求的法律依据。磋商请求必须向争端解决机构和有关理事会、委员会进行通报。

【协定文本摘录】

《关于争端解决规制及程序的谅解》第 4 条磋商

Understanding on Rules and Procedures Governing the Settlement of Disputes

Article 4

Consultation

3. If a request for consultations is made pursuant to a covered agreement, the Member to which the request is made shall, unless otherwise mutually agreed, reply to the request within 10 days after the date of its receipt and shall enter into consultations in good faith within a period of no more than 30 days after the date of receipt of the request, with a view to reaching a mutually satisfactory solution. If the Member does not respond within 10 days after the date of receipt of

the request, or does not enter into consultations within a period of no more than 30 days, or a period otherwise mutually agreed, after the date of receipt of the request, then the Member that requested the holding of consultations may proceed directly to request the establishment of a panel.

...

7. If the consultations fail to settle a dispute within 60 days after the date of receipt of the request for consultations, the complaining party may request the establishment of a panel. The complaining party may request a panel during the 60-day period if the consulting parties jointly consider that consultations have failed to settle the dispute.

8. In cases of urgency, including those which concern perishable goods, Members shall enter into consultations within a period of no more than 10 days after the date of receipt of the request. If the consultations have failed to settle the dispute within a period of 20 days after the date of receipt of the request, the complaining party may request the establishment of a panel.

...

11. Whenever a Member other than the consulting Members considers that it has a substantial trade interest in consultations being held pursuant to paragraph 1 of Article XXII of GATT 1994, paragraph 1 of Article XXII of GATS, or the corresponding provisions in other covered agreements, such Member may notify the consulting Members and the DSB, within 10 days after the date of the circulation of the request for consultations under said Article, of its desire to be joined in the consultations. Such Member shall be joined in the consultations, provided that the Member to which the request for consultations was addressed agrees that the claim of substantial interest is well-founded. In that event they shall so inform the DSB. If the request to be joined in the consultations is not accepted, the applicant Member shall be free to request consultations under paragraph 1 of Article XXII or paragraph 1 of Article XXIII of GATT 1994, paragraph 1 of Article XXII or paragraph 1 of Article XXIII of GATS, or the corresponding provisions in other covered agreements.

二、专家组程序

如果争端不能在磋商程序中得到解决，那么申诉方可以向争端解决机构提出设立专家组的请求。专家组程序是 WTO 争端解决中最重要的程序之一。DSU 共 27 条，其中有关专家组程序的条款就有 11 条之多，可见一斑。根据有关规则，专家组应在提出设立专家组请求之后的 45 日内设立，并在 6 个月之内向争端各方提出报告。在紧急情况下，专家组提出报告的期限则缩短为 3 个月。

在专家组程序中，有以下几个问题值得特别关注：

（一）专家组的设立与组成

根据 DSU 第 6 条的规定，专家组的设立遵从“反向协商一致”原则，即一旦争端方提出设立申请，专家组最终应该是自动设立的。针对设立专家组的申请，争端解决机构最迟应该在将该请求列入争端解决机构正式议程的会议之后的下一次会议上成立专家组。这一规定意味着，在该请求列入争端解决机构正式议程的会议上。被诉方可以阻挠或否决专家组的设立，但在下一次会议上，专家组的设立是自动的，这时被诉方不再有权否决专家组的设立。

专家组成员一般由秘书长指定，除非反对方能够给出令人信服的理由，否则其反对意见将不会被考虑。此外，DSU 第 8 条规定了专家组成的资格问题，拥有专家资格的人主要包括了如下三类：现任或前任政府官员，GATT 或 WTO 官员，以及贸易方面的学者与律师。同时，专家组程序也有相应的回避制度，除非当事方同意或不持异议，专家组成员不应是争端当事方与争端第三方的公民。若案件涉及发展中国家，在该发展中国家的要求下，专家组成员中应当至少有一名成员来自发展中国家。专家组成员在案件审议过程中，应以个人身份任职。政府或成员方不应对专家组成员作出指示或施加影响，干扰专家组成员公正判案。为了保障专家组成员审案时的独立、公正，DSU 还专门制定了《行为守则》来规范专家组成员审案时的行为。

【协定文本摘录】

《关于争端解决规制与程序的谅解》第 8 条专家组组成

Understanding on Rules and Procedures Governing the Settlement of Disputes

Article 8

Composition of Panels

1. Panels shall be composed of well-qualified governmental and/or non-governmental

individuals, including persons who have served on or presented a case to a panel, served as a representative of a Member or of a contracting party to GATT 1947 or as a representative to the Council or Committee of any covered agreement or its predecessor agreement, or in the Secretariat, taught or published on international trade law or policy, or served as a senior trade policy official of a Member.

2. Panel members should be selected with a view to ensuring the independence of the members, a sufficiently diverse background and a wide spectrum of experience.

3. Citizens of Members whose governments (6) are parties to the dispute or third parties as defined in paragraph2 of Article 10 shall not serve on a panel concerned with that dispute, unless the parties to the dispute agree otherwise.

4. To assist in the selection of panelists, the Secretariat shall maintain an indicative list of governmental and non-governmental individuals possessing the qualifications outlined in paragraph 1, from which panelists may be drawn as appropriate.That list shall include the roster of non-governmental panelists established on 30 November 1984 (BISD 31S/9), and other rosters and indicative lists established under any of the covered agreements, and shall retain the names of persons on those rosters and indicative lists at the time of entry into force of the WTO Agreement. Members may periodically suggest names of governmental and non-governmental individuals for inclusion on the indicative list, providing relevant information on their knowledge of international trade and of the sectors or subject matter of the covered agreements, and those names shall be added to the list upon approval by the DSB. For each of the individuals on the list, the list shall indicate specific areas of experience or expertise of the individuals in the sectors or subject matter of the covered agreements.

5. Panels shall be composed of three panelists unless the parties to the dispute agree, within 1days from the establishment of the panel, to a panel composed of five panelists. Members shall be informed promptly of the composition of the panel.

6. The Secretariat shall propose nominations for the panel to the parties to the dispute. The parties to the dispute shall not oppose nominations except for compelling reasons.

7. If there is no agreement on the panelists within 20 days after the date of the establishment of a panel, at the request of either party, the Director-General, in consultation with the Chairman of the DSB and the Chairman of the relevant Council or Committee, shall determine the composition of the panel by appointing the panelists whom the Director-General considers most appropriate in accordance with any relevant special or additional rules or procedures of the covered agreement or covered agreements which are at issue in the dispute, after consulting with the parties to the dispute. The Chairman of the DSB shall inform the Members of the composition of the panel thus

formed no later than 10 days after the date the Chairman receives such a request.

8. Members shall undertake, as a general rule, to permit their officials to serve as panelists.

9. Panelists shall serve in their individual capacities and not as government representatives, nor as representatives of any organization. Members shall therefore not give them instructions nor seek to influence them as individuals with regard to matters before a panel.

10. When a dispute is between a developing country Member and a developed country Member the panel shall, if the developing country Member so requests, include at least one panelist from a developing country Member.

11. Panelists' expenses, including travel and subsistence allowance, shall be met from the WTO budget in accordance with criteria to be adopted by the General Council, based on recommendations of the Committee on Budget, Finance and Administration.

（二）专家组的职权范围

专家组的职权范围（terms of reference）是专家组审理案件的基础，只有职权范围内的事项专家组才有管辖权。DSU 第 7 条规定："专家组应按照（争端各方引用的适用协定名称）的规定，审查（争端方名称）在……文件中提交争端解决机构的事项，并提出调查结果以协助争端解决机构作出该协定规定的建议或裁决。"据此，专家组的职权是由争端方的意愿决定的，各争端方援引的协定，就构成专家组在案件审查中的权限范围。

DSU 第 7 条还规定，争端各方在专家组设立后 20 天内可就专家组职权范围另行作出约定。此外，在特定情况下，DSB 可授权其主席在遵守第 1 款规定的前提下，与争端各方进行磋商，制定专家组的职权范围。在此种情况下，应将专家组的职权范围散发全体成员，若议定的不是职权范围，则任何成员均可在 DSB 中提出相关的任何问题。

（三）专家组的评审标准

根据 DSU 第 11 条的要求，专家组应当对其审议的事项作出客观的评估，评估又可以分为事实评估与法律评估，并据此提出相应的建议或裁决可以依据的其他调查结果。而这一客观评估要求，不可避免的将涉及评审标准问题。在乌拉圭回合中，美国曾要求提出专家组应适度尊重各国政府所作出的合适的

（proper）事实认定和合理的（reasonable）法律解释，但由于各国担心美国将利用此类“评审标准”继续维持其单边措施并据此束缚专家组的手脚，“DSU 是否应纳入审议标准”的问题也因此成为乌拉圭回合谈判中的关键争议点之一。其中，美国要求“两反一保”的三个贸易救济措施均应纳入审议标准，从而使 DSB 更为尊重国内调查当局的意见，但日本等深受美国单边贸易救济之害成员对此坚决反对，最终各方妥协，仅仅将评审标准写入《反倾销协定》第 17.6 款中。①

（四）专家组的审理程序

DSU 的第 12 条和附件 3《工作程序》对专家组的案件审理程序作了明确的规定，包括专家组的时间程序、工作程序、证据等问题。

在时间程序方面，专家组应当在 6 个月内（从专家组组成和职责范围确定之日起到最终报告提交争端各方时止）作出裁定并出台相应的报告。对于紧急案件，审限为 3 个月。如果专家组认为不能在这段时间内完成报告，那么应书面通知 DSB 其延迟的原因及预计提交报告的时间，但无论如何，从专家组成立到向成员散发报告的时间不能超过 9 个月。此外，在案件审理过程中，投诉方可以请求专家组随时中止其工作，但是请求中止的时限不得超过 12 个月，同时 DSU 对专家组的程序、DSB 的决定、建议和裁决的实施等所规定的时限应作相应的延长。如果发展中成员作为被诉方，DSU 规定：应给予其充分的时间以准备和提交论据。

一般情况下，专家组工作程序的主要流程包括以下几个阶段。第一次开庭审理之前，争端各方应向专家组提交书面文件。申诉方应当将书面陈述先行提交专家组，然后被诉方再行提交。但是，专家组与争端方协商一致后，双方也可同时提交书面陈述。在实践中，专家组还会要求提供陈述概要，主要是因为书面陈述的篇幅往往很长。在第一次庭审过程中，申诉方、被诉方和第三方对案件进行陈述；各方提出书面反驳意见，并在第二次开庭中进行口头答辩。然后相互提问，专家组也可以提问。如果当事方提出科学性或者技术性的问题，专家组可以

① 葛壮志：《WTO 争端解决机制法律和实践问题研究》，法律出版社 2013 年版，第 114 页。

向这方面的专家进行咨询或者任命专家提供咨询报告；专家组向各方散发报告的陈述部分（只包括事实和相关争议，不包括最终的结论和裁决），要求争端方在两周内对报告提出意见；专家组向各方分发包括裁定和结论的中期报告，并给予当事方一周的时间进行审查；专家组对报告进行审核，并与争端各方再次举行会议；向争端各方散发最终报告，并在 3 周内将报告散发给所有 WTO 成员方。

DSU 中并没有关于证据列举、认定等方面的规定，仅仅在附录 3 中规定在专家组第一次会议前，双方应将各自的事实即论辩以书面形式提交。因此，有关证据规则内容主要见于实践之中，其中最重要的就是举证责任分担问题。

（五）专家组报告的通过

DSU15 条所规定的中期审议阶段结束后，是专家组报告通过的程序。DSU 第 16 条对此进行了规定：为了使各成员方对专家组报告有充足的时间进行考虑，DSB 在报告散发之日起 20 日内不能考虑通过该报告。但是，在报告散发之日起 60 日内，报告应该在 DSB 会议上通过。也就是说，报告应当自散发之日起 20 日至 60 日内通过，但是有两个例外：一是争端一方已经正式将其上诉决定通知 DSB；二是 DSB 协商一致不通过该报告。在第一种情况下，上诉完成之前，专家组报告不会被考虑通过。第二种情况基本上不会发生，因为根据反向协商一致原则，专家组报告几乎是自动通过的。

专家组报告通过程序无损于各成员就专家组报告发表意见的权利。各成员如果对专家组报告有反对意见，应至少在 DSB 开会讨论通过报告的 10 日前，提出解释其异议的书面理由，以供 DSB 散发给其他 WTO 成员。各成员有权充分参与专家组报告通过程序，其意见应被充分记录在案。

【协定文本摘录】

《关于争端解决规制及程序的谅解》第 16 条 专家组报告的通过

Understanding on Rules and Procedures Governing the Settlement of Disputes

Article 16

Adoption of Panel Reports

1. In order to provide sufficient time for the Members to consider panel reports, the reports shall not be considered for adoption by the DSB until 20 days after the date they have been circulated to the Members.

2. Members having objections to a panel report shall give written reasons to explain their objections for circulation at least 10 days prior to the DSB meeting at which the panel report will be considered.

3. The parties to a dispute shall have the right to participate fully in the consideration of the panel report by the DSB, and their views shall be fully recorded.

4. Within 60 days after the date of circulation of a panel report to the Members, the report shall be adopted at a DSB meeting[①] unless a party to the dispute formally notifies the DSB of its decision to appeal or the DSB decides by consensus not to adopt the report. If a party has notified its decision to appeal, the report by the panel shall not be considered for adoption by the DSB until after completion of the appeal. This adoption procedure is without prejudice to the right of Members to express their views on a panel report.

三、上诉审议程序

专家组作出裁决后，如果申诉方认为专家组的法律解释或结论错误，可以提出上诉并随之启动上诉审议程序。

（一）上诉机构组成

DSU 第 17 条第 1 款至第 3 款详细规定了上诉机构的组成情况。具体而言，

① If a meeting of the DSB is not scheduled within this period at a time that enables the requirements of paragraphs 1 and 4 of Article 16 to be met, a meeting of the DSB shall be held for this purpose.

上诉机构由 7 人组成，其中 1 人担任主席，由成员选举决定。主席任期 1 年，但经成员决定可连任 1 次。DSB 所任命的上诉机构人员任期 4 年，每人可连任 1 次。名额一旦空缺，即应补足。但是如果被接替者任期未满，则接替者只在余下的时间任职。

上诉机构审理案件实行轮换制，按照上诉机构工作程序具体实施。按照轮换制分工，应考虑随意选择、不可预见及机会均等原则。任何一个上诉案件均由 3 人负责审理，其中 1 人经选举担任本案主席，负责协调案件审理的整个过程，主持听证会和有关会议并协调起草上诉机构报告。对于案件的决定应完全由这 3 人作出，其他决定则由上诉机构集体作出。但在实践中，由于案件负担较重，上诉机构秘书处的律师会帮助上诉机构成员对上诉案件所涉及的法律问题进行法律研究，并提出一些建议。

上诉机构由具有公认权威并在法律、国际贸易和各适用协定所设主题方面具有公认专门知识的人员组成。上诉机构的成员通常具有广泛的代表性。按照 DSU 的相关规定，上诉机构的成员不隶属于任何政府，不应从任何国际组织、政府组织、非政府组织或私人那里接受或寻求指示，也不得参与审议可能导致利益冲突的争端。

【协定文本摘录】

《关于争端解决规制及程序的谅解》第 17 条 常设上诉机构

Understanding on Rules and Procedures Governing the Settlement of Disputes

Article 17: Appellate Review

Standing Appellate Body

1. A standing Appellate Body shall be established by the DSB. The Appellate Body shall hear appeals from panel cases. It shall be composed of seven persons, three of whom shall serve on any one case. Persons serving on the Appellate Body shall serve in rotation. Such rotation shall be determined in the working procedures of the Appellate Body.

2. The DSB shall appoint persons to serve on the Appellate Body for a four-year term, and each person may be reappointed once. However, the terms of three of the seven persons appointed immediately after the entry into force of the WTO Agreement shall expire at the end of two years, to be determined by lot. Vacancies shall be filled as they arise. A person appointed to replace a person whose term of office has not expired shall hold office for the remainder of the predecessor's term.

3. The Appellate Body shall comprise persons of recognized authority, with demonstrated expertise in law, international trade and the subject matter of the covered agreements generally. They shall be unaffiliated with any government. The Appellate Body membership shall be broadly representative of membership in the WTO. All persons serving on the Appellate Body shall be available at all times and on short notice, and shall stay abreast of dispute settlement activities and other relevant activities of the WTO. They shall not participate in the consideration of any disputes that would create a direct or indirect conflict of interest.

（二）上诉机构审议的范围与时间限制

DSU 第 17 条第 5 款规定，自当事方正式通知其上诉决定之日，到上诉机构报告散发 WTO 成员，一般不应超过 60 日。此外，涉及紧急情况的案件，例如涉及易腐货物，还应当尽量加快程序。如果不能在 60 日内提交报告，应书面通知 DSB 迟延的原因，以及提交报告的估计期限。但整个上诉程序不得超过 90 日。截至 2018 年 6 月 30 日，WTO 争端解决机制进入上诉审议程序的案件中，上诉审议程序最长达到了 395 日，平均时限也超过了 90 日，达到了 125 日。[①]可见，在实践中存在大量超过 DSU 规定上诉审议时限的情况。

DSU 第 17 条第 6 款规定了上诉机构审议的范围。依据相关规则，上诉机构只审查专家组报告中的法律问题和法律解释，对于事实的认定应由专家组作出。然而，在实践中法律问题和事实问题的界限并不明确。例如，专家组根据 DSU 第 11 条是否对有关事实进行了客观评估，应属于法律问题。对于上诉中提到的专家组报告中的法律问题和法律解释方面的错误，上诉机构都应当提出

① See WTO ANALYTICAL INDEX of DSU–Article 17 (Jurisprudence), Table showing the length of time taken in Appellate Body proceedings to date, access at: https://www.wto.org/english/res_e/publications_e/ai17_e/dsu_art17_jur.pdf.

处理意见。但是，对于上诉中没有提及的法律问题，上诉机构不能裁决。上诉机构可以维持、修改或撤销专家组报告的法律观点和结论。在上诉涉及多个法律问题的情况下，上诉机构可以分别作出维持、修改或撤销的决定。

【案例摘录与评析】

《WTO 分析索引》DSU 第 17 条（法理）

WTO ANALYTICAL INDEX
DSU–Article 17 (Jurisprudence)

1.5 Article 17.6: scope of Appellate review
1.5.1 "issues of law ... and legal interpretations"
1.5.1.1 Factual findings versus legal findings

6. In EC–Bananas III, the Appellate Body identified several findings of the Panel as being factual findings and thus outside its scope of review:

> "On the first issue, the Panel found that the procedural and administrative requirements of the activity function rules for importing third-country and non-traditional ACP bananas differ from, and go significantly beyond, those required for importing traditional ACP bananas. This is a factual finding. ...
>
> ...
>
> It is, however, evident from the terms of its finding that the Panel concluded, as a matter of fact, that the de facto discrimination did continue to exist after the entry into force of the GATS. This factual finding is beyond review by the Appellate Body. Thus, we do not reverse or modify the Panel's conclusion in paragraph 7.308 of the Panel Reports.
>
> ...
>
> In our view, the conclusions by the Panel on whether Del Monte is a Mexican company, the ownership and control of companies established in the European Communities that provide whole sale trade services in bananas, the market shares of suppliers of Complaining Parties' origin as compared with suppliers of EC (or ACP) origin, and the nationality of the majority of operators that 'include or directly represent' EC

(or ACP) producers, are all factual conclusions. Therefore, we decline to rule on these arguments made by the European Communities."①

7. In EC – Hormones , the Appellate Body made a distinction between factual② and legal findings and stressed that factual findings "are, in principle, not subject to [its] review":

"Under Article 17.6 of the DSU, appellate review is limited to appeals on questions of law covered in a panel report and legal interpretations developed by the panel. Findings of fact, as distinguished from legal interpretations or legal conclusions, by a panel are, in principle, not subject to review by the Appellate Body. The determination of whether or not a certain event did occur in time and space is typically a question of fact; for example, the question of whether or not Codex has adopted an international standard, guideline or recommendation on [one of the growth hormones at issue] is a factual question. ... The consistency or inconsistency of a given fact or set of facts with the requirements of a given treaty provision is, however, a legal characterization issue. It is a legal question."③

...

15. In US – Softwood Lumber V , the United States submitted that one of the issues raised by Canada on appeal – whether the United States' investigating authority exercised its discretion in calculating wood chip offset revenue for Tembec in an "objective" and "even-handed" manner –

---

① Appellate Body Report, EC–Bananas III, paras. 206, 237 and 239.

② Examples of factual findings that the Appellate Body have refrained from reviewing are Appellate Body Report, EC–Bananas III, paras. 206; 237 and 239; Appellate Body Report, Australia–Salmon, paras. 259-261; Appellate Body Report, Japan–Agricultural Products II, para. 98; Appellate Body Report, India–Quantitative Restrictions, paras. 143-144.

③ Appellate Body Report, EC–Hormones, para. 132. See also, *inter alia*, Appellate Body Report, *US–Upland Cotton,* where the Appellate Body dealt with the scope of an appellate review under Article 17.6 of theDSU and recalled its previous findings in *EC–Hormones*. In particular, the Appellate Body stated that:

"[p]ursuant to Article 17.6 of the DSU, appeals are 'limited to issues of law covered in the panel report and legal interpretations developed by the panel'. To the extent that the United States' arguments concern the Panel's appreciation and weighing of the evidence, we note from the outset that the Appellate Body will not interfere lightly with the Panel's discretion 'as the trier of facts'. At the same time, the Appellate Body has previously pointed out that the consistency or inconsistency of a given fact or set of facts with the requirements of a given treaty provision is ... a legal characterization issue'."

Appellate Body Report, *US–Upland Cotton*, para. 399. See also Appellate Body Report, *US–Anti Dumping Measures and Oil Country Tubular Goods*, para. 195.

was a factual issue and, accordingly, beyond the scope of appellate review. The Appellate Body first noted that United States did not dispute the general proposition that an investigating authority must make its determinations in an objective and even-handed manner, as the Panel had found that the USDOC did in this case, but did not find such an obligation in Article 2.2.1.1 of the Anti-Dumping Agreement. The Appellate Body disagreed with the United States since, in its view, the issue raised by Canada was a question of law. For the Appellate Body, "[t]he fact that such an 'obligation [is] not found in Article 2.2.1.1' is not dispositive. Whether a particular approach of an investigating authority is, or is not, even-handed is, ultimately, a matter of the 'legal characterization'① of facts and, as such, a matter of law".②

（三）上诉机构案件审议具体程序

直接争端方对专家组报告拥有上诉资格。第三方拥有一定的书面陈述权利，但并不具有直接对专家组报告进行上诉的权利。争端方一旦决定上诉，应当书面通知 DSB，并将所有文件同时送交案件所有参与方，同时向 WTO 秘书处提交上诉通知。上诉通知应包括专家组报告的名称、上诉的性质、专家组报告在法律问题和法律解释方面的错误。上诉机构的案件审理程序由上诉方提出书面陈述，被上诉方书面陈述与听证会等环节构成。

上诉方提出书面陈述。上诉方应当在提出上诉通知后 10 日内，向秘书处提交其书面陈述，同时送交其他参加方。其内容主要包括：对上诉依据的准确表述，包括专家组报告在法律问题和法律解释方面的具体错误，以及支持上诉主张的法律观点；对所依据的有关协议和其他法律渊源规定的准确表述；要求上诉机构作出裁决的性质。

被上诉方书面陈述。被上诉方应当在上诉通知提出后 25 日内，向秘书处提交书面陈述，同时将该陈述送交其他参与方。其内容主要包括：反对上诉方书面陈述的法律观点，对上诉方书面陈述中每个依据的接受或反对，所依据的法律的列举，要求上诉机构所作裁决的性质。

听证会。上诉机构一般应当在上诉通知作出后 30 日内召开听证会，确定

① Appellate Body Report, EC–Hormones, para. 132.

② Appellate Body Report, US–Softwood Lumber V, para. 163.

听证会日期后应尽早通知参加方。在召开听证会时，一般由上诉方先进行陈述（opening statement），再由被上诉方和第三方分别进行陈述。紧接着，各方就上诉问题进行辩论，上诉机构也会在辩论时针对双方观点提出各种问题，要求各方以口头或书面形式回答。在辩论结束后，各方按照顺序宣读最后陈述（closing），但实践中也有当事方放弃进行最后陈述的做法。

（四）上诉报告的通过

上诉机构报告的通过同样采用“反向一致”的表决方式。具体而言，在上诉机构报告散发给 WTO 成员后 30 日内，DSB 应当在会议上对该报告进行表决，除非 DSB 经协商一致不通过该报告，否则 DSB 应当通过该报告。这与专家组报告的表决通过类似，表明了上诉机构报告几乎是自动通过的，除非胜诉方也选择否决报告，并且眼看报告无法通过而不采取任何措施。不过，在 DSB 会议上，WTO 各成员仍有权发表意见，不过成员的意见并不影响报告的通过。

【协定文本摘录】

《关于争端解决规制及程序的谅解》第 17 条上诉机构报告的通过

Understanding on Rules and Procedures Governing the Settlement of Disputes

Article 17: Appellate Review

Adoption of Appellate Body Reports

14. An Appellate Body report shall be adopted by the DSB and unconditionally accepted by the parties to the dispute unless the DSB decides by consensus not to adopt the Appellate Body report within 30 days following its circulation to the Members.① This adoption procedure is without prejudice to the right of Members to express their views on an Appellate Body report.

① If a meeting of the DSB is not scheduled during this period, such a meeting of the DSB shall be held for this purpose.

四、执行程序

WTO 争端解决机制的裁决对争端方具有法律约束力。但是，由于 WTO 争端解决机构不具有强制执行裁决的权力，因此裁决的执行主要依靠被诉方在争端解决机构的监督下自觉进行。如果申诉方认为裁决并未被被诉方执行或执行程度未满足裁决要求，申诉方可以向争端解决机构申请就被诉方执行问题进行审查和裁决。专家组的这种审查也可以向上诉机构上诉。此外，若被诉方认定裁决未得到执行或未完全得到执行，申诉方也可以向争端解决机构申请进行报复。因此，WTO 争端解决机制相较于普通争端解决机制，在执行程序方面反映出较为独特的特点。一套完整的 WTO 执行程序，包括成员方通报履行意愿、确定履行合理期限、执行措施异议、补偿措施、授权报复等环节。按执行程序设置目的的区别，执行程序又可以分为执行监督程序，以及补偿与中止减让这两个部分。

（一）建议或裁决履行监督

执行监督程序的设置目的，在于促使专家组报告或上诉机构报告能够得到迅速的执行。DSU 第 21 条规定了 DSB 对建议和裁决履行的具体监督措施。

1. 履行意愿通报

根据其要求，在专家组或上诉机构报告通过后的 30 日内举行的 DSB 会议上，有关成员应将执行建议和裁决的意愿通知 DSB。这一规定实际上是要求败诉方对执行裁决表态，在实践中基本上没有出现败诉方在会议上明确拒绝执行裁决的情况。

2. 履行合理期限

裁决和建议应当迅速被实施，但是若立即实施不切实际，则应确定一个合理的执行期限。合理期限可以由有关成员自己提出，并经 DSB 批准。若不能确定，当事方可以在报告通过后 45 日内经过协商确定期限；若不能达成一致，则应该在报告通过后 90 日内通过仲裁程序来确定这一期限。一般情况下，这种仲裁请求由胜诉方提出，当事方在决定仲裁后10日内确定仲裁员（可以是一人，也可以是几人），将人选通知WTO总干事。总干事通知仲裁员，并且在该仲裁员同意后开始仲裁。

另外，根据DSU第21条第4款的规定，执行期限的确定有一个最后的期限，即从专家组设立之日起不得超过15个月。若由于专家组或上诉机构不能如期完成报告而延长了时间，则应在15个月之外加上所延长的时间，但所有时间相加一般不应超过18个月。

3. 执行措施异议

根据DSU第21条第5款和第6款的规定，如果争端当事方对于是否存在执行建议和裁决的措施，以及执行建议和裁决的措施是否符合相关协议的要求存在分歧，这类争端应诉诸争端解决程序处理，包括求助于原案专家组。专家组一般应该在争端提交之后的90日之内发布报告。也就是说，DSU第21条规定了争端方对执行裁定或建议的异议处理程序，这一程序也被称为“第21.5条程序”。该程序中专家组的权限范围通常会按照DSU第7条的规定来处理，专家组在审案时，不限于先前程序中所提出的主张、观点和事实。在实践中，当事方可以针对该程序所发布的报告提起上诉。

（二）补偿与中止减让

补偿与中止减让，则是在迫不得已的情况下，对于不执行或不完全执行裁决的成员方所进行的合法制裁与报复的授权与规制的严格限制规则。

1. 补偿措施

如果败诉方未能在合理的期限内执行DSB的建议和裁决，则应投诉方请求，败诉方必须在合理期限届满前与被诉方就补偿所涉及的部门或协定进行补偿谈判。补偿针对的是执行裁决的合理期限过后，这些措施仍不能修改或取消的情况，这时，由于该成员继续实施这些措施会给成员造成影响，因此需要对此做出补偿。补偿的方式不是金钱给付，而是通过降低特定产品的关税、修改其他贸易领域的减让等方式，给受到影响的成员提供更多的贸易机会。补偿具有自愿性。

2. 中止减让

DSU 第 22 条第 2 款至第 9 款明确规定了中止减让或授权报复的各项具体规则。

如果在合理期限届满后的 20 日之内，争端方仍然没有达成令人满意的补偿协议，投诉方可以请求争端解决机构授权中止对各有关协议的减让或其他义务，这即为通常所说的报复程序。败诉方对申诉方拟报复数额或程度有异议的，可以根据 DSU 第 22 条第 6 款的规定请求仲裁。

中止减让的部门应该与利益受损或丧失的部门相同。具体分为以下几种情况。其一，如果投诉方认为相同部门的中止减让或其他义务实际不可行或者没有效果，可以寻求中止同一协议项下的其他部门的减让或其他义务，这也即跨部门中止减让。其二，如果投诉方认为同一协议项下其他部门的中止减让或其他义务不可行或没有效果，且情况严重，可以寻求中止另一有关协议项下的减让或其他义务，这也即跨协议中止减让。跨协议中止减让和跨部门中止减让统称为交叉报复。

争端解决机构授权的报复程度应等同于利益丧失或受损的程度。若适用协定禁止中止减让或其他义务，则 DSB 不得授权此类中止。DSB 应当在合理期限结束后 30 日内审议胜诉方的请求，授权报复，此时适用的决策机制仍然是“反向一致”。

按照 DSU 第 22 条第 7 款的规定，确定贸易报复额度的仲裁员并不涉及审查中止减让和其他义务的性质。仲裁作出的仲裁裁决具有终局性，有关各方不得寻求第二次仲裁。仲裁裁决应当迅速通知 DSB，以便其作出中止减让或其他义务的授权。在补偿或报复期间，DSB 应当继续监督裁决的实施情况

需要额外指出的是，报复只是一种临时性安排，如果违反措施已经取消，或者被诉方已经对受影响的利益提供了补偿办法，或者争端双方已经达成满意的解决办法，报复就应当中止。

总之，WTO 争端解决机制为多边体制的正常运行提供了强力保障。这一执行机制体现出了 WTO 争端解决程序既往不咎的特点与价值取向，在后续惩罚与救济措施方面存在不足，并在一定程度上导致了某些成员方屡次恶意违反 WTO 义务的不当行为。但是，总体来说，这一具有法律约束力和强制执行力的机制，为 WTO 争端解决机制的良好运行奠定了坚实的基础。

【案例摘录与评析】

一、中国诉欧盟紧固件反倾销争端案

EUROPEAN COMMUNITIES – DEFINITIVE ANTI-DUMPING MEASURES ON CERTAIN IRON OR STEEL FASTENERS FROM CHINA
(WT/DS397/R)

VII.FINDINGS

A. RELEVANT PRINCIPLES REGARDING STANDARD OF REVIEW, TREATY INTERPRETATION AND BURDEN OF PROOF

...

1. Standard of Review

7.2 Article11 of the DSU provides the standard of review for WTO panels in general.Article11 imposes upon panels a comprehensive obligation to make an "objective assessment of the matter", an obligation which embraces all aspects of a panel's examination of the "matter", both factual and legal.①

7.3 Article17.6 of the AD Agreement, which sets forth the special standard of review applicable to disputes under the AD Agreement, provides:

"(i) in its assessment of the facts of the matter, the panel shall determine whether the

① Article 11 of the DSU provides in part: "The function of panels is to assist the DSB in discharging its responsibilities under this Understanding and the covered agreements. Accordingly, a panel should make an objective assessment of the matter before it, including an objective assessment of the facts of the case and the applicability of and conformity with the relevant covered agreements, and make such other findings as will assist the DSB in making the recommendations or in giving the rulings provided for in the covered agreements."

authorities' establishment of the facts was proper and whether their evaluation of those facts was unbiased and objective.If the establishment of the facts was proper and the evaluation was unbiased and objective, even though the panel might have reached a different conclusion, the evaluation shall not be overturned;

(ii) the panel shall interpret the relevant provisions of the Agreement in accordance with customary rules of interpretation of public international law.Where the panel finds that a relevant provision of the Agreement admits of more than one permissible interpretation, the panel shall find the authorities' measure to be in conformity with the Agreement if it rests upon one of those permissible interpretations."

Taken together Article11 of the DSU and Article17.6 of the AD Agreement establish the standard of review we will apply with respect to both the factual and the legal aspects of the present dispute.

7.4 Thus, we will find the challenged anti-dumping determination to be consistent with the AD Agreement if we find that the EU investigating authorities established the facts properly and evaluated them in an unbiased and objective manner, and that the determinations in question were based on a permissible interpretation of the relevant treaty provisions.① In our assessment of the matter, we must limit our review to the "facts made available in conformity with appropriate domestic procedures to the authorities of the importing Member", in accordance with Article17.5(ii) of the AD Agreement.We will not undertake a *de novo* review of the evidence before the investigating authority during the proceeding, and will not substitute our judgement for that of the EU investigating authorities even though we might have made a different determination were we examining the evidence that was before the investigating authorities ourselves.

7.5 The Appellate Body has clarified a panel's standard of review of the facts pursuant to the above provisions in the following terms:

"It is well established that a panel must neither conduct a *de novo* review nor simply defer to the conclusions of the national authority.A panel's examination of those conclusions must be critical and searching, and be based on the information contained in the record and the explanations given by the authority in its published report.A panel must examine whether, in the light of the evidence on the record, the conclusions reached by the investigating authority are reasoned and adequate.What is 'adequate' will inevitably depend on the facts and circumstances of the case and the particular claims made, but several general lines of inquiry are likely to be relevant.The panel's scrutiny should test whether the reasoning of the authority is coherent

① See below, paragraphs 7.6~7.8.

and internally consistent.The panel must undertake an in-depth examination of whether the explanations given disclose how the investigating authority treated the facts and evidence in the record and whether there was positive evidence before it to support the inferences made and conclusions reached by it.The panel must examine whether the explanations provided demonstrate that the investigating authority took proper account of the complexities of the data before it, and that it explained why it rejected or discounted alternative explanations and interpretations of the record evidence.A panel must be open to the possibility that the explanations given by the authority are not reasoned or adequate in the light of other plausible alternative explanations, and must take care not to assume itself the role of initial trier of facts, nor to be passive by 'simply *accept[ing]* the conclusions of the competent authorities.'"① (Footnote omitted.)

...

B. TERMS OF REFERENCE OF THE PANEL

7.11 The European Union argues that a number of the claims addressed in China's first written submission are not within the Panel's terms of reference either because (1) they were not identified in China's panel request consistently with the requirements of Article6.2 of the DSU, or (2) they were not subject to consultations.China responds that all the claims that the European Union argues are outside the Panel's terms of reference are in fact within the terms of reference.

7.12 Given the significant number of terms of reference objections raised by the European Union, and in order to avoid repetition, we consider it appropriate to outline at the outset the legal standard under which we will assess such objections.We will then apply that standard to the specific objections raised by the European Union below, when we address the claims to which each specific objection pertains.

7.13 The first set of terms of reference objections raised by the European Union pertains to China's panel request.We note that under Article 7.1 of the DSU, it is the complaining party's request for establishment of a panel – that is, the panel request—that determines the terms of reference of a WTO panel.Article6.2 of the DSU provides, in relevant part:

> "The request for the establishment of a panel shall be made in writing.It shall indicate whether consultations were held, identify the specific measures at issue and provide a brief summary of the legal basis of the complaint sufficient to present the

① Appellate Body Report, United States–Investigation of the International Trade Commission in Softwood Lumber from Canada–Recourse to Article 21.5 of the DSU by Canada ["US–Softwood Lumber VI (Article 21.5–Canada)"], WT/DS277/AB/RW, adopted 9 May 2006, para. 93.

problem clearly."

Therefore, a panel request must identify the sp*ecific measures at issue* and must provide a *brief summary of the legal basis of the complaint sufficient to present the problem clearly*. Together, these two elements constitute the "matter referred to the DSB", which forms the basis of a panel's terms of reference under Article 7.1 of the DSU.It is important that the panel request be sufficiently clear for two reasons:first, it defines the jurisdiction of the panel, since only the matter(s) raised in the panel request fall within the panel's terms of reference;and second, it serves the due process objective of notifying the parties and potential third parties of the nature of a complainant's case.① To ensure the fulfilment of these objectives, a panel has to examine the panel request carefully "to ensure its compliance with both the letter and the spirit of Article6.2 of the DSU".②

7.14 The Appellate Body's analysis in *Korea – Dairy* offers guidance as to how a panel should address the issue of whether a panel request provides "a brief summary of the legal basis of the complaint sufficient to present the problem clearly" in accordance with Article6.2 of the DSU.First, the issue is to be resolved on a case-by-case basis.③ Second, the panel must examine the panel request very carefully to ensure its compliance with both the letter and the spirit of Article6.2 of the DSU.④ Third, the panel should take into account the nature of the particular provision at issue – *i.e.*, where the Articles listed establish not one single, distinct obligation, but rather multiple obligations, the mere listing of treaty Articles may not satisfy the standard of Article6.2.⑤

7.15 Thus, with respect to the European Union's argument that certain claims addressed in China's first written submission were not identified in its panel request consistently with the requirements of Article6.2 of the DSU, we shall base our assessment on the principles outlined above. This will require us, in each instance, to consider the text of China's panel request to determine whether it identifies the specific measure, and provides a brief summary of the legal

① Appellate Body Report, Brazil–Measures Affecting Desiccated Coconut ("Brazil–Desiccated Coconut"), WT/DS22/AB/R, adopted 20 March 1997, DSR 1997:I, 167, p. 22; Appellate Body Report, United States–Continued Existence and Application of Zeroing Methodology ("US–Continued Zeroing"), WT/DS350/AB/R, adopted 19 February 2009, para. 161.

② Appellate Body Report, European Communities–Regime for the Importation, Sale and Distribution of Bananas ("EC–Bananas III"), WT/DS27/AB/R, adopted 25 September 1997, DSR 1997:II, 591, para. 142.

③ Appellate Body Report, Korea–Definitive Safeguard Measure on Imports of Certain Dairy Products ("Korea–Dairy"), WT/DS98/AB/R, adopted 12 January 2000, DSR 2000:I, 3, para. 127.

④ Appellate Body Report, Korea–Dairy, para. 130.

⑤ Appellate Body Report, Korea–Dairy, para. 124.

basis of the complaint, and potentially whether the European Union has been prejudiced by the formulation of the panel request.Moreover, as stated by the Appellate Body, compliance with the requirements of Article6.2 of the DSU must be demonstrated on the basis of the text of the panel request read as a whole, and defects in the panel request cannot be cured in the subsequent submissions of the parties.①

7.16 The second set of terms of reference objections raised by the European Union relates to consultations. The European Union asserts that some of the claims which it acknowledges are sufficiently set out in China's panel request, are nonetheless outside the Panel's terms of reference because they were not subject to consultations.In support of its assertions, the European Union refers to alleged inadequacies in China's request for consultations and/or asserts that no consultations took place with respect to certain claims.

7.17 This portion of the European Union's terms of reference objections raises the question of the relationship between a complaining party's request for consultations and the panel's terms of reference.We note that the DSU does not contain a provision that directly addresses this issue. Article4 of the DSU, entitled "Consultations", provides in relevant part:

> "4. Any request for consultations shall be submitted in writing and shall give the reasons for the request, including identification of the measures at issue and an indication of the legal basis for the complaint. ...

7. If the consultations fail to settle a dispute within 60 days after the date of receipt of the request for consultations, the complaining party may request the establishment of a panel.The complaining party may request a panel during the 60-day period if the consulting parties jointly consider that consultations have failed to settle the dispute."(emphasis added)

Article 17 of the AD Agreement also contains provisions regarding consultations between WTO Members in disputes under that Agreement, providing in relevant part:

> "17.1 Except as otherwise provided herein, the Dispute Settlement Understanding is applicable to consultations and the settlement of disputes under this Agreement ...
>
> 17.3 If any Member considers that any benefit accruing to it, directly or indirectly, under this Agreement is being nullified or impaired, or that the achievement of any

① Appellate Body Report, United States–Countervailing Duties on Certain Corrosion-Resistant Carbon Steel Flat Products from Germany ("US–Carbon Steel"), WT/DS213/AB/R and Corr.1, adopted 19 December 2002, DSR 2002:IX, 3779, para. 127.

objective is being impeded, by another Member or Members, it may, with a view to reaching a mutually satisfactory resolution of the matter, request in writing consultations with the Member or Members in question.Each Member shall afford sympathetic consideration to any request from another Member for consultation.

17.4 If the Member that requested consultations considers that the consultations pursuant to paragraph3 have failed to achieve a mutually agreed solution, and if final action has been taken by the administering authorities of the importing Member to levy definitive anti-dumping duties or to accept price undertakings, it may refer the matter to the Dispute Settlement Body ('DSB')."(emphasis added)

7.18 Thus, Article4.4 of the DSU provides that a request for consultations has to identify the measures at issue and indicate the legal basis of the complaint.Article 4.7 of the DSU, in turn, stipulates that if parties fail to settle the dispute within 60 days from the receipt of the consultations request, the complaining party may request the establishment of a panel.Article17.1 of the AD Agreement states that the DSU applies to the consultations and the settlement of disputes that arise under the AD Agreement.Article17.3 of the AD Agreement provides that if a Member considers that any benefit accruing to it, directly or indirectly, under the AD Agreement is nullified or impaired, or that the achievement of any objective is impeded by another Member, it may request consultations with the Member concerned.Article17.4 states that if parties fail to settle the dispute through consultations, the complaining Member may refer the matter to the DSB to seek the establishment of a panel.Finally, Article17.5 provides that the DSB would, in such a situation, establish a panel to resolve the dispute.

7.19 In our view, none of these legal provisions supports the proposition that a complaining Member is precluded from identifying in its panel request claims not specifically identified in its request for consultations.Article6.2 of the DSU requires that a panel request must indicate whether consultations were held, but neither it nor any other provision of the DSU indicates that the scope of the request for consultations determines the precise scope of the subsequent panel request.

7.20 We note that the effect of a complaining Member's request for consultations on a panel's terms of reference has been discussed extensively in prior panel and Appellate Body reports.In *Canada – Aircraft*, for instance, the respondent argued that certain claims raised with respect to measures that were not identified in the complaining Member's request for consultations fell outside the panel's terms of reference.The panel rejected this argument.The panel underlined the fact that a panel's terms of reference were determined by the complaining

Member's panel request, adding that as long as the request for consultations and the panel request concerned the same "dispute", the claims raised in the panel request would fall within its terms of reference even if they were not raised in the request for consultations.In the panel's view, "this approach [sought] to preserve due process while also recognising that the 'matter' on which consultations are requested [would] not necessarily be identical to the 'matter' identified in the request for establishment of a panel".① It follows from this reasoning that the scope of a request for consultations and that of a panel request do not have to be identical.The panel's findings on this particular issue were not appealed.

7.21 A similar issue arose in *Brazil – Aircraft*.The respondent in that case argued that certain subsidy programmes not identified in the complaining Member's request for consultations were not within the panel's terms of reference, even though they were identified in the panel request. The panel noted that under the DSU, the terms of reference of a WTO panel were determined by the complaining Member's panel request, not its request for consultations.While acknowledging the importance of the consultations in terms of clarifying the situation between the parties to the dispute, the panel nevertheless reasoned that "to limit the scope of the panel proceedings to the identical matter with respect to which consultations were held could undermine the effectiveness of the panel process".② According to the panel:

> "[A] panel may consider whether consultations have been held with respect to a 'dispute', and that a preliminary objection may properly be sustained if a party can establish that the required consultations had not been held with respect to a dispute. We do not believe, however, that either Article4.7 of the DSU or Article4.4 of the SCM Agreement requires a precise identity between the matter with respect to which consultations were held and that with respect to which establishment of a panel was requested."③ (emphasis added)

On appeal, the Appellate Body agreed with the panel's reasoning:

① Panel Report, Canada–Measures Affecting the Export of Civilian Aircraft ("Canada–Aircraft"), WT/DS70/R, adopted 20 August 1999, upheld by Appellate Body Report WT/DS70/AB/R, DSR 1999:IV, 1443, para. 9.12.

② Panel Report, Brazil–Export Financing Programme for Aircraft ("Brazil–Aircraft"), WT/DS46/R, adopted 20 August 1999, as modified by Appellate Body Report WT/DS46/AB/R, DSR 1999:III, 1221, para. 7.9.

③ Panel Report, Brazil–Aircraft, para. 7.10.

"We do not believe, however, that Articles4 and 6 of the DSU, or paragraphs 1 to 4 of Article4 of the SCM Agreement, require a precise and exact identity between the specific measures that were the subject of consultations and the specific measures identified in the request for the establishment of a panel.As stated by the Panel, '[o]ne purpose of consultations, as set forth in Article4.3 of the SCM Agreement, is to 'clarify the facts of the situation', and it can be expected that information obtained during the course of consultations may enable the complainant to focus the scope of the matter with respect to which it seeks establishment of a panel.' We are confident that the specific measures at issue in this case are the Brazilian export subsidies for regional aircraft under PROEX. Consultations were held by the parties on these subsidies, and it is these same subsidies that were referred to the DSB for the establishment of a panel. We emphasize that the regulatory instruments that came into effect in 1997 and 1998 did not change the essence of the export subsidies for regional aircraft under PROEX."① (footnote omitted, italic emphasis in original, underline emphasis added)

7.22 More recently, the Appellate Body, in *US – Upland Cotton*, underlined the importance of not allowing the request for consultations to inappropriately limit the scope of the dispute, observing:

"As long as the complaining party does not expand the scope of the dispute, we hesitate to impose too rigid a standard for the 'precise and exact identity' between the scope of consultations and the request for the establishment of a panel, as this would substitute the request for consultations for the panel request.According to Article7 of the DSU, it is the request for the establishment of a panel that governs its terms of reference, unless the parties agree otherwise."② (footnotes omitted, emphasis added)

7.23 In *Mexico – Anti-Dumping Measures on Rice*, the respondent argued that the complainant had broadened the scope of the legal basis of the complaint in the panel request compared with the request for consultations and asked the panel to find that the claims associated with the new legal provisions cited in the panel request were outside the panel's terms

① Appellate Body Report, Brazil–Export Financing Programme for Aircraft ("Brazil–Aircraft"), WT/DS46/AB/R, adopted 20 August 1999, DSR 1999:III, 1161, para. 132.

② Appellate Body Report, United States–Subsidies on Upland Cotton ("US–Upland Cotton"), WT/DS267/AB/R, adopted 21 March 2005, DSR 2005:I, 3, para. 293.

of reference.The panel declined the request, stating:

"In our view, the fact that certain provisions were added to the list of alleged violations in the request for establishment compared to the request for consultations is a consequence of the consultation process which serves the purpose of clarifying the facts of the situation enabling the complainant to focus the scope of the matter with respect to which it seeks the establishment of a panel.It does not mean that no consultations were held on the matter, as the only difference between the request for consultations and the request for establishment consists of the fact that a number of closely related legal provisions alleged to have been violated were added.The measures remained the same and so did the legal basis for the complaint, as is evident from the narrative provided in the request for establishment.In our view, consultations were thus held on the matter on which the establishment of a Panel was requested.We therefore reject Mexico's request in this respect." ①

The Appellate Body upheld the panel's findings in this regard.The Appellate Body recalled its previous findings on this issue and pointed out that the reasoning of prior reports regarding the difference between the scope of the request for consultations and the panel request with respect to the specific measures at issue equally applied to the difference between these two documents with respect to the legal basis of the complaint.The Appellate Body emphasised that the role of consultations was to allow the exchange of information necessary to refine the contours of the dispute, as a result of which the complaining Member might reformulate its claims in its panel request.According to the Appellate Body:

"[It] is not necessary that the provisions referred to in the request for consultations be identical to those set out in the panel request, provided that the 'legal basis' in the panel request may reasonably be said to have evolved from the 'legal basis' that formed the subject of consultations.In other words, the addition of provisions must not have the effect of changing the essence of the complaint."② (emphasis added)

① Panel Report, Mexico–Definitive Anti-Dumping Measures on Beef and Rice, Complaint with Respect to Rice ("Mexico–Anti-Dumping Measures on Rice"), WT/DS295/R, adopted 20 December 2005, as modified by Appellate Body Report WT/DS295/AB/R, DSR 2005:XXIII, 11007, para. 7.43.

② Appellate Body Report, Mexico–Definitive Anti-Dumping Measures on Beef and Rice, Complaint with Respect to Rice ("Mexico–Anti-Dumping Measures on Rice"), WT/DS295/AB/R, adopted 20 December 2005, DSR 2005:XXII, 10853, para. 138.

7.24 Based on the foregoing, we consider that there does not have to be precise identity between China's request for consultations and its panel request, either with regard to the specific measures at issue or with regard to the legal basis of the complaint.As long as the request for consultations and the panel request concern "the same matter" or, put differently, as long as the legal basis of the panel request "may reasonably be said to have evolved from the legal basis identified in the request for consultations", a claim not specifically identified in China's request for consultations, but properly identified in the panel request, will fall within our terms of reference.

7.25 Finally, with regard to consultations, we recall that China, in Exhibit CHN-65, submitted a list of questions that were allegedly sent to the European Union prior to consultations and were discussed during consultations.China submitted this document in response to the factual assertion made by the European Union that some claims identified in China's panel request were not discussed during consultations.① This raises the question of what determines the scope of consultations between the parties to a dispute:the request for consultations or what is actually discussed in such consultations?We note that this particular issue also arose in *US – Upland Cotton*.The factual circumstances presented in *US – Upland Cotton* were very similar to those presented in these proceedings.The complaining party in that dispute presented to the panel a list of questions that had been submitted in writing to the respondent during consultations. In determining whether the complainant had broadened the scope of the dispute in its panel request, the panel took this list into consideration in considering what had actually been discussed during the consultations between the parties.② The Appellate Body, however, disapproved the panel's actions in this regard, concluding that panels should limit their analysis regarding the scope of consultations to the written request for consultations.The Appellate Body considered that to examine what happened in consultations would be contrary to Articles4.6 and 4.4 of the DSU, which provide, respectively, that consultations shall be confidential and that the request for consultations be made in writing and notified to the DSB.The Appellate Body also noted that often it would be difficult for a panel to find out what was discussed in consultations because there is

---

① The European Union objected to the submission of this document by China and requested a decision from the Panel on this matter. The Panel's decision allowing the submission, but noting that the decision was "without prejudice to our consideration of [the exhibit's] relevance to, or the weight we may accord to it in our consideration of the preliminary jurisdictional objections raised by the European Union" was sent to the Parties on 7 May 2010. See Annex H.

② Panel Report, United States–Subsidies on Upland Cotton ("US–Upland Cotton"), WT/DS267/R, Corr.1, and Add.1 to Add.3, adopted 21 March 2005, as modified by Appellate Body Report WT/DS267/AB/R, DSR 2005:II, 299, para. 7.61.

no public record of those discussions and parties often disagree about what was discussed.[①]

7.26 Taking the Appellate Body's reasoning into consideration, we find that it would not be appropriate to look into what was actually discussed between China and the European Union in the consultations between the parties, and we will therefore limit our analysis regarding the scope of consultations to the text of China's request for consultations.

...

C. CLAIMS REGARDING COUNCIL REGULATION NO. 1225/2009 (THE BASIC AD REGULATION) AS SUCH

...

7.43 We note that the premise for the European Union's preliminary objection with respect to China's claims under Articles6.10, 9.3 and 9.4 of the AD Agreement is the allegation that the specific measure at issue, *i.e.*, Article9(5) of the Basic AD Regulation, addresses only the imposition of anti-dumping duties, whereas the three provisions of the AD Agreement cited by China concern the determination of dumping margins or the establishment of the level of anti-dumping duties.[②] Since, according to the European Union, the specific measure at issue does not address the calculation of dumping margins, the European Union argues that claims under the provisions of the AD Agreement which deal with the calculation of margins fall outside our terms of reference.

7.44 In this regard, we agree with China that the European Union confuses the identification of the claims in the panel request with the arguments that are to be developed in the subsequent panel proceedings.We find it relevant and important in this regard that the European Union dedicates a significant portion of its substantive arguments regarding these three claims to its effort to demonstrate that Article9(5) of the Basic AD Regulation does not concern the calculation of dumping margins and therefore does not fall within the scope of the obligations set forth under these three provisions.Indeed, it is clear to us that whether Article9(5) of the Basic AD Regulation is limited to the imposition of dumping duties, or also relates to the calculation of dumping margins or the establishment of the level of anti-dumping duties, is a disputed matter that must be resolved as part of the substance of this case, rather than a matter to be assumed in the context of resolving a preliminary objection.[③] We note that this argument is the only basis for the European Union's terms of reference objection in this context.We therefore find that China's

① Appellate Body Report, US–Upland Cotton, para. 287.

② See, European Union, first written submission, paras. 53, 54, 58 and 62.

③ We note that we do not mean to suggest that we agree with European Union's characterization of China's claims as concerning the calculation of dumping margins, but that even assuming this to be the case, the scope of Article 9(5) of the Basic AD Regulation is not so clear as to preclude us from considering them.

claims under Articles 6.10, 9.3 and 9.4 of the AD Agreement are within our terms of reference.

【本案评析】

以上案例节选自 2009 年中国诉欧紧固件反倾销争端案专家组报告。该案对专家组权限问题进行了分析。专家组在报告中详细地梳理了争端解决实践中相关案例关于专家组职权范围的核心论述。

二、中国诉美国禽肉限制措施争端案

UNITED STATES - CERTAIN MEASURES AFFECTING IMPORTS
OF POULTRY FROM CHINA
(WT/DS392/R)

VII. FINDINGS

A. PRELIMINARY ISSUES

1. Terms of reference of the panel

...

(i) Background

7.3 As indicated above, the United States argues that consultations were not requested under the *SPS Agreement*. China's consultations request reads in the relevant parts as follows:

"In addition, although China does not believe that the US measures at issue restricting imports of poultry products from China constitute sanitary and phytosanitary measures ('SPS measure') within the meaning of the *Agreement on the Application of Sanitary and Phytosanitary Measures* ('*SPS Agreement*'), *if it were demonstrated that any such measure is an SPS measure, China also requests consultations with the US pursuant to Article11 of the SPS Agreement*. In particular, to the extent any such measure is demonstrated to be an SPS measure, China considers that the measure is in breach of the US obligations under the *SPS Agreement*, including but not limited to Articles2.1-2.3, 3.1, 3.3, 5.1-5.7, and 8 thereof.

Generally, to the extent it is demonstrated that any such measure is an SPS measure, China is concerned that the US measure may violate Articles2.1, 2.2, 5.1-5.4, and 5.6 of the *SPS Agreement*, because any SPS measure is not based on a proper assessment of the particular risks presented and is not supported by sufficient scientific evidence. China is also concerned that any such measure, to the extent not applied with respect to similarly situated imports from other

Members, may violate Articles2.3 and 5.5 of the *SPS Agreement*. Moreover, China is concerned that any SPS measure fails to observe the provisions of Annex C of the *SPS Agreement* with respect to the operation of control, inspection and approval procedures, and may therefore violate Article8 of the *SPS Agreement*. Additionally, China is unaware of any basis on which any such US measure is justified under international standards, guidelines or recommendations, or otherwise, consistently with Articles3.1 and 3.3 of the *SPS Agreement*. Finally, China is unaware of any basis on which such US measure is justified by Article5.7 of the *SPS Agreement*, if applicable." (emphasis added)

...

(ii) Arguments of the parties

7.12 Although China's consultations request does refer to Article11 of the *SPS Agreement*, the United States argues that China's conditional language means that consultations were not actually requested.① The United States explains that China first stated in its consultations request that it does not believe that the measures at issue fall within the *SPS Agreement*. China then stated that if it were demonstrated that any such measure is an SPS measure, it also requests consultations with the United States pursuant to Article11 of the *SPS Agreement*. The United States argues that as China stated that it does not believe that the relevant measures are SPS measures, China also rendered it clear that the imposed condition for a request for consultations pursuant to Article11 of the *SPS Agreement* had not been fulfilled. The United States therefore submits that the only conclusion that can be reached is that the condition was not fulfilled and thus that no request pursuant to Article11 of the *SPS Agreement* was made.②

...

(iii) Analysis by the Panel

7.25 The Panel is therefore called upon to determine whether China's use of the conditional tense in its consultations request means that China has *not* requested consultations under the *SPS Agreement* and whether that would deprive the Panel of jurisdiction to hear China's claims under the *SPS Agreement*. We note that there is substantial jurisprudence on the relevance of the consultations request and the holding of consultations to a panel's terms of reference. However, the implications of using the conditional tense in a consultations request have never been

① Paragraph 6 of China's consultations request reads: "In addition, although China does not believe that the US measures at issue restricting imports of poultry products from China constitute sanitary or phytosanitary measures ('SPS measure') within the meaning of the Agreement on the Application of Sanitary and Phytosanitary Measures ('SPS Agreement'), if it were demonstrated that any such measure is an SPS measure, China also requests consultations with the US pursuant to Article 11 of the SPS Agreement ..."

② United States' request for a preliminary ruling, para. 20.

considered by previous panels or the Appellate Body.

The relevance of the consultations request and the holding of consultations to a panel's terms of reference.

7.26 A panel's terms of reference, as provided for in Article7.1 of the DSU[①], are generally set in the Panel Request which must follow the rules set forth in Article6.2 of the DSU.[②] Additionally, the Appellate Body has explained that "as a general matter, consultations are a prerequisite to panel proceedings"[③] and has underscored the importance and benefits of consultations. In particular the Appellate Body has pointed out that consultations serve to help the parties assess the strengths and weaknesses of the case, narrow the scope of differences between them and reach a mutually agreed solution. In addition, consultations provide the parties with an opportunity to define and delimit the scope of the dispute.[④]

7.27 Consultations are regulated in Article4 of the DSU. Article4.2 of the DSU provides that "[e]ach Member undertakes to ... afford adequate opportunity for consultation regarding any representations made by another Member concerning measures affecting the operation of any covered agreement taken within the territory of the former".

7.28 The Appellate Body also observed in *Brazil – Aircraft,* that "Articles4 and 6 of the DSU ... set forth a process by which a complaining party must request consultations, and consultations must be held, before a matter may be referred to the DSB for the establishment of a panel".[⑤] In

---

① Article 7.1 of the DSU states that the standard terms of reference, unless otherwise agreed by the Parties shall be:"To examine, in the light of the relevant provisions in (name of the covered agreement(s) cited by the parties to the dispute), the matter referred to the DSB by (name of party) in document . . . and to make such findings as will assist the DSB in making the recommendations or in giving the rulings provided for in that/those agreement(s)"

② Appellate Body Report, Guatemala–Cement I, paras. 69-76; see also Appellate Body Report, US–Carbon Steel, paras. 125-127.(explaining that the identification of the specific measure and the legal basis of the complaint in the Panel Request comprise the "matter referred to the DSB".)

③ Appellate Body Report, Mexico–Corn Syrup (Article 21.5–US), para. 58.

④ Appellate Body Report, Mexico–Corn Syrup (Article 21.5–US), para. 54. Appellate Body Report, Brazil–Aircraft, para. 131. We note that in certain instances panels and the Appellate Body have recognized that a responding party may be considered to have waived its objection to a lack of consultations if it does not object in a timely manner. Appellate Body Report, Mexico–Corn Syrup (Article 21.5–US), para. 63 (dealing with a lack of consultations request under Article 21.5 of the DSU); Appellate Body Report, US–FSC, paras. 165-166. However, the United States objected to China's consultations request upon receipt of the request for consultations, at the DSB meeting where the panel was established, and directly to the Panel during the timeframe set forth for requesting preliminary rulings. Therefore we do not consider "waiver" as a possible basis for why China's claims under the SPS Agreement, might be included in our terms of reference.

⑤ Panel Report, Brazil–Aircraft, para. 7.10 (citing) Appellate Body Report, EC–Bananas III, para. 142.

that same proceeding, the panel had considered that because the DSU essentially requires the DSB to establish a panel automatically upon request of a party, a panel cannot rely upon the DSB to ascertain that requisite consultations have been held and to establish a panel only in those cases.[①] Accordingly, the panel determined "that a panel may consider whether consultations have been held with respect to a 'dispute', and that a preliminary objection may properly be sustained if a party can establish that the required consultations had not been held with respect to a dispute."[②]

7.29 The requirements that apply to consultations requests are set out in Article4.4 of the DSU, which provides, in relevant part, that "[a]ny request for consultations shall be submitted in writing and shall give the reasons for the request, including identification of the measures at issue and an indication of the legal basis for the complaint".

7.30 We note that the term "legal basis of the complaint" has not been interpreted in respect of Article4.4 of the DSU. The Appellate Body has, however, interpreted the same term as used in Article6.2 of the DSU to mean the claim made by the complaining party.The Appellate Body has also clarified that a claim sets forth the complainant's view[③] "that the respondent party has violated, or nullified or impaired the benefits arising from, an identified provision of a particular agreement".[④] Given the nearly identical language in Article4.4 of the DSU, we consider that this understanding could also be applied to the term "legal basis for the complaint" in Article4.4.

7.31 Article4.4 of the DSU however requires the consultations request to include an "indication of the legal basis of the complaint" while Article6.2 of the DSU requires the panel request to "provide a brief summary of the legal basis for the complaint sufficient to present the problem clearly".

7.32 In this respect, China argues that "indication" of the legal basis of the complaint

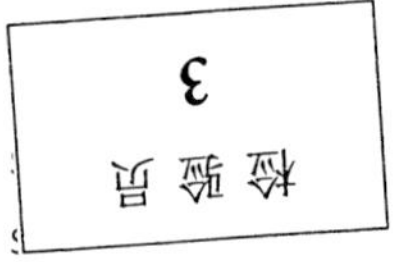

es significantly less than what is required under Article6.2, i.e. "identify

issue and provide a brief summary of the legal basis for the complaint

problem clearly". In China's view, an "indication" under Article4.4 is a "hint

nformation from which more may be inferred" while Article6.2 requires a description that is "sufficient" meaning adequate for a certain purpose, enough, to present the problem clearly.China considers that this difference reflects the heightened burden of panel requests under Article6.2 of the DSU and the understanding that the legal basis of a claim often

① Panel Report, Brazil–Aircraft, para. 7.10.

② Appellate Body Report, US–Oil Country Tubular Goods Sunset Reviews, para. 162.

③ Appellate Body Report, Korea–Dairy, para. 139.

④ China's response to Panel question No. 6.

evolve during the course of consultations.[①] China thus submits that it had met the burden of providing as "indication" in terms of Article4.4 of the DSU.[②]

7.33 The United States agrees that an "indication" of the legal basis does not require that all the claims be spelled out in the consultations request. However, the United States argues that this distinction is not pertinent to the issue of whether claims under the *SPS Agreement* are within the Panel's terms of reference, because, in its view, China's consultations request plainly states China's view that the United States' measure is not subject to the *SPS Agreement*.[③]

7.34 In describing how a panel must examine a panel request for consistency with the obligations in Article6.2 of the DSU, the Appellate Body has noted that the panel request must be examined as a whole and in light of attendant circumstances.[④] Given the relationship between the consultations request and the panel request, the shared language in Article4 and Article6.2 of the DSU, the similar purposes of the two requests, i.e. to delimit the scope of the dispute, and the need to interpret both provisions in a harmonious way[⑤], we find the Appellate Body reasoning pertinent for the analysis of the consistency of consultations requests with the obligations of Article4.4 of the DSU as well.

7.35 The Panel is aware that in making its analysis of whether a particular claim was included in the consultations request, it should not inquire as to what actually occurred during consultations. The panel in *Korea – Alcoholic Beverages* correctly noted that "[t]he only requirement under the DSU is that consultations were in fact held ... [w]hat takes place in those consultations is not the concern of a panel".[⑥] The Appellate Body explained in *US – Upland Cotton*

---

① China's response to Panel question No. 6.

② China's response to Panel question No. 6.

③ United States' response to Panel question No. 6.

④ Appellate Body Report, Korea–Dairy, paras. 124-127; also Appellate Body Report, US–Carbon Steel, para. 127.

⑤ The Appellate Body has recognized the applicability of the principle of effectiveness (*ut res magis valeat quam pereat*) in the interpretation of the covered agreements. This principle was first discussed in Japan–Alcoholic Beverages II, para. 24. In US–Gasoline, the Appellate Body noted that this principle obliges a treaty interpreter to give meaning and effect to all the terms of a treaty. (Appellate Body Report, US–Gasoline, p. 23). In light of the interpretative principle of effectiveness, the Appellate Body in Argentina–Footwear (EC) ruled that it is the duty of any treaty interpreter to "read all applicable provisions of a treaty in a way that gives meaning to all of them, harmoniously." [Appellate Body Report, Argentina–Footwear (EC), para. 81]. The Appellate Body further held in Korea–Dairy that Article II:2 of the WTO Agreement expressly manifests the intention of the Uruguay Round negotiators that the provisions of the WTO Agreement and the Multilateral Trade Agreements included in its Annexes 1, 2 and 3 must be read as a whole. (Appellate Body Report, Korea–Dairy, para. 81).

⑥ Panel Report, Korea–Alcoholic Beverages, para. 10.19.

that examining what took place in the consultations would seem contrary to Article4.6 of the DSU, which provides that "[c]onsultations shall be confidential, and without prejudice to the rights of any Member in any further proceedings". Finally, the Appellate Body noted that, there is no public record of what actually transpires during consultations and parties will often disagree about what, precisely, was discussed.①

7.36 Therefore, the Panel will inquire whether China indicated the *SPS Agreement* as a legal basis for its complaint in its consultations request and in doing so will look at that consultations request as a whole and in light of the attendant circumstances. However, the Panel will not use as a basis for its determination what either party alleges took place during consultations.② Therefore, while we will consider the exchange of letters in April 2009 – which are precisely about the scope of China's consultations request – we will not consider any questions posed or answers given during the consultations.

Whether China has requested consultations pursuant to the *SPS Agreement*

7.37 The United States focuses its argumentation on China's statement that it does not believe that the United States' measures are SPS measures and that it is requesting consultations with the United States pursuant to Article11 of the *SPS Agreement* "if it were demonstrated that any such measure is an SPS measure".

7.38 According to the United States, a "conditional" request for consultations under Article11 of the *SPS Agreement* does not amount to an "actual" request for consultations pursuant to Article11 of the *SPS Agreement*.③ Most importantly, the United States contends that it would have no way of knowing whether the condition had been satisfied and that China's request had become operative.

7.39 Although the language in China's consultations request and, in particular, the reference to a "demonstration" that the measures in question are SPS measures, is not the most artful, the Panel, further to the abovementioned jurisprudence, should not look at one phrase in the consultations request in isolation, but rather examine the consultations request as a whole and in light of the "attendant circumstances". This means that the Panel needs to consider the consultations request in its entirety and place the SPS references in the context of the rest of the consultations request. Additionally, the Panel will consider whether the exchange of letters are part of the "attendant circumstances" of the consultations request.

---

① Appellate Body Report, US–Upland Cotton, para. 287.

② Although China, in its first written submission, refers to its questions to the United States and what actually took place during consultations, given the Appellate Body findings in US–Upland Cotton, we will not base our decision on what one party or another says occurred during consultations.

③ United States' Preliminary Ruling Request, para. 19.

7.40 With respect to the rest of the consultations request, the Panel notes that China's consultations request deals with US measures affecting the importation of poultry products from China into the United States.[①] Additionally, in paragraph1 of the consultations request, China states that it "is concerned that Section727, in conjunction with the overall US regime for regulating imports of poultry products places restrictions on the import from China of poultry products that are inconsistent with the United States' WTO obligations".[②] The Panel is of the view that it is reasonable to interpret this reference to the overall regime for the importation of poultry products to be a reference to the PPIA as well as its implementing regulations, especially given China's reference, in the immediately succeeding paragraph to 9CFR§381.196[③] as one of several US regulations that cannot be implemented because of Section727. There is no dispute among the parties that the PPIA and the regulatory regime set up pursuant to its mandate are SPS measures.

7.41 China's consultation request, after outlining the legal basis for its complaint with respect to Articles I and XI of the GATT1994, includes, in paragraphs6 and 7, controversial language where it specifically references the *SPS Agreement*.

7.42 It appears to the Panel that China was attempting to challenge Section727 under the GATT1994 and the *Agreement on Agriculture*, and, in the alternative, under the *SPS Agreement* in the event the United States argued that Section727 is an SPS measure within the scope of the *SPS Agreement*. It thus seems to the Panel that China wanted to ensure that the *SPS Agreement* was within the Panel's terms of reference in such a case. Rather than being confusing, this seems consistent with the panel's reasoning in *Korea – Commercial Vessels* that "if a complaining party wishes to pursue claims in respect of a given measure under multiple provisions, whether complementarily or alternatively, not only is it *permitted* by Article6.2 of the DSU to refer to all of those provisions in its request for establishment, but it is *required* to do so".[④] The Panel is of the view that the same logic should also apply to consultations requests.

7.43 Given the surrounding context, the Panel is of the view that China's consultations request did "indicate" an SPS basis for its complaint, even if that basis, seen in isolation, was qualified in somewhat unclear conditional language.[⑤] In that respect, it is important to note that

① China's consultations request, WT/DS392/1, opening paragraph.

② China's consultations request, WT/DS392/1, para. 1.

③ Code of Federal Regulations, 9 Ch. III, Food Safety and Inspection Service, USDA (1-1-08 Edition).

④ Panel Report, Korea–Commercial Vessels, subparagraph 29 of para. 7.2. Recall our discussion above on the relevance of Article 6.2 jurisprudence to an understanding of similar obligations in Article 4.4.

⑤ We do note that upon receipt of the United States' letter, China could have filed an amended or supplemental consultations request which would have eliminated any doubt on the part of the United States and avoided spending time and resources on this matter.

although there are many similarities between Articles4.4 and 6.2 of the DSU and they should be interpreted in an harmonious way, the obligation on a Member in its consultations request is to "indicate" the legal basis for the complaint whereas the obligation in the panel request is to provide a "brief legal summary of the legal basis of the complaint sufficient to present the problem clearly". Therefore, an indication is something less than a summary sufficient to present the problem clearly. While the Panel does not wish to be perceived as encouraging WTO Members to present their problems confusingly in their consultations request, it does seem that there is a bit more leeway in how WTO Members phrase complaints in a consultations request *vis-à-vis* the clarity required in a panel request which is the final word on the scope of the dispute.①

7.44 Additionally, if we move beyond the consultations request itself to an examination of the "attendant circumstances" and include in that examination the exchange of letters between the United States and China, China's intentions and the United States' understanding thereof, becomes even clearer.

7.45 We note that China's letter advises the United States that its understanding is not correct and goes on to say that:

> "Through its request for consultations (WT/DS392/1), China has requested consultations under Article11 of the *SPS Agreement* to cover a contingency, namely the demonstration that any of the listed measures is an SPS measure. To that end, China will shortly provide the United States with written questions requesting the United States to provide answers during the consultations concerning the nature and status of measures identified in the consultation request. Thus, China has indeed requested, and the United States and China will engage in, a consultation that fully addresses relevant questions concerning whether any of the U.S. measures are SPS measures within the meaning of the *SPS Agreement*. The parties will also consult on the questions regarding the various claims under the *SPS Agreement* applicable to such measures, as stated in China's consultations request."②

---

① We note that China also brings up whether the United States was "prejudiced" by the supposed confusion in the consultations request (China's first written submission, para. 173). Although some panels and indeed even the Appellate Body have delved into the issue of prejudice, we note that the Appellate Body has also found that jurisdiction is a fundamental prerequisite for lawful panel proceedings. (Appellate Body Report, US–Carbon Steel, para. 127.) Therefore it is our view that non-compliance with the various provisions that set forth how to establish a panel and its terms of reference cannot be overcome by a lack of prejudice to the respondent.

② China's letter of 28 April 2009. Exhibit CN-38.

7.46 As noted by the United States itself, the Appellate Body has concluded that "consultations provide the parties an opportunity to define and delimit the scope of the dispute between them".① Accordingly, if through consultations the complaining party obtains a better understanding of the operation of a challenged measure such that additional provisions of the covered agreements become relevant, it may reformulate its complaint to include these other provisions, even from covered agreements not mentioned in the consultations request, so long as the legal basis in the panel request may reasonably be said to have evolved from the legal basis that formed the subject of consultations.

7.47 We also recall the reasoning of the panel in *China – Publications and Audiovisual Products,* pursuant to the Appellate Body's conclusions in *Mexico – Anti-Dumping Measures on Rice,* that:

> "[I]n some circumstances, a claim based upon a WTO provision of a covered agreement which was not contained in the request for consultations, can nevertheless be considered to be within a panel's terms of reference. If through consultations the complaining party obtains a better understanding of the operation of a challenged measure such that additional provisions of the covered agreements become relevant it may reformulate its complaint to include these other provisions so long as the legal basis in the panel request may reasonably be said to have evolved from the legal basis that formed the subject of consultations.②

① Appellate Body Report, Mexico–Corn Syrup (Article 21.5–US), para. 54.

② Panel Report, China–Publications and Audiovisual Products, para. 7.115 citing Appellate Body Report, Mexico–Anti-Dumping Measures on Rice, para. 138 where it stated:

"A complaining party may learn of additional information during consultations—for example, a better understanding of the operation of a challenged measure—that could warrant revising the list of treaty provisions with which the measure is alleged to be inconsistent. Such a revision may lead to a narrowing of the complaint, or to a reformulation of the complaint that takes into account new information such that additional provisions of the covered agreements become relevant. The claims set out in a panel request may thus be expected to be shaped by, and thereby constitute a natural evolution of, the consultation process. Reading the DSU, as Mexico does, to limit the legal basis set out in the panel request to what was indicated in the request for consultations, would ignore an important rationale behind the requirement to hold consultations—namely, the exchange of information necessary to refine the contours of the dispute, which are subsequently set out in the panel request. In this light, we consider that it is not necessary that the provisions referred to in the request for consultations be identical to those set out in the panel request, provided that the 'legal basis' in the panel request may reasonably be said to have evolved from the 'legal basis' that formed the subject of consultations. In other words, the addition of provisions must not have the effect of changing the essence of the complaint."

7.48 It seems to us that what has happened in this case is that China merely forecasted its expectation of obtaining a better understanding of the operation of the challenged measures and that the *SPS Agreement* might be relevant in the consultations request rather than simply waiting to reveal the possibility of an SPS claim in the Panel Request. The Panel finds it difficult to sustain a reading of Articles4 and 6 of the DSU whereby a complainant could make no reference to the possibility of an evolution of its claims in its consultations request and nevertheless have those claims included in the terms of reference of the panel, yet a complainant who did mention them would have them excluded.

7.49 In light of the above, the Panel therefore concludes, examining the consultations request as a whole, that China, in its Consultation Request, indicated that the *SPS Agreement* would serve as the basis of its claims, albeit in a conditional manner. Additionally, an examination of the attendant circumstances, most notably the exchange of letters prior to consultations taking place, supports the conclusion that the *SPS Agreement* was indicated as a basis for China's claims. Accordingly, the Panel finds that China did request consultations *inter alia* pursuant to Article11 of the *SPS Agreement* and that, therefore, China's SPS claims are within its terms of reference.

(iv)Conclusion

7.50 The Panel therefore disagrees with the United States' contention that China did not request consultations under the *SPS Agreement* and finds that China did request consultations pursuant to Article11 of the *SPS Agreement,* indicated the various provisions of that Agreement that were the basis for its claims, and that, therefore, China's SPS claims are within its terms of reference.

2.Whether the Panel may rule on an expired measure

(a) Background

7.51 The United States has contended, and China agreed,① that Section727 expired on 30 September 2009, i.e. two days after the deadline for China's first written submission. This raises the question of whether the Panel should make findings on a measure that is no longer in force. We note that the United States has not requested the Panel not to make findings on an expired measure.② Nevertheless, the Panel believes that before going ahead and examining the WTO consistency of Section727 pursuant to China's various claims, we need to decide whether we may make rulings and recommendations on a measure that is no longer in force.

① United States' first written submission, para. 2; China's response to Panel question No. 11.

② See United States first written submission, para. 93. The United States argues that the Panel only needs to consider China's claims under Article XI:1 of the GATT 1994 and any needed defence under Article XX(b) in order to resolve this dispute.

(b)Arguments of the parties

7.52 The United States alleges that Section727 has expired[①] and thus has been supplanted by Section743.[②] The United States further argues that any funding restriction imposed by Section743 has been lifted as a consequence of the Secretary of Agriculture's issuance of a letter to the US Congress on 12 November 2009.[③] As indicated above, the United States has not requested the Panel not to rule on Section727.

7.53 China does not contest that Section727 is no longer in force. For China, though, the expiration of Section727 has no bearing on the Panel's terms of reference, as Section727 expired after the Panel was established and its terms of reference were set. China contends that measures expiring after the establishment of a panel or during the panel process have repeatedly been found by panels and the Appellate Body to be within a panel's jurisdiction. As an example, China argues, in Indonesia – *Autos,* the panel rejected Indonesia's argument that the National Car program was a moot issue because it had expired. In doing so, China explains, the panel referenced several GATT and WTO disputes where measures included in the terms of reference were terminated after the commencement of the panel proceedings, and where panels nevertheless went on to make findings in respect of those measures.[④] China submits that this approach has been followed in subsequent disputes, such as *EC – Selected Customs Matters* and *US – Upland Cotton.* China stresses that, in *US – Upland Cotton*, the Appellate Body noted that "GATT and WTO panels have frequently made findings with respect to measures withdrawn after the establishment of the panel [and] [i]n none of these cases has a panel or the Appellate Body premised its decision on the view that, *a priori*, an expired measure could not be within a panel's terms of reference".[⑤]

(c) Analysis by the Panel

7.54 The Panel will therefore determine whether it should rule on an expired measure. The Appellate Body explained in *EC – Bananas III* (*Article21.5 – Ecuador II)*, "once a panel has been established and the terms of reference for the panel have been set, the panel has the competence to make findings with respect to the measures covered by its terms of reference". The Appellate

① United States' first written submission, para. 62.

② United States' first written submission, para. 68.

③ United States' first written submission, para. 74. The letter can be found in Exhibit US-45.

④ China refers to the Panel Report, Indonesia–Autos, para. 14.9, citing Panel Report, US–Wool Shirts and Blouses and GATT disputes EEC–Dessert Apples, EEC–Apples (US), EEC–Apples I (Chile), US–Canadian Tuna, EEC–Animal Feed Proteins and US–Section 337. China's response to Panel question No. 11.

⑤ China refers to the Appellate Body Report, US–Upland Cotton, footnote 214. China's responses to Panel question No. 11.

Body thus concluded that it is "within the discretion of the panel to decide how it takes into account ... a repeal of the measure at issue".[①] It is therefore within our discretion to decide whether to make findings on Section727.

7.55 We note that, in the past, panels have decided to make rulings on expired measures where the respondent Member had not conceded the WTO inconsistency of the measure and the repealed measure could be easily re-imposed.[②] In our view, this is precisely the case of Section727 since the United States does not concede the alleged WTO inconsistency of Section727 and the appropriations legislation in the United States is of an annual nature. Section727 reiterated the language of a previous annual appropriations provision with identical wording, Section733, and it has now expired and a new provision, Section743, has been adopted to address FSIS access to appropriated funds for activities regarding China's equivalence application. Although we acknowledge that Section743 does not share the same language as Section727 and its predecessor, Section733, we consider that if we were to refuse to make findings on the expired measure – Section727 – the Panel might be depriving China of any meaningful review of the consistency of the United States' actions with its WTO obligations, while allowing the repetition of the potentially WTO inconsistent conduct. This would certainly call to mind the "moving target" scenario which the Appellate Body in *Chile – Price Band System* stated that a complainant should not have to face.

7.56 The Panel will thus proceed to make findings on the WTO consistency of Section727 which is within its terms of reference. Nevertheless, the Panel recognizes that it would not be appropriate to make recommendations pursuant to Article19 of the DSU with respect to a WTO-inconsistent repealed measure that has ceased to have legal effect.[③] Indeed, if the Panel finds that Section727 was inconsistent with any of the provisions of the covered agreements within its terms of reference, it would be pointless to ask the United States to bring Section727 into conformity with those covered agreements since the measure is no longer in force.

(d)Conclusion

7.57 The Panel therefore concludes that it will proceed to make findings on the WTO-consistency of Section727 which is within its terms of reference.

---

① Appellate Body Report, EC–Bananas III (Article 21.5–Ecuador II), para. 270.

② Panel Report, India–Additional Import Duties, paras. 7.69-7.70.

③ Appellate Body Report, US–Certain EC Products, para. 81; Appellate Body Report, US–Upland Cotton, para. 272; and Appellate Body Report, EC–Bananas III (Article 21.5–Ecuador II), para. 271.

【本案评析】

以上案例节选自中国诉美国禽肉限制措施争端案专家组报告。专家组报告中对专家组权限问题进行了分析。该案专家组讨论了专家组职权范围中的其他情况，并在此基础之上，审查过期失效的贸易措施是否在专家组的审查范围之内的问题。

三、欧共体涉及肉类产品及其制品（荷尔蒙）措施争端案

EC-MEASURES CONCERNING MEAT AND MEAT PRODUCTS
(HORMONES)
(WT/DS26/AB/R、WT/DS48/AB/R)

V. The Standard of Review Applicable in Proceedings Under the SPS Agreement

110. The European Communities appeals from certain findings of the Panel① upon the ground that the Panel failed to apply an appropriate standard of review in assessing certain acts of, and scientificevidentiary material submitted by, the European Communities.② The European Communities claimed,more specifically, that:

... the panel erred in law in not according deference to the following elements of the EC measures:

- the EC's decision to set and apply a level of sanitary protection higher than that recommended by Codex Alimentarius for the risks arising from the use of these hormones for growth promotion;

- the EC's scientific assessment and management of the risk from the hormones at issue; and

- the EC's adherence to the precautionary principle and its aversion to accepting any increased carcinogenic risk.

The panel also erred in law because it:

- assigned a high probative value to the scientific views presented by some of the five scientific experts chosen by it(and to the views of the technical expert appointed by CodexAlimentarius);

- disregarded in effect or distorted the scientific evidence presented by the EC and

① US Panel Report, paras. 8.124, 8.127, 8.133, 8.134, 8.145, 8.146, 8.194, 8.199, 8.213 and 8.255; Canada Panel Report, paras. 8.127, 8.130, 8.136, 8.137, 8.148, 8.149, 8.197, 8.202, 8.216 and 8.258.

② EC's appellant's submission, para. 140.

its scientific advisors, and systematically considered the scientific views of the panel appointed experts or even a minority of those experts, of higher probative value than the scientific evidence presented by the EC scientists;

- based its legal interpretations and findings on a number of critical issues on the majority of scientific views presented by its own appointed experts, instead of limiting itself to examining whether the scientific evidence presented by the EC was based on "scientific principles" [as required by Article 2:2 (of the SPS Agreement)].①

111. In the view of the European Communities, the principal alternative approaches to the problem of formulating the 'proper standard of review' so far as panels are concerned are two-fold. The first is designated as "de novo review". This standard of review would allow a panel complete freedom to come to a different view than the competent authority of the Member whose act or determination is being reviewed. A panel would have to "verify whether the determination by the national authority was 'correct' both factually and procedurally".② The second is described as "deference". Under a "deference" standard, a panel, in the submission of the European Communities, should not seek to redo the investigation conducted by the national authority but instead examine whether the "procedure"required by the relevant WTO rules had been followed.③

112. Clearly referring only to an appropriate standard of review of factual determinations by the domestic authorities of a Member, the European Communities submits that the principle of deference has been embodied in Article 17.6(i) of the Anti-Dumping Agreement, which reads as follows:

17.6 In examining the matter referred to in paragraph 5:

(i) in its assessment of the facts of the matter, the panel shall determine whether the authorities' establishment of the facts was proper and whether their evaluation of those facts was unbiased and objective. If the establishment of the facts was proper and the evaluation was unbiased and objective, even though the panel might have reached a different conclusion,the evaluation shall not be overturned;

113. The European Communities further urges that the above-quoted standard, which it describes as a "deferential 'reasonableness' standard"④ is applicable in "all highly complex factual situations, including the assessment of the risks to human health arising from toxins and

① EC's appellant's submission, para. 139.

② EC's appellant's submission, para. 122.

③ EC's appellant's submission, para. 123.

④ EC's appellant's submission, para. 128.

contaminants"[①], and should have been applied by the Panel in the present case.

114. The first point that must be made in this connection, is that the SPS Agreement itself is silent on the matter of an appropriate standard of review for panels deciding upon SPS measures of a Member. Nor are there provisions in the DSU or any of the covered agreements (other than the Anti-Dumping Agreement) prescribing a particular standard of review. Only Article 17.6(i) of the Anti-Dumping Agreement has language on the standard of review to be employed by panels engaged in the "assessment of the facts of the matter". We find no indication in the SPS Agreement of an intent on the part of the Members to adopt or incorporate into that Agreement the standard set out in Article 17.6(i) of the Anti-Dumping Agreement. Textually, Article 17.6(i) is specific to the Anti-Dumping Agreement.[②]

115. The standard of review appropriately applicable in proceedings under the SPS Agreement, of course, must reflect the balance established in that Agreement between the jurisdictional competences conceded by the Members to the WTO and the jurisdictional competences retained by the Members for themselves.[③] To adopt a standard of review not clearly rooted in the text of the SPS Agreement itself,may well amount to changing that finely drawn balance; and neither a panel nor the Appellate Body is authorized to do that.

116. We do not mean, however, to suggest that there is at present no standard of review applicable to the determination and assessment of the facts in proceedings under the SPS Agreement or under other covered agreements. In our view, Article 11 of the DSU bears directly on this matter and, in effect, articulates with great succinctness but with sufficient clarity the appropriate standard of review for panels in respect of both the ascertainment of facts and the legal characterization of such facts under the relevant agreements. Article 11 reads thus:

---

① EC's appellant's submission, para. 127.

② On the other hand, as suggested by the United States, we must note the *Decision on the Review of Article 17.6 of the Agreement on Implementation of Article VI of the General Agreement on Tariffs and Trade 1994*, which states:

Decide as follows: The standard of review in paragraph 6 of Article 17 of the Agreement on Implementation of Article VI of GATT 1994 shall be reviewed after a period of three years with a view to considering the question of whether it is capable of general application. (underlining added)

This Ministerial Decision evidences that the Ministers were aware that Article 17.6 of the *Anti-Dumping Agreement* was applicable only in respect of that Agreement.

③ See, for example, S.P. Croley and J.H. Jackson, "WTO Dispute Panel Deference to National Government Decisions, TheMisplaced Analogy to the U.S.Chevron Standard-of-Review Doctrine", in E.-U. Petersmann (ed.), *International Trade Law andthe GATT/WTO Dispute Settlement System* (Kluwer, 1997) 185, p. 189; P.A. Akakwam, "The Standard of Review in the 1994Antidumping Code: Circumscribing the Role of GATT Panels in Reviewing National Antidumping Determinations" (1996), 5:2 *Minnesota Journal of Global Trade* 277, pp. 295~296.

"The function of panels is to assist the DSB in discharging its responsibilities under this Understanding and the covered agreements.Accordingly, a panel should make an objective assessment of the matter before it, including an objective assessment of the facts of the case and the applicability of and conformity with the relevant covered agreements, and make such other findings as will assist the DSB in making the recommendations or in giving the rulings provided in the covered agreements. Panels should consult regularly with the parties to the dispute and give them adequate opportunity to develop a mutually satisfactory solution." (underlining added)

117. So far as fact-finding by panels is concerned, their activities are always constrained by themandate of Article 11 of the DSU: the applicable standard is neither de novo review as such, nor "total deference", but rather the "objective assessment of the facts". Many panels have in the past refused to undertake *de novo* review①, wisely, since under current practice and systems, they are in any case poorly suited to engage in such a review. On the other hand, "total deference to the findings of the national authorities", it has been well said, "could not ensure an 'objective assessment' as foreseen by Article 11 of the DSU".②

118. In so far as legal questions are concerned - that is, consistency or inconsistency of a Member's measure with the provisions of the applicable agreement - a standard not found in the text of the SPS Agreement itself cannot absolve a panel (or the Appellate Body) from the duty to apply the customary rules of interpretation of public international law.③ It may be noted that the European Communities refrained from suggesting that Article 17.6 of the Anti-Dumping Agreement in its entirety was applicable to the present case. Nevertheless, it is appropriate to stress that here again Article 11 of the DSU is directly on point, requiring a panel to "make an objective assessment of the matter before it,including an objective assessment of the facts of the case and the applicability of and conformity with the relevant covered agreements ...".

119. We consider, therefore, that the issue of failure to apply an appropriate standard of

---

① Panel Report, *United States-Underwear*, adopted 25 February 1997, WT/DS24/R; Panel Report, *Korea-Anti-DumpingDuties on Imports of Polyacetal Resins from the United States*, adopted 27 April 1993, BISD 40S/205; Panel Report, *United States-Imposition of Anti-Dumping Duties on Imports of Fresh and Chilled Atlantic Salmon from Norway*, adopted 27April 1994, ADP/87; and Panel Report, *United States-Initiation of a Countervailing Duty Investigation into Softwood LumberProducts from Canada*, adopted 3 June 1987, BISD 34S/194.

② Panel Report, *United States-Underwear*, adopted 25 February 1997, WT/DS24/R, para. 7.10

③ DSU, Article 3.2.

review, raised by the European Communities, resolves itself into the issue of whether or not the Panel, in making the above and other findings referred to and appealed by the European Communities, had made an "objective assessment of the matter before it, including an objective assessment of the facts ...". This particular issue is addressed (in substantial detail) below.① Here, however, we uphold the findings of the Panel appealed by the European Communities upon the ground of failure to apply either a "deferential reasonableness standard" or the standard of review set out in Article 17.6(i) of the Anti-Dumping Agreement.

【本案评析】

以上案例节选自欧共体涉及肉类产品及其制品（荷尔蒙）措施争端案上诉机构报告。在该案中，申诉方美国认为欧共体第 96/22 号政令禁止在牲畜饲料中使用荷尔蒙或特定激素物质，而这使得来自美国肉类产品及其制品受到了限制或禁止，并构成了相应的限制或禁止措施，该案上诉机构对专家组的一般评审标准进行了重点的分析。

四、美国影响羊毛编织衫和外套进口的措施争端案

china – measures affecting the protection and enforcement of intellectual property rights (WT/DS362/R)

VII. FINDINGS

A. COPYRIGHT LAW

...

(vi) procedural issue

7.140 China emphasizes that the United States bears the burden of proof of this "as such" claim.② China alleges that the only evidence that the United States has offered is the text of Article 4(1) of the Copyright Law itself.③

7.141 The Panel notes that the United States provided more evidence than the text of the provision.In any case, the Panel recalls the following statement in the Appellate Body Report in *US – Corrosion-Resistant Steel Sunset Review*:

① Paras. 131-144 of this Report.

② China's rebuttal submission, paras. 227-229.

③ China's rebuttal submission, paras. 266-268.

"When a measure is challenged 'as such', the starting point for an analysis must be the measure on its face. If the meaning and content of the measure are clear on its face, then the consistency of the measure as such can be assessed on that basis alone. If, however, the meaning or content of the measure is not evident on its face, further examination is required ..." ①

7.142 In the present case, the Panel's review of the Copyright Law, in particular Article 4(1), on its face, shows that the measure is sufficiently clear to conclude that the United States has made a primafacie case of inconsistency. Article 5(1) of the Berne Convention (1971) provides that Members shall ensure that authors shall enjoy in respect of their works the rights specially granted by that Convention. Article4(1) of the Copyright Law provides that certain works shall *not* receive the protection of that Law and that Law provides the rights specially granted by that Convention.Whilst the Panel has not accepted all the United States' allegations regarding the range of works that fall within Article 4(1), that does not undermine the basic finding of an inconsistency.

【本案评析】

以上节选自美国影响羊毛编织衫和外套进口的措施争端案上诉机构报告。该案上诉机构认为，国内法中通行的"谁主张谁举证"的做法，同样适用于 WTO 的争端解决实践。

五、中国关于特定出版物及视听娱乐产品所采取的影响贸易权和分销服务措施案

CHINA – Measures affecting trading rights and distribution services for certain publications and audiovisual entertainment products

(WT/DS363/R)

VII. FINDINGS

A. GENEAL ISSUES

1.Burden of proof

7.1 We recall the general principles applicable to burden of proof in WTO dispute settlement,

① Appellate Body Report in US–Corrosion-Resistant Steel Sunset Review, para. 168.

i.e., that a party claiming a violation of a provision of a covered agreement by another Member must assert and prove its claim.[①] We also recall that any party who asserts a fact, whether the claimant or the respondent, is responsible for providing proof thereof. This is in conformity with generally accepted canons of evidence in civil law, common law, and, in fact, in most jurisdictions, that the burden of proof rests upon the party, whether complaining or defending, who asserts the affirmative of a particular claim or defence. If that party adduces evidence sufficient to raise a presumption that what is claimed is true, the burden then shifts to the other party, who will fail unless it adduces sufficient evidence to rebut the presumption.[②]

7.2 These general canons also apply in WTO dispute settlement, such that once a complaining party has made a prima facie case, the burden of proof moves to the defending party, which must in turn counter or refute the claimed inconsistency.[③] The Appellate Body explained, in Canada – Dairy (Article21.5 New Zealand and US II) that:

> "as a general matter, the burden of proof rests upon the complaining Member. That Member must make out a prima facie case by presenting sufficient evidence to raise a presumption in favour of its claim. If the complaining Member succeeds, the responding Member may then seek to rebut this presumption. Therefore, under the usual allocation of the burden of proof, a responding Member's measure will be treated as WTO-consistent, until sufficient evidence is presented to prove the contrary."[④]

7.3 It is also well to remember that "a prima facie case is one which, in the absence of effective refutation by the defending party, requires a panel, as a matter of law, to rule in favour of the complaining party presenting the prima facie case"[⑤].

7.4 The Appellate Body also has clarified that in the context of WTO dispute settlement "[a] prima facie case must be based on "evidence *and* legal argument" put forward by the complaining party in relation to *each* of the elements of the claim.A complaining party may not simply submit evidence and expect the panel to divine from it a claim of WTO-inconsistency. Nor may a complaining party simply allege facts without relating them to its legal arguments."[⑥]

7.5 Precisely how much and precisely what kind of evidence will be required to establish such

① Appellate Body Report on US–Wool Shirts and Blouses, p. 16, DSR 1997:I, 323 at 337.

② Appellate Body Report on US–Wool Shirts and Blouses, p. 14, DSR 1997:I, 323 at 335.

③ Appellate Body Report on EC–Hormones, para. 98.

④ Appellate Body Report on Canada–Dairy (Article 21.5 New Zealand and US II), para. 66.

⑤ Appellate Body Report on EC–Hormones, para. 104.

⑥ Appellate Body Report on US–Gambling, para. 140.

a presumption will necessarily vary from measure to measure, provision to provision, and case to case.[①]

7.6 Given this general rule, it is the complainant in a given case who initially bears the burden of proof to establish a prima facie case of inconsistency of a measure with a provision of a WTO covered agreement, before the burden of showing consistency with a provision or defending it under an exceptional provision (e.g. Article XX of the GATT1994) shifts to the defending party.

7.7 In the present case, therefore, it is the United States who has the initial burden of proof to establish a prima facie case of alleged inconsistencies of China's measures with the various provisions it has cited, including China's Protocol of Accession, Article XVI and XVII of the GATS and Article III:4 of the GATT1994. With respect to the US claims regarding China's trading rights commitments in the Protocol of Accession, China, as the party making an affirmative defence of its measures under Article XX(a) of the GATT1994, bears the initial burden of proof.

【本案评析】

以上案例节选自中国关于特定出版物及视听娱乐产品所采取的影响贸易权和分销服务措施案专家组报告。该案专家组对于争端解决程序中"谁主张、谁举证"这一举证责任的适用进行了详细阐述。

六、中国原材料出口措施争端案

CHINA – MEASURES RELATED TO THE EXPORTATION OF VARIOUS RAW MATERIALS (WT/DS394/R, WT/DS395/R , WT/DS398/R)

VII. FINDINGS

7.209 China does not contest that any of these products are subject to quotas under the 2009 measures.However, China considers that the complainants have failed to establish a violation under Article XI:1 of the GATT1994 because they failed "to establish China's non-compliance with the terms of Article XI:2(a) with respect to the export quotas on all of the products at issue."[②] China argues that the chapeau to Article XI:2 "links the scope of application of the obligation in Article XI:1 to the further requirements in Article XI:2(a)-(c)" by providing that Articles XI:1 shall

① Appellate Body Report on US–Wool Shirts and Blouses, p. 14, DSR 1997:I, 323 at 335.

② China's first written submission, para. 350; China's second written submission, para. 36.

"not extend to" the types of export restriction described in Article XI:2.[①] Accordingly, it requests the Panel to reject the complainants' claims on the basis that they failed to demonstrate that the quotas at issue do not "fall[] within Articles XI:2(a), (b), or (c)" and thereby demonstrate that a violation should apply.[②] China finds support for this in what it asserts was the Appellate Body's treatment in similar provisions, namely Article27.2 of the SCM Agreement and GATT Articles II:1(a) and II:1(b) of the GATT1994 in *India – Additional Import Duties*.[③]

7.210 The complainants reject this view, arguing that the Appellate Body made clear in *US – Wool Shirts and Blouses* that the provisions under Article XI:2 are "affirmative defences" and that the burden is therefore on the respondent – and not the complainant – to demonstrate that Article XI:2 is somehow applicable.[④] China characterizes the Appellate Body's statement as "obiter" and no longer applicable in light of an evolving "taxonomy" adopted by the Appellate Body.[⑤]

7.211 The Panel finds itself at odds with China's view that the Appellate Body statement in *US – Wools Shirts and Blouses* regarding Article XI:2 is not applicable to the matter at hand.The Appellate Body was clear in its statement on the operation of Article XI:2(c)(i), stating:

> "Articles XX and XI:(2)(c)(i) are limited exceptions from obligations under certain other provisions of the GATT1994, not positive rules establishing obligations in themselves. They are in the nature of affirmative defences. It is only reasonable that the burden of establishing such a defence should rest on the party asserting it".[⑥]

---

① China's first written submission, para. 353.

② China's first written submission, para. 353; China's second written submission, para. 29.

③ China's first written submission, paras. 354-357. China refers to Article 27.2 of the SCM Agreement, which provides that "[t]he prohibition of paragraph 1(a) of Article 3 shall not apply to … other developing country Members … subject to compliance with the provisions in paragraph 4". The Appellate Body concluded that the "prohibition of Article 3.1(a)" would only "apply" if the complainant demonstrates non-compliance with Article 27.4. See Appellate Body Report, Brazil-Aircraft, para. 141. China's first written submission, paras. 358-359; referring to Appellate Body Report, India–Additional Import Duties, paras. 153 and 190.

④ Complainants' joint opening oral statement at the first substantive meeting, para. 128. United States' second written submission, para. 205; European Union's second written submission, paras. 42-46; European Union's opening oral statement at the second substantive meeting; Mexico's second written submission, para. 210.

⑤ China's second written submission, paras. 31-36.

⑥ Appellate Body Report, US–Wool Shirts and Blouses, p. 16, DSR 1997:I, 323, at p. 337; see also GATT Panel Report, EEC–Dessert Apples, para. 12.3; GATT Panel Report, Canada–Ice Cream and Yoghurt, para. 59.

7.212 The Panel sees no basis to conclude that the logic applicable to Article XI:2(c)(i) would not apply as well to the separate subparagraph, Article XI:2(a), which falls under the same chapeau paragraph.In addition, as the European Union also points out, China's interpretation would suggest that a complainant might need to demonstrate that other GATT provisions, such as GATT Articles XII, XVIII, XX or XXI, are also inapplicable.①

7.213 Accordingly, the Panel concludes that the burden is on the respondent (China in this case) to demonstrate that the conditions of Article XI:2(a) are met in order to demonstrate that no inconsistency arises under Article XI:1.With this in mind, the Panel will consider below the complainants' claims that China subjects the exportation of bauxite, coke, fluorspar, silicon carbide and zinc to quotas inconsistently with its obligations under Article XI:1.

【本案评析】

以上案例节选自中国原材料出口措施争端案专家组报告。对于WTO争端解决机构在争端解决程序中"谁主张、谁举证"这一举证责任的适用，该案专家组进行了详细阐述。

【延伸阅读】

一、相关典型案例

1. China—Measures Related to the Exportation of Various Raw Materials, (WT/DS394, WT/DS395, WT/DS398)

2. European Communities—Definitive Anti-Dumping Measures on Certain Iron or Steel Fasteners from China, (WT/DS397).

3. China—Measures Affecting Trading Rights and Distribution Services for Certain

① See European Union's second written submission, para. 12. In addition, the Panel considers the nature of Article XI:2 is distinct from the positive obligations contained in Article 27 of the SCM Agreement, or the special relationship that exists between GATT Articles II and III in respect of duties and charges as border measures and internal charges. Like the European Union, the Panel agrees that the particular interpretation of Article was influenced in India–Additional Import Duties by the "strong link" between Article II:2(a) and Article III:2. A challenge under Article III:2 should not be allowed to avoid the burden to show that the conditions of that provision are met by instead presenting its claim under Article II:1(b), and then requiring the respondent to prove that the charge is actually consistent with Article III:2 [and therefore with the exception in Article II:2(a)] (See European Union's second written submission, para. 19).

Publications and Audiovisual Entertainment Products, (WT/DS 363)

4. United States—Definitive Safeguard Measures on Imports of Certain Steel Products, (WT/DS252)

5. China—Measures Affecting the Protection and Enforcement of Intellectual Property Rights, (WT/DS 362)

6. United States—Final Anti-Dumping Measures on Stainless Steel from Mexico, (WT/DS 344)

7. Canada—Certain Measures Concerning Periodicals, (WT/DS 31)

二、相关学术论著

1. 黄东黎、杨国华:《世界贸易组织法: 理论·条约·中国案例》, 社会科学文献出版社 2013 年版。

2. 杨国华:《WTO 中国案例评析》, 知识产权出版社 2015 年版。

3. 韩立余:《既往不咎——WTO 争端解决机制研究》, 北京大学出版社 2009 年版。

4. 龚柏华:《WTO 二十周年: 争端解决与中国》, 上海人民出版社 2016 年版。

5. 任媛媛:《WTO 争端解决机制中的仲裁制度研究》, 法律出版社 2015 年版。

6. 吕微平:《WTO 争端解决机制的正当程序研究——以专家组证据规则和评审标准为视角》, 法律出版社 2014 年版。

7. Peter Van den Bossche, *The Law and Policy of the World Trade Organization: Text, Cases and Materials,* Cambridge University Press, 2017.

8. Ralph H. Folsom, *Principles of International Litigation and Arbitration,* West Academic Publishers, 2016.

9. Gregory C. Shaffer, Ricardo Meléndez-Ortiz, *Dispute Settlement at the WTO: The Developing Country Experience*, Cambridge University Press, 2010.

10. Chad P. Bown, Joost Pauwelyn, *The Law, Economics and Politics of Retaliation in WTO Dispute Settlement (Cambridge International Trade and Economic Law),* Cambridge University Press, 2010.

三、相关网络资源

https://www.wto.org/english/res_e/publications_e/ai17_e/dsu_e.htm.